THE
LIVING FEMALE WRITERS

OF THE

SOUTH.

THE

LIVING FEMALE WRITERS

OF THE

SOUTH.

EDITED BY THE AUTHOR OF

"SOUTHLAND WRITERS."

"Quos fama obscura recondit."
ÆNEID v. 302.

PHILADELPHIA:
CLAXTON, REMSEN & HAFFELFINGER,
819 & 821 MARKET STREET.
1872.

Republished by Gale Research Company, Book Tower, Detroit, 1978

Entered according to Act of Congress, in the year 1871, by
CLAXTON, REMSEN & HAFFELFINGER,
in the Office of the Librarian of Congress at Washington.

STEREOTYPED BY J. FAGAN & SON, PHILADELPHIA.

A Firenze Book

Library of Congress Cataloging in Publication Data

[Tardy, Mary T   ] ed.
The living female writers of the South.

Reprint of the ed. published by Claxton, Remsen &
Haffelfinger, Philadelphia.
Includes index.
1. American literature--Southern States. 2. Ameri-
can literature--Women authors. 3. American literature
--19th century. I. Southland writers, Author of.
II. Title.
PS551.T35   1976   811'.4'08   75-44070
ISBN 0-8103-4286-3

To

JOHN R. THOMPSON,
VIRGINIA,

JAMES WOOD DAVIDSON, A.M.,
SOUTH CAROLINA,

HON. W. G. McADO,
GEORGIA,

CHARLES DIMITRY,
LOUISIANA,

*A Quartette of Southern Authors who have ever kindly encouraged
and judiciously advised the "Female Writers of the
South:" This Record of them is*

Respectfully Dedicated.

CONTENTS.

PAGE

INTRODUCTORY... 1

KENTUCKY.

MRS. CATHARINE A. WARFIELD. *S. A. D*............................ 17
MISS ELIZA A. DUPUY. *S. A. D*....................................... 28
   DAGUERREOTYPE FROM A DEAD MAN'S EYE. *N. Y. Ledger*.......... 31
ROSA VERTNER JEFFREY.. 33
   Extract.—FLORENCE VALE. A Poem...................................... 38
AGNES LEONARD... 39
   FRA DIAVOLO. Poem.. 43
   ANGEL OF SLEEP. Poem.. 44
SARAH M. B. PIATT.. 46
   PROEM: TO THE WORLD. *A Woman's Poems*............................... 47
   MY WEDDING-RING. Poem. *Nests at Washington, and Other Poems*... 48
   THE FANCY BALL. *Galaxy Magazine*.................................... 48
NELLY MARSHALL. *Charles Dimitry*....................................... 49
   QUESTIONS. Poem.. 50
   ALDER-BOUGHS. Poem.. 51
   A WOMAN'S HEART.. 52
FLORENCE ANDERSON... 53
   FLORENCE ANDERSON, THE POET. Poem, by *Mary R. T. McAboy*... 54
   THE WORLD OF THE IDEAL. Poem... 54
MRS. CHAPMAN COLEMAN AND DAUGHTERS. *Eliza Lee*...... 56

	PAGE
MRS. ROCHESTER FORD	57
AUNT PEGGY'S DEATH-BED. *Grace Truman*	58
MRS. MARIE T. DAVIESS	62
HARVEST HYMN. Poem	65
VALUE OF PERMANENCE IN HOME AND VOCATION. *Extract*	66
VIRGINIA PENNY	67
SALLIE J. H. BATTEY	68
DREAMS. Poem. *Southern Magazine*	69
ALICE McCLURE GRIFFIN	70
SPIRIT LANDSCAPES. Poem	70
M. W. MERIWETHER BELL	71
THE VALLEY LILY'S MESSAGE. Poem	72

LOUISIANA.

SARAH A. DORSEY	74
A TEXAN PRAIRIE. *Recollections of Allen*	78
AGNES GRAHAM, Reviews of. *N. Y. Round Table*	79
REFUGEEING. *Lucia Dare*	80
GOVERNOR ALLEN. *Recollections of Allen*	81
THE LAURIES AT HOME. *Lucia Dare*	81
MARIE BUSHNELL WILLIAMS. *M. F. Bigney*	85
PLEASANT HILL. Poem	87
THE LEGEND OF DON RODERICK. *Editor N. O. Times*	89
THE ENCHANTED TOWER OF TOLEDO. Poem. *N. O. Sunday Times*	91
THE LAST WILD FLOWER. *N. O. Sunday Times*	95
ANNA PEYRE DINNIES	98
THE WIFE. Poem	100
THE LOVE-LETTER. Poem	103
THE BLUSH. Poem	104
JULIA PLEASANTS CRESWELL	105
THE MINSTREL PILOT. Poem	108
M. SOPHIE HOMES	110
THE DREAM-ANGEL. *Scott's Magazine*	116
ELIZA LOFTON PUGH. *Margaret C. Piggot*	118
ST. PHILIP'S	120

PAGE

ELIZA ELLIOTT HARPER... 121
  I'LL COME IN BRIGHT DREAMS. Poem............................. 122

MARY WALSINGHAM CREAN................................... 123
  SANTA CLAUS. Poem... 124
  BRONZE JOHN AND HIS SAFFRON STEED. Poem......... 125

MRS. JOSEPHINE R. HOSKINS................................. 127

SUSAN BLANCHARD ELDER. A. P. D........................ 128
  CLEOPATRA DYING. Poem...................................... 130

MRS. M. B. HAY.. 132
  ASPASIA. Sonnet. Crescent Monthly........................... 132

GERTRUDE A. CANFIELD. M. B. Williams................. 133
  IN THE TRENCHES.. 134

ELLEN A. MORIARTY... 136
  AN OLD STORY. Poem.. 137

MRS. E. M. KEPLINGER... 138
  OVER THE RIVER. Poem.. 139

MRS. LOUISE CLACK. G. Augusta Canfield................. 141
  GRANDMOTHER'S FADED FLOWER. Poem................. 143

MARY ASHLY-TOWNSEND....................................... 144
  EBB AND FLOW. "Xariffa's" Poems............................. 146
  CREED. "Xariffa's" Poems...................................... 146

MRS. FLORENCE J. WILLARD................................... 148
  RIP VAN WINKLE. Poem.. 149

JEANNETTE R. HADERMANN.................................. 150

CATHARINE F. WINDLE.. 151
  WHY DO I LOVE HIM? Poem.................................. 152
  NOVELS AND NOVELISTS. Extract. N. O. Sunday Times.... 152

MRS. A. M. C. MASSENA... 154

MARY TERESA MALONY... 154
  DEAD IN THE STEERAGE. Poem.............................. 155
  A HOME OF LANG SYNE. Poem............................... 156

A CRESCENT CITY COTERIE, VIZ.:............................. 157
  MATILDA A. BAILEY... 157
  FLORENCE BURCKETT... 158
  MARY CRESAP.. 158
  ALICE DALSHEIMER.. 158

B

PAGE

MARY GREEN GOODALE 159
SARAH C. YEISER 161
SAMUELLA COWEN 161

GEORGIA.

MARY E. TUCKER. Autobiography 163
HUGGING THE SHORE. Poem 170
KINDNESS. Poem 170

MARGIE P. SWAIN. W. G. McAdo 170
VANITAS. Poem 172
THE LAST SCENE. Poem 173
THE SENTINEL OF POMPEII. Poem 174

KATE A. DU BOSE 175

LOULA KENDALL ROGERS 177
THE HEALING FOUNTAIN. Poem 179

EMMA MOFFETT WYNNE 180
LIFE'S MISSION. Cragfont 181

ANNIE R. BLOUNT 183
UNDER THE LAMPLIGHT. Prize Poem 185

MARIA J. WESTMORELAND 188
THE UNATTAINABLE. Scott's Magazine 189
TALKING. Scott's Magazine 191

MARIA LOU EVE 193
SINCERITY IN TALKING. Extract. Prize Essay 193

KATE C. WAKELEE 194
TO THE MEMORY OF CAPTAIN HERNDON. Poem. Godey's Lady's
Book 195

CARRIE BELL SINCLAIR 196
"UNKNOWN." Poem 198

MRS. BETTIE M. ZIMMERMAN 200
CHRISTMAS TEARS. Poem 200

SALLIE M. MARTIN 202
CHARLOTTE CORDAY. Women of France 203

CLARA LE CLERC 204

PAGE

MRS. BESSIE W. WILLIAMS.. 205
AFTER THE BATTLE. *Ciaromski and his Daughter*..................... 205

LOUISE MANHIEM, (MRS. HERBERT.) *R. J.*................... 207
ON DRESS. *Southern Illustrated News*............................... 208

MRS. REBECCA JACOBUS... 211

MRS. MARY A. McCRIMMON...................................... 212
FLORIDA. Poem. *Literary Crusader*................................. 213

MRS. AGNES JEAN STIBBES....................................... 214
REV. A. J. RYAN, THE GOLDEN-TONGUED ORATOR............. 214

MISS FANNY ANDREWS.. 216
A PLEA FOR RED HAIR. *Godey's Lady's Book*...................... 218
PAPER-COLLAR GENTILITY.. 221

MARIA J. McINTOSH... 223

KATE CLIFFORD KENAN.. 229
THE DOCTOR. *"Violetta and I."*................................... 230

MARY LOUISE COOK. *Emma Moffett*............................... 232

CORNELIA BORDERS. *"H."*... 233

MRS. EPPIE B. CASTLEN. *W. G. McAdo*........................... 234
AUTUMN DAYS. *"Chiquita's" Poems*................................ 235

MRS. A. P. HILL. *Mrs. Colquitt*.................................... 236

MRS. MARY F. McADO... 237
ONEIROPION. Poem.. 238

THEODOSIA FORD... 239

JANIE OLLIVAR... 240
MORNING DREAMS. Poem. *Southern Field and Fireside*........... 240

JULIA BACON.. 240
WILL'S A WIDOWER... 241

E. W. BACCHUS... 242
CHARLES DICKENS. Poem. *Baltimore Home Journal*.............. 242

ALABAMA.

PAGE

MADAME ADELAIDE DE V. CHAUDRON............................... 244

MISS KATE CUMMING... 245

MRS. ANNIE CREIGHT LLOYD 247

MRS. E. W. BELLAMY.. 248
    FOUR OAKS. Reviews. *W. T. Walthall*... 248
    A SUMMER IDYL. Poem. *Land We Love*...................................... 251
    TRANSITION. Poem. *Land We Love*... 253

MARY A. CRUSE.. 255
    WAKING OF THE BLIND GIRL BY THE TONES OF THE GRAND ORGAN.
    "Cameron Hall.".. 257

LILIAN ROZELL MESSENGER... 261
    THE OLD WHARF AT PINE BLUFF. Poem. *N. Y. Home Journal*..... 262

SARAH E. PECK... 264

JULIA L. KEYES. *G. P. K*... 265
    TO MY ABSENT HUSBAND. Poem.. 266
    A DREAM OF LOCUST DELL. Poem. *Southern Field and Fireside*..... 268

AUGUSTA J. EVANS... 270
    MACARIA, Review of. *James R. Randall*....................................... 273
    ST. ELMO, Review of. *Jerome Cochran, M.D*.................................. 276

I. M. PORTER HENRY... 281
    RIMMER. Poem. *Land We Love*.. 282

CATHERINE W. TOWLES... 283

MRS. JULIA SHELTON, (LAURA LORRIMER.).............................. 285
    THE FEVER-SLEEP. A Prize Poem. *Southern Field and Fireside*..... 285

MRS. OCTAVIA WALTON LE VERT... 291

MARY WARE. *S. E. Peck*.. 292
    CONSOLATION. Poem. *Home Monthly, (Nashville.)*....................... 293

MRS. E. L. SAXON.. 294
    MY VINE. Poem. *N. O. Sunday Times*... 295

S. S. CRUTE.. 296

ANNA FREDAIR.. 296

CAROLINE THERESA BRANCH. *Rev. Dr. Myers*....................... 296

BETTIE KEYES HUNTER.. 297
    A MOTHER'S WISH. Poem. *Baltimore Home Journal*.................... 297

MISSISSIPPI.

PAGE

SALLIE A. VANCE. *M. E. B*.. 299
THE TWO ANGELS. Poem.. 300
GUARD THINE ACTION. Poem....................................... 301

MRS. MARY STANFORD... 303
MY NEW-YEAR'S PRAYER. Poem. *Southern Monthly, (Memphis.)*.... 305

MRS. S. B. COX... 307
SPIRIT-WHISPERINGS. *N. O. Sunday Times*........................ 309

ELIZA J. POITEVENT.. 311
A CHIRP FROM MOTHER ROBIN. Poem. *N. O. Picayune*............ 313
THE ROYAL CAVALCADE. Poem...................................... 314

MARY W. LOUGHBOROUGH.. 315

FLORIDA.

MARY E. BRYAN... 316
ANACREON. Poem.. 324
MISERERE. Poem.. 326
BY THE SEA. Poem. *Mobile Sunday Times*....................... 329
THE FATAL BRACELET.. 331
HOW SHOULD WOMEN WRITE? *Southern Field and Fireside*......... 335

FANNY E. HERRON.. 340
THE SIEGE OF MURANY. *Extract. Mobile Sunday Times*........... 340

MRS. M. LOUISE CROSSLEY....................................... 342

AUGUSTA DE MILLY... 343
"IMPLORA PACE." Poem.. 344
"FLORIDA CAPTA." Poem... 345

TENNESSEE.

MRS. L. VIRGINIA FRENCH....................................... 347
"MAMMY:" A HOME PICTURE OF 1860. *Land We Love*............... 352
THE BROKEN SENTENCE. A Tribute to the late Lieut. Herndon...... 354

PAGE

MRS. ANNIE CHAMBERS KETCHUM. *Mary J. S. Upshur*........ 357
A MOTHER'S PRAYER. Poem. *N. Y. Churchman*........................ 358
REQUIEM. Poem.. 360
UNDER THE LEAVES. *"Lotus."*.. 362

MRS. CLARA COLES.. 364
SABBATH MORN. *"Clara's" Poems*...................................... 365

ADELIA C. GRAVES.. 366
HUMAN SOVEREIGNTY; OR, EVERY MAN A KING. Poem. *Scott's Magazine* 369

MRS. MARY E. POPE.. 371
THE GIFT OF SONG.. 372

MARTHA W. BROWN... 374
"THOU ART GROWING OLD, MOTHER." Poem............................... 374

AMANDA M. BRIGHT.. 376

ANNIE E. LAW. *W. G. McAdo*... 377
MEMORIES. Poem.. 377

VIRGINIA.

MRS. MARGARET J. PRESTON.. 379
OLD SONGS AND NEW, Review of. *London Saturday Review*............ 379
BEECHENBROOK, Review of. *N. Y. Round Table*........................ 380
BEECHENBROOK, Review of. *Field and Fireside*....................... 382
MRS. PRESTON'S POETRY, Review of. *Wm. Hand Browne*................ 385
NON DOLET. Sonnet. *Old Songs and New*.............................. 386
UNDERTOW. Sonnet. *Old Songs and New*............................... 387
ACCEPTATION. Poem. *Beechenbrook*.................................... 387
THE LADY HILDEGARDE'S WEDDING. *Old Songs and New*............... 388

MRS. S. A. WEISS. *Charles Dimitry*.................................... 391
THE BATTLE EVE. Poem. *Southern Literary Messenger*............... 393
CON ELGIN. Poem. *Susan Archer Talley's Poems*..................... 394

MRS. CONSTANCE CARY HARRISON. *Charles Dimitry*.............. 398

MISS M. J. HAW.. 399

MRS. MARY WILEY... 400
A BUNCH OF FLOWERS. Poem. *Southern Literary Messenger*........ 400

PAGE

MISS M. E. HEATH.. 401

VIRGINIA E. DAVIDSON.. 402

MRS. J. W. McGUIRE.. 403

MISS SALLIE A. BROCK... 404
WHAT IS LIFE? Poem. *Metropolitan Bend*............................ 407

MISS SUSAN C. HOOPER... 409
THE OCCUPATION OF RICHMOND... 411

MATILDA S. EDWARDS... 414

MRS. MARY McCABE......., ... 415

MISS MARY J. S. UPSHUR... 416
MARGARET. Poem. *Southern Literary Messenger*.................. 418

MISS SARAH J. C. WHITTLESEY.. 420

HELEN G. BEALE.. 421

MRS. CORNELIA J. M. JORDAN. *Charles Dimitry*.................... 423
FALL SOFTLY, WINTER SNOW, TO-NIGHT. Poem....................... 426
FLOWERS FOR A WOUNDED SOLDIER. Poem. *Magnolia Weekly*...... 427

LAURA R. FEWELL.. 428
A VIRGINIA VILLAGE — 1861. *Scott's Magazine*..................... 428

LIZZIE PETIT CUTLER.. 430
SPIRIT-MATES. *Household Mysteries*.................................... 431

MARY E. WOODSON.. 433

M. VIRGINIA TERHUNE, (MARIAN HARLAND.)............................ 433

MRS. WM. C. RIVES. *S. D.*... 436

MARY TUCKER MAGILL.. 438

MISS EMILY V. MASON.. 439

MARY EUGENIE McKINNE. *A. W. H.*...................................... 440

NORTH CAROLINA.

MARY BAYARD CLARKE. *Judge Edwin G. Reade*.................... 442
APHRODITE. Poem. *Mosses from a Rolling Stone*.................... 449
GRIEF. Poem. *Land We Love*.. 451
LIFE'S FIG-LEAVES. Poem. *Land We Love*.............................. 453

PAGE

MRS. MARY MASON.. 454

CORNELIA PHILLIPS SPENCER... 454

FANNY MURDAUGH DOWNING. *H. W. Husted*.................... 455
SUNSET MUSINGS. Poem.. 456

VIRGINIA DURANT COVINGTON.. 458

MARY AYER MILLER. *Mary B. Clarke*................................. 459

MRS. SARAH A. ELLIOTT... 460

FRANCES C. FISHER... 461
VALERIE AYLMER, Review of. *T. Cooper De Leon*.............. 461

SOUTH CAROLINA.

SUE PETIGRU KING... 463
A LOVER'S QUARREL. *Sylvia's World*............................ 464

CAROLINE GILMAN.. 468

CAROLINE H. JERVEY. *Jeanie A. Dickson*........................ 469
JULIA SLEEPING. Poem.. 470
A SUMMER MEMORY.. 472

CAROLINE A. BALL.. 473
THE JACKET OF GRAY. Poem.. 473

MARY S. B. SHINDLER.. 475

JULIA C. R. DORR.. 477

ESSIE B. CHEESBOROUGH.. 478
RENUNCIATION. Poem. *Crescent Monthly*...................... 478

MISS ALICE F. SIMONS... 479

MARY SCRIMZEOUR WHITAKER.. 480
THE SUMMER RETREAT OF A SOUTHERN PLANTER........ 482

FANNY M. P. DEAS... 484

MARGARET MAXWELL MARTIN.. 485
MY SAVIOUR, THEE! Poem... 487

MRS. M. A. EWART RIPLEY... 488

MRS. CATHARINE LADD... 489

PAGE

CLARA V. DARGAN.. 491
JEAN TO JAMIE. Poem... 493
SLEEPING. Poem. *Southern Field and Fireside*............ 495
FLIRTING WITH PHILIP. *Philip : My Son*..................... 495

MARIAN C. LEGARE REEVES................................... 498
INGEMISCO, Review of. *C. W. Hutson*...................... 498
RANDOLPH HONOR, Review of. *Round Table*................ 500

FLORIDE CLEMSON... 502

ANNIE M. BARNWELL.. 503
ON SOUTHERN LITERATURE. *Scott's Magazine*............ 504

MARY CAROLINE GRISWOLD................................... 505
THE WHITE CAMELIA. Poem.................................. 505

MISS JULIA C. MINTZING. *Charles Dimitry*............... 506
VICTOR AND VICTIM. Poem................................... 507
GŒTHE AND SCHILLER. *Land We Love*..................... 508

JEANIE A. DICKSON.. 512

MRS. LAURA GWYN. *Ex-Governor B. F. Perry*............ 513
MY PALACE OF DREAMS. Poem................................ 513

MISS CATHARINE GENDRON POYAS......................... 515
SONNET. *Year of Grief, and Other Poems*................ 516

SELINA E. MEANS... 517

LOUISA S. McCORD.. 518

MRS. MARY C. RION... 518

MARYLAND.

ANNE MONCURE CRANE.. 519
EMILY CHESTER, Review of. *E. P. Whipple*............... 519
EMILY CHESTER, Review of. *Geo. H. Hilliard*............ 520
EMILY CHESTER, Review of. *Gail Hamilton*............... 521
OPPORTUNITY, Review of. *Paul H. Hayne*................ 523
WORDS TO A "LIED OHNE WORTE." Poem.................. 526
WINTER WIND. Poem. *Galaxy Monthly*................... 527
FAITH AND HOPE. *Opportunity*.............................. 527

LYDIA CRANE.. 529
KÖRNER'S BATTLE PRAYER.................................... 529
C

PAGE

ELLIE LEE HARDENBROOK.. 530

GEORGIE A. HULSE McLEOD.. 531
    MINE! *Thine and Mine; or, The Stepmother's Revenge*.................... 532
    THE LOST TREASURE. Poem... 532

EMMA ALICE BROWNE... 533

ESTELLA ANNA LEWIS... 534
    THE FORSAKEN. Poem. *Records of the Heart*............................... 535
    THE GRIEF OF ALCÆUS. Poem. *Sappho.—Act II*........................... 538

HENRIETTA LEE PALMER.. 539
    THE STRATFORD GALLERY, Review of. *Atlantic Monthly*................ 540

MRS. EMMA D. E. N. SOUTHWORTH.. 541

MISS ELIZA SPENCER.. 542
    A MARYLAND FARM-HOUSE. *Mary Ashburton*............................ 542

TAMAR A. KERMODE... 543
    GIVE US THIS PEACE. Poem... 543

ELEANOR FULLERTON.. 544
    SO LONG AGO. Poem.. 544

TEXAS.

FANNY A. D. DARDEN.. 546
    THE OLD BRIGADE. Poem... 546
    CHECKMATE. Poem.. 548

MRS. S. E. MAYNARD.. 549
    CLEOPATRA TO MARC ANTONY. Poem. *Crescent Monthly*........... 550

MAUD J. YOUNG... 551

MOLLIE E. MOORE. *Colonel C. G. Forshey*................................... 555
    THE RIVER SAN MARCOS. Poem.. 556
    STEALING ROSES THROUGH THE GATE. Poem............................. 560
    MINDING THE GAP. Poem... 561

FLORENCE D. WEST... 565
    THE MARBLE LILY. Poem. *Land We Love*.................................. 565

ALPHABETICAL INDEX.

A BORIGINAL Portfolio, 9.
Acceptation, (Poem,) 387.
Adrienne, 410.
Adhemar, 536.
After the Battle, 205.
Agnes Graham, (Review of,) 79.
Albert Hastings, 480.
Alder-Boughs, (Poem,) 51.
Alpurente, Dr. F. R., 157.
Alfriend, F. H., 8.
Altorf, 12.
Alone, 434.
Alida, 489.
Allen, Governor, 81.
Alston, Edith, 159.
Alston, Washington, 479.
"American Pulpit," Sprague's, 151.
American Courier, 294.
American Poets and their Favorite Poems, 406.
Alma Grey, 369.
Allworth Abbey, 541.
Amaranth, The Southern, 406.
Anacreon, (Poem,) 324.
Ann Atom, 150.
Anderson, Florence, 53.
Anderson, Florence, the Poet, (Poem,) 54.
Anderson, Dr. Leroy H., 503.
Andrews, Fanny, 216.
Ancient Lady, 515.
Angel of Sleep, (Poem,) 44.
Angoisse, 26.
Answered, (Poem,) 159.
Ante-Bellum, 232.
Antethusia, 237.
Arnold, Matthew, 152.
Appleton's Journal, 461.
Arria, 119.
Arcturus, 489.
Army Argus and Crisis, 247.
Ashhurst, Lady of, 30.
Ashleigh, 30.
As By Fire, 50.

Aspasia, (Sonnet,) 132.
Ashmead, Rev. Wm., 151.
Ashes of Roses, 410.
At Last, 435.
Atlantic Monthly, 540.
Aunt Abby the Irrepressible, 448.
Autobiography of an Actress, 9.
Aunt Charity, 161.
Aunt Kitty, 224.
Aunt Phillis's Cabin, 9.
Aunt Peggy's Death-bed, 58.
Autumn Dreams, 235.
Autumn Days, (Poem,) 235.
Auchester, Charles, 492.
Ayer, General Henry, 459.
Azile, 4.
Azélee, 161.

B ACON, Julia, 240.
Bacchus, E. W., 242.
Baden, Frances Henshaw, 541.
Bagby, G. W., 8.
Bailey, Matilda A., 157.
Baker, Gen. Mosely, 546.
Ball, Fancy, (Poem,) 48.
Ball, Caroline A., 473.
Ball, Isaac, 473.
Ballard, J. J., 549.
Banner of the South, 214.
Baring, Mrs. Charles, 12.
Barber, Miss C. W., 184, 283.
Barnwell, Annie M., 503.
Barnwell, Thomas Osborn, 503.
Bartow, Gen. Francis S., 239.
Battle Eve, The, (Poem,) 393.
Battle of Manassas, 447.
Battey, Sallie J. H., 68.
Battey, Manfred C., 68.
Beale, Helen G., 421.
Beale, Wm. C., 421.
Beauseincourt, 25.
Bell, M. W. Meriwether, 71.
Bell, Captain Darwin, 72.

Bellamy, Mrs. E. W., 248.
Beechenbrook : A Rhyme of the War, 380–382.
Beechwood Tragedy, The, 399.
Benny, 359.
Bennett, Martha Haines Butt, 10.
Bertha the Beauty, 420.
Bessie Melville, 256.
Betts, Mary Wilson, 4.
Betts, Morgan L., 4.
Beulah, 271.
Beverley, 309.
Béverley, Jr., 309.
Beverly, Elise, 542.
Bigby, Mary Catharine, 6.
Bigney, Mark F., 4, 148.
Bibb, Thomas, 106.
Blake, Mrs. Daniel, 13.
Blackwell, Rev. John C., 414.
Blanchard, General A. G., 128.
Blind Alice, 225.
Blount, Annie R., 183.
Bloody Footprints, 403.
Borders, Cornelia, 233.
Bowdre, Judge P. E., 234.
Branch, Caroline Theresa, 296.
Branch, Rev. James O., 297.
Brace, Ned, 241.
Bradley, Thomas Bibb, 107.
Brenan, Joseph, 123.
Brewer, Sarah, 5.
Bridal Eve, 541.
Bride's Fate, 541.
Bride of Llewellyn, 541.
Brigand's Bride, 138.
Bright Memories, 531.
Bright, Amanda M., 376.
Brockenborough, Judge, 403.
Brock, Miss Sallie A., 404.
Broken Sentence, The, 354.
Brother Clerks, The, 145.
Bronze John and his Saffron Steed,(Poem,) 125.
Browne, Wm. Hand, 312, 385.
Browne, Emma Alice, 533.
Brown, Martha W., 374.
Brown, R. B., 374.
Burckett, Florence, 158.
Bryan, Mary E., 316.
Bryan, Madeline T., 189.
Bunch of Flowers, A, (Poem,) 400.
Bug Oracle, The, 420.
Burwell, W. M., 5.
Burke, T. A., 183.
Buds from the Wreath of Memory, 296.
Busy Moments of an Idle Woman, 463.
" Byrd Lyttle," 14.
By the Sea, (Poem,) 329.

CAIUS Gracchus, 518.
Callirhoé, 5.
Callamura, 108.
Calhoun, John C., 502.

Caldwell, Howard H., 491.
Cameron Hall, 256.
Canfield, Gertrude, A., 133.
Caruthers, Wm. A., 8.
Carra, Emma, 214.
Castlen, Eppie Bowdre, 234.
Castlen, Dr. F. G., 234.
Carrie, 505.
Carrie Harrington ; or, Scenes in New Orleans, 111.
Carnes, Rev. J. E., 553.
Cary, Constance, 398.
Cary, Archibald, 398.
Casper, 458.
Cave Life in Vicksburg, My, 315.
Celeste ; or, The Pirate's Daughter, 30.
Charleston Daily News, 473.
Charlotte Corday, 203.
Charms and Counter-Charms, 225, 227.
Charles Morton ; or, The Young Patriot, 477.
Charity, Aunt, 161.
Ciaromski and his Daughter, 205.
Chaudron, Madame Adelaide De V., 244.
Cheesborough, Miss Essie B., 478.
Cheesborough, John W., 478.
Checkmate, (Poem,) 548.
Chesney, Esther, 491.
Cheves, Langdon, 518.
Chester, Emily, (Reviews of,) 519–521.
Chirp from Mother Robin, A, (Poem,) 313.
Chiquita, 235.
Chicora, 9.
Changed Brides, 541.
Christmas Guest, 542.
Christmas Tears, (Poem,) 200.
Christmas Holly, 435.
Child of the Sea, 536.
Citizen : Miles O'Reilly, 168.
Clack, Mrs. Louise, 141.
Clara, 196.
Clara's Poems, 364.
Claiborne, Ferdinand, 303.
Claudia, 491.
Clarke, Mary Bayard, 442, 460.
Clarke, Colonel Wm. J., 442.
Cleopatra to Marc Antony, (Poem,) 550.
Cleopatra Dying, (Poem,) 130.
Clemson, Floride, 502.
Clytie and Zenobia ; or, The Lily and the Palm, 449.
Coleman, Mrs. Chapman, 56.
Coleman, Eugenia, 56.
Coleman, Judith, 56.
Coleman, Sallie, 56.
Coles, Mrs. Clara, 364.
Colquitt, Mrs., 237.
Cochran, Dr. Jerome, 272, 276.
Come to Life, 492.
Coming Home, 492.
Common Sense in the Household, 435.
Coquette's Punishment, 30.
Cotting, Doctor, 165.

Constantine, 171.
Constance, 205.
Concealed Treasure, 30.
Conspirator, The, 29.
Conquest and Self-Conquest, 225, 226.
Confederate Dead, 242.
Cook, Mary Louise, 232.
Cocke, William Archer, 415.
Consolation, (Poem,) 293.
Con Elgin, (Poem,) 394.
"Confederate Notes," 417.
Cordova, 553:
Correspondence of Mr. Ralph Izard, 12.
Corinth, and other Poems, 425.
Cousin Kate, 229.
Cousin, Victor, 152.
Cousins, The, 225.
Courtland, Miss, 415.
Covington, Virginia Durant, 458.
Cox, Mrs. S. B., 307.
Cragfont, 180.
Crane, Anne Moncure, 519.
Crane, Lydia, 529.
Crane, Wm., 529.
Country Neighborhood, 29.
Courier, Louisville, 39.
Cowden, Mrs. V. G., 7.
Cowen, Samuella, 161.
Creed, (Poem,) 146.
Creole, 154.
Creola, 161.
Crescent Monthly, 132, 246, 550.
Crescent, New Orleans, 309.
Creswell, Julia Pleasants, 105.
Creswell, Judge David, 107.
Crescent City Coterie, A, 157.
Cresap, Mary, 158.
Crean, Mary Walsingham, 123.
Creight, Annie P., 247.
Cruel as the Grave, 542.
Crittenden, Life and Times of J. J., 57.
Crimes that the Law does not Reach, 463.
Crossbone Papers, 144.
Cross, Jane Tandy Chinn, 3.
Crown Jewels, The, 182.
Crossley, Mrs. M. Louise, 342.
Crossley, J. T., 343.
Cruse, Mary A., 255.
Cruse, Sam, 255.
Cruse, Wm., 255.
Crute, S. S., 296.
Cumming, Miss Kate, 245.
Curse of Clifton, 541.
Cushing, E. H., 559.
Cutler, Mrs. Lizzie Petit, 430.

DALE, Salvia, 158.
Dalsheimer, Alice, 158.
Daguerreotype from a Dead Man's Eye, 31.
Daisy Dare, and Baby Power, 37.
Dacotah; or, Legends of the Sioux, 8.
Dana, Charles E., 475.

Darden, Fanny A. D., 546.
Daughter, The Planter's, 30.
Darlington Southerner, 492.
Dargan, Clara V., 491.
Dargan, Dr. K. S., 491.
Davis, I. N., 284.
Davidson, Virginia E., 402.
Davidson, J. W., 493.
Daviess, Marie T., 62.
Daviess, Captain Samuel, 63.
Daviess, Jos. Hamilton, 63.
Dawson, Rev. John E., 236.
Day-Spring, 486.
Devereux, Thomas P., 442.
Dead Heart, 30.
Dead in the Steerage, (Poem,) 155.
Deas, Mrs. Anna Izard, 12.
Deas, Fanny M. P., 484.
Deems, Rev. Dr., 454.
Deeds, The Lost, 30.
De Milly, Augusta, 343.
Deen, Ethel, 343.
De Leon, T. C., 461.
Destiny, 479.
De Vere, Lalla, 202.
Deserted Wife, The, 541.
Diary of a Southern Refugee during the War, 403.
Dictionary of Similes, Figures, Images, Metaphors, etc., 264.
Dickens, Charles, (Poem,) 242.
Dickson, Jeanie A., 512.
Dickson, Dr. Samuel Henry, 512.
Dimitry, Charles, 393, 398, 426, 512.
Dimitry, Alexander, 5.
Dixie, (Poem,) 457.
Divorce, The, 30.
Dinnies, Anna Peyre, 98.
Dispatch, Richmond, 433.
Discarded Daughter, 541.
Doctor, The, 230.
Dorsey, Sarah A., 74.
Dorsey, Anna H., 14.
Downing, Fanny Murdaugh, 455.
Downing, Charles W., 455.
Dorr, Julia C. R., 477.
Dorr, Seneca M., 477.
Dorr, Zulma, 477.
Dreams, (Poem,) 69.
Dreams, My, 518.
Dream of Locust Dell, (Poem,) 268.
Dress under Difficulties, 217.
Duncan Adair; or, Captured in Escaping, 4.
Du Bose, Kate A., 175.
Du Bose, Charles W., 175.
Du Ponte, Mrs. Sophie A., 5.
Du Ponte, Durant, 5.
Dupuy, Eliza A., 28.

EARLS of Sutherland, 214.
Ebb and Flow, (Poem,) 146.
Eastman, Mrs. Mary H., 8.

Edwards, Major John D., 317.
Edwards, Matilda S., 414.
Edwards, Rev. A. S., 414.
Edwards, General S. M., 414.
Edgar, Rev. John T., 365.
Edgefield Advertiser, 492.
Edenton Sentinel, 420.
Ellis, Colonel John, 18.
Ellis, Thomas G., 29.
Ellett, Mrs. E. F., 486.
Eliot, George, 22.
Elder, Susan Blanchard, 128.
Elder, Charles D., 129.
Ellen Leslie, 225.
Ellen; or, The Fanatic's Daughter, 7.
Ellen Fitzgerald, 129.
Elzey Hay, 216.
Elliott, Mrs. Sarah A., 460.
Elliott's Housewife, Mrs., 460.
Ellen Campbell; or, King's Mountain, 488.
Elma South, 478.
Empty Heart, The, 435.
Emerson, 152.
Emma Carra, 214.
Emma Walton, 30.
Emily Herbert, 225.
Employments of Women, 67.
Enchanted Tower of Toledo, (Poem,) 91.
Eoland, 401.
"Estelle," 374.
Error, Fatal, 30.
Etna Vandemir, 68.
Evans, Augusta J., 270.
Evans, Mrs. E. H., 10.
Evans, Miss Mary, 400.
Evans, Dr. M. H., 400.
Eve, Maria Lou, 193.
Evening Star, The, (Poem,) 185.
Evenings at Donaldson Manor, 225.
Evangeline, 137.
Evening Post, New York, 462.
Evil Genius, The, 30.
Evelyn, Wm. M., 492.
Ewart, James B., 488.
Exhortation to the Inhabitants of the Province of South Carolina, 11.
Extracts from "Florence Vale," (Poem,) 38.
Exiles, Huguenot, 30.
Eyrich, A., 148.

FADETTE, 502.
Fancy Ball, The, (Poem,) 48.
Faith and Hope, 527.
Fairfax, Ruth, 214.
Fairfax, Monimia, 398.
Fairfax, Thomas, 398.
Fair Play, 542.
Fall Softly, Winter Snow, To-night, (Poem,) 426.
Family Secret, 30.
Fatal Error, 30.
Family Doom, 541, 542.

Fallen Pride, 541.
Fashionable Life, 9.
Fatal Bracelet, The, 331.
Fatal Marriage, The, 541.
Fielding, Fanny, 416.
Fewell, Laura R., 428.
Fever-Sleep, The, (Poem,) 285.
Filia Ecclesiæ, 76.
First Love, (Poem,) 162.
Fisher, Frances C., 461.
Fisher, Colonel Charles F., 461.
Finley, Miss Julia, 285.
Five Hundred Employments adapted to Women, 67.
Flirting with Philip, 495.
"Florence Vale," Extracts from, (Poem,) 38.
Flori, C. de, 502.
Florence Anderson, the Poet, 54.
Floral Year, The, 99.
Floral Wreath, 489.
Florida, (Poem,) 213.
Florida Capta, (Poem,) 345.
Florida, 457.
Florence Arnott, 225.
Floyd, General John, 237.
Floyd, Mary Faith, 237.
Florine de Genlis, 416.
Flowers of Hope and Memory, 424.
Flowers and Fruit, 486.
Flowers for a Wounded Soldier, (Poem,) 427.
Ford, S. Rochester, 57.
Ford, Theodosia, 239.
Forever Thine, 491.
Fortune Seeker, 541.
Foote, Mary E., 371.
Forgiven at Last, 150.
Forrester, Dr. Alexander, 151.
Forlorn Hope, 157.
Forest City Bride, The, 194.
Fortune's Wheel; or, Life's Vicissitudes, 234.
Forrest, Life of General Bedford, 371.
Forecastle Tom, 477.
Forsaken, The, (Poem,) 535.
Forshey, Colonel C. G., 565.
Four Oaks, (Reviews of,) 248.
Fra Diavolo, (Poem,) 43.
Frazer, Martha W., 374.
Fredair, Anna, 296.
French, L. Virginia, 316, 347.
Furman, Prof. Samuel, 480.
Furman, Richard, 480.
Fullerton, Eleanor, 544.
Fuller, Violet, 544.

GALLAWAY, Colonel M. C., 261.
Galaxy, The, 436.
Gan Eden, 446.
Gardner, Colonel James, 322.
Garnet; or, Through the Shadows into Light, 247.
Georgia Gazette, 196.

George Balcombe, 438.
Gerald Gray's Wife, 463.
Gertrude Glenn, 292.
Gipsy's Prophecy, The, 541.
Gibbs, Dr. R. W., 294.
Giddings, Joshua R., 366.
Gift of Song, The, (Poem,) 372.
Gilman, Caroline, 468.
Gilman, Rev. Samuel, 468.
Gift-Book, Mrs. Gilman's, 468.
Give us this Peace, (Poem,) 543.
Gleanings from Fireside Fancies, 50.
Glenmore, Addie, 70.
Glenelglen, 340.
Glover, Wilson, 469.
Goodale, Mary Green, 159.
Goetzel, S. H., 7, 245.
Gœthe and Schiller, 508.
Grace Truman; or, Love and Principle, 57.
Gray, Amy, 14.
Grandmother's Faded Flower, (Poem,)143.
Grace and Clara, 225.
Graves, Adelia C., 366.
Graves, Z. C., 367.
Grief of Alcæus, (Poem,) 538.
Griswold, Mary Caroline, 505.
Griswold, Hon. Whiting, 505.
Griffin, Alice McClure, 70.
Griffin, Geo. W., 2, 70.
Guard Thine Action, (Poem,) 310.
Guardian, Southern, 491.
Gwyn, Mrs. Laura, 513.
Gulf City Home Journal, 247.

HADERMANN, Jeannette R., 150.
Hagar; or, The Lost Jewel, 247.
Halleck, Fitz-Greene, 47.
Hamilton, Gail, 521.
Hancock, Mrs., 68.
Hansford, 8, 438.
Harland, Marian, 433.
Harper, Eliza Ellis H., 121.
Harper, Dr. James D., 121.
Harp, The Southern, 476.
Harp, The Northern, 476.
Hart, Prof. John S., 224, 226.
Harrison, Constance Cary, 398.
Harrison, Burton N., 398.
Harvest Hymn, (Poem,) 65.
Harris, Edmund, 292.
Hardenbrook, Ellie Lee, 530.
Haunted Homestead, 541.
Hawes, Alice, 434.
Hawes, Samuel P., 433.
Hawes, M. Virginia, 433.
Haw, Miss M. J., 399.
Hay, Mrs. M. B., 132.
Hay, Rev. A. L., 132.
Haywood Lodge, 322.
Hayne, Paul H., 523.
Heart History of a Heartless Woman, 463.
Heath, Miss M. E., 401.

Helen Courtenay's Promise, 470.
Heart Whispers; or, Echoes of Song, 197.
Heart Drops from Memory's Urn, 420.
Heart Histories, 157.
Hemans, Felicia, 154.
Hentz, Caroline Lee, 6.
Helemar; or, The Fall of Montezuma, 537.
Healing Fountain, The, 179.
Hester Howard's Temptation, 26.
Henry, Ina M. Porter, 281.
Henry, George L., 282.
Heroism of the Confederacy, 148.
Hermine, 129.
Herron, Fanny E., 340.
Herbert, Mrs., 207.
Heydenfeldt, Judge, 211.
Herbert Hamilton; or, The Bas Bleu, 420.
Heriolt, Edwin, 489.
Hidden Heart, 420.
Hidden Path, 434.
Hildegarde, 128.
Hill, General D. H., 503.
Hill, Mrs. A. P., 236.
Hilliard, Hon. Henry W., 233.
Hilliard, Hon. Geo. H., 520.
Hillyer, Rev. John F., 549.
Hill, Judge Edward Y., 236.
Holmes, Rev. Wm., 202.
Holcombes, The, 8, 439.
Holt, Harry, 204.
Holt, Polly, 204.
Home of Lang Syne, A, (Poem,) 156.
Homes, M. Sophie, 110.
Homes, Luther, 116.
Home Monthly, 276, 417.
Hope, Ethel, 281.
Home and Abroad, 437.
Hooper, Miss Susan C., 409.
Hosmer, Harriet, 454.
Hospital Life in the Army of the Tennessee, 245.
Houston Telegraph, 558.
Household Mysteries, 430.
Houghton, Colonel R. B., 319.
Household of Bouverie, 22.
How Women can Make Money, 67.
How should Women write? 335.
Howard, Samuel, 468.
Howard, Caroline, 469.
Howard, Helen, 492.
How He won Her, 541.
Hulse, Dr. Isaac, 531.
Huguenot Daughters, 515.
Hughes, Judge Beverley, 307.
Hugging the Shore, (Poem,) 170.
Hull, Angele De V., 7.
Human Sovereignty; or, Every Man a King, (Poem,) 369.
Huguenot Exiles, 30.
Hume, Mrs. Sophie, 11.
Hutson, Mrs. Mary, 12.
Hutson, C. Woodward, 498, 501.
Huxley, Prof., 152.

Hunter, Mrs. Fanny E., 165.
Hunter, Judge John, 165.
Hunter, Bettie Keyes, 297.
Hunter, A. M., 297.
Husks, 434.
Husbands and Homes, 434.
Husted, H. W., 455.
Helen Gardner's Wedding-Day, 435.

IDE Delmar, 478.
  " I 'll come in Bright Dreams," (Poem,) 122.
"Implora Pace," (Poem,) 344.
In a Crucible, 120.
India; or, The Pearl of Pearl River, 541.
Indian Chamber, and other Poems, 21.
India Morgan; or, The Lost Will, 194.
Ingemisco, (Review,) 498.
Inez: A Tale of the Alamo, 271.
In the Trenches, 134.
Ivy Leaves from an Old Homestead, 531.
Iztalilxo, The Lady of Tula, 348.

JACOBUS, Mrs. Rebecca, 211.
  Jacobus, J. Julien, 211.
Jacqueline, 128.
Jacket of Gray, (Poem,) 473.
Jackson, "Stonewall," 379.
Jeffrey, Rosa Vertner, 33.
Jeffrey, Alexander, 34.
Jephthah's Daughter, 368.
Jenkins, D. C., 5.
Jessie Graham, 225.
Jean to Jamie, (Poem,) 493.
Jervey, Caroline Howard, 469.
Jervey, Louis, 469.
Jones, Dabney, 204.
Jones, General Samuel, 498.
Jordan, Mrs. Cornelia J. M., 423.
Jordan, Francis H., 424.
Journal, Louisville, 414.
Joseph the Second and his Court, 244.
Jourdan's Cook-Book, Mrs., 188.
Judith, 294, 492.
Junkin, Margaret, 379.
Junkin, Rev. George, 379.
Julia Sleeping, (Poem,) 470.

KALOOLAH, 549.
  Kampa Thorpe, 248.
Kenan, Kate Clifford, 229.
Kermode, Tamar A., 543.
Keplinger, Mrs. E. M., 138.
Keplinger, Samuel, 138.
Ketchum, Mrs. Annie Chambers, 357.
Key, Francis Scott, 115.
Keyes, Julia L., 265.
Keyes, Colonel Washington, 297.
Keyes, Joseph M., 297.
Kimball, Mrs. Leonard, 311.
Kindness, (Poem,) 170.
King's Stratagem, The, 538.
King, W. H. C., 139.

King, Henry, 463,
King, Judge Mitchell, 463.
King, Mrs. Sue Petigru, 463.
Kitty's Tales, Aunt, 225.
Knickerbocker Magazine, 463.
Knights of the Horseshoe, 8.
Körner's Battle Prayer, (Poem,) 529.

LA Tenella, 445.
  Lacy, General Edward, Life of, 517.
Lady of Virginia, A, 403.
Lady of Ashurst, 30.
Lady Hildegarde's Wedding, 388.
Lady of the Isle, 541.
Ladies' Southern Florist, 518.
Ladies' Home, 357.
Ladies' Home Gazette, 202.
Lady Tartuffe, The, 539.
Ladd, Mrs. Catharine, 489.
Lalla De Vere, 202.
Lamartine, 536.
Lanman's Adventures in the Wilds of America, 106, 255.
"Land We Love," 281.
Lansdowne, 421.
La Roche, Dr. Rene, 19.
Last Days of the War in North Carolina, 454.
Last Scene, The, (Poem,) 173.
Last Wild Flower, The, 95.
Latona, 68.
Latienne, 242.
Lauries at Home, 81.
Laura Lorrimer, 285.
Law, Miss Annie E., 377.
Le Vert, Mrs. Octavia Walton, 178, 291.
Le Vert, Dr. Henry S., 291.
Lee, Eliza, 516.
Lee, Rev. S. M., 414.
Lee, Robert E., 379.
Lee, Mary Elizabeth, 13.
Lee, Eleanor Percy, 7.
Lee, Edith, 158.
Lee, General, and Santa Claus, 142.
Le Clerc, Clara, 204.
Le Clerc, 161.
Legare, Hugh S., 151.
Legend of Don Roderick, 89.
Leila Cameron, 176.
Leola, 177.
Legend of Sour Lake, 553.
Leisure Moments, 10.
Letters to Relatives and Friends on the Trinity, 476.
Letters of Eliza Wilkinson, 468.
Letter addressed to Mrs. Woodhull, A, 297.
Lennox, Mary, 232.
Leonard, Agnes, 39.
Leonard, Dr. O. L., 39.
Leroy, 503.
Leverett, 166.
Lewis, Estella Anna, 534.
Lewis, S. D., 534.

Little Episcopalian, 256.
Literary Crusader, 321.
Literature, Studies in, 70.
Lily of the Valley; or, Margie and I, 14.
L'Inconnue, 240, 348.
Lloyd, Mrs. Annie Creight, 247.
Lloyd, Wm. E., 247.
Living Christianity Delineated, 12.
Locust Dell, 265.
Lochlin, 171.
Logan, Mrs. Martha, 12.
Lola, 182.
Lofty and the Lowly, 225.
Lost Heiress, 541.
Loew's Bridge, A Broadway Idyl, 169.
Lotus, 357.
Lost Deeds, The, 30.
Lost Diamonds, 484.
Lewis, Colonel John L., 121.
Life of General Lee for Youth, 440.
Life and Campaigns of General Lee, 415.
Life's Mission, 182.
Life's Curse, 30.
Life and Writings of Mrs. Jameson, 128.
Life of M. M. Pomeroy, 169.
Life's Changes, 294.
Light and Darkness, 430.
Linda Lee, 460.
Lily, 463.
Little Match-Girl, The, 484.
Loughborough, Mary W., 315.
Louisville Journal, 35, 39, 170, 414.
Lost Treasure, (Poem,) 530.
Love Letter, The, (Poem,) 103.
Love's Stratagem, 127.
Love's Labor Won, 541.
Lover's Quarrel, A, 464.
Lucia Dare, 79.
Lucy Ellice, 137.
Luola, 459.
Lyle Annot, 294.
Lyle Currer, 343.

McABOY, Mrs. Mary R. T., 54.
McAdo, W. G., 170, 377.
McAdo, Mrs. Mary F., 237.
McBride, Mrs. Julia, 317.
McClure, Dr. Virgil, 71.
McCabe, Mrs. Mary, 415.
McCabe, James D., Jr., 415.
McCord, Louisa S., 518.
McCord, D. J., 518.
McClanahan, Saml. G., 513.
McCrimmon, Mrs. Mary A., 212.
McGuire, Miss J. W., 403.
McGuire, Rev. John P., 403.
McIntosh, Maria J., 223, 229.
McIntosh, Major Lachlan, 224.
McIntosh, Captain James M., 224.
McKinne, Mary Eugenie, 440.
McLeod, Georgie A. Hulse, 531.
McLeod, Dr. A. W., 531.
McMahon, Colonel J. H., 374.
D

McMahon, Mary Ann, 488.
McPhail, Rev. G. Wilson, 421.
Mabbit Thorn, 419.
Macaria; or, Altars of Sacrifice, 273.
Madison, Virginia, 405.
Madison Family Visitor, 284.
Magill, Mary Tucker, 438.
Magnolia Weekly, 343.
Maiden Widow, 542.
Malony, Mary Teresa, 154.
" Mammy : " A Home Picture of 1860, 352.
Manheim, Louise, 207.
Mara, 171.
Marble Lily, The, (Poem,) 565.
March, Prof. F. A., 422.
Mardis, Hon. Samuel Wright, 161.
Margaret, (Poem,) 478.
Marshall, Annie Mary, 157.
Marshall, Humphrey, 49.
Marshall, Nelly, 49.
Marie's Mistake, 154.
Maria del Occidente, 3.
Marguerite; or, Two Loves, 448.
Mary Bunyan; or, The Dreamer's Blind
    Daughter, 58.
Mary Austin; or, The New Home, 14.
Mayfield, Millie, 110.
Martin, Mrs. Sallie M., 202.
Martin, George W., 202.
Martin, Margaret Maxwell, 485.
Martin, Rev. William, 485.
Mary Ashburton, 542.
Maryland Farm-House, 542.
Mason, Emily V., 439.
Mason, Mary, 454.
Massena, Mrs. A. M. C., 154.
Masonic Signet and Journal, 284.
Matthews, Cornelia Jane, 423.
Matthews, Edwin, 423.
Mayflower, Minnie, 489.
May Rie, 123.
Maynard, Mrs. S. E., 549.
Means, Selina E., 512.
Means, Dr. T. Sumter, 518.
Mendelssohn's Songs, 492.
Mépsisé, (Poem,) 159.
Memories, (Poem,) 377.
Men, Women, and Beasts, 39.
Meredith, Rev. Thomas, 200.
Merton, 30.
Meta Gray, 225.
Messenger, Lilian Rozell, 261.
Metcalfe, Amanda, 376.
Metcalfe, Barnett, 376.
Methodism; or, Christianity in Earnest,
    486.
Meriwether, Dr. Charles Hunter, 71.
Messenger, Southern Literary, 8, 418.
Miller, Mary Ayer, 459.
Miller, Willis M., 459.
Mine, 532.
Minding the Gap, (Poem,) 561.
Mintzing, Miss Julia C., 506.

Minor, B. B., 8.
Minor Place, 296.
Miriam, 434.
Miss Barber's Weekly, 284.
Missing Bride, 541.
Mobile Sunday Times, 205, 247, 340.
Moffett, Emma, 180.
Moffett, Major Henry, 181.
Mollie Myrtle, 39, 241.
Montanas, The, 68.
Minstrel Pilot, The, (Poem,) 108.
Miserere, (Poem,) 326.
Miriam, 401.
Moore's Anecdotes and Incidents of the
    War, Frank, 197.
Moore, Miss Mollie E., 295, 555.
Moore, Dr., 517.
Moriarty, Ellen A., 136.
Moriarty, Eliza, 136.
Mina, 98.
Morna, 489.
Mosely, Mrs. Mary Webster, 9.
Motherhood, (Poem,) 158.
Mother's Wish, A, (Poem,) 297.
Mother's Prayer, A, (Poem,) 358.
Morton House, 461.
Morna Elverley; or, Outlines of Life, 458.
Morning Dreams, (Poem,) 240.
Moss-Side, 434.
Mosses from a Rolling Stone, 443.
Motte Hall, 478.
Mother-in-Law, 541.
Mühlbach, L., 245.
Muni Tell, 70.
Murray, Hon. Miss, 446.
Murdaugh, Hon. John W., 455.
Mrs. Hill's New Cook-Book, 236.
Myths of the Minstrels, 536.
My Saviour, Thee, (Poem,) 487.
My Roses: A Romance of a June Day, 352.
Mystery of Cedar Bay, The, 324.
My Cousin Anne, 133.
My Penny Dip, 145.
Mysterious Marriage, 30.
Myrtle Blossoms, 39.
My Wedding Ring, (Poem,) 48.
Mystery, 189.
Myers, Rev. Dr., 296.
My Palace of Dreams, (Poem,) 513.

NALLEY, Rev. G. W., 414.
    Nation, 68.
National Quarterly Review, 537.
Nashville Christian Advocate, 4.
Nameless, 457.
Natchitoches Times, 323.
Neale, Flora, 531.
Neale, Nellie, 401.
Nereid, The, 237.
Neighborhood, Country, 30.
Nelly Bracken, 357.
Nemesis, 434.
Neria, 428.

Nests at Washington, and Other Poems,
    47.
New Year's Prayer, My, (Poem,) 305.
New Orleans Mirror, 4.
New York Ledger, 31.
New York Evangelist, 58.
New York Tribune, 168.
New York Sunday Times, 168.
" Nobody Hurt," 455.
Non Dolet: a Sonnet, 386.
Norton, Mrs., 3.
Norfolk Herald, 418.
" None but the Brave deserve the Fair,"
    281.
Not a Hero, 119.
Nothing Unusual, 492.
Novels and Novelists, (Extract,) 152.
Nott, Dr. Josiah C., 517.
Nott, Prof. Henry Junius, 517.
Novelettes of a Traveller, 517.

OCCUPATION of Richmond, The, 411.
    O'Hara, Theodore, 34.
Old Brigade, (Poem,) 546.
Old Songs and New, 379.
Old Landlord's Daughter, 14.
Old Story, An, 137.
Old, Old Story, The, 531.
Ollivar, Janie, 240.
On Dress, 208.
Oneiropion, (Poem,) 238.
Opportunity, (Review,) 523.
Osborn, Colonel Wm. C., 233.
Our Little Annie, 492.
Our Refugee Household, 142.
Outlaw's Bride, 30.
Over the River, (Poem,) 139.
Old Wharf at Pine Bluff, (Poem,) 262.
Overall, J. W., 5, 115, 312.

PALMER, Henrietta Lee, 539.
    Palmer, Dr. J. W., 539.
Palmer, Rev. B. M., 4, 75.
Palmer, Mary Stanly Bunce, 475.
Paper-Collar Gentility, 221.
Parke Richards, 428.
Partisan Leader, The, 8, 438.
Parted Family, and Other Poems, 476.
Pastimes with my Little Friends, 10.
Pastor's Household, 176.
Patterson, Mary, 303.
Pearl Rivers, 311.
Pearl; or, The Gem of the Vale, 247.
Peck, Sarah E., 264.
Penny, Virginia, 67.
Perry, Ex-Governor B. F., 513.
Perfect through Suffering, 457.
Percy, Charles, 18.
Percy, Sarah, 18.
Perine, Mary Eliza, 164.
Perine, Edward M., 164.
Perdita: a Romance of the War, 433.
Petit, Lizzie, 430.

Petigru, John James L., 463.
Planter's Daughter, 30.
Planet Lustra, The, 26.
Pleasant Hill, (Poem,) 87.
Phemie's Temptation, 435.
Philip Arion's Wife, 39.
Philanthropist, 403.
Principle and Policy, 403.
Piatt, Sarah M. B., 46.
Piatt, John J., 47.
Piggot, Margaret, 120.
Pinckney, Miss Maria, 13.
Pleasants, John Hampton, 105.
Pleasants, Governor James, 105.
Pleasants, Hugh R., 105.
Pleasants, Tarleton, 106.
Plea for Red Hair, A : by a Red-Haired Woman, 218.
Pocahontas : A Legend, 9.
Pope, Mrs. Mary E., 371.
Pope, Lieutenant W. S., 371.
Poe, Edgar Allan, 3, 8, 316.
Poe's Literati, 3, 534.
Poems by Two Sisters of the West, 21.
Poems by Rosa, 34.
Poems by Mary E. Tucker, 168.
Poems by Matilda, 415.
Poetry of Travelling in the United States, 468.
Poet-Skies, and Other Experiments in Versification, 502.
Poitevent, Miss Eliza J., 311.
Popinack, 458.
Porter, Ina M., 281.
Porter, Judge B. F., 281.
Poyas, Catharine Gendron, 515.
Praise and Principle, 225.
Preston, Margaret J., 357, 379.
Preston, Colonel J. T. L., 380.
Prentice, Geo. D., 2, 70.
Prentiss, S. S., 29.
Prince of Seir, The, 377.
Progression ; or, The South Defended, 114.
Proem : To the World, 47.
Pugh, Eliza Lofton, 118.
Prairie, A Texan, 78.

QUESTIONS, (Poem,) 50.
Queen of Hearts, 138.
Quillotypes, 144.

RACHEL'S What-Not, 100.
Raids and Romance of Morgan and his Men, 58.
Ramsay, Mrs. Martha Laurens, 12.
Rayon d'Amour, 68.
Random Readings, 100.
Rankin, McKee, 149.
Rankin, Rev. Jesse, 459.
Randall, James R., 273.
Randolph Honor, (Review,) 500.
Reade, Judge Edwin G., 442.
Reeves, Marian C. Legare, 498.

Recollections of a New England House-keeper, 468.
Recollections of a Southern Matron, 468.
Recollections of Governor Allen, 74.
Reedy, Captain James, 299.
Reflected Fragments, 4.
Refugeeing, 80.
Refugitta, 398.
Records of the Heart, 534.
Reginald's Revenge, 420.
Register, Mobile, 461.
Reginald Archer, 526.
Reid, Christian, 461.
"Reliquæ," 13.
Religious Poems, 486.
Rena, 343.
Reminiscences of Cuba, 448.
Reminiscences of York, by a Septuagenarian, 517.
Renunciation, (Poem,) 478.
Requiem, (Poem,) 360.
Retribution, 541.
Rion, Mrs. Mary C., 518.
Ring, My Wedding, (Poem,) 48.
Richards, Rev. Wm., 175.
Richards, T. Addison, 176.
Richardson, M., 142.
Rimmer, (Poem,) 282.
Rip Van Winkle, (Poem,) 149.
Richmond : Her Glory and her Graves, 425.
Ritchie, Anna Cora Mowatt, 9.
Ripley, Julia Caroline, 477.
Ripley, Wm. Y., 477.
Rivals, The : A Tale of the Chickahominy, 399.
Richmond during the War, 404.
Rives, Mrs. Wm. C., 436.
Rives, Hon. Wm. Cabell,,436.
River, San Marcos, (Poem,) 556.
Ripley, Mrs. M. A. Ewart, 488.
Ripley, Colonel V., 488.
Riverlands, 492.
Roadside Stories, 282.
Romance of Indian Life, 8.
Romance of the Green Seal, 25.
"Rosa," 34.
Robinson Delmonte, 534.
Round Table, 79, 148, 244, 248, 276, 376, 435, 499, 500.
Rose and Lillie Stanhope, 225.
Rose-Bud, 468.
Ross, John, 29.
Rogers, Norman, 110.
Rogers, M. Louise, 342.
Rogers, Dr. C., 179.
Rogers, Loula Kendall, 177.
Royal Recluse, 12.
Royal Cavalcade, The, (Poem,) 314.
Ruined Lives, 368.
Rutledge, Emma Middleton, 13.
Ruth, 236.
Ruth Raymond ; or, Love's Progress, 468.
Ryan, Rev. A. J., 436.

Russell's Magazine, 463.
Ruby's Husband, 435.

SCOTT'S Magazine, 180.
Scanland, Dr. S. E., 42.
Scrimzeour, Sir Alexander, 480.
Seaton, Gales, 445.
Seals, John, 321.
Sea-Drift, 502, 531.
Seclusaval; or, The Arts of Romanism, 368.
Secret Chamber, 30.
Secret, Family, 30.
Seemuller, Mr., 526.
Sentinel of Pompeii, The, (Poem,) 174.
Sergeant Dale, 273.
Shackelford, W. F., 98.
Shaw, Dr. John, 115.
Shindler, Mrs. Mary S. B., 475.
Shindler, Rev. Robt. D., 476.
Shelton, Mrs. Julia, 285.
Sheppard, Elizabeth Sara, 492.
Sibyl, 202.
Siege of Murany, (Poem,) 340.
Sigoigne, Madame, 20.
Silverwood: a Book of Memories, 380.
Simkins, Colonel Arthur, 492.
Sisters, The, 183.
Simonton, Anna Frances, 516.
Sincerity in Talking, 193.
Sinclair, Carrie Bell, 196.
Sinclair, Rev. Elijah, 196.
Simms's War Poetry of the South, 281.
Simms, W. Gilmore, 12, 438, 485.
Simons, Alice F., 479.
Sketches of Southern Literature, 415.
Sleeping, (Poem,) 495.
Smith, Rev. B. M., 434.
Smith, Robert White, 165.
Smith, Rev. Geo. G., 503.
Smiley, Matilda Caroline, 414.
So Long Ago, (Poem,) 544.
Sonnet, 516.
Sophisms of the Protective Policy, 518.
Southworth, Mrs. Emma D. E. N., 541.
Southern Poems of the War, 440.
Southern Society, 422.
Souvenirs of Travel, 292.
Souvenirs of a Residence in Europe, 437.
Southern Girl's Homespun Dress, 197.
Southern Villegiatura, A, 80.
Southern Opinion, 403.
"Southland Writers," 6.
South Carolina Gazette, 10.
South, The, 128.
Southern Monthly, The, (Memphis,) 127, 304, 365.
Southern Literary News, 161.
Southern Literary Companion, 184, 284.
Southern Field and Fireside, 268, 273, 285.
Southern Literature, On, 504.
Spencer, Dr. D. M., 366.
Spencer, Miss Eliza, 542.

Spencer, Cornelia Phillips, 454.
Spirit-Mates, 431.
Spirit-Landscapes, (Poem,) 70.
Spirit-Whisperings, 309.
Spotswood, Dr. John C., 296.
Standing Guard, 531.
Stanford, Mrs. Mary, 303.
Stranger's Stratagem; or, The Double Deceit, 420.
St. Philip's, 120.
St. Elmo, 276.
Stark, A. B., 169.
Stella Letters, 538.
Stephens, Hon. Alexander H., 234.
Stealing Roses through the Gate, (Poem,) 560.
Stibbes, Mrs. Agnes Jean, 214.
Stilling, Margaret, 400.
Still Faithful, 492.
Stonewall Jackson's Way, 539.
Stockton, Rev. Thomas H., 10.
Stratton, Catharine, 489.
Stratford Gallery, (Review,) 540.
Studies in Literature, 2, 70.
Student of Blenheim Forest, 14.
Sturdevant, Captain Joel, 28.
Sturges, Mr., 419.
Stuart Leigh, 448.
Sunnybank, 435.
Summer Memory, A, 472.
Summer Idyl, A, (Poem,) 251.
Summer Noonday Dreams, 392.
Sunset Musings, (Poem,) 456.
Summer Retreat of a Southern Planter, 482.
Swain, Margie P., 171.
Swift, Miss, 106.
Sylvia's World, 463.
Sybil Huntingdon, 477.

TALES for the Freemason's Fireside, 284.
Tales of the Weird and Wonderful, 26.
Tale of the Pearl-Trader, 26.
Tales and Legends of Louisiana, 87.
Tales and Ballads, 468.
Talking, 191.
Terhune, M. Virginia, 433.
Terhune, Rev. E. P., 434.
Tears on the Diadem, 14.
Tenella, La, 445.
Temperance Crusader, 204.
Temperance Lyre, 477.
Ten Years Outre Mer, 538.
Thine and Mine; or, The Stepmother's Reward, 531.
Thackeray, Wm. Makepeace, 463.
Thomas, Sarah Brewer, 5.
Three Bernices; or, Ansermo of the Crag, 376.
Three Golden Links, 284.
Think and Act, 67.
Thompson, John R., 8.

Thoughts about Talking, 193.
Thou art Growing Old, Mother, (Poem,) 374.
Timothy, Lewis, 10.
Timrod, Henry, 492.
To the Memory of Captain Herndon, (Poem,) 195.
To my Absent Husband, 266.
Townsend, Mary Ashly, 144.
Townsend, Gideon, 144.
Townsend, Cora, 144.
Towles, Catherine W., 283.
Towles, Hon. John C., 284.
Trials of May Brooke, 14.
Trials of an Orphan, 294.
Transition, (Poem,) 253.
Triumphs of Spring, 446.
Triumphant, 503.
Treatise on Gardening, 12.
Tried for her Life, 542.
Tucker, Mary E., 163.
Tucker, Beverly, 8, 438.
Tucker, Judge St. George, 438.
Three Beauties, 541.
Two Sisters, 541.
Two Lives; or, To Seem and To Be, 225.
Two Angels, The, (Poem,) 300.
Two Heroines; or, Freaks of Fortune, 549.
Types of Mankind, 517.

UNDER the Stones, 144.
Under the Lamplight, (Poem,) 185.
Under the Oaks, 401.
Unattainable, The, 189.
Unknown, (Poem,) 198.
Unknown, 517.
Under the Leaves, 362.
Undertow: a Sonnet, 387.
Upshur, Mary J. S., 416.
Upshur, Wm. Stith, 416.
Upshur, Judge Abel P., 416.

VALERIE Aylmer, 461.
Vance, Sallie Ada, 299.
Vanitas, (Poem,) 172.
Van Voorhises, 144.
Van Wickle, J. C., 144.
Vanquished, (Review,) 40.
Vashti; or, Until Death Us do Part, 280.
Vendel, Emile de, 244.
Verses of a Lifetime, 468.
Vernon Grove; or, Hearts as They Are, 469.
Victor and Victim, (Poem,) 507.
Virginia Zulaine, 12.
Violet; or, The Cross and Crown, 225, 228.
Violetta and I, 229.
Viola, 455.
Vine, My, (Poem,) 295.
Virginia, 403.
Vick, Captain Joseph, 440.

Village, A Virginia, (1861,) 428.
Vivia; or, The Secret of Power, 541.

WAGGLE, Sam, 157.
Waddell, John, 440.
Walker, Judge Alexander, 5, 144.
Wallis S. Teakle, 447.
Wakelee, Miss Kate C., 194.
Waking of the Blind Girl by the Tones of the Grand Organ, 257.
Walthall, Major W. T., 245, 248.
Walker, Miss, 296.
Walker, Judith Page, 436.
Walker, Colonel Francis, 437.
Warfield, Mrs. Catharine A., 17.
Ward, Hon. John, 225.
Ware, Mary, 292.
Way it all Ended, The, 433.
Weiss, Mrs. S. A., 391.
Weimar, 552.
Welby, Amelia B., 3.
West, Florence D., 565.
Westmoreland, Maria J., 188.
Westmoreland, Dr. W. F., 189.
What is Life? (Poem,) 407.
Whig, Richmond, 417.
Whipple, E. P., 519.
Whitaker, Mary S., 480.
Whitaker, Daniel K., 5, 481.
Whitaker, Lily, 482.
Whittlesey, Miss Sarah J. C., 420.
White, Thomas W., 8.
Whiting, General John, 6.
Why do I Love Him? (Poem,) 152.
White Camelia, The, (Poem,) 505.
Wife, The, (Poem,) 100.
Wife's Victory, 541.
Willard, Mrs. Florence J., 148.
Williams, Marie Bushnell, 85.
Williams, Josiah P., 86.
Williams, Dr. R. D., 129.
Williams, Mrs. Bessie W., 205.
Will's a Widower, (Poem,) 241.
Wiley, Mrs. Mary, 400.
Windle, Mrs. Catharine F., 151.
Windle, Geo. W., 151.
Windle, Mary J., 151.
Wind Whispers, 348.
Winter Wind, (Poem,) 527.
Wilson, L. M., 280.
Wood Notes, 449.
World of the Ideal, (Poem,) 54.
Words to a "Lied ohne Worte," (Poem,) 526.
Woman in America: Her Work and her Reward, 225.
Woman an Enigma, 225.
Women of France, The, 203.
Women, Employments of, 67.
Women, Five Hundred Employments adapted to, 67.
Woman: Her Education, Aims, Sphere, Influence, and Destiny, 369.

" Women of the South," by Mary Forrest, 57, 347, 391.
Worthington, Jane Taylor, 9.
Woodbine, Jenny, 183.
Wreath of Rhymes, A, 116.
Woodson, Mary E., 433.
Wynne, Emma Moffett, 180.

X ARIFFA, 144.
Xariffa's Poems, 145.
XIXth Century, 458.

Y ALE Literary Magazine, 473.
Yeiser, Sarah C., 161.

Yeiser, Dr. Philip, 161.
Yule, 434.
Young Housewife's Counsellor and Friend, 454.
Young Sailor, 477.
Yorkville Enquirer, 479.
" Year of Grief," 515.
Young, Mrs. Maud J., 551.

Z AIDEE, 505.
Zimmerman, Mrs. Bettie M., 200.
Zena Clifton, 262.
Zenaida, 53.

INTRODUCTORY.

THIS record of the "Living Female Writers of the South" is intended to embody the names and works of all those ladies who have written for publication, and been recognized as "writers" in the Southern States.

Few of the "writers" sketched have made a profession of literature; that is, have made writing the means whereby they earn a subsistence. From the Southern portion of the United States come the most popular of the Female Novelists of America.

Although literature in the South is in its youth, there is a bloom of youthful vigor and glowing enthusiasm about it, giving promise for the future. Yet dilettanteism — the treating literature as if it were the amusement of an idle hour, instead of a most grave and serious pursuit, on the right following of which, to a great extent, our people's intellectual life depends — has been the bane of Southern literature; this, and the eulogy of many editors, whose politeness and amiability would not let them see the mischief they were doing. It is incumbent upon the press of the South to try to redress this evil; to stimulate those who write tolerably, to write well if they can; and those who write well, to write better; and gently but firmly to repress those who have mistaken their vocation.

What has given the literature of France its brilliancy, that of Germany its depth of learning, and that of England its clear rationality, but the presence of a competent and exigent criticism?

In this collection will be found record of Southern writers, good, bad, and indifferent. I have not pretended to pick the chaff from the wheat. I have made record of such writers as have written and published sufficient to form a volume, and told the world who they are, and what they have done, and left it to conclude what it has a right to expect from them in the future.

The pages following show that in the South we have creative art; but we have not that art of criticism which comes from culture and study.

It is but meet and right to give a superficial glance at those "female writers of the South" who are no longer among the living; and of those of whom little is known, who may be among the living.

The enterprise of the South in journalism can hardly be complained of, if we estimate it by the number of efforts made.

The late George D. Prentice, distinguished as poet and journalist, (born at Griswold, Conn., on December 18, 1802, removed to Louisville, September, 1830, and on the 24th day of November following published the first number of the *Louisville Journal*: died January 21, 1870,) by private correspondence, and timely notices in his Journal, caused many a blossom of poetry to blow in hearts that might otherwise only have worn a purple crown of thistles. Of many of these poets the pages following bear record. George D. Prentice exercised a wide influence in the field of literature. To quote from Mr. George W. Griffin's "Studies in Literature:"* "The affluence of Mr. Prentice in genius and in equipments of education seemed to be wellnigh endless. He was as generous in the beneficent use of his intellectual wealth as he was great in the magnitude of its possession. Those who knew him intimately, during his editorial career in Louisville, can easily call up from the storehouse of memory a hundred examples of his judicious, unstinted, and benevolent kindness to young aspirants for fame."

---

* Second edition, revised, (Claxton, Remsen & Haffelfinger,) Philadelphia, 1871.

The lovely song-bird "Amelia" was one of Mr. Prentice's most noted protégées.

AMELIA B. WELBY, whose maiden name was Coppuck, was born in the town of St. Michael's, Md., in 1821, and died at Lexington, Ky., May 2, 1852. When she was about fourteen years of age, her father removed to Kentucky. She married, in 1838, Mr. George B. Welby, of Louisville. Through Mr. Prentice, "Amelia's" poems were introduced to the public.

A collection of her poems was published in 1844, which passed through four large editions. In 1850, Appleton & Co., New York, published her poems in one handsome volume, illustrated.

Edgar A. Poe, in his "Literati," says: "Mrs. Welby has nearly all the imagination of Maria del Occidente, with a more refined taste; and nearly all of the passion of Mrs. Norton, with a nicer ear, and equal art. Very few American poets are at all comparable with her in the true poetic qualities. . . .

"There are some poets in America (Bryant and Sprague, for example) who equal Mrs. Welby in the negative merits of that limited versification which they chiefly affect — the iambic pentameter; but none equal her in the richer and positive merits of rhythmical variety, conception, invention. They, in the old routine, rarely err. She often surprises, and always delights, by novel, rich, and accurate combination of the ancient musical expression."

An author, whose books achieved popularity of the purest and rarest type — "books that are the evident product of intellect and culture; full of vigor, as well as the most delicate grace and perception — the portraiture showing the graphic and true lines of a master, and her works all touched with the issues of a refined, womanly, and religious spirit"*—has recently been called from her ministry here to a heavenly home. I allude to

JANE TANDY CHINN CROSS, who was born in Harrodsburg, Ky., in 1817, and died in the same town, October, 1870.

* Mary Forrest.

At a youthful age Miss Chinn was married to James P. Hardin, of Kentucky. He died in 1842, leaving his widow with three children. In 1848, Mrs. Hardin was married to the Rev. Dr. Cross, who survives her.

With her husband, she made a tour to Europe, and corresponded with the *Nashville Christian Advocate*. This series of letters was published under the title of " Reflected Fragments." It was about 1851 before Mrs. Cross commenced writing for publication.

Her books are four volumes for children, and " Duncan Adair; or, Captured in Escaping;" "Azile: A Story," Nashville, 1868.

Mrs. Cross wrote a great deal for periodicals, in prose and verse, and translated in a masterly manner, from the Spanish of Florian, " Gonzalvo de Cordova; or, The Conquest of Granada."

" Azile," her most ambitious effort, is a quiet story, straightforward, growing in interest to the close. The scene of the first part is in Dresden. There is some fine-art criticism, and a deal of information about the customs and habits of the German people, their amusements and recreations. The scene is transferred to the Southern States at the beginning of the war, (1860,) and ends with the first battle of Manassas. Mrs. Cross's picture of life in the South, during that time of revulsion and enthusiasm, is true in conception. Her style was clear, smooth, and lively; and knowing Jean Paul, she was an enthusiastic admirer of him.

The minor writers of Kentucky, who have no mention in this volume, and are not among the living, are few in number. Among the dead may be mentioned MARY WILSON BETTS. She was born about 1830, near Maysville, Ky. At the time of her marriage (1854) to Morgan L. Betts, editor of the *Detroit Times*, she was one of the most popular of the younger writers of the South. "Mrs. Betts was widely admired as a young poet whose writings gave promise of decided excellence." She died suddenly, September 16, 1854.

The New Orleans Mirror — a literary journal established by Mark F. Bigney, a poet and journalist, (at this time editor of the *New*

Orleans Times, was a medium for the *début* of several of the female writers of the South. I believe the suspension of this weekly paper was caused by the war. There have been a vast number of literary journals started in New Orleans — short-lived — and it would be of little benefit to attempt to enumerate the titles. Frequent mention is made in the following pages of the Sunday issues of the New Orleans daily papers, which contain much that is worthy of preservation in a more permanent form. D. C. Jenkins, Judge Walker, Alexander Dimitry, J. W. Overall, M. F. Bigney, D. K. Whitaker, W. M. Burwell, Durant DuPonte, and other less known writers are employed editorially on the New Orleans press.

There are several authors resident in Louisiana, of Northern birth, who have made the Pelican State their home, and might be classed as among the writers of the South, whose names do not appear in this volume.

SARAH BREWER, born in Wilbraham, Mass., 1793, came South over fifty years ago, to establish institutions for the education of the daughters of the South. She married Captain David Thomas, of Jackson, La., and after his death, in 1849, removed to New Orleans, which she made her home. In 1857, Mrs. Thomas crossed the Atlantic, and made a tour of England, Scotland, Ireland, France, etc., and prepared for publication (J. B. Lippincott & Co., Philadelphia, 1860) " Travels in Europe, Egypt, and Palestine."

Mrs. Thomas is the oldest living female writer of the South — nearly eighty years of age. She has an earnest desire to aid in building up a Southern literature. She has on hand MSS. for a volume of poems, collected from periodicals to which she occasionally contributed. New Orleans is her home.

Since this volume has been printed, Mrs. SOPHIE A. DuPONTE, *née* Brook, of New Orleans, has published a translation of " Callirhoé," (Claxton, Remsen & Haffelfinger, Philadelphia,) one of the novels of Maurice Sand, son of Madame Dudevant, of whose *nom de plume* he has claimed inheritance. Mrs. DuPonte's translation is excellent. Mrs. DuPonte is the wife of Durant DuPonte, of the New Orleans press.

Georgia, styled the "Empire State," is certainly the empress of the Southern States as regards the number of female writers, and from having been the home of the most successful literary journals of the South, and whose literary light burned brighter and longer.

In the "SOUTHLAND WRITERS," published in 1869, a brief notice is made of MARY CATHARINE BIGBY, born in Newnan, Ga., and resident in that charming town; the author of many gems of verse, and several prize poems. Mrs. Bigby died at Newnan, July 23, 1870.

Alabama's literary journals have been few and of brief existence. The people of this State are a commercial rather than a literary people; and, to quote the language of the late Hon. Alexander B. Meek, poet and historian, "Until a taste for the fine arts is excited, when that mighty, slumbering attribute of the mind — its only immortal part — the ideal, is stirred, and not till then, may we hope for a native literature; a literature that shall redeem and illustrate this cotton-growing region. All previous efforts will be a wasteful dissemination of pearls. You might as well scatter, with the vain hope of vegetation, the delicate seed of the chrysanthemum or the dahlia upon the sandy slopes of the Chandeleur Isles."

A few periodical works have been maintained in Alabama for a time, by the efforts of an exalted purpose upon the part of the publishers; but they have met with no adequate and spirited patronage, and have ceased to exist, and soon been forgotten.

Alabama has had authors — now not among the living — of whom we are proud. Meek, from the southern part of the State; from Middle Alabama, Pickett; and Jere Clemens, from a northern county, were a distinguished trio.

" A very distinguished and sweet daughter of Southern literature was CAROLINE LEE HENTZ. She was the daughter of General John Whiting, of Massachusetts, and in 1825 married Mr. Hentz, who was at one time a professor at Chapel Hill College. Her destiny was cast with the South, where she preferred to live, and to end a delicate existence, amid the magnolia flowers, whose pure and gentle zephyrs mingled their aroma with her dying breath. Her productions are pure fiction, simple and true, drawn from the heart, and highly illustrative of the unstained elements of Southern society, manners, and morals. They are domestic tales, which reflect the best features of home life, and are true, because drawn from the fountains of nature. The authoress does not strike for the bolder region of historic romance, but relies upon a truthful and appreciative sense of the affections, which she handles with delightful delicacy." *

Mrs. Hentz passed many useful years in Alabama; first, at Locust Dell, near Florence, Ala., (of which homestead her elder daughter charmingly sang in after years,) where she was in charge of a female academy for nine years — afterward at Tuscaloosa, and then for three years at the pleasant town of Tuskegee. Mrs. Hentz died in 1856, at Columbus, Ga.

Mrs. ANGELE DE V. HULL, who resided in Mobile, and died there, was a favorite contributor for several years to *Graham's Magazine* and other literary journals. She was a sister of Mrs. Adelaide De V. Chaudron, a sketch of whom opens the record of living female writers of Alabama.

In Natchez, the gay-society town of Mississippi in years agone, the lovely, lively ELEANOR PERCY WARE was a belle among noted belles. Miss Ware was the younger sister of Mrs. Catharine A. Warfield, and author jointly with her of the "Wife of Leon, and other Poems," published in 1843, and the "Indian Chamber, and other Poems," (1846.) She married Mr. Henry Lee, a native of Virginia, and resided in Hinds County, Miss., where she died in 1849.

In 1860, S. H. Goetzel & Co., of Mobile, published "Ellen; or, The Fanatic's Daughter," a novel, by Mrs. V. G. COWDEN. This lady was a resident of Mississippi. Her book was not a success.

Virginia, the "Old Dominion" State, is well known for the production of statesmen, jurists, historians, and authors. "The Knights of

* William Archer Cocke, of Virginia.

the Horseshoe " — an interesting tale, founded on colonial life in Virginia in the days of Governor Spottiswoode, in which the author, William A. Caruthers, of Virginia, has given some fine illustrations of the manners, habits, and tastes of the old Virginia settlers — has seemed to me as the Alpha of Virginia fiction.

Judge Beverly Tucker produced two very attractive novels, one of which, " The Partisan Leader," acquired considerable notice during the late war, on account of its political prescience. His nephew, a brave and gallant man with gifted genius, was the author of an interesting historic novel, entitled "Hansford: A Tale of Bacon's Rebellion," and it is a pleasure to tell the readers of the South of a niece of this latter, and grand-niece of the former, who has recently published her first book, " The Holcombes."

The *Southern Literary Messenger*, published in Richmond, under the editorial care of Thomas W. White — the first number published in 1835, and the last in 1864 — was the longest-lived monthly of the South. To this magazine there was a bright constellation of contributors. Its editors, after Mr. White, were B. B. Minor, E. A. Poe, John R. Thompson, George W. Bagby, and F. H. Alfriend; and its contributors embraced the names of men and women now well known wherever the English language is read.

Among the authoresses of Virginia, not elsewhere noted, mention must at least be made of Mrs. MARY H. EASTMAN, daughter of Dr. Thomas Henderson, of the U. S. A., and wife of Captain S. Eastman, of the U. S. A. She was born at Warrenton, Fauquier County, Va. While she was a child, her parents removed to the City of Washington, where she lived until the time of her marriage, which took place at West Point, in 1835. As a companion of her husband at Fort Snelling and other frontier stations, Mrs. Eastman enjoyed excellent opportunities of studying the Indian character, which she has graphically depicted in her four works relating to the Aborigines of America, viz.:

1. Dahcotah; or, Legends of the Sioux. New York, 12mo, 1849.
2. Romance of Indian Life. Philadelphia, 8vo, 1852.

3. Aboriginal Portfolio, illustrated by S. Eastman, U. S. A. 4to, 1853.

4. Chicora, and other Regions of the Conquerors and Conquered. 4to, 1854.

Besides these, Mrs. Eastman, in 1852, published a novel entitled "Aunt Phillis's Cabin," intended as a response to Mrs. Stowe's "Uncle Tom's Cabin." The sale of this book reached eighteen thousand copies in a few weeks. In 1856, she published "Fashionable Life," a novel, the motto of which was—"*But the world! The heart and mind of woman! Every one would like to know something about that!*" Mrs. Eastman has been a frequent contributor to magazines, etc.

Mrs. MARY WEBSTER MOSELY, wife of John G. Mosely, of Richmond, and daughter of Robert Pleasants, wrote for various periodicals, and was highly esteemed for her virtues and literary accomplishments. Her only published work was "Pocahontas," a legend, with historical and traditional notes; issued in 1840. Mrs. Mosely died in Richmond, in 1844, aged 52 years.

Mrs. ANNA CORA MOWATT RITCHIE has been frequently sketched as a Southern authoress, and I am proud to place the name of so gifted a woman upon my pages. Anna Cora Ogden was born in Bordeaux, France, in 1818. When sixteen years of age, she was married to James Mowatt, of New York, a lawyer of wealth and culture. For a history of her eventful and heroic life, the reader is referred to her "Autobiography of an Actress," published first in 1855. Mr. Mowatt died in 1851.

In 1854, Mrs. Mowatt became the wife of William F. Ritchie, at that time editor of the *Richmond Enquirer.*

Mrs. Ritchie published numerous plays and novels that were successful. She died in England, July 26, 1870.

Mrs. JANE TAYLOE WORTHINGTON, wife of Dr. F. A. Worthington, of Ohio, and daughter of Colonel Lomax, of the U. S. A., was a native of Virginia. By the frequent changes of residence involved in military service, she was afforded large opportunities for observation and social and intellectual culture, but she always retained a strong

2

attachment for her native State, and nearly all her writings in prose and verse appeared in the *Southern Literary Messenger* of Richmond. She died in 1847.

Mrs. MARTHA HAINES BUTT BENNETT, born in Norfolk, Va., was the author of several successful volumes. "Leisure Moments," a collection of short tales, essays, and sketches, was published in New York in 1859. She contributed to various periodicals.

In 1865 she was married to Mr. N. J. Bennett, of Bridgeport, Conn

In 1866, Mrs. Bennett published a volume for children, entitled "Pastimes with my Little Friends," (New York, Carleton.) She died in New York in 1871.

Mrs. E. H. EVANS, a sister of the Rev. Thomas H. Stockton, and the wife of Dr. M. H. Evans, of Amelia County, Va., published a volume of poems, (Philadelphia, 1851, 12mo,) and was a contributor to magazines. She is the mother of Mrs. Mary Wiley, who is sketched among the living female writers of Virginia.

The "Old Dominion" State has had a few other female writers who are worthy of mention, whose literary works were popular and attractive, but whose addresses, amid the mighty changes of a few years, it has been impossible to ascertain.

South Carolina has been quite as fruitful of endeavors to establish literary journals as her Southern sisters, and quite as unfortunate, if judged by the financial standard alone. Literary success has often been good, while the financial was not; and in general, the former has been far ahead of the latter.

Journalism in South Carolina dates back about a hundred and thirty years. Its protagonist — to use that word in Mr. Petigru's sense of it — was Mr. Lewis Timothy, who in Charleston established *The South Carolina Gazette*, in the year 1731. Literary periodicals have been less successful, financially speaking, than the political; less than agricultural; and less, if possible, than religious. Experiments, however, have been made in a large variety of spheres, from the heaviest to the lightest; from grave to gay; from the orthodox doctrinal utterances of Church organs, to the flippant *on dits* of village gossip; from the *Magnolia* (not grandiflora) of Mr. Whitaker, to the sweet little *Rosebud* of Mrs. GILMAN; from the solid learning of Legare's *Southern Review*, to the *niaiseries* of Sargent's *Brazen Nose*. In earlier times there were *The Columbian Herald*, *The South Carolina Museum*, *The Monthly Magazine*, *Heriot's Magazine*, and *The Southern Literary Journal* of Mr. Carroll; not to mention some half literary and half political issues. Then there were *Whitaker's Magazine*, or magazines, and afterward *Russell's*. Mrs. Gilman's *Southern Rose* bloomed for a while. Besides, Mr. Simms did earnest and effective work in *The Southern Literary Gazette*, *The Cosmopolitan*, *The Magnolia*, his *Southern and Western Magazine and Review;* and did heroic work on *The Southern Quarterly Review*. All of these lived only for a time. Not one of all the above — and this list of the dead is not complete, and many were meritorious in their way — not one is now living.

In those past days, the great mass of pen-work was done by men. Few of the gentler sex ventured into print. It was not the style. The life of ease, elegance, and leisure, for ladies, in those statelier times, was full of noble and beautiful deeds; but few of those ladies cared for literary laurels, and many seemed to shrink with native delicacy from the *bruit* of authorial notoriety. The number of female writers in the past of the "Palmetto State" is small. About a dozen names, of the few dozens who have written for newspapers, are all that have become authors; and several of these never wrote a line for publication, but their letters or writings were given by others to the world after their lives had closed.

The earliest name that we meet is that of Mrs. SOPHIE HUME, whose "Exhortation to the Inhabitants of the Province of South Carolina, to bring their Deeds to the Light of Christ and their own Consciences," seems to be a pious book, and one of a woman thoroughly in earnest. She dates this volume at "Charles Town, in South Carolina, the 30th of the Tenth Month, 1747 ;" and it was published at Bristol, in England, in 1750. Her "Epistle to the Inhabitants of South Carolina" appeared in 1754, London.

A few years later, in 1760, appears the second name. This is Mrs. MARY HUTSON, *née* Woodward, whose good works live after her in the shape of a small volume — "Living Christianity Delineated in the Diaries and Letters of two Eminently Pious Persons, lately deceased, viz., Mr. Hugh Bryan, and Mrs. Mary Hutson, both of South Carolina." The book is divided into two parts, the second pertaining to Mrs. Hutson.

A decade later, 1770, appeared a "Treatise on Gardening," which had been written by Mrs. MARTHA LOGAN, in her seventieth year.

Later, Mrs. ANNA IZARD DEAS appeared as the editor of the "Correspondence of Mr. Ralph Izard, of South Carolina, from the year 1774 to 1804," which she prefaced with a short memoir of her father. A second volume is still unpublished.

In 1811 was published Dr. David Ramsay's "Memoirs of Mrs. MARTHA LAURENS RAMSAY, with Extracts from her Diary." Of this excellent lady — a daughter of Mr. Henry Laurens, of Revolutionary fame — Mr. Simms says: "Her letters to her son at college are models of their kind. She was a matron and a mother of rare excellence of character, of pure nature, of vigorous thought and fine taste, and richly deserving of that title of strong-minded woman which is so much abused at the present day. Her mind had strength without pretension, grace without flippancy or conceit; and she wrote her morals at once from heart and head, not from the latter alone, and feeling the faith which she so earnestly professed, and conscious of the truth in all the lessons which she taught."

In the earlier years of the present century figured in Charleston society Mrs. CHARLES BARING, a lady of the great banker's family, an actress and author, who wrote "Altorf," "The Royal Recluse," "Virginia Zulaine," and possibly some other dramas. Dr. Simms, who met Mrs. Baring in her old age, says: "She had been a successful actress, and even in her latter days she carried herself with the air of a tragedy queen who had been trained in the excellent but stately school of the famous Siddons."

The subject-matter of Miss MARIA PINCKNEY's work in defence of nullification principles, indicates the force and character of her vigorous and practical mind.

Under the touching and appropriate title of "Reliquæ" are embodied the poems of Mrs. DANIEL BLAKE, *née* Emma Middleton Rutledge. Sprung from a line most illustrious in a State of historic renown, this lady, a daughter of Major Henry M. Rutledge, and grand-daughter both of Arthur Middleton and of Edward Rutledge, whose names grace the Declaration of Independence, was born in 1811, and died in her native Charleston in 1853. Nature, which gave her personal beauty, rare elegance of manner, and unequalled loveliness of disposition, added a childlike unconsciousness, which made her the only one unaware of her great charms, and gave her the divine gift of song. The character of her poetic principle is that vital sympathy with the outer world, which the true poet alone knows. As she herself so happily expresses it, she seemed to hold

> "The fibres of a hidden chain,
> That, linked by thousand sympathies,
> In close communion can enwreathe
> Insensate things with those that breathe;
> .   .   .   .
> As if pure spirit stooped to hold
> Commerce with child of mortal mould."

One rises from the perusal of this dainty volume with a consciousness of something sweetly sad, but fresh and hopeful; with a feeling like the memory of sad music heard at morning, in spring, amid the smiles and odors of early violets. The tone, the thoughts, and the spirit of the book are all the reflex of an accomplished, refined, and gifted Southern woman.

The name of Miss MARY ELIZABETH LEE, her delicacy of constitution, her superb endowments, her physical suffering, her early death, the hue of mingled melancholy and hope that tinges all her genius and her life, these are all fresh in the memories of the host of friends who knew and appreciated her in Charleston. Her "Poems" were published in

1851, two years after her death. She died in her thirty-ninth year, at her home, in Charleston. She had contributed to most of the literary journals of the South, in her day — to *The Southern Rose*, *The Orion*, and *Whitaker's Magazine*, of her native State, and to others not entirely literary.

Besides the "living writers" noted in this volume, there are a few not mentioned on account of the impossibility of obtaining data for a sketch, etc.

Mrs. ANNA H. DORSEY is, I believe, a native of Baltimore. She has been writing for over twenty years, (without any notice of herself or writings, in the numerous "cyclopædias of literature.") She has written dramas, poems, novels, tales and essays, a great many stories for young people, and in all she has shown considerable talent and research. "The Trials of May Brooke," "Tears on the Diadem," "The Old Landlord's Daughter," etc., are the delight of school-girls. Nearly all of the Catholic periodicals have articles from her pen, for she is a most prolific writer.

"The Student of Blenheim Forest," second edition, was published in 1867, (John Murphy & Co., Baltimore.) This story is sad, but beautiful. It opens in Virginia, at Blenheim Forest, the elegant residence of Colonel Clavering, on the banks of the Rappahannock River. The elegant diction and refined taste displayed in this book commend it to cultivated readers.

"The Lily of the Valley; or, Margie and I: and other Poems," by Amy Gray, (Baltimore, Kelly & Piet, 1870.) This little volume contains the first fruits of the imagination of a lady of Maryland, who published the book "to aid in the education of destitute little girls of the South, orphaned by the late war."

"Byrd Lyttle" is the *nom de plume* of a lady of Baltimore, who has contributed charming sketches to Southern magazines, and published one small volume, "Mary Austin; or, The New Home," (Alfred Martien, Philadelphia, 1870.) This book is inscribed to the "Sunday-school Scholars of Memorial Church, Baltimore."

These and perhaps a few others, whose names we find as contributors to the numerous ephemeral periodicals of the past, make up the total of the small number of "female writers" that figure in the literature of the Southern States who are not mentioned in our volume.

The data of this work are correct, and reliable, and carried to the present time. The errors that appeared in the "Southland Writers," I have endeavored to correct. I can only hope this book may meet with as many kind friends as did that, and be of more benefit to our infant Southern Literature.

MOBILE, *June*, 1871.

LIVING
FEMALE WRITERS OF THE SOUTH.

KENTUCKY.

MRS. CATHARINE ANN WARFIELD.

"Genius does what it must, and Talent does what it can."

THESE words of Mr. Lytton sprung involuntarily to our lips when we turned away from the hospitable door of Beech-moor, on the occasion of a recent visit to its gifted mistress. She stood at the door, looking wistfully after our departing carriage, and we watched the calm, gracious, matronly figure, with its well-poised, haughty head, until the last wave of the beautiful white hand was shut from our eyes by the thick groups of spruce and fir-trees which stud the borders of the carriage-drive. The grass was fresh and dewy, glittering with water diamonds, and the tufts of pink and white peonies, the fragrant lilies and early spring roses grouped upon the lawn, filled the morning air with perfumes. As we passed through the gate, the breeze wafted to us a strong breath from the trestled honeysuckle and jasmines that overhung, canopied, and completely curtained in the back porch which adjoined Mrs. Warfield's apartments. It was a sigh of farewell from a spot where we had passed two happy months, — a period for remembrance, when, like the hero Gottreich, of Jean Paul's little tale, we come to make up our " Remembrances of the best hours of Life, for the hour of Death," — when we, too, mean to cheer " ourselves " at our last hour with the views of

3

17

a happy life, and to look back from the glow of evening to the brightness of the morning of our youth; — then we will recall our visit to Beechmoor, and the friendship of its mistress. We will remember the hours of frank intercourse and honest communion of heart and soul passed under the shade of those clambering jasmine vines. So few people in this world are thoroughly true, — so few are thoroughly refined, — so few are thoroughly sympathetic, — so few are thoroughly educated. The author of "The Household of Bouverie" is all of these. It was like awakening from a beautiful dream to go away from that deep inner life, with the continual intoxication of that soulful society, back into the bustling, fretting, hurrying world of travel ; — to look away from the soft dark-gray eyes, radiating emanations from a spirit so warm and so strong, — eyes so full of vitality, both mental and sensuous, — into the hard, rapid, eager eyes of money-changers and souls engrossed in thoughts of traffic and material life. During this visit we learned many facts connected with our subject.

Charles Percy, a captain of the British army, was one of the early colonists of Louisiana. He married his third wife, a lady of Opelousas. His descendants are numerous in Mississippi and Louisiana.

Sarah Percy was married first to Colonel John Ellis, a man of wealth and influence at Natchez, Miss. After his death, she married Nathaniel A. Ware, a lawyer from South Carolina, — a man of profound learning and well versed in science, particularly in Botany, but a man full of eccentricities and naturally very shy and reserved in character. His domestic trials rendered him bitter and outwardly morose, even to his friends, sometimes even to his children. He was a philosopher of the school of Voltaire, a fine scholar, with a pungent, acrid wit, and cool sarcasm, which made him both feared and respected by those brought into collision with him. He lived to be old, and died of yellow-fever, near Galveston, Texas, where he had invested his means very extensively in lands. He was a handsome man, his features marked, — his nose aquiline, his mouth small and compressed, his eyes of a bright blue, his complexion pure and fair as a young girl's, his cheeks freshly colored, his brow white as a lily, — a very venerable-looking man, with long, thin, white locks falling on his neck; his forehead was very high, very prominent, and very narrow. He wrote two works on Political Economy, which made some reputation for him among the class of men who take interest in such reasonings. He was a man of mark, though not much beloved—out of his own family circle. He wrote also a "*geographical*" novel. His wife, who was very young when left a widow by Colonel Ellis, had borne Major Ware two daughters, Catharine and Eleanor; but at the birth of the latter, family proclivity inherited from her father declared itself, and the charming, attractive young woman never recovered her reason, from the delirium of puerperal fever. Major and Mrs. Ware were then living near Natchez. There was the loudest expression of sympathy and regret on the part of her many friends, by whom Mrs. Ware was greatly beloved, but after trying every medical suggestion that the South could afford, Major Ware was compelled to take his suffering wife to Philadelphia for better advice; — her two children by her first marriage were already there. Her son was at college at Princeton, N. J.; her daughter, Mary Ellis, the wife of Dr. Rene La Roche, of Philadelphia.

Now the father had to take charge of his two helpless little girls, so sadly deprived of their mother's tender care. He was passionately devoted to his little daughters, never content to have them away from him; and he did the best he could for them. They had wealth and friends, but it was lonely for the little things, wandering about from place to place, as their father's wretchedness led him to do, in his restless, weary life, — never long separated from the stern, peculiar scholar, whom they could not comprehend, except in his intense tenderness and earnest anxiety to bring them up as lovely, refined ladies should be educated.

There was only eighteen months' difference between the sisters; Catharine was the elder, but Eleanor was so bright, so clever, and so active, that she always took the lead, wherever they might happen to be. They were nearly of one size. Eleanor was a beautiful child; Catharine's face was not so regular in feature, and she had not her sister's brilliant complexion. Catharine had the Percy eye, dark-gray with black lash; she was like her mother, dark-haired and brunette. Eleanor was a picture to see; her eyes were as blue as heaven, her features statuesque, her hair black, with a purple tinge. Catharine was shy, sensitive, easily abashed, and readily provoked to tears — a sad, pensive child; Eleanor was self-reliant, gay, dancing like a sunbeam. So Catharine readily yielded the *pas* to her younger sister, and believed more devoutly than any one else in Eleanor's superiority, both physical and mental. She retained through life the same feeling of homage to her sister, and still believes Eleanor to have been more gifted than herself. These children had a singular training. Their father taught them a good deal himself, and he always provided them with the best masters, when he would sometimes make a prolonged halt in Philadelphia or elsewhere, for the purpose of their better instruction. They had a good many strange experiences. Their principal governess was a Mrs. Mortimer, an English lady, for whom they always expressed great affection. Some winters they spent in their native South; some summers they would be in Florida, some in the North. Then Ellen was placed at school at Madame Sigoigne's, in Philadelphia. Catharine would not go to school; she ran away and returned to her sister's house, which was only a few squares from the school. Madame came soon after in great agitation, in search of the truant, but the girl hid herself in a wood-closet, and wept so unrestrainedly when discovered, that the dismayed friends had to give up the point, and Major Ware had to take her back again to himself. He rented a suite of rooms now, and supplied her with books and masters. Then he went through a careful course of reading with her in English classics and in French ; teaching her to scan English prosody, and furnishing her, thus, with most invaluable and rare learning. Eleanor came to them every Saturday. She learned everything with facility; she played delightfully on her small harp, that her father had ordered from Erard, made expressly for her use. She danced like a fairy ; talked French like a native. She was a bright, beautiful, inevitable child. Catharine shrunk timidly from the world, into which, however, she was frequently forced to go. Her elder sister's house was the centre of a gay and fashionable circle; the reunions at Madame Sigoigne's and Dr. La Roche's were frequented by the most distinguished persons, both native and foreign. Madame Sigoigne, an emigrée from St. Domingo, was a marchioness of France by birth, and at that time there was a very brilliant circle of French exiles in and near Philadelphia. All strangers brought letters to her, and to her nephew, Dr. La Roche. Mrs. La Roche was a great favorite in this circle, and so Catharine and Eleanor were obliged to see much of the fashion and gayety of Philadelphia. Eleanor liked it very much ; she was always a little queen in society, kind and warm-hearted, generous, but *tant soit peu* capricious, and rather tyrannical, perhaps, over her more timid sister. Catharine advised Eleanor. The love between these sisters was peculiar and beautiful. They absolutely seemed to have but one soul. Their intercourse was as frank and unreserved as that of a penitent and father confessor. They never had a thought or an emotion from each other in all their lives. Their hearts were absolutely bare to each other's gaze, — they hid not even weaknesses from each other. Nothing could be more perfect than the confidence and friendship between them. The oneness of sympathy was wonderful. They did everything together. At an early age, they began to write little tales and poems together. Catharine married, at an early age, Mr. Elisha Warfield, of Lexington, Kentucky. Eleanor was necessarily separated a good deal from her; but they vowed to spend at least some months together every year, and they wrote to each other nearly every day. We have had some of these letters in our hands — some of Eleanor's later letters to her sister; graphic word-pictures, descriptive of thought and every passing shade of feeling.

Catharine lived a quiet, domestic life, absorbed in the rearing of her family of six children, in Lexington, some years, and afterward near it, on a farm she purchased for the sake of country air. She devoted herself to her children; her only recreation was in her pen. She and Eleanor had always kept up their habit of writing poems and other matter. It was instinct with them. Their father, getting possession of some of their poems, had a volume published in 1845 — "Poems by Two Sisters of the West." These were received with some favor by the public. Then another volume was published in 1846 — "The Indian Chamber, and other Poems." The sisters were gratified by the reception of their writings, and had planned out a number of tales and poems to be collated, when suddenly Eleanor died at Natchez, in her thirtieth year. When told by her weeping niece, according to solemn promise made that she would inform her aunt "if danger was near," her first words were, "Oh, what a blow for Catharine!" Her last thoughts, after bidding farewell to her husband and her four little children, were for her sister — far away in Lexington. She charged her niece and her husband with messages of loving words and consolation for *Catharine;* then gave directions for her funeral, received extreme unction from the hands of Bishop Chanche, (the family were Roman Catholics,) and died tranquilly. The news of Eleanor's death prostrated Catharine, both physically and mentally. She was now alone — her elder half-sister, Mrs. La Roche, was dead after great suffering — her brother was dead — and now Eleanor. — She was frantic in her grief; there never has been any consolation for her save in the hope of Immortality and the restitution of those whom she still loves and longs for. Her father died! Blow after blow had stricken her into the dust. She abandoned even her pen — it "*reminded her of Eleanor.*" Years after her sister's death, her niece, who had supported "Eleanor's" dying head upon her bosom, — the eldest daughter of her only brother, — visited her. There was much weeping and much talking of the beloved dead; and then the niece opened the closed drawer which contained the manuscripts of the two sisters, and prevailed upon Catharine to review some of them with her. Thus the pen, so long unused, was taken up again, and shortly after, Mrs. Warfield published "THE HOUSEHOLD OF BOUVERIE" — one of the most remarkable novels ever written by an American woman. It may challenge comparison with any novel, American or English, in originality, style, and diction.

The portrait of Erastus Bouverie is as original and peculiar as that of Gœthe's Mephistopheles. Indeed, it is only with the works of great masters that one can think of comparing this book. It is a vain attempt to review it or do justice to its merits in such a brief article as this. It is a work that will *endure*, and will grow in the favor of scholars. Of living female authors, we can only class Mrs. Warfield with George Sand and George Eliot. She holds her pen with like mastery; her conceptions are Shakspearean. The only American author whom she at all resembles in diction, is Hawthorne. Many pages of the "Household of Bouverie" might be interleaved with his without detection of difference of style in the writers. It is perhaps a fault in this book to have put the "Diary of Camilla" as an appendix. It should have been inserted in the body of the book; — but this Diary, in itself, is quite perfect. Mrs. Warfield is always Southern in opinion; and so her writings have had sectional prejudice to contend against. Herself a slave-owner and possessor of large landed interests in Texas — birth, instinct, education, sympathy, and interest bind her to the fortunes of her own people. She has been unfortunate, like all the rest of the South, and has lost very heavily in the recent war. Her spirited war-lyrics were frequently on the lips and stirred the pulse of the Confederate soldiers. Her love of country, like all the rest of her sensations, is a *passion*. She has no transient nor frivolous emotions; there is nothing light or ephemeral about Mrs. Warfield. She feels profoundly, or not at all. Matters that fret and disturb, or interest lighter natures, do not move her. She passes over them with calm, icy indifference. The majority of people bore her; though she is kind to all of God's creatures, few interest her much. She lives almost like a recluse. There are a few friends who visit her constantly, who esteem it a high privilege to be the recipients of her graceful hospitality. She is a very Arab in her ideas of the duties connected with bread and salt. But her 'friends are few; even they are admitted only to intimacy — never to familiarity. She preserves always a certain reserve and decorum of life, if we can phrase it so, in speaking of such a very simple and unaffected manner as hers is. She is always conscious of her *own value* in God's universe, in the presence of humanity; though she kneels low enough before the Creator. This gives her an equipoise and tranquillity of manner, which is soothing and full of repose. One feels how strong she is, and yet so gentle, — a strong, fertile, tropical nature, never weak, rarely cold, always creative, and emanating sensuous vitality at every breath. She delights, physically, in light, warmth, and perfumes. The temperature of her apartments is kept always at an almost equatorial grade of warmth; any but semi-tropical beings would be oppressed by such an atmosphere as seems almost absolutely necessary for her existence. She is like the Greeks in her detestation of cold and darkness. She is very impressible to atmospheric influences — being "akin with Nature." She feels the electricity in the air long before the thunderstorm bursts, and suffers until the lightnings flash out and the rain breaks through the clouds charged with electric fluid.

Mrs. Warfield's voice is singularly pleasant in speaking — full, soft, low, and vibrating — with a wonderful chromatic scale in its flexible tones. The sounds alone compel one's attention; like the playing of an instrument of music, the register and tone are delightful to the ear. She reads finely, and one of the greatest pleasures in frank companionship with her, is a habit she has frequently, in the pauses of conversation, of turning to her table, upon which always lies a number of books, and taking up a favorite volume, either of prose or poetry, without any exordium, beginning to read portions from it, making exquisite comments and criticisms as she reads. We recall hours spent in that way over Praed, Lowell, and others, which were delightful.

There is freshness, breadth of color, and warmth about her in everything. She is rather below the medium height, five feet three inches in stature, now inclining to *embonpoint*. Her hands are studies for an artist — very beautiful. Her head is set rather haughtily upon her shoulders — she is very erect — and it is rather tossed back as she moves. Her head is well shaped, looking larger than it really is, from the heavy mass of very black hair, now slightly streaked with gray, which seems as if it would bow her head with its weight. She usually wears, in spite of this great mass of tresses, a small point, *à la Marie Stuart*, of lace, black or white. Her eyes are dark-gray, shadowed by black lashes; her brow is beautiful; nose, straight, fine, and delicate, with dilating nostrils. Mouth is large and very mobile, — it is her most expressive feature, — but not regularly handsome; her chin is rather heavy, showing strong vitality and physical power, though not coarse, nor square. Her appearance is striking and attractive; genius is stamped in every lineament, and sorrow too. Her life has not been happy, — neither are her writings. She is by nature a dramatist, and a great tragic writer. She is not to be judged by the small tastes and petty rules of ordinary minds. She belongs, by birthright, to the highest order of human genius, and has sat at the feet of the masters who have sung powerfully of the "guilt, the crimes, and the misery of humanity, as well as of the eternal beneficence and glorious compassion of God."

Mrs. Warfield is never commonplace — neither is she always pleasing. She indulges little in fancy — her imagination is wonderful — her pictures sometimes seem to have a lurid glow, and have a strange fascination. Though occasionally *nearly* melo-dramatic, she is never extravagant, nor exaggerated, holding her passion in rein always; this belongs to the retinue of her nature. Her flights are always assured and steady — one never feels alarmed about them; she sails like an eagle — does not skim like a swallow, but will swoop down when she is ready, with a perfect precision. She handles her pen always *en maître*. Her books will bear study and close criticism — they are lessons of art; her periods have that beautiful rhythm which marks the sentences of the noblest writers, and yet she writes with ease; there is no effort visible — indeed, there is no effort ever in her writings! She writes without exhaustion; frequently without any need for review or correction; page after page is traced by her rapid pen, and flung aside without further care. She has written all her life — so that she does not prepare a book, or has not yet done so, for any special publication; — she puts her hand in her drawer of manuscripts, and selects a book, a poem, or a tale, as may be needed. She never sits down to manufacture a book — she writes because she *must*. "Genius does what it *must*, and Talent does what it *can*."

We do not think that Mrs. Warfield's power has been fully developed to the public — the extent and variety of her pen is yet unknown. She has in MSS. volumes equal, if not superior, to the "Household of Bouverie," yet entirely dissimilar. Some day they will all be placed before the public — then Mrs. Warfield will take her right position in the world of letters.

There is one marked peculiarity in Mrs. Warfield's writings. It is their perfect — we will not say purity, for it is a higher quality — it is the perfect chastity of mature womanhood. Amour with her is always firmly constrained, controlled by womanly modesty, subordinated to duty and to womanly pride. The truest, highest, noblest instincts of womanhood are those developed in her characters; she never disparages, degrades, or defames her own sex. Her women are not perfections; — they are not icy; — they are sensuous, capable of passion, emotional, not above trial or temptation, but they are true and pure. The character of Camilla Bouverie teaches the happiest lessons of noble womanhood: women ought to become better after receiving such an ideal; and so of Miriam Hartz — of Bertie. How different this conception of Bertie is from what would have been a French conception of a young girl's developing nature. What snow-flakes with a rosy flush over them, are those sisters of Bertie, and the mother, and Cecelia, and Lilian! worthy grand-daughter of Camilla Bouverie! Only a woman of noblest conceptions and finest instincts could have imagined these characters — a woman who reverenced herself and *her sex*. Even in the heroine of the "ROMANCE OF THE GREEN SEAL," though there seems to have been a shallowness of nature and some obliquity of moral sight, the instincts were pure. Mrs. Warfield has published no mere love story; not that she could not have written it — her poems have passion enough, — but that she did not choose to write it, and her taste shrinks from exposure and flaring analysis of a passion she believes congruous only with youth. Dreams are over with her; — the experiences of life have been very sad and very bitter.

"Beauseincourt" was suggested by some incidents which occurred during a visit to Florida, in Mrs. Warfield's early childhood, which made a deep impression on her susceptible nature. The character of Marcelline is drawn from actual fact, as well as the fearful death of

4

Colonel La Vigne — even to the having his eye picked out by vultures, as he lay dead three days in the swamp. Eleanor had intended making this story up into form, and it was rather a fond fancy upon her sister's part, which induced her to do it, after Eleanor's death.

Mrs. Warfield has a volume of "Tales of the Weird and Wonderful," written by her sister and herself — in manuscript, which are very remarkable. Her own tale of "The Planet Lustra" will compare with anything of E. A. Poe's, in imaginative power ; and her sister's "Tale of the Pearl-Trader" is very beautiful. We hope Mrs. Warfield may be induced to print these stories. Another novel, called "ANGOISSE," is very fine ; and another called "Hester Howard's Temptation" interested us deeply. She has also a novel in verse, nearly finished, in the style of "Aurora Leigh." She has written numbers of tales, sketches, poems ; some have been printed in newspapers, magazines, etc., and many she has still in manuscript.

Mrs. Warfield has been reproached for presenting such analyses of crime and criminals, as she has seemed to prefer as studies of art, in her two published novels. If we had the space, we would copy fairly and reiterate what Bulwer has already so well said in his "Word to the Public" written as an appendix to his "Lucretia."

"Thus it will be perceived that in *all* the classic, tragic, prose-pictures, preceding our own age, criminals have afforded the prominent characters, and crime the essential material.

"The tragic fiction is conceived — it has taken growth — it may be destined, amid the comparative neglect of the stage, to supply the lessons which the tragic drama has, for a while, abandoned. Do not fetter its wanderings from free search after truth through the mazes of society, and amid all the contrasts of nature. If it is to be a voice to the heart, an interpreter of the secrets of life, you cannot withhold from it the broadest experience of the struggle between good and evil, happiness and woe.

"'Hunc igitur terrorem animi, tone brasque necesse est.'

"Terror and compassion are the sources of the tragic writer's effects ; the destructive or pernicious power of intellect corrupted into guilt, affords him the natural means of creating terror for the evil, and compassion for its victims."

Thus argues one of the great masters of modern fiction, — and, reasoning from *his* premises, one can recognize great moral teachings in the incidents which cluster around Erastus Bouverie, and Prosper La Vigne. Intellect without moral goodness is nothing worth, — a love all selfish is a blasting fire, baleful to itself and all within the circle of its influence. Is there no lesson taught in that portrait sketched in with Occagna-like power, of that brilliant, bad, selfish man, Erastus Bouverie?

Is there not a Brahminical love of life in all its forms, and a stern reiteration of the cry against Cain — in Prosper La Vigne's story? Those books teach morals that underlie all humanity and teach the lessons *grandly*, if not charmingly.

Mrs. Warfield can sing syrens' songs when she chooses. In these two books she has preferred to strike in men's ears, the startling clang of the iron fasces of the Lictors leading the way into the Hall of Judgment.

" BEAUSEINCOURT " is her latest publication, — that book is simply an episode of a larger work, entitled, originally, " The retrospect of Miriam Montfort," which was considered too long for the Press — and therefore mutilated by having the beginning and the end summarily cut off. Mrs. Warfield intended to work these fragments up into another volume, but we doubt whether her failing health will permit her to carry out this infusorial scheme. We have read the work, as it was originally composed, and have no hesitation in saying, that Mrs. Warfield did herself great injustice in this decapitation of her book. She composes usually in the form of the English three-volume novel; the truth is, she is not American, either in her genius, tastes, or knowledge of literature. She is neither fast nor superficial; sensational she is, because she is dramatic by nature, and *is* a Poet writing prose. Like Gœthe, with her every emotion, every incident finds its vent in rhyme; and to one whom she honors sufficiently to allow of entrance into her inner life, the glancing over her books of MSS. poems is a revelation of her entire life. It is very probable that the extent of her ability may never be known during her mortal life. " They learn in suffering what they teach in song,"— and at her door the god of silence stands ever with his finger on his lip; honored and worshipped, no irreverent hand will be allowed to lift the veil which falls before the inner life.

It is very unjust to such a writer as Mrs. Warfield, to attempt to give any idea of her powers by cutting out a paragraph, or an occasional poem, and setting it at the end of such an article as this, — and I refuse to do it. " In all good works," Ruskin says, " Every part is connected, so that any single portion is imperfect when isolated." This is just the case here—one knows not what, or where to choose. In this Abyssinian butchery of cutting a steak from a living animal, and holding it up as a sample of meat, we feel more inclined to take what comes first to hand. Mrs. Warfield excels in descriptions of storms. The storm in "Beauseincourt," page 94, is very fine; and the storm on the lake, in her little tale dubbed by the publisher "The Romance of the Green Seal," (a name reminding one involuntarily of champagne wine,) is very remarkable.

"All human work is necessarily imperfect," * and our friend is only human. Her life has not been gay—her books are sad. She has lived too much out of the world. In this day a writer must study men, as well as books—a woman's life is necessarily limited, and a wounded heart seeks quiet and isolation. If Mrs. Warfield had the large experience of cities and men that "George Sand" and "George Eliot" have had, she would write with them. As it is, her genius is sometimes morbid, but it is always—*genius.* Her war-songs can be read in the collection of "Southern Poems of the War," made by her friend, Miss Emily V. Mason.

Mrs. Warfield resides on a farm in Peewee Valley, near Louisville, Kentucky.

June, 1868. †

———o○⦂⦂○o———

ELIZA A. DUPUY.

MISS DUPUY, perhaps one of the most widely known of the authors of the South, is the descendant of that Colonel Dupuy who led the band of Huguenot exiles to the banks of James River. Colonel Dupuy's grave is still exhibited in the old church whose ruins consecrate the ancient site of Jamestown. Her maternal grandfather was Captain Joel Sturdevant, who raised a company at his own expense, and fought gallantly throughout the war of the Revolution. Miss Dupuy is also related by blood to the Watkins family of Virginia. One of her best novels is founded on the story of "The Huguenot Exiles;" many of the incidents therein are drawn from family tradition. Miss Dupuy was born in Petersburg, Va. After the death of her father, her family experienced heavy reverses of fortune, and this girl, then a handsome, stately, dark-haired maiden, with a spirit

* Ruskin.

worthy of her lineage, stepped boldly forward to aid in the support of her younger brother and sister. She was competent to teach. She became a governess in the family of Mr. Thomas G. Ellis, of Natchez, where she had charge of the education of his daughter, now known as the author of several books, publishing under the name of "Filia." Miss Dupuy found a pleasant home here, where she was thrown continually into the society of such women as Eleanor and Catherine Ware, and such men as S. S. Prentiss, John Ross, Boyd, and Bingaman. Natchez at that time boasted a brilliant circle of wit and intellect, and the handsome young governess, with her dignified reserve and noble pride, was one of its ornaments. Miss Dupuy began to write very early. While at Natchez she wrote the "Conspirator," and read it aloud to her little circle of friends and admirers. Eleanor Ware and she used to have grand literary symposiums, where they would read their productions to each other and to gentle Mrs. Ellis, who sympathized warmly in their tastes, and little "Filia" would often hide in a corner to listen.

With some difficulty Miss Dupuy succeeded in getting her "Conspirator" published. It is a story of the conspiracy of Aaron Burr. It was successful — over 25,000 copies of this novel have been sold. She now devoted much of her time to writing, and gradually was enabled to give up the irksome confinement of a teacher's life. She taught after this in a "Country Neighborhood," near Natchez, where she wrote her novel of that name. She has written constantly ever since. She was unfortunate in the failure of her publisher and the consequent loss of her copyrights, which would have supplied her now with a handsome income. She has always been wonderfully industrious, a patient worker, and very exacting of herself. She labors usually about four hours every morning, and her MSS. are only corrected when sent to the printer. Her physical health has been firm and vigorous, else she could never have endured such a drain upon her mental powers. She is a tall, large, nobly developed woman, with healthy nerves — *mens sana in corpore sano*. She has always been calm, firm, simple, but reticent in nature and deportment, — a woman everywhere respected and often much beloved. She has preserved her friends through life unchanged. She is a friend in the rainy days of existence as well as in sunshine — immaculate, pure, high-principled and companionable; her features are large and well moulded, Greek in outline; her eyes blue; and her hair, which was very abundant in early womanhood, rippling and satiny, fell in ebon waves, a flood of tresses, below her knee. She wore it usually in a broad, heavy braid around her head, like a diadem, while a multitude of ringlets streamed over her cheeks; the crown of hair a coiffure not unsuited to her large head and stately frame. She moves softly and tranquilly, but decidedly. Her voice is sweet and pleasing in tone, but distinct and clear in its low articulation. She has been engaged for several years past in writing for Bonner's "Ledger." She is bound by contract to furnish Mr. Bonner with a thousand pages annually. She is really a *littérateur* by profession, and an honest and faithful one. In consequence, she improves in her writings. She is faithful to her art. Her recent novel of "The Evil Genius," furnished to the *Ledger*, is regarded by many persons as the best of her numerous writings. It is very difficult to make a selection from such abundant material, and scarcely necessary, as Miss Dupuy's novels are so generally popular.

She resides now at Flemingsburg, Kentucky.

She says, in a letter to a friend, these remarkable words, in answer to a question: "As a Southern woman, I would sooner have thrust my hand in a blazing fire, as the Roman youth did, than have taken a pen in it, to throw discredit on my own people."

None who ever knew her intimately, could conceive of Miss Dupuy's failing in any duty, toward God, or friends, or country.

The following is a list of the novels furnished to the "New York Ledger": "The Lost Deeds," "Mysterious Marriage," "White Terror," "Outlaw's Bride," "Life Curse," "Warning Voice," "Secret Chamber," "Family Secret," "Lady of Ashhurst," "Fatal Error," "Evil Genius," and "The Dead Heart;" and she has published in book-form, — "Merton; a Tale of the Revolution," "The Conspirator," "Emma Walton, or Trials and Triumphs," "The Country Neighborhood," "Celeste, or The Pirate's Daughter," "The Separation," "The Divorce," "The Coquette's Punishment," "Florence, or The Fatal Vow," "The Concealed Treasure," "Ashleigh," "The Planter's Daughter," and "The Huguenot Exiles."

October, 1868.

THE DAGUERREOTYPE FROM THE DEAD MAN'S EYE.

One bright morning, toward the close of September, Arden strolled to a nook, a mile above the fall, filled with rocks and water-plants; and he became so absorbed in transferring them to his sketch-book, that time passed insensibly on. The hours from dawn till eleven he reserved to the claims of his art; the remainder of the day was devoted to other less entrancing labors. It was his usual custom to bring with him a basket containing his frugal breakfast, but this morning he had forgotten it, and toward ten o'clock he discovered that he was very hungry. Reluctantly closing his portfolio, he turned his loitering steps toward the cottage, pausing every few moments to catch some new beauty in the flitting shades of light upon the hill-sides.

Suddenly there was a noise—a trembling of the earth around, and fragments of glass and wood were thrown into the air. One wild glance showed him that the domed roof was blown from the cottage, and, casting down all that impeded his steps, he ran with wild speed toward the scene of the disaster. But he was half a mile distant, and many moments elapsed before he reached the entrance of the cottage. Swiftly passing through the hall, he found the door which separated Carlyle's laboratory room from the body of the house, thrown from its hinges, and with inexpressible anguish he saw his cousin lying amid the wrecks of his apparatus, utterly lifeless. To raise him up, scan his lineaments, and sink down in utter hopelessness, was the work of a moment; for he who had studied every phase of death as an artist, saw its unmistakable impress upon the features of the fallen man. Yet there was an expression of resistance and anguish upon them, which forbade the idea that he had perished from the effects of the explosion.

In his wild agony, Arden called loudly on Carlyle's name; but, alas! on earth he would never more respond to that call. He lifted him up, and placed him upon a large chair; as he did so, he saw, with dilating eyes, that a stream of blood welled slowly from his throat. A brief examination satisfied him that his cousin had not perished from the explosion, but that a sharp weapon had severed the jugular vein at one blow. Then he knew that he had been murdered, and a sickening sense of self-accusation overcame him. He had brought him there, in spite of all the warnings which should have turned him from his purpose. A sudden tremor came over him, and cold drops gathered on his brow; for he remembered that he had lured his kinsman to that lonely spot; he was next heir to property which many thought had been unjustly bestowed upon Carlyle to his own injury; they were alone in the house, and he might be accused of having compassed his death.

He looked wildly around for help. His eyes fell upon the box containing the plates which Carlyle had shown him a short time before. Their conversation flashed upon his mind; and he rushed to his own room, to remove the instrument with which he took daguerreotypes, in the faint hope that he might gain a clue to the murderer, by taking a picture of the eye of the dead man. Those orbs which scarcely yet had begun to glaze in death, might be made to shadow forth the form on which they had last gazed, and thus reveal the dread secret of his tragic fate.

With incredible speed, Arden placed the lens at the proper focus, took the prepared plate, and adjusted the figure of the dead man. The light from above fell upon the ghastly form, with the life-stream slowly welling over the snowy linen of his shirt-bosom, and he could have cried aloud in the agony of his soul at that fearful sight; but this was no time to give way to emotion; he must to work to save himself from the foulest suspicion that ever darkened the fame of a man. Magnifying the eye to its utmost extent, with trembling hands, he closed the aperture, and awaited the result. Twenty was counted more from the rapid pulsations of his heart, than from any effort of his own, and he removed the plate.

Excited as he was, he submitted the picture to the usual chemical tests with extreme care, though he scarcely hoped for any successful result to the experiment. It was alone suggested by the desperate circumstances in which he was placed, and with feverish doubt he watched the lines as they appeared upon the highly polished surface. To his unbounded amazement, the eye was delineated bold and clear, and upon the surface of the retina was visible a distinctly outlined head! Using a powerful magnifying glass, he saw that it was the face of a young and singularly lovely girl, with heavy braids of hair falling low upon her cheeks. The large eyes were filled with mingled compassion and terror, and the half parted lips expressed the extremity of horror.

Arden gazed in amazement and incredulity, though he held before his eyes the mute evidence of his skill; here was a nearly perfect picture of a creature so lovely that under other circumstances his artist soul would have bowed before her as the realization of his fairest ideal of woman. Could this creature indeed have dealt the fatal blow which deprived his kinsman of life? Could nature create a being so fair, and yet deny those finer impulses which should move one of such perfect mould? But if she had not committed the deed, why was she here, why should her lovely face have been the last object on which the eyes of the dead man rested?

While this scene progressed, Arden was so intensely excited that he was unconscious that others had reached the scene of action, and were watching his movements with intense eagerness. As he first turned the head toward the light, three persons entered the apartment; they uttered exclamations of surprise and horror at the terrible scene which met their view, they gazed with him on the fair image he had so wonderfully obtained, but the preoccupied artist was unconscious of it all. If they touched him, he shook of their grasp, but gave no heed to them,— when they questioned him, he heard them not. His senses seemed frozen into unconsciousness by the awful shock his nervous system had received. But one idea possessed him: to gain a clue to this mysterious deed, for which he, in all probability, would be held accountable.

ROSA VERTNER JEFFREY.

ROSA VERTNER JEFFREY was born Rosa Vertner Griffith.
Her father, John Griffith, lived near Natchez, was a man of
elegant culture, and wrote very pretty little tales and poems, many of
his Indian stories having been published in the first-class Annuals,
years ago, and several of them highly complimented in England,
("The Fawn's Leap," and "Indian Bride," were quite celebrated.)

Rosa inherits her talents from him; his brother, Wm. T. Griffith,
was one of the most eminent lawyers at the bar of Mississippi, in his
day. All of the Griffiths are gifted, having graceful manners — were
charming people. "Rosa" is a granddaughter of Rev. Dr. James
Abercrombie, whose memory is highly revered in Philadelphia, and
indeed throughout the United States, as an Episcopal minister. Her
mother, who was a Miss Abercrombie, was beautiful and accomplished,
but died early, leaving four little children; and it was then that Rosa's
maternal aunt, Mrs. Vertner, adopted her, and was all that an own
mother could be. Her early childhood was passed at a beautiful
country place near Port Gibson, Miss., called "Burlington," and
owned by her adopted father. She loved that home as she has never
loved another, "for the attachments of imaginative children to localities are stronger than those formed in after-life." Some idea of her
attachment to that lovely spot may be formed by the perusal of her
beautiful poem, "*My Childhood's Home.*" When only ten years of
age, she was taken to Kentucky for the purpose of completing her
education, and the parting from "Burlington" was her first sorrow.
She was educated at the seminary of Bishop Smith, at Lexington, Ky.;
was married, at the early age of seventeen, to Claude M. Johnson, a
gentleman of elegant fortune.

A friend of Rosa from childhood, says: "Rosa was one of the most
beautiful women, physically, that I ever knew; her head and face were
perfect as a Greek Hebe. She is large and full, with magnificent bust
and arms; eyes, real violet-blue; mouth, exquisite, with the reddest
lips; and perfect features; her hair, dark-brown, glossy, curling and
waving over a nobly proportioned brow. She is bright, gay, joyous,
and perfectly unaffected in manner, full of fun and even practical
jokes, and with the merriest laugh." Such was Rosa the girl.

After the death of Mr. Johnson, leaving her with four children, she resided with her adopted parents until her marriage to Alexander Jeffrey, Esq., a native of Edinburgh, Scotland.

In 1850, under the signature of " Rosa," she became a contributor to the "Louisville Journal," of which Geo. D. Prentice was editor. A great number of her poems appeared in this journal, although from time to time she contributed to the principal literary journals of the country. In 1857, her poems were published in a volume by Ticknor & Fields, Boston, and elicited from the press throughout the country the warmest tributes of praise.

The following pretty complimentary notice of " Poems by Rosa," was written by the lamented hero-poet, Theodore O'Hara : —

"If in the general distribution of blessings, Providence has been impartial, and so bestowed its favors as to equalize the condition of human beings, there are instances in which exceptions seem to occur that utterly overthrow the idea of universal equity. The author of these exquisite lyrical gems furnishes an example in point. Young, beautiful, accomplished, with every enjoyment which health can covet, or admiration afford, or fortune procure, she might have been denied, without injustice, those brilliant gifts which often alleviate the ills of poverty, or light the darkness of misfortune. But Nature, as if to illustrate the munificence of her bounty, and signalize the object of her favor by a prodigality of blessings, has bestowed upon Mrs. Johnson, in addition to great personal beauty, gentleness of disposition, vast fortune, and all the joys of domestic life, the lofty attributes of genius. We have read this volume with the deepest pleasure. There is scarcely a line which does not breathe the inspiration of true poetry. There is no pretension, no straining after effect, no stilted phraseology, seeking in its pompous flow to dignify, by mere word-draping, trivial commonplace impressions, but a genuine outpouring of that exquisite sensibility which gives to the occurrences of daily life the fascination of romance. We have seldom seen developed in a higher degree that subtile power which clothes with a mantle of tenderness and beauty every object which it touches. Memory and imagination mingle their trophies in the lovely pictures which she paints ; and so faultless is the skill with which they are blended, that some of these poems seem an exquisite tissue of interwoven light and shade. The style is easy and glowing, the language chosen with scrupulous taste, — or rather not chosen at all, for it seems to be but an atmosphere of the thoughts which it envelops, — the imagery is striking and appropriate, and always perfect in its analogies ; the sentiment tender and noble, reflecting in beautiful harmony the radiance of intellect with the cheering warmth of true womanly feeling.

"Among the poems which specially excited our admiration we may mention 'The Sunset City,' which is one of the most magnificent specimens of descriptive poetry we have ever read. Every line seems to glow with brilliant gems, and over all is thrown a gorgeous emblazonry of fancy which dazzles and deludes the mind by its sparkling splendor. 'The First Eclipse' is a poem in blank verse, of greater length and of much higher order. In it, the author conceives and describes the lofty mission of science, its noble elevation above the commoner pursuits of life, its glorious achievements and rewards, although the instrument by which its triumphs were accomplished may pass unnoted from the memory of men. The crowning jewel of the casket is 'The Frozen Ship.' This beautiful story exhibits the highest order of poetic merit. The argument is most happily conceived, the surroundings are all grouped with perfect propriety, and the gradual evolution of the denouement is most artistically wrought. The piece abounds in graphic, life-like descriptions, in delicate tenderness of expression and exquisite beauty of sentiment. . . .

" In perusing these poems and contemplating their countless infinity of gems, we lose the power to discriminate in the general and dazzling impression of their brilliancy, like the Chaldee shepherd, who has gazed upon the starry splendors of the firmament till his overpowered vision can distinguish but one unbroken sheen of glory."

In the spring of 1864, Mrs. Jeffrey published, through Sheldon & Co., New York, a novel entitled "Woodburn," of which we give the following review.

(*From the "Louisville Journal."*)

" Woodburn: A Novel. — Several weeks ago, in announcing this work as forthcoming, we said:

" ' Where its scene is laid, or what its plot is, or who is its hero or heroine, are points upon which the public as yet have received no inkling; but those who are acquainted with the genius and taste of the fair authoress must feel assured, that, in respect to the scene and plot, as well as in all other respects, the production will be brimful of charm. Her legion of admirers feel a world of curiosity respecting the work, but no solicitude. They confide implicitly, as they well may, in her rare and beautiful powers.'

" We are now able to say that this implicit confidence was not misplaced. It has been nobly justified: Woodburn, in respect to the scene and plot, as well as in all other respects, is indeed brimful of charm. In support of this judgment, we beg to adduce the following notice from the Hartford *Courant*, which is one of many favorable notices that we might cite, and which throws quite as much light on the scene and plot and principal characters, as we think a person who has not read the novel is entitled to receive.

" ' It is refreshing to meet, in these days of the sensational Braddon-Wood school of fiction, a story possessing so much real ability as " Woodburn." The scenes are, for the most part, laid at the South; and the many fine pictures of its sunny landscapes, with which the book abounds, relieve the intense interest of the story. Most of the characters are drawn with great cleverness, and a few in such clear outlines that we feel assured we have met them in real life. The hero and heroine, Mr. Clifford and Ethel Linton, are fine characters. Both possess the noblest qualities of mind and heart, and the reader will be in love with them from the first. The villain of the story, who bears the harsh-sounding name of Basil Thorn, is a *real* villain. For unmitigated scoundrelism and remorseless hatred it would be hard to match him. His miserable death in the woods is a relief to us. Rachel Thorn, a sort of Becky Sharp, but without Becky's triumphs, is a powerfully drawn character. One of the best personages in the book is the narrator herself, Amy Percy — bright, shrewd, honest — a girl who, disappointed in her first love, does n't believe in breaking her heart therefor. The plot is ably managed, and the secret that hangs about Doctor Foster and the maniac, is so skilfully concealed until the denouement, that it is impossible to guess at it. There is much acuteness displayed in many of the author's reflections and observations. Her style is clear, compact, and animated, and with occasional exuberance reminding us of Miss Prescott. "Woodburn" will add largely to Mrs. Jeffrey's fame, and in the difficult field of fiction-writing she will take high rank.'

"This is very high praise, but not too high. It is rather below than above the merits of 'Woodburn.' The fascination of the story is complete. No reader who crosses the threshold will pause short of the recesses which enshrine the mystery. Nor is the style unworthy of the story. On the contrary, the story blazes in the style like a gem in its setting. 'Woodburn' is a success. Considered as a first effort in the field of fiction, it is a brilliant success."

Here is a word-picture of the heroine: —

"Ethel Linton was the most superb beauty I ever saw. At that time past the bloom of early youth, being twenty-five, yet her loveliness had ripened — matured — losing not freshness, yet gaining depth and tenderness of expression, in its growth to full perfection. She was tall and elegantly formed, — a wavy, graceful figure, yet so round, there were no harsh angles there to mar its stately symmetry; fair, very fair, with large, lustrous hazel eyes, into whose clear depths you might gaze long and earnestly, and while gazing, feel as well assured that the soul within was a temple of purity and truth, as in watching the stars, we know those blue steeps which they adorn are boundary-lines to a world of angels. The features were regular, yet not with the severe perfection of a Grecian statue. And it was the ever-changing lights and shades of expression, that constituted Ethel's chief attraction; — the glow, the beam of intellect, the bewitching smiles or laugh of gayety — at times almost childish in its ringing merriment, and then, a shadow of mournfulness flitting over her face, eclipsing its light like wreaths of purple vapor, that sometimes start suddenly across the glory of a summer sky, breaking into shimmering gleams the glow of sunshine on some enchanting landscape, yet shading it so softly, so dreamily, that we know not which to deem most lovely, the living picture bathed in light, or shadowed by its veil of purple cloud. My sister's hair was her crowning beauty. Golden-brown, silky, and abundant, it rippled in shining waves over her white brow, and, braided into a mass at the back of her regal head, shone like a halo — illuminating her whole form."

Here is a beautiful stroke of pathos:

"Still, Cecil Clare continued to preach — Sunday after Sunday rising up with that white, still face, whose very calmness told a tale of fearful, inward struggle; and once, when the prayers of the congregation were requested for Pearl, (when the fever was at its height,) his voice grew so low and tremulous, we knew that it swept over a well of unshed tears, like the sad waiiing wind of Autumn, when through some lone valley it comes, with a sobbing sound, drearily sweeping over deep, still waters."

And here are acute reflections:

"Poor, dear, beautiful Ethel! — if they could only have met before her first miserable marriage! Yet when I suggested this to Cecil Clare the other day, he looked very grave, and said: ' Don't suppose, because events are contrary to what our feeble judgment may deem best, that it is so, or that we could better the order of things by arranging them to suit ourselves; for, by cultivating such thoughts, we put our little mite of earthly wisdom up in opposition to that Almighty One who never has erred and never can err. Had your cousin met Mr. Clifford in her early youth, they might not have been congenial in disposition and temper, as they now appear to be, for she has doubtless been softened and strengthened by early trials; and, though we know nothing of his history, there is a sad, firm, calm look about Mr. Clifford, which indicates that he has borne some heavy weight of sorrow patiently, and met reverse of fortune bravely as a man — resignedly as a Christian. Perhaps they both needed this to make them what they now are, and (if destined for each other) it is far better they never met until now; for God orders all things well. Suppose you, or I, or any other human being, had the government and direction of everything, even on this little globe of ours (to say nothing of the boundless universe) for one day, how would it end? In misery, confusion, and ruin. Let us not then presume, in the weakness of human folly, to doubt the wisdom of God.' "

Mrs. Jeffrey has several novels in MS., and a poem which she thinks possesses more merit than anything she ever wrote, entitled "Florence Vale." Claxton, Remsen & Haffelfinger, Philadelphia, publish in the winter of 1870, "Daisy Dare, and Baby Power," a poem illustrated.

Mrs. Jeffrey's residence is Lexington, Kentucky.

October, 1870.

EXTRACTS FROM "FLORENCE VALE."*

I have been blest, — so fully blest — that, basking in the light
Of purple joy — grief was to me like a wild stormy night
To those who sweep silk curtains back, and watch the shut-out gloom
Amid the rosy atmosphere of a luxurious room.

I knew that death was in the world, and woe, and bitterness,
But — insolent in happiness — I thought of sorrow less
Than children think of cold, who gaze on painted polar seas
'Mid Syrian roses — 'neath the shade of balmy citron-trees.

And when it came — Heaven dealt the blow with an unsparing hand :
I dreamed in Eden; to awake 'mid wastes of burning sand.
Life's dreary waste, which 'neath a load of hate, I've wandered through
Weary, as 'neath his Saviour's curse, speeds on the "Wandering Jew."

As scattered graves, that dot with gloom the eastern traveller's way,
So grief and pain do sadly mark life's high-road as we stray;
And for that time has Memory raised an altar of regret,
Among the joys, along my path, like golden mile-stones set.

A glorious type of womanhood, whose very waywardness
Beguiled my lips ere they could chide, to smile on her bliss.
A nature with no hidden shoals, but clear as waves that show
To mariners, through crystal deeps, the coral-reefs below !

I hate, aye, loathe, the very thought, that Love's blest name is given
To passions scarce more like to it than Hell is like to Heaven.
By one, the feelings are refined, as streams are purified
In sparry caves, or shining sands, through which they ofttimes glide.

The other is like some foul spring, where (lured by thirst) we drink,
To find a noxious, burning tide, with ashes on its brink,
And lo ! it doth pollute the soul, as erst the God-cursed Nile
With waves of blood the sunny lands of Egypt did defile.

And from that time, above the wreck of hopes so bright and blest,
Within my heart revengeful hate upreared his snaky crest,
And on each tender, prayerful thought a foul pollution shed,
Like blood upon a battle-field, staining the daisies red.

* These extracts are taken at random from the MSS. poem.

AGNES LEONARD.

THIS lady was born in Louisville, Kentucky. She is a daughter of Dr. O. L. Leonard, celebrated as a "mathematician." He practised medicine in the city of Louisville for many years; yet, desirous of giving his children the best possible educational advantages under his direct supervision, he gave up his practice as a physician, and took charge of the Masonic College, at La Grange, Ky., and was afterward President of the Henry Female College, at New Castle, Ky. At the age of thirteen, Agnes began to write for the press. Her first article was a short effort at versification, which was published in the Louisville "Journal," and noticed by George D. Prentice, the godfather of so many Southern writers, as follows:

"A young girl, twelve years of age, sends us a piece of poetry, written when she was only ten. Though hardly worthy to be published, it indicates the existence of a bud of genius, which, properly cultivated, will expand into a glorious flower."

Since this *début*, Miss Leonard has written almost constantly, under the *nom de plume* of "Mollie Myrtle," but of late years under her own name. In 1863 a collection of her earlier efforts appeared in book-form, under the title of "Myrtle Blossoms." There was nothing unusual in the volume, the merit being of a negative order. Some of the poems were very good; one critic saying: "These poems are so harmonious, as almost to set themselves to music."

Miss Leonard's mother died when she was a small child, and her father remaining unmarried, and very indulgent, Miss Agnes led a roving, gypsying sort of life, following her own inclinations, and studying persons rather than books.

Miss Leonard contributed to the Chicago "Sunday Times," in 1867, a series of articles, entitled "Men, Women, and Beasts," and also contributed regularly to the "Sunday Tribune" of said city, and the Louisville "Sunday Courier." Carleton & Co., of New York, published in 1867 a novel from her pen, entitled "Vanquished," which is to be followed by a sequel, under title of "Philip Arion's Wife."

Miss Leonard's *personnel* is thus sketched by a prominent author of our Southern country:

"I can bring her very distinctly before my 'mind's eye,' in her tall and slender grace. She is youthful in appearance and in reality, and possesses a face almost as perfect as a Greek bas-relief, and full of power and passion, with capabilities both of sweetness and satire. Her conversational powers are brilliant, yet tinged with melancholy, which some might mistake for bitterness. Sensibility and pride are the two distinctive expressions of her features; and like many enthusiasts, she has found the world she lives in but 'Dead-Sea apples' to the taste. In some of her essays there is deeper pathos and keener wit than are to be met with·in her pleasing novel, 'Vanquished.' The poem, 'Angel of Sleep,' is full of singular abandon and beauty."

From the numerous notices of "Vanquished," I make extracts from a candid review that appeared in the "Chicago Tribune":

"'Vanquished' may be considered Miss Leonard's first sustained work, and her real *début* before the literary world at large. It is not a gracious task at any time to criticise the first effort of a *débutante* in any department of art, and it is especially ungracious in literature; but a very candid perusal of 'Vanquished' has convinced us that, while the *début* may not be a success of enthusiasm, it is a success far more pronounced and positive than that achieved by the majority of young writers of fiction, and that she has secured a position with her first book which she may make permanent for the future, by the exercise of the increased skill in construction, and the power of condensation which experience will give to her.

"The story of 'Vanquished,' concisely stated, is the struggle of life,—the conflict which is fought on each individual battle-ground between inclination and duty. The ground-work of the story has been skilfully laid. The characters are introduced in quick succession, and many of them are drawn with a faithfulness and distinctness of outline which stamps them at once as portraits. Her characters all bear the impress of probability, without a trace of the exaggerated, high tragic, and melo-dramatic tone which pertains to most of the heroes and heroines of latter-day fiction. Some of them, such as the cynical Rashton, Dr. Kent, the inquisitive Mr. Bagshaw, and his homely but delightfully domestic wife; Philip Arion, the minister; Bernice Kent, who is the real heroine of the story, and Olive, are complete and harmonious in their portraiture, and never lose their identity. There are others, such as Oswald Kent, Aurelia, his sister, and the Brainards, who are connected with every phase of the story, and yet are very imperfectly sketched. Still others, introduced as accessories, having no relation to the general movement of the story, such as the Murdlains, the Bonnivets, the Mortimer Browns, the Melbournes, and others, are very happy instances of character painting, with a very few touches of the brush. A few illustrations of this will explain what we mean. George Bonnivet was the kind of man that a certain class of women prey upon remorselessly, tormenting the poor fellow to death, and then bestowing any amount of posthumous praise upon the victim's memory, wearing their widow's weeds complacently, and declaring that 'he was the best of men.' John Meggs, whose standard of perfection was apple-pie, and saw 'apple-pie personified in Miss Leila;' Mr. Lyons, who was 'a mature young man of twenty-five,' or 'a youthfully disposed person of forty, it was doubtful which;' Mrs. Murdlain, without whom 'Murdlain was a cipher; with her, their representation of society was not to be scorned. Mr. Murdlain, minus Mrs. Murdlain, was nothing. Mr. Murdlain, plus Mrs. Murdlain, was the first member of an equation, to be finished with immensity.'

"The movement of the story is kept well in hand, and the real *dénouement*, the relation between Olive and Dr. Rashton, is very skilfully concealed until the proper moment. The most acute reader would hardly suspect the key which is to explain the connection between characters, and the final unfolding of the plot and disposition of the people who have been moving upon the stage. This is one of the principal charms of the book — this utter concealment of *motif*, and its disclosure just at the right time to the reader, without having offered a hint of its nature, or betrayed a clue which might have weakened the interest in the story.

"There is one respect in which 'Vanquished' differs from almost every other work of fiction. We can scarcely recall one written by a young lady, in which the author has not treated us to a very glowing description of scenery, drawn out with painful minuteness, and devoted to 'fine writing;' to personal pictures, in which each picture is limned for us, commencing with the hair and ending with the toes, and in which we get the exact shade of the tresses, the color of the eyes, the length of the nose, and the curve of the lips; and to mysterious toilet accounts, in which we get the color, texture, and material of the lady's or gentleman's wardrobe, as the case may be, with an extra touch of the technicalities of the language of fashion, in the case of a bride or bridegroom. Miss Leonard has had the good sense to omit all this. There is not a single description of scenery in the book. . . . . . She makes her characters describe themselves by their manners and their conversation, by the oddities and eccentricities which in real life distinguish men and women from each other, and by their actions in public and private. In the majority of cases, she has been very successful, and the result is, people are quite as sharply pictured as if she had given us the nationality of the nose, the cut of the sleeve, or the size of the slipper. Her work is nearly all subjective; a study of characters rather than of faces, of mental struggles, trials, aspirations, ambitions, and motives, rather than of physical surroundings or objective scenes.

"A prominent feature in Miss Leonard's book is her frequent departure from the thread of her story — a straying out as it were from the beaten path into the fields — for the purpose of moralizing. These little dissertations are thoroughly healthy in their tone, often displaying a very keen insight into character, and are logical in treatment, although not always carried out

6

to their final result, as in some of the conversations between Bernice and
Dr. Rashton. But, on the whole, they are terse, aphoristic, and pleasant, and
throw her characters into stronger relief. We give a few of them at random.

"'Pain is an old story. We realize this after a time. We grow to understand by slow degrees that only the inconsiderate are confidential concerning
their sorrows. Only the weak have groans extorted from them by the agony
of mere heart-ache.'

"'Your talisman is Tact. Do not forget. You may consider this a plat-
itude, nevertheless it is a truth. After Goodness, a woman's greatest possession is Tact; then Beauty, then—Intellect. The last is in most cases super-
fluous in any unusual development. The first two are indispensable. You
may be forgiven for being a fool, if you are a graceful one; but you will
never be forgiven if you lack Tact.'

"'Duty is grand and Religion is glorious, but does not the human heart,
steady and pure as it may be, and mounting on love-flights often as it dare,
want a human sympathy perfectly indulged to make it healthful?'

"'We are in the midst of trifles that death may make relics of.'

"'So with mind. Experience disciplines it so gradually, it develops so
silently and imperceptibly, that we do not realize its growth until some bitter
experience bursts its calyx, and we marvel at what seems to be its sudden
maturity. We say sorrow has matured, whereas sorrow has simply expanded
the faded petals that joy would perhaps have kept hidden, but whose
growth joy as well as sorrow has assisted.'

"Miss Leonard has an admirable vein of humor, and a very skilful use
of the weapons of satire; summed up, 'Vanquished' may be pronounced a
success. The plot is well constructed; the movement of the story is regular;
the *dénouement* is skilfully sprung upon the reader, the characters are drawn
from life, and depend for their interest upon their own merits, without the
false coloring of improbability, exaggeration, or sensation, which are the
prevailing attributes of latter-day fiction; the style is pleasant and sketchy,
and an air of refinement pervades the whole book. It has many of the
faults which seem to be inseparable from all young writers, but experience
will undoubtedly point them out, and suggest the method of curing them.
We see no reason why Miss Leonard should not attain a very high position
in the literary world."

On the 29th of October, 1868, Miss Leonard was married to Dr. S.
E. Scanland, formerly of Kentucky.

Her varied accomplishments will adorn the domestic circle, as they
have already the social and literary circle.

October, 1869.

"FRA DIAVOLO."

"Fra Diavolo," that was the play;
  And the night was a glorious night in May.
  Stars on her brow, and bloom at her feet,
  And the breath of her west winds warm and sweet;
  That was without; within, the light
  Of dancing eyes and of jewels bright,
  And radiant faces, proud and fair,
  Outshone the rays of the gaslight's glare,
  And a strange, sweet perfume filled the air
  From the fragrant flowers I wore in my hair.

Well, there, in a front-row box, were we,
  As fond and happy as lovers could be;
  And on my libretto he wrote his name,
  And under it, " *Chérie, je vous aime;* "
  And my brain went round with the maddening play,
  And the 'wildering joy of that night in May;
  While the crimson glowed in my burning cheek,
  As I looked a love that I could not speak.

"Forever and ever, love of mine,
  Forever and ever I am thine;
  The sun shall fade and the stars shall wane,
  And my heart cry out for return in vain;
  Yet ever and ever its troth shall be,
  Beloved, plighted but to thee."
  These were the words, on that night in May,
  That were said in the pauses of the play;
  These were the words that rang in my heart,
  And made themselves of my soul a part.

And I asked in the glow of the joyous hours
"Was there ever a love on earth like ours?"
"Never, O queen of my heart," he replied,
"Never, my beautiful spirit-bride,
  Never a feeling so pure and true,
  Never a woman so lovely as you."
"Fra Diavolo!" that was the play,
  And the night was a glorious night in May;
  Three years ago—oh, what an age it seems,
  With its roseate hues of vanished dreams!

Three years ago! Ah, the love has fled;
The lást red spark of its flame is dead,
And vainly we search each other's face
For the olden charm and the olden grace;
And we think of the past with an icy chill
Which is very unlike the olden thrill,
Which shook our hearts that night in May,
When "Fra Diavolo" was the play.
We are so cold, the past is dead,
And the last red glow of love has fled.

And we smile at the feeling that thrilled us then,
When we see it in other women and men;
And we sigh "*Eh bien!* they must one day learn
How short a time love's red-fires burn."
Ah, yes, we are older and wiser now —
Too wise for the follies of youth, I trow;
Yet, would to Heaven, that night in May,
When "Fra Diavolo" was the play,
And on my libretto you wrote your name,
And under it, "*Chérie, je vous aime!*"
Might come again, to fade no more,
Till I close my eyes on the earthly shore.

ANGEL OF SLEEP.

Angel of Sleep! I am weary and worn,
Faint with the burden of life I have borne,
Eager for all that thy presence can bring,
Folding me under thy sheltering wing,
Shutting my eyes to the dull glare and heat,
Closing my ears to the unquiet street,
Taking me out from the bustle and strife,
Giving a death that is sweeter than life.

Angel of Sleep! All the day's work is done;
Weariness surely thy blessing has won;
Nearer, come nearer, thy beautiful wing
Visions of peacefulness ever can bring,
Dreamings that over my worn spirit lie—
Star-glory over a pale moonless sky,

Quietude soothing an overtasked brain,
Hushing the cry of importunate pain.

Angel of Sleep! I am tempted and tried;
Lay your hands over the wounds in my side;
Wounds that are deeper and wider, I ween,
Than any that mortal eyes ever have seen.
I am so weary, too weary to weep;
Come to me, beautiful Angel of Sleep,
Soothe me to slumber, and keep me at rest,
And stifle the heart that beats in my breast.

Angel of Sleep! Success is a dream,
Fame but a bubble on life's rushing stream;
Love is a mirage that beckons afar,
Friendship the gleam of a pale distant star;
Faith a vague rainbow that arches the sky
Over the spot where the storm-ruins lie;
Hope a red torchlight that brightens the way;
Sorrow the measure of life's rainy day.

Fain would I rest, blessed Angel of Sleep;
Rest, though to-morrow I wake but to weep;
Rest while my heart in my bosom I smother,
Knowing one day is like unto another,
Seeing no change in the long years that creep,
Shadow-like over the Future's Great Deep;
Shadows of vessels with gayly-filled deck,
Barques that the breakers are ready to wreck.

Over and over the story is told;
Told to the youthful and proved by the old,
Burden and sorrow, and bustle and strife,
Hope and despair the sad story of life;
Yet oh, my beautiful Angel of Sleep,
Over my spirit your loving watch keep;
Wave your white wings that the tempest may cease,
And slumber give unto my weariness peace.

SARAH M. B. PIATT.

A SOUTHERN critic and poet, doubtless desiring to be considered as one on whom the "mantle of genius" of E. A. Poe has fallen, in a series of "critical nibbles," placed Alice Cary HIGH among the "lady poets" of America, saying: "Alice Cary has written more *good* poetry than any lady in America,"— continuing:

"There is but one other Southern poetess who can be compared to Alice Cary, and that one is Sallie M. Bryan. Miss Bryan is the more imaginative — Miss Cary the *more touching* of the two. The former is passionate . . ."

He concludes by naming Miss Bryan as one whose name will live as long as there shall exist a record of American letters.

We agree with this "critic" in his high estimate of Sallie M. Bryan.

Sarah Morgan Bryan was born two or three miles from Lexington, Ky., August 11th, 1836. Her grandfather, Morgan Bryan, was one of the pioneers of the State, and the founder of Bryan's Station, well known in the early Indian struggles. Her family was related to Daniel Boone. Her mother (who is represented to have been a lovely and beautiful woman) having died while she was a child less than eight years old, she lived with her aunt, Mrs. Annie Boone, at New Castle, Ky., and received her education principally at the Henry Female College, long a favorite Southern institution at that place. While yet a very young girl, she interested many who knew her with a poetic gift which in one so young seemed marvellous. Her first published poem was contributed without her knowledge by one of her cousins to a newspaper at Galveston, Texas, and she was afterwards prevailed on to allow her girlish writings to appear in the *Louisville Journal*, from whose columns they gained a wide circulation and popular recognition, especially throughout the South. The late Fitz

46

Greene Halleck was one of the first to notice and admire her poetic genius, and having been pleased with one of her earlier poems in the *New York Ledger*, he took pains to make inquiry and learn her address; he then wrote her a note, which is so pleasantly characteristic and so brief that it may not be improper now to make it public.

Guilford, Conn., ——, 1858.

DEAR LADY: No doubt you often receive letters requesting your own autograph. May I reverse the medal and ask you to accept the autograph of one who admires exceedingly your —— [the name of the poem]. I remain, dear lady, your obedient servant,

FITZ GREENE HALLECK.

In June, 1861, Miss Bryan was married to Mr. John James Piatt, a poet of " exceedingly great promise," and resided with her husband in Washington City until last year ('67). In 1864, Mr. Piatt published a small volume at New York, entitled "Nests at Washington, and Other Poems," which included some of the later poems of Mrs. Piatt. But since her marriage she has written comparatively little, occasional poems by her having been published, during the year or two past, in the various magazines. Her later poems, which are generally very artistic, brief, and delicately turned, with a sort of under-current dramatic element in them often, as the reader will observe in the poem of "The Fancy Ball," have been recently published (1871) by J. R. Osgood & Co., under the title "A Woman's Poems."

Mrs. Piatt's home is now in Cincinnati, Ohio.

December, 1868.   △

PROEM.

TO THE WORLD.

Sweet World, if you will hear me now:
   I may not own a sounding lyre,
And wear my name upon my brow
   Like some great jewel full of fire.

But let me, singing, sit apart,
   In tender quiet with a few,
And keep my fame upon my heart,
   A little blush-rose wet with dew.

MY WEDDING-RING.

My heart stirr'd with its golden thrill
   And flutter'd closer up to thine,
In that blue morning of the June
   When first it clasp'd thy love and mine.

In it I see the little room,
   Rose-dim and brush'd with lilies still,
Where the old silence of my life
   Turn'd into music with "I will."

Oh, I would have my folded hands
   Take it into the dust with me;
All other little things of mine
   I'd leave in the bright world with thee.

THE FANCY BALL.

As Morning you'd have me rise
   On that shining world of art;
You forget! I have too much dark in my eyes —
   And too much dark in my heart.

"Then go as the Night — in June:
   Pass, dreamily, by the crowd,
With jewels to match the stars and the moon,
   And shadowy robes like cloud.

"Or as Spring, with a spray in your hair
   Of blossoms as yet unblown;
It will suit you well, for our youth should wear
   The bloom in the bud alone.

"Or drift from the outer gloom
   With the soft, white silence of Snow:"
I should melt myself with the warm, close room;
   Or my own life's burning. No.

"Then fly through the glitter and mirth
   As a Bird of Paradise."
Nay, the waters I drink have touch'd the earth;
   I breathe no summer of spice.

"Then!" Hush; if I go at all,
(It will make them stare and shrink,
It will look so strange at a Fancy Ball,)
I will go as Myself, I think!

---oo⦂⦂oo---

MISS NELLY MARSHALL.

THE subject of this sketch is the daughter of the distinguished General Humphrey Marshall, of Kentucky, celebrated in the annals of the South as a soldier and a statesman. She was born in Louisville, Kentucky, in the year 1847.

From her earliest childhood, Miss Marshall's intellectual development was remarkable, and her first compositions, though, as was natural, abounding in the crudities that mark the early efforts of all young writers, foretold that mental power and strength which have since won for her so many warm admirers and true friends. But those abilities which, in another, would have been carefully and tenderly nurtured, were, in her, subjected to the pruning-knife of opposition, and hence her talent may be said to have grown like the prairie-rose, climbing and clinging and blossoming at its own sweet will.

Reared in the strictest seclusion, and allowed only the freest communion with Nature, she has grown into womanhood with the trusting confidence of childhood in her heart and beautifying her character. She is described as *petite* in stature, delicately proportioned, and with large gray eyes and wavy light-brown hair.

Miss Marshall is perhaps one of the most popular writers in the South and West, although, as yet, her intellectual power is, as it were, undeveloped. Her friends claim and expect more marked manifestations of talent than she has yet given, and, judging by what this young lady has already accomplished, we think we may safely assert that they will not be disappointed.

The circumstances that led Miss Marshall to abandon the retirement in which she had hitherto lived, were very sad. The war, which brought devastation and desolation to so many homes in Kentucky, passed by "Beechland" with an unsparing hand. Unexpected trials, sickness, death, adversity, assailed that once merry household; and as a member of the shadowed and grief-stricken circle, Miss Marshall was compelled to resort to her pen, to stand in the breach between those

7

most dear to her and misfortune. Miss Marshall's first volume was published in 1866, "Gleanings from Fireside Fancies," by Sans Souci. "As By Fire," a novel, published in New York in 1869, was successful —giving promise of future success. At Frankfort, Kentucky, February 13th, 1871, Miss Marshall was married to Mr. McAfee.

1869.   CHARLES DIMITRY.

QUESTIONS.

Why are the days so drearily long?
Why seems each duty a terrible task?
Why have my red lips hushed their glad song?
Why?—thro' the distance I hopelessly ask!

Why are the sunbeams ghastly and dim?
Why have the flowers lost their perfume?
Why wails my heart a funeral hymn?
Why do my tears all my smilings entomb?.

Was I predestined a child of despair?
Must all my brightest hopes soonest decay?
Must all my castles be reared in the air,
And hope, taking wings, speed fleetest away?

Will he forever be haughty and cold?
Never once melting 'neath love's sunny smile?
Memories—sweet mem'ries of glad days of old—
Teach me again how his heart to beguile!

Has the bright past no brightness for him?
Is the warm love that he cherished quite dead?
Ah, love's gay visions have grown strangely dim!
Holdeth his heart a new passion instead?

If this dark knowledge of misery be mine;
If the hope of his truth, because brightest, be fleetest:
Then, come, beloved Death!—I'll gladly be thine;
And of all Love's embraces thine own shall be sweetest!

ALDER–BOUGHS.

Shake down, oh, shake down your blossoms of snow,
   Green alder-boughs, shake them down at my feet;
Drift them all over these white sands below,
   Pulsing with perfume exquisite and sweet ;
And 'neath their kisses it may be my heart,
   Frozen and cold all these long dreary years,
Into fresh being may longingly start,
   Melting its ice into passionate tears:

Tears that must flow like a wide gulf between
   Two hearts that loved in the days long ago;
Days, when these alder-boughs nodding were green,
   Flecked, as they now are, with blossoms of snow:
Days, when my lover and I were both young,
   Both full of constancy, passion, and love;
Roaming and dreaming these wild woods among,
   While a blue May sky bent smiling above.

Days that are dead as the dead in their graves;
   Days whose sweet beauty and perfume have passed,
Like the white foam-fret on Ocean's green waves,
   Buoyant and lovely, but too frail to last.
And as we bend o'er the cold forms of those
   Who have gone early to Death's sombre sleep,
Folding their hands as to welcome repose,
   Thus have I come o'er these dead days to weep.

So bend low, oh, bend low! alder-boughs green,
   Till I can catch at your blossoms of snow;
Nodding like hearse-plumes so soft in the wind
   Over these smooth stretching white sands below!
Never again while I live, alder-boughs,
   Will I your snow-blooms and verdant leaves see;
But when I lie dead and cold in my grave,
   I pray God they'll blossom and fade over me!

A WOMAN'S HEART.

From "As By Fire."

Fanny Evesham was jealous as Gulbeyez, and the bitterness of her indignation against beautiful, innocent Electra amounted almost to passion. But it was not a jealousy prompted by love. It was simply the gangrene of wounded vanity, that her husband should not find her so irresistible that disloyalty to her charms would be impossible. Woman's heart is a deep and wonderful mystery, and it is not for the world, with the presumption of a Dædalus, to attempt to solve it by a process of metaphysical or philosophical investigation. Dædalus was ingenious artist enough to make the labyrinth of Crete, but the intricacy of a woman's emotions would be a riddle which I question if Œdipus himself could solve. In unhappiness of the heart they are seldom faithful to themselves! In the hour of physical or social trials they stand forth in the arena magnanimous, unflinching — nothing sordid is mingled with their enthusiasm; but let a woman's heart once resign itself to the sway of vanity, and she is already as irredeemably lost as if she trod the red-hot tesselations of the Vulcanian regions. No "Eden-born motives," no noble surroundings, no lofty altitudes, can her soul harbor or appreciate. Thenceforth she is a creature whose debasing passions will cast her from any exalted position she may occupy, or may have striven to attain. And of all errors into which she may fall, this love of flirtation, this contemptible vanity which would gratify itself at the cost of the purest and most ennobling emotions of which the heart is capable, is most defamatory to her character as a wife, a mother, or a woman. She makes herself the puppet for a mocking multitude; she blights and degrades herself by a contemptible assumption of affection which she does not in reality entertain; she pollutes the altars of love and friendship with the ashes of a dead heart; she sets an example of evil to the sweet, fresh natures about her, which will doubtless beguile many into a like commission of folly — which, after all, terminates in mortification, chagrin, repentance, and regret. Yet at this shrine of pollution Mrs. Evesham bowed herself down an humble votary, and the sin of her beguilement reared its serpent crest above her.

FLORENCE ANDERSON,

Of Glen Ada, near Harrodsburg, Ky.

WE subjoin the following brief sketch of one, who, from the un-eventful and subjective character of her life, protests that she is not a theme for the biographer.

Florence Anderson is a Virginian by birth, a Kentuckian by adoption. Descended from families which for many generations had combined the highest attributes of scholar, soldier, and gentleman, men who from the dawn of our country's history had counted it no loss to peril all save *honor* in defence of that country's liberties, Miss Anderson inherited, as her birthright, a love of learning, of honor and true glory.

She had no teacher but her father. Her infant steps were steadied by him, as his hand guided her onward and upward to the fair temple of Knowledge. Deeply imbued as his own mind was with the love of classic lore, it was not strange that he should teach his docile and ambitious pupil a deep sympathy with his tastes. Before a dozen summers had blossomed over her, she had read Virgil and Horace; had felt her heart thrill at the recital of the mighty deeds of heroes, had wept o'er Hector slain, and fallen Troy. In "Zenaida," Miss Anderson's earliest work, the frequent, familiar allusions to classic subjects, and the use of words of classic derivation in preference to the more rugged and vigorous Saxon, were noted as defects in her style by more than one kindly critic.

The book* was written as a contribution to a little paper, edited by a sister and herself to enliven the winter evenings, in a quiet country home. Read aloud by that sister's voice of music, now mute forever, the imperfections of "Zenaida" were overlooked by its too partial judges, and the book was published before the more chastened and corrected taste of the writer had had time to prune its too great luxuriance. Its flattering reception by an indulgent public would, doubtless, have stimulated the young authoress to renewed exertion in the field of romance, had not the war absorbed her sympathies, and paled the light of the unreal by the glare of the actual. In Miss Anderson's ideal of true development, the artist is ever subordinate to the woman, the woman to the Christian. She turns from the profound speculations and beautiful theories of philosophers and sages with more confiding

* "Zenaida," published by J. B. Lippincott & Co., Philadelphia, 1859.

faith in the Christ, the True Light; recognizing Him as the Saviour of all mankind, but preëminently the Friend of woman. Believing as she does that the aim of life should be rather to make the whole life a poem, divine in its beautiful harmony, than to write poetry, her poems are to be judged more as the spontaneous expression of an emotional condition of the mind than as the labored effort of her muse. She has sung as the birds sing, because the song in her heart demanded a voice.

The following personal description is from the graceful pen of a sister-poet, Mrs. Mary R. T. McAboy, of Paris, Ky.

FLORENCE ANDERSON,

THE POET.

Thro' the fair summer-time she came to me
As bright birds flit to grace a crumbling shrine,
Or like a blossomed vine with graceful twine,
That drapes with young, fresh life a leafless tree, —
She came, like Undine rising from the sea,
Yet so ethereal, in the soft sunshine,
She seemed to me half mortal, half divine,
So fair she was in maiden purity.
I clasped her small white hand; she read to me
From Poet, rapt to his divinest theme,
And still she shone, as in a golden dream,
The while she shared his nectared ecstasy.
And then I said, her heart is like the snow,
That reddens in the sunset's reddest glow.

ROSEHEATH, Ky., April 16, 1866.   M. R. M.

THE WORLD OF THE IDEAL.

[Das Ideal ist das einzige Paradies aus welchem wir nicht getrieben werden können.]

On spirit world! by thy golden streams,
I sit in a trance of delicious dreams;
A magical flush in the air doth rest,
Soft as the tint on the sea-shell's breast.

The summer ne'er fades in thy shady bowers,
And long, bright branches of clustering flowers

Trail thick over paths by the river's side,
Wooed, wooed by the murmurs of the tide.

There is no sun in the blue above,
And yet a glow, like the light of love,
Diffuses its radiance over all,
And binds the spirit in magic thrall.

The air is stirred by a faint, soft breeze,
There's a sound like the humming of myriad bees,
And oft to the listening ear doth float
The exquisite swell of a song-bird's note.

No friendship ever may enter there
That would feel a taint in the soft pure air;
No lover intrude on the hallowed spot,
Whose vows, are unheeded and forgot.

No votary kneel on thy holy sod,
Whose soul is traitor to his God;
Nothing unholy, nothing untrue,
Can dwell 'neath that arch of stainless blue.

But friends, whose tender and loving smile
Can all remembrance of grief beguile,
Walk with the spirit, and share its joy,
Unmixed with envy's base alloy.

And poets tune their mystic lyres
Where slumber sacred, hidden fires,
And, skilled in music's subtlest lore,
Unfathomed depths of the soul explore.

To the fair aurora-tinted heights
Of the world beyond they wing their flights
And stand and beckon from their bands
The angels of the immortal lands.

They sing of beauty, of love, of youth,
The value of life, the power of truth,
Of all things holy, of all things pure,
Which shall eternally endure.

Such bowers of rest do the angels plan
For the earth-worn, weary soul of man;
And none have the power to disinherit
From its world of dreams the Ideal spirit.

MRS. CHAPMAN COLEMAN AND DAUGHTERS.

MRS. COLEMAN is more widely known as a woman of society, and as the daughter of the late John J. Crittenden, of Kentucky, than as an author. She was born at Frankfort, the capital of the State. Her educational advantages in early life were not such as are now enjoyed by the young ladies of the present day; but they were *the best* that Kentucky at that time afforded. At her father's house she met with the most distinguished men of the State, and grew up among the thinkers and talkers of the day.

In 1830, Miss Crittenden married Mr. Chapman Coleman, of Louisville, and resided in that city, the centre of a gay and brilliant circle, until her husband's death, in 1850. Mrs. Coleman is a most brilliant conversationalist. A friend, who has been intimate with her for over thirty-seven years, says: "She has always been ambitious of attaining to distinction and the highest degree of excellence in everything she attempted. Her duties as a daughter, a wife, a mother, a sister, a friend, have always been performed in the most conscientious and admirable manner."

Mrs. Coleman has been the mother of seven children, and from their birth she ever devoted herself to their education. After her husband's death she went to Europe, and lived in Germany for the purpose of educating her children. She studied with them, and mastered the French and German languages, with what success, the clever translations from both languages, given to the world by herself and daughters, best testify. Eugenia, Judith, and Sallie Coleman assisted the mother in these translations, of which the series of romances of Mrs. Mühlbach, relating to "Frederick the Great," are best known. The Misses Coleman are lovely, refined, and charming young ladies, full of grace and culture; how could the daughters of such a mother fail of being otherwise?

Mrs. Coleman's knowledge of literature is extensive and accurate. She has a prompt and bright judgment, and her industry and energy are invincible. Could she be induced to give her own thoughts to the world of readers, they could not but be delighted with their originality, cleverness, and her piquant style.

Since her return from Europe, Mrs. Coleman has resided principally in Baltimore. She was one of the select committee sent from Baltimore to petition President Johnson in behalf of Mr. Jefferson Davis, then in prison.

56

Mrs. Coleman has published recently a Life and Times of her father, the Hon. J. J. Crittenden, (J. B. Lippincott & Co., Publishers, Philadelphia, 1871,) one of the distinguished men of the country — as she is, and has always been, regarded as one of the most distinguished among the brilliant women of Kentucky.

1869.   E. L.

——∘∘ːⓈː∘∘——

S. ROCHESTER FORD.

MRS. FORD, whose maiden name was Rochester, was born at Rochester Springs, Boyle county, Kentucky, in 1828.

She was the eldest of three daughters, and only in her fourth year when her mother died. "This loss was providentially supplied by the judicious supervision of her maternal grandmother, a woman of great mental and physical vigor, who devoted herself to her grandchildren with true motherly interest. Accustomed herself to out-door exercise, the management of a farm, and the superintendence of a large family, and being withal a woman of highly religious character, she appreciated and enforced the kind of training which is now apparent in the strong characteristics of our writer." * From the same authority we get the following:

"Her advantages for acquiring Biblical knowledge were rather unusual. She was a lover of books and a close student. Her uncle, Rev. J. R. Pitts, occupied an adjacent farm, and gave her free access to his library and counsel. She cultivated the acquaintance of clergymen, especially those of her own denomination, and took an intelligent and deep interest in the study of the distinguishing principles of their theology. In this way she laid the foundation of the skill with which she has since defended the faith of her people."

She married the Rev. S. H. Ford in 1855, who was at that time pastor of a Baptist church in Louisville, Ky. A short time after his marriage, Rev. Mr. Ford became proprietor of a religious monthly, called the "Christian Repository," which he conducted with success until the "war-cloud burst."

Mrs. Ford commenced her literary life by contributing to this magazine, in the pages of which first appeared "Grace Truman; or, Love and Principle."

This work was published in 1857, by Sheldon & Co., of New York, and gracefully dedicated to "Elizabeth T. Pitts, my loved and venerated grandmother, who, beneath the weight of eighty years, still

8   * "Women of the South," by Mary Forrest.

cherishes, with clear conception and unabated zeal, those principles which, in orphan childhood, I learned from her lips."

This book had a very large sale.

In 1860, through the same publishers, appeared Mrs. Ford's second book, — "Mary Bunyan, the Dreamer's Blind Daughter," — a tale of religious persecution. Says the *New York Evangelist*:

"The simple incidents of Bunyan's life, his protracted imprisonment, his heroic endurance and lofty faith, are of themselves full of the deepest and most thrilling interest. It needed only the picture of his blind daughter, Mary, in her gentleness and patience under sore misfortune, to give completeness to the tragic yet noble scenes in which Bunyan figures, so modestly yet grandly conspicuous. The author of the volume before us has carefully gathered up such historical facts — and they are, fortunately, numerous and well authenticated — as could throw light upon her subject, and has employed them with great sagacity and effect in the construction of her story."

During the war, Mrs. Ford was a refugee in "Dixie." For some time, in the later part of the war, Rev. Mr. Ford was stationed in Mobile. "The Raids and Romance of Morgan and his Men,"* which appeared serially in a weekly paper, was published by S. H. Gœtzel, Mobile, in 1864, on dingy paper, with "wall paper" covers, but had a large sale, and was read and re-read by camp-fires and firesides. Mrs. Ford is now residing in Memphis, where her husband is editing the "Southern Repository," a monthly journal.

March, 1868.

AUNT PEGGY'S DEATH-BED.

Wasted by disease, worn out with the strife of life, a calm, patient sufferer lies upon the bed of death. She knows her hours are almost ended, and as she feels the shadow of death stealing gently over her, her countenance becomes more and more radiant with the light of heaven.

'T is a little cottage room, — neat, yet very plain; its whitewashed walls, and snowy window-curtains, and nicely dusted chests, and old-fashioned bureau with its bright brass knobs, all attest the hand of care.

In the right-hand corner, near the fireplace, stands a low bed, with its clean pillows and blue yarn coverlet, and on that bed lies a resigned sufferer,

* An edition was published by Sheldon & Co., New York, 1866.

breathing out her mortal life. She is sleeping now; for the anodynes have done their work of mercy, and all pain is for the time entirely lulled.

Beside the bed are two watchers, silent, lest the slightest noise might disturb the sleeper. One holds the old attenuated hand in hers, and gently notes the ebb and flow of the wellnigh spent life-current. The other is seated by her side, watching with anxiety every changing expression of the earnest face.

The sleeper wakens, opens her eyes, and looks intently round the room, as if in search of some one whom she had been long expecting. Not finding the object of her lengthened gaze, she asked, in a low, feeble voice:

"Hain't he come yit?"

"No, Aunt Peggy, not yet."

"An' won't he come dis mornin', Miss Gracey, don't you think? I wants so much to see him."

"Yes, Aunt Peggy, I am looking for him every minute."

"I hopes he will; for I wants to talk wid him once more afore I goes. He'll surely come by-'m-by; he never misses a day."

"Yes, Aunt Peggy, I know he will come," she answered, bending over her, and giving her a cup of cold water. "He will be here, I am sure, in a few minutes; Mr. Holmes has gone to town for some medicine for you, and he will come with him."

"Med'cin's no more use for me, Miss Gracey. I'se almos' done wid dis airth, bless de Lord; my time is come to go and be at rest. I tink before de sun sets dis day, I shall be far away from here in my Massa's house."

"Do you feel any pain now, Aunt Peggy?" said Fanny, approaching nearer and taking the wasted hand in hers. She looked up as if she did not understand the question.

"Does anything hurt you now, Aunt Peggy?" she repeated, bending over her, and speaking in a louder tone.

"No, no, Fanny dear. I feels no more pain now; it's all gone, an' I think I'll never have any more on this airth; an' I'se sure I'll not have any in heben."

As the old woman uttered these words of hope and resignation, they both felt her words were true; that soon the spirit which was now so faintly animating that sinking frame would be released from its clay prison-house, to be forever at rest in the paradise of God.

"Can I do anything for you, Aunt Peggy?" she asked, as she saw the old servant direct her eye to the little table at the foot of the bed.

"Jest a leetle drop of water, dear; I feels so hot here," and she laid her hand on her breast; "an' raise dis ole head a leetle higher, chile, dat I may see him when he comes. An', Miss Gracey, draw dat curtin a bit to one side, to let de light in, for my eyes is a-growin' dim. I wishes he'd come."

Her requests were attended to. She was raised, and supported by pillows in the bed, so as to have a full view of the door.

"Dat will do, Fanny dear; I kin see him now, if he comes afore my sight is gone."

Fanny turned aside to hide her grief as the old servant spoke of the unmistakable signs of approaching death. Aunt Peggy had been to her a friend since the day she had first seen the light of earth. She had watched over her as if she had been her own child; and often had her kind hands supplied her childish wants, and her kind words consoled her childish sorrows. And in after-years, too, she had given her aid and comfort when her heart was sorely stricken; had pointed out, in her own homely way, the path to those joys that fade not — that possession which is "undefiled, and that passeth not away."

Mrs. Holmes, who had every day come to see the faithful old servant, entered the room. As soon as she caught a glimpse of her face, she read therein the evidences of approaching dissolution. Going to the bedside, and taking up the wan hand, she leaned down and asked her how she felt.

"I 'se almos' home, Miss Jane," and a faint smile for a moment parted her parched lips.

"And are you happy, Aunt Peggy, in the prospect of so soon standing in the presence of your great Judge?"

"Yes, yes, Miss Jane, I 'se very happy. I has nothin' to fear. My Saviour will ans'er for me when I 'se called to give my account. He has died for me, and his death has took away all my sins."

She stopped short for want of breath. Her respiration was becoming gradually more and more difficult. She folded her hands, and, closing her eyes, remained perfectly still for several minutes. Then looking anxiously up at her mistress, who was still by the bedside, she said, feebly:

"I wishes he would come."

"She speaks of Edwin, I suppose," said Mrs. Holmes, addressing herself to Grace.

"Yes; she has several times expressed a desire to see him."

Just then footsteps were heard through the half-open door. The old woman, her hearing apparently rendered more acute by the great anxiety of her mind, seemed to catch the sound instantly, and turning her head on the pillow, said in a strong, clear voice:

"He 's comin' now! I hear his step," and her eye lighted up with an expression of earnest expectancy.

"An' so you 's come at last," she said, looking up into his face as he stood by her bedside, and making an effort to extend her hand to him. He perceived her intention, and immediately, with the gentleness of a woman, took her wasted hand, and pressed it within his own.

"And how do you feel now, Aunt Peggy?"

"I 'se very happy now, Massa Ed. I 'se so glad you 's come. I thought I shouldn't see you agin, maybe, for I 'se almos' gone. I 've jes been tellin' Fanny here, dat before de sun goes down I shall be in my Massa's house."

Mr. Lewis felt her words were true. He saw that the spirit could not much longer linger in its frail tenement.

Mr. Holmes mixed the medicine he had brought from Dr. Denny, and offered it to her.

She shook her head slowly. "It's no use now, Massa John; it won't do no good."

"But take it, Aunt Peggy; it will keep you from suffering."

She reached out her hand in the direction of the cup, but she had not strength to take it. Mr. Holmes elevated her head, and she swallowed about half of the mixture; and then, as if exhausted by the effort, she fell back upon the pillows. The frill of her cap was thrown back from her forehead, revealing her gray hair; her gown was opened about the throat, and her bosom was partially bared, for she had complained of a great burning within, which nothing they could give her would allay. One hand rested on her breast, the other lay extended by her side. Not a muscle moved; her breathing became low and lengthened; and as they looked upon her, they felt it must be death. She had remained some time in this state of stupor, while every breath was thought to be her last, when, suddenly arising, she unclosed her eyes, and fixing her gaze upon Mr. Lewis, who stood next her, she motioned for him to come nearer. He leaned over to catch her words. She seemed to be waiting for him to speak. He put his lips close to her ear, and said:

"Do you feel that His rod and staff comfort you, Aunt Peggy?"

Gathering up her whole energy, as if for the final struggle, she answered, in a voice which was understood by all present:

"Yes, yes; I fear no evil, bless de Lord. De grave has no terrors for me; and the sting of death is took away! I can say wid de 'postle, 'I has fought a good fight; I has kept de faith,' and I know dare is a crown laid up for me in heben, which my Saviour will soon place on dis poor ole head."

"Your trust in the Lord Jesus Christ is sure and steadfast, Aunt Peggy; no clouds to hide his face from you."

"No, no; my Saviour is wid me, an' his smile fills me wid joy. Christ died for poor sinners like me, an' he is willin' and able to save all dat comes unto him."

Her voice failed her, so that she could not proceed further, and she remained motionless, with her eyes fixed upon Mr. Lewis, as if desirous of saying something more to him. At length she continued:

"Go on, Massa Ed, to preach the gospel of Christ to sinners; never give it up. Try to build up de little church, and God will help you."

Her eyes passed from one to another, and rested at last upon Mr. Holmes.

"Go on, Massa John, in de way you has set out; you, and Fanny, and Miss Gracey. You has all been kind to me, and I 'se sorry to leave you; but I 'se going home, and you 'll all come arter me soon. Den we shall never part no more. I bid you all farewell," and she moved her powerless hand slightly toward them. Each one approached the bedside, and clasped the death-cold hand, while tears bedewed their cheeks.

"Good-bye," she murmured to each pressure.

They watched her as her breath grew fainter and yet more faint; a slight shudder passed through her frame, a gasp, and all was still! Her spirit had gone up to dwell on high.

For some moments not a word was spoken. Each one stood gazing on the lifeless form before them with sorrowful heart; for she who lay there, wrapped in the mantle of death, had been a friend to each — to all.

MRS. MARIE T. DAVIESS.

MRS. DAVIESS is of pure Revolutionary stock. Her two grandsires, Capt. George Robards and Col. John Thompson, having fought through the war for Independence, married fair and excellent daughters of the Old Dominion, of which all parties were natives, and soon after removed to Kentucky, settling on adjoining plantations. Drawn together by the common memories of their service in the field, their acquaintance ripened into warm intimacy, which had the not uncommon result of an alliance by marriage between the two families. In 1807, Miss Robards and John B. Thompson were united in marriage, and, after a short residence on their farm, removed to Harrodsburg, where they ever after resided, Mr. Thompson practising successfully his profession — the law, — occasionally serving in the Legislature of his State. He was a member of the Senate when the cholera swept over the land in 1833, taking him among its victims. The death of Mr. Thompson, in the prime of life and usefulness, seriously contracted the horizon of his family's future; but a proud and energetic mother did all within her power to keep this sad reverse from interfering with their substantial good. She gave her four sons liberal educations, and her daughters such opportunities as the village school afforded, which was then, and is now, among the best in the West. The sons were all educated in their father's profession, and the eldest, John B. Thompson, the only one that entered into public life, was for many years a representative of Kentucky in Congress, and, while Lieut.-Governor of the State, was elected, at the death of Henry Clay, to fill his seat in the Senate of the United States. Mrs. Daviess's opportunities for the acquirement of social distinction were of the finest. Residing in Harrodsburg, which every summer for many years was a resort of fashion and gayety, she was brought in constant contact with the *élite* of Southern and Western society that for six months of the year thronged this "Saratoga of the West." Doubtless, in the scattered homes of this smitten region, when their now sobered tenants dwell on the happy days of "lang syne," Miss Marie Thompson has ever a place in the revived tableaux.

In 1839, Miss Thompson was married to William Daviess, son of Capt. Samuel Daviess, and nephew of Col. Joseph Hamilton Daviess, a gentleman of worth, of fine address and remarkable colloquial powers. He was educated for a lawyer, but never practised. He entered upon a public career with great zest and promise of reward to his ambition, but, falling into wretched health, resigned his place in the State Senate, and has since contented himself with rural pursuits; and seldom does a roof-tree shelter a more hospitable home or a more agreeable family circle than does the one of Hayfields.

Mrs. Daviess's writings, especially poetry, were not, as now is frequently the case, the result of her training in belles-lettres, but simply the overflow of feeling and fancy that would not be repressed. Her coming before the public was not with the intention of ever writing professionally, nor the pursuit of the *ignis fatuus*, fame.

A bridal compliment to a friend was so kindly received, that, by request from one and another editor, Mrs. Daviess threw out many waifs of beauty on the passing current of journalism, seldom under her own name, but signed by such name as the passing fancy suggested. Her effusions were extensively copied, and complimented for their smooth flow of rhyme and almost redundant beauty of expression. "The Nun" was the most elaborate poem she ever published. Most of Mrs. Daviess's MSS. and copies of her published articles were destroyed by an accident, and we have but few poetical specimens to choose from. "A Harvest Hymn" breathes a spirit of gratitude to Him who sends his seedtime and harvest alike upon the just and the unjust, and which we should all feel, whether we abide on the mountain-tops of prosperity or in the valley of humility.

For some years after her marriage, if the fountain of Mrs. Daviess's pen flowed at all, it was like some of those strange streams that sink beneath the earth's surface, and wind on their way unseen, yet gathering strength and purity to reappear in and fertilize fresh fields. The first fruit of Mrs. Daviess's revived authorship which I met were "Roger Sherman — A Tale of '76," and "Woman's Love," both very well conceived and sustained stories. But her strong conviction that the plain, practical duties of life should command, if necessary, the whole of every woman's time, seems to have tinged the very holiday hours she secured by extra exertion for the exercise of her taste; and of late her writings seem to have been a kind of photograph of her every-day life. She received from the Kentucky State Agricultural Society a premium for the essay on the "Cultivation and Uses of Chinese Sugar-Cane," a product she was the first to introduce into the State, prophesying it would, as it has, become a staple of the West. Subsequently, she was awarded a diploma for an essay upon some literary theme by the National Fair, held in St. Louis a few years ago. For some time she has been special contributor to several leading agricultural papers. Among them, Colman's "Rural World," of St. Louis, and "Cultivator and Country Gentleman," Albany, N. Y. Her letters in these journals are among their most charming features, and the most useful exercises of a fluent pen. Viewed from one standpoint, all literature can be divided into two classes, the writers of Art, and the writers of Nature. In one, the composer is admired as a master-architect, who has ingeniously fettered together base, shaft, and cornice; where thoughts stand like pillars carefully hewn, and whose figures adorn them, as curiously-wrought carving these columns. In the other class, we look upon the author as a friend, who, with absorbing conversation, beguiles us into a walk, and all the while points out to us the charms of the landscape spread out before us; showing us the mist-enveloped truths that rise like blue hills in the distance, but lingering on the familiar things that surround us; descanting with as much grace on the usefulness of the herb as the beauty of the flower; commenting with equal interest on the value to commerce of the distant river which bears on its waters the produce of our own and foreign lands, and the meanderings of the babbling brook that, fretting over the rocky ledges, descends into the peaceful valley on foamy wings.

Mrs. Daviess belongs to the latter class, and can please her readers as well with explanation of the useful as descriptions of the beautiful, often blending the two together in a manner we think quite her own.

Mrs. Daviess is a living refutation of the world-wide charge of the incompatibility of literary and housewifely tastes. You might surprise many of her neighbors with the information that she "wrote for publication." She has always seemed to mingle literary habits so easily with the overwhelming cares of a large family, that we hope that genius as well as water will find its level, and that she will some day find leisure for a free exercise of her pen, and we see her take a prominent place among the "Southland Writers."

1868.

HARVEST HYMN.

"And ye shall eat neither bread, nor parched corn, nor green ears, until the selfsame day that ye have brought an offering unto your God : *it shall be* a statute for ever throughout your generations." — LEV. xxiii. 14.

The Hebrew reapers on their blades leaned and gazed o'er the plain
Wet with the toil-drops from their brow as from a summer's rain ;
Then, tho' upon their dreary minds the vision clear arose
Of home, and all its smiling group, and evening's sweet repose,
They gathered of their harvest fruits, and ere the trump that woke
From every hill and grassy glade its wild thanksgivings spoke,
They from ten thousand altar-fires sent to the bending skies
The incense of their grateful hearts in harvest sacrifice.

And smiled the eye of heaven more bright on ancient Palestine,
Than it is wont in summer hours on our fair land to shine —
Did genial rains fall freer there, or the fresh, lifeful breeze
Come with more stirring hopes to them from wide commercial seas
Than unto us — or had they hearts more glad, or arms more strong,
Than has our free land's sturdy race — that we have not a song,
Or altar-fire, or trumpet-note, at harvest home, to call
Forgetful hearts to thankfulness to Him who giveth all ?

Come ! if the temple hath no voice that claims that task of love,
Come round the household altar now, and yield to Him above
Thanks for the treasure garnered in ; ask for the strength again
To reap where'er His kindness spreads the golden harvest plain ;
And pray thy nation may not prove ungrateful as that race,
That Heaven may never make thy home a bare and blighted place ;
That, tho' a conq'ror tramples now o'er Judea's courts and plains,
No tyrant step shall stain our land or scar her sons with chains.

VALUE OF PERMANENCE IN HOME AND VOCATION.

(EXTRACT.)

Another fruitful cause of discontent lies in what phrenologists term locality. Coupled with that, and almost as pernicious in its influence upon our characters, is the want of a feeling of permanence in our vocations.

It was a great day for human progress when the revolutionary axe was laid to the law of primogeniture, that bitter root whence sprang all the unjust and baneful usages of aristocracy; yet it was a pity that with the genealogical tree should perish the many fair virtues that clustered in its shade, as love of home, pride of name, and fealty to kindred blood. It is an animating thought to the spirited younger brother, that he has an equal interest in the honors and name of his sire; and that, when the sire has been gathered to his rest, law will give him an equal interest in his heritable goods. Yet it is a shame because no law entails the homestead on the name — that the place which a father's pride and mother's taste have combined to render a paradise, should have none but a salable value in their children's eyes. So with our callings. It is a proud thing to feel we are not born serfs to any soil or condition — that, by virtue of our own good deeds, and in the strength of our own will, we may rise to any station in our country's scale of honor; and yet it is sad to feel that almost all our homes, and talents, and vocations are, like Chinese junks, ever floating, and that all we have and are can be had at a price. Ay, there is purity, and should be strength, in the tie that binds us to the homestead. The family that realizes its present to be its future home for all time to come, will not be drones or idlers, dreamers or speculators, in the many El Dorados that lure the sanguine to ruin.

The trembling grandsire will plant, because he knows his fair young grandchild shall gambol in the shade of his cherished tree; the young will sow, because they shall reap; and thus, planting and tending together, make strong the bonds that hold, by happy associations, all to the old hearth-stone. In a like manner, a faith in the permanence of our vocations conduces to skill and proficiency, and generates an honorable emulation to excel in that craft with which we know our name and memory shall ever be identified. And this feeling of permanence in our homes and vocations gives higher tone to our moral nature. Knowing that upon the acquaintances of to-day we are to depend for the courtesies and kindness that must sweeten our evening hours of life, we allow our hearts to throw out their tendrils freely, nor fear they shall be rudely broken. Cordiality and benevolence take, in our intercourse with our kind, the place of formality and selfishness; and, instead of a restless desire to find how we can make all we meet subserve our interests, we know no higher pleasure than basking in the sunshine of gratitude which our own unselfish service of our kind has caused to light and glow around us. Living under these influences, the homes that are now so often profaned by the reckless steps of vice and the hideous voice of discord would become what they should be, the highest, purest type a Christian knows of heavenly rest. Then should we understand that feeling which makes it unsafe to give voice to the songs of Switzerland in the ears of her exiled soldiery; the sentiment that makes the stricken foreigner beg his way back to his "Vaterland;" the unquenched desire that sends the outcast Jew in his death-hour to lay his bones in the desolate land of his faith.

———oo;o;oo———

VIRGINIA PENNY.

MISS PENNY was born at Louisville, Kentucky, 1826. She is a graduate of the Female Seminary at Steubenville, Ohio.

Her published works are as follows:

1st. *Employments of Women.* A Cyclopedia of Women's Work. Boston. 12mo. 1863.

2d. *Five Hundred Employments adapted to Women.* Philadelphia: J. E. Potter & Co., publishers. 12mo. 1868.

3d. *Think and Act.* A Series of Articles on Men and Women, Work and Wages. Philadelphia: Claxton, Remsen & Haffelfinger. 12mo. 1869.

4th. *How Women can Make Money,* Married or Single, in all Branches of the Arts and Sciences, Professions, Trades, Agricultural and Mechanical Pursuits. Cr. 8vo, pp. 500. Springfield, Mass., 1871.

The subject-matter of these volumes is the same.

" Miss Penny has earned the sober gratitude of women, and men interested in the lot of women, by the labors of many years in the hardest and least remunerative fields of service. She is no orator, politician, or manager, but a delving, drudging worker. With a patience that only the most profound faith could have sustained, and an industry that only a deep enthusiasm could have kept from flagging, she has devoted herself to the task of collecting and assorting facts bearing on the subject of woman's work and wages. What work women did or could do; the amount of training demanded for it; the number of hours daily that must be devoted to it; the conditions and circumstances attending on its performance; its effect on health, spirits, and disposition; the average amount of its remuneration; the prospect it opened; in short, every particular that was interesting or important in a practical point of view, she endeavored to ascertain. . . . Miss Penny's style is not especially brilliant or attractive, but is interesting; and, better than all, her essays are sober, wise, and important."—*Nation, November* 18*th,* 1869.

March, 1871.

———◦◦⋛⋚◦◦———

SALLIE J. H. BATTEY.

MRS. SALLIE J. HANCOCK BATTEY was born at Evanside, Kentucky, about fourteen miles from the city of Louisville, at an old homestead which has been the property of her family since the State was a wilderness. She was married at an early age to Mr. Hancock, and was a widow a few years afterward, and for ten years devoted herself to the education of her daughter, and the profession of literature. As an author Mrs. Hancock was industrious, and won laurels and friends. She has written considerable in prose and verse, under the name of "Latona," for the Louisville journals, and magazines North and South. For some time she edited a magazine. Has published three books, namely, two novels, and one volume of poems.

1st. *Etna Vandemir.* A Romance of Kentucky and "The Great Uprising." New York. 1863.

2d. *The Montanas; or, Under the Stars.* New York, 1867.

3d. *Rayon d'Amour.* Poems. Philadelphia, 1869.

Mrs. Hancock has been called the "Minstrel of the West."

A poet, in an address to her, thus alludes to her poems:

> "Not thine to sing the sage's lore,
>   Nor yet to hymn polemic creed :
>   Thy song supplies a nobler need,
> And touches chords untouched before."

In 1870, Mrs. Hancock was married to Mr. Manfred C. Battey, formerly of Buffalo, N. Y., now of Washington, D. C.

Her address is Evanside, near Jeffersontown, Ky.

March, 1871.

DREAMS.

> "We are such stuff
> As dreams are made of, and our little life
> Is rounded with a sleep."
>
> SHAKSPEARE.

Golden ripples on the wall,
Linger while the shadows fall:

Eden visions trailing far,
Through the sunset gates ajar;

Diamond anchors on Time's strand,
Tracery of the Almighty hand;

Death and sleep its counterpart,
Mutely crossing hand and heart:

Things that are, and things that seem,
Through the pearly gates of dream,

Strangely blent by God's decree
In a dual mystery.

Thus, when sorrow's night has shed
Blight for living, pall for dead,

Fairer forms of light are born;
Suns cross o'er the dark to morn;

Dreams are mirrored life to be,
Heaven in an earthly sea:

Stars at play, amid the sand,
Chime in chorus deep and grand;

Spirit symbols here and there,
Tell us God is everywhere.

ALICE McCLURE GRIFFIN.

POEMS, by Alice McClure Griffin — Cincinnati, O., Rickey & Carroll, 1864, — was the simple title of a 12mo volume of 126 pages. This volume is composed principally of verses that have appeared in the columns of papers and magazines, over the signature of "Muni Tell" and "Addie Glenmore."

In a preface the reader is informed that "the entire book was written when the author was between fourteen and twenty years of age."

Alice McClure was born in Boone County, Kentucky — the only daughter of Dr. Virgil McClure, also a native of Kentucky. Her mother is a descendant of Burns, the poet, and the author of several novels. Alice McClure graduated at the Wesleyan Female College, Cincinnati, at the age of sixteen. Her father at this time removed to Newport, Ky., where Miss McClure was married, on the last day of 1861, to Mr. G. W. Griffin, author of "Studies in Literature" — a revised edition published by Claxton, Remsen & Haffelfinger, Philadelphia, 1871.

Since their marriage, they have resided in Louisville. Mrs. Griffin writes occasionally for various periodicals. The following poem was thought to be very beautiful by the late George D. Prentice.

SPIRIT LANDSCAPES.

Not those bright scenes that charm the human eye
With rich material beauty, glowing forth
In bold relief of landscape — beauty drawn
Of earthly hills and towering mountains high,
Or tangled vales, or native murmuring streams,
Whose rippling music echoes from the cliffs
And high ascents that hedge their waters in;
Nor yet the flowery fields, nor meadows rare,
Where, 'mid the perfumed shades and grassy slopes,
The ruminating herds seek sweet repose,
Or gambol sportively in frolic free!

70

Not those, ah, no! though e'er so fair and bright,
Can fill the spirit's ken with full delight;
No earthly scenes, though e'er so finely wrought,
Can charm the vision of exalted thought.

Imagination dreams of realms refined,
Of scenes of beauty charted on the mind,
Where, in unrivalled loveliness, appears
The spirit landscape of the inner spheres; —

Where poesy sheds upon the fields of sense
Sweet ideal flowers of wit and eloquence;
And mountain thought looks up to genius, high
Enthroned upon the clouds of virtue's sky; —

Where, softly as a summer rainbow, seems
The blending colors of affection's beams;
And, bright as stars that gem the brow of night,
Resplendent aspiration sheds her light; —

And love, and truth, and holy, high resolve,
Within their orbits gracefully revolve;
And through the system of religion roll
Around their centre the inspired soul.

These are the scenes that charm the spirit's eye,
More than terrestrial views of richest dye;
And lovelier far than earth and sea combined
Is the bright spirit-landscape of the mind!

March, 1869.

———∘o⫯⦿⫯o∘———

M. W. MERIWETHER BELL.

MISS MERIWETHER is a native of Albemarle County, Virginia. She was born in that wild, beautiful spot, called the North Garden, and from childhood drew inspiration from its lovely mountains, and sang to the ripple of its streams.

She is the second daughter of Dr. Charles Hunter Meriwether, and is descended maternally from old Virginian families.

She is a genius, and "lisped in numbers" from earliest childhood. When only nine years of age, some of her verses were sent to a Virginia paper, as specimens of precocious rhymes, and were published, puffed, and copied into various papers.

After the death of her father, occurring when the subject of this notice was twelve years old, the family removed to Kentucky.

In 1858, Miss Meriwether married Captain Darwin Bell, and from the time of her marriage has resided in Christian County, Kentucky. Post-office, Garrettsburg.

Mrs. Bell has been termed the "Poetess of the Flowers." She writes quaint and suggestive prose.

March, 1871.

THE VALLEY LILY'S MESSAGE.

O valley lily, pure and pale,
 Ring out a silver chime
From all your pearly bells, and lend
 Your music to my rhyme.

With odorous sighs and tears of dew,
 Peal out the tender tale;
And tell him all I whispered you
 Down in the mossy vale.

Tell him the royal rose is bright,
 The stately lily fair;
The tulip wears a robe of light,
 The jasmine scents the air.

But on their beauty if he looks,
 Oh, tell him, then, of this:
The rose her inmost leaves unfolds
 To the wanton zephyr's kiss.

And the white lily, saintly fair,
 Like Danaë of old,
Spreads out her snowy lap to catch
 The yellow sunbeam's gold.

The gaudy tulip boldly woes
 The butterfly and bee,
And the jasmine flings her twining arms
 Round every shrub and tree.

But the valley lily hides away
  In places cool and dim;
Under the shadowy leaves, and keeps
  Her sweetness all for him.

Thus tell him, sweetest messenger;
  Ring o'er the silver chime:
His heart must listen if you lend
  Your music to my rhyme.

LOUISIANA.

SARAH A. DORSEY.

I N alluding to the "Recollections of Henry W. Allen," an intimate friend of Mrs. Dorsey thus speaks of her:

"To comprehend the organization that gave being to this book, one must have known the author — a woman highly strung, and yet calm; nervous, and yet courageous; sensitive, and yet not susceptible; and strongly practical and considerate of the common usages of life. For one of such poetic taste, such ardent fancy, and withal devoted in no ordinary degree and with no common fidelity to her duties, her friends, her country, and her God, she possesses in an extraordinary degree the faculty of friendship, so to speak — that pure disinterestedness of soul which enables its possessor to put aside all selfish considerations in behalf of its objects of regard, and to separate from any warmer or more sentimental feeling the affection that may so legitimately exist between the sexes.

"She had known Governor Allen from her childhood, is twenty years his junior, and was actuated in his service not only by friendship and zeal, but a sort of hero-worship, which our late disastrous struggle was well calculated to arouse in the Southern breast."

Sarah Anne Ellis was born on her father's plantation, just below Natchez. Her parents also had a residence in the suburbs of that city, where she was brought up. Her parents were both young and very wealthy, belonging to the oldest and most influential families in Mississippi and Louisiana. Her mother was Mary Routh; her father, Thomas George Percy Ellis. She was the eldest child, born before her mother was sixteen; therefore, being rather an earnest, grave sort of a child, her mother always declared "Sarah was much older than she was." Her parents were both gay, and much beloved in society. Her mother was a very lovely woman, and her father was very gifted and brilliant. He died very suddenly at an early age. Sarah was his idol, being the only daughter with two sons, until a girl was born three weeks before his death. She adored her father; his death made a deep and ineffaceable impression on her, even at the early age of nine years.

74

The dim outlines of the groundwork of "Agnes Graham's" family story were Mrs. Dorsey's own. Her great-grandfather, grandmother, and aunts suffered in that terribly mysterious dispensation of God. The earliest recollection of Mrs. Dorsey recalls her grandmother, a beautiful, stately woman, with exquisite hands and moulded form, an inmate of her father's house, hopelessly melancholy, possessing everything that the prestige of birth, and rank, and wealth could give; but the "skeleton in the closet" was always there, and for years this dreadful thought pursued her, even from childhood, as it had all of her family (her gifted aunts as well), making their inner lives deeper and more thoughtful than the life of most people.

Her mother married Gen. Charles G. Dahlgren, afterward of the C. S. A., brother to the now Federal Admiral. Sarah was passionately fond of books, and was most carefully educated by her mother and stepfather. She had every advantage that money could procure. Her youth was very gay at Natchez, noted as the "society town" of the South. We are told that Mrs. Dahlgren entertained charmingly, in true, open-hearted Southern manner. She died of *disease of the heart*, in 1858.

In 1853, Miss Sarah Ellis was married to Samuel W. Dorsey, of Tensas Parish, La.

From earliest youth, in common with most *thinking* Southerners, she has been deeply interested in the laboring class, and can say honestly, in the face of Heaven, she has devoted every faculty she possesses to their improvement, so far as she could, while she owned them. This she did as a matter of duty. She now does what she can for them as a matter of humanity. Every Sunday, in her plantation-home in Tensas Parish, she has a class of from fifty to sixty scholars of negroes. She teaches them to read and write, and religion. She is an Episcopalian, and believes a full ritual the only way to interest or reach these masses. Her husband lost nearly a quarter of a million of dollars by the war. They took their negroes to Texas during the "struggle for Confederate independence." Some of the experiences of Louise Peyrault (in "Lucia Dare") were real. Indeed, most of the Southern incidents in this book are true, most of the characters from life. The scenes in Natchez are merely idealized; any old resident can locate them.

Mrs. Dorsey began to write for the press by accident,—a lucky one was it for the public. Writing on business to the New York *Churchman*, she ventured to answer a question propounded in that paper concerning the use of the choral service and full ritualism for negroes. She had adopted the full ritual, and had herself adapted the American liturgy to some of the cathedral services and music of the Anglican Church, and wrote her experience of five years' use of this musical science to the *Churchman*. The editor published her letter, and, in a subsequent number, another, signing the articles "Filia Ecclesiæ," daughter of the church. She liked the name and has ever since retained it.

Mrs. Dorsey has lived almost equally at Natchez and on Lake St. Joseph, where her family have had their plantations since the first settlement of the State.

All of Mrs. Dorsey's writings are Southern in tone and character, and have nationality, and are valuable, inasmuch as they are true pictures of that phase of Southern existence which is over and will soon be forgotten in the misery into which our unhappy country is plunged.

Mrs. Dorsey is passionately fond of study, but has necessarily been a woman of society and of the world, all her life. The friend, once before quoted, speaking of her memory of what she read, as illustrated in her " Recollections of Governor Allen," remarks :

"'The writer of *this book* has so 'encyclopedic a mind,' so to speak, that her daily conversation is quite as much strewn with the result of her reading as are the pages here recorded. I have sometimes, when in her society, been reminded of Sidney Smith's remark about memory — when he termed it a wondrous engine of social oppression. Yet is she frank, eager, and artless as a child."

Her married life has been smooth and unruffled. She recognizes all of God's goodness to her, having had more than " the fourteen happy days of the Moorish monarch."

During the war, Mrs. Dorsey spent two years in Texas. While there, she aided in nursing in a Confederate hospital, and did such work for the church as she could. She travelled twice from Texas to the Mississippi River by land, once with her husband, two overseers, and several hundred negroes. The measles broke out among them ; they had a very distressing time, and buried the poor creatures all along the road. They were frequently compelled to encamp for days and weeks at a time. She had a tent made of a piece of carpet, but it did not always protect them, as it was not water-tight. Mr. Dorsey had to leave her to go after some negroes in the northern part of the State, and she was alone with the overseers and negroes for ten days in the immense pine forests of Winn Parish.

In 1860, Mrs. Dorsey sent to New York, to be published for gratuitous distribution, the choral services she had arranged and used so successfully among her negroes for years. The now Bishop of Florida had charge of this for her, but the intended publisher failed, and the war came, and the service remained unpublished. She is an enthusiastic Episcopalian, and was a dear friend of the lamented Bishop-General Leonidas Polk. She is very much interested in the establishment of an order of deaconesses, connected with the church in New Orleans, which was her reason for making Agnes Graham (in the novel heretofore alluded to) end as one. This effort she desires to make in obedience to a promise exacted from her by Bishop Polk, on his last visit to her, in 1860, "that she should do everything in her power, as long as she lived, toward the establishment of a Sisterhood of Mercy in New Orleans." The bishop considered this a matter of primary importance to the *Church* and *Protestantism*.

During the war, Mrs. Dorsey's house was burned in a skirmish, and several men killed in her flower-gardens.

She is a highly accomplished lady, reading six languages, though by no means a pedant—a musician, performing on the harp with the same exquisite taste as "Agnes Graham" is described·as doing. We quote the passage:

"The young lady, after passing her fingers lightly over the strings of the harp, took her seat and played a brilliant, merry polka. . . . Striking a few modulations upon the strings, the music changed from the gay polka movement to a slow, plaintive measure. The red lips parted, and breathed most touchingly the exquisite melancholy strain of Schubert's 'Wanderer.' The song ended, the chords swelled on the air. She sang the scena and aria from Der Freischütz, '*Wie nahte mir der Schlummer bevor ich ihn gesehn.*' It is a gem of music, and it was sung to perfection. The joyous allegro movement at the close, '*All meine Pulse schlagen,*' was admirably rendered."

She uses her pencil like a born artist!   And yet Mrs. Dorsey is by no means a "literary lady," as that term is often used, priding herself much upon her domestic qualities, being a capital nurse for the sick, a good teacher, an excellent housekeeper, and, when it is necessary, a superb cook.

In 1866, Mrs. Dorsey published, through M. Doolady, New York, "Recollections of Henry Watkins Allen, Brigadier-General Confederate States Army, Ex-Governor of Louisiana," of which volume the private secretary and friend of Governor Allen thus speaks:

"It is the most faithful and thorough portrait of him that could be drawn, the best word-likeness that has been produced this century. It is accurate in point of fact; it is full in materials; it is tasteful in arrangement. The coldest critic cannot deny it the merit of sincerity and strict adherence to truth. The most exacting literary critic would stultify himself if he were to say that he found no beauties in the style, no pathos."

Reading a copy of this volume after a friend of the author has read and wept over it, we find many passages "pencilled," with remarks made on the same. Speaking of the burial of a brother of Henry Allen on the prairie of Texas, the author says (pp. 26 & 27):

"It is a pleasant resting-place, — one of those Texan prairies, — they are so thick with bloom and verdure. In that dry atmosphere the wild flowers seem peculiarly fragrant. Bulbs abound — hibiscus, glowing crimson; narcissi, a sort of blue narcissus with a golden centre; ornithigalliums of fine-rayed corollas double as daisies, white, with chalices of tender lilac bordered with green, so delicate they droop in the plucking; crimson poppy mallows, hanging their heads heavily, as Clyte did hers in the Greek sculptor's thought, on their long, slender, hairy footstalks; purple iris, small, Tyrian-dyed, flecked with white and gold dots; larkspurs, pink, and white, and blue; pale, flesh-colored prairie-pinks; long, full racemes of straw-colored cassias; great bunches of light papilionaceous blossoms, set in ovate leaves of light olive-green; starry heleniums; coreopsis too, yellow, eight-cleft, darkening into brown-red disk florets; foxgloves, white and violet-spotted; pink and purple campanaulas, cymes of golden bloom, like English wall-flowers; paniales of downy, azure, four-petalled blossoms, like Swiss forget-me-nots; bull-nettles, with prickly runcinate leaf, guarding a tender, snow-white, soft bloom, which rivals the Indian jasmine in its exquisite fragrance and graceful beauty. All sorts of salvias, verbenas, mints, and wild balms grow profusely on those prairies, mingled with the delicate, fine-leaved, close-creeping vines of the lemon-colored and pink-blossomed, vanilla-scented sensitive plants (mimosas), and the rich green of the musquite and gamma grasses, making a lovely covering even over graves. And above all this blossoming earth stretches out a vast dome of clear blue sky, vast as the horizon on the 'wide, open sea.'"

To which the friend pencils: "*She writes* con amore *here. There is not a flower among all of those mentioned that she has not painted to the life.*"

In 1867, "Lucia Dare," a novel, was published in New York. This is in part a war novel. The pictures of Southern life are well drawn, and some of the characters interesting and vividly portrayed. Annie Laurie especially is a very lovely creation, and Grace Sharpe a strongly drawn one. A great fault in this novel is too many characters. A novel should have three or four prominent characters around which the interest of the narrative should centre — they must be brought prominently forward, and made the chief actors. From the opening of this novel, I thought Lucia Dare was to be the chief actor, and her brother's fate to remain a mystery until the close of the volume; but the story is wrought out differently, and with much interest too, although the reader recognizes Lucia's brother (Gerald) as soon as he appears. A revised edition of "Lucia Dare," with omitted chapters of much interest, may possibly be shortly published.

In 1869, Claxton, Remsen & Haffelfinger, Philadelphia, published "Agnes Graham." This is a revision of "Agnes" — a novel which was published serially in the "Southern Literary Messenger," 1864, and was reviewed in the New York "Round Table" thus:

"This is a story of our own day, a genuine presentation of life — under circumstances, however, which may be considered a little exceptional. The scenes are laid principally in the South, and there is a warmth of imagination about some of the descriptions which lead one to think that they are colored and sometimes magnified beyond the measure of nature. But the characters are admirably drawn: there is scarcely one which does not seem to have a living counterpart; they are all consistent with truth, and in harmony with each other. Every woman who has been to school has seen one such girl as Agnes Graham; and her conduct during the scene in the playground — which is very well described — plainly betokens the power, self-control, and rigid sense of right which distinguish the noble girl through life. Left an orphan, she passes her vacations with her Aunt Eleanor, to whom she is devotedly attached. This aunt is a gentle, pure, good woman, suffering under the weight of a sorrow which no human aid can mitigate or remove; and between her son Robert and Agnes Graham a strong affection springs up, to which the outer world sees no objection. Robert goes to Germany to study medicine, and returns about the time that Agnes finishes her education, to claim his bride. But, before giving her consent to their marriage, Aunt Eleanor deems it necessary to impart to each of the young people a terrible family secret, which might forever preclude the possibility of their being united. Robert determines to make Agnes his wife at all hazards, and the whole weight of the inevitable sacrifice falls upon her. The finger of God had placed an impassable barrier between them, and she had no alternative but to part from him. An opportunity occurs for Agnes to accompany some other relatives to Italy, where a life of trial and intense mental anguish awaits her. . . . . Her whole conduct and bearing through life, her struggles with sorrow which knows no healing and spreads like a pall over her whole existence, are depicted in a manner which shows that the author has an appreciation of genuine pathos which appeals at once to the heart of her readers. . . . . 'Filia' possesses many of the most important qualifications for a good novelist, and her faults are only those of immaturity."

Mrs. Dorsey has recently written a novel that will, we think, attract great attention from the reading world and the "critics." It will be entitled "A Southern Villegiatura."

REFUGEEING.

On our way to Texas, Louise and her little ones, all the slaves, and I. . . .
We lead the strangest life, cousin, and — 'camp out,' as they call it, every night, take our meals, gipsy-fashion, by the roadside. We have tents — Louise and I; but the negroes threw away their tents as too cumbrous, and they content themselves with bowers, or lairs, built up of pine branches. It is very picturesque. We stop for the night, usually at sunset, near a stream of water. The wagons are drawn up in rows; children, old women, and bed-clothes emptied out of them, and then such a motley scene of confusion you could not imagine — everybody so busy; our tents hoisted while Louise and I sit on a log or fallen tree-trunk, and survey the excited multitude of negroes building up their green booths, shaking out their blankets, rattling skillets and frying-pans over the numerous fires which spring up as if by magic. Louise showed me the 'fire-horn' of the negroes, a small end of cow's-horn filled with half-burned cotton lint, and a jack-knife and a piece of common flint. The children race about like mad things, joyful to escape from the confinement of the wagon. Louise's little ones play with the tiny darkies; she does not pretend to keep them asunder. 'The little negroes are not wicked,' she says, in answer to my remarks on this point. 'They are very good to my children, and I like my little ones to love these little slaves. Why, *I* love the poor creatures, Lucia.' And so she does. Every evening she goes about among her slaves, seeing after the sickly and delicate ones.

GOVERNOR ALLEN.

"Allen was singularly earnest in nature. His intellect was very quick and bright. If a jest or an amusing anecdote was repeated to him, he would seize the point instantly, and his merry laugh would ring out with all the enjoyment of a child. But he had himself no innate sense of humor, no appreciation of what Mr. Ruskin calls 'the grotesque.' The simplicity of his nature, on this point, was amusing, and produced, sometimes in those who loved him most, a sort of tender, wondering, smiling pity; because, from the lack of this inherent consciousness of the ludicrous, he was sometimes betrayed into the assumption of positions that in other men would have been ridiculous. The incongruity, however, never striking him, he would do and say peculiar things, that would make people smile, with such entire *bonhommie*, such singleness of purpose, honesty of heart, and open warmth of expression, as Sir William Hamilton expresses it, '*such outness*' of truth, and goodness, such high ideal perception of romantic sentiment, and so much clever, shrewd, practical, intellectual ability shining through everything, that, while he was often peculiar, frequently amusing, he never was absurd or frivolous! Though sometimes he seemed *vain*, he was never *affected*. He was honest even in his foibles. If he had had any sense of humor, he would not have *seemed vain*. People that are gifted with a quick perception of wit and humor, instinctively avoid placing themselves in what they fancy might be '*a ridiculous position.*' Their vanity is deep, perhaps, but it is hidden. It is a sensitive nerve, that warns them, and preserves them from peculiarity. They are sensitive to ridicule, and fear being 'laughed at.' Allen never had that fear; he never for an instant supposed anybody *would laugh at him*. He liked the badinage and railleries of a friend; they amused him, even at his own expense. Allen never saw anything amusing in his making a desperate charge at Shiloh, with his head bound up in white cotton! He considered it all *en règle*. It was the best to be done, under the circumstances!"

THE LAURIES AT HOME.

(*From "Lucia Dare."*)

"The 'Charmer,' for so was fancifully named the boat that had transported Lucian up the broad river, reached Natchez just at sunset. Lucian found a carriage and servants of Mr. Laurie's waiting for him at the landing 'under the hill.' When the carriage—it was an open brette (the fashionable *afternoon* carriage for driving at Natchez)—reached the top of the long hill, at least five hundred feet in height, round which the road wound on an inclined plane up to Natchez 'on the hill,' Lucian, chancing to look behind him, could

11

not refrain from uttering an exclamation at the beauty of the view. The coachman, thinking that Lucian spoke to him, checked his horses. Lucian stood up in the carriage and looked down to the river, rolling its vast volume of waters at the foot of the bluffs. The village of Natchez, under the hill, was clustered close to the water's edge; the bluffs rose precipitously, garnished with pine-trees, and locusts, and tufted grasses; the vista here terminated in Brown's beautiful gardens, gay with flower-beds and closely clipped hedges. Far away over the river stretched the broad emerald plain of Louisiana, level with the stream, extending for many, many miles, its champaign chequered with groups of white plantation-houses, spotted with groves of trees, rich in autumnal beauty, glowing with crimson, gold, and green, softened by veils of long gray moss. This plain was dotted with lovely lakes, whose waters shone in the slanting rays of the declining sun like so many great rubies in a setting of smaragdus. The sun went down quickly, as he does at sea, a round, red fire-ball, while light splendid clouds of purple, pink, lilac, and gray on the blue, blue heavens refracted the ascending, slender, quivering rays of the disappearing orb, the type of Deity in all natural religions, the Totem of the Natchez Indians.

"The 'Charmer' was moving off, under full head of steam, up the river, and a number of skiffs and small boats were plying about over the broad Mississippi. Lucian gazed with delight on all this beauty; then seeing the night coming on fast, he bade the coachman drive on. They had some distance to go — nearly two miles out of the suburbs — before they could reach their destination. They drove rapidly up the streets of the village, for the town itself was scarcely more than through the suburbs, of handsome residences, whose gardens, all adjoining and dovetailed into each other, almost realized the descriptions of Damascus, that queen of the desert, with its triple chain of gardens, its necklaces of 'paradises.' Lucian was confused and excited by the rapid motion of the carriage, rushing on through acres of bloom, perfume, foliage, and verdure; passing here and there the glimmering white pillars of stately houses, in most of which lamps began already to burn and glow, and throw out long, narrow shafts of penetrating light on the darkness, glittering through the glossy shining leaves of the evergreen *lauri-mundi*, the native almond-laurel, and casting a cheering radiance over the wayfarer as he passed along. Notes of music, and singing of sweet voices, and the gay laughter of little children, sounded on his ear and died into silence instantaneously as the carriage rolled by.

"Beloved city — bright city of 'the Sun!' — how often have I paced with child's feet the road that Lucian was now travelling over, and listened, as he did, but more lingeringly, to the sounds of gentle human life stirring within thy peaceful homes! How often have I thanked God for my beautiful childhood's home — for my precious Southern land — for its sunshine, its verdure, its forests, its flowers, its perfume; but, oh! above all, for the loving, refined, intelligent, gentle race of people it was my great, my priceless privilege to be born among — a people worthy to live with — yes, *worthy to die for*. The stern besom of war has swept over you, beloved Natchez. Your fairest homes have been desolated, your lovely gardens are now only remembrances. Your family circles are broken up; your bravest sons are sleeping in the dust of death, or weeping tears of bitterness in exile; your daughters, bowed down with penury and grief, are mourning beside their darkened firesides; your joyous households transferred to other and kindlier lands; the forms of my kindred faded into phantoms of the past; strangers sit now in the place that once was mine; but yet thou art lovely, still lovely in thy ruin, in thy desolation. City of my heart — city of my love — city of my childish joy. Oh, city of my dead!

"The carriage stopped suddenly at a gate, the footman swung it open, the two leaves flew back with a clang, the carriage proceeded at a slower pace through an avenue, or rather wound through 'a piece of woods' that an Englishman would call a park. It was almost a hundred acres of primeval forest-trees, under which the red-man had often danced, consisting for the most part of oaks, — white, red, and water oaks, — with mixture of hickory, gum, maples, magnolias, and the cucumber-tree, with its umbrella-like top, its immense leaf, and the enormous white vase seated in the centre of radiating foliage like a huge chalice of perfume, handsomer even than its sister, the magnolia grandiflora.

"Natchez is in the temperate, not the tropical zone; so there is exaggeration in the fanciful descriptions of its climate and productions, as given by Chateaubriand and Lady Georgiana Fullerton; but it is a warm, bright, sunshiny place, with marked and changeful, though not extreme transitions of temperature and seasons. Its pleasant, gently rolling hills and dells are laughing and gay with blossoming trees and shrubs; the old earth breathes forth flowers from every rough pore—not heavy, stupefying, deeply-colored tropical bloom — but great luxuriance of fresh, delicately tinted blossoms of all hues and forms, spreading successively their capricious, flaunting beauty, mantling the old mother anew with every morning's light. The wild flowers there are worthy of being the subject of Adelbert Dietrich's delicate pencil, or of Miss Prescott's glowing word-painting. One need only describe faithfully what exists, not attempting to heighten or exaggerate with human imagination or invention what God has made so lovely, to paint attractive pictures of those 'magnolia' hills and of the park through which Lucian was now being driven:

"When the carriage entered the smaller circle of fencing that enclosed the house and gardens, the noise of the wheels grating on the gravel of the drive caused the heavy doors of the portal to fly open, and Margaret and Jenny, forestalling the decorous servant, emerged from the gloom and advanced to welcome the traveller. Margaret looked like a fairy standing in the moonlight, her red-brown hair clouded about her; and Jenny, who was as usual all dusk, except the curd-like teeth and shining eyes, might have passed very well for her attendant dwarf. Jenny was small of her age and had elfish ways. Her peculiarities of appearance were heightened on this occasion by costume: she sported a large white apron with a wide ruffle, much too long for her, really borrowed from Betsy for the purpose of adornment; a white handkerchief tied on her head, turban-fashion, tall as a dervish's cap, a long strand of blue glass beads around her neck, a pair of immense gold ear-rings, and her broadest and widest grins.

"'This way, Lucian, this way,' said Margaret; 'not up the staircase;' leading him, as she spoke, beneath the flight of stairway which led up into the gallery of the first story. Margaret led him then through a hall level with the ground, paved with black and white marble, which ran under the arch of the stairways.

"'Here they all are, in here. You know this is such a queer old Spanish house! You'll soon find out all about it, though it *is* puzzling at first.'

"The newly arrived guest was kindly received by Mr. Laurie and Annie, who were sitting alone near a blazing wood fire in the family parlor. The nights were too chilly for the blind man, even for that early period of the fall.

"'Come to the fire, Lucian,' he said; 'one gets cool riding, and this old house of Guyoso's is damp as a basement, almost.'

"Lucian looked around with some curiosity at the rather old-fashioned, quaint furnishing of the apartment they were sitting in it. It was handsome, but not new. On the wall just opposite hung the portrait of a man in full armor — a dark, oval face, handsome and swarthy. Annie saw his glance. 'That,' she said, taking up a lamp and holding it so that the light could fall on the picture, — 'that is a portrait of Bienville, by Champagne. Bienville was a relative of my family. Here is another of Guyoso, the Spanish Governor of Mississippi.'

"'Has n't he got a long nose?' interrupted Margaret, disrespectfully.

"'Here's another of Stephen Minor, who was second in command under Spanish domination.'

"'Do you like his uniform, Lucian?' asked Margaret.

"'It is all red, with yellow facings, and see the big star on his breast!'

"'Here is some gold plate belonging to Vidal, that he brought from Spain to the colony. His whole dinner-service was gold — *is* gold, I should say; his descendants, our neighbors, still use it on grand occasions.'

"'And who is this?' asked Lucian, as he examined a small miniature hanging below the portrait of Bienville.

"'That,' said Annie, 'is a likeness of our grand-uncle, Philip Noland, who disappeared in 1807, and was never heard of again. He was a lieutenant in the navy of the United States; his wife lost her reason from grief at his prolonged absence. She had just been married — was barely more than a child in years at the time she eloped with and married Philip against the will of her family. We have some of his letters still extant. He seems to have been an intellectual, but not a good man, from all I can learn. His wife still survives; she is over sixty years old now, and has been harmlessly insane since she was sixteen. She lives here, Lucian, in one wing of the house. You may probably see her. Though she is constantly attended by a faithful nurse, and can rarely be persuaded to quit her room, or even her couch, sometimes she becomes restless and wanders over the house : her mind is usually in a mazed state. We do not confine her at all ; it has never been necessary ; we only watch her ; she goes where she likes usually. Patty is always with her, but Aunt Jane is so old she does not want to go about much; she dislikes strangers. It is one never-ceasing cry from her lips after her husband. No matter what she may be talking about, in a little while she begins to moan for Philip and ask where he is — to wonder that he does not come. "Philip stays so long ! he never used to," is her constant cry. To think that has been going on for fifty years ! The love of the woman has survived everything — youth, beauty, reason. Human hearts are fearful things to play or trifle with.'"

————∘○⟨⊙⟩○∘————

MRS. MARIE BUSHNELL WILLIAMS.

MRS. M. B. WILLIAMS is a native of Baton Rouge, La. Her father, Judge Charles Bushnell, came to this State from Massachusetts within the first decade after the purchase of Louisiana had been accomplished, and in due time married into a Creole family of substantial endowments and high repute. Judge Bushnell was well and favorably known at the bar of Louisiana. He was a gentleman of great legal erudition; but, though devoted to his profession, he found time to cultivate the general branches of literature, and to participate in their elegant enjoyments.

His favorite daughter, Marie, early manifested a studious disposition. She was a fair, bright-eyed, spiritual girl, of more than ordinary promise. Though slight in figure, she was compactly formed. Her features were cast in nature's finest mould, and her clear dark eye and smooth fair brow were radiant with intellectual light.

When this description would apply to Miss Bushnell, she became the *élève* of Alexander Dimitry, whose fame as a scholar has since become world-wide. The management of a pupil so richly dowered with God's best gifts was a pleasing task to the professor, and he soon imparted to her not only the fresh instruction which she required, but a deep and profound reverence for learning akin to that which he felt himself.

This relation of teacher and scholar continued for several years, and was not severed till Miss Bushnell became a complete mistress of all the principal modern languages. Indeed, the range of her studies was quite extended, and we hazard very little in saying that she was, when they were completed, the most learned woman in America.

At length, when she had rounded into perfect womanhood, physically as well as mentally, the honor of an alliance with her was sought by many of the proudest and wealthiest gentlemen of Louisiana. The successful suitor proved to be Josiah P. Williams, a planter of Rapides, and from the date of her marriage, in 1843, she resided near Alexandria, on Red River, with the exception of a brief experience of refugee-life in Texas when the war was at its height, until 1869, when she removed to Opelousas, La.

As a wife, and the mother of an interesting family of children, Mrs. Williams performed her whole duty. But though the domestic virtues found in her a true exponent, they by no means lessened her interest in literary pursuits. For her own amusement and that of a choice *coterie* of literary friends — her constant visitors — she was accustomed to weave together legends of Louisiana, both in prose and verse, which soon established her reputation among those who were admitted into the charmed circle. She, however, had no fancy for the plaudits of the world. For years she refused to appear in print, but when at length a few of her articles found their way into literary journals, she was at once admitted to an assured position among judges as a singer and a teacher. With a vast fund of acquired knowledge; a mind original, philosophic, and sympathetic; a fancy at once brilliant and beautifully simple, added to a mastery of language when force of style was found necessary, and an easy, happy facility in all the lighter phases of literary effort,— Mrs. M. B. Williams will yet, when the world knows her merits and does her justice, take her place among the first of the distinguished women of America.

We have not before us any complete list of the productions of her pen, nor shall we attempt any critical analysis of those specimens which are to follow this article. They shall be left to the good taste and judgment of our readers, with a full confidence that they cannot fail to please.

We shall merely say, in conclusion, that Mrs. Williams suffered severely by the reverses which marked the latter years of the "lost cause." The death of her husband was her first great sorrow: the destruction of her beautiful residence, "The Oaks," by the vandal followers of Banks in his Red River raid; the wounding of one son; the untimely death of another; the material misfortunes which reduced her from affluence to poverty,— all followed in such disheartening succession, that few indeed could have borne up under such a series of calamities. But her faith was strong. She could look religiously through the storms of the present into the calm and glory of that peace which is to come. Few have ever met reverses with greater fortitude, or fought the battle of life more bravely. For years past she has been a constant and valued contributor to the New Orleans "Sunday Times," and while her writings have proved her a brilliant thinker, they show no traces of egotistic grief. The sorrows by which she has been surrounded are mourned by her only as sorrows common to the whole desolated South.

Mrs. Williams has in preparation, to be published in a volume, "Tales and Legends of Louisiana," in a lyrical poem — a poem which we hope will introduce her talents to the whole country, making her name familiar as a "household word."

As a translator from the French, German, and Spanish, Mrs. Williams is deservedly successful, her translations from the German language being very felicitous and faithful.

1868.   MARK F. BIGNEY.

PLEASANT HILL.

Roll my chair in the sunlight, Ninetta,
　　Just here near the slope of the hill,
Where the red bud its soft purple clusters
　　Droops down to the swift-flowing rill.

See the golden-hued wreaths of the jasmine,
　　Like stars, through yon coppice of pine,
While the fringe-tree its white floating banners
　　Waves out from the blossoming vine.

How the notes of the mocking-bird, ringing
　　From hillside and woodland and vale,
Greet the earliest flush of the morning
　　With trills of their happy love-tale!

Ah! beauty and music and gladness,
　　Ye follow the footsteps of spring;
The breeze, in its pure balmy freshness,
　　Seems fanned from some bright angel's wing.

Look yonder and see, little daughter,
  Where locust-trees scatter their bloom,
Have the pansies, in velvet-eyed sadness,
  Peeped yet through the turf near the tomb?

Nay, then, turn not aside, my Ninetta;
  The grave of our Walter should gleam
In the earliest flush of the spring-time —
  The glow of the autumn's last beam.

For he loved them, the flowers and sunshine,
  The birds, and all beautiful things;
But he loved best the dim purple pansy
  That over his resting-place springs.

Ah! just there, where that laurel is glancing,
  Just there, in that sink of the dell,
Came a surge of the deadliest combat,
  Sweeping on in its terrible swell.

And I saw him, my darling, my treasure,
  My boy with the sunlighted hair;
I could see the proud sweep of his banner,
  And the smile that his lip used to wear!

Ah! he led them, how bravely, Ninetta!
  His voice, with its silver tones, pealed
Through the hurtling storm of the battle.
  As it swept o'er the blood-streaming field.

I watched a strange wavering movement,
  I watched from yon low cottage-door,
Till a riderless horse bounded upward —
  Then I lay with my face to the floor.

There he lies now, my sunny-haired darling,
  My boy with the frank, fearless eyes!
And I fancy to-day that they watched me
  From the depths of the shadowless skies.

Ah! watching his sorrowful mother,
  And watching this sorrowful land,
That his heart's crimson life-tide had moistened
  For the tread of a fanatic band.

What! in tears? Ah! my gentle Ninetta,
　Your mother has mourned for her child
With none of that womanly weakness
　That softens an anguish too wild.

But I look at his grave in the sunlight,
　And my heart in its radiance grows strong,
For he died in the flush of his triumph,
　And not in this tempest of wrong.

Yes, he fell in the heat of the battle,
　Nor dreamed of the thraldom and shame
Which have blasted this fair Southern valley
　With breath of their ravening flame.

And his grave, oh! thank God, is a freeman's!
　Ay, freely the flowers may wave;
No foeman those garlands of honor
　May tear from the sleep of the brave.

Ah! take me within, my Ninetta;
　My gallant young soldier sleeps well;
And ere the first glow of the summer,
　I too must lay down in the dell.

[THE LEGEND OF DON RODERICK.

In the ancient annals of Spain, Don Roderick, "*ultimo Ruy de los Godos,*" occupies a conspicuous position. The royal city of Toledo was his abode, and strange indeed are the marvels told of it by the old monkish chroniclers. In this city were the necromantic tower of "Pleasure's Pain" and the wondrous "Cave of Hercules," the latter of which extended from the centre of the city beneath the bed of the Tagus and for three leagues beyond. Toledo is declared to have been founded by Tubal, the son of Japhet and grandson of Noah; but whether this be so or not, its existence certainly runs back to a very remote period, and its history is full of marvels. Around it are curious vaults and subterraneous habitations, supposed to have been the retreat of the inhabitants in case of invasion or through fear of floods. "Such a precaution," says the worthy Don Pedro de Roxas, in his History of Toledo, "was natural enough to the first Toledans, seeing that they founded their city shortly after the deluge, while the memory of it was still fresh in their minds."

In the posthumous works of Washington Irving, published by his relative,
12

Pierre M. Irving, the curiosities of Toledo are treated of at considerable length, connected as they are with the legend of Don Roderick. The place had always a necromantic tendency, the diabolical mysteries of magic having been taught there for many centuries. This was indeed so much the case, that the neighboring nations defined magic as the *Arte Toledana*.

Irving gleans from the venerable Agapida many mysteries relative to the Magic Tower of Toledo, which he relates with great unction. The tower, he says, "was round, and of great height and grandeur, erected upon a lofty rock, and surrounded by crags and precipices. The foundation was supported by four brazen lions, each taller than a cavalier on horseback. The walls were built of small pieces of jasper and various colored marbles, not larger than a man's hand, so subtly jointed, however, that but for their different hues they might have been taken for one entire stone. They were arranged with marvellous cunning, so as to represent battles and warlike deeds of times and heroes long passed away; and the whole surface was so admirably polished that the stones were as lustrous as glass, and reflected the rays of the sun with such resplendent brightness as to dazzle all beholders."

We have written the foregoing as an appropriate introduction to a poem, entitled "The Enchanted Tower of Toledo," written by Mrs. M. B. Williams, one of the very best of the female writers of America. This poem was written at "The Oaks," a beautiful place in Rapides Parish, near Alexandria, in June, 1861. Since then, The Oaks, and the delightful home to which they gave their name, have been swept away by the storm of war that passed over our beloved land, and nothing remains of them now save sad and desolate reminders of the past.

Soon after a notice appeared in this journal of "Irving's Spanish Papers and other Miscellanies," Mrs. Williams wrote to us as follows: "By the way, what is that legend of Don Roderick, mentioned in the late collection of Irving's fugitive pieces? I hope he has not anticipated me, for in 1861 I wrote a poem (never yet published) on one of the adventures of that monarch, which I found in some musty old Spanish legends, never translated in this country." With a modesty as creditable to her as her genius, Mrs. Williams adds: "If the great master has anticipated me, my work will lose its only merit, originality."

On this point we feel inclined to take issue with the writer. Her poem loses nothing by comparison with the felicitous prose description by him whom she has reverently termed "the great master." Indeed, the stately march of her rhythmic periods brings the romance of the old legend into far bolder relief than it could possibly be presented by the best of prose. — *Editor N. O. Times.*]

THE ENCHANTED TOWER OF TOLEDO.

> "En este torre los Reyes
> Cada uno hecho un canado,
> Porque lo ordinare ansi
> Hercules el afamado,
> Que gano primero a Espana
> De Gerion gran tirano."
> (*Romances neuvamento sacados Lorenco de Sepulveda.*)

"Here we meet thee, King Rodrigo! outside of the city's wall,
For the words my lips must utter on no other ear can fall;
Thou descendant of the Godos, crowned and sceptred King of Spain,
Thou must listen to the warders of the Tower called Pleasure's Pain.

"In the first days of this kingdom, when Alcmena's godlike son
From Geryon's bloody thraldom all this pleasant land had won,
Midst Toledo's orange-bowers he by strong enchantment's might
Raised this tower from base to summit in one single summer's night!

"Earthly hammers were not sounded, but a passing rush of wings,
And the sword of bright Orion down its starry scabbard flings;
Men grew pale, and women fainted, for the midnight air was filled
With such sounds that earthly daring in each mortal breast was stilled.

"But the dewy moon dawned brightly, and the giant's task was done;
Pale he looked and sighed right sadly in that golden summer sun:
'I have locked the Tower of Magic — bid each future king of Spain
Bolt and bar the dreadful secret, lest he win a bitter pain.'

"There no human foot must wander — there no human eye must scan,
Till the tower and secret perish from the memory of man;
Fate may send some daring spirit: let him pause and ponder long
Ere he does his name and country such a deadly, grievous wrong.

"King Rodrigo, we have spoken! never did we speak in vain,
For each king has left his token on the Tower of Pleasure's Pain;
Twelve good locks are on the portal; thine will make the fateful one.
Sire! thy royal hand must place it ere the setting of the sun."

Laugheth loud the King Rodrigo — "Certes, thou hast care for me;
But these marvels, gentle warder, I am strangely pressed to see;
Never spell of darkest danger but some Christian knight's devoir
Was to break the curst enchantment, tho' 't were locked in magic bar."

Looketh round the King Rodrigo: "Knights, ye fight for love and laws,
And ye deal your blows right stoutly for the sake of Holy Cross;
But to-day we war with magic in the Tower of Pleasure's Pain;
He whose heart beats scant measure, let him shun the coward's shame."

Looketh up the King Rodrigo; still his haughty crest of pride
Sought not aid from earth or heaven, but the fears of both defied;
And his bright eye laughed right gayly, and his lips curled scornfully,
As he marked his comrades shudder, and their heads droop mournfully.

"Woe unto thee, King Rodrigo! woe to all the Spanish land,
When the sacred guard is broken by a monarch's impious hand!"
And the hoary warder kneeleth, with his gray head in the dust:
"Woe to him whose path of power lieth o'er a trampled trust!"

"King, we crave thee pause and hearken." Loud the stately footstep rung,
Louder still the scornful laughter — "We must work ere set of sun;
And we pray thee, pious warder, tho' thou lend'st no helping hand,
Not with idle fears of dotage thus to daunt my gallant band."

On the brazen lions couchant rose the tower like a dream;
Jasper walls and diamond turrets lave the sunset's latest beam;
Twelve good locks are on the portal, and, though struck with might and main,
Morning's sun rose on the workers ere the inner court they gain.

There unrolls the strangest vision: pictured walls surround a dome,
Anadyomene smiles downward from her shell upon the foam,
And the builder's twelve great labors all in precious stones are wrought,
Every figure on the fabric with a weird-like motion fraught.

On a couch of Indian iv'ry rests a giant's marble form,
And upon its lifeless bosom, lo! a lettered scroll is borne,
Golden-lettered, and it readeth to the king's astonished eyes:
"Woe to thee, O reckless monarch! thou hast gained the couch of sighs.

"Thou, O traitor! thou art fated for this kingdom's overthrow;
Thou, whose impious hand would conquer secrets which no man should know,
Read thy fate in yonder casket; let the magic web unfold;
Man, thy kingly state must nerve thee till the dreadful tale is told."

From a casket, gem-enwoven, floated forth a web of white,
And upon its snowy surface, lo! a pictured summer night;
Sweepeth broad the silvery Tagus, and the shadows of the trees
Rest upon the starlit waters, rippled by the evening breeze.

And 'neath orange-boughs, dew-laden, drooping to the water's side,
Stands a maiden idly dreaming, casting flowers o'er the tide;
Seeking in the stars above her, in the river at her feet,
Symbols of that first dear fancy whose divine unrest is sweet.

Scarce a child, and scarce a woman, yet a woman's stately grace
Lent pride to the broad, white forehead; though, on the enchanting face
Lingered still the smile of childhood, that she learned before her speech,
When her visions were as sinless as the blossoms in her reach.

But a moment—and the thicket parts before a heavy tread;
Shrinks the maiden, and her features quiver with a mortal dread;
Mail-clad knight now stands before her, with his barred visor down,
But above his head appeareth semblance of a golden crown.

Oh, the pantomime of terror which the magic canvas gave!
How the mail-clad knight low pleaded! how the maiden seemed to rave!
Till, with gesture of defiance, like a hawk upon its prey,
In his grasp he seized the maiden, and the picture passed away.

"By God's truth," cried King Rodrigo, and his anger, like a flame,
Reddened, and he clenched his gauntlet—"By God's truth, 'tis bitter shame!
Who the traitor knight that ventures thus to do this deadly wrong?
Would to heaven he stood before me; knightly spurs were his too long."

From the casket slowly rises plaintive sighs and anguished wail—
Woe! woe! for the lost Florinda; ye have read her piteous tale;
Woe for the dishonored maiden! woe for the dishonored knight!
Spain! O Spain! thy days are numbered! sinks thy fame in endless night!

"Traitor! ravisher! Rodrigo—read thy kingdom's blasted fate!"
Then the web again unrolleth—lo! the Moors are at the gate,
And the Christian tocsin soundeth, but the Paynim horde pour in;
Holy cross and knightly helmet sinking with the battle's din.

Shrill the Tecbir's war-cry ringeth, kettle-drum and atabal
But above the din of battle rose a woman's frenzied call:
"Curses on thee, King Rodrigo! to revenge my deadly wrong,
I have called the Paynim army, and the Crescent waxeth strong.

"King Rodrigo! King Rodrigo! on thy soul the curse be laid
Of a Christian maiden ruined, of a Christian land betrayed.
God will judge between us, monarch, for the closing day draws near,
And before His throne of justice, lo! I bid thee, king, appear!"

Then, with wild, unearthly laughter, down the magic web was sent;
Sounds of forms of nightmare terror through the dim court came and went;
Standeth firm the King Rodrigo — on their knees his knightly band —
Yet his mortal terror speaketh in blanched brow and trembling hand.

"Ha, good knights! ye seem too fearful; yet, if magic web speaks truth,
Here stand I a traitor monarch, faithless knight, and lost to ruth.
St. Iago! but the mummers played their part with right good will,
For I hear the Moorish cymbals, and the woman's shriek rings still!"

And his trusty sword he lifted: "While this brand my arm can wield,
I can conquer all these omens in the first good battle-field!"
Loud then scoffed the King Rodrigo: "Book of Fate shall ne'er enclose
Such a page of shame and sorrow — not for me such train of woes."

Forth from the enchanted tower quickly passed the knightly train,
Crashed the iron doors behind them, and the locks sprung on again;
With a torch within its talons, sweeping round in circling flight,
Lo! a golden eagle lighteth on the tower's topmost height.

With its wings it fanned the fire, till the rushing flames burst forth,
And a jet of burning crimson sprang up to the farthest north;
Quick replies the lightning flashes — loud the answering thunder rolls;
Downward sink the couchant lions — like a scroll the tower unfolds.

Deep within its burning centre, lo! a funeral banner stood,
And upon its midnight surface naught save one great wave of blood;
But the wave surged up and downward, till a crimson, fiery flash
Swept the tower from base to summit, and it sank with heavy crash.

  .   .   .   .

Years of pride, of shame, of anguish o'er the Spanish land have passed,
And in yonder field of battle Christian rule hath struck its last.
By the Guadalete's waters, discrowned, dying, and alone,
Roderick lies, his bitter anguish far too deep for tear or moan.

O'er his dying vision floateth all that wondrous web of fate —
Falsest knight, dishonored monarch sueth Heaven's grace too late,
For above the din of battle rose that summons high and clear:
"God shall judge between us, traitor! — at His throne, O King, appear!"

THE OAKS, *June* 19, 1861.

THE LAST WILD FLOWER.

Down in sheltered hollows, or by hillsides, blooms, from November to the first severe cold of December, the last wild flower of our Louisiana forest — the saponaria or gentian.

There can be nothing more exquisite than the clear sapphire of these fairy bells, rising from the sombre brown of dead grass and faded leaves. So bright, so intense in hue, that it needs little stretch of imagination to fancy them flakes of the clear blue sky fallen on earth. We have seen them, when the winter has been early, rising from snow-drifts, their tender, delicate corolla peering above the wintry shroud, a very eye of hope, shining with brighter and purer lustre through the chill and gloom of earth.

Flowers sometimes read us a lesson that needs no headings to make it comprehensible to our hearts, for its text was written in the garden of Eden; but in the flush of spring, the plenty and gorgeousness of summer, this lesson is incomplete. Its highest moral reaches us through the storms and dark-ness of winter, when we shrink and shiver in cutting blasts, which seem to give fresh vitality to some of the frailest and most delicate creations on God's earth. The idea of an Omnipresent protection, adjusting itself to every need, somehow presents itself to the mind, and we shelter and nestle under the very thought.

The gentian, too, always a favorite, is now to us a reminiscence of an event which, two winters ago, made us very sad.

In journeying to and fro across the Sabine, one cold day in December, we met on its banks, at Burr's Ferry, a refugee train, which, like ourself, was detained on the Louisiana side until some repairs had been made on the ferry-boat, to enable us to make the "traverse" with safety in that tempest-uous weather. Any one who has ever crossed the Sabine in wind and storm knows well what a dreary, desolate, dangerous crossing it is. Primitive enough, too, with its ropes stretched from bank to bank, by which the ferry-man steadies his boat and shapes its course. Should it break, down would sweep the frail craft into the wild reaches of the river, and, nine chances to ten, either upset or sink there.

A common danger establishes an immediate sympathy between utter strangers, and by the time the leaky ferry-boat was ready for its first load we knew the names, the hopes, the fears of the whole party, and even their destination. We entered, too, with the liveliest interest into the solicitude of an aged couple for the comfort of their invalid daughter — an only child. She was a beautiful girl of about seventeen or eighteen, and one glance at her pallid, sharpened features, told us that she was nearer the end of her last journey than her devoted parents seemed to realize. We had heard of her before, — "the Lily of A——," as she was called, — heard of her beauty, accomplishments, and wealth, and we listened with profound compassion to the tale told by one of her friends — a tale which showed how little all the rich gifts of nature or fortune had availed to shield her from that common lot of humanity — sorrow.

We have no time or space to dwell on particulars. Like many others in Louisiana, where the war was carried on in the very yards or parks of the planters, she had seen her lover, the gallant Captain F——, fall in a skirmish not ten paces from her door.

The shock, coming upon a constitution more than delicate, had hastened its decay, and the Lily of A—— faded slowly beneath one of those inscrutable maladies that have hitherto perplexed and baffled all medical skill.

More from the restless fancy of an invalid than from any fear of an invading army, she had persuaded her parents to join the refugees from the neighborhood, and they were now *en route* for Mexico.

She was made as comfortable on the leaky boat as circumstances would admit, but the waves dashed over the low sides and saturated her wrappings. In moving her hand restlessly over the side of the boat, a handsome emerald ring dropped into the river. She held up her hand with a faint smile. "All," she said; "I might have made this sacrifice to destiny with a better grace some years ago. It was exceeding happiness that always sought to propitiate fate; but I gave up my treasures long since." And she shivered and complained of the piercing cold as a wave, larger than the rest, swept over the boat, almost swamping it.

With difficulty we reached the other side, and warming ourselves by a large fire built by some German emigrants who were camped on the bank, we then made preparations to pass the night in an uninhabited hut by the roadside. A large fire was kindled on the hearth, blankets hung against the walls to keep out the wind, and every means in our power used to shield the invalid at least from exposure. But she insisted on lying near the open door, gazing across the swollen, turbid stream at the gloomy pine-forest on the Louisiana side. Her large, sad eyes filled by degrees with tears, but by a strong effort she kept them back, and gently but firmly resisted all her parents' entreaties to be moved from her exposed situation.

"Let me look a little longer," she pleaded; "remember, I may never see it again. Do you know, I understand now those Polish exiles near A——, who had brought a little piece of their native soil to lay over their hearts when they died. *Pour avoir encore des reves de la patrie,* they said. Dear Louisiana, I never knew before how I loved you." And she lay back exhausted for some moments.

Suddenly her eyes were attracted by a flower growing on the sloping bank near the water's edge. "Get it for me," she cried, eagerly. We plucked it, a long, beautiful spray of gentian, and laid it in her hand.

"How beautiful! how more than beautiful!" she murmured; "so triumphant over blight, decay, and even death itself; so redolent of hope and promise; so full, too, of the old happy time." And she pressed it passionately to her lips with low, indistinct murmurs.

"Mamma"—turning to her mother—"do you remember the little tuft of gentian near the summer-house at Bienvenue, how it blossomed through the frost; and when a heavy fall of snow at last destroyed it, the blue of the petals was as bright, its texture as silky as if living and growing? Beautiful Bienvenue! I almost wish I had not left it. Do you think the orange-tree at my window is dead to-day, for this is a piercing wind?" Her mother turned aside, almost unable to answer.

"Thank you," she said to us, "for the gentian. Flowers are my passion, and this one, coming to me to-day, amid all this dreariness, seems to have brought back the blue sky, hidden by those heavy storm-clouds."

As night came on, shiverings, and at last delirium, seemed to point to a speedy termination of the young life that was now visibly ebbing fast away in that lonely log hut on the Sabine. Dumb and paralyzed by their crushing grief, the parents sat beside her, while pitying friends employed themselves in kind offices. The dying girl seemed unconscious of all her surroundings; she was once more in her Louisiana home, babbling of the flowers she had loved and tended, and of the little gentian by the summer-house. No sad or troubled memory seemed to intrude on her peaceful, happy visions. The dead might have been with her, but they were once more living and loving.

From the tents of the German emigrants near, at times swelled up some song or chant, which seemed to harmonize with the sick girl's dreams, for she would smile faintly and listen. The deep, mellow voices at last struck into that saddest of all sad melodies — "Die langen, langen Tag."

Some memory must have been evoked from the profound depths of that wail of a breaking heart, for she moved restlessly, and whispered, "My lone watch-keeping." But in a second the peaceful look came back, and half raising the gentian she still held convulsively in her hand, the broken Lily of A—— was among the fadeless flowers of the Eternal River.

Thence comes it that the gentian, to us, is full of hope and memory.

13

ANNA PEYRE DINNIES.

THIS accomplished daughter of the South, known so long as a poet by the sweet, wild title of "Moïna," * was born in Georgetown, South Carolina.

Her father, W. F. Shackelford, an eminent lawyer of that State, removed, with his youthful daughter, from that city to Charleston, where he placed her under the care of the Misses Ramsay, daughters of the celebrated Dr. D. Ramsay. Inheriting from her father a talent for poetry and a delicacy of taste, she also received from him the encouragement of her youthful genius, and the development of her refined and graceful word-painting.

At the early age of fourteen, her young heart was given to J. C. Dinnies, a gentleman of New York, but then settled in St. Louis, Mo., and, preferring the white flowers of true affection and manly worth to the lonely laurel crown, "Moïna" encircled her fair brow with an orange wreath, and her young life with a true, devoted love.

Though married to one capable of monopolizing all her thoughts and worthy of all her young heart's devotion, still, in her hours of leisure, Mrs. Dinnies found a delight in expressing in words the deep feelings of happiness that welled up from her poetic soul; and sweet as the notes of a happy bird were the songs which issued from the serene and quiet home of the youthful poet-wife.

Many of her published pieces were written before her marriage, though they still hold a high and honored place in American literature. The history of the "Charnel Ship" has been read and admired by youthful hearts and sober heads; yet few dreamed that a child had penned those thrilling words "which filled each heart with fear."

A number of Mrs. Dinnies's most valuable manuscripts were destroyed by fire in St. Louis — among them a long poem, nearly finished, in six cantos, and several tales ready for publication; but too happy to write for fame, and only caring to speak in song when feeling prompted

---

* Mrs. Dinnies adopted the signature of "Moïna" when quite young. Since the close of the war, Reverend Father Ryan, author of "The Conquered Banner," and other poems, has used the same pseudonym.

98

imagination or suggested subjects worthy of her pen, " Moïna " sought not to retrieve the loss.

In November, 1846, Mr. Dinnies removed to New Orleans, and it was during their residence in the Crescent City that there fell upon the heart and home of the poetess a shadow which, as yet, neither time nor friendship has ever brightened. To her had been given the sweet task of watching the opening mind of a lovely gifted daughter — one who inherited all her parents' nobleness and worth, and who, had she been spared, might well have shared her mother's laurels. But this bright young creature, this idol of a mother's heart, this fair reality of a poet's dream, was called in her earliest girlhood from earth to heaven. Over this broken flower, " Moïna " bowed her head in anguish; but engraving upon her daughter's tombstone the sacred, consoling words, "Sursum Corda," she wrote the same upon her heart. And in the sweet sad songs of " Rachel," we have seen and felt that, though a mother's heart be crushed, a poet's " soul is lifted upward " on the wings of grief and resignation. Mrs. Dinnies's poetry, like everything connected with this gifted woman, breathes of refinement and imagination, mirroring forth the purity of her heart and the high culture of her poetic nature. Always sweet and melodious, it rings at times with martial tones and thrilling eloquence, capable of arousing the soldier's enthusiasm for his country, or the fond devotion of woman for all that is good and holy. She does not deal in a profusion of words — for it seems to be her peculiar talent to find the fittest expression for her beautiful ideas — thus allowing them to shine forth in all their native strength, through their graceful coloring of language.

But it is at home that Mrs. Dinnies realizes her own beautiful illustration of the white chrysanthemum; or rather it is in that charmed setting that the gifted poetess appears as the " peerless picture of a modest wife," beaming with love and tenderness upon her husband's home and heart, and shedding upon all who enter the circle of her influence the charms of intellect and the blessings of woman's kindly heart.

In 1847 appeared the only volume Mrs. Dinnies has published. " The Floral Year," in the style of an annual, was published in Boston. The volume is entirely original. Its design is novel and happy. It consists of one hundred poems, arranged in twelve collections. Each one of these illustrates a bouquet of flowers, such as may generally be culled in the garden or the green-house during its appropriate month ;

and the flowers in each bouquet are illustrated individually and collectively. Thus the charm of unity is added to the beautiful fancies and pure sentiments that are thus thrown upon the waters like a garland from the garden of the Muses.

One reviewer said: "'The Floral Year' may be justly considered as a work of art throughout. By its design, the flower is adapted to the sentiment, and the sentiment to the poem. When the one is of a character that rises to passion, the other is distinguished by power of thought, feeling, and expression. But when the sentiment is of a gentle or negative sort, the poem is remarkable for its simplicity, beauty, and melody."

While residing in St. Louis, in 1845, Mrs. Dinnies edited a newspaper, "The Chaplet of Mercy," for a Fair for the benefit of orphans. The contents of this paper were entirely original, and some of the most distinguished writers of the country contributed. After removing to New Orleans, several years elapsed without her publishing anything, except a few fugitive pieces in the newspapers. In 1854, she contributed a series of didactic articles, under the head of "Rachel's What-Not," to the "Catholic Standard," a weekly journal edited by her husband; and also a series of "Random Readings," consisting of short extracts from various authors, with comments or reflections by herself.

Just before the war, Mrs. Dinnies commenced calling in the stray children of her brain, intending to place them in some kind of order, and perhaps publish them in one or more volumes. She had revised and transcribed about twenty tales, when New Orleans was captured, and the arrest of Mr. Dinnies and imprisonment, by order of Gen. B. F. Butler, caused her to put aside her design for more prosperous times. Mr. Dinnies's health — first broken during his imprisonment at Forts Jackson and Pickens — continued to decline until he became a confirmed invalid; and her heart and thoughts were so occupied by the condition of his health, that she lost all interest in everything save the means of restoring his constitution. In a poem, written when she was little more than a child, she seemed to have a prevision of her fate. "These lines have much sweetness, and flow from a deep fountain of earnest feeling."

> "I could have stemmed misfortune's tide,
> And borne the rich one's sneer;

Have braved the haughty glance of pride,
   Nor shed a single tear ;
I could have smiled on every blow
   From Life's full quiver thrown,
While I might gaze on thee, and know
   I should not be ' *alone !* '

"I could — I think I could have brooked,
   E'en for a time, that thou
Upon my fading face hadst looked
   With less of love than now ;
For then I should at least have felt
   The sweet hope still my own,
To win thee back, and, whilst thou dwelt
   On earth, not been ' *alone !* '

"But thus to see from day to day
   Thy brightening eye and cheek,
And watch thy life-sands waste away,
   Unnumbered, slow, and meek ;
To meet thy look of tenderness,
   And catch the feeble tone
Of kindness, ever breathed to bless,
   And feel I 'll be ' *alone !* ' —

"To mark thy strength each hour decay,
   And yet thy hopes grow stronger,
As filled with heavenward trust, they say,
   ' Earth may not claim thee longer : ' —
Nay, dearest ! 'tis too much ; this heart
   Must break when thou art gone ;
It must not be — we may not part —
   I could not live ' *alone !* ' "

Mrs. Dinnies is a resident of the Crescent City, where she is beloved and revered by her friends.

"There are few American writers whose productions have met with more uniform approbation than the poems of Anna Peyre Dinnies. Entirely free from affectation, they never offend the critic by the inflated or the meretricious. On the contrary, they are distinguished by the correct elegance that is the characteristic of some minds in letters, as it is the trait of high breeding in society. Nor does it in her appear to be the result of study or of art, but it sits gracefully upon her, as if it sprung naturally from intuition," says a writer in the "Southern Literary Messenger."

A poet, in noticing her poems, says: "They are full of feeling, expression, melody, and their words fall upon the heart like distant music, awakening the startled memories of all life's pleasant things, and flinging over the soul its fine net of captivating sounds. Her images are clear, her expression free, as if the heart itself were touched by the contemplation of its own bright and fanciful creations."

The writer quoted above says: "We would style her writings *the poetry of the affections*. Not deficient in imagination, but abounding more in the every-day emotions of life than those which depend upon unusual events to call them into play, the heart, especially the female heart, is the instrument upon which she delights to show her skill, and its chords vibrate to her touch as freely and truly as the harp gives forth its melody to the master's practised hand.

"The thoughtful Shelley defines poetry to be 'the expression of the imagination.' To the feeling Moïna, it is the language of the heart. She utters its syllables in tones of sweetness, frames its sentences with the nice perceptions of art, and speaks with the energy of deep emotion. Her style is seldom diffuse, and rarely redundant in tropes and figures. Who cannot recall to his mind the bright days of his early youth, when the keen and refined perceptions of the soul, with all the freshness of a vernal morn, were first awakened to the glories and the beauties of nature; when the universe was a great volume, every page of which was eloquent with a deep and mysterious lore, filling the whole soul with astonishment and delight; when the heart thrilled to all external influences, as the Æolian strings that are hung amid the trees respond in melody to the soft-breathed wooings of the passing zephyr? And feeling thus, the world of Moïna is the heart — the heart is her universe — the heart the great volume whose pages she loves to illustrate.

"The strong fountains of passion burst from their hidden depths at her command, and pour forth their floods of tenderness, disdain, or scorn. The gentle streams of sentiment rise at her behest, and flow in gladness and beauty through her strain. 'The cataract of thought' comes rushing up from the recesses of the soul. The pleasant dreams of fancy awaken at her call. Love, hope, faith, and confidence glow in her songs; while pride, ambition, scorn, and despair are admirably portrayed in some of her effusions. The lighter emotions, possessing in themselves less of the poetic, are not often the subjects of her choice. The ludicrous she seems to avoid as undignified, and the sarcastic as unfeminine. The wild and mysterious excite her fancy, and lead it to speculations upon primal causes, which result in poems of a highly religious character. The beautiful in nature and art also leads her to the contemplation of the Divine Author of all beauty, and awakens melodies filled at once with hope, devotion, and faith in a brighter world. The flowers fill her with sweet associations and glowing fancies. The winds whisper of danger, and teach her own dependence upon a Higher Power. The stars, the clouds, the moonbeams, all hold strange companionship with her spirit, bearing it afar from earth. Music touches the sealed fountains in her bosom, and excites or saddens according to the strain. Deeds of daring, acts of magnanimity, feelings of gratitude, all create the poetic inspiration. These are the *materiel* from which she culls, combines, and arranges her fancies into verse."

1868.   Mrs. S. B. E.

THE LOVE-LETTER.

The full-orbed moon
In regal splendor proudly tracked the sky;
And the fair laughing flowers of early June
Slept, fanned by Zephyr as he floated by;
The night was hushed, but beautifully clear,
As though enchantment late had wandered there,
And left her charm unbroken; so profound
The deep tranquillity that reigned around.

Close to an open casement, which o'erhung
The quiet scene, there pensively sate one,
Who gazed, not on the loneliness thus flung
Over the earth beneath, but sad and lone,
Held converse with her soul.

She was not fair;
Beauty had set no impress on her brow,
Nor genius shed his heaven-caught lustre there;
Yet there was one who loved her, and whose vow
Was met with all that tenderness which dwells
Only in woman's heart; those fancy spells
That poets dream of.

Now within her hand
She clasped a letter; every line was scanned
By the pure moonbeams round her brightly thrown;
She murmured half aloud, in love's own tone,
His last and dearest words; her warm tears fell
Upon that line, and dimmed the name she loved so well!

"Cease not to think of me," yet once again
She read — then answered in this heartfelt strain:

I could not hush that constant theme
  Of hope and reverie;
For every day and nightly dream,
Whose lights across my dark brain gleam,
  Is filled with thee.

I could not bid those visions spring
  Less frequently,
For each wild phantom which they bring,
Moving along on fancy's wing,
  But pictures thee.

I could not stem the vital source
  Of thought, or be
Compelled to check its whelming force,
As ever in its onward course
  It tells of thee.

I could not, dearest! thus control
  My destiny,
Which bids each new sensation roll
Pure from its fountain in my soul
  To life and thee.

THE BLUSH.

"An outward and visible sign of an inward and spiritual grace."

Was it unholy? Surely no!
  The tongue no purer thought can speak,
And from the heart no feeling flow
  More chaste than brightens woman's cheek.

How oft we mark the deep-tinged rose
  Soft mantling where the lily grew;
Nor deem that where such beauty blows
  A treacherous thorn's concealed from view.

That thorn may touch some tender vein,
  And crimson o'er the wounded part,
Unheeded, too, a transient pain
  Will flush the cheek and thrill the heart.

On Beauty's lids the gem-like tear
  Oft sheds its evanescent ray;
But scarce is seen to sparkle, ere
  'T is chased by beaming smiles away.

Just so the Blush is formed and flies,
  Nor owns reflection's calm control;
It comes — it deepens — fades and dies —
  A gush of *feeling* from the soul!

JULIA PLEASANTS CRESWELL.

A WONDERFULLY clever writer!" exclaimed a critic, one who was well acquainted with her writings. The poetry of Mrs. Creswell is full of sweetness and gentleness; and, as has been said of Felicia Hemans's poetry, so can we truly say of the verse of the subject of this notice, viz.: "That it is of a soft, subdued enthusiasm, breathing, moreover, throughout such a trusting and affectionate spirit, that it must ever find a welcome and a rest in all true, loving hearts."

Mrs. Creswell has a right to expect an inheritance of talent on both sides of her house. Her father belonged to the Pleasants family, of Virginia, which has contributed several distinguished names to the annals of that State. John Hampton Pleasants, of Richmond, who fell in the famous Ritchie duel; Governor James Pleasants, among the dead; and Hugh R. Pleasants,* among the living, are not unknown to fame. The Pleasants are from Norfolk, an old family of England, which I judge, from its recurring in the pages of Macaulay and other historians occasionally, maintained an honorable position centuries back. The first emigrants to this country embraced the tenets of William Penn, and for more than a hundred years his numerous descendants, who have spread all over the United States, preserved that faith. Everything concerning the history of so gifted a woman as Julia Pleasants Creswell is interesting, and the following, relating to her ancestors, is of interest: "John Pleasants," says my Virginia correspondent, "emigrated to this country in the year 1665, the 'animus mirabilis' of Dryden, and settled in the county of Henrico. He left two sons: the younger inherited the estate called Pickernockie, now owned by Boyd and Edmond, on the Chickahominy. From this his descendants were called 'Pickanockies.'"

From this younger branch of the family sprung the names I have mentioned above. The Pleasants blood has been blent with some of the finest old families in Virginia — the Jeffersons, the Randolphs, the Madisons.

My correspondent says: "The family have generally been very hon-

* Died in 1870.

est people, and quite remarkable for intelligence; very few of them, however, have been distinguished in public life, their besetting sins being indolence and diffidence!"

Tarleton Pleasants, Mrs. Creswell's grandfather, was a highly educated and accomplished gentleman, to judge from his finely written letters. He was ninety-four years old when he died. His means were limited, and Mrs. Creswell's father left his home in Hanover county at the age of sixteen to push his own fortunes. He sojourned awhile in the Old Dominion State as printer's boy, and then as sub-editor. The Territory of Alabama was then attracting the Western world, and he went thither, landing at Huntsville, one of the earliest settlers. His popular manners won him golden opinions from all, and he was elected to the office of Secretary of State, Thomas Bibb being at that time Governor of the State. Mr. Pleasants married the second daughter of the Governor.

Julia was the second child of the marriage. Soon after his marriage, Mr. Pleasants abandoned politics, and engaged in mercantile life. Ex-Governor Bibb owned immense estates, and Julia was, so to speak, reared in the lap of luxury. Mr. Pleasants wrote with ease and facility, having a fondness for the pursuit. From childhood Julia was fond of fashioning her thoughts in rhyme, and her father fostered the inclination. He was especially solicitous to secure to his children all the advantages of which, in some measure, his own youth had been deprived, and Julia was indeed fortunate in having for eight years the instruction of a very superior woman. With pleasure I give the meed of praise to one of the many teachers with whom "teaching" is a noble employment, not mere drudgery, who deserve a great reward for their well-doing, albeit they seldom receive it in this life. Miss Swift (from Middleton, Vermont) was a remarkable woman — one who always acted on the broad ground that learning is dear for itself alone; and in her admirable school no prizes were held out to cause heart-burnings and deception — no dreadful punishments to intimidate the fearful and appall the wicked. The consciousness of having done well was the only reward, and the sweet satisfaction of knowledge gained the happiness. Miss Swift was selected by Governor Slade, of New York, to take charge of a Normal school, designed for the education of teachers for Oregon. Says Charles Lanman, in his "Adventures in the Wilds of America " — 2 vols. 1854 — alluding to the subject of this sketch :

"But of all the impressions made upon me during my visit to Huntsville, the most agreeable by far was made by Julia Pleasants, the young and accomplished poetess. She is as great a favorite in the entire South, as she is in this, her native town, and is destined to be wherever the thoughts of genius can be appreciated. She commenced her literary career by contributing an occasional poem to the 'Louisville Journal.' . . . . . Born and bred in the lap of luxury, it is a wonder that the intellect of Miss Pleasants should have been so well disciplined, as its fruits, in spite of their unripeness, would leave one to suppose it had been. But death having recently made her an orphan, and taken from her side a much-loved sister, she has been schooled in the ways of Providence, as well as of the world, and now, when she strikes the lyre, it responds chiefly in those tones which find a resting-place in her sorrowing heart. Like Mrs. Hemans, Miss Pleasants is a thinker and writer of high order, and her mission upon earth cannot but be both beautiful and profitable."

Miss Pleasants' cousin, Thomas Bibb Bradley, a gifted, ambitious, ardent, and aspiring young poet, who died at an early age, ("a brilliant bud of promise was cut off in him,") first drew her poems from their obscurity, and startled her timid bashfulness by launching them upon the "sea of publicity." The generous spirit of George D. Prentice found kind and tender things to say of her timid fledglings of the imagination.

Mr. T. B. Bradley gathered up some of his own and his cousin's poems, and brought out a joint volume in 1854. Mrs. Creswell says, in alluding to this volume:

"The book was not creditable to me, and still less so to my cousin. My own poems were disfigured by misprints, and only one in the book is a fair sample of my cousin's brilliant powers. He was younger than myself, and at that age when a writer falls readily into the style of the last author he has been reading. . . . . There is one poem in the book — 'My Sister' — giving the full sweep of his wing, which the lovers of true music will not willingly let die. I have no hesitation in saying that it challenges criticism, and is, without doubt, one of the most perfect poems in our language."

Miss Pleasants was left an orphan by the simultaneous death of her parents, after which she resided several years with her grandmother, Mrs. Bibb. Here she lost her sister Addie, about whom she sang her sweetest songs. In 1854, she was married to Judge David

Creswell, a man of talents, and a native of South Carolina. Judge Creswell was a wealthy planter near Shreveport, La., but lost his wealth by the war, and has resumed the practice of the law.

Mrs. Creswell has a volume of poems ready for publication. Claxton, Remsen and Haffelfinger, of Philadelphia, in 1868, published a novel written by her, entitled *Callamura*.

"Greenwood," the home of Mrs. Creswell, is near Shreveport, La. Here she is the centre of a happy circle, surrounded by a quartette of children, of whom the only daughter, named Adrienne, (the *nom de plume* under which Mrs. Creswell first published,) having inherited the poetic temperament, at the early age of ten dabbles in "rhymes."

1868.

THE MINSTREL PILOT.

On the bosom of a river
Where the sun unloosed its quiver,
Or the starlight streamed forever,
    Sailed a vessel light and free:
Morning dewdrops hung, like manna,
On the bright folds of her banner,
While the zephyr rose to fan her
    Softly to the radiant sea.

At her prow a pilot, beaming
In the hues of youth, stood dreaming,
And he was in glorious seeming,
    Like an angel from above:
Through his hair the breezes sported;
And as down the wave he floated,
Oft that pilot, angel-throated,
    Warbled lays of hope and love.

Through those locks, so brightly flowing,
Buds of laurel-bloom were blowing,
And his hands, anon, were throwing
    Music from a lyre of gold:

Swiftly down the stream he glided,
Soft the purple waves divided,
And a rainbow arch abided
    On his canvas' snowy fold.

Anxious hearts, with fond emotion,
Watched him sailing to the ocean,
Praying that no wild commotion
    'Midst the elements might rise:
And he seemed some young Apollo,
Charming summer winds to follow,
While the water-flag's corolla
    Trembled to his music sighs.

But those purple waves, enchanted,
Rolled beside a city haunted
By an awful spell, which daunted
    Every comer to her shore:
Nightshades rank the air encumbered,
And pale marble statues numbered
Lotus-eaters, where they slumbered,
    And awoke to life no more!

Then there rushed with lightning quickness
O'er his face a mortal sickness,
While the dews in fearful thickness
    Gathered o'er his temples fair;
And there rolled a mournful murmur
Through the lovely Southern summer,
As that beauteous Pilot-comer
    Perished by that city there.

Still rolls on that radiant river,
And the sun unbinds his quiver,
On the starlit streams forever,
    On its bosom as before;
But that vessel's rainbow banner
Greets no more the gay savanna,
And that Pilot's lute drops manna
    On the purple waves no more!

M. SOPHIE HOMES.

("*Millie Mayfield.*")

THE subject of the present sketch, Mrs. Mary Sophie Shaw Homes, was born in Frederick City, Maryland; but having resided in Louisiana nearly all her life, she claims it as the State of her adoption. She is the daughter of Thomas Shaw, of Annapolis, Md., who for over twenty years filled with honor the situation of cashier of the Frederick County Branch Bank of Maryland, and was a man beloved and highly respected by all who knew him. On her mother's side, her ancestors were good old Maryland Revolutionary stock, two of her great-uncles having fallen, in defence of their rights as freemen, at the battle of Germantown. After her father's death, which happened when she was quite a child, her mother removed with her family to New Orleans, where Mrs. Homes has since resided. She has been twice married: her first husband, Mr. Norman Rogers, dying in the second year of their union, she was left a widow at a very early age, and her life has been one of strange vicissitudes; but by nature she is energetic, resolute, and determined, and although not hopeful, is very enduring; and, as a friend once said of her, "possesses the rare qualification of contentment in an humble position, with capacities for a most elevated one."

She appeared before the literary world of New Orleans under the *nom de plume* of "Millie Mayfield," in 1857, as a newspaper contributor of essays, sketches, and poems, which (to quote from one of the leading journals of New Orleans, the "Daily Crescent") "could not fail of attracting attention from the unmistakable evidences of genius they displayed, the poetry being far above mediocrity, and the sketches spirited and entertaining;" so that when, in the same year, her first published volume in prose, entitled "Carrie Harrington; or, Scenes in New Orleans," made its appearance, the public was prepared to give it a most favorable reception. Of this book, Mrs. L. Virginia French thus wrote: "This is a most agreeable and readable book. . . . . The style is easy, natural, and unostentatious. . . . . . There is a vein of genial humor running through the whole book."

A writer in the " New Orleans Crescent " reviews " Carrie Harrington ; or, Scenes in New Orleans : "

"This is a new and charming work by a Southern lady — the maiden effort, I may say, in novelistic literature, by one who is already favorably known to our State as a sweet poetess; for few are they who have read and not been pleased with the truthful emanations in harmonious numbers from the accomplished pen of ' Millie Mayfield.'

"Having just risen from a careful perusal of it, I can honestly pronounce it a work replete with refreshing thoughts, expressed with a flowing happiness of diction, supplying, at this season of the year particularly, a great desideratum, as all can't-get-aways and even run-aways across the lake will admit.

"This the writer is constrained to confess, despite his predisposition to be hypercritical, — he had almost said unfriendly to it, because, perhaps, of its being the production of a petticoat, — an institution spreading, as all the world knows, pretty considerably nowadays, — when he sat down to glance at its contents. Agreeably surprised, he was taught a lesson of the supreme folly of preconceived impressions, which he will not easily forget. The authoress of Carrie Harrington has in this novelette — if I may so term it, being in one volume, and yet as suggestive of thought and promotive of reflection, if not as well calculated to enchain attention and challenge admiration as many three-volumed novels written by established favorites of the reading public, and which, for the most part, answer to a charm Pollok's description of one, viz., 'A novel was a book three-volumed and once read, and oft crammed full of poisonous error, blackening every page, and oftener still of old deceased, putrid thought, and miserable incident, at war with nature, with itself and truth at war; yet charming still the greedy reader on, till, done, he tried to recollect his thoughts, and nothing found but dreaming emptiness,' — in this little work, I say, she has given an earnest of the possession of talent of a very high order in this branch of light literature. There is nothing *labored* about it — a great blessing to readers; for elaboration, when apparent, is generally painful, at least to me. The characters spring into existence in rapid succession — take and keep their places, while the individuality of each is maintained with tolerable integrity, and seemingly drawn from life by one who has diligently exercised the faculty for observation. I would not, however, be understood to say that in their portrayal there are no inequalities — no inelegancies — no infelicities — no redundances; or that she is *au fait* in their introduction : better marshalling there might have been, which accomplishment can only be attained by practice, for there is no royal road to perfection, even for *women*, gifted as they are with intuition.

"Many of the scenes, though far from being faultless, sparkle with talent, and talent is something; but here and there she betrays a want of *tact*, and *that*, while not absolutely talent, is everything in every undertaking; for, as somebody has somewhere said, sententiously, 'talent is power—tact, skill; talent is weight—tact, momentum; talent knows what to do—tact, how to do it; it is the eye of discrimination, the right hand of intellect,'—and so it is slipping into one's good graces as a billiard-ball insinuates itself into the pocket. The story is pleasingly simple and purely domestic—opening not in the hackneyed style to which so many of our novelists are notoriously addicted; such as a 'solitary horseman' was approaching a wood in time to rescue some beauty in distress, etc.; or, as a 'handsome stranger,' apparently on the shady side of thirty, leg-weary and foot-sore, arriving about sunset at a village inn, just in season to play the eavesdropper to a conversation, in which he learns wonders regarding himself, etc.

"The hall-door bell of Judge Loring's aristocratic mansion being vigorously rung, announces a visitor whose business would seem not to brook delay—and so it proves; for in waddles the pussy, fussy, garrulous, go-a-headative Mrs. Percival, with her everlasting exclamation of 'Lawful sakes alive!' to the great dismay and disgust of the haughty beauty, Isabelle Loring, who happens at home alone, with her hair in paper against an entertainment to be given in the evening, at which she fondly anticipates the conquest of Horace Nelson's heart. In no very amiable mood, but with many an unfriendly wish, does the proud girl hastily brush herself into presentableness, and descends to the parlor, where, with a smile that would rival that of a seraph in glory—though with sorrow be it observed, expressly got up for the occasion by hypocrisy—she greets her visitor, who is all impatience to declare her mission.

"Unromantic, plain, matter-of-fact, coarsely spoken is Mrs. Percival—blunt to rudeness, and generous to a fault; and while indulging a vulgarity indigenous to her nature, and peculiarly offensive to 'ears polite,' displaying a heart as large as creation—so that we cannot help loving her, and owning that 'even her failings lean to virtue's side.' In speech—and she is flippant enough in all conscience—she is a second edition of Mrs. Malaprop, constantly mispronouncing and misapprehending words; for example: she talks complacently of her 'morey-antic,' (moire antique;) says 'swarry' when she would say soirée; 'infermation' for inflammation; 'portfully' for portfolio, and so forth. Isabelle Loring has received a liberal education—contracted grand ideas of upper-tendom, and being surpassingly beautiful, womanlike, requires no ghost from the grave to tell her so. Devoted to dress, magnificent in foreign airs, and inordinately fond of admiration, reminding us, in the matter of pride, and in that only, of Pauline Deschappelles, for there the likeness ends—as Pauline is not without redeeming points—and, when crossed in desire, in some respects, of Lady Sneerwell. I have been thus particular, as these personages—the very antipodes of each other—play respectively important parts in the story.

"Mrs. Percival blurts out her errand in her accustomed manner, which is one of mercy, and is referred to mamma, who is at Aunt Langdon's, whither

Mrs. Percival directs her hurried steps, and in her haste almost runs foul of Miss Letty at the street-door — a malicious piece of dry-goods, unworthy of the institution of calico, and rejoicing in the twofold occupation of dressmaker and scandal-monger. Miss Letty, in giving vent to her envy, bristles up and talks waspishly of Mrs. Percival's low origin, much to the edification of Isabelle, who is jealous of the exceeding loveliness of Mrs. Percival's only daughter and child, Ella. Ella, the pure-minded, the devoted, whom we could have wished had been made the heroine instead of Carrie, all beautiful and dutiful as she is, as we have often wished, when reading the 'Ivanhoe' of Scott, that the high-souled Rebecca had been preferred to the less interesting Rowena.

"Ella, like Isabelle, is enamored of Horace Nelson, but widely different are their loves; the one modestly conceals, the other coquettishly displays. At a party where they all meet, they discover that they are rivals, and, as it would seem to Ella, without hope of success on her part. The effect of this discovery is the loss of the roses from her cheek, which her mother observing and mistaking the cause, talks funnily enough of dosing the love-stricken girl with salts! Not a bad idea, by-the-by; we have faith in salts and senna, even for the correction of the malady of love. A heavenly creature is Ella, notwithstanding that she is the child of vulgar parents of mushroom growth into opulence! Horace Nelson is a fine young fellow, the scion of a family amply endowed with pride of birth, and dependent on a rich, gouty old uncle, who, in his bitter hostility to parvenuism, insists on his nephew marrying a full-blooded aristocrat on pain of disinheritance. Hard as is the alternative, the noble youth declares his love to Ella and his independence of the uncle, goes to woo the fickle goddess in the auriferous fields of California and Australia, returns with a pocket full of rocks, and marries the ever-faithful Ella.

"Carrie Harrington and her brother Robert are left unexpectedly in a deplorable state of orphanage, when the good Mrs. P. opportunely appears, takes the distracted Carrie home with her, intending to adopt her, where, thanks to the excellent nursing of Ella, the health of the bereaved one is in due time re-established. The brother goes to sea. No sooner is Carrie herself again than she is afflicted with conscientious scruples as to eating the bread of idleness, and, after a scene, resolves to seek a public-school teachership, which, by the aid of Mr. Percival, she obtains, and makes acquaintance at the same time with a highly mercurial lady (Katy), who makes merry at the expense of the school-board with a wickedness of elegance richly meriting castigation. This, it is needless to add, refers to days of yore; for, as the Frenchman would say, *nous avons change tout cele maintenant.* Out of this acquaintance there grows a warm and lasting friendship between Carrie and Katy. The gouty old uncle, disgusted with the plebeianism of his nephew's amatory proclivities, proposes marriage to Isabelle, who, out of sheer spite to the same individual, accepts.

"They cross the lake, and meet at one of the watering-places, the Percivals,

15

Carrie, and Katy, and there marvel on marvel occurs.   Edward Loring owns the soft impeachment to Carrie, who, nothing loth, frankly reciprocates.   Isabelle heartlessly neglects her lord, who is hopelessly confined to his bed — suffers some French count to make illicit love to her, and elopes with him to find a watery grave.   The shock of this elopement accelerates the death of the old uncle, who, before dying, recognizes in Carrie his grandchild.   A portion of his vast wealth she of course inherits, and becomes the loved wife of the happy Edward Loring.   Robert returns from a prosperous voyage, sees and straightway falls in love with Katy, who, like a sensible widow that she is, and none the worse for being '*second-hand,*' takes compassion upon him after the most approved fashion, and 'all goes merry as a marriage-bell.'

"Such is an outline of the story.   In conclusion, I cannot help expressing my admiration of Katy; she is the very '*broth*' of a woman, brimful of fun, talks like a book, dealing extensively in refined irony, and often dropping remarks which fall and blister like drops of burning sealing-wax.   Sometimes, however, her drollery outstrips her discretion and overleaps the boundary of propriety, acquiring a broadness hardly blameless, as in the quotation somewhat profanely applied, the hoop-fashion being the subject of conversation: 'Though their beginning was small, yet their *latter end* should greatly increase.'   The scenes and passages I would especially commend for truthfulness and raciness, are those of love between Carrie and Edward; of bathing, when one of the girls roguishly cries out, 'A shark!' and Mrs. P. innocently sits on the *emplatre* of a French woman ; and of the *bal masque*, at which the count, who, like Esau, 'is a hairy man,' is caught toying with the bejewelled finger of Isabelle.

"The work, as I have already intimated, though not without blemishes, evidently bears the marks of genius, a little too freakish, at times, it is true; and if, as I understand, it was written for amusement, rather than with a view to publication, it is a highly creditable effort, and bespeaks a talent whose cultivation it would be a pity, if not a crime, to neglect."

In 1860, she published a volume in verse, in defence of the South, entitled " Progression; or, The South Defended," "which was a most remarkable production for a female ; evincing deep research and strong analytical and logical reasoning capacities — besides breathing the very soul of patriotism and devotion to her native land."

That she loves her native South with the whole strength of her poetic temperament, a short quotation from one of her poems will show :

> "O Fairy-land! Dream-land! O land of the South,
> What nectar awaits but the kiss of thy mouth —
> Balm-breathing, soul-sweet'ning, as fancy distils
> The perfume thy golden-rimmed chalice that fills !

There are many that sing of the land of the vine,
And chant the wild legends of myth-peopled Rhine,—
That catch from the blue waves of Arno a tone,
Or hymn the low dirges of foam-crested Rhone,—
That join in the 'Marseillaise' war-cry of France,
Or blow forth a blast of the days of the lance
And the tournament — then breathe a tender love-strain
Of troubadour tinkling his heart's secret pain
On the answering strings of a well-thrumm'd guitar:
But grander, yet sweeter and holier far
Are the cadences floating o'er thee, happy clime!
To sound through the far-reaching arches of Time,
Dear land of the sunbeam, when minstrels shall bring
Forth the melody slumb'ring upon thy gold string!
Oh, waken thee, harpists! and tell all the worth
That lies hushed on the sweetly-toned lyre of the South!"

Her fugitive poems and sketches, scattered broadcast and with a lavish hand, would, if collected, fill several volumes. Some newspaper critic, in speaking of her poetry, says: "We might select some single lines from many of the fugitive pieces of this sweet singer of the South that the painter's pencil could not make more perfect; and others that, in singular beauty of thought, will compare favorably with anything found in the language."

She was — besides writing for many other papers at home and elsewhere — a constant contributor, for over two years, to the New Orleans "True Delta," whose literary editor,* himself a poet and critic of well-known abilities, has pronounced her, "undeniably, the finest female lyrist in the Southwest."

Her poetic talent seems to have been inherited from an elder brother of her father's, — Doctor John Shaw, of Annapolis, Md., — whose poems and letters of travel were published after his death for the benefit of his widow, many of the most interesting reminiscences being furnished by his college "chum" and bosom-friend, Francis Scott Key, the author of the "Star-spangled Banner."

But, although descended from one of the oldest families in the land, her life has not passed without care, and much time that she would like to devote to literary pursuits has to be more practically employed in fighting the great battle of life. It is a matter of surprise with those who know her, how she ever could have written so much with so many other things to engross her; but, to quote her own words:

*John W. Overall.

> "*Life without trials!* — who would give
>   The cares that make him wise,
> To be the useless drone that hives
>   No honey as he flies?
> Why, Nature in her mighty book
>   This wholesome lesson shows —
> That e'en the thistle's thorny crook
>   Can blossom as the rose."

She was married to Mr. Luther Homes in 1864, and continues to reside in New Orleans. In 1870, a volume of her fugitive poems was published by J. B. Lippincott & Co., Philadelphia, entitled "A Wreath of Rhymes."

1869.

THE DREAM-ANGEL.

And now the Dream-Angel soared once more over sloping roofs, tall chimneys, spires, domes, and brick-and-mortar cages. Where in the vast city will she first bend her glances? See, through yon partially raised dormer-window, the full moonlight streaming, falls on the couch of a slumbering youth. It is an humble attic in which he rests; its walls are bare, its cot meagrely furnished; but that coarse pillow caresses a head where ideality and lofty thought have imbedded their priceless jewels on the brow's broad surface.

Bend lower, spirit; look into that imaginative brain, and deep down into that warm glowing heart. No garret's bounds can crib their longings; no raftered roof holds down their high desires and lofty aspirations. 'T is Nature's child you look upon — and towering mountains, starry heights, singing brooklets and flowery dales, are his inheritance. Oh! guard well the poet's dream — let not the stains of earth mar its brightness!

Tenderly the Dream-Angel binds o'er his brow a chaplet of the mystic witch-hazel, softly singing through its leaves as she does so:

> Breathe here "a spell," mysterious plant —
> Let dreams embody his soul's deep want!

The unplastered walls of the little attic crumble down, and he stands on a wood-crowned upland, which slopes gently away, terminating in a green valley and fairy lake. The tinkling bells of browsing cattle, mingling with the ripple of laughing brooklets, float through the golden atmosphere, which no visible sun illumines, but soft, rosy, and purple clouds, with gilded edges and inward glow, like the fire shut up in the opal's heart, wave gentle folds over the burnished blue heaven. The air is sleepy with the odorous breath of flowers, and golden-winged beetles hum a drowsy drone as they rest on the tall silken grasses that wave green banners over the dancing streamlet. A thick wood, with its interlacing leaves and branches, shuts out this paradise from the noisy world, and fairy shapes flit through the green recesses, or dip their clustering ringlets in the limpid lake ; while starry eyes peep over the rosy hedges, and taper-fingers rain showers of jasmine-buds upon eyelids slumbering on the mossy banks, or in the bowers where clematis and sweet-brier twine their stars and fragrance. No sounds are heard from out the playful host but laughter musical ; they look their love, and speak with flowers their pure thoughts.

And now, a band of dimpling, blushing nymphs have twined a wreath of amaranth, and, circling around him in a mazy dance, they place it on his brow ; while soft through the hushed air a dreamy cadence floats, and unseen harps and voices blend a witching strain :

> Come! come! come!
> Come to our bowers of light,
>   O son of the morning-land!
> Dreary and dark is the baneful night
>   That shrouds the world's cold strand.
> 'Tis suspicion, and doubt, and wrong
>   That engender the earthly cloud;
> But come to the bowers where faith is strong,
>   And the sorrowing head 's ne'er bowed.
>   Come! come! come!
>
> Come! come! come!
> Come with a heart of youth —
>   Come with an eye of fire,
> Drink of the fount of immortal Truth,
>   And quench each gross desire!
> 'Tis the glow of generous thought
>   That golden lights our sky;
> And love makes our music — melody wrought
>   By the spirit's harmony!
>   Come! come! come!
>
> Come! come! come!
> Here, the words you breathe,
>   Here, the thoughts that burn
> Will spring into living flowers, to wreathe
>   Thy Hope's now mouldering urn!
> Lay down thy petty cares;
>   Cast off thy sin's dark yoke;
> And cool thy brow with ambrosial airs,
>   Whose echoes grief never woke!
>   Come! come! come!

"Where? where?" exclaimed the youth, starting from his pillow with kindling eye and flushing cheek; "oh, where will that glorious dream be realized?"

"In heaven!" softly whispered the Dream-Angel, as she floated out on the moonbeam.

——oo;o;oo——

ELIZA LOFTON PUGH.

ELIZA LOFTON PUGH, *née* Phillips, is a native of Louisiana, though of French and Irish extraction; and few, who have any acquaintance with her, fail to recognize, both in manner, conversation, and appearance, the prominent characteristics of the races from which she sprang; few either, who, recalling her father, fail to remember in him the true type of the "Irish gentleman" — a man well and widely known throughout the State, generous, brave, and hospitable, endearing himself to all ranks by his *bonhommie* of manner, which, united to his talents and energy, made him a successful politician. To fine qualities of mind and heart he united the gifts of a ready narrator, and that talent, not uncommon to his countrymen, of rendering himself the "life of convivial gatherings." To all who knew and loved Colonel Phillips this sketch of his daughter among the literati of the South will not prove uninteresting. Alas! that an early death snatched from him the gratification of realizing in the woman the fond predictions of the early promise of the child. From her infancy she evinced a constitution so remarkably fragile, that it caused her devoted mother many an hour of sad reflection — particularly sad, as she discovered that as the powers of her mind were being rapidly developed, the inspiration of the soul seemed wearing away the body. She lived in a world of her own creation, surrounded by images of her own fancy. Her conversation has ever been remarkable for its originality and freshness, which has rendered her from childhood interesting to persons of all ages.

Reared in the almost entire seclusion of home — bereft one by one of its inmates and the companionship of those endeared to her not less by the closest ties of relationship than a warm and earnest sympathy in the passion of her life, — she became prematurely thoughtful as the companion of her widowed mother, in the absence and marriage of an only sister. At the age of ten she wrote a little story, in which the precocity of her inventive genius was apparent. She also evinced great talent in the extreme force of her descriptions, the elevation of her sentiment, and the poetic beauty of her language.

After a careful home education, she completed her course under the able direction of Miss Hull, whose seminary at that time had no rival in the confidence of the people of the South. Miss Hull, in speaking of her, said:

"She came to me under high encomium from Mrs. M., a friend of mine, who said: 'You will find in her an apt pupil, an eager student, a patient, untiring reader. She possesses talent which will do you much credit.' I next day welcomed the pupil thus introduced, into my seminary, and surveyed her with interest, but with some disappointment. In the pale, slender, delicate child, with stooping shoulders, and grave, unattractive face, only enlivened by a pair of dark, thoughtful eyes, I saw slight indication of the mind, which, however, an early examination into her studies satisfied me was of no ordinary promise."

Two years of close application to study, and the advantage of free access to the private library of her preceptress, and to which was added the privilege of unrestrained communication with the finely cultivated mind of her teacher, closed the educational course of Eliza Phillips.

She returned home to devote herself to her still secret passion for her pen.

Married at the age of seventeen to a son of the Hon. W. W. Pugh, of Louisiana, she passed the first three years of her married life on her husband's plantation; where, in its unbroken solitude, without the solace of her favorite authors, without other companionship than that of her family, she first acquainted her friends with her efforts at authorship.

Blelock & Co. published a novel, entitled "Not a Hero," in 1867, which was written by Mrs. Pugh at the beginning of the war, or at the time when the war-cloud was gathering in its wrath. Short sketches, "literary and political," were published in the "New York World," "New Orleans Times," and other journals of less note, under the *nom de plume* of "Arria."

Improved in health and appearance, she now devotes herself to the pursuit which has, from her childhood, taken so strong a hold upon her fancy; but to the exclusion of no single duty, either as daughter, wife, or mother.

At the time of the present sketch, Mrs. Pugh is but in the spring season of her womanhood, and, we predict, of her authorship.

The quaint, grave child has developed into the gay, sprightly woman, presiding with a graceful hospitality in her unpretending home, endearing herself to her old friends, and recommending herself to new acquaintances, by an engaging manner, quickness of repartee, and a display of many of the happiest qualities of heart, which she inherits in no slight degree from her father, while in manner, gesture, and appearance the French extraction unequivocally proclaims itself. Giving all her spare moments to her pen, and to a careful supervision of her only child, she has not permitted her literary life to cast the shadow of an ill-regulated household on those who look to her for their happiness, or to cloud for an instant the sunshine of home. She has not sunk the woman in the author, and has unhesitatingly declared her purpose to relinquish the pleasure of her pen should a word of reproach from those she loves warn her of such a probability. Yet to all who know her, that domestic circle proves that a combination of the practical and literary ·may be gracefully, pleasantly, and harmoniously blended.

Mrs. Pugh has a novel now in the press (1871) of Claxton, Remsen & Haffelfinger, Philadelphia. It is entitled "In a Crucible."

1868.   MARGARET C. PIGGOT.

ST. PHILIP'S.

There was no scenery in or around St. Philip's, at least none so called; no mountains, around whose summits the rosy mists of morning might gather; no hills, over whose green slopes the flocks of lazy Southdowns might graze; no jagged cliffs, against which a heavy rolling sea might thunder its eternal harmonies; though miles and miles away the arrowy river flowed with deepening current into the Mexican Gulf, broadening near its outlet, flattening at its edges, and the sedgy margin running out into great stretches of marshy ground. Higher up, in and around St. Philip's, it flowed sluggishly through steep banks in the summer-time, swelling angrily with winter floods and tides, and rushing hoarsely along, its current broken here and there into eddies around a clump of stunted willows bedded in the sand, or sweeping out into broad curves, with the sunlight dancing over it, and the comfortable country-houses mirrored in its still, glassy surface just at sunset.

The country was not picturesque, but would have delighted the eye of the agriculturist in its rich grain-fields, luxuriant hedges, and well-kept gardens. There were wide, open commons, filled with browsing cattle; fat pasture lands, where the sleek, thoroughbred stock of the plantations ranged, chewing their cuds contentedly under shade-trees under the summer heat, and lowing gently as they followed the narrow pathway, cropping as they went to the milking-pens — evening shadows gathering the while, and the shrill chirp of insects growing clamorous as the sun descended. Yet there was beauty in the aspect of the landscape — a beauty to satisfy even a fastidious taste. If there were neither hills nor mountains, there were clouds, that, evening after evening, piled themselves in fantastic masses against the setting sun, and whose outlines stood out, bold and clear, against the western light. There were gorgeous strips of coloring too — painted skies, with the sun sinking down like a huge red ball in the midst: sunsets that equalled anything for richness of hue that the human eye ever beheld. There was deep, sombre blue in the evening skies that Poussin had striven vainly to paint; and a glint in the golden sunlight pouring over river, wood, and field, that Claude could never match! There was a softness in the air when the October mists rolled over the woodlands, and autumn moonlight silvered the earth, that even the passionate heart of the poet could not breathe, and that hushed the fevered pulse while the planets glowed in the dusky canopy overhead. There were stretches of forest, with giant oaks, and whispering poplars turning their silver-lined leaves to the light, — slender sumach, that blushed red under autumn skies,— broad-spreading magnolias,— immortal bays, filling the air with their faint, subtile breath,— hawthorns, powdered in the spring like crusted snow, and flashing scarlet with the first frost that ripened the berries on its stems. Here you sometimes stumbled over sloping mounds, where, underneath the shadows of these great Western forests, the bones of the red men lie bleaching with the centuries that roll over them — dead, indeed, since their rest is undisturbed by the march of civilization, whose gigantic proofs stare us in the face in this latter day. The roadside grew up thickly with purple heather; and flaunting lilies of scarlet and yellow, covered flat, marshy plains, while graceful water-lilies hung silent in the summer noon, spreading dark-green, glossy leaves over the water, where tiny fish swam in and out, and where, through the summer nights, the frogs croaked, and ugly, spotted snakes coiled among the reeds.

ELIZA ELLIOTT HARPER.

MRS. ELIZA ELLIOTT HARPER, a daughter of Colonel John L. Lewis, of Claiborne Parish, La., was born in Jones County, Georgia, in September, 1834, and moved to Louisiana with her parents in 1846, which State has been her home since.

Mrs. Harper's life has not been eventful — as she is wont to say, " the lines have fallen to her in pleasant places." At an early age, she married Dr. James D. Harper, and resides at Minden, Claiborne Parish, La. Mrs. Harper's early publications were in the " Louisville Journal," over the signature of " Sindera."

1870.

I'LL COME IN BRIGHT DREAMS.

Yes, I'll come in bright dreams, love,
  I'll come to thee oft,
When the light wing of sleep
  On thy bosom lies soft:
When, wearied with care, love,
  Thou seekest repose,
And with thoughts of the dear one
  Thy fond bosom glows.
When the tear-drops of nature
  Beam bright on the flower,
Reflecting the sky gems,
  I'll come to thy bower.

Yes, I'll come in bright dreams, love,
  I'll come and we'll stray
'Mid the beauties of dream-land,
  And 'twill ever be May;
For the sound of thy voice
  Is the coo of the dove,
And no gale can be soft
  As thy whispers of love.
Be thy lips the billows,
  And mine, love, the beach.
And thus fondly caressing,
  The dream-land we reach.

Yes, I'll come in bright dreams, love,
  And oh! if it be
That "life's but a dream,"
  I'll dream, love, with thee.
Yes, dream 'neath the heaven
  Of thy dark, beaming eye,
Nor e'er from its starlight
  My spirit would fly.
Then I'll come in life's dream, love,
  And bright will it be;
It cannot know sorrow,
  If spent, love, with thee.

MARY WALSINGHAM CREAN,

WELL known to the Southern muses by the simple *nom de plume* of "May Rïe," was born in Charleston, S. C., but has been from infancy a resident of the Crescent City. Her career as a writer commenced as a school-girl, and opened with a series of lively, dashing, and piquant articles, prose and verse, communicated to the "Sunday Delta" when under the control of the gifted Joseph Brenan. Much interest prevailed for a time over the gay and graceful incognita.

She continued for several years a frequent contributor to the same paper, winning a local popularity seldom attained at the first steps of a literary career.

Late political troubles came, the writers of the "Delta" were scattered, and "May Rïe's" harp remained long silent, or was only struck in secret, to sing of sorrow or of patriotic devotion.

The cloud of national strife swept past. The subject of this sketch, like many others, was reduced to a position of need, and again resumed her pen, but no longer as a pastime.

She entered upon her career as a paid writer for the New Orleans "Sunday Times," and for two years has been a regular weekly contributor to its pages, also appearing occasionally in other journals and magazines.

Of mingled English and Irish extraction, Mary Walsingham combines in her nature the best characteristics of the two nations of Albion and Erin, tempered by a high degree of American sentiment. In her, a strong though golden chain of solid English sense ever gracefully reins in those coursers of the sun, Irish wit and passion; and the real and ideal, whether they ascend alternately, like the celestial twins, or rule together, like Jove and Juno, reign in harmonious duality, each retaining its proper limits, and one ever preserving the other from deficiency or excess. No collection of her writings has yet been made in book-form.

Miss Crean is writing a novel of "Life in the Old Third." Years ago, the lower and oldest part of the city of New Orleans was called the "Third Municipality." It is entirely French — unique and old-fashioned both in build and the manners and customs of its inhabitants — and furnishes as good a scene and material for romance as any of the cities of the Old World. Miss Crean resided in the "Old Third" in her childhood, and an original and highly entertaining

123

book must be her effort. She also has in preparation a volume of criticisms of Southern writers.

1869.

SANTA CLAUS.

O Santa Claus! dear Santa Claus!
  Long years have waned and things have changed
Since o'er the roof-tree's wintry floss
  With dancing heart my glances ranged,
And strained to view thy silver wheel,
  Or mark thy chariot 'gainst the sky,
Or hear thy tiny frosted heel
  With stealthy step go swiftly by,
    Along the roof-tree's fringing floss,
    O Santa Claus! dear Santa Claus!

Thou elfin friend, of fame benign,
  And ruddy glow and genial glee!
What radiant, fairy hopes were mine
  That found their central sun in thee!
What cavern'd stores of Christmas joys,
  What thrilling mines of wealth unseen,
Thou darling dream of girls and boys,
  Went rolling in thy chariot's sheen,
    Along the roof-tree's glittering floss,
    O Santa Claus! dear Santa Claus!

How dear the smoke-wreath's misty blue,
  How bright the ruddy kindling hearth!
How prized the chimney's magic flue
  Which bore thy cherished form to earth!
What sleepless hours — what throbbings wild —
  What thrilling hopes around us clung,
As murmuring breeze, or swallow mild
  Some echo on the midnight flung
    From off the roof-tree's fringing floss,
    O Santa Claus! dear Santa Claus!

And hark! I hear the merry horn —
  The merry, clattering, jingling chime

That usher'd in the crystal morn,
　The jovial hours of that sweet time;
The thrilling bursts of laughter clear —
　The frantic song of joy and mirth —
The hearty, ringing Christmas cheer
　Around the stockings on the hearth,
　　Beneath the roof-tree's waving floss,
　　O Santa Claus! dear Santa Claus!

I see the forms at rest for years —
　Our starry household-idols then —
Arise from out the mist of tears,
　To light our mourning hopes again;
And sever'd hearts, and sunder'd hands,
　And perish'd ties, how sweet of old!
And faded hopes, and broken bands,
　Unite from out oblivion cold,
　　Beneath the roof-tree's fringing floss,
　　O Santa Claus! dear Santa Claus!

But, no! our dearest hopes and forms
　Are with thy perish'd glories pale,
Thou sweetest charm of childhood's charms,
　And childhood's brightest fairy-tale!
They beat no more in music-bars,
　The jocund minstrelsy of earth,
But softly beam like happy stars
　Above our lonely Christmas hearth,
　　Beneath the roof-tree's fringing floss,
　　O Santa Claus! dear Santa Claus!

BRONZE JOHN AND HIS SAFFRON STEED.

Came riding forth on a charger bold,
　From the land of the citron-bloom,
A stalwart knight, with a lance of gold,
　And a dancing yellow plume:
His shield was of bronze, and his helmet high;
Of flame was his breath, and of fire his eye;
And swift was the flight of the charger by
　Of this knight with a yellow plume!

Away and away, o'er wood and wold —
  O'er city and mountain high!
Sharp was the flash of that lance so bold,
  And the glance of that fiery eye!
Here was a body, and there was a bier;
For he fell'd one here, and slew one there:
"Away to the feast of death elsewhere!"
  Sang the knight as he clattered by.

Rap, rap, rap! on the city wall —
  Rap, rap! and "What! ho! indeed!
Who is there?" quoth the warden tall.
  "*Bronze John and his Saffron Steed.*"
Quoth the warden grim, "And who may you be?
And come you from the North countrie,
Or from the pestilent South," quoth he,
  "Bronze John and your Saffron Steed?"

Rap, rap, rap! on the city gate,
  And "Open, thou fool, to me!"
Quoth the bold Don John, with his lance in wait:
  "I come from the South countrie —
The challenging knight of the Brazen Shield —
And I summon this fortress to quickly yield!"
"First I'd see thee dead!" quoth the warden chield,
  And grinning, clattered the key.

Then back drew the knight on his charger bold,
  And lifted his javelin keen;
One blow on the gate with his barb of gold,
  And where was the warder then?
Here was a body, and there was a bier;
The captain was here, and the sentinel there.
"A king is Bronze John, and his sceptre's his spear,"
  Sang the knight as he mounted again.

And "Hey! for the land of the South," he laughed,
  "The land of the citron-bloom!
And the potent knight of the yellow shaft,
  And the floating yellow plume!
A king is Bronze John — his steed is Death —
Of fire is his eye, and of flame his breath,
And his lance is the doom of the foe," he saith,
  "Bronze John and his saffron plume!"

NEW ORLEANS, Sept., 1867.

MRS. JOSEPHINE R. HOSKINS.

HOW true is it that true worth and genius are like the violet, hiding from public gaze, and only discovered by its perfume, that cannot hide itself always! The subject of this article is like a " violet," as modest and unassuming as talented, and on that account not well known, for true merit goes unrewarded, while glitter mounts high on Parnassus, and sits there for a time.

Mrs. Hoskins is by birth a New-Yorker, but has resided in the South for over thirty years, and known and loved "Southland" best of all other lands. Her father was a Frenchman, born of Italian parents; he came to the United States just before the war of 1812, entered the army, and served with some distinction under General Macomb, and after the close of the war was enrolled, by special compliment for services rendered, in the regular army. Her mother was a native of Philadelphia. . . .

Mrs. Hoskins's life has been fraught with many lights and shadows, changes and vicissitudes, interspersed with sorrows that fall more frequently to the few. When in her twenty-sixth year, she was obliged to succumb to a disease which she had fought and conquered through mere force of will and natural energy ever since her childhood. By degrees it reduced her to the position of a cripple, confining her to the boundaries of four walls, and giving her a sufficient amount of suffering of various kinds to learn to "possess her soul in patience," as she expresses it. For over twenty years she has been thus afflicted, and during that time she has had trials of a far heavier kind; and yet the true woman remains, kind, gentle, and uncomplaining, pervaded with that peace which passeth human understanding.

Mrs. Hoskins first wrote for publication during the last illness of her husband, in 1858; but not knowing the pathway that led to print, and being too timid to ask the way, having no confidence in her own powers, it was not until the publication of the "Southern Monthly," (Memphis,) in 1860, shortly after making New Orleans her home, that she found courage to send her articles to that journal. " Love's Stratagem," a novelette, printed in the December number (1861) and succeeding number of that monthly, was far superior to anything of the kind that appeared in that magazine. It was not so much the plot as the language, so chaste and beautiful. "Jacqueline," her *nom de plume*, made a reputation with her first contribution, which was increased by the publication of an essay on the "Life and Writings of Mrs. Jameson," in two articles, which, though it seemed to treat of a criticism likely to be understood but by a favored few in a country where galleries of art are not, yet it was of the literature that creates them. Her timidity caused her to veil her *personelle*, and who Jacqueline was remained a mystery! The capture of the city of New Orleans blockaded her avenue to print, and she remained silent and idle during the war, until, shortly after the surrender, John W. Overall started a literary journal in the city of New Orleans, called "The South," to which she contributed under the *nom de plume* of "Hildegarde," discovering that "Jacqueline" was known to some of her friends. That journal was a "publication of a few days" — I verily believe, "dying of dulness."

Writing is very painful as a mechanical effort to her, although, from her graceful sentences and fluent style, one would hardly think so. She has contributed to the "Catholic World," and other magazines. Though going into the "afternoon of life," God has preserved to her in a singular manner the heart-elasticity, in many things, of youth. She says:

"My trouble is to realize time, rather than feeling, and to learn how to grow old gracefully."

1869.

SUSAN BLANCHARD ELDER

IS the daughter of General Albert G. Blanchard, late of the C. S. A. She was born in an extreme Western frontier military post, where her father, then a captain in the United States service, was stationed to watch the border Indians, and her childhood was passed amid scenes and incidents that naturally arise in such a situation. Her mother died while she was yet very young, and for many years hers was the sad experience of an unloved orphan, for she was soon separated from her father's care.

She was educated in the world-noted public schools of the city of New Orleans; cultivation taught her to appreciate art, and her education thoroughly developed a mind of no ordinary capacity.

While quite young, she became the wife of Charles D. Elder, of New Orleans; and when the changed duties from a daughter's secluded home to a wife's and mother's cares fell to her lot, she met them firmly, and cheerfully fulfilled their requirements.

Mr. Elder, when New Orleans was captured by the Federals, went into the Confederacy with his family, and, like many others, sought from place to place a home of safety for his young and helpless family. In Selma, Ala., they remained some time — and their house was almost a hospital for sick and wounded soldiers at one time.

Since she was sixteen, she has contributed to the press, at first short poems and little pictures of life to different newspapers. "Babies," "The First Ride," etc., were full of pathos and beauty, while her poems were outpourings of a young, pure heart overflowing with love and an admiration of the beautiful. "Hermine," her *nom de plume*, always attracted attention to her articles. Much of her patriotic enthusiasm for military distinction must be ascribed to her young days at the West, also her love of the wild and stupendous in Nature. There is great simplicity in her style, and tenderness of feeling in all that she writes. A tinge of melancholy sometimes colors her song; but may not its source be traced to that poetic temperament so touchingly described by L. E. L., and her early want of a mother's tenderness?

She wrote only occasionally, until war came upon our land, when the first battle-cry seemed to renew all her childhood's memories, and her muse poured forth streams of patriotic feeling, appealing to all, and inspiring many hearts.

After the "surrender," she returned to New Orleans, and gracefully conforms to their changed circumstances, devoting much time to the education of her children and those increased household cares to which our Southern matrons have been called since the war. As a woman, she is peculiarly gentle in her manners and refined in her tastes: even in conversation her language is well chosen, and her words harmonious and elegant. She is still quite youthful. Mrs. Elder's most ambitious prose effort is a tale called "Ellen Fitzgerald," embodying some of the events in the life of the late lamented Dr. R. D. Williams, the Irish patriot and poet, who died at her house in

17

Thibodeaux, La., before the war, and full of Southern scenes and feelings. I am told that it would make a duodecimo volume of over 400 pages. She published a portion of this tale in the "Morning Star," a Catholic weekly, published in the Crescent City.

1868.   A. P. D.

CLEOPATRA DYING.

Glorious victim of my magic!
  Ruined by my potent spell,
From the world's imperial station
  Have I dragged thee down to Hell!
Fallen chieftain! unthroned monarch!
  Lost through doting love for me!
Fast, on shades of night eternal,
  Wings my soul its flight to thee!

Cæsar shall not grace his triumph
  With proud Egypt's captive queen!
Soothed to sleep by aspic kisses,
  Soon my heart on thine shall lean.
Soon my life, like lotus-blossoms,
  Swift shall glide on Charon's stream;
Clasped once more in thy embraces,
  Love shall prove an endless dream.

Iris! Charmian! Bind my tresses!
  Place the crown above my brow!
Touch these hands and take these kisses —
  Antony reproves not now!
Gods! my lips breathe poisoned vapors!
  They have struck my Charmian dead!
Foolish minion! durst precede me
  Where my spirit's lord has fled?

None shall meet his smile before me,
  None within his arms repose;
Be his heart's impassioned fires
  Quenched upon my bosom's snows!
None shall share his burning kisses
  Ere I haste me to his side!
Octavia's tears may prove her widowed —
  Cleopatra's still his bride!

See, my courage claims the title!
  Closer pressed the aspic fangs —
Memories of his quickening touches
  Sweeten now these deadly pangs!
Honor, manhood, glory's teachings —
  All he bartered for my smile!
Twined his heart-strings round my fingers,
  Vibrant to a touch the while;

Followed fast my silver rudder,
  Fled from Cæsar's scornful eye,
Heeded not his bleeding honor,
  Glad upon my breast to lie!
Then I snared him in my meshes,
  Bound him with my wily art,
From the head of conquering legions
  Snatched him captive to my heart.

Wild his soul at my caresses!
  Weak his sword at my command!
Rome with fury saw her mightiest
  Bowed beneath a woman's hand!
Noblest of the noble Romans!
  Greatest of the Emperors three!
Thou didst fling away a kingdom,
  Egypt gives herself to thee!

Sweet as balm; most soft and gentle
  Drains the asp my failing breath!
Antony, my lord! my lover!
  Stretch thy arms to me in death,
Guide me through these deepening shadows!
  Faint my heart, and weak my knee!
Glorious victim! ruined hero!
  Cleopatra dies for thee!

MRS. M. B. HAY.

MRS. HAY, well known throughout the South by her poems and prose, which display talent, sometimes lacking in finish and study, was born in New York, but her parents removed to Kentucky during her infancy, and she was raised in the South.

She is descended from English and Irish parentage. Her mother's father was Scotch, by name of Wilson, and a relative of the celebrated "Christopher North." She is related, on her father's side, to General Andrew Jackson, to whom she is said to have a strong family and personal resemblance. She was married at the age of sixteen to the Rev. A. L. Hay, and accompanied her husband, who went as missionary to the Indians, among whom she spent eight years.

Her life has been spent in arduous duties, and writing has been only an occasional recreation. She has not had the leisure to devote to her pen, to cultivate imagination or indulge in æsthetic taste. She has written many articles of practical or local interest, having been obliged, by circumstances, to lay aside inclinations and taste, and consequently has wooed the Muse but occasionally.

Mrs. Hay has gained considerable reputation as a teacher of mathematics, and has written an arithmetic, which was highly complimented by the professors who examined it.

Mrs. Hay is at this time a resident of Shreveport, La.

The following sonnet, which appeared in the first number of the "Crescent Monthly," New Orleans, received many merited encomiums.

ASPASIA.

Aspasia! fair Miletian, thou art wreathed
   With all a woman's heart can wish, the dower
   Of classic beauty fair, illumed with power
Of intellect. From thy red lips are breathed
Wisdom's deep tones, to woman scarce bequeathed.
   Fame brings thee brilliant wreaths of jewels rare,
   To wind with passion-flowers amid thy hair;
With Love's rich wine thy heart's deep thirst relieved.
Yet lackest thou the gem whose glorious sheen
   Would o'er them all a heaven-born splendor roll—

The gem that from Cleomene's pale brow doth gleam —
The virgin whiteness of a holy soul.
Her crown of pure white lilies shall as diamonds beam:
Upon thy brow shall rest shame's darkest scroll.

1869.

————∞⚬⚭⚬∞————

GERTRUDE A. CANFIELD.

MRS. GERTRUDE AUGUSTA CANFIELD is a native of Vicksburg, Miss. She was born in 1836, and on the second marriage of her mother, removed with her to the Parish of Rapides, La., where she has since resided. In 1859 she married, and her husband, the gallant Major Canfield, was killed in leading a desperate charge at the battle of Mansfield, April 8th, 1864. No man in Rapides was more universally liked and respected than Major Canfield, and the tribute of honor to his memory was general and spontaneous throughout the parish where he had resided and practised his profession — the law.

Few among our war-stricken people have suffered more deeply than Mrs. Canfield. The loss of husband and children, the utter destruction of all her property, the necessity of providing for the wants of a helpless family, would have utterly overwhelmed a woman of less energy than herself. To this last circumstance (the struggle for support) is owing, in a great measure, the shortness and infrequency of her published writings. The few which have appeared in the "Louisiana Democrat" and New Orleans "Crescent" are marked by a sentiment and sensibility of a true poetic order. They convey the idea of culture, and a fancy which only scatters these slight lyrics from an abundance which will yet mature a work of more depth and pretension.

But it is from Mrs. Canfield's unpublished writings that her friends draw the clearest prestige of her future literary success.

A novel yet in manuscript (the publication having been delayed for a time) is marked by a force, a pathos, and a purity which must give her a high place among Southern writers. It is a tale which none but a woman could have written, from the insight it gives into a woman's heart and hidden springs of action; but it is also filled with characters and details masculine in their grasp of thought and treatment. When "My Cousin Anne" is published, we feel confident that the author will receive her reward, in part at least. We add purity as the crowning grace, for among the sensational and *decollété* writings of the present day, her mode of creation comes to us as a new revelation.

Mrs. Canfield's lyrics are, many of them, spirited and good. They do not appear to be the result of deep thought and careful combination, but spontaneous outbursts which seek rhythmical cadences as the natural music of the song. What she has done already is nothing but an imperfect interpretation of powers, to which we look for more sustained effort and fuller work.

1868.   M. B. W.

IN THE TRENCHES.

It was on a cold sleety night of March, 1865, that in one room of a large tenement-house in Richmond a good fire and bright light were burning — a circumstance worthy to be " made a note on," such luxuries as fire and light not being by any means common in the beleaguered capital, where wood was scarce and dear, coal scarcer and dearer, and money (that would buy anything) scarcest and dearest of all. The lights were " tallow dips," it is true, but they were tolerably numerous, and judiciously disposed to give as much brilliancy to the scene as possible ; and the red glow of the fire was, on so cold and dark a night, a luxury and beauty of the first order. Nor was this all. The light shone upon a pretty picture of household comfort, such as no one would have expected in a tenement-house in Richmond in 1865 ; that last dreadful year of our dreadful struggle, when the exhausted and undermined Confederacy tottered to its fall ; when want was rife in palaces, and gaunt famine crouched on fireless hearths where, till then, the cheery blaze and the hospitable feast had never lacked.

The building of which we write had not been originally a tenement-house, but the residence of an opulent family whom the chances and changes of war had driven from their home, leaving behind them all the comforts and luxuries to which they had been accustomed ; so that the room was prettily and even elegantly furnished.   In the centre of the room was a table, and on that table — oh, sight rare and delectable ! — was arranged a supper that would have rejoiced the soul of an epicure even in long past and almost forgotten " good times."

White sugar, heaped in snowy profusion, a rare old china bowl, real coffee — none of your wretched substitutes of rye, potatoes, corn-meal, etc., but the genuine Mocha — shed its grateful aroma through the bright tin spout of the coffee-pot on the hearth ; the white china tea-pot flanked it on the other side, while at the foot of the table stood a juicy ham ; golden butter occupied the centre ; white rolls and biscuits, sweet-cakes and preserves filled up the intervals, and fragrant honey shed the odor of summer-flowers on the wintry air.   How on earth, I hear my incredulous readers exclaim, did such a number of good things meet together in Richmond, in 1865?   It happened in this wise : The tenement-house was crowded from attic to cellar with refugees from all parts of the adjacent country, and each one had contributed her quota to the feast. One had given the sugar, nearly half the small quantity brought from home, and jealously hoarded in case of sickness; another had spared the coffee from a sick husband's hospital stores; another had sent the juicy ham smuggled in from the country by a faithful contraband; and the pickles, preserves, honey, etc., came from similar sources. Kind and generous hearts! Of their little, each had spared a portion to enhance the young wife's innocent festival. Old Virginia! immortal Old Virginia! cypress mingles with and overshades her laurels, and her soil sounds hollow with the graves of her noblest sons; but, at least, she has a glorious record to show; and beside the red blazonry of her world-famed battle-fields shines the gentler and more tender, yet equally eternal lustre of her heroic women's deeds of love and charity. And the little feast, contributed from a dozen generous sources, is in honor of one of Virginia's brave defenders — one who had spent all the nights of this cold, sleety March in the trenches before Petersburg — who slept, if he slept at all last night, on the cold, wet ground; but who should press to-night, please God! a softer, warmer couch.

The long-desired, long-solicited furlough is granted at last; and to-night the husband rejoins the wife, not seen for six long months. A few brief days of happiness they will share, even amidst war's universal desolation — forgetting the past, defying the future, they will be happy in the present. No wonder the young wife's eyes glisten, and her cheek flushes, and her breath comes quick and hurried, as she glances now at the clock, now at the table, and anon, with a fonder, more lingering look, at a tiny cradle drawn close to the glowing hearth, in which sleeps a chubby boy of four months old. Four months old, yet never seen by his father! Oh, what pure delight to show her boy, her first-born, to the author of his being! — to witness the father's proud joy! — to share his rapturous caresses! Tears of exquisite happiness — "the rapture trembling out of woe" — stole down the young wife's cheek as she bent beside her infant's cradle, and breathed her lowly, heart-felt "Thank God!" At that instant her ear caught the distant sound of approaching wheels — she knew it was near the hour when the last train from Petersburg would be in: doubtless her husband was a passenger in that train — doubtless it was his vehicle now drawing near. Yes; she is right — the carriage stops before the house — there is a knock at the street-door — it opens, and steps ascend the stairs — nearer — nearer — nearer yet.

She starts to her feet, and, with neck outstretched, fixed eye, and ear intent, she stands like a statue of expectation. But when the step pauses before her door, with one bound she is across the room, and, without waiting for a knock, throws the door open, prepared to fling her arms around her husband's neck. A stranger stands before her — he places a small slip of paper in her hand, and turns away. He is a messenger from the telegraph office — it is a telegraphic dispatch. She opens it — what does she read? "Your husband was killed in the trenches before Petersburg this afternoon at three o'clock."

No more — no less! No more was needed to hurl her from a heaven of happiness to a hell of woe — no less could tell the tale! In the trenches! While she prepared to welcome her long-absent with light, and warmth, and feasting — with tenderest caresses, joyous smiles, and the sweet laughter of his unseen child, *he* lay dead in those cold, dreary trenches! There slain — there buried! Never after to be seen by her — never again to have his clay-cold lips pressed by the frenzied warmth of hers — never to lay a blessing on his infant's head! Dead in the trenches! While the words of thanksgiving yet trembled on her lips, came the sudden tempest, uprooting her every hope — the stern, relentless answer of inexorable destiny to her prayer. What wonder if, with the wild, piercing shriek of desperate woe that rang through every corner of the startled house, there went out from that darkened soul all hope, all faith, all religion? Draw the curtain in mercy over such a scene! Into how many desolated homes — could we, Asmodeus-like, have looked during those terrible four years — should we have beheld the same fatal message carry horror and despair to millions of anguished hearts? And can these things ever be forgotten or forgiven? "Vengeance is mine," saith the Lord; "I will repay it." "How long, O Lord, *how long!*"

———oo:o:oo———

ELLEN A. MORIARTY.

WE believe, firmly, that there is much in a name, and are as often attracted by the name of a writer as the title of the article. The name of "Moriarty" is attractive and inviting.

Miss Moriarty came to America when very young; was educated in the North, and, on leaving school, came to the South, and has resided here for nine years, no inconsiderable portion of her life.

Miss Eliza Moriarty, well known in the North as a poet of much promise, is a sister to the subject of this article.

Miss Ellen Moriarty writes cleverly. Her poems are generally "hasty," but, with some corrections, do very well, and now and then she is brilliant. Her stories are excellent. We think that she is a better prose-writer than a poet; but as a poet, far above mediocrity. We look forward to seeing Miss Ellen ranking very high among the writers of the country; and with close application and study, it will not be a great while before her name will be lauded as a "rising star" in the horizon of literature. Her modesty and quiet dignity has kept her from being paraded conspicuously before the world; but we still hope and expect that good time to come when true merit will not go unrewarded, and "glitter" be given its true place.

Miss Ellen Moriarty has contributed to various periodicals, North and South; recently to Miles O'Reilly's "Citizen," under her own name and various *noms de plume* — "Evangeline" and "Lucy Ellice" among others.

She is now living near Baton Rouge, La.

1868.

AN OLD STORY.

Ah! my love, how many a day
  I have gone down to the ocean-side,
And lingered there, till in twilight gray
  The sunshine sank in the darkening tide.
And I'd watch the white sails come and go,
  And hear from afar the mariner's song;
And I'd weep, I'd weep, for I loved you so,
  My heart was sad, and the days were long.

Ah! my love, when the proud ship bore
  Your true love from the land away;
You did not dream, ere the year was o'er,
  The one you loved would that love betray.
But a mother's sighs, and a sire's command,
  And the yellow gold in the balance hung,
And a faithless heart and a faithless hand
  Were bartered away by a faithless tongue.

My love! my love! and we met once more
  'Mid the light and song and the merry dance;
But the hope and the joy of the past were o'er,
  And I shrank from the gleam of your scornful glance.
How I loathed the diamonds that decked my brow,
  How my soul turned sick in the pomp and glare;
I had won them all with a broken vow —
  Won them! — to purchase a life's despair!

18

MRS. E. M. KEPLINGER.

(" *Queen of Hearts.*")

MRS. E. M. KEPLINGER, whose maiden name was Patterson, is a native of Baltimore, Md., of German descent by the paternal line. Her parents died when she was so young, she has no recollection of them, and amid the miseries of orphanage she began the life which seems to have ever been shaded by sorrow. Gentle, yielding, and sensitive in her nature, she has felt more keenly the harshness of fate; and there is a sadness in her face which plainly shows she has suffered.

At an early age she was married in Mobile to Samuel Keplinger, of Baltimore.

Amid all the chilling realities of life, Mrs. Keplinger seems to have lived in the ideal, and through all her sad years she has been wedded to the beautiful in art and literature. Her mind, naturally brilliant, has been well stored with the gems of learning, and the productions of her pen have acquired for her a desirable position among the "writers of the Crescent City."

Her first poem, "The Brigand's Bride," written in the eighteenth year of her age, and published some time after in the "Southern Ladies' Book," attracted notice; and from the time of its publication her effusions have been welcomed for the beauty, feeling, and grace they embody.

For many years Mrs. Keplinger has been a teacher in the public schools of New Orleans. Her amiability and warm heart have won for her a large circle of admiring friends, and as she possesses a character noted for firmness, she has the rare ability to retain old friends under all vicissitudes of fortune, while her worth and intelligence are constantly enlarging friendship's shining band.

A true Southern woman, during the "reign of Butler" in New Orleans she resigned her position as teacher, her only means of support, and went to the uncertainty and privations of a life in the *Confederacy.* Like an angel of mercy, she labored faithfully in the hospitals, and many a dying prayer breathed her name, and many a living soldier has cause to bless the tenderness of heart that bade her willing feet into those wards of disease and death.

After the surrender of the Confederate troops she returned to New Orleans, poor, broken in spirits by the defeat of her hopes, and more saddened with the terrible scenes she had witnessed. Her talents procured her a friend and a patron in the lamented W. H. C. King, who paid her liberally for contributions to his paper, the "Sunday Times." A critic, in noticing her contributions, speaks of "Queen of Hearts" as the "genial, touching, and sweetly natural." Yet "Queen of Hearts" has not written for fame; but for "lucre." Her contributions to the "Sunday Times" were written under many disadvantages, most of them when her energies were exhausted, her brain weary with a day of care in the school-room. Writing for pleasure and writing from necessity are very different; and Mrs. Keplinger's efforts need polishing and pruning.

1869.

OVER THE RIVER.

'T was a beautiful land! It arose in my dream,
    Verdant, and varied, and flashing in light;
Choral with songs of many a stream,
    That sung itself on to the ocean of night.

Ferryman, ferryman, row me across
    To that beauteous land on the other side:
This river!—it runs like a wave of floss
    Through the beauteous land mine eye hath descried.

O'er the calm waters gliding away,
    Lightly the rower sways to the oar;
Ha! my warm cheek is moist with the spray:
    Nearer we draw to the beautiful shore!

The glorious land which appeared to my view —
    Its zephyry clouds like mountains below,
Floating far down the ether of blue,
    Golden, and crimson, and azure, and snow.

And the river's still singing e'ermore to the sea,
    Or sleeping in shade while the bright stars look down,
Hushed by the sound of their own melody,
    Giving back to the night-queen her silvery crown.

What is this change that comes over my sight?
  Where are the fields and the forests of pride?
Where are the valleys all glowing in light?
  The beauteous land which mine eye hath descried.

Ah, *these* are pure waters! No more shall I thirst!
  The cooling wavelet, it meeteth my hand;
Out from the hill-side the clear drops burst;
  I stoop! but it fades in the bedded sand.

I must tarry awhile! We will moor the bark here—
  Crossing the river at eventide;
Far distant those beautiful shores appear,
  Which seemed but to border the river's side.

Well! I must on. 'T is a desolate way;
  Night cometh, too! Ah! where is the land?
How distant! how dim! how it fadeth away!
  It seemed by this winding river spanned.

Chill comes the north wind; I falter! No light!
  Still wander I on. No gleaming of day;
The beautiful land fades afar from my sight;
  Surely those mists must have led me astray!

"Ah! there's a river far darker than this—
  Shrink not! Its waves bear thee out to the shore
Of the beautiful land—to thy vision of bliss;
  They who have crossed it return nevermore.

"Shudder not, traveller! No ill doth betide
  Thy bark on the shores of that perilous sea;
High rolls the wave, but sure is the guide
  Who waits on the banks of that river for thee."

Back o'er the waters my vision flits by!
  False were the meteors that led me astray;
My beautiful land, with its bright gilded sky,
  I sought it all over life's desolate way.

MRS. LOUISE CLACK.

THE subject of this sketch, Mrs. Louise Clack, of New Orleans, is a Northerner by birth; but having been from her infancy associated with the South by the ties of interest and relationship, she was, in feeling, a Southerner, even before her marriage, at a very early age, with Mr. Clack, of Norfolk, Va., made her in heart and soul indissolubly united to our country and our people. Since her marriage, her constant residence at the South, her love for its people, and her devotion to and sufferings for its cause, have made her, to all intents and purposes, a Southerner, and fully entitled to a place among Southern writers.

Up to the commencement of the war, the current of her life glided on as smooth and smiling as a summer sea. The wife of a prosperous lawyer in New Orleans, her time was passed in the pursuit of innocent pleasures, in dispensing elegant hospitalities among her numerous friends, and in the delightful cares of wifehood and maternity. It is well said that "the happiest nations have no history;" and if this be true of nations, it is certainly no less true of individuals.

When "halcyon broods over the face of the deep;" when not a storm disturbs the deep serenity of the soul; when not a cloud so large as a man's hand glooms on the horizon of the future — what then can the historian or the biographer find to say? But when calamity comes; when danger threatens; when the "times that try *men's* souls" are upon us, and we see the spirit of a "weak woman" arise in the majesty of its strength to confront disaster and battle single-handed with adverse fortune, what nobler theme could poet or historian desire? Such is an epitome of the life we would portray; a life, alas! too like in its leading features to the lives of thousands more of our unfortunate countrywomen during and since the late terrible struggle. When Beauregard's call for aid rang trumpet-like through the length and breadth of our land, Col. Clack raised and equipped a battalion of volunteers, and hastened to join our hard-beset army at Corinth. From that time the subject of our sketch endured what many another anguished heart was at the same time suffering. To know that the one cherished idol of her soul was severed from her side, exposed daily, hourly, to desperate danger; never to know what moment might bring the tidings of his death; to lie down at night with the unspoken but heartfelt prayer that morning might not bring the dreaded tale; to rise at morning from dreams haunted by visions of battle and slaughter—with the awful thought that night might close over her a widowed mother, and alas! after hoping, fearing, dreading, praying for three long years, at last came the fatal blow which, as no fears could hasten, so no hopes, no prayers could avert.

Col. Clack fell at the battle of Mansfield, in the desperate charge made by Minton's brigade on the enemy's batteries, when many a hero's soul passed from the bloody field to the arms of attending seraphs. When the sad news reached his widow, she was a refugee from New Orleans. To the pangs of her awful bereavement were added those of exile. It was while in this desolate and forlorn condition that her first literary work was produced. Until now, beyond an ardent love for, and a keen appreciation of the beauties of literature, she had no claim to the title of "literary;" but now an intense longing for "something apart from the sphere of her sorrow"—something that should lift her out of, wrench her away from the ever-present, torturing subject of her regrets, together with pecuniary necessity, induced her to prepare a volume for the press. "Our Refugee Household" was the result — a book which unites, in a charming manner, the sad experiences of the writer with the loveliest creations of fiction and fancy. It is a string of pearls strung on a golden thread. The varied characters and changing fortunes of the little "Refugee Household;" the heart-breaking trials and imminent perils to which they were exposed, form a groundwork of intense interest, upon which the lively fancy of the writer has erected a superstructure of fairy-like beauty and elegance. In addition to her first work, Mrs. Clack has also published a Christmas storybook for children, which bears the title of "General Lee and Santa Claus" — a tiny volume, which unites in its limited space sound patriotic feeling with the frolic fancies so dear to little folks. And she has, we believe, now in press a much more elaborate work than either of the above; one which we hope will place her fame on an enduring pedestal for the admiration of posterity.

November 5th, 1870, (since the above notice was written,) Mrs. Clack was married to Mr. M. Richardson, of New Orleans.

With this brief sketch, we present to our readers the following specimen of her poetical powers, which will, of itself, speak sufficiently in their praise, without the addition of a word from us.

THE GRANDMOTHER'S FADED FLOWER.

"Oh, grandmother dear, a masquerade ball!
   A ball, I do declare!
I'll robe myself rich in costume of old,
   In a train, and powdered hair."

And a beautiful girl of sixteen years
   Knelt by her grandmother's chest;
While that stately dame, in a high-backed chair,
   Smiled at each timely jest.

Brocades, and silks, and satins antique
   Were strewn in confusion rare
Round the fair young girl, while diamond and pearl
   She wound in her bright brown hair.

"What's this? what's this?" she jestingly cried,
   Holding high a faded flower;
"Why treasure it here, my grandmother dear,
   With relics of bridal dower?"

"My child, it is dearer far to me
   Than silk, or satin, or pearl;
For it 'minds me well of vanished hours,
   Of hours when I was a girl.

"Ay, well I remember the day, 'lang syne,'
   When my first love, last love — gone —
Came to my side with this then fresh flower;
   'Twas a beautiful spring-like morn.

"But he's gone before — yes, many a year!
   Hush, Flo! the pearls are thine;
I'll meet him yet in perennial spring:
   Don't crush the flower — it's mine."

And the fair girl gazed in mute surprise
   At the tear and flushing cheek;
Kissed the tear away, then her thoughts stray
   To the ball of the coming week.

   .   .   .   .

The ball is o'er — a pure white bud
   Flo folds to her throbbing breast;
She has learned the power of the faded flower
   She found in her grand-dame's chest.

1869.   G. A. C

MRS. MARY ASHLY TOWNSEND.

THE genius, gracefulness, and spirit which characterized certain contributions published in the "New Orleans Delta," over the *nom de plume* of "Xariffa," sixteen or seventeen years ago, when that journal was conducted by Judge Alexander Walker, excited much interest and curiosity at the time in literary circles, as to the identity of the no less modest than gifted writer.

An eager inquiry at last discovered that "Xariffa" was a young lady just passing the threshold of womanhood; and that though connected by ties of kindred with many of the oldest and best families in Louisiana, and thoroughly imbued with the taste, sentiments, and ideas of Southern society, she was by birth and education a Northerner. A native of New York, Mrs. Townsend was of the ancient and honorable stock of the Van Wickles, of New Jersey, and the Van Voorhises, of Duchess County, New York. Her mother, the daughter of Judge J. C. Van Wickle, of Spotswood, New Jersey, is a lady of fine mind herself, and distinguished for her elegance of manner and generous hospitality. She is still living at Lyons, New York, the birthplace of "Xariffa." In the very bloom of her literary fame and promise, Miss Van Voorhis formed a matrimonial alliance with Mr. Gideon Townsend, an energetic and intelligent gentleman, who, though of an active and business character and much absorbed in the struggles of commercial life, always manifested a warm sympathy with and high appreciation of the literary tastes and pursuits of his talented wife.

The happy and congenial couple now live in New Orleans, surrounded by a most interesting family, including a bright little daughter, who is already an authoress at the age of thirteen,* and gives promise of unusual brilliancy and vigor of intellect. Since her first appearance in the "Delta," Mrs. Townsend, or rather "Xariffa," as she prefers to be known in her literary relations, has been a regular contributor to many of the leading journals and magazines of the day, and a successful essayist in some of our ablest Reviews. In the "Delta," the "Crossbone Papers," which were widely copied and commended; "Quillotypes," a series of short essays, which were attributed,

---

* "Under the Stones," by Cora Townsend. Published in New York, 1867.

144

on account of their vigor and power, to the pen of one of the opposite sex, excited special attention and admiration. "My Penny Dip," a humorous tale or sketch, was published throughout the country and ascribed to various authors, and, returning at last to New Orleans, reappeared in the "True Delta" as "My Penny Dip, by Henry Rip," a fit name for so bold an appropriator of the product of another's genius.

In 1859, Derby & Jackson, New York, published "The Brother Clerks, a Tale of New Orleans, by ——," which was Mrs. Townsend's first book. It was moderately successful.

In 1870, J. B. Lippincott & Co., Philadelphia, published "Xariffa's Poems" — a collection of one hundred poems. The volume is tenderly inscribed "To my Mother." It was favorably reviewed by many pleased critics. One writer, comparing "Creed" with the poet laureate's "Maud," states:

"Mrs. Townsend is by no means passionless; but her passion is not obtrusive, and, therefore, it never offends the most fastidious taste. She has, what is better and higher than passion — what is a well-spring of truer poetry — an infinite fountain of purely human tenderness and sympathy. She has, too, that divine melancholy that sweet suggestive sadness, which Poe declares to be the soul of poetry. As to style, she especially excels in richness and variety of coloring."

"Xariffa's" poems, while they are emotional, never degenerate into mere sentimentality. In the volume we have that tenderness, grace, and sweetness, the soft, clear, sunny charm, and the inborn and inwoven harmony, which are latent to the poetic constitution of Mary Ashly Townsend.

We cannot, however, in the narrow compass of this sketch, enumerate the many productions of Mrs. Townsend's pen. Besides prose sketches, she ranks high as a poetess. Her poems evince originality, imagination, taste, and power of harmonious versification. Some specimens of these, which accompany this sketch, will give an idea of her poetic gifts and powers. We confess, however, to a preference for her prose writings. In pleasant sketches of character and scenery, in quiet humor and gentle satire, her smooth, even style and euphonious yet vigorous sentences never fail to enlist interest, to hold the attention of the reader, and to leave a most agreeable impression of the sound sense and pure heart of the accomplished writer. It is much to be regretted that family cares and duties should deprive the public,

19

and especially her immediate circle of friends and admirers, of the more frequent enjoyment which her pleasant contributions to our periodical literature must always afford to those who can appreciate and admire genius, wit, high mental and moral culture, and good taste, so happily blended with all the social and domestic virtues, as they are in the subject of this sketch.

1870.

EBB AND FLOW.

I.

The morn is on the march — her banner flies
In blue and golden glory o'er the skies;
The songs of wakening birds are on the breeze,
The stir of fragrant zephyrs in the trees;
Waves leap full-freighted to the sunny shore,
Their scrolls of snow and azure written o'er
With hope, and joy, and youth, and pleasures new,
While surges fast the sands with jewels strew —
    The tide is in.

II.

The stars shine down upon a lonely shore;
The crested billows sparkle there no more;
Poor bits of wreck and tangled sea-weed lie
With empty shells beneath the silent sky.
Along the shore are perished friendships spread,
In Hope's exhausted arms lies Pleasure dead;
A life lies stranded on the wreck-strewn beach,
The ebbing waves beyond its feeble reach —
    The tide is out.

CREED.

I.

I believe, if I should die,
And you should kiss my eyelids when I lie
  Cold, dead, and dumb to all the world contains,
The folded orbs would open at thy breath,
And from its exile in the Isles of Death
  Life would come gladly back along my veins.

II.

I believe, if I were dead,
And you upon my lifeless heart should tread,
  Not knowing what the poor clod chanced to be,
It would find sudden pulse beneath the touch
Of him it ever loved in life so much,
  And throb again warm, tender, true to thee.

III.

I believe, if on my grave,
Hidden in woody deeps or by the wave,
  Your eyes should drop some warm tears of regret,
From every salty seed of your dear grief
Some fair, sweet blossom would leap into leaf
  To prove death could not make my love forget.

IV.

I believe, if I should fade
Into those mystic realms where light is made,
  And you should long once more my face to see,
I would come forth upon the hills of night,
And gather stars like fagots, till thy sight,
  Led by their beacon blaze, fell full on me!

V.

I believe my faith in thee,
Strong as my life, so nobly placed to be,
  I would as soon expect to see the sun
Fall like a dead king from his height sublime,
His glory stricken from the throne of Time,
  As thee unworth the worship thou hast won.

VI.

I believe who has not loved
Hath half the treasure of his life unproved;
  Like one who, with the grape within his grasp,
Drops it, with all its crimson juice unpressed,
And all its luscious sweetness left unguessed,
  Out from his careless and unheeding clasp.

VII.

I believe love, pure and true,
Is to the soul a sweet, immortal dew
    That gems life's petals in its hours of dusk:
The waiting angels see and recognize
The rich Crown-Jewel, Love, of Paradise,
    When life falls from us like a withered husk.

———ooᛝᛝoo———

MRS. FLORENCE J. WILLARD

IS the authoress of a novel published in London in 1862, and in 1869
republished with the imprint of A. Eyrich, New Orleans—entitled
"The Heroism of the Confederacy; or, Truth and Justice," by Miss Florence J. O'Connor, which was the maiden name of Mrs. Willard.

She is a native of Louisiana, and, before the war, contributed to the
"Mirror," a paper edited by Mr. Mark F. Bigney, now editor of the
"New Orleans Times." She has contributed lengthy poems to the
New Orleans "Sunday Times," signed with her initials, ("F. J. W.")
In 1869, she published a volume of poems in Canada. She was in
Paris during the late siege.

A Northern paper thus reviews "*her*" novel:

"The picture she draws of Louisiana society before the war is gorgeous in
the extreme. All day long 'in halls of polished marble, with beautifully
carved doors, which an inhabitant of the Orient might envy,' women robed
in point-lace and diamonds, and more beautiful than an angel's dream, and
men of a *distingué*-ness altogether beyond words, discuss, in language which
the benighted Northern mind finds it difficult to comprehend, politics, love,
and war, the excellence of slavery, the crimes and insolence and treachery
of the black-hearted Yankee, the long-suffering patience and magnanimity
of the down-trodden South. Around them, respectfully admiring and drinking deep draughts of political wisdom from their sparkling converse, stand
eager representatives of the titled aristocracy of Europe, glad to be recognized as their social peers — among whom a real French count and an un-
doubted English earl are conspicuous by their flashing coronets and their
chivalric disregard of grammar. In deference to these distinguished — we
beg Miss O'Connor's pardon, *distingué* — foreigners, much of the conversation
is conducted in French of singular impurity and incorrectness; in fact, it
appears to be of that variety known in New Orleans as bumboat French —
whereupon the Gallic nobleman shows he can be as resplendently ungram-
matical in his own sweet tongue as in the ruder speech of perfidious Albion.

No one talks for less than half an hour at a time, and it seems to be a point of honor with each to use only the longest words; and the only pauses in the eloquent strife are when the doors of the *salle à manger* (there were no dining-rooms in that favored land) were thrown open, disclosing 'banquets that the most fastidious disciple of Epicurus,' etc. etc. So 'the hours rolled on in revelry' until the war-cloud bursts: the tocsin peals, and so does the Southern hero. The brilliant pageant vanishes, and in its stead we have the hideous apparition of the beast Butler and the monster Farragut."

In conclusion, as a sample of Mrs. Willard's verse, we offer the following lines on "Rip Van Winkle," written after seeing Mr. McKee Rankin perform that part:

RIP VAN WINKLE.

I.

More, alas! than Rip Van Winkle
    Waken from a sleep of woe,
To find all they loved and cherish'd
    Have forgot them long ago.
Not alone in Sleepy Hollow
    Is this painful scene or change;
But o'er all the earth are Derricks —
    Gertrudes live where women reign.

II.

Oh! how often has one harsh word
    Rent asunder human tie,
And sent forth a lonely outcast
    'Neath the bitter blast to die.
Rip Van Winkle is but type of
    Those who wake from *feeling's* sleep,
Finding all is disappointment
    Where'er death or change doth creep.

III.

Twenty years! this surely long is;
    I would give my *best* friends ten:
Were I not forgotten wholly,
    They were not the sons of men.

All have slept who wake to sorrow;
  Aching limbs and frosty head
Come not with Time's icy imprint
  But when true affection's dead.

IV.

Poor Rip found his musket rusty;
  It fell from his weak grasp down;
But he found e'en hearts decaying
  When he reach'd his native town;
And he found the snows of winter
  Had not only strew'd his head,
But the graves of the departed,
  Sleeping with the silent dead.

V.

Happy they, who, like Van Winkle,
  Find true hearts with them, and pass
In a foaming cup forgiving,
  Holding to their lips the glass.
Though in age and tatter'd garments
  He quaff'd on unto the end,
Hoping "friends live well and prosper,"
  The cup, until the last, his friend.

December, 1870.

JEANNETTE R. HADERMANN.

"FORGIVEN AT LAST," a novel, (Philadelphia, 1870,) the first book of Miss Jeannette R. Hadermann, who resides near Lake St. Joseph, Tensas Parish, La. This novel was a "first book," and, it has been stated, was partly autobiographical. It was received with some favor, sufficiently so to invite another effort. Miss Hadermann's contributions to the New Orleans "Sunday Times," under the pseudonym of "Ann Atom," are excellent and well-written sketches.

Miss Hadermann was born in New Jersey, the younger daughter of an Episcopal clergyman, who removed to Natchez, Miss., while the subject of this notice was a child, where he was for some time a professor in Jefferson College.

February, 1871.

CATHARINE F. WINDLE.

MRS. CATHARINE FORRESTER WINDLE is the daughter of the Rev. William Ashmead, deceased. At the time of his death, Rev. Mr. Ashmead was pastor of the Second Presbyterian Church of Charleston, S. C., and was eminent as a pulpit orator and *littérateur*. The reputation and characteristics of this distinguished clergyman are perpetuated in a biographical sketch in Dr. Sprague's " American Pulpit," as well as by a memorial tablet in the church alluded to. The elaborate inscription of the latter is from the pen of the lamented Hugh S. Legare, of South Carolina. A duplicate of this tablet is erected in the First Presbyterian Church of Lancaster, Pennsylvania, over which congregation Mr. Ashmead at one time presided, and which last-named State was the birthplace of his daughter Catharine. Mrs. Ashmead, who was a daughter of Dr. Alexander Forrester, of Wilmington, Delaware, was noted for her literary tastes and talents. The natural heritage, therefore, of the subject of this notice was a fondness for letters. At an early age, Miss C. F. Ashmead commenced her literary publicity at the North, where she was educated, as a contributor to " Graham's " and " Sartain's " magazines, then highly popular serials of light literature. Subsequently, she published a volume of poems.

In February, 1849, she married Mr. George W. Windle, of Wilmington, Delaware, and they immediately afterward became residents of New Orleans. From this time until 1861, Mrs. Windle wrote at intervals for the " Delta " and " True Delta."

Mr. George W. Windle was a brother of Miss Mary J. Windle, favorably known years ago as an author, but who for fifteen years has been a hopeless invalid, residing in Washington, D. C.

The experiences of the war (during which four years she aided the cause of the South to the extent of her power), which added to her greater maturity of years and character, seem latterly to have deeply impressed Mrs. Windle with the earnestness of life. The serious religious and social problems of the marvellous age in which we live have attracted her interest, and, in such measure as circumstances have permitted, have instigated of late her efforts both of the pen and otherwise. In 1865, she gave a public lecture in New York and elsewhere, to advance a new and peculiar theory, "that woman is deputed by Nature to accomplish the perfection of the human race."

Mrs. Windle is a disciple of Victor Cousin and Jouffroy in philosophy, and a student of the writings of Herbert Spencer, Matthew Arnold, Professor Huxley, and Emerson.

Mr. Windle died in Shreveport, La., April, 1870. Since her husband's death she has resided in New Orleans.

The following is a specimen of her earlier poetical compositions:

WHY DO I LOVE HIM?

"Why do I love him?" Search the unfathomed well
To find the sources whence its waters swell;
Explore the mines, whose richest veins untold
Give the first promise of their hidden gold;
Or seek in ocean for its parent stem
Whereon once grew the polished coral gem.

"Why do I love him?" Ask the evening star
To waft its story from the realms afar;
Or bid the flower that decorates the earth
Relate the wondrous history of its birth;
Or call departed spirits to return,
And bear the tale of their untrodden bourne.

"Why do I love him?" Let a mother tell
Wherefore it is she loves her child so well;
Let awful Deity assign a cause
For loving man, a recreant to His laws;
But vainly ask not woman to impart
The mystic secret of her plighted heart.

NOVELS AND NOVELISTS.

EXTRACT.

... The person of real culture beholds in fiction the highest of all arts —
that through which not only human character and life may be justly represented, as these have thus far in the progress of the race exhibited themselves
in their various phases, but also as the fitting mirror of that sublime philosophy which underlies the incidental experience of all the individuals and

generations of mankind—linking them as well together in one common brotherhood, as uniting them by the ties of vivid relationship to the stupendous universe of Infinite wisdom. In proportion to true mental (or shall I rather say moral?) advancement, fictitious narrative affords enjoyment solely as it is created in accordance or otherwise with this, its lofty delegation. Its chief capacity of giving pleasure to the highest order of taste consists in its presenting those tenderer and diviner touches of nature by which the whole world is made kin; nay, by which the whole system of worlds are conjoined with our humanity, ennobling and elevating it from the connection with a scheme of such magnitude and evident completeness.

Of such novels we have had but few. Previously to this day of unique development in which we live, they have never hitherto been produced, nor could they earlier have met with any appreciative readers. They are the growth of a new era of scientific discovery, of religious thought and conviction, and of prophetic promise for mankind. Even now, portions of them—those, perhaps, which constitute in reality their exquisite merit—are overlooked, or sometimes even condemned by persons whose insight has not reached to their grand moral plane: readers not yet permeated with the new spiritual influence of an exalted humanitarianism, of which the suggestion in such fictions appears to them an absurdity, or a heresy, as the case may be, and not, as it truly is, the certain presage of the prevalence ultimately of a divine magnetism of general philanthropy and of reverence of our kind—the destined forces to regenerate our national globe. The novelist himself has undergone the "new birth" who has been able to insert such touches in his pages. And something of the same renovation must have been experienced by his reader before his productions can be properly appreciated. The freemasonry of his labor has its spiritual password, requiring initiation. The subtle depths in the human essence which he hath explored, and the soundings whereof he hath wrought in verisimilitude in his creations, only the responsive mind recognizes as faithful copies of latent gems existing in the invaluable mine of our common humanity, that shall one day come to light universally in the race, to glorify and exalt its future generations, and verify its relationship with Deity.

Of the many fictions of Dickens, that which is incomparably his greatest production is held in proper estimation by but few. The author himself, however, I believe, would have claimed the "Tale of Two Cities" as his masterpiece, for he must have had a consciousness of its grandeur while writing it, and felt that he was employing his art under an unusual inspiration. But among the countless admirers of his novels, how small a number are there who would name this work, if called upon to designate their favorite in the long catalogue of his novels! And yet, while neither in force nor in vigor, as a whole, has he written anything at all equal to it, the conception of Sidney Carton's self-sacrifice to the guillotine in order to save his successful rival, is the sublimest suggestion in the entire range of fiction. . . . It stands

20

alone among the creations of the novelist, both for the most exquisite pathos worthily (instead of mawkishly) applied, and for the full exhibition of the sublime, as pertaining to our humanity. It indeed deserves the appellation of a new evangel.

———o○;○;○○———

MRS. A. M. C. MASSENA.

MRS. MASSENA has published one book, entitled "Marie's Mistake," Boston, 1869. This work is presumed to be partly autobiographical.

Mrs. Massena's pseudonym is "Creole," and she has written considerable for various papers, and edited a paper in the interior of Louisiana. With her, "writing" is a profession, and she has *vim* and energy to succeed.

She was born in New Orleans, July 4th, 1845, and made her *début* as a writer in 1864.

She resides in the parish of Plaquemine.

1871.

———o○;○;○○———

MARY TERESA MALONY.

MRS. MALONY is a remarkably ready writer — the mechanical construction of her verse is not always faultless, but nevertheless possesses the true ring of genius. Her frequent contributions to the New Orleans "Times," dated San José, Cal., over her full name or initials, have been extensively copied by the newspaper press from Maine to California. Mrs. Malony is a great admirer of the poems of Felicia Hemans, and some of her productions are too much imitations of the verse of this gifted lady. Her "stately verse" is very fine, as are her descriptive pieces. On account of the length of these poems, we are unable to quote.

Mrs. Malony, whose maiden name was De Lacy, was born in Manchester, England, in 1839. While she was an infant her parents removed to New Orleans. The choirs of the Mississippi River, the hush of whose anthem dies on the lips of the Crescent City, were heard first after her cradle song. Here was she married; here were her five children born — (like Mrs. Hemans, she has four sons;) — and at this time, sojourning in the "Golden Land," San José, California, she looks forward longingly to an early return to the "home of lang syne," within sight and hearing of the "Big River."

1871.

DEAD IN THE STEERAGE.

Seven years old, and the delicate rays
  Of shaded Italian skies
Faded then out from a dear smiling place —
  Her childish, beautiful eyes.

She was but poor, with the foreign speech
  Of her parents' kindred land —
Strangers, and sorrowful, standing each
  Just holding a small dead hand.

The engine clanked — they were going slow —
  The waters grew shallow and green;
They made her a grave, when the ship "lay to,"
  In the Mexican hills between.

Her coffin was boards of the roughest pine,
  Unflowered, untinted of hue,
But over and under they did entwine
  A flag of the starry blue.

Into the long-boat lowered it — then
  The plash of the oars dipped low,
Bearing it over the soft waves, when
  The sun was brightest at glow —

When the sun was brightest, at summer glow,
  That never would set for her;
The shoal was broad, like a glad young brow,
  And the bay-washed shells astir.

Like pulses of some child-heart at play
  With the tides and throbs of life,
There's where they made her a grave that day,
  Far, far from the days of strife.

SAN JOSÉ, CAL.

A HOME OF LANG SYNE.

My father planted the China trees
   That cover its old roof o'er,
And brothers and sisters played in the breeze
   That wandered by its door.
But some are gone far over the seas,
   And some will play no more;
They're laving their wee tired feet in the waves
   That wash Eternity's shore.

Well I remember the creeping vines,
   With their blossoms purpling through,
And the roses, that laughed to the summer winds,
   And the violets sweet, that grew
Near the little glass door, with its clear white panes,
   That charmed the sunlight through
On the pine floor in shading stains,
   With many a varying hue.

And the dim old loft, with its books "galore,"
   That many an hour beguiled
With their pictures of grim old kings of yore,
   And many a legend wild.
And then the charms of the other old loft,
   All sweet with the new-mown hay,
That tempted my wandering feet so oft
   To find where the hens would lay.

And the wild, wild songs we used to sing,
   Coming from school in the field;
Oh! the joy that in their tones did ring
   No music on earth will yield.
And the old oak-trees that grew in a clump
   That we were afraid to pass,
Where the "ghost" who reigned might be only a stump,
   And the sounds the waving of grass.

Don't you remember, dear L——, the night
   That we had to pass it by —
All the prayers we said — and the fright
   We suffered — you and I —

And how closer together we pressed,
  Walking as fast as we could?
Ah! how happy we were — and blessed,
  When we were past the wood.

How many woods, darker and drear,
  We meet in the journey of life,
With no clasping hand to quiet our fear,
  But all alone in the strife!
But we may remember the prayers we said,
  And walk straight on to the *right*,
Until we come to the edge of the wood,
  And enter Eternity's light.

———o-o°:♀:°o-o———

A CRESCENT CITY COTERIE.

THERE is much literary feeling in the city of New Orleans, and numerous writers there reside. The literary journals — the "Sunday Times" and the "Picayune" in particular — have always paid liberally their corps of *special* contributors. Among these writers, I will make mention of those not otherwise noted, who are prominent as promising *littérateurs*.

———

MATILDA A. BAILEY.

Mrs. Bailey has for over two years been a regular contributor to the "Times." A series of sketches entitled "Heart Histories," by "Forlorn Hope," have been very popular. Notwithstanding the adjective prefixed to the beautiful pseudonym, her articles are the embodiment of "hope." She has also written comic articles under the name of "Sam Waggle," which were attributed to a masculine pen.

Mrs. Bailey is a daughter of Dr. F. R. Alpurente, a physician of New Orleans, where she was born.

FLORENCE BURCKETT.

This young lady, yet in the "spring-time of life," writing, under the graceful pen-name of "Edith Lee," prose sketches, made her *début* in the "Times" about the same time as Mrs. Bailey and Mrs. Dalsheimer, in 1868.

Miss Burckett is the daughter of a merchant of New Orleans — was born in Vicksburg, Miss., and removed to the Crescent City in her childhood.

MARY CRESAP.

Mrs. Cresap was born in Kentucky. Her maiden name was Annie Mary Marshall. She was early married.

For twenty years Mrs. Cresap has lived in New Orleans. Many of her poems have appeared in "Godey's Lady's Book," also in the New Orleans papers. She possesses dramatic talent, and has written several parlor dramas for the amusement of her friends.

ALICE DALSHEIMER.

Mrs. Dalsheimer is a native of the Crescent City. Her contributions to the "Times," principally poetical, under the name of "Salvia Dale," have elicited encomiums and encouraging predictions of future success. She is a teacher. The following verse is from a poem printed in the "Times" in the summer of 1870.

MOTHERHOOD.

Two little arms around my neck,
　　In artless, fond caressing;
Two little lips upon my own
　　Sweet baby-kisses pressing;
Two sparkling eyes that beam with love
　　Which knows no doubt or fearing;

A cooing voice that whispers soft
　Some lisping words endearing:
These, these the spells that banish care,
　Life's sweetest solace bringing,
And gratefully I clasp the joy
　From motherhood upspringing.

MARY GREEN GOODALE.

A quiet, almost a hidden life, leaves but little to be told which could possibly interest the public. Six years of incessant ministry in sick-rooms leaves few traces upon a life save those of sorrow or care.

Since Miss Goodale first began to write verse — at the age of twelve — every emotion of her soul has found its most natural expression in verse. Under the name of "Edith Alston," her poems have appeared in the journals of the day. She is a regular contributor to the "Picayune" — is a native of the city of New Orleans — expects to publish a volume of poems. I give two of her recent poems.

MÉPSISÉ.

There was a spring, to which at dawn of day
　I went, and quaffs of sweetest coolness drew;
Then walked with firmer feet along the rugged way,
　Till day had fled, and softly fell the dew.

Another draught at evening's quiet hour,
　Sent pleasant dreams to thread my gentle sleep,
Till every weary limb had gained new power
　To climb the morrow's hills, however steep.

One eve, the sun in more than gorgeous flame
　Had sunk to let the night o'erspread the sky,
When I, full languid, to the fountain came —
　Alas! its bed, its very source was dry!

ANSWERED.

I.

Pray for you? do I not always pray? Why,
　If it be cold, for you I ask for heat —
　Or if it should storm, that it may not beat

Upon you defenceless. I wake and cry
At night to God, that His angels may fly
    Unto you to keep you, finding it sweet
    To be so near before Him. Spirits may greet
When the body is distant. To be nigh,
None saying "Nay!" these hearts would mount so high
    They could not be reached. God, if it were meet,
    Could have it thus. When shall we turn our feet
Into the same path? Time moves so slowly —
And still, it will be yet, before we die —
    And then our joy will be so full — complete!

II.

But in all these years — through this delay,
    Will our God forget us, keeping so near
    As we do? We say "Thy will," yet just here
We sob, before whispering "be done." The way
A child looks into mother eyes, to say
    Her fond heart — so I; that I may see clear
    Some faint wish arise, some kind thought appear,
To teach me what to ask, for you — my stay —
My one earth-comfort. How can I repay
    This love? Must I never show you how dear
    To me is your footfall — smile — at the mere
Shadow of your passing? Some birds use clay
To build their nests: if so, I'm sure I may
    Make earth-love lift me to a higher sphere.

III.

Your letter seemed to me a white-winged dove,
    And it lies on my breast all night and day.
    How I wish that I could in my turn say
All my heart answers, so perfect in love,
So full in devotion! How can I prove
    All these things to you, now you are away —
    No one else reads my heart — ay, although the fray
Of cloth shows its texture, I do not move
With their questions. Has not every grove
    Some glad bird to sing in it? So is the play
    Of your thoughts on my soul. Will you say, Nay,
If I ask you for more — to sound above
The world's din and care — all interwove —
    The sweet, with the bitter — *love* — when I pray?

SARAH C. YEISER.

Sarah C. Yeiser, born Smith, is a native of Vermont. She came South in girlhood. In 1847 she married Dr. Philip Yeiser, of Alexandria, La.

Mrs. Yeiser has been a successful teacher in New Orleans for many years. Her contributions to the "Crescent," of New Orleans, were signed "Azélee;" yet her *nom de plume* of "Aunt Charity" is more familiar to Southern readers.

As a woman of scholastic attainments, Mrs. Yeiser deserves notice. Being a lover of God's grand handiwork, she has made the material world her lifelong study, and her familiarity with the science of nature is equalled by few scholars of either sex.

SAMUELLA COWEN.

MRS. COWEN is the posthumous daughter of the Hon. Samuel Wright Mardis, member of Congress from the State of Alabama, and an eminent lawyer. She was born May 6th, 1842. While an infant, her family removed to New. Orleans, where Samuella grew up, was educated, and was married.

From an early age she evinced a talent for literary composition. Her first novelette was written for the "Mirror," a literary paper conducted by Mr. Bigney, the present editor of the New Orleans "Times."

During the war, Mrs. Cowen made Richmond her sojourning place, as her husband was in the Virginia army. It was here she made her literary talent of monetary value by writing for the "Southern Literary News." A novelette, entitled "Creola," attracted attention, and was reviewed in several newspapers. "As the production of a young, untrained, and inexperienced writer, it evinced more than ordinary talent."

While writing for the "Illustrated News," Mrs. Cowen adopted the pseudonym of "Le Clerc," which she has ever since retained.

She is a resident of New Orleans. The following was published during the "war:"

April, 1871.
21

FIRST LOVE.

Like a tender violet bursting
  In the early morn of spring,
Like the blush of dawn in summer,
  When the humming-bird takes wing,
Is the young heart's first awaking
  From its calm and peaceful rest,
When begins the stir of passion
  In the warm and throbbing breast.

Now the cheek grows rich in blushes,
  And the eyes, with fitful light,
Seem to stray in search of Eden —
  Seem to seek for something bright.
And a thousand mysteries solemn
  Cling around the gentle soul,
Like a rose-bud in the morning
  Ere its crimson leaves unroll.

First love! ah, who has not felt thee
  Thrill within their bosom's core,
And wept burning tears of passion
  When its first sweet dream was o'er.
Like a streamlet, clear as crystal,
  With the sunbeams on its breast,
While the south wind, wreathing dimples,
  Shows a gentle heart's unrest.
'T is a star which rises early,
  Sinking soon to rise no more;
'T is the dew-drop on the flower
  Ere its blooming life is o'er.

First love! ah, we well remember
  Well, too well, that witching hour
When our soul in tender rapture
  First divined thy magic power;
Like a soul enshrined in ocean,
  Far from beaten track or shore,
Thou of tears dost make a treasure,
  But thy spell returns no more.

GEORGIA.

[AUTOBIOGRAPHY.]

MRS. MARY E. TUCKER.

YES! seven *cities* claimed the honor of being the birthplace of the immortal "Homer" *after he was dead*. I, who am still living, have the credit of being born in three *States,* not to speak of countless numbers of *cities*.

Georgia, State of my adoption — the Empire State of the South! proud would I have been had thy red hills given me birth; but — I was not born there.

New York, because Staten Island had the honor of being the birthplace of my noble father, whose ancestors, the Huguenots, left France because of their devotion to a *principle*, thinks that I should have been born there: I was not.

Providence, Rhode Island, the place of my mother's nativity, *intends* claiming me upon the plea that I have Yankee ingenuity and perseverance; but — I was not born there. Rhode Island is too small a State to claim me.

That I was born, is an undeniable fact. My father says that Cahaba, Alabama, is the place of my nativity.

Alabama—"Here let us rest!"—the beautiful name which was given *my State* by the Indian chieftain who, driven by the cruel white man from his native home, sought with his tribe to find peace and rest in the flower-land bordering on the beautiful river which still bears the name of "Alabama." The Indian found no rest — neither did I: in that respect the Indian and I resemble each other.

Posterity may wish to know in what year the light of my genius burst upon the world. My enemies pronounce me somewhere near forty years of age; my friends declare I do not look a day over twenty. Our family Bible was destroyed by the Yankee or negro incendiaries during the late "rebellion" — I use the word "rebellion" sarcastically, for I was a REBEL, and I glory to own it — therefore, unless I choose to tell my age, posterity will never be the wiser. The Bible

163

said, before it was burned: "The 6th day of November, 1838, Mary E. Perine saw the sorrowful light of day."

My mother! Holy influences surroun'd me. No cord of memory thrills at the sacred name of mother: only in dreamland have I seen her. She, the beautiful child of song — loving and beloved, pure as the flowers she cherished — died that I might live.

They buried her under the orange-trees, and often, while a tiny child, have I sought the jasmine-covered grave, and wept for the love of mother.

"Mary Eliza, beloved wife of Edward M. Perine, died in the twentieth year of her age.

> " ' Many daughters have done virtuously,
> But thou excellest them all.' "

That is all. What more can I wish? It is enough to make me venerate anything in the shape of woman who bears the sacred title of *mother*.

My father! It is said I am especially fond of gentlemen. Why should I not be? My father was a gentleman; and, judging all men by him — my standard of a true, honorable, noble image of the Almighty's master-piece — how can I keep, if simply out of respect for my father, from loving his sex? My father! That one word contained my child-world. He was to me *all* — mother, father, sister, brother, and everything except grandmother; for I had a grandmother, and my earliest recollection is of a kind of buzzing in my ear as she vainly essayed to rock me to sleep in my little cradle. How could I go to sleep, when she would not hush talking? I remember distinctly that, exasperated to frenzy, I told her that if she did not let me alone I would make Uncle Wiley, our negro carriage-driver, cut her head off and throw her in the river.

The power of conversing is a gift greatly to be desired, but I certainly do not wish my children to inherit the fully developed organ of language of their great-grandmother.

Perhaps I do wrong to mention the only failing, if the gift of language can be called a failing, that my grandmother possessed. I could fill volumes with her virtues. I can never forget her untiring and unselfish devotion to me as a child, and to my own little ones, who, when her cords of memory quavered with age, took my place in the heart of the dear old lady; and I seemed to her what my dead mother once had been. No — when I want an example of faith, hope, love, and charity, I have only to look upon my grandmother.

I suppose I must have been a very precocious child, for I know that I read the "Pilgrim's Progress," and the "Arabian Nights' Entertainments," and made love to my father's clerks before I was six years old.

When I was eight years of age, my father married Miss Fanny E. Hunter, daughter of Judge John Hunter, formerly of Selma, Alabama, who was well known during his life throughout the Southern States.

The sister of my step-mother married Col. Robert White Smith, of Mobile. Mrs. Smith was, a few years ago, one of the most beautiful ladies I ever saw, and is still very lovely. After my father's marriage, my grandmother went to Milledgeville, Ga., to take possession of some property which came to her on the death of her brother. I, of course, accompanied her. In Milledgeville, I was chiefly noted for my mass of peculiarly colored hair, which strikingly resembled the tendrils of the love-vine, which grows so plentifully in the marshes of the South, my light-blue pop-eyes, and also for my large feet and hands, which seemed to be forever in my own way, and in the way of everybody else. "They say" that I used to be a rhymist then — perhaps I was. I only know that every time I climbed a tree, or hid my grandmother's spectacles, I was called bad or mischievous. Now, when my olden pranks are alluded to, they are termed the "eccentricities of genius." I was, of course, sent to school. Being considered fearless and venturesome, I was selected, together with a young classmate from the botany class, to search in the woods for wild flowers as specimens to be analyzed. We liked botany, but preferred zoölogy, and returned to the school-house with rare specimens. When the teacher opened the box, what was his astonishment and consternation to find it filled with tiny toads, which jumped out and covered the floor, and also a young owl, for which I had taken pains to climb into a hollow tree, to the detriment of my dress!

Poor old Doctor Cotting! he was blessed with a deal of patience, but the frogs proved too much for him, and I was sent home with a message that nothing but the grace of God could do anything with me.

As Topsy says, "I growed up," until I became a fair and goodly tree, as far as size was concerned. My father came to see me, and concluded that I, his eldest hopeful, needed pruning and training. For that purpose he brought me to New York. During my journey, I characterized myself, much to the mortification of my father and step-mother, by drinking lemonade from my finger-bowl, calling nut-crackers pinchers, and blanc-mange pudding — all owing to the want of proper training. I am glad now that my early years were spent with a poor grandmother instead of a wealthy father, for the economy practised in her household gave me habits of frugality which I would not otherwise have possessed, and which proved invaluable to me during the war.

My father placed me in a boarding-school in New York, where I remained one year only; for I was fond of the creature comforts, and as I only received the flow of the soul, I left in disgust. My indulgent parent then placed me in the "polishing mill" of Mrs. Leverett, who still has her school in Eighteenth Street; and to that establishment I am indebted for the elegance of manners for which I am so justly noted.

Here let me mention that Mrs. Leverett was all to me that a tender, gentle mother could have been. She praised my talents, which she, even then, although I could not realize it, seemed to think I possessed; reproved me for my faults, and gently strove to correct or eradicate them. Mrs. Leverett's daughters were also very kind to me, and I remember with gratitude how they seemed to take the ignorant, rough Southern girl into their hearts.

At last I was sent home accomplished.

I was young, rich, and as for looks, why, I could pass in a crowd of ugly girls.

Of course I fell in love. What fool does not? I did not marry the object of my adoration. I fell in love again: this time I married, after first saying to my intended:

> "No, thou art not my first love:
> I had loved before we met;
> And the music of that summer-dream
> Still lingers round me yet.
> But thou, thou art my last love,
> My dearest, and my best;
> My heart but shed its outer leaves
> To give thee all the rest" — CABBAGE.

After my marriage, my husband took me to his home in Milledgeville, Ga., where we lived with his mother for one year. They were all kind to me, and I loved them, but I was glad when my husband said that I should preside over a home of my own.

The next year a little birdling came to cheer our nest, "My Gentle

Annie," my dark-haired child, whose deep-blue eyes and sad glances seem ever before me. Then came "Little Mary," the one the preachers call an "imp of mischief" — a white-haired fairy foundling, so loving, and so full of fun.

Perhaps I was happy then : I do not know, but I think I was; any way, we lived peacefully until the war commenced. It brought sorrow to all our land ; and I need not speak of its consequences to me, one of the million sufferers.

When the struggle ended, my father and my husband said they had lost *all*.

It is said, that to become a Christian, one must be born again : poets and Christians resemble each other, for

"Poeta nascitur non fit;"

and I know that the suffering I endured during, and after the close of the war, must have been the pangs of my second birth, which created a poetic nature I am sure I did not before possess.

Leaving my home and little ones, with the full, free consent of my husband, and the approbation of my father, I came to New York, (I cannot speak of the sorrowful parting from my babies,) to seek my fortune as a journalist, and also to procure a publisher for a volume of poems which I had written at various times.

It would be useless to tell how I struggled with poverty, but never lost my precious hope and faith ; and how, in time, I found and made friends by scores, Republicans and Democrats, who completely ignored the political question, and gave me not only encouragement, but work, for which they paid me well. Say what you will about the cold, heartless nature of the true-born Northerner, I *know* by sweet experience, that, beneath the crust of snow, deep hidden in their hearts there blooms the fragrant flower of sympathy, whose perfume gladdens the heart of the homeless, when the outward ice is thawed by the knowledge that one is worthy, industrious, and not totally devoid of brains.

Need I say that I succeeded ? and that those who advised me to remain at home and cook and wash dishes, (two kinds of work I could never endure,) and turned their heads the other way when they saw me, now greet me with smiles and say, "I always knew you would succeed, you were so persevering." True, I am still away from my home and those I love, but soon, very soon, I hope to be with my dear ones, never to leave them again until the Great Master calls me to join my mother in that glorious land where all is love.

I have given you a brief outline of my eventful life, in which I have stated the leading facts only. Hundreds of pages could I fill with my journeyings over the United States, and incidents which I am sure would prove interesting; but you remember the old adage, that " shoe-makers' children always have to go without shoes; " so I, who am con-stantly employed in writing the lives of others, cannot spare time to elaborate my own history. So I will only add, that if ever I become famous, it will be owing to the *blessing*, not the *curse — necessity.*
1868.

In 1867, M. Doolady, New York, published Mrs. Tucker's first vol-ume — "Poems." The "New York Tribune" says of this volume:

"A volume of *Poems*, by Mary E. Tucker, published by M. Doolady, is apparently of Southern origin, and derives a certain interest from its expres-sion of Southern feelings during the war, and its allusions to the sufferings of the South since the restoration of peace. At the same time, it is not intended to exert a sectional influence, much less to nourish the sentiment of contempt and hate for the lovers of the Union. Nor is there any consider-able portion of its contents devoted to themes of local interest; but, on the contrary, they are drawn from the general experience of life, and depict the emotions which arise from its vicissitudes in a mind of more than ordinary sensitiveness. The poems are the effusions of an excitable nature with an ear attuned to the melodies of rhythm, and an experience familiar with the gradations of joy and sorrow. They do not pretend to be the exponents of deep thought, or to have been prompted by the highest impulses of the imagination. With their modest claims, they need not be brought to the test of an austere judgment; and their frequent sweetness of versification, and their pleasant, if not brilliant fancies, entitle them to a respectable place in the poetry of feeling and aspiration."

"Miles O'Reilly's " paper, "The Citizen," welcomes this volume thus:

"Mrs. Tucker has prefaced this dainty little volume with her own portrait, and on first opening the book we wondered why she had published either the portrait or the poems. But between the two there is a striking resem-blance. After looking at the face for a little, you grow to like it for its kind, pleasing, truthful, womanly expression. And so, too, the verses, though they are not, strictly speaking, beautiful, improve vastly upon acquaintance. They are true and sincere in sentiment, and sufficiently smooth in versifica-tion. There is no affectation, no unhealthy sentimentality about them; but many of them possess a simple, touching pathos that is infinitely above the simulated sorrow so dear to the school-girl mind."

Says Professor A. B. Stark, of Tennessee, in a notice of this volume:

"In the poems we find ample evidence of the poet's Southern origin and sympathies. But before reading the poems, we look at the preface — it is rude to skip the preface, the little, private, confidential foretalk the author wishes to have with the reader — and find it modest, naïve, and winning, disarming one of the power of harsh criticism. Hear her:

"'Out of a simple woman's heart these rivulets of rhyme have run. They may not be great, nor broad, nor deep. She trusts they are pure. She wrote these verses often in sorrow, perplexity, and distress. . . . She will feel rewarded if, though these buds and flowers be not very beautiful, they give to any soul the perfume of simple truthfulness and genuine feeling.'

"Well, her poems are neither broad, nor deep, nor brilliant. If you look into her volume for new ideas, philosophic thought, glowing imagery, deep insight into passions and motives, or an intense love of nature, you will be disappointed. But they are pure, simple, natural — the outgushings of a true woman's heart, sympathetic, kind, loving, truthful. While reading them, you feel that you are in communication with an innocent, noble-hearted, Christian woman. There is no cant, no twaddle, no morbid sentimentality — a negative merit, always appreciated by a healthful reader. Her volume belongs to that respectable class of books which afford pleasure, comfort, and recreation; in their brief life doing some good, but no harm; cheering some lonely, heart-sick wanderer; sending out into the darkness a single ray of heavenly light, which may guide some poor, benighted soul amid the pitfalls of sin; adding one sweet note to the grand symphony of joy and praise and thanksgiving swelling up from the hearts of all that are glad, and pure, and innocent on earth."

"Loew's Bridge, a Broadway Idyl," a brief poem, was published by the same publisher, and attracted a great deal of attention. The poet views the moving throng on Broadway from Loew's Bridge,* a large aërial structure at the intersection of Broadway and Fulton Street, where the thoroughfare is continually thronged with vehicles of all kinds, rendering it almost impossible for pedestrians to pass.

Mrs. Tucker has been a most industrious writer, contributing regularly to "The Leader," "Ledger," and other New York papers. Her latest ambitious effort was a "Life of Mark M. Pomeroy, Editor of the La Crosse Democrat, a Representative Young Man of America" — Carleton, publisher, New York, 1869.

1869.

* This bridge has been recently taken down.

_2

HUGGING THE SHORE.

"Do you think you will hug the shore, captain, to-day?"
Asked a saucy young flirt, with a smile;
  With a crimson flush was dyed her cheek,
And over her brow swept the roseate hue,
While her eyes revealed in their dancing blue
  All the lips declined to speak.

The captain glanced at the distant shore,
  And then at the maid awhile:
The shore was distant, and she was near,
And the rose-tint deepened, as he said, "Dear,
  I'll neglect the shore to-day!"

And around her waist crept the captain's hand—
It was so much better than hugging dry land!
And he said, glancing over the vessel's bow,
"The ship is hugging Cape Hatteras now,
  But I'll hug the Cape of May."

KINDNESS.

One single word of heart-felt kindness
  Oft is worth a mine of gold;
Yet how oft we, in our blindness,
  The most precious wealth withhold.

Like soft dews on thirsting flowers,
  It revives the drooping heart;
And its magical, blest showers
  Is the soul's best healing art.

Oh! however sad and lonely
  Life's dark, sterile path may be,
One, one single kind word only
  Causeth all its gloom to flee.

How can we know of the troubles
  That must rack another's soul!
All must know that empty bubbles
  Of life's cares o'er all heads roll.

Then, forgiving and forgetting,
  Let for aye the kind word fall;

Only our own sins regretting
With a charity for all.

Then this life will be a pleasure,
When we all speak words of love;
For we know our earthly measure
Will be more than filled above.

———∘∘⦂⊙⦂∘∘———

MISS MARGIE P. SWAIN.*

THIS young writer is a native of Taliaferro County, in the State of Georgia; but in early life she became a resident of Alabama. Her home is with her adopted parents, Mr. and Mrs. E. J. Swain, of Talladega County,

The great civil war, at its inception in 1861, found Miss Swain, then scarcely entered on her teens, a pupil of White Chapel Female Seminary, near Talladega. At a period of life when most young girls are busying themselves with lessons in geography or algebra, her daring mind actually planned and executed "Lochlin," a regular "romaunt of the war," in iambic verse. It was completed, and put through the press at Selma, Alabama, at an age younger than that at which a vast majority of the poets have made their way into the publication vestibule of the temple of fame. The first edition of this poem abounded with typographical and other errors, resulting in great part from the manifold difficulties experienced by publishers as results of the war. In this first edition, the poem was entitled "Mara," for which the young authoress has substituted "Lochlin" in a new edition about to be published.

Since the publication referred to in 1864, Miss Swain has spent a portion of her time at school; has mastered an extensive course of literary and historical reading, and has written many other poems, soon likewise to be given by her publishers to the world. The most considerable of these is "Constantius," an historical drama of the times of the immediate successors of Constantine the Great. We venture the prediction that Miss Swain's "Constantius" will prove a decided triumph in the difficult art of dramatic composition, and a faithful portraiture of Roman life in the fourth century. Her minor poems,

---

* Miss Swain was married at Rome, Ga., January 15th, 1871, to Mr. Mosely, editor and proprietor of the Rome "Daily."

sufficient of themselves to form a respectable volume in point of size, display great versatility of powers, range of information, rhythmical aptitude, and rare poetic beauty.

And yet all these works of her genius have been produced while she has so constantly been seen in the school-room, or the gay circle of thoughtless companions, that it is wonder to those who know her best how or when they were written. This fact is of itself a high commentary on the force of her genius, and creates higher hopes for her future great and lasting eminence in literature. A manifest improvement in her later productions is visible; and as she has before her all of that period of life when the full maturity of her intellectual powers may be expected to be realized, other works, surpassing those already produced, may be confidently expected.

In January, 1871, Miss Swain was literary editress of the Rome (Ga.) "Gazette."

In person, Miss Swain is about the medium height, of fair complexion, handsome spirited features, and hazel eyes, that, when interested in conversation, glow with singular brilliancy. In conversation, she seldom attempts to display those powers which she seeks to wield through her pen; but when occasionally interested by a congenial companion, her conversation is peculiarly instructive and fascinating. If she can happily steer clear of the maelstrom of matrimony, and life and health be spared to her in the pursuit of literary renown, we confidently predict for her an eminence in the world of letters not excelled by that of any of her countrywomen — and we even hope that she may surpass them all.

1869.   ————————   W. G. McADO.

VANITAS.

Ah, vainly we sigh for the summer
  That dwells in the land of fair flowers;
And vainly we strive for the pleasures
  And the bliss of happier hours!

For joy is a flower that bloometh
  At morning, and fadeth at night;
The mem'ry thereof is outblotted
  By thoughts which each day brings to light.

Care roots up the planting of pleasure;
  The heart is the seat of all woe;
The worst of all pains is its throbbings,
  Those pains that kill life as they go.

Love rises, entrances, and leaves us,
　　And hopes drift like leaves before wind;
All bright things and sweet take their leavings,
　　But sorrow remaineth behind.

How vain are the dreams which we cherish —
　　Those dreams in the dark future's mines;
They melt as the foam of the ocean,
　　And die like the music of rhymes!

When all things we have that are given,
　　Satiety is but the crown;
And while in the chase of strange visions,
　　In death's darkened vale we go down.

Then, oh! for a land of all beauty,
　　Where dwelleth the light of old days —
The soul is not cheated by falseness,
　　And joy has bright, genuine rays.

THE LAST SCENE.

The last gun had sounded defiance to foes,
　　Each sword in its scabbard was lying;
Each vet'ran stood sternly, and thought on his woes,
　　And wept that his country was dying.

Our rifles were stacked, and our cannons were laid
　　In graves o'er which heroes were weeping;
We gazed on our banners the last time displayed,
　　And envied those then 'neath them sleeping.

Our chieftain and hero in sorrow passed by,
　　Yet proud — 'neath its pall never drooping;
We loved him — we cheered, yet our shout rose not high;
　　Our hearts were to destiny stooping.

We saw our proud banner, now conquered, fall low,
　　And that of the foe rise above it;
We felt that its folds should wave o'er us no more,
　　And wept — for then most did we love it.

We looked on our squadrons bowed down 'neath despair,
　　And thought on the dead clothed in glory;
Gazed, through blinding tears, on our country's black bier,
　　And longed to lie down with the-gory!

We thought on our glory — our loved ones afar —
　　The long years of toils and of dangers;
Then trembling, clasped hands, we worn brothers in war,
　　And proudly we parted 'mid strangers!

THE SENTINEL OF POMPEII.

Dr. Guthrie tells us a touching story of the fidelity of a Roman soldier at the destruction of Pompeii, who, although thousands fled from the city, remained at his post, because dishonorable to abandon it without being relieved, and died a death of useless, but of heroic devotion. He says: "After seventeen centuries they found his skeleton standing erect in a marble niche, clad in its rusty armor, the helmet on its empty skull, and its bony fingers still closed upon its spear."

Thick darkness had lowered, Vesuvius had sounded,
　　The flame of his wrath arose high in the sky;
Dense volumes of thick smoke the mountain surrounded,
　　And lay like a pall over doomed Pompeii.

Far, far in the distance the peal of his thunder
　　Vibrated, and shook the firm earth with its sound;
While, to his hot centre the mount rent asunder,
　　Red rivers of lava in fierceness poured down.

And thousands were gazing in fear and in horror,
　　And thousands, inured to it, dreamed not of doom;
But soon e'en the fearless beheld with deep sorrow
　　That ashes the city — themselves, would entomb.

Like snow-flakes, those ashes of dire desolation
　　Came thick, fast, and stifling, with burning-hot stones:
While momently grander the fierce conflagration
　　Loomed up in the distance, with death in its tones.

And near to the gate that looked out on the mountain,
　　A sentinel stood with his spear, keeping guard;
He saw the hot lava boil up like a fountain,
　　And heavily roll on the city toward.

He thought of his dear wife alone in her anguish,
  The helpless ones weeping beside her in fear;
"Yet not e'en for sweet love must duty e'er languish,"
  He murmured, and clasped again tightly his spear.

The hours passed slowly — none came to relieve him;
  He called to his leader: "How long must I stay?"
Yet not for his life would that soldier deceive him,
  But stood to his post through that terrible day.

He saw the dark ashes entombing the city;
  He saw them rise up inch by inch to his chin;
He looked on the burning flood, and in deep pity
  He uttered one prayer for his home, and was dead.

The city was covered, the lava flowed over,
  And beauty and manliness, childhood and age,
And rich things and beauteous now to discover,
  Were buried below by Vesuvius' rage.

Years, long years have passed, yet that sent'nel is standing,
  All helmeted, now disinterred, near his post;
And pilgrims, aweary at Pompeii landing,
  Look on him, the strangest of all her strange host!

———oo°•°oo———

KATE A. DU BOSE.

MRS. DU BOSE is the eldest daughter of Rev. William Richards, of Beaufort District, S. C. She was born in a village in Oxfordshire, England, in 1828. Shortly after her birth, the family came to the United States, and settled in Georgia, but removed in a few years to their present home in Carolina.

In 1848, she was married to Charles W. Du Bose, Esq., an accomplished gentleman, and lawyer of talent and ability, of Sparta, Georgia, where they still reside.

Mrs. Du Bose was educated in Northern cities, but for some years was a teacher in Georgia, her adopted home.

At an early age, she gave indications of a love of letters, and had she chosen to "break the lance" with professional contestants for literary honors, she must have won distinction and an enviable fame. But as a bird sings because it must find vent for its rapture, or as the heart will overflow when too full for concealment, thus with her writings. Her productions have been given to the public from time to time, through journals and magazines, generally under the *nom de plume* of "Leila Cameron." Some of her best poems appeared in the "Southern Literary Gazette," published in Charleston, and edited by her brother, Rev. William C. Richards, now a resident of Providence, R. I. The "Orion Magazine," of Georgia, was also favored with contributions from her pen, and in its columns appeared the prize poem, entitled "Wachulla," the name of a famous and wonderful fountain near Tallahassee, Florida. This poem was deservedly popular, and if the spirit of the fountain had chosen a nymph from its own charmed circle to sing the praises of "beautiful Wachulla" and its surroundings, the lay could not have gushed up from a heart more alive to its beauties and attractions than that of its talented author.

In 1858, Mrs. Du Bose's first volume was published by Sheldon & Co., New York. This is a prose story for the young, entitled, "The Pastor's Household "— a story of continuous interest, displaying narrative and dramatic power. The portraiture of "Lame Jimmy," one of the prominent characters — "a meek, silent boy," with pale face, and a look of patient suffering upon his young features — is admirably drawn ; and as we *see* him, as he bends over his desk at school, with his large eyes full of the light of intellect, poring over his books, we triumph in the truth that God sometimes gives the poor boy, in his threadbare coat, the princely endowments of mind which may win him distinction among the "world's proud honors," and crown him a king among men.

As a member of a large family, all remarkable for intellectual acquirements, Mrs. Du Bose has been much favored in procuring an early and thorough cultivation. One of her brothers, Rev. William C. Richards, is not only widely known as a popular editor and writer, but is also the author of the "Shakspeare Calendar." Another brother, T. Addison Richards, of New York, the poet and artist, is the principal of the "School of Design for Women," established within the walls of Cooper Institute, New York.

In her elegant home, where unpretending piety and domestic love are combined with refined and cultivated tastes, seen in all the surroundings, and where the patter of children's feet is heard, and their happy laugh echoes through its walls, Mrs. Du Bose forms the centre of attraction to a circle of friends, as well as that of home, and wears with equally charming grace the triple name of wife, mother, and author.   1867.

LOULA KENDALL ROGERS.

L EOLA, a well-known *nom de plume*, falls on the ear softly, musically, " as if the very personification of that ideality which extracts inspiration from the whispering wind, the song of birds, the blush of flowers, the lightning's flash, and the thunder's roar."

Miss Kendall is a graduate of the Wesleyan Female College, of Macon. In the home of her childhood, a charming country-seat in Upson County, Ga., there are so many lovely spots in her native county, so many " glen echoes " where one might imagine her a nymph " calling to sister spirits of the greenwood," we do not wonder that the gift of poesy is hers.

Her ancestors were from North Carolina, and there is probably no family whose authentic history can be more closely traced through every period of the annals of that State. Her great-great-grandfather, who signed his name Joseph Lane, Jr., as far back as 1727, died at his residence on the Roanoke, in 1776. His youngest son, Jesse Lane, emigrated to Wilkes, near Oglethorpe County, Ga., and his descendants are dispersed through all the Western and Southern States; Gen. Joseph Lane, a candidate for the Vice-Presidency of the United States in 1860, and ex-Governor Swain, of Chapel Hill, North Carolina, being among the number. One of his daughters married John Hart, son of Nancy Hart, the famous heroine of the Broad River Settlement, and one of his grand-daughters was wife of Judge Colquitt, Senator from Georgia in 1847. Thus brought into close relationship with many of the highest families of the South, the subject of this sketch inherited the spirit of patriotism that prompted them to make any sacrifice, however great, for the welfare of their country. We do not know that we can introduce her in a more acceptable manner than by inserting here the following extract of a letter written by her without any thought of its publication, (1862.) Speaking of herself, she says:

" I have always been a child of nature and lover of poetry ever since I can remember, though it is pleasure enough for me to lurk among flowers, to listen to their heart-voices, and remain *silent* while drinking with intoxicating delight the sweets of far more gifted worshippers. Occasionally I cannot resist an inclination to snatch my own little harp from its favorite bed of violets; but its rustic strains are simple, and not worthy of being placed among the productions of those whose gifted pens have gained for them a reputation more enduring than gold. My first poem was written at eight years of age, a grand attempt, which mamma carefully preserved. At dreaming fourteen, I went to Montpelier Institute, once under the supervision of Bishop Elliott, and its fairy groves, sparkling streams, and 'moonlit palaces' grew more dear when I fancied them the abode of viewless beings who told me of all things holy and beautiful. My composition-book was filled with wild, weird imagery, and the geometrical figures on my slate frequently alternated with impromptu verses, which are still kept as souvenirs of that dear old place. Two years in Macon College (where prosaical studies and life's sterner realities crossed my path) almost obliterated the silly dream of my childhood; a dream of *fame*, which now has utterly departed, for I have long since ceased to pursue a shadow so far beyond my reach. I write for those who love me — that is all; but if these wild flowers, gathered among the hills and streams of my native land — these untutored voices that speak to me from each nestling leaf, are able to dispel *one* single cloud among the many that overshadow our country, I have no right to withhold them.

. . . .

"There is no lack of talent in our bright Southland; but, under the sunlight of prosperity, it has never yet been brought out in all its strength."

Of these "wild flowers and these untutored voices" we shall have but little to say, preferring to let them speak for themselves. She writes prose and poetry with equal facility, and her letters are models of literary composition; for here she expresses herself with that gentle warmth and modest freedom that characterizes her conversation. As Mrs. Le Vert somewhere expresses it: "She seems to dip her pen in her own soul and write of its emotions." In company she is plain and unassuming, being wholly free from pedantry and pretension; and yet she possesses great enthusiasm of character — the enthusiasm described by Madame De Staël, as "God within us, the love of the good, the holy, and the beautiful."

"Leola" was quite a student, and accomplished much, though her advancement would probably have been greater had she possessed such a literary guide and friend as G. D. Prentice was to Amelia Welby. But, as has been said of another, when we consider the great disadvantages she must have labored under on an isolated plantation, far from public libraries, and far from social groups of literary laborers and artists, it seems to us that her writings reveal the aspirations of a richly endowed genius and the marks of a good culture.

"Leola" is also exceedingly domestic, being, as she says, gifted with "a taste for the *substantial* as well as the poetry of life;" a proof that poetry and the larder are not always separate companions, but may exist together on very amicable terms. The productions of "Leola" consist of fugitive pieces dashed off under the inspiration of the moment, many of them being published in the newspapers of the day. We would "as soon think of sitting down to dissect the bird whose song has charmed us, as to break upon the wheel of criticism poems springing so much from the *heart-side* of the author."

Since the end of the war, Miss Kendall has become the wife of Dr. C. Rogers, and lives near Thomaston, Upson County, Georgia.
1868.

THE HEALING FOUNTAIN.*

"A nameless unrest urged me forward; but whither should I go? My loadstars were blotted out: in that canopy of grim fire shone no star. I was alone, alone! A feeling I had that there was and *must* be somewhere a Healing Fountain. From the depths of my own heart it called to me, Forward! The winds, and the streams, and all nature sounded to me, Forward!"—CARLYLE'S *Sartor Resartus.*

On, on she wandered all alone, o'er deserts vast and dim,
No hopeful ray to light the gloom, no spirit-soothing hymn;
The wearied heart no goal had found, all dark the future seem'd;
"There *must* be rest *somewhere*," she cried, and nought the toil deem'd.

Black shadows clung around the heart once filled with childlike trust,
And tempters whispered in her ear, "*Thy spirit is but dust!*"
Then she long'd to know, poor orphan child, if in another sphere
She ne'er must meet with Lilly, to dwell forever there?

If the spirit's voice must ever cease, with life's dull care and pain;
If the midnight toil, her searches for Egeria's fount were vain?
Beulah! thy childhood's sacred haunts are truthful guides for thee;
There rove at twilight's solemn hour, and lowly bend the knee.

Yon lofty mountain's gilded height looks upward to the sky,
E'en Nature's simplest voices tell the soul can never die:
Then leave thy desert vast and dim, where erring feet have trod;
Each streamlet here, each bud and flower will speak to thee of God!

But onward still, O child of toil! by storm and tempest tossed;
Thy burning feet are wandering on, till childhood's faith is lost!
The scorching beam of summer sun poor Hagar scarce could bear,
With no fount to slake her fever-thirst, no waters gurgling there,

* Written after reading "Beulah," 1859.

Till words of confidence and trust her parching lips express'd;
Then joyfully an angel came, and gave her peaceful rest:
So Beulah might have found the balm to lighten every care —
A spring to heal her aching heart — by strong and earnest *prayer.*

The Healing Fountain! Pure and bright those ripples near us gleam;
We need not roam o'er burning sands to quaff its crystal stream:
Its whispering music oft we hear, a star shines from above,
Illuming all with holy light — that star is Heaven's love.

EMMA MOFFETT WYNNE.

CRAGFONT is the title of a neat, unpretending volume, from the publishing house of Blelock & Co., New York, issued in 1867.

The title-page stated that the book was by "a young Southern lady." It was the first production of Emma M. Wynne, of Columbus, Georgia.

Like the majority of Southern books, "Cragfont" has been indiscriminately praised by well-meaning but injudicious friends, whereas true criticism, while it might pain for a time, would in the end assist the youthful *débutante* on the field of literature.

"Cragfont" is a book of promise. From the remarks of two readers of this book, we cull the criticisms we give.

A writer in "Scott's Magazine," of Atlanta, praised:

"Not sustaining carping Zoilus in his ill-nature, we think, with another, upon whose brow the greenest of laurel is still triumphantly worn, that 'to point out too particularly the beauties of a work is to admit tacitly that these beauties are not wholly admirable.' 'Cragfont' is not without errors, such as all young writers are betrayed into; but the flashings of genius so visible throughout the book overshadow and outweigh the faults, which, after all, are only the 'peccadilloes of the muse.' The plot of the book is finely conceived, the invention strong and vigorous, while imagination, that primary and indispensable requisite in a writer, like the touch of Midas, gilded every object that presented itself. The style is classical and elegant. The author seems to excel in the delineation of female character. They are all particularly fine and well sustained.

"The heroine, Isabel Grattan, never grows commonplace, while the gay, sprightly Lizzie Armor wisely refrains from attempting a part too heavy.

"While dealing in classical lore and antiquities, perhaps, a little too freely, there is a depth of tenderness and pathos running through the whole, that would tell at once it came from a woman's heart."

A lady criticizes "Cragfont" thus:

" In the first place, I began at the beginning and read the title-page. The little quotation from Cousin, and the longer one from Mrs. Browning, each came in for a share of study. I knew that these mottoes contain frequently the key to the whole matter which follows; and so would I do 'Cragfont' justice, and read these too. The second contained a hint which I resolved to profit by — to

> " ' Gloriously forget ourselves, and plunge
> Soul forward into the book's profound.'

Very profound I have proved it — that is, some parts of it. The fair author evidently admires Miss 'Beulah' Evans, and follows hard after the celestial flights of that learned lady. The title is not appropriate; it might just as well be styled New Orleans, or New York, since the scenes are laid principally in these two cities, and 'Cragfont' only appears briefly in two chapters. This 'ancestral mansion' is a 'stylish' country residence for an American; but perhaps in Tennessee they do live in 'turreted castles,' and perhaps they have 'rooks' in Tennessee, also. I don't know much about the ornithology of that State, but I had an idea rooks were confined to England. However, this may be merely a 'poetic license' to prove the unmistakable and indisputable aristocracy of our hero, as rooks are supposed to favor with their presence only the *ancien régime*.

" ' Cragfont' contains a variety of information, and a variety of languages, and a series of essays or dissertations on various subjects are scattered through the book. It exhibits talent and promise of future excellence; but, in itself, is hardly a successful novel or book of essays — a 'half-way performance.' The writer, we feel confident, will yet make a worthy offering to Southern literature."

The author of "Cragfont," Mrs. Emma Moffett Wynne, was born in Alabama, in 1844. Her father, Major Henry Moffett, removed to Columbus, Ga., a beautiful city on the banks of the Chattahoochee, before she had completed her fourth year. She was very fortunate in having her steps first directed in the paths of learning by the accomplished and talented authoress, Mrs. Caroline Lee Hentz, under whose tuition she was placed at the age of five years.

In her fifteenth year, she went to the well-known Patapsco Female Institute, near Baltimore, entered at once the senior class, and graduated the following year with much honor to herself, receiving a gold medal for proficiency in French. The following fall of 1860 she spent in New York, at the Spingler Institute, perfecting herself in music, French, Italian, etc. Owing to the "state of the country," she returned home early in the spring, (1861.)

During the war, she occasionally contributed to the "Field and Fireside," published at Augusta, under the *nom de plume* of "Lola." She was married in May, 1864, to Major V. W. Wynne.

Mrs. Wynne, being young, with native talent and habits of study, will, without doubt, enrich the literary world with many productions of rare merit. She has recently published an historical romance in some way connected with Maximilian, the late Emperor of Mexico— a tragic subject well suited to her pen—entitled "The Crown Jewels."

In personal appearance, Mrs. Wynne is exceedingly prepossessing; and this, combined with an elegance and vivacity of manner, renders her both attractive and fascinating.

1870.

LIFE'S MISSION.

The mission of life is not always lofty, yet the duty of its accomplishment is none the less imperative. The account is required of the one talent as surely as of the five. The mountain is too steep and rugged save for men of stern mould; yet in the valley the fields "are waiting for the laborers." How mistaken is the reasoner who would reserve to the sterner sex all those feelings of ambition, the reaching upward for higher and holier things! How many of gentler natures have felt the unsatisfied longing for more knowledge, more power over their own minds! When we go, with Mrs. Hemans, Mrs. Browning, and Jean Ingelow, through all the chambers of the soul, and listen to the music of their songs, we feel that within our hearts whole volumes of sweet poetry exist; the power to word it alone is wanting. Just as those we love so dearly are never in this life quite near enough to us; we would have them closer—heart to heart, soul to soul; this mortal body stands between. In our dreaming of the other world, we sometimes think that perhaps by our joy there will be these yearnings satisfied; the spell of silence will be broken, and our own poetry, sweet, beautiful, heavenly, will fill our hearts.

ANNIE R. BLOUNT.

MISS BLOUNT is a native of Richmond County, Va. She commenced writing for her own pleasure and amusement at an early age, and many of her juvenile productions appeared in print under various signatures.

She graduated at Madison Female College, Madison, Ga., with the very highest honors the institution could confer; the president stating to the trustees and audience that she was the most perfect scholar he had ever graduated.

After her graduation, although very young, Miss Blount assumed the editorial conduct of a literary paper, which, under her auspices, rapidly grew into public favor, and was widely circulated. Miss Blount, besides being literary editress of the "Bainbridge Argus," (which position she held for two years,) contributed to other Southern literary journals. She received a prize offered by a literary paper published in Newbern, N. C., for "the best story by any American writer."

Mr. T. A. Burke, then editor of the "Savannah News," thus alluded to her success:

"An examining committee, composed of W. Gilmore Simms, the eminent novelist, Rev. B. Craven, President of the Normal College, N. C., and John R. Thompson, editor of the 'Southern Literary Messenger,' have awarded the first prize, a one-hundred-dollar gold medal, to 'Jenny Woodbine,' *alias* Miss Annie R. Blount, of Augusta, Ga., 'for the best story,' to be published in a Southern paper. We know Miss Blount well, and her success as a writer, both of prose and verse, is what her decided talent induced us to expect She is young — probably the youngest writer of any reputation in the country, North or South — and, with proper study and care, she has much to expect in the future."

This story, "The Sisters," was printed in 1859, in the "Newbern Gazette." Miss Blount has received numerous prizes for poems and novelettes, offered by various papers. In the summer of ——, she was invited by the trustees and faculty of Le Vert College, Talbotton, Ga., to deliver an original poem at their annual commencement. An enthusiastic gentleman, in a notice of the "Commencement," says:

"It was the privilege of the large audience to listen to a poem from Miss Annie R. Blount, of Augusta. Her subject seemed to be, 'The Power of Woman.' The reading elicited extraordinary interest. . . . . It is impossible for me to give any just idea of the poem, and I will conclude by saying, if I am ever called to the battle-field, I want the fair author to be there to read the concluding lines at the head of my column."

The next summer, Miss Blount delivered a poem at the "College Temple" Commencement, Newnan, Ga. After the reading of the poem, the faculty of College Temple conferred on her the degree of "Mistress of Arts."

In 1860, Miss Blount collected her poems and printed them in a book. The volume was dedicated to Hon. Alexander H. Stephens, under whose kindly auspices it was published. Considering the unsettled state of the times, the book sold well, and was highly complimented by the press. The following notice of the volume is from the pen of that graceful writer, Miss C. W. Barber, then editress of the "Southern Literary Companion":

"While looking over some book-shelves in our new home, the other day, we came, unexpectedly, across a volume of Miss Blount's poems. We had never seen the book before, and sat down at once 'to read, to ponder, and to dream.' Annie Blount has, in this unassuming volume, established her right to the laurel-wreath. She may now lay her hand confidently upon it, and few will dispute her right to its possession. We were not prepared to find so many gems in so small a casket; we did not know that so sweet a bird carolled amid the magnolia groves of the South.

"Letitia E. Landon won for herself a deathless fame in England and America. Wherein are her poems so greatly superior to Miss Blount's? Both have dwelt much upon the varied emotions of the human heart; sometimes it is hopeful, sometimes disappointed love that they sing about. At Annie Blount's age, Letitia Landon had certainly written nothing sweeter, deeper, or in any respect better than this volume of poems contains. Before she died upon the coast of Africa, she had, of course, gone through a wider range of experience than Annie Blount has yet done, and every phase of human life develops in us all some latent power. But, even in her last poem — an address to the 'North Star,' written only a few hours before her death — there is nothing superior to the following, which we copy from Miss Blount's Poem entitled, 'The Evening Star':

" 'Where dwellest thou, my young heart's chosen one ?
What glorious star can claim thee as its own?
If it be true that when the spirit flies
From earth it nestles in the starlit skies,
What orb is brightened by thy radiant face?
Methinks in yonder Evening Star I trace
The light which circled o'er the brow I love,
And fixed my wayward heart on things above.

  .   .   .   .

Sweet Evening Star, brighter than all the rest,
Thou art the star my infancy loved best;
And still the fancy-dream my bosom swells,
That there, with thee, my loved one's spirit dwells:
I'll clasp the dear delusion to my breast,
That it may quell this wild and vague unrest,
And though from native land I wander far,
I'll turn to thee with love, bright Evening Star.' "

Miss Blount resides with her brother in Augusta, Ga.
1869.

UNDER THE LAMPLIGHT.

A PRIZE POEM.

Under the lamplight, watch them come,
  Figures, one, two, three;
A restless mass moves on and on,
  Like waves on a stormy sea.
      Lovers wooing,
      Billing and cooing,
Heedless of the warning old,
Somewhere in uncouth rhyme told,
  That old Time, Love's enemy,
Makes the warmest heart grow cold.
See how fond the maiden leaneth
  On that strong encircling arm,
While her timid heart is beating
  Near that other heart so warm;
Downcast are her modest glances,
Filled her heart with pleasant fancies.
  Clasp her, lover! — clasp her closer —
  Time the winner, thou the loser!

24

He will steal
From her sparkling eye its brightness,
From her step its native lightness;
   Or, perchance,
Ere another year has fled,
Thou may'st see her pale and dead.
   Trusting maiden!
   Heart love-laden,
    Thou may'st learn
That the lip which breathed so softly
  Told to thee a honeyed lie;
That the heart now beating near thee
   Gave to thee no fond return —
   Learn — and die!

Under the lamplight, watch them come,
  Figures, one, two, three;
The moon is up, the stars are out,
  And hurrying crowds I see —
   Some with sorrow
   Of the morrow
    Thinking bitterly;
   Why grief borrow?
   Some that morrow
    Ne'er shall live to see.
  Which of all this crowd shall God
   Summon to his court to-night?
  Which of these many feet have trod
   These streets their last? Who first shall press
  The floor that shines with diamonds bright?
   To whom of all this throng shall fall
    The bitter lot,
   To hear the righteous Judge pronounce:
   "Depart, ye cursed — I know ye not!"
   Oh! startling question! — *who?*

Under the lamplight, watch them come,
  Faces fair to see —
Some that pierce your very soul
  With thrilling intensity:
   Cold and ragged,
   Lean and haggard —
    God! what misery!
See them watch yon rich brocade,
By their toiling fingers made,
  With the eyes of poverty.

Does the tempter whisper now:
"Such may be thine own!"—but *how?*
Sell thy woman's virtue, wretch,
And the price that it will fetch
  Is a silken robe as fine—
   Gems that glitter—hearts that shine—
    But pause, reflect!
     Ere the storm shall o'er thee roll,
     Ere thy sin spurns all control—
And the price that it will bring
  Though with jewels bright bedecked,
  Thou wilt lose thy self-respect;
   All the good will spurn thy touch,
    As if 't were an adder's sting,
    And the *price* that it will bring
     Is a ruined soul!
  God protect thee—keep thee right,
  Lonely wanderer of the night!

Under the lamplight, watch them come—
  Youth with spirits light;
His handsome face I'm sure doth make
  Some quiet household bright.
   Yet where shall this lover,
   This son, this brother,
    Hide his head to-night?
  Where the bubbles swim
  On the wine-cup's brim;
   Where the song rings out
   Till the moon grows dim;
  Where congregate the knave and fool,
  To graduate in vice's school.
   Oh! turn back, youth!
    Thy mother's prayer
    Rings in thy ear—
     Let sinners not
     Entice thee there.

Under the lamplight, watch them come,
  The gay, the blithe, the free;
And some with a look of anguished pain
  'T would break your heart to see.
   Some from a marriage,
    Altar, and priest;
   Some from a death-bed,
    Some from a feast;

Some from a den of crime, and some
Hurrying on to a happy home;
Some bowed down with age and woe,
Praying meekly as they go;
Others — whose friends and honor are gone —
To sleep all night on the pavement stone;
And losing all but shame and pride,
Be found in the morning a suicide.
Rapidly moves the gliding throng —
List the laughter, jest, and song.
   Poverty treads
     On the heels of wealth;
   Loathsome disease
     Near robust health.
   Grief bows down
     Its weary head;
   Crime skulks on
     With a cat-like tread.
Youth and beauty, age and pain —
Vice and virtue form the train —
Misery, happiness, side by side;
Those who had best in childhood died,
   Close to the good — on they go,
   Some to joy, and some to woe,
     Under the lamplight —
     Watch them glide,
On like the waves of a swelling sea,
On, on, on to Eternity.

MARIA J. WESTMORELAND.

MARIA ELIZABETH JOURDAN is the third child and second daughter of Colonel Warren Jourdan and Mary J. Thornton, his wife — all Georgians. Mrs. Jourdan, at the ripe age of fifty-four years, has in preparation a practical " Cookery Book," which will be peculiarly adapted to the wants of young and inexperienced housekeepers.

With Maria Jourdan, music was a passion. Having been so fortunate as to have always enjoyed the tuition of skilful masters, she became a proficient in the art, and, unlike most married ladies, she has never given up her favorite amusement, but devotes much time to familiarizing herself with the various operas.

Miss Jourdan's *alma mater* is the Baptist College located at La Grange — as it is also that of her not less gifted sister, Mrs. Madeline T. Bryan, who writes charmingly, both in prose and verse. A few weeks after the completion of her seventeenth birthday, Maria Jourdan became the wife of Dr. W. F. Westmoreland, of Atlanta, where she resides. During the war, Mrs. Westmoreland composed two very creditable dramas, which were entitled "The Soldier's Wife" and "The Soldier's Trials," and were performed at the Atlanta Athenæum. The proceeds of the plays were donated to the destitute wives and children of those Atlantians who were in the Virginia army.

Mrs. Westmoreland has a talent for essay writing and reviews. Her reviews of Owen Meredith's "Lucille" and Mrs. Browning's "Aurora Leigh" caused many to read those poems who would never have had that pleasure but for the rapturous praise pronounced by her upon these poems. She contributed to "Scott's Monthly" characteristic essays — conversational in style, abounding in humor, wit, and satire — under the signature of "Mystery."

Mrs. Westmoreland has ready for the press a novel, to be published anonymously. She also contemplates publishing her "Essays" in a gala suit of "blue and gold."

Atlanta, 1869.

THE UNATTAINABLE.

That indefinable longing — that hopeless yearning after what we have not — that craving of the human heart which is never satisfied — that irrepressible desire to go forth into the Invisible — to live in the ideal, forgetting and forgotten — to roam from star to star, from system to system, only holding intercourse with the unseen spirits that dwell in this imaginary world! Twelve hours of such existence were worth a whole lifetime tamely spent in eating, drinking, and sleeping! We are taught that reason and judgment are more to be desired and cultivated than all the other mental faculties, while imagination is the least desirable, and, if indulged in, produces a listless inertia, which erects an ideal standard of life, leading us into untold vagaries and idiosyncrasies. But, in the words of Mrs. Browning:

> "If heads
> That hold a rhythmic thought must ache perforce,
> For my part, I choose headaches."

So, if imagination, on this *je ne sais quoi*, can carry us beyond this "vale of tears" — can stop for a moment Ixion's fatal wheel — can make Tantalus, in spite of his thirst, essay his efforts for water — then give us the ideal — let us dwell in the imaginary. First let us consider — what are we born for? A purpose. What do we live for? — vainly pursuing that will-o'-the-wisp, Happiness, which, while we grasp it, glides through our fingers, and is gone. We die — hoping to reach heaven. Since Adam's expulsion from the Garden of Eden, human nature, in every age, in every clime, and under all circumstances, has been the same. Empires have risen and fallen — men tempted and overcome — women flattered and betrayed — martyrs in every cause have perished on the rack and at the stake. And what is the cause of it all? Is it not that uncontrollable desire to "o'erleap our destinies," and penetrate the realms of the unknown? We are undoubtedly born to fill some niche in the great walls of the world; but where that vacancy is, few of us discover until too late, or, having found, still fewer go to work in real earnest to fulfil their allotted destinies. That "life is real, life is earnest," too few of us appreciate; and that we are all rather blindly following some phantom, some ideal of the soul, is too palpably true to be controverted. There is implanted in every human breast, with any aspiration at all, a heart-felt craving that will not be stilled — a something that preys upon our very lives as the vulture upon the vitals of Prometheus. It seeks to go beyond our present life, and fain would pierce the dim shades of futurity, hoping to find in its winding mazes that phantasm which did not reveal itself in the past, and which the present denies.

These phantoms rise up from the shrine of ambition, and every other passion to which mankind are prone. Does it not seem strange, that with all the lights of the past before us, we should so often be deluded? Is it not stranger still that we should trust this *ignis fatuus*, knowing it has lured so many unwary pilgrims to destruction — these spectres, that lead us blindly on, and elude our very grasp when we stretch forth our hands to clasp them? Each individual fancies himself the fortunate one who is to escape disappointment and sorrow — whose bark is to sail upon an unruffled sea, propelled by propitious gales — still hoping to evade the fatal whirlpool, until he is irretrievably lost in its circling eddies. This "Wandering Jew," this restive demon is never at ease. Take the first mentioned of these phantoms — these invisible giants that crush as they bear you onward: Ambition, for example. It is a monster of frightful mien, a fiend incarnate, which sacrifices everything to gain its ends. It heeds not the cries of orphans, nor the prayers of widows. It sheds with wanton hand the blood of the brave, and gazes on the criminal with defiant scorn. It snatches from men their morals, from women their virtue. It turns love into hate — rends asunder family ties — disrupts governments — toils unceasingly on, ever on, and levels everything in its march to victory. Argus-eyed, it watches to add more victims to its list. The night is engrossed with plots which the day shall execute. When, at last — having forfeited honor, principle, friends, name, and everything worth living for — this proud Lucifer reaches the topmost round of the ladder of fame, dragging its weary victims after it, we find, alas! too late, that the dream of our lives, the *Ultima Thule* of our hopes, "like Dead-Sea fruit, turns to ashes on our lips." By ambition, angels fell; and it cannot be expected that poor, frail mortals should win where seraphs failed.

TALKING.

What shall we talk about, then? — and how? Every one has felt the power of words, and been moved to tears or convulsed with laughter by their touching pathos or ready wit. The charm and fascination of talking well refines and polishes men, while it elevates women. How delightful, upon the occasion of a dinner party, to have some one present who can relate an anecdote, repeat a poem, propose an appropriate toast, or sing a song! It is said that at those "club" parties in London, years ago, where the most brilliant wits of the day were wont to assemble to enjoy "a feast of reason and a flow of soul," the participants would study assiduously their speeches for a week before attending, thereby rendering them perfectly sparkling. Of course, then, the ready wit and unexpected puns, etc., would but increase their brilliancy. It is a well-known fact that Sheridan always prepared himself before attending those parties, at which he would meet the most polished wits. The "Noctes Ambrosianæ" of Edinburgh might be re-enacted in more parts of the world than one, if every one would only give a little more attention to these matters.

But the "almighty dollar" is the curse, the Mephistopheles of Americans; and even now I can hear some excessively practical person exclaiming, "What's the use of it?" "What will it pay?" Why, the use of it is to cultivate the agreeable, and make that life which is but a span — a troubled dream at best — pass as pleasantly as possible. If it does not pay you, it will yield a rich harvest to your children. Just think how much more agreeable life would pass, should the whole world wear its "company face" all the time, instead of going about growling and scowling about everything! But, while you must cultivate your conversational powers, do not ignore the fact that the peculiar charm in entertaining lies not so much in talking yourself as in touching upon some favorite topic of the person addressed, and in listening in the most deferential manner. This was Madame Récamier's *forte*. She was very beautiful and attractive, but did not converse nearly so well as many of those brilliant women of Paris during her day; but she possessed sufficient tact to touch the right chord in others, and, with her lovely eyes resting upon their faces, and seemingly drinking in every word as though it had been inspired, she entered into their conversation *con amore*, and left each one under the impression that he was her *beau idéal* of manly perfection. Does not this go far in proof of the doctrine that men love pretty, silly women, who can hand them their slippers and *robe de chambre,* and draw them a cup of tea, ten times more than they do an intellectual woman, who can be a companion for them. It is a melancholy fact that highly cultivated and intellectual women only call into existence a kind of cold admiration from the other sex; and while their hearts are breaking and longing for love and sympathy, they find that it is all bestowed upon some little weak, namby-pamby, dependent creature, who does not nor cannot appreciate it. And thus time flies by on lightning wings, and we stand upon the very brink of eternity before we know that we have lived, or understand the duties and demands of life.

The Countess of Blessington is represented as a great talker, but so sparkling and witty that she always drew around her the most cultivated and polished men. On the contrary, while Madame de Staël is conceded to have been the most gifted female writer who ever lived, in conversation she harangued rather than entertained, until, intellectual as she was, the men would actually fly from her. Her excessive vanity sometimes placed her in very ridiculous positions. Everybody is familiar with the story of herself and Napoleon, when she asked him who was " the greatest woman in France? " and his reply, "She who bears the most children, and gives to France the greatest number of soldiers." Her vanity led her to suppose that the Emperor would say, " Why, Madame de Staël, of course." On another occasion she and Madame Récamier were conversing with Talleyrand ; or, to use his own expression, he was " sitting between *wit* and *beauty*." Madame de Staël propounded the following question : " Monsieur Talleyrand, if Madame Récamier and yourself and myself were taking a little excursion upon the Seine, and the boat were to capsize, which one of us would you attempt to rescue? " Like a genuine Frenchman, he replied : " I should endeavor to rescue both." A little piqued at his reply, Madame de Staël said : " Well, you know you would have some preference ; which one of us would you save? " He replied again : " I should extend a hand to each one." Irritated beyond concealment this time, Madame de Staël said angrily : " Tell me ! which one would you rescue ? You know it would be impossible to save both." True to his French nature, Talleyrand gallantly replied : " You, who know everything, Madame de Staël, should know that also." Thus he extricated himself from his embarrassing position by complimenting (and justly, too) her intellect. This is a specimen of ready wit which is rarely found.

Nothing can more finely portray the power of words than the famous speech of Napoleon to his army, just preceding the battle of the Pyramids, in which he said : " Soldiers ! from those summits forty centuries contemplate your actions ! " Do you suppose they would have been fired with the enthusiasm and patriotism which made them conquering heroes, if he had said : " Boys ! that huge pile of rocks are gazing at you? " Never ! Then, if there be such a charm and fascination in conversing well, let us all ignore that which is vulgar and commonplace, and cultivate to the highest extent the " unruly member."

MISS MARIA LOU EVE.

WHAT this lady has published has attracted attention, and gives promise of future excellence in some work of an extended character. Miss Eve has received several prizes for essays. The prize essay furnished to "Scott's Magazine" in 1866, entitled, "Thoughts about Talking," was very readable.

Miss Eve was born at Woodville, near Augusta, Ga. She has contributed occasionally articles to various Georgia journals, and has two novels in manuscript, which may never delight this generation of readers. Writing, with her, has been an occasional amusement only. Her residence is in Richmond County, Ga.

1869.

SINCERITY IN TALKING.

And *apropos* of the foundations of talking, there is also an old-fashioned idea, now nearly obsolete, *nous avons change tout cela,* that they should rest more or less upon truth as their basis; and despite all theories to the contrary, there is a certain satisfaction in feeling that we may rely implicitly upon the statements that are made to us, especially upon professions of esteem or regard.

We all carry with us into the business transactions of life a certain alloy of skepticism, and receive each statement with a few grains of allowance, not feeling bound to believe that each flimsy fabric will last until we are tired of it, simply because told so by the obliging shopkeeper; but in the social relations of life there are some things that we would like to receive upon faith. If we could only believe all the pleasant things told us by our friends, what a charming world would this be! And when our particular friend, Mrs. Honeydew, tells us she is delighted to see us, have we any right to question her sincerity merely because we happened to overhear her say, "Those tiresome people again?" We had no business to hear what was not intended for us. Why should we go peering behind the scenes, where all is so fair and specious on the outside?

If we should all commence telling the truth at once, what a grand smash-up of the great social machine! What a severing of long-standing friendships — what a sundering of ties! Madam Grundy would hang herself in despair. If I should tell my dear friend, Araminta, that her new bonnet is horrid — simply because she asks me how I like it, and that is my honest opinion — would she ever speak to me again ?   Or would you endure the presence of the man, though he were your best friend, who should tell you that your two-forty nag shuffles in his gait? Alas! which of us would not, like True Thomas, have refused the gift of the "lips that could never lie"?

Yet, let us not linger too long on the wrong side of the embroidery frame, picking flaws in the work, but only see to it that our fingers weave no unworthy figures on the canvas.

What a wonderful thing, after all, is this matter of talking! Words — words! Deeds are as nothing to them. It is said that love requires professions — but friendship demands proofs in the form of actions. But was it by deeds of kindness or devotion that whimsical, prating old Jack Falstaff so endeared himself to the heart of Prince Hal as to call forth that most touching and suggestive tribute, "I could have better spared a better man," upon hearing that his old boon companion was killed? We can better spare the man who has saved our life than the one who makes it pleasant by his society, the pleasant companion who made it worth the saving. Blessed forever be the art of talking; and blessed be the men and women who, by their pleasant, sunshiny talk, keep the heart of this gray-haired old world as fresh as ever it was in its prime. The pleasant talkers, may their shadows never grow less!

MISS KATE C. WAKELEE.

MISS WAKELEE is one of those talented women who have yet to make a literary career. A friend of hers says: "Of all shrinking and modest women, Miss Wakelee is most so." For twelve years she has written constantly, but, mimosa-like, has shrunk from the ordeal of publication. A story from her pen appeared in the "Saturday Evening Post," Philadelphia, and one in the "American Union," Boston. In 1863, the novelette of "India Morgan; or, The Lost Will," was a successful competitor for a prize offered by the "Southern Field and Fireside" newspaper. A novelette entitled, "The Forest City Bride," a tale of life in Savannah and Augusta during the war, furnished to "Scott's Magazine," was a lifelike narrative. Miss Wakelee is very natural indeed in her delineations of life and manners.

Before the war, Miss Wakelee wrote only to please her friends. The following tribute to the brave commander of the ill-fated steamship "Central America," printed in Godey's "Lady Book," December, 1858, was from her pen :

TO THE MEMORY OF CAPTAIN HERNDON.

A song for the brave—let it roll like the sea
  From every red lip that has pillowed a prayer,
From every warm heart gush boundless and free,
  Re-echoed by angels through viewless air,
Wide spreading in beauty, and swelling with might,
From the east to the west, on the wings of the light.

An anthem of praise for the hero who stood,
  Undaunted and firm, in the battle of death—
Below him, deep thund'ring, the boiling flood,
  Above him, in fury, the wild tempest's breath;
No thought of himself, despair, or the grave,
While there was a woman his mercy could save.

A single thought stirred his heart's quivering strings—
  He heard, for a moment, the music of home;
His brain madly reeled, while his straining eyes gazed
  Unblenched on his fate—a swift-speeding doom.
His livid lips set, and his white brow grew pale;
But his hand nobly wrought, his soul did not quail.

Down, down in the depths of the deep he may lie,
  The spot all unmarked to the swift passer o'er,
But his name, like a star, shall be set in the sky,
  And *woman* forever his mem'ry adore:
Bright angels descend to his pillow at even,
There keep watch until Earth shall melt into Heaven.

Like most of our Southern women, Miss Wakelee is comparatively impoverished, and her pen must become a "mighty instrument."

Miss Wakelee was born in Connecticut, a great-granddaughter of Governor Law, of that State; but she has lived so long in Georgia, has so thoroughly identified herself with the interests of that State and the South, that no one ever remembers she was not to the "manor born."

Miss Wakelee is elegantly educated, polished in manners, of a cheerful and sympathizing temperament, making her, as a gentleman remarks, the friend and favorite of everybody. She is charming in conversation, and her manuscript is neat and legible.

Her home is in Richmond County, Georgia—a county that is noted for the intellect of the fair daughters thereof.

  1869.

CARRIE BELL SINCLAIR.

A CHARLESTON journal calls Miss Sinclair "one of the sweetest muses that ever warbled the simple history of a nation's dead." By her many patriotic poems she is best known.

Miss Sinclair has passed nearly all of her life in Georgia, which is her native State, having been born in Milledgeville, the capital of the State. Her father, the Rev. Elijah Sinclair, a Methodist minister, was a native of South Carolina, as was her mother, and had just entered upon his ministerial labors as a member of the Georgia Conference when Carrie was born. The Rev. Mr. Sinclair was of Scotch descent, his mother being a sister of Robert Fulton, the inventor of the first steamboat. He labored faithfully as a minister of the gospel until within a few years of his death, when failing health compelled him to leave the pulpit. At the time of his death, the Rev. Mr. Sinclair was teaching a school for young ladies in Georgetown, S. C. He left his widow and eight daughters — the eldest only married. Carrie Bell was a child at this time, and felt this great sorrow as only one who is possessed of a poetic temperament can feel. Some three years after the death of her father, a younger sister died, and his grave was opened that the child's dust might mingle with his. It was upon this occasion that Carrie Bell penned her first rhymes, telling her childish sorrow in song. Soon after, her mother removed to Augusta, and then she commenced her literary career, writing because she could not resist the spell that lingered around her, and not that she had any desire to venture upon the road to fame. Her first appearance in print was in a weekly literary paper published in Augusta, "The Georgia Gazette," under signature of "Clara."

In 1860, she published a volume of poems in Augusta, of which says a reviewer : "Here and there the poetical element glitters through like the sunlight between fresh green leaves, and shows that she possesses some of the elements necessary for success.

> " 'If the mind with clear conceptions glow,
> The willing words in just expression flow.'

If the *débutante* has not given us a tree capable of sheltering us beneath its branches, she has at least presented us with some modest flowers, which we may gracefully wear on our breasts."

Shortly after the publication of this volume, she went to Savannah to reside, and, although not entirely abandoning the field of letters, yet she felt that new duties claimed her attention, and she could not be content to tread only the flowery fields of poetry and romance while war waged its wild desolation around her; and she turned her attention to the wants of the soldiers, and, when she wielded the pen, it was that she might in some way aid in the cause of her bleeding country, or record the deeds of her brave heroes in song and story. Of one of Miss Sinclair's poems, "The Southern Girl's Homespun Dress," the following remarks were made in "Frank Moore's Anecdotes and Incidents of the War, North and South":

"The accompanying song was taken from a letter of a Southern girl to her lover in Lee's army, which letter was obtained from a mail captured in Sherman's march through Northern Alabama. The materials of which the dress alluded to is made are cotton and wool, and woven on the hand-loom, so commonly seen in the houses at the South. The scrap of a dress, enclosed in the letter as a sample, was of a gray color, with a stripe of crimson and green, quite pretty, and creditable to the lady who made it."

Since the close of the war, Miss Sinclair has been busy with the pen, and has contributed to most of the leading journals of the South and many in the North and West. For over two years she has been a regular contributor to the "Boston Pilot," from which widely circulated journal many of her poems have been copied into English and Irish papers.

The kind welcome extended to Miss Sinclair's first volume of poems served not only to lay the foundation of a literary life, but it has been the stepping-stone to the success that has crowned her later efforts, for had the harsh sentence of the critic fallen upon her earlier productions, a naturally timid and sensitive nature would have shrunk from the ordeal of again facing the public.

A second volume from Miss Sinclair will shortly appear, entitled, "Heart Whispers; or, Echoes of Song." A journal, noticing the advent of this volume, thus alludes to the poems and the poet:

"Miss Sinclair's poems abound with vigor, pathos, and the current of genuine poetic sentiment, united with almost faultless versification, breathing the ardor of true affection, and those deep-thrilling touches of patriotic sentiment that make the tendrils of the warm Southern heart to cling with redoubled fondness around the once happy and prosperous sunny South. What, for instance, could be more touching than the following little incident, which gained her so many commendations and so much silent admiration. Strewing flowers over the graves of the Confederate dead in the cemetery near Augusta, she came upon one with a head-board bearing the simple inscription, 'Unknown.' Then and there she wrote the beautiful poem ('Unknown'). This she framed, wreathed with a chaplet of flowers, and placed on the grave of the unknown defender of the Southern cross."

"UNKNOWN."

Written upon visiting the Graves of the Confederate Dead, in the Cemetery, Augusta, Ga.

I stood beside a little mound,
   Marked by an humble stone,
And read the soldier's epitaph,
   In the one word — " Unknown ! "
Not e'en a name to tell of him
   Who slept so sweetly there —
No name o'er which loved one could bend
   To drop affection's tear.

The only one who sleeps " unknown "
   Among the many brave;
" *Somebody's darling*," though, I know,
   Sleeps in that soldier-grave !
Perchance to some poor mother's heart
   He was the only joy !
Perhaps that mother waited long
   To welcome home her boy !

Perhaps a gentle sister, too,
   Prayed for him night and day,
And watched with anxious heart to greet
   The loved one from the fray;
Or it may be, some maid, whose love
   To him was yet more dear,
Is weeping now with grief for him
   Who sleeps so sweetly here !

Upon each little white slab here
   Is traced some soldier's name,

And proudly do we love to tell
  Their glorious deeds to Fame!
But ah! 't is sad indeed to stand
  Beside this humble stone,
And read *no name* — and know that one
  Is sleeping all "*unknown!*"

To know that there are loving hearts
  Who 'd give their all to-day
To stand beside this grave, where sleeps
  Their soldier-boy in gray!
But 't is enough to know that he
  For our dear country died;
And stranger hands can twine fair flowers
  Above this spot in pride.

Ah! here are many soldier-graves —
  He does not sleep alone!
And though *no name* of him is traced
  Upon this simple stone,
There is a spotless scroll above!
  And on that snowy page
Hath angel-hands for the "*unknown*"
  Recorded name and age!

AUGUSTA, GA., Feb. 2, 1867.

Miss Sinclair has wooed the Muses amid many of the toils and perplexing cares of every-day life, and often the harp has been tuned to song when the soul echoed only to notes of sorrow. With the stern duties of life around us, and all its bitter trials to meet, not even the poet's heart can always be tuned to sweet melody; but the "Psalm of Life" must be sung in sad as well as sweet numbers. But God has willed that the child of *genius* should be the child of sorrow too; for suffering and song go linked hand in hand as twin sisters.

Miss Sinclair is now residing in Philadelphia, (1871.)

1869.

MRS. BETTIE M. ZIMMERMAN.

THE "Southern Illustrated News," published at the capital of the "Confederate States," was an excellent "*war* literary journal," though not much of the "illustrated!" In this paper many excellent articles appeared from writers hitherto unknown to the public, and many writers made their *début* therein. As some one has remarked, "many ladies turned to writing as a refuge from anxiety." Several of the writers of the "News," whose first effusions appeared in its columns, are now "high" on the steps of "fame's ladder," and are not only welcome, but *well-paid* contributors to Northern literary journals.

It was in 1863 that the "News" contained creditable poems by "Mrs. B. M. Z——" and the following year, the "Southern Field and Fireside" (Augusta) published some poems from the same pen.

Mrs. Zimmerman is by birth a North-Carolinian, and daughter of the late Rev. Thomas Meredith, an eminent divine of the Baptist denomination. Some years since she was married to R. P. Zimmerman, of Georgia, since which time she has resided in that State. For several years she made the beautiful city of Augusta her home, but the shadow of death there fell upon her life, clouding its brightness; for in its lovely, peaceful "city of the dead" sleeps her boy, to whom she alludes in the beautiful poems, "Three Years in Heaven" and "Christmas Tears."

During and since the close of the war she has lived in Atlanta — "that monument of a conqueror's wrath," which is now, phœnix-like, rising from the ashes of desolation in renewed youth and beauty.

Mrs. Zimmerman possesses a taste and talent for literature, and writing, with her, has been a pleasing pastime merely, she only lacking the study and application to make a name in the "book of Southern literature."

1869.

CHRISTMAS TEARS.

But one little stocking hangs to-night
　Upon my chimney wall,
Swinging its little, nerveless foot,
　Where the fitful shadows fall.

But one to-night! Seven years gone by,
   Another hung in the light—
Another heart throbbed by my side
   On each happy Christmas-night.

But one little sock for Santa Claus
   To fill with his bright gifts rare—
One pair of hands at early dawn
   Now searching for treasure there!

The mated socks lie folded away,
   And the darling feet are cold;
The little hands, like lily-leaves,
   Lie hid in the grave-yard old.

The radiant eyes, and warm, red lips,
   To dust have mouldered away:
The glad, young heart will greet no more
   The light of a Christmas-day.

Then, is it strange that my heart will turn,
   With its weight of unwept tears,
And yearn with a ceaseless longing
   For the light of by-gone years?

That a shadow comes with the dawning
   Of each happy Christmas-time,
Marring the perfect melody
   Of this age-resounding chime?

Alas! my heart must ever be sad,
   And the blinding tear-drops fall,
When I miss the little stocking
   Once hung on the Christmas-wall.

26

MRS. SALLIE M. MARTIN.

SALLIE M. MARTIN is a native of South Carolina, the first and only child of Elnathan L. and Jane Wallace Davis. Her father died when she was an infant, leaving her to the care of his early bereaved and youthful widow. To the careful and loving training of her mother is due whatever she may accomplish in the future, whether of literary fame, or the successful practising of domestic virtues.

After the death of Mr. Davis, his widow and daughter resided with her grandfather, Rev. William Holmes, a gentleman of means and influence, not only in Fairfield District, his home, but throughout many portions of the State.

"Sallie" was instructed nearly entirely by her mother at home, for it was only at intervals and for short periods at a time that she was sent to school. When she was ten years of age, her grandfather became unfortunate in business, so as to cause an almost entire loss of property, and removed to Georgia, accompanied by Mrs. Davis and her daughter. Having resided in Georgia the larger part of her life, she is as much devoted to her adopted as to her native State.

In 1860, she was affianced to Mr. George W. Martin, a gentleman of talent, connected with the press of Atlanta, and then, for the first time, turned her attention to literature; at his solicitation, publishing short articles in 1861. In 1863, she was married — a youthful bride — for she is very young, and has, we hope, a long and brilliant future before her.

She contributed to various journals of the "Confederacy," over the signature of "Sibyl." Her most ambitious effort was a novelette, entitled, "Lalla De Vere," written in 1864.

Mr. Martin, having been in the Confederate service for three years, was in Selma with the "Chattanooga Rebel," — a daily journal of considerable reputation and ability,— designing to bring out the novelette of "Lalla De Vere" in book-form. His paper, binding, etc., and his person, were captured, and for many weeks his wife was ignorant of his fate. "Lalla De Vere" was published in the "Ladies' Home Gazette," a journal published in Atlanta, (1867.)

As a writer, Mrs. Martin's style is chaste and elegant, never flippant. Her essays are superior to her narratives.

A series of articles, entitled, "The Women of France," composed of sketches of "Madame Roland and the Empress Josephine," "Joan d'Arc and Charlotte Corday," "Héloise and Marie Antoinette," that appeared in "Scott's Magazine," are, we think, the best articles that have appeared from the pen of "Sibyl."

CHARLOTTE CORDAY.

In Charlotte Corday we find none of the religious enthusiasm which supported Joan d'Arc. If she believed in God at all, it was a sentiment wholly separated in her mind from any connection with her earthly mission. She did not feel herself called by any superior power to lay down her life for her country. The mighty power to do so lay in her own individual strength. Think what stern resolve must have gathered day by day in her mind, as she sat with her father in the assembly of the exiled deputies, where, without one thought that her striking beauty was calling forth admiration, she was slowly but surely nerving her heart and hand to strike the blow which should rid France of a tyrannical monster !

So little did she value her life in comparison to the welfare of her country that, after she had sheathed her blade in the cruel and wicked heart of the hideous Marat, rather than lose the opportunity of witnessing with her own eyes the effect this deed would have upon the people for whose good it was executed, she made no attempt whatever to escape, though she might readily have done so. It was a grand, a noble sight, to see a beautiful woman of twenty-five selling her own life that she might take that of an old and loathsome wretch whose race was wellnigh run. There was no fire, no impulse in the cool, deliberate act for which she had calmly made every preparation, as well as for the consequences. There was no battle-cry of "On to victory and glory," to lead her on; but only the "still small voice" within her own heart, of "Liberty to France !" Ah ! little did she dream that her apt reply to the president of the tribunal before which she was tried, would be handed down from one generation to another ! He asked how it was that *her* first blow reached the heart of Marat — if she had been practising beforehand. "Indignation," she calmly said, "had roused my heart, and it showed me the way to his." It was so quietly, so simply expressed, yet spoke such volumes. So absorbed was she in her own patriotic devotion to the cause of liberty, that she was not even aware of the deep and glowing passion which her beauty and valor awakened in the breast of the unfortunate Adam Lux, who deemed no life so sweet as the death which his beloved had suffered, and so prayed that he might but perish as she did, which happiness to him was granted.

The scaffold, the cord, the block, had no terror for the heroic Charlotte. Only her womanly delicacy suffered at the exposure of her person to the vulgar gaze of the crowd. Even when her beautiful head, with its wealth of matchless hair, was severed from the body, the still soul-lit eyes opened and cast a look of indignation upon the ruthless executioner who dared to buffet her now lifeless cheek. Well did she win the name of heroine. Justly is she entitled to rank among the illustrious women of her country.

CLARA LE CLERC.

THIS young lady is favorably known in a limited circle as a "charming writer of prose." She is an Alabamian by birth, although the early years of her childhood were passed in Mississippi. Several months after her ninth birthday, her parents moved to the "Empire State," (Georgia,) and in one of the many pleasant little towns of the noble old State has she ever since resided.

Entering school at the age of eleven, she remained a close student until she graduated, a few days before her eighteenth birthday. During her scholastic life, every spare moment was devoted to her pen, and oftentimes her vacations were passed in *scribbling*.

Her first story was entitled, "Popie Weston." Very few of her writings have ever found their way into print. When she was fifteen years of age, Dabney Jones, the great temperance lecturer, begged a short story, which appeared in "The Temperance Crusader," then edited by Mrs. Mary E. Bryan.

In 1865, she wrote a series of "Reveries" for the "Southern Literary Companion," under the signature of "Harry Holt;" also replies, "Old Maid Reveries," by "Polly Holt." Since that time she has contributed to "Scott's Magazine," "Miss Barber's Weekly," "Child's Delight," and "Burke's Weekly for Boys and Girls." Some of her friends affirm that she possesses the faculty of pleasing children to a greater extent than almost any one of the present day.

Miss Le Clerc has been, as assistant teacher, sheltered beneath the wing of her *alma mater* since her graduation, which *alma mater* is "College Temple," at Newnan, Georgia.

1869.

MRS. BESSIE W. WILLIAMS.

A MONG the Southern writers, there are many who never published a line until the disastrous state of affairs consequent upon the close of the war found them compelled to earn a living; and the pen, a delight in happier and prosperous days, was chosen by many as a means of livelihood. Articles written for the pleasure and amusement of a limited circle now saw light, that otherwise would never have been printed.

Mrs. Bessie W. Williams ("Constance") has not published a great deal, but in what she has published, in "Scott's Magazine" and "The Mobile Sunday Times," we think we see germs of great promise for future excellence. She may be now a "half-fledged birdling, but her wings will soon be sufficiently grown, and she will fly high."

Her real, breathing, moving life has been so full of stirring events, so made up of deepest sorrows and sweetest joys, that not until recently has she felt she could quietly sit down and write her thoughts.

Mrs. Williams is a native of the town of Beaufort, State of South Carolina. She is the daughter of Lieutenant-Colonel Johnson, of "Hampton's Legion," who nobly yielded up his life on the field of the "First Manassas." The three names, Bee, Bartow, Johnson, were among the first which became immortal in the Confederate struggle for independence. Her husband was Henry S. Williams, of Marietta, Georgia, where she now resides. At the youthful age of twenty-one, Mrs. Williams was a widow. If it were possible for her to devote her time to reading and studying, we think, candidly, that as a writer she would take a high place among the literati of our country.

The following extract is from the concluding chapter of "Ciaromski and his Daughter," published in the "Mobile Sunday Times."

1869.

AFTER THE BATTLE.

Oh! what words can describe, what language can depict the horrors of a battle-field? Fearful it is when the booming of the cannon, the clash of arms, the shouts of commanders, the cheering of the men, and the wild neighing of steeds, in a horrible medley, rend the skies; but when these sounds have passed away, when the bloody work is finished, and we are left alone with the dying and the dead — then the human tongue fails, and language is powerless to portray.

On such a scene as this the setting sun now casts his last, lingering rays. The snow-covered plain, which in its spotless purity his early beams had gilded, now lies crimson and reeking with the blood of the slain. The battle is over — the cries of victory have died away in murmuring echoes among the hills; and here, resting from their toils, lie the weary laborers in this bloody field.

All gory and mangled they lie. Some, whose hearts are beating still, though the tide of life is fast ebbing away; and others with the moisture of death upon their brows, his stiffening hand upon their limbs.

Oh, fond mother! here you will find your darling, the pride of your heart, him whom you have borne in your arms and pressed to your bosom. Come, look upon him now! Is this cold, lifeless form, with matted locks and distorted features, your gallant, fair-haired boy?

Loving wife! here too is your husband, the father of your children, the strong arm upon which you leaned, the true heart where you ever found love and sympathy; the lips are cold now — they return not your kiss.

Devoted daughter! come, seek thy father, for he too lies here! See, the gray locks are stained with blood, and the eyes are dim and sightless. Place thy hand upon his heart — it beats no more! Then he is dead, and from thy life hath passed away one of its greatest blessings. Long, long wilt thou mourn the loss of his protecting love — that love which was born in thy birth, and grew with thy growth, unselfish, untiring.

Yes; husbands, sons, fathers, lovers, brothers — all lie upon the red plain, weltering in their blood. My heart grows sick within me as I gaze upon the scene of carnage. O sun! withdraw thy lingering rays; and do thou, O night! envelop with thy sable mantle and shut out from my sight the horrid spectacle!

LOUISE MANHIEM.

(Mrs. Herbert.)

MISS MANHIEM was born in Augusta, Georgia, in 1830. Her mother, whose maiden name was De Pass, was born in France, and emigrated to America when a child. She was a woman of fine endowments, and possessed great strength of character, which she constantly displayed in the judicious training of a large family of children amid the severest struggles of poverty. All of her children are men and women of eminent virtues and genius. Her five daughters are known in their social home-circle as writers: the two elder employ the pen merely as a means of pleasing recreation; the three younger have made it a means of pecuniary benefit. Their two brothers, the Hon. Judge S. and Elcan Heydenfeldt, are men whose eminence is too well known to the world to require notice from us otherwise than as the talented brothers of five gifted sisters.

The father of the three younger daughters (their mother having married the second time) was of Scotch and Irish descent; and though far more proud of his American birth, he often asserted with chivalric pride that the "blood of the Bruces" flowed in his veins. He was a man of quick, nervous temperament, and, though not having leisure to enter into "authorship," genius often rose superior, and the "poet" triumphed over the laborer. He died in his forty-fifth year. His talents were transmitted to his eldest child, Louise Manhiem, the subject of this sketch.

Miss Manhiem became Mrs. Herbert in 1853, but her husband dying immediately after his marriage, (three days,) she sought consolation in her studies. A few years after, she accompanied her brother to Europe, where he wished to educate his children, and where she remained for two years, visiting the principal cities of the Old World.

Mrs. Herbert is now in California, and urges in her pleasant, forcible letters emigration to that "grand and splendid country." Although separated by oceans, we hope and expect many pungent and pleasing articles will cross the Atlantic to brighten and gladden our firesides.

Mrs. Herbert possesses a lively, genial disposition, is a fluent talker, and fond of cheerful company, preferring the more congenial mind of learned men to the more versatile and light companionship of her own sex. Under all circumstances, she is an agreeable companion.

In person, she is of medium height, well formed, and peculiarly graceful. She has a little spice of temper, (as, by-the-by, all the sisters have, but one;) but she possesses a noble nature and kind heart, which we hope will beat long enough to add much to the general happiness and the wisdom of mankind.

Mrs. Herbert has never published a volume, her contributions being to the magazines and literary journals of the day. She is a splendid French scholar, translating that language with ease and fine diction.

1869.   R. J.

ON DRESS.

Finished at last — sealed, directed, post-stamped! Very well — tie on your bonnet — fling on your shawl. Oh, never mind! don't stop to coax on those tedious gloves, pray! You have a long way to go, and you can put them on as you walk along. You are not the Countess of Blessington, you know; and now you have no tedious brothers to preach and tyrannize.

It is true that the race of slovenly blue-stockings is fast dying out, and I, for one, certainly do admire to see a woman who "goes in thoroughly for dress." Not, indeed, the order of painted popinjays or peacock tribe, who, bedecked in all the ornament for which she can find space, and brilliant in every coloring of the rainbow, spends her time in strutting from one mirror to another, admiring the effect of its charming *tout ensemble* — keeping the white hands constantly busy brushing off specks, arranging a stray ringlet or rebellious lock, (sometimes too with the *pomatum* which happens to be most handy, and not particularly odorous or perfumed should the digestion be impaired or the dentist's rooms unfrequented,) pulling out a puffing, a crumpled frill, a tumbled flounce, a creased ribbon, a crushed collarette or undersleeve; re-fastening a brooch, re-adjusting a bracelet, or re-arranging belt or buckle:— one of those "*gentle* creatures," who, upon an accident in the crowded street, where her trailing skirts are out of place and out of taste, deserving any amount of ill luck — if not ill treatment — from some awkward boot or spur, cannot forbear an expression of peevish regret, or a flash of malignant anger from beneath the "fringed lashes" at the miserable, luckless offender. No! not one of these worshippers at the feet of fashion, but one of those majestic and queenly or graceful and delicate creatures whom you involuntarily turn to look upon again — those who, once robed with due regard to delicacy of texture, to harmonious blendings of color, and an exquisite adaptation of form and propriety of contrast — above all, the suitableness of the color and costume to the peculiar style of personal adornment — never think again of their dress except as a common accessory to their general appearance, which, being persons of intelligence and refinement generally, they are too highly bred to allow a spectator to perceive occupies them unduly. Supposed to be wealthy, they are all the more assiduous, when not so in reality, to suppress all those little demonstrations that might give rise to the suspicion of an excess of personal vanity, or the presumption that the coarser and more material features of existence occupy the greater part of their time or concern. And nothing is more grateful to the feelings, nor more delightful to the eye, even to a woman — and how much more must it be to a man! than to witness, upon many of those little, and sometimes annoying and irremediable misfortunes to the *toilette* of a lady that are so frequent upon the street or in the crowded " party-room " — what is more admirable and soothing than to notice the gracious bend, the charming deprecatory shake of the gracefully set head, protesting against your self-reproach and excuses — the brilliant bit of jest, if proximity permit, in the sweet and gentle smile that assures you, better than words, that " it is not of the least consequence, and can be easily remedied! " I can fancy such a woman exciting a tender reverence, and being the one any man would feel " delighted to honor " — or a woman either.

Yes; I am much inclined to say, with the vast majority, such important and ferocious personages as *Dr. Johnson, Dean Swift, Christina of Sweden, and Lady Mary Wortley,* notwithstanding — "*Vive la mode!*" but I might add, with double enthusiasm, "*Vive le bon gout!*" The world would, indeed, be an ugly place, if *all* the women wore tumbled or limp skirts, soiled collars pinned awry, shoes unlaced, and fingers stained with ink; for, in this age of educational advancement, two-thirds at least of our charming, clever women may very justly lay claim to "blue-stockingism," or the more attractive title of *littérateur.* Or it would be a very monotonous world if *every* face, oval, or round, or long — if *all* brows, high or low, prominent or receding, square or round, massive or delicate — were adorned with hair worn in long, rich ringlets, like *Madame Roland,* or short, charming *frieze,* like pretty *Nell Gwynn,* or *à l'Impératrice* or *à la Grec* — very carelessly done too; the end trailing behind, no matter whether the neck upon which it rests be wrinkled and yellow and freckled, or whether it be *à la Eugenie* or *à Marie Antoinette,* the loveliest necks ever possessed by mortal woman, except, perhaps, poor *Anne Boleyn* — the two last food for the axe! Alas! what may yet be the fate of the third?

There is one singular fact, however, with regard to careless women, which, being paradoxical, will have its objectors, I know, but which long experience and close observation has taught me is correct beyond a doubt, or with few exceptions. It is this: that many of those women who are the most seemingly indifferent to personal appearance, are the very ones whom

27

attention to the rules and taste in the arrangement of costume would vastly improve, and who, after all, are the most inordinately vain of all women!

I have said above, the order of slovenly "blue stockings" had become almost extinct. There is, however, a remnant of the school who act upon a new principle. I suppose it used to be that carelessness saved time, and dirt, trouble. Ablution has certainly become a universal and imperative necessity of the age. But carelessness is now viewed from a new stand-point by the disciples of the reformed school. They have taken their cue from such poetical licenses as "Beauty unadorned is adorned the most!" "Sweet simplicity!" "Charming negligence!" "Delightful indifference to personal appearance!" "Entrancing abandon!" and the like hackneyed hyperboles.

And the phrases are well enough after all, time, place, and circumstances corresponding or considered. The careless simplicity — even the extreme approach to negligence and abandon, or recklessness, and rebellion against all accepted rules of propriety in costume, pose, and style that certainly became the "fairest *Adelaide*" — gave a bewitching air of *espièglerie* to that loveliest hoyden, *Laura* — or that enhanced the divine grace of the proud, silent, beautiful *Myra* — heightened the dazzling attractions of the brilliant and haughty *Semiramis*, or the daring, passionate, bewilderingly entrancing *Cleopatra*, are all well enough. *These* trespassers may carry it off grandly triumphant in the very face of rules of art or propriety, but woe to the miserable, mistaken mediocrity, personal or mental, that ventures to follow where these daring, self-confident guerillas and pioneers undertake to lead!

It *is* a pity their imitators could not "see themselves," etc., etc. And yet, there are moments when verily, in spite of their intense silliness, I could not help but pity their discomfiture and crushing disappointment.

I once knew a beauty who used to take half an hour extra at her *toilette* to arrange a curl upon her forehead so as to give it the appearance of accident. Chance did first reveal to her keen, artistic perceptions that it enhanced her charms. Her lover admired it, too; and she availed herself of the hint. She was much complimented upon the "*sweet*" pet straggler, and it received all sorts of caresses and encouragements from every slender hand that dared the familiar approach to that queenly brow; and when, with an enchanting little *moue* of impatience, and a still more enchanting blush and smile, accompanying an *espiègle* glance at me, who was in the secret, she would attempt to push back the intruding lock, she was immediately besieged with intercessions to permit the pretty trespasser to remain.

It came about, then, that shortly after that, when spending some weeks at a gay country-place, I chanced to be cognizant — unwillingly — of an attempt to imitate this illustrious "renegade curl," on the part of one of these *indifferents* — these lovers of "interesting simplicity," who "did n't care the least in the world *how* they looked!" and whose broad, majestic brow and quiet face, that was almost plain in its grave repose, and which *did* look far more interesting, and decidedly more soft and feminine, crowned by her smooth, glossy wealth of braids, than in artificially tumbled locks.

It followed naturally enough, then, that the poor thing was most desperately, but unconsciously teased by her artless companions' constant attempts to force the deserter back to his proper quarters, and fasten it all the more securely for fear of new attempts at insubordination, for "Hermine looks hideous with that strand always in her eyes. How on earth came your hair so uneven, Hermine?" "To make that set for your sister Claudia?" "But you should have taken it from the back hair, dear!" They were also lavish in their condolences concerning the "stiff" quality of the little "twist," or, as the more irreverent termed it, "pig-tail," and positive in their assurances that it would become pliable as soon as it "grew out" again. I pitied the poor girl's flushes of impatience and pallors of suppressed anger, annoyance, and disappointment, though sometimes the by-play was comic enough. But the innocent gravity of my face then and there was a *chef-d'œuvre* of self-restraint — a fitting and commendable holocaust to — charity!

————oo:o:oo——

MRS. REBECCA JACOBUS

WAS born at Cambridge, S. C., February 22, 1832. She is younger sister of Louise Manhiem. During her infancy, her parents removed to Augusta, Ga., where they remained until she reached her eleventh year, when her father, dissatisfied with his vocation, and craving that sphere of life which his poetic imagination pictured in the wilds of Florida, emigrated to that lovely land. The versatile beauty, sombre gloom, and grandeur of its scenery, awoke the talent of his second daughter, and threw into her after-life an impassioned love of solitude and nature.

Mrs. Jacobus was educated by her eldest brother, Judge Heydenfeldt, and graduated at the principal seminary in Montgomery, Ala., with credit.

She married, in 1852, J. Julien Jacobus, a good and talented man, who, contrary to the general rule, was proud of his young wife's literary ability, and who now and then took pleasure in inditing poems complimentary to her genius. The reverent affection with which he regarded her to the end of his short life is the noblest panegyric we can offer her in the character of wife and mother — the hearth of home being the truest means by which to test the higher attributes of a good and gifted woman. In her home circle, her virtues shine pre-eminent, and sanctify the genius which they adorn. Death, however, soon entered this happy home, and gathered two lovely children to his breast, casting a deep gloom over the young mother's life, which a few years later was deepened by the death of her husband, who fell while defending his home and his country on the bloody plain of Shiloh. Death claimed few nobler victims than this young and talented man, who had already given bright promise of future pre-eminence in his profession as a member of the Georgia bar.

The deep devotion which Mrs. Jacobus pays to the education of her three promising children elicits our especial admiration. She is a woman of medium height, is slight and well formed, has regular features; she is habitually pale, and her face wears a thoughtful expression when in repose; her manner is quiet and retiring, and there is an atmosphere of marked refinement pervading her every movement.

Mrs. Jacobus is a Jewess by birth, (as are all the five sisters,) and, with that native pride so inherent in the Hebrew people, she brings up her children in accordance with the Jewish faith. (Her father was a Presbyterian.)

Mrs. Jacobus is still young, and though her life has been early clouded with sorrow, we hope she will yet emerge from her voluntary seclusion, and we confidently expect much that is good, true, and beautiful from her pen.

Her home is in Augusta, and she promises a book to the world at a not distant day.

1869.

MRS. MARY A. McCRIMMON.

MRS. McCRIMMON has done much for Southern letters; has been editress of several literary journals; in 1859, edited the "Children's Department," in the "Georgia Temperance Crusader," and during the war, edited an "Educational Monthly" at Lumpkin, Georgia, her then residence. She was also among the prominent contributors to the "Southern Illustrated News," her sketches and poems being much admired by the readers of that journal, which had an extensive circulation in camp as well as at the firesides of the readers of the "Southern Confederacy."

Since the close of the war, Mrs. McCrimmon, we are informed, has married a Mr. Dawson, and removed to Arkansas.

As one of the constant "workers in the mine of literature," we could not well omit the name of this lady, although obliged to furnish such an incomplete notice as this.

———————

FLORIDA.

Land of beauty — blooming ever
  In the golden summer sun;
Land of perfume — blighted never
  By the borean blast; where one
Unfading, dreamy spring-time still
Lies like a veil on plain and hill.

Soft the shadows slowly creeping
  Through thy dim and spectral pines;
Pure thy lakelets, calmly sleeping,
  Save a few light, rippling lines,
When the white water-lilies move,
And fairies chant their early love.

Far in ether, stars above thee
  Ever beam with purest light;
Birds of richest music love thee;
  Flowers than Eden's hues more bright;
And love — young love, so fresh and fair,
Fills with his breath thy gentle air.

Oh, land of beauty — clime of flowers —
  Scenes of precious memory!
Thine are the happy "by-gone hours"
  Which made all of life to me;
When every moment was, in joy, an age —
A volume concentrated in a page.

But, land of beauty, blooming ever
  'Neath the fairest summer-sky,
I may see thee more — ah! never--
  Never hear thy soft wind's sigh;
Yet in my heart thou evermore must dwell;
Then land — dear land of beauty, fare thee well!

    1860.

MRS. AGNES JEAN STIBBES.

RUTH FAIRFAX, a favorite contributor of novelettes, poems, and sketches to Father Ryan's paper, the "Banner of the South," published in Augusta, is known by a few friends to be Mrs. Stibbes, at the present time residing in Savannah. Mrs. Stibbes was born in South Carolina. She commenced writing for publication when about sixteen years of age, and was married at seventeen years to a gentleman of Georgia.

Until the late war, her life was one bright scene; but; in common with her Southern sisters, all of her property was swept away, her home desolated, and wanting the "necessaries of life," she wrote the first chapters of the " Earls of Sutherland " (afterward published in the "Banner of the South ") to pass away in pleasant thoughts the hours that were otherwise so frightfully real. During the war, she contributed novelettes and sketches to the "Field and Fireside," under the *nom de plume* of " Emma Carra."

REV. A. J. RYAN,

THE GOLDEN-TONGUED ORATOR.

I have seen him, the poet, priest, and scholar! I have seen him — yea, and not only sat with hundreds of others listening to the holy words of love that fell from his lips, not only made one of many to whom his words were addressed, but I have listened to words of kindness and admonition, addressed to *me alone;* and this is not all. I have clasped his hand, gazed into the unfathomable depths of those clear blue eyes, seeing there a blending of the tenderest pity and almost superhuman love with the shadow of a deep sorrow.

The majesty of his holy office loses nought of its mysterious grandeur when explained by his lips. As he cries, "Ours is the royal priesthood!" behold that radiant smile! It illumines his pale face as does a sunbeam the pure and graceful lily, and the glorious thoughts, fresh from his soul, breathe sweet incense to our hearts! Would that mine were the privilege of daily kneeling at his feet, and, while his hand rests on my bowed head, have him invoke God's blessing upon me.

I listened lingeringly to the last words that fell from his lips, treasuring them up in my heart, and then turned away, grieving that I could see him, hear him no longer; and yet I bore away with me, fresh from his lips, a fervent "God bless you!" that has hovered round me like a halo of glory, brightening my pathway through the weary world.

.   .   .   .

The earth has seemed greener, the sky bluer, the sun brighter since my interview with him; and still, in imagination, I can see his delicate pale face, the beautiful brown, waving hair, and glowing, soul-lit eyes — eyes that look down into one's heart, seeking the real feelings of the soul — eyes that tell of holy thought, of tender love for all mankind — eyes that speak of a strong soul struggling with the frail tenement of clay, beating her wings, longing to be free!

.   .   .   .

I can even now see him before me, as he stood then, his hands clasped, his head thrown back, and a smile of rare beauty brightening his pure face as he exclaimed, with a ring of holy exultation in his voice; "And upon this rock will I build my Church, and the gates of hell shall *never* prevail against it."

This is no fancy-sketch, but a bright reality, and yet I have not done justice to him of whom I speak.

MISS FANNY ANDREWS.

(*Elzey Hay.*)

THIS record of " Southern Writers" would be incomplete without mention of a young lady, the daughter of an able legal gentleman of Washington, Georgia, and herself born and educated in the State, who has, since the close of the war, been a frequent contributor to the periodical literature of the country, under the pseudonym of " Elzey Hay."

Until recently, " Elzey Hay " was " Elzey Hay " merely.

Miss Andrews believes that " the great beauty of anonymous writing is to protect one against bores and the other annoyances of a small reputation, till one can claim the advantages of a great one."

Her identity was published to the world without her knowledge, and she feels diffident in appearing among " Southern Writers " with that mask which separated her from the public thrown aside.

As she expresses the matter in a recent article, we prefer to use her words :

"Under all circumstances, it is wisest to feel one's ground first, before advancing boldly upon it, and for a timid or reserved person there is nothing like a pseudonym, which throws a veil over one's identity, and stands like a tower of defence to shield one's private life from the invasions of public curiosity. If by the public were meant merely that vague assembly of individuals which makes up the world at large, one would care very little about it, save in so far as one's interest was concerned in pleasing its taste; but each one of us has a little world of his own, bounded by the circle of his personal acquaintance, and it is the criticism of this public that literary novices dread. Within this circle there is always some one individual who, to young female writers in particular, is the embodiment of public opinion. One could not write a line without wondering what this person would think of it, if the blessed anonymous did not come to one's aid. Safe behind this shield the most timid writer may express himself with boldness and independence."

From my first acquaintance with the articles of " Elzey Hay," I felt the identity of such a sparkling, piquant writer could not long remain concealed.

Sometimes I am almost tempted to call her the "Southern Fanny Fern," but "Elzey" is a woman, and "Fanny" a bloomer, perhaps! Both excel in a peculiar style—so bright, witty, caustic; but the wit of "Elzey Hay" is as keen as a Damascus blade and as polished. Fanny Fern's wit reminds one of a dull, spiteful, little penknife. The former "holds the mirror up to nature;" the latter caricatures it. The one laughs merrily and good-naturedly at the faults and follies of mankind; the other sneers at them. "Elzey Hay" is a great favorite with her own sex; Fanny Fern is not. In one, we recognize the champion of *the* sex, in the other a "Woman's Rights lecturer." But both are a terror to the "lords of creation." They deal stinging blows to domestic tyrants, would-be exquisites, and pretence generally; the small weaknesses and foibles of the "lords of creation" are not dealt with tenderly. Satire is a powerful weapon in cutting off the excrescences of society. Juvenal and Pope and Thackeray effected some good in their day. So will "Elzey Hay."

"Elzey Hay" has been a frequent contributor to Godey's "Lady's Book," and "Scott's Magazine," (Atlanta.) "Dress under Difficulties," a paper concerning the "fashions in Dixie during the war," which appeared in Godey's "Lady's Book," for July, 1866, is "Elzey Hay's" most widely read article.

Her first *début* as a writer was in the "New York World," shortly after the close of the war, in an article entitled "A Romance of Robbery," exposing some infamous proceedings of the Bureauites at a village in Georgia. She assumed the character of a Federal officer in this instance. She has also been correspondent for other New York papers under "masculine signatures." We venture to predict that, if she lives, Miss Andrews will be widely known, and "sparkling Elzey Hay" be as familiar as a household word in the homes of our land.

Her home is in the charming town of Washington, where Miss Andrews is one of the attractions, entertaining with her delightful conversations, for she converses as well as she writes.

28

A PLEA FOR RED HAIR.

BY A RED-HAIRED WOMAN.

There has always existed an unconquerable, and it seems to me unreasonable prejudice against red hair among the nations of Northern Europe and America. In vain do physiognomists, phrenologists, physiologists, or any other *ologists*, declare that the pure old Saxon family, distinguished by red heads and freckled faces, is highest in the scale of human existence, being farthest removed from the woolly heads and black faces of the African or lowest race; the world positively refuses to admire red heads and freckled faces, or to regard them as marks of either physical or intellectual superiority. In vain are nymphs, fairies, angels, and the good little children in Sunday-school books, always pictured with sunny tresses; the world is so perverse that it scorns in real life what it pronounces enchanting in books and pictures. Now this inconsistency is the main cause of quarrel that we red-heads have against the rest of the world. Little does it advantage us that our hair is thought bewitching on the angels in picture-books, while it is sneered at on our own heads in drawing-rooms. Willingly would we resign the ideal glories of sylphs and angels to our dark-haired sisters, if we could in return share some of the substantial glories they enjoy in real life. The world is too inconsistent: while our *crowning* feature seems to be acknowledged as the highest type of ideal beauty, it is at the same time regarded as a trait of positive ugliness in real life. No painter ever made a black-haired angel. Men's ideas of celestial beauty seem to be inseparable from the sunny ringlets that dance round azure eyes like golden clouds floating over the blue canopy of heaven. I challenge any of my readers to name a single poet or painter who has ventured to represent angel or glorified spirit with black hair. Even the pictures and images of our Saviour — with reverence I speak it — are generally represented with some shade of yellow hair, and surely all that relates to Him must come up to our highest ideas of perfect loveliness. If red hair were really such a bad thing, why should the inhabitants of heaven be always painted with it? Who would think of representing even the lowest of the angels with a red nose? And yet in real life red heads meet with little more favor than red noses.

Poets are as friendly to red hair as painters. Milton describes his Adam and Eve —

> " The loveliest pair
> That ever since in love's embraces met;
> Adam, the godliest man of men since born
> His sons; the fairest of her daughters, Eve " —

both as red-haired.

"His fair large front, and eyes sublime, declared
    Absolute rule; and *hyacinthine locks*
    Round from his parted forelock manly hung
    Clustering, but not beneath his shoulders broad;
    She, as a veil, down to the slender waist
    Her unadorned golden tresses wore."

Milton's admirers will doubtless be shocked at the idea of a red-headed Adam and Eve, and consider the accusation a slander on the poet; but substitute the epithet auburn, golden, or *hyacinthine*, and nobody's taste is offended. Poets always take care to observe this nice distinction, and their readers are satisfied, few ever stopping to consider that *auburn* is only a polite name for one kind of very red hair. The difference is simply this: what is golden or auburn hair on a pretty woman, is blazing red on an ugly one; and people are apt to like or dislike it, according as they see it connected with pretty faces or plain ones. After gazing at a portrait of the beautiful Queen of Scots, one is enraptured with auburn ringlets; after beholding a picture of her ill-favored rival, Elizabeth, one is equally out of humor with *carroty hair*. The force of prejudice in this matter is strikingly illustrated in the case of two sisters — the one very pretty, the other very plain, who once spent some time in the house where I was boarding. Though the hair of both was precisely the same color, that of the younger, or handsome one, was always called *auburn*, the other *red*. A lady one day had the kindness — some people are very fond of making such pleasant little remarks — to tell the ugly one that her hair was not near so pretty a color as that of her sister. The person addressed made no reply; but, when the polite lady had departed, told me that she was wearing frizettes made of her pretty sister's curls, which had been cut off during an attack of fever.

On first thoughts, it may seem strange that red hair is nowhere held in such contempt as among those races of whom it is most characteristic; but this results from the general disposition of mankind to depreciate what they have, and overrate what they do not possess. In France, Spain, Italy, all the nations of Southern Europe, nothing is so much admired as the most fiery red hair — called by a more poetical name, of course; while a dark-browed Mexican, whose stiff, wiry locks bear greater resemblance to the tail of a black horse than anything else in nature, will all but fall down and worship the beauty of any happy possessor of sunflower tresses. "Coma Bella, Coma Blanca," are the pleasing sounds which greet the ear of a red-headed woman on landing in Mexico, as she finds herself surrounded by an admiring group of natives; doubly pleasing by contrast to the less flattering remarks which she has been accustomed to hear from Americans or Englishmen. Châteaubriand seems to have found it impossible to reconcile his ideas of the beautiful and poetical with the presence of sable tresses, for he describes the hair of his Indian heroine, Atala, as a *golden* cloud floating before the eyes of her lover!

If poets and painters are the friends of red hair, novelists are its mortal foes. It is the business of these latter to make the ideal approach the real, and their highest excellence consists in making the one so like the other that one can scarcely tell them apart. They take advantage of the prevailing prejudice against red hair to paint their worst characters with it. Tittlebat Titmouse and Uriah Heep are a perpetual slander upon red-headed people. The character usually ascribed to these last, and with much truth, is entirely out of keeping with that ascribed by the great romancers to their villains. Red-haired people are generally high-tempered, impulsive, warmhearted; and, though it may not become a red-headed woman to say so, I do not think I have ever known one to be either a fool or a coward. Such characteristics are entirely at variance with the low, sneaking craftiness of Uriah, or the sottish imbecility of Titmouse. It always seemed to me that the latter ought to have been drawn with a certain pale, sickly shade of sandy hair, which looks as if it might once have been red, but had got faded, like a piece of bad calico, from constant using. Uriah, on the other hand, should have stiff, straight, puritanical locks, with a dark, sallow complexion, and green eyes. There are some people who look as if they had lain in the grave until they had become mouldy, and then risen to wander about the world without ever getting dry or warm again. Uriah Heep belongs to this class, and should have nothing about him so warm and bright as a sunny head.

One reason for the common dislike of red hair may be found in the fact that it is often accompanied by a red or freckled face, neither of which is exactly consistent with our ideas of the most refined and delicate beauty. But is it not unfair to lay the faults of the face and complexion upon the hair? Nobody objects to black hair because it sometimes accompanies a dark, muddy complexion; and, upon the whole, I think brunettes oftener have bad complexions than blondes. After all, there are as many pretty faces framed in gold as in jet. There are three golden threads from the head of Lucretia Borgia preserved in the British Museum on account of their rare beauty. It is said that Cleopatra had red hair; the beautiful Mary of Scotland certainly had it, and the present Empress of France is crowned with something which is cousin-german to it; and this seems to be the secret of the present triumph of blondes. Whenever a reigning beauty happens to be crowned with the obnoxious color, prejudice dies out for a time, and light hair becomes the fashion, as at present. Brunettes are in despair, and red-headed women have their revenge. *Modes* are invented, such as frizzing and crimping, which do not at all become raven tresses, but render golden locks bewitching. There are started all manner of devices for giving dark hair a golden tinge. Gilt and silver powders are used without stint, while some devoted worshippers of fashion submit to the ordeal of lying with their hair in dye for thirty-six hours, and then run the risk of making it blue, green, or purple, as did their worthy prototype, Tittlebat

Titmouse, in his famous attempt at the reverse and more common operation.

But these wayward freaks of fashion never last long. So soon as the
belle, whose beauty in spite of red hair cheated people into the belief that
she was beautiful because of it, becomes *passé*, or out of fashion, and some
sable-tressed rival succeeds to her triumphs, the old prejudice revives. The
pretty names of auburn, golden, sunny are dropped, and red hair falls into
such disrepute that any charity schoolboy will fly to arms if the odious epithet is applied to his pate. Men and women are unconscious of the power
there is in a pretty face; they are influenced by it involuntarily. Many an
ugly fashion gains ground just because pretty women will look so pretty in
spite of it, that others are deluded into the belief that the fashion is itself
graceful and becoming. Thus it is with red hair; some of the reigning
belles of Europe having been supplied with it by nature, and making a
virtue of necessity, have brought it in fashion. Let the rest of us make the
most of the triumph they have won, and pray that a dark-haired empress
may not ascend the throne of France till we are too gray to care what our
hair was in the beginning. The ascendency we enjoy at present cannot
endure forever, that is certain; for though the world may submit to the dic-
tates of fashion for a season, she has a spite against red hair at the bottom,
and will make war on it to the end of time. When eternity begins, as it
seems pretty generally conceded that angels have — well, I won't offend the
reader by saying *red* hair, but certainly something very like it, if poets and
painters are to be credited — it is to be hoped that our triumph may then
prove more lasting.

PAPER-COLLAR GENTILITY.

"Ward's patent reversible, perspiration-proof paper collar, warranted, by
the chemicals used in its composition, to equal in polish the finest linen finish, and to rival in durability the best," etc., etc.

What a commentary on the age in which we live! What a catalogue of
shams and vulgarities! "Fine linen finish," a sham upon raw material;
"reversible," a slander on personal neatness; "perspiration-proof," an in-
sult to friendly soap and water, the only honest means that nature has provided for making a man thoroughly "perspiration-proof." The present has
often been called an age of shams, and who can question the justice of the
accusation, when we see a "patent, reversible," many-sided sham, boldly
asserting itself as such, and obtaining public favor through the very hollow-
ness of its pretensions?

Considered merely in themselves, without reference to their usual accom-
paniments, paper collars are comparatively small affairs, scarcely worth singling

out for special reprehension, from among the greater shams to which the age is addicted, but they are significant of much beyond themselves. They are the outward and visible signs of an inward and by no means *spirituelle* state of things, which is not *chic*, as the Parisians say. They are suggestive of a small shopkeeper, second-rate boarding-house state of society, where frowsy young ladies in pink ribbons sing sickly ballads to amorous dry-goods clerks, and ogle, at the sentimental parts, some slender swain in shining paper collar and soiled kid-gloves. They are suggestive of plated forks and printed cards of invitation; of bad cigars and cheap perfumery; of suspiciously large and showy brooches, stuck into not always the most immaculate of shirt-bosoms; — and worse than all, they are suggestive of a mind to save washing-bills; of a desire to keep up the "outward and visible signs" of decency without the "inward and spiritual grace;" of a whited-sepulchre style of toilet, content to be all rottenness and corruption within, if it is beautiful enough without; of a class of men who can stay three weeks from home on a box of paper collars. Think of a man's going to spend Christmas at a country house, with his baggage in his pocket; think of his deliberately turning the soiled side of a "patent reversible *perspiration-proof*" in toward his skin; what liberties may we not suspect him of taking with the invisible and unmentionable parts of his toilet? Imagination shrinks from exploring farther the recesses of such a whited sepulchre.

Paper collars are typical of a class of men, as well as a state of society. A cast-off "patent reversible perspiration-proof" gives as clear an insight into the habits and manners of the wearer, as the comparative anatomist can obtain from a tooth or a bone of any other animal. The individual distinguished by the "Professor at the Breakfast Table" as the *Kohinoor* is a perfect specimen of the paper-collar class, and I am as well satisfied that he wore a "patent reversible perspiration-proof," enamelled and embossed on both sides, as if the "Professor" had taken special care to inform us of the fact. The man of thorough paper-collar breeding is essentially one of the "fellers." He always has very sleek, greasy hair, carefully curled, and perfumed with cinnamon or bergamot, and is much addicted to light kid-gloves, always a little soiled. He wears a huge seal ring on his little finger, (his nails are never clean,) and a miraculous brooch, with perhaps studs to match, in his shirt-bosom. From his vest-pocket dangles a bulky chain, with a quantity of big seals, secret-society badges, etc., at one end, and possibly, a watch at the other. His coat and pants are in the latest fashion, his boots are glossy as a mirror, but who shall dare to say what is under them?

His habits vary slightly in different localities, but not enough to destroy the unity of the species. North of the Potomac, he talks through his nose, and says, "I calc'late;" farther South, he drawls his vowels, puts his knife into his mouth when he eats, and tries to talk literary on magazine stories and Miss Evans's novels. As to business pursuits, the Northern type of the *genus paper-collaris* is usually a merchant's clerk, or a small tradesman in the dry-goods line; the Southern, a country beau, who puts on a clean shirt every Sunday, to go "sparking" among the girls. The species is chiefly indigenous to large commercial towns, and always flourishes best where laundresses' fees are highest. It is very widely diffused, however, and exists, with slight variations, under all vicissitudes of civilization and nationality, and individuals may readily be detected, even when the most prominent mark of the species is wanting. Circumstances may have placed certain individuals beyond the reach of paper-collar influences, but they have paper-collar souls, all the same as though they carried the outward badge of the species round their necks.

There is a class below, as well as one above, paper collars — an honest, humble, hard-working class, in homespun shirts, without collars — a class perfectly free from vulgarity because perfectly free from pretension. The two extremes of society are, perhaps, the only classes entirely free from vulgarity, in the proper acceptation of the word. The one, because it pretends to nothing which it is not; the other, because it pretends to nothing at all. In Europe the peasantry are treated with more familiarity by the aristocracy than the *bourgeoisie;* and of all the lower strata of American society, the least vulgar, because the least assuming, are, or rather *were,* the negroes of the South. The ignorance and simplicity of these people kept them below pretension, and therefore above vulgarity. The idea of a respectable old "Uncle," as old "Uncles" were once, in a paper collar, is as preposterous as the thought of General Lee or Wade Hampton in the same guise. Extremes often meet, and in many respects the lowest stratum of society is less removed from the highest than are the intermediate, or paper-collar classes. The only difference between the homespun-shirt man and the paper-collar man is the difference between a good piece of stout brown wrapping-paper and the bill of a broken bank. The one is good for all it pretends to; the other is good for nothing at all.

——oo⦙⊕⦙o-o——

MARIA J. McINTOSH.

MARIA J. McINTOSH was born in 1803, at Sunbury, Liberty County, Georgia. Sunbury is forty miles south of Savannah, on the sea-coast of Georgia. In a reminiscence of this spot, Miss McIntosh thus records her impressions:

"Sunbury was beautifully situated, about five miles from the ocean, on a bold frith or arm of the sea, stretching up between St. Catharine's Island on the one side and the main land on the other — forming apparently the horns of a crescent, at the base of which the town stood. It was a beautiful spot, carpeted with the short-leaved Bermuda grass, and shaded with oak, cedar, locust, and a flowering tree, the Pride of India. It was then the summer resort of all of the neighboring gentry, who went thither for the sea-air. Within the last twenty years it has lost its character for health, and is now a desolate ruin; yet the hearts of those who grow up in its shades still cling to the memory of its loveliness, — a recollection which exists as a bond of union between them, which no distance can wholly sever. Its sod, still green and beautiful as ever, is occasionally visited by a solitary pilgrim, who goes thither with something of the tender reverence with which he would visit the grave of a beloved friend."

The house of Major Lachlan McIntosh, the father of the subject of this sketch — who had been commissioned in the American army of the Revolution — was a stately old mansion, commanding a full view of the water; and here the first twenty years of her life were spent.

"The remembrance of the generous hospitality, the graceful society, the luxuriant beauty of nature that displayed itself in and around the family mansion, is vivid in the mind of our author, and shows itself in the fervor and enthusiasm of her language whenever she writes of the land of her childhood." *

At an academy in Sunbury, which dispensed its favors to pupils of both sexes, Miss McIntosh received all of her education for which she is indebted to schools. After the death of her parents, Miss McIntosh passed much of her time with a married sister, who resided in New York, and afterward with her brother, Captain James M. McIntosh, of the U. S. Navy, whose family had also removed to that city. In 1835, Miss McIntosh was induced to sell her property in Georgia, and invest the proceeds in New York securities. The commercial crisis of 1837 caused her to lose; to awake from her life-dream of prosperity — bankrupt.

"By an almost universal dispensation of Providence, which ordains means of defence and support to the frailest foundation of animal life, with the new station was granted a power of protection, of pleasure, and maintenance, unknown to the old. New feelings and powers came into life." . . .*

A friend advised her to attempt a juvenile series of books, and suggested "Aunt Kitty" as a *nom de plume*. Two years after the loss of her property, Miss McIntosh had completed her first book, — a small volume, bearing the marks of a feeling, religious mind, and written in

* Professor John S. Hart.

a pleasant, easy style, suitable for children, and was entitled "Blind Alice." For two years the manuscript of this little volume lay alternately on the table of the author and the desk of publishers. At last, in January, 1841, it was published anonymously. Its success was complete. With renewed energy she resumed her pen, and finished "Jessie Graham," a work of similar size and character, which was published in the summer of the same year. "Florence Arnott," "Grace and Clara," and "Ellen Leslie," all of the same class and style, appeared successfully and at short intervals, the last being published in 1843.

These five works are generally known as "Aunt Kitty's Tales." They met with great success, and were republished in England with equal success. They are simple tales of American life, told in graceful and easy language; conveying a moral of beauty and truthfulness that wins love at once for the fictitious character and the earnest writer.

The following are Miss McIntosh's volumes. In addition, she has contributed many tales to the different magazines.

6. Conquest and Self-Conquest. 1844.

7. Woman an Enigma; or, Life and its Revelations. 1844.

8. Praise and Principle. 1845.

9. The Cousins. A tale for children. 1845.

All of these works appeared anonymously. The following were published with the name of the author.

10. Two Lives; or, To Seem and to Be. 1846. (Seven editions of this work were published in less than four years.)

11. Charms and Counter-Charms. 1848.

12. Woman in America; her Work and her Reward. 1850.

13. Evenings at Donaldson Manor; or, The Christmas Guest. 1850. (A collection of tales.)

14. The Lofty and the Lowly. 2 volumes. 1852.

15. Emily Herbert; or, The Happy Home. 1855.

16. Rose and Lillie Stanhope; or, The Power of Conscience.

17. Violet; or, The Cross and Crown. 1856.

18. Meta Gray. A juvenile tale. 1858.

* "In 1859, Miss McIntosh, in company with her nephew, (the Hon. John Ward, American Minister to China,) and his family, sailed for Liverpool. After spending some months in pleasant wanderings about

* Mary Forrest's "Women of the South."

29

England and France, Miss McIntosh, in company with Mrs. Ward and her children, settled quietly down in one of the picturesque valleys of Geneva, Switzerland.   Here, in the society of a few genial friends, and in tender and worshipful communion with the great heart of Nature, she gathered strength and inspiration, and memorized much valuable material for future labors.   At the beginning of 1860 she returned to New York, where she now resides."

Miss McIntosh's books have been translated into French, and have sold largely in England, France, and on the Continent.

I will give notices of several of her books, from high critical authorities.

"Conquest and Self-Conquest" was of a more ambitious character than any of her previous works, which were published anonymously. In the April number of the "Southern Literary Messenger," (1844,) a correspondent, in a "gossip about a few books," commences thus:

"Who can have written the little book called 'CONQUEST AND SELF-CON-QUEST; OR, WHICH MAKES THE HERO?' I have read it with a delight that no book of its class has inspired me with since 'Sandford and Merton,' 'The Parent's Assistant,' 'Popular Tales.'   Amid the numberless and worthless tomes of trash that have in recent times superseded those glories of English literature just named, it is meat and drink to one who relishes an exquisite blending of the sweet with the useful to find such a treat as this 'Con-quest and Self-Conquest.'   It is a story of an American boy, who, after an early education at home, under the eye of a judiciously fond mother, went, at eleven years of age, to a grammar school; fought, was beaten; grew stronger in body and principles; won the heart of his adversary; entered the navy; and there, in a career of virtue and honor, proved how unnecessary vice or ferocity is to a high place among the sons of maritime glory.   Except Miss Edgeworth and the author of 'Sandford and Merton,' I do not know a writer who has so happily portrayed true heroism."

"WOMAN AN ENIGMA.* This is an attempt to delineate, not moral prin-ciples that are well defined — not religious duties that are more easily de-picted — but the ideal, impalpable, varied substance of woman's love.   The first scene in the book opens in a convent in France, where young Louise waits upon a dying friend, and the friend leaves her ward as an affianced bride to her brother, the Marquis de Montrevel.

"The vow is duly made between the noble courtier and the trusting girl. Louise is then taken to Paris by her parents, and introduced into fashionable life with its gayeties and seductions, while the Marquis is absent on his estate.

* Professor John S. Hart.

The new world of pleasure has no effect on the novicé, save so far as it stimulates her to excel, that she may be the more worthy of her husband's love. She mingles in the dance to acquire grace, in the *soirée* to learn the styles of fashionable life — and all for the sole purpose of being the better fitted to be the companion and wife of the high-born noble. But the absent lover hears of the brilliant life of his so lately timid girl, and, ignorant of the mighty power that impels her to the exertion, scorns the supposed fickleness that will give to the many that regard which he had hoped to have won exclusively for himself.

"Then follows the portion of the work which most perfectly pictures the author's idea of womanly love. The earnest toil of the poor girl for the pittance of a smile that is rewarded by jealousy with a sneer; the passionate pride of the wounded woman; the stern sorrow of the man; and the final separation, are all true to the instincts of that master feeling."

"CHARMS AND COUNTER-CHARMS.* In this work the author seems to have concentrated the strength of her artistic and womanly nature. It is threaded with veins and nerves, as if she had dipped her pen in living hearts and written on and on because the elastic tide would flow. It impresses one with a painful sense of reality, and at the same time with a conflicting sense of unnaturalness, not of highly wrought fiction, but of *intense truth*. The plot is complicate, but well defined and sustained. Questions of vital import are involved, and worked out with a will and fervor which leave their indelible record upon the memory of the reader.

" Euston Hastings, the hero, belongs, we should say, to the German type of organism and temperament. A ' dark man,' the philosopher Alcott would call him, with luminous phases. A man of strong will and rare physical and spiritual magnetism; skilled in metaphysical disquisition, worldly-wise, skeptical, and sufficient; lofty and cold as a mountain peak to the many, but to those who interest him, or whom for any reason he would interest, warm, winsome, and low-voiced as the sigh of a summer twilight; a man of whom we can most of us say we have known *one* such in a lifetime; one whom we admired and deprecated; a sphere that was not loud nor discordant, but deep and unserene; a spirit that knew its power and loved to test it, though in the process it stirred and troubled many waters.

"Evelyn Beresford, a young girl of warm heart and generous impulses, the pet and sunbeam of her father's house, marries Euston Hastings, and is borne along his fiery orbit, ignoring, to meet his exactions, one after another, the finer and holier instincts of her nature, till at last she reaches a point from whence she must retrace her steps or lose all. Stifling the cry of her agonized heart, she goes forth from his home, with her frail life in her hand, and Euston Hastings, left alone with the memory of her love and prayerful vigils, for the first time awakes to a sense of 'heart within and God o'erhead.'

* Mary Forrest.

Penitent and subdued, he seeks out the fugitive, and a new union, based upon the sympathy and fitness of divine appointment, secures to both the happiness which had well-nigh been wrécked forever."

"VIOLET; OR, THE CROSS AND CROWN. This work is marked by fine delineations and dramatic power, no less than by simplicity and pathos.

"The story unfolds with a wild shipwreck scene on the coast of New Jersey. A sweet babe, the only living thing upon the stranded vessel, is found lashed to an upper berth, while its dead mother lies, white and cold, beneath the water on the cabin floor. The burial scene upon that desolate shore — the group of rude wreckers, and the lone waif child — the still sleeper in the rough deal box — the 'dust to dust' of the sublime service, mingling with the hoarse roar of the ocean — is singularly impressive. The book is full of such pictures.

"The foundling is claimed by one of the wreckers, and taught to look upon him and his coarse companions as her natural protectors. While yet very young, by one of the coincidences occasional to real life, inevitable to romance, she is thrown into the presence of her true father, who, unconscious of their tender relation, yet impelled by an undefinable instinct, adopts his unknown child. She is baptized Violet Ross, in memory of his angel wife — her mother — and removed from the lawless wreckers to a refined and luxurious home. But amid the amenities of her new position, one thought haunted and distressed her: she is *not* Violet Ross, the daughter of her noble foster-father, but Mary Van Dyke, and must still say 'father' to the repulsive wrecker, and 'mother' to the wrecker's wife; they have a first claim, and may at any time recall her. The good pastor tells her that every human creature must bear a cross on earth who would wear a crown in heaven, and that this is her cross. That night the angels record the vow of the beautiful girl to bear cheerfully and unfalteringly the burden imposed upon her; and then commences a life of sacrifice, and a series of events which give to the book a peculiar and deep interest. Many a bruised heart has lifted itself hopefully in the light of little Violet's smile and the strength of the promise, thus happily presented, 'Bear the cross, and ye shall wear the crown.' " [*]

[†] "Miss McIntosh restricts herself in the characters of her story, and selects only the common ones of practical life, as though anxious for the principle alone, and the fiction that would draw the reader off from the moral is discarded. In her quiet pages there never occurs the extreme either of character or passion. It is only the system of conscience — the rule of right — the law of God that is portrayed; and the more marked characters, or the more easily delineated beauties and feelings of life and nature, are left with a rigid indifference to those whose design is to please more than to instruct.

"Yet the reader, when the book is closed, and he has gone to his daily labor, or mingles in social life, finds lingering in his brain and warming in

[*] Mary Forrest's "Women of the South."   [†] Professor John S. Hart.

his heart, a true principle of honor and love that is constantly contrasting itself with the hollow forms by which he is surrounded; and if he fails to bear himself up to that high ideal of principle which he feels to be true, he still walks a little nearer to his conscience and his God; and long after the volume is returned to the shelf and forgotten, a kindly benediction is given to the noble influence it excited. And thus will it be with the author who lives in the hearts and not in the fancy of her readers. And long after she is returned to the great library of the unforgotten dead, a blessing, wide as her language and fervent as devotion, will descend on the delineator of those lofty principles that showed the nobleness of simplicity and the holiness of truth."

KATE CLIFFORD KENAN.

VIOLETTA AND I; by "Cousin Kate." Edited by M. J. McIntosh. Boston. 1870.

The motto of this little volume is from Longfellow:

>   " . . . Gentleness and love and trust
>   Prevail o'er angry wave and gust."

This is a beautiful story of the Southern sea-side. It is short, and reads very much as if it were a study for a more ambitious book of the future. The style will remind the reader of "Aunt Kitty's Tales," of her earlier works. The chapter giving an account of Maggie's "want to learn physic, and practice, and have a gig, and a man to beat the mortar, and do like her father and Thomas, and not her mother and Violetta," shows that "Cousin Kate" has humor in her composition. The "good doctor" is a pathetic study — poetry delineated in the character of a country doctor.

The story purports to be a grandmother's history of her girlhood. The picture of the little Otilia and the old doctor — companions, "babyhood" and "old age" — is charming, and gives evidence of pathetic power possessed by the young author. The old doctor was growing old —

"Much of his old wit and dry humor left him also; and he seemed like some good husbandman, who will shortly set out on a journey. The little Otilia, in her shy, dreamy way, seemed to be a better companion to him than any other; and often the two would sit together in the office porch, and Otilia would sing to him sometimes little hymns, sometimes broken parts of a German chant that she had heard from her old nurse — the hazy sunlight, as it fell upon the pair, showing often that both had fallen asleep; and I said to myself as I saw them, that the pure heart of the child rested against the pure heart of the man; for through all of life's warfare could there be any more simple, more tender, than this gray-haired father? I think, when he entered heaven, the little children, who love the guileless and the good, must have led his feet by the golden river, and never known how he was old and weary in this world before he came to theirs, so little had the years touched the true heart."

Miss Kate Clifford Kenan is the daughter of Mr. M. J. Kenan, of Milledgeville, Ga. She is young, and resides with her parents in the city mentioned. Mrs. Kenan (whose maiden name was Spalding) is a native of the sea-coast of Georgia, near Darien, and is related to the McIntosh family, who settled there in the early days of colonization. The distinguished authoress, Miss Maria J. McIntosh, was an intimate friend of the family of Mr. and Mrs. Spalding — Mrs. Kenan's parents in her girlhood — and her noble heart testifies its love and remembrance of the past by ushering into the literary world the first book of Miss Kate Kenan — "Violetta and I."

Miss Kenan's early life was spent on the sea-coast of Georgia; and the graphic sketches of sea-coast adventure and existence, of peril and rescue, are the results of her own experience and observation. About ten years ago, when Miss Kenan's family removed from the sea-coast to Milledgeville, she was hardly more than a child. Her vivid pictures of sea-side life are the result of her early impressions when she daily gazed at "old ocean," and sometimes, in the language of Byron,

" . . . laid her hand upon his mane."

Miss Kenan has furnished numerous verses and prose sketches to various newspapers.

THE DOCTOR.

When I recall the kind of practice this dear old gentleman did, I am often troubled at the force of an unpleasant truth. I often had to own to myself that he would not have stood very high at this day, for he believed physic a humbug, and nature the best doctor; and though I never doubted, when he was telling me so, that he was right, yet many learned men have arisen, and many learned things are now in fashion; and it is clear to me my father did not practise as they do. The older he grew, the fewer medicines did he carry in his square chest; and I sometimes thought his dear memory was failing him. He prescribed frequently "fresh air" and "fresh water." Once I feared he had made the wife of a Dutch skipper very angry. She brought her little child to my father's office, and for the life of me I could not tell which was its head and which its feet, as it lay across her bosom, so completely was it enwrapped in shawls. I saw a queer little smile in the corner of my father's eye, as he commenced unrolling the wrappings, until he came to a poor little, smothered, white face — all the while listening to a crowd of ailments. To my surprise, he handed the little thing over to me, and bade me sit with it in the sunshine; and, as I carried it out, I heard him say to the mother, "Sunshine, madam; that's the first prescription, and don't cost a cent; fresh water, madam, that's the next, and fully as cheap — not a thimbleful to start it crying, with no beneficial effects, but a tubful, madam, enough to wet the whole of its skin at once." And then I heard a great oath from my father, — for he sometimes said such things when very much excited, though he always expressed his regret afterward for having done so. The oath now, it seems, was because the little morsel I held in my arms so tightly, for fear the sunshine would melt it, or the sea-breeze coax it away, ate "things" just as the burly skipper and his wife did — a fact which the honest Dutchwoman told with great pride. Though I am certain my father would not have wounded the feelings of a humming-bird, yet it sounded wickedly to me when he said, "Madam, with such a taste, I fear your child will not be content with milk and honey, which is, I hear, the simple diet of a better world." When she comprehended him fully, I heard her sobbing gently, and my father's old, kind manner returning, he told her that we had Bible doctrine for milk for babes, and not strong meat; and when she had gone away hugging the little one up to her motherly heart, and stopping every now and then to kiss it, I said, "Father, how could you make her cry about the babe?" and he said, as he drew me on his knee, smoothing the curly locks so like his own: "Sweet heart, did I ever make thee cry but for thine own good? Tears shed for innocent error are not bitter; only conscious guilt draws burning tears. When thy little hands lifted the young mocking birds from their nest last spring, and I told thee how the mother would grieve for her lost nestlings, thy tears fell fast; but they were quenched, dear little heart, when I restored them to their nest. So with yonder poor woman. She lifted her baby from the proper place where God had put it, and she only cried to see what she had done, as thou didst; but she will not cry any more, for only mismanagement ailed the babe, and she will bear in mind what I told her concerning it." And several months after, the same woman came; but the baby was so rosy I hardly knew it. Wherever a patch of sunshine fell, it crawled over the floor toward it, and once I saw it trying to catch a beam which slanted in through the lattice; and I thought my father must have given it some drugs; but he only said, "Nay, thou little medicine-chest, not any of thy drugs!" And afterward, as was his common habit when he could think of nothing else to tell Thomas to do, he lifted me on his knee, and bade him burnish the instruments — those instruments that his dear old hands never touched if he could help it, and which he kept as bright as silver, but always locked up in the skeleton case.

MARY LOUISE COOK.

IN 1869, a novel, entitled "Ante-Bellum; or, Southern Life as it Was," was published by J. B. Lippincott & Co., Philadelphia. "Mary Lennox" was the name given as the author; and it was dedicated to "the friends of the South." "Ante-Bellum" was, as the title would imply, a story of Southern life before the war, naturally portrayed, written in a simple style.

A Georgia writer reviewed this novel in a long criticism:

"The name itself calls up so many happy memories of Eden-like homes, holidays, and pastimes that we are prepared to be pleased before the book is epened. After that, the history of an orphan girl, who wrought out her life to a successful issue of happiness and love by a simple adherence to the rules of duty and Christian kindness, enchains the heart as scene after scene of Southern life is unfolded. As the author, with a master-hand, portrays some scene so lifelike to memory, you think your own experience has been turned into history, and chronicled by some sympathizing friend."

A writer in a Northern paper, in a review of "Ante-Bellum," writes thus:

"The South owes the author a debt of gratitude for the beautiful word-painting she has given of many Southern scenes of ante-bellum memory. . . . The sentiment of the book is elevating and exquisitely chaste and refined; and her sensible and timely views upon home education for girls are calculated to be of benefit. Our greatest objection to the book is, that its political tendency is to keep alive the spirit of discord and dissension which exists between the North and the South, by appealing to sectional pride and prejudice; but its excellent rhetoric and ethics almost compensate for this."

This latter criticism disarms itself, as it arises simply from the prejudice of the writer's own mind; and any impartial reader would free the author of "Ante-Bellum" from the charge of attempting, in its pages, to fan the flames of useless strife, though the love of the South and devotion to her speaks throughout the book.

Mrs. Cook — the owner of the pseudonym "Mary Lennox" — is a native of the State of Georgia, and has for a number of years resided in Columbus. Her maiden name was Redd. She was left an orphan at an early age, and was married, when quite young, to Mr. James C. Cook, a planter.

Poetry, music, painting, and all that is elevating and refining, are a part of her nature. Surrounded, as she is and has been, with every luxury, and occupying a high social position, writing, with Mrs. Cook, has been and is an expression of her soul which could not be kept back. She writes because she cannot help it. On the walls of her home one sees evidence of her skill as an artist. "Ante-Bellum" is Mrs. Cook's only published book. She is, at present, contributing short poems and stories to different Southern journals.

1871.   E. M.

---∘∘⦂𝕺⦂∘∘---

CORNELIA BORDERS.

THE subject of this sketch is a native Georgian, and was reared in the village of Hamilton, that nestles between abrupt hills, which give to the surrounding scenery a wild and picturesque appearance. There, beside flowing waters and mountain slopes, and in the midst of valleys rich with forest growth, she rambled in her youth and saw the gorgeous sunsets that are only seen in such a region. She loved nature, and her rambles amidst these scenes deepened and intensified her feelings. The amusements that so generally attract the young did not interest her so much as books and the companionship of her own thoughts. Her parents encouraged her love of books; and her father (the late Colonel William C. Osborn), with rare judgment, selected such works for her as would give strength to her character and deepen her moral sentiments. The strength of character, firmness of purpose, and noble resolution that distinguish her, are due (next to the training of her mother, a very superior woman,) to the course of reading that she pursued at an early age.

Miss Osborn accompanied the family of Hon. Henry W. Hilliard
30

to Europe, when that gentleman was appointed Minister to Belgium, being a near relative of Mrs. Hilliard. Soon after her return from Europe, she was married to Augustus Borders, Esq., a lawyer. Some time after their marriage they removed to Texas, where Mr. Borders died. Mrs. Borders, after her husband's death, removed to Houston, and devoted much of her time to writing.

At the close of the war, she returned to Columbus, Ga., where she now resides. Mrs. Borders has recently completed a work entitled "Fortune's Wheel; or, Life's Vicissitudes," which is ready for publication. Several distinguished gentlemen who have perused the MS. pronounce it superior to anything issued from the South for years.

The Hon. Alexander H. Stephens writes:

"I have given the work a careful perusal from the beginning to the end. The best evidence of my opinion of its merits is that I was interested in it from the first line to the last. In my judgment the work has real merit. As it progresses it becomes more interesting; after a while it becomes exceedingly so. The moral of it surpasses any work of the kind I have read lately; no one can read it without benefit."

H.

MRS. EPPIE B. CASTLEN.

AMONG the candidates for poetical honors of the female writers of the South — who from her youth, her energy, her genius, and the rapidity with which she conceives and executes her committal to language of those inspirations which overflow her soul like a river, indicates plainly the prominence she is destined to hold in Southern literature — is Mrs. Eppie Bowdre Castlen.

Mrs. Castlen is the daughter of Judge P. E. Bowdre and his wife, — née Miss Labuzan, of Augusta, Ga. — and the wife of Dr. F. G. Castlen, of Macon, Ga. Her birthplace was Thomaston, Ga. Her parents lived for a short time during her girlhood in New Orleans; and, being of French blood and Gallic temperament, her recollections of that Franco-American city are of the most agreeable character. It was here, on the borders of that mighty river which bears deservedly the title of "Father of Waters," that her girlish muse first found expression in words.

Within the past two years, writing as she always does, not for fame, but, to use her own expressive phrase, because she cannot resist the inclination to put her ideas in words, she has contributed to several literary journals of the South.

In the autumn of 1870, D. Appleton & Co., New York, published the poems produced within the past two years by Mrs. Castlen, in a handsome volume, entitled "Autumn Dreams; by Chiquita"—the latter being Mrs. Castlen's pseudonym. This volume is illustrated by a steel engraving of the charming face of the authoress.

Mrs. Castlen has for several years resided in Macon, Ga. Her home is ·one of the loveliest in that city, situated on the beautiful "Hill" crowned with many elegant mansions. Already her active brain has planned, and her cunning hand is executing, another literary task, which promises to eclipse "Autumn Dreams;" and from her youth, her genius, her thoroughly awakened ambition, we may safely predict for her a high rank among the "Southern Writers" of the future.

October, 1870.   W. G. M.

AUTUMN DAYS.

"The melancholy days are come — the saddest of the year!"
The berries have to scarlet turned ; and bare, and brown, and sere,
Hard beaten by the fretful rain, the harvest fields appear.

Unfolded lie the grand and gorgeous glories of the wood!
And on the hillside, where the blue-eyed flowers in beauty stood,
The Autumn-hued vines lowly bend to meet winds strong and rude.

Like Summer rain the golden leaves in showers patter down,
Adorning gnarled and knotted roots with nature's brilliant crown,
Not heeding moans, nor winds, nor storms, that tell of Winter's frown.

Or on the clear, bright bosom of the ever murmuring stream
They softly lie, and kiss with crimson lips the waves that gleam,
And dance, and rise, and swell, and tremble 'neath the Moon's pale beam.

Upon projecting, barren rocks, 'midst mountain wilds its home,
The fierce, defensive, bristling pine, with stiff and spiral form,
In scanty dress a guardian stands, and proudly meets the storm.

And patriot chief, thou grand old oak, thou monarch brave and true!
How much of human feeling (since from acorns small you grew,)
Has ebbed and flowed? — How much of grandeur, space and time seen you.

The heart has felt the beauty of the Summer woods — of gales
That wav'd the leaves and blossoms, blushing in the lowly dales,
And these sweet, thornless treasures, lost, the sad heart still bewails.

A morn of beauty soon will rise! nor over Summer's bier,
Nor folded, faded petals, shall we drop the hopeless tear, ,
Sweet flowers, bright days, will come again ; — the *gladdest* of the year.

MACON, GA., January 14th, 1870.

MRS. A. P. HILL.

MRS. HILL is the author of a valuable book on "Cookery," published by Carleton, New York, 1870.

"Mrs. Hill's New Cook-Book" is the title of a handsome duodecimo volume of over four hundred pages, every receipt in which has been tested by experienced practical housekeepers. The directions in the culinary art are interspersed with an occasional sentiment, showing that the authoress has a taste for literature as well as for the delicacies of the table.

Mrs. Hill has prepared, by request of the church of which she is a member, a biography of the Rev. John E. Dawson, of the Baptist denomination. She has also contributed, under the name of "Ruth," to various religious publications.

Mrs. Hill, whose maiden name was Dawson, was born in Morgan County, Ga., early in the century. Her parents were Virginians. Her husband was the late Edward Y. Hill, Judge of the Superior Court of Georgia, and at one time nominated for the gubernatorial chair of Georgia. His death at the noontide of life left his widow with the care and training of several children. Faithfully has she discharged her duties as a judicious mother. Two noble sons were killed during the war between the sections. Bereft of her stay, her fortunes shattered in the general wreck, Mrs. Hill accepted with becoming dignity and fortitude her position. With praiseworthy self-reliance she set about the compilation of her book of domestic receipts. Her experiment has proven a success. Although in feeble health and advanced in years, she still exhibits a spirit of enterprise and progress truly striking. She now holds the position of Superintendent of the "Orphans'. Free School," which she organized, and which numbers nearly two hundred pupils, located at Atlanta, Georgia.

November 30th, 1870.   MRS. COLQUITT.

————oo°⦿°oo————

MRS. MARY F. McADO.

MRS. McADO—the wife of Colonel W. G. McAdo, of Milledgeville, Ga.—is the granddaughter of General John Floyd, who commanded the Georgia troops in the war with the Creek Indians in 1813–14, and is the daughter of General Charles R. Floyd, of Camden County, Georgia, who died prematurely in 1845, when the subject of this notice was in early girlhood. Mrs. Floyd died shortly after her husband, and on the youthful Mary Faith devolved the onerous duties of superintending the household. For that reason, her education at schools was not as complete as it would have been had her parents lived; but her indomitable energy has achieved perhaps more than if she had been more favored in this respect. She is an accomplished scholar, profound in her knowledge of books and of human nature.

At a youthful age, Miss Floyd married Mr. Randolph McDonald, of St. Mary's, who died of yellow fever at Savannah, in 1854. In 1858, the young widow was married to Colonel W. G. McAdo, at that time Attorney-General of the Knoxville Circuit in Tennessee. During the "war between the States," Colonel McAdo removed his family to Georgia, and now resides in Milledgeville. Husband and wife are congenial—being studious in their habits, fond of books, the possessors of a large library, and both somewhat addicted to authorship.

Mrs. McAdo (whose literary pseudonym "Mary Faith Floyd" is simply her maiden name) is the author of many small poems. She is also a frequent contributor, both in prose and verse, to several magazines and papers of the day, and is the author of two romances of merit — "The Nereid," whose scene is her native sea-coast of Georgia, and "Antethusia," which embodies her impressions of Eastern Tennessee, where she resided from 1858 to 1862. Of the two performances last mentioned it is idle to speak.

The public will soon have an opportunity of judging for themselves of their merits. They possess originality of style and matter, and being located in fields hitherto unexplored by the busy legion of fiction writers. Mrs. McAdo has other and more serious literary undertakings projected; and her energy scarcely allows a day to intervene between planning and executing in such cases.

She possesses one remarkable characteristic — an administrative capacity so active and comprehensive that her literary labors do not detract from the bestowal of all the attention to the comforts of her large household, which the best of housewives are accustomed to vouchsafe.

1871.

ONEIROPION.

Drifting in an eternity of space,
  My soul all quivering and naked lay
Upon the undulating waves of time,
  In the full blazing heat of a noonday.

Clay casket locked in opium's dreamy trance,
  My spirit on glad pinions now set free,
Like ship, all sails unfurled, and rudderless,
  Breasted the great deep with untrammelled glee.

The billowy waves that broke on foaming cliffs
  Were slaves, not masters, to its bounding speed —
On, on, forever on in trackless space
  It sped, a living, quivering, wavering reed.

Now diving deep to famed old coral halls,
  Then gliding o'er Old Ocean's sparkling floor,
Then spreading its swift wings through Æther's dome,
  It soared to distant spheres ne'er reached before.

Finite in infinite like a scroll unrolled,
  And cloud empurpled banners edged with gold,
Borne up on breezy wings of endless time,
  Displayed earth's deathless names by Fame enrolled.

Quivering with hope my soul all naked lay,
    And sought to find its name there graven in light,
But clouds rolled up between, with darkened folds,
    And hid the banners in the gloom of night.

In darkness deep desponding, my soul fled,
    Once more rocked on the roaring billows deep,
Till, lost 'mid icy breakers of despair,
    It sank in dreamless shroud of endless sleep.

O Time! O Waves! What care to ye or yours
    How many naked panting souls must lie
Wailing upon thy bleak and rocky shores,
    Lost in thy deafening roar their piercing cry?

August, 1870.

----oo:o:oo----

THEODOSIA FORD.

WRITING for children is in itself an art, and in the South there are writers who are directing their talents to amuse and instruct the children of their section. Among this number, deserving of mention, is Mrs. Theodosia Ford, who has been a contributor to the "Riverside Magazine" and "Burke's Monthly for Boys and Girls." Her sketches have been copied by the press generally. She writes over her initials.

Mrs. Ford is a native of Savannah, a sister of General Francis S. Bartow, of Georgia — who fell at the first battle of Manassas — and the widow of the Rev. Dr. Ford, for many years rector of St. Paul's (Episcopal) Church, in Augusta, Ga.

Mrs. Ford's home is at Woodstock, in the neighborhood of Cave Spring, which is her post-office. Mrs. Ford has been compelled by ill health to give up a school for young ladies, of which she was principal, and to rely upon her pen.

A charming little volume of Christmas Stories and Tales is now (1871) in the press of Claxton, Remsen & Haffelfinger, Philadelphia.

JANIE OLLIVAR.

L'INCONNUE was the signature to poems "brief and charming" that appeared for the years between '61 and '65 — that awful time of war and devastation — in the "Southern Field and Fireside," a weekly literary journal published in Augusta, Georgia.

The unknown was a young lady of Augusta, Miss Janie Ollivar.

Here is one of her poems. A critic said of these verses: "The last stanza is one of the sweetest in the language. Truly the morning-glories have shaken much freshness into her songs."

MORNING DREAMS.

How sweetly rests the fervid cheek
　Upon the dimpled arm!
These purple morning-glories seek
　To break her slumber's charm.

They clamber to her casement wide,
　To watch her in her sleep,
And with the sunlight, side by side,
　In her visions creep.

She smiles! How little seems to wake
　Her smiles. To me it seems
As if these morning-glories shake
　Their freshness through her dreams.

"L'Inconnue's" harp is seldom heard now. Since the close of the war she has "obliged Mr. Benson" by taking his name.

———o-o:o:o-o———

JULIA BACON.

MISS BACON is not as well known as a writer as she deserves to be. She is a native of Macon, Ga., and has always resided in her native State. She has published prose and verse under several *noms de plume*, the most popular of which is "Mollie Myrtle." Miss Bacon possesses a keen sense of the ridiculous, and excels in humorous articles. This disposition is inherited, for "Ned Brace," of the "Georgia Scenes," was a kinsman of hers. She has been highly complimented for her descriptions of scenery. She has a novel ready for publication. Resident of Howard, Taylor County, Georgia. (1871.) The following verses have been extensively copied by the press throughout the country.

WILL'S A WIDOWER!

The night-bird sings her plaintive song,
　　Will's a widower!
On zephyr's wing 'tis borne along,
In simple wood-notes clear and strong,
　　Will's a widower!

Methinks a tone of sadness dwells
　　In that wild, simple lay;
And mournful is the tale she tells
　　Beneath the moon's soft ray.

Poor widowed Will! we grieve to hear
　　Will's a widower!
But mourn not for the lost one dear,
The living only need our care.
　　Will's a widower!

Perchance in some sequestered grove,
　　His life may sweetly glide,
If he consents to take and love
　　Another birdie bride.

Go tell him this, and cease to sing
　　Will's a widower!
And let us hear in early spring
Your echoes through the forest ring,
　　Will's *no* widower!

31

E. W. BACCHUS.

A POEM, entitled "The Confederate Dead," published in 1866 — signed "Latienne" — struck the popular fancy, and was copied into the newspapers of the South most extensively. These lines are to be found in several compilations of Southern poems of the war.

"Latienne" has published other poems, in several journals, of different grades of merit. We give herewith a few stanzas from a poem written at the occasion of the late Charles Dickens's visit to the United States.

> We see his creatures, — form, dress, face, —
>   And hear the tales they tell;
> Know every one's accustomed place
>   And trick of gesture, well;
> Here, Peggoty, with honest brow,
>   Gives welcome blunt and true;
> There, Turveydrop's majestic bow
>   O'erwhelms us with adieu.
>
> We gaze with loving vision, while
>   Draws near, with gentle grace,
> Dear Agnes, with her heav'nly smile,
>   And calmly noble face;
> But turn from Pecksniff with disgust,
>   The hand of Pinch to shake,
> And leave Uriah in the dust,
>   A spurned and writhing snake.
>
> .   .   .   .
>
> We bend, a childish couch above,
>   And hear the shore's long sighs,
> As, drifting from the arms of love,
>   The heir of Dombey dies.
>
> We enter Bleak House with a smile,
>   For Esther's smile is there;
> We linger by the ancient pile
>   Where Dedlock's glories were.
> As poor Miss Flite for judgment looks
>   To Heav'n's high court, do we,
> Half wondering that its patience brooks
>   An earthly chancery.

Ah! wondrous is the power which breathes
　　Such life in forms of art,
And with a band of shadows wreathes
　　The universal heart;
Which speaks with voice whose music thrills
　　In echoes, o'er and o'er,
The list'ning ear, that eager fills,
　　Yet ever asks for "more."

Far dearer than the conq'ror's fame
　　Is his that mirrored lies—
With every echo of his name—
　　In moved and tender eyes;
Nor civic crown need covet he,
　　Whose arms far reaching span,
And bind in common sympathy
　　The brotherhood of man.

"Latienne" is the pen-name of Miss Lizzie W. Bacchus, a native of Wilmington, N. C. During the late war, the family of Miss Bacchus became refugees, and settled in Savannah, Ga., where they now reside. The subject of this notice is a teacher at Eufaula, Ala.

ALABAMA.

MADAME ADELAIDE DE V. CHAUDRON.

THIS lady, who stands unsurpassed as translator of the now famous Mühlbach novels, is a resident of Mobile. Her father was Emile de Vendel, a teacher of some distinction in a country where teaching is regarded as one of the professions, and where intellect, education, and birth are principally valued as the "open sesames" of good society. Adelaide de Vendel was married at an early age to Mr. West, of St. Louis: he was a lawyer by profession. After his death, she resided in Mobile, where she contracted a second marriage with Mr. Paul Chaudron. Left again a widow, she was compelled by misfortune to adopt her father's honorable occupation, and being well qualified by her talents and accomplishments, she assumed the charge of a seminary for young ladies, a position she still fills.

She is known as an author principally from her translation of the "Joseph II." of the Mühlbach novels, and also for her compilation of a series of readers and a spelling-book, during the late war. These were published in Mobile, and adopted in the public schools of that city; they are regarded as really excellent text-books.

The "Round Table," a journal not usually too favorable in its judgment of Southern authors, speaks thus of the translation of the "Joseph II. and his Court":

"The translation of this volume is unusually praiseworthy. Some small things might be said by way of criticism, but we pass them in deference to its general superiority. A translator is to be tested by the success with which the spirit of the original is preserved in the translation. To translate words is a simple task, but to re-embody the original work in its spirit in the translation is the work of genius. Madame Chaudron, to achieve this result, has dared to assume the responsibility of a free translation, and has succeeded."

244

S. H. Goetzel, of Mobile, publisher and bookseller, had published before the war a number of books in a style and on a scale never before attempted in the Southern States; but having to contend with the many difficulties as a pioneer in this field of enterprise, he had realized little profit from it when the "Confederate" war broke out, paralyzing all pursuits not military in character.

In the course of the war the demand for other than military books began to revive. The Federal blockade cut off the Southern States from all of the ordinary sources of supply. Soldiers in camp or garrison, and still more in the hospital, began to crave for something to read. Anxious hearts at home felt the lack of the stimulus or diversion of literary novelty even more than in ordinary times. It was then that Mr. Goetzel's acquaintance with contemporary German literature suggested to him the bright idea of introducing to the "Confederate" public the fascinating sensationalism of the Mühlbach novels, previously unknown to either English or American readers. "Joseph the Second and his Court" was the first English version of any of these (audaciously styled) "historical novels," which have since become so popular in America. It was issued in four parts or volumes, and had a great run. *

Mrs. Chaudron is appreciated in the society of Mobile. She has fine conversational powers, an excellent memory, and a happy faculty in imparting ideas and knowledge gathered from general reading; her fine musical powers make her an acquisition to any circle; but her *specialité* is decidedly the acquisition of foreign languages.

1869.

———o◦⦂⦂◦o———

MISS KATE CUMMING.

MISS CUMMING hardly can be classed as a "writer" in the professional interpretation of that term, "Hospital Life in the Army of the Tennessee" being her only contribution to the literature of the country.

Miss Cumming is of Scotch descent, and has resided in Mobile since childhood.

"Hospital Life in the Army of the Tennessee" was published by John P. Morton & Co., Louisville, Kentucky, in 1866. Says a reviewer:

---

* For these facts I am indebted to Major W. T. Walthall.

"At the first glance over the title-page of this book, the reader will, very likely, form an opinion of it from the work written by Miss Florence Nightingale after the Crimean War. But Miss Cumming's book is of a very different character. Miss Nightingale confined herself almost entirely to her life in the hospitals at Scutari and its vicinity, and gave minute directions upon the subject of nursing the sick and wounded, the management of hospitals, and general clinical treatment. Miss Cumming aims to do more than this. She was constantly with the army in the field, received the wounded in nearly every action, and assisted in organizing the field hospitals in the memorable campaigns in Tennessee, Kentucky, and finally in Georgia, when the army was retreating. She has told the story in a plain, straightforward manner, made up from the diary kept through the war; and has presented a very fair history of the operations of the Western army under Bragg, Johnston, and Hood. To the soldiers of the Army of the Tennessee, and to their relatives and friends, this book contains much that is interesting. An heroic woman leaves her comfortable home in the Gulf City, and offers her services as a matron in the corps of field-nurses. She devotes her whole time to the care of the sick and wounded soldiers, sees to the cleansing of their hospital wards, attends to their food, and often with her own hand prepares delicacies for those prostrate with wounds or burning with fever. But she is not located in some interior village, where everything is quiet, and food plenty; her place is in the field. She follows the army in all its wanderings, prepares lint and provides stimulants when a battle is expected, and establishes temporary sick-wards in the first building to be had, when the battle has been fought and the wounded are being brought in. For four years Miss Cumming followed this army-life, and every evening, after the fatigues of the day, spent a few moments over her diary, recording the incidents that transpired around her, 'all of which she saw,' to paraphrase the expression of Cæsar, 'and a part of which she was.'

"The book is almost a transcript of that field-diary. It has been but little altered, and still bears evidences of haste in some parts, as if the words were written just before starting for Dalton or Atlanta, when the army was retreating; and of fatigue in others, as if jotted down after being all day ministering to the sick. But while some may complain of this crudity, if we may so call it, there can be no doubt that this adds very much to the spirit or piquancy of the book. Its main beauty is, that the words convey all the force and testimony of an eye-witness, or even of an actor in the events recorded."

MRS. ANNIE CREIGHT LLOYD.

ANNIE P. CREIGHT, in 1863, published several short articles in prose and verse in the "Gulf City Home Journal," of Mobile, her first appearance in print. The editor of that journal, in alluding to Miss Creight's contributions, remarked:

"Miss Creight has put in our hands, with evident trepidation and timidity, several short papers. We saw some faults, but we thought that they could be remedied by a little encouragement, and we gave them to the public. We thought if we would assist the bird to learn to fly, that it would fly very well after a while."

And the editor truly prophesied, for since that time Miss Creight has made for herself quite a to-be-envied place among "Southland writers." Her first novelette appeared in the "Army Argus and Crisis," Mobile, and was entitled "Garnet; or, Through the Shadows into Light;" which was followed by "Hagar; or, The Lost Jewel," which we consider superior to any of her published novelettes. These novelettes have had the honor of republication in the columns of a Mississippi paper, since the close of the war.

In the summer of 1867, Mrs. Lloyd was the successful competitor for a prize offered by the "Mobile Sunday Times" for the best romance; "Pearl; or, The Gem of the Vale," being the title of the successful novelette.

Miss Creight was born in Abbeville, South Carolina: she is yet young in years, and with careful study and judicious pruning of her narratives will accomplish something worthy of herself and her country. At an early age, Miss Creight removed to Mississippi; was educated in Aberdeen, where she graduated in 1859; deprived of parents, she came to Mobile, Alabama, and shared the home of an uncle; in 1866, she was married to William E. Lloyd, and resides in Mobile, occasionally writing as a recreation.

1869.

MRS. E. W. BELLAMY.

MRS. E. W. BELLAMY ("Kampa Thorpe") has not, as yet, accomplished a great deal in the literature of her country, but what she has published she has cause to be proud of. Her novel "Four Oaks" was published by Carleton, New York, 1867. The "Round Table," New York, under the impression that "Kampa Thorpe" was of the masculine gender, thus alludes to "Four Oaks":

"This is a story of every-day life, in which all the incidents are probable, and, what is yet more rare, the characters are all perfectly natural. A number of men and women, differing in age though not in station, are brought together on terms of pleasant acquaintanceship, and there is a more liberal allowance than usual of intelligent men and brainless nonentities, of sensible women and those torments of modern society, women of an uncertain age on the lookout for husbands; and although there are no diabolical villains, there are mischief-makers enough to occasion unpleasant complications, which, together with mysterious miniatures and family secrets, combine to sustain an interest which the events of the story would not otherwise suffice to keep alive.

"The scene opens in the pleasant town of Netherford, where, after a severe round of introductions to the forefathers and relatives of the heroine, we are presented to a charming, good-hearted, and beautiful girl, a little spoiled, rather self-willed, and somewhat too self-reliant, but so true and honest, so free from all the vices which attach to the fashionable and fast young lady of the present day, that we are grateful to the author who awakens our interest for a woman equally endowed with vitality, modesty, and common sense. There is an absence of all romance about a life passed among such restless and ill-assorted people as form the society of Netherford, but the author has refrained from giving us any exaggerated or extravagant scenes; he is thoroughly consistent and natural, and his imagination has evidently been greatly assisted by personal observation."

And a Southern editor and critic of experience (Major W. T. Walthall) thus reviews the book:

"We have subjected this volume to careful reading — a reading much more careful than we are in the habit of giving to any new novel.

"We confess having commenced 'Four Oaks' with some nervous apprehensions — fear lest it might prove like too many books by Southern authors, which task the ingenuity of an indulgent reviewer to effect an awkward compromise between candor and charity in the expression of his opinion. They have to be 'damned with faint praise,' or eased off with unmeaning platitudes. 'Four Oaks,' we are happy to say, is not one of such books. We have read it through with continually increasing interest, and have laid it down with that paradoxically pleasant regret which busy people rarely have the luxury of feeling in finishing a book — regret that it is ended.

"Considering the temptations held out by the examples of some of the most successful novels of the day, 'Four Oaks' is to be commended almost as much for what it is *not*, as for what it is. It is not a 'sensational' story. There is not a battle, nor a duel, nor a ghost, nor a murder, and but one pistol-shot in it. [We do not object to a reasonable use of these elements of interest in a novel, but it is very refreshing to meet with one that can be just as interesting without them.] It has no violations of the letter or the spirit of the seventh commandment — no sentimental apologies for vice — no poetic idealization of acts and passions which in the honest language of the Scriptures are called by homely names that would be inadmissible in elegant fiction. Without a particle of prudery or pretension, it is imbued with the very atmosphere of purity — purity not *inculcated*, but taken for granted. To say that the author is a lady, *ought* to be sufficient to make all this follow as a matter of course; but, unfortunately, some of the lady novelists of this generation have taught us a different lesson.

"Nor does the author of 'Four Oaks' delight in twisting and torturing human passions and feelings into agonies of strange attitudes and fantastic developments. Her characters are men and women, with loves, hates, hopes, fears, joys, sorrows, faults, and follies, like those of other people.

"Neither is 'Four Oaks' a device for showing off the learning of the author. She shows the effects of culture, but not its processes. There is, perhaps, rather too much botany in one of her chapters, but this is an exception to the general rule.

"Again, 'Four Oaks' is neither political, polemical, nor philosophical. Thoroughly Southern as it is, the word 'Southern' scarcely occurs in it, nor is there anything said of patriotism, or chivalry, or the sunny South, or the peculiar institution. Its locality is defined only by its general tone, spirit, and the language, manners, and usages of the people who figure in it. It has no theory to maintain, nor any 'mission' to fulfil.

"It is needless, however, to specify the negative merits of 'Four Oaks,' when it has so many that are positive. It is a story of every-day life. Its materials and its style are of the most unpretending sort. We are introduced in the early chapters into the society of a pleasant little circle of people in 'the town of Netherford,' on the 'banks of the Ominihaw,' and these people constitute nearly all the personages of the story. The heroine is far from being a model of propriety. She is full of faults and foibles, which some-

32

times provoke the friendly reader and make his interest and sympathy tremble in the balance for a moment, but she is sure to carry away his heart in the end. Her education is lamentably imperfect when she is first introduced. She likes picnics and dancing better than books, has never read even 'The Lady of the Lake,' and 'The Burial of Sir John Moore' is new to her; but she has a heart, and an honest one, and she is witty and beautiful. Herein, as we think, the author again shows good sense. We have a great respect for plain women. They often make admirable nurses, friends, mothers, sisters, and even sweethearts and wives for those who are indifferent about beauty, but they do not answer for heroines of romance. Even Jane Eyre has to marry a blind man. But Harry Vane is not only beautiful — she is bewitching in every sense. We may vow that she is unworthy of being loved, but she wins ·us back in the course of the next minute, and binds us faster than ever. The progress of her character, and the quiet but steady growth of its improvement, are among the most interesting features in the book ; and yet there is no parade made of it. The art of the artist is admirably concealed.

"We have never read anything more thoroughly and unaffectedly natural than the characters, the conversation, and incidents of this book. It exhales the very odor of the groves, the fields, the forests, and the ancestral homes of Virginia or the Carolinas; and yet, as we have already said, neither Virginia nor Carolina is mentioned. There are no tedious and elaborate descriptions of scenery or analyses of character: the touches that set them before us so vividly are imperceptible. The humor of some passages is delightful. It must be a dull soul — totally insensible to mirth — that can read unmoved such scenes as the account of the first meeting of the Quodlibet, or that of Mr. Dunbar's courtship, or his prescription of 'earthworms and turpentine,' or some others that might be specified.

"But it is in the love-scenes of 'Four Oaks' that its chief charm consists. Trite as is the theme, it is still that which stirs most deeply the human heart, and has the most universal attraction for human sympathy. We have often seen its influences depicted with more power, but never with so much of exquisite grace, delicacy, and fidelity, as in this book. Without a particle of sentimentality to repel the most fastidious taste, it unites all the truth and tenderness of the sentimental school with the sparkle of the gayer and lighter sort, and touches of exquisite delicacy, which could proceed only from a woman's pen, and which may be appreciated, but scarcely described or ana--lyzed.

"We forbear to say anything more in praise of 'Four Oaks.' What we have said is not said from any undue partiality, for we know the writer only by reputation — scarcely even by name. We are sensible, too, of some faults in her book. It has, to a certain degree, that fault from which scarcely any lady writer — perhaps none — is entirely free: the fault of diffuseness. But then, there is this difference: the works of most women (and perhaps of most men too) would be improved by reducing them to one-fifth of their dimensions; in the case of 'Four Oaks,' we could not possibly *spare* more than one-fifth. There is an artistic fault in the too rapid introduction of characters in the beginning. The mind of the reader is confused, and one has to look back for explanation oftener than we like in the hurry of novel-reading.

"The sum of the whole matter is, that 'Four Oaks' is the most delightful book that we have read for a long time. It is the very book to be read aloud either by the winter fireside or the summer seaside, with one congenial listener, or a circle of such listeners, and to leave all parties more genial, more happy, more thankful to the Creator for his good gifts, more charitable toward his creatures. It is very rarely that we could conscientiously recommend the author of a new novel to repeat the effort, but in this case we very much hope that 'Four Oaks' is only the beginning of a series. 'Kampa Thorpe' has not mistaken her vocation."

Mrs. Bellamy is a widow, and is a teacher in a seminary at Eutaw, Greene County, Alabama. Her essays contributed to the "Mobile Sunday Times" are beautiful and elegant articles, and we imagine she is an ardent lover of "nature and nature's God."

1869.

A SUMMER IDYL.

When woodlands spread their denser screen,
  And wheat is reap'd on sunburnt plains;
When apples blush for looking green,
  And berries ripen in the lanes;

When bees go robbing clover-fields,
  And barefoot truants wade the brook,
Or 'neath the shade the forest yields
  They seek them out some breezy nook;

When summer weaves her slumb'rous spell
  Of dreamy murmurs, lulling care,
Till Thought lies dormant in his cell
  To watch the castles rise in air;

What vocal rover haunts the land,
  Roaming adown the dusty walks,

Or in the stubble takes his stand,
  And loudly of the harvest talks?

From sylvan coverts far and near
  A name is called from morn till night,
And questions asked in accents clear
  About the crop of Farmer White;

That vague, mysterious crop of peas
  The gleaners of the feather'd gown
Are waiting eagerly to seize
  When "Bob" shall lay his sickle down.

O Bob, Bob White! where doth he dwell?
  And wherefore do they call his name?
And who is he?—can any tell?
  Can any whisper whence he came?

Have any seen him on the hills,
  Industrious at the dawn of day?
Have any spied him by the rills,
  Dozing the noontide hours away?

Perchance he is akin to Kate
  Who did the deed without a name,
Or that poor Will whose luckless fate
  The twilight babblers oft proclaim.

"A man of words, and not of deeds,"
  He dwells in an unreal clime,
And takes his ease in sunny meads,
  Unjostled by the march of time.

In those fair realms beyond the stream,
  That parts the infant from the man,
I see this farmer in a dream,
  With kindly eye and cheek of tan;

A jolly wight, who loves his pipe,
  And knows the cunning speech of birds,
But parleys o'er his peas unripe
  To teach his reapers human words.

An echo from old Babyland,
  His name, across the vanish'd years
By summer breezes lightly fann'd,
  Brings happy thoughts bedew'd with tears,

What tireless rambles through the wood,
　　What revels round the bubbling spring,
By slopes whereon the stout oaks stood,
　　And held the grape-vine for a swing!

O summer days! O summer joys!
　　That come not as they came of old;
Their charm still lingers in the voice
　　Now piping from the sunlit wold.

Wherefore be blessings on the bird
　　That warbles with such magic art;
What time his "airy tongue" is heard,
　　The past illuminates the heart!

JULY, 1868.

TRANSITION.

"BRILL ON THE HILL," ALA.

How soon will end the Summer days!
　　Though thick and green the forest-leaves,
Already Autumn's golden haze
About the woods and hilly ways
　　A veil of tender radiance weaves.

Oh! what is in the Autumn sun,
　　And what is in the Autumn air,
Makes all they shine and breathe upon,
Ere yet the Summer days are gone,
　　Look so exceeding sweet and fair?

E'en weeds, that through the Summer rain
　　Grew wanton, and o'ertopped the flowers, —
Rude children of the sunburnt plain, —
Bud out and blossom, not in vain,
　　Around the Summer's faded bowers.

For long ago the violets fled,
　　The pansy closed its purple eye,
The poppy hung its uncrowned head,
And on the garden's grass-grown bed
　　The lily laid her down to die.

No more the roses bud and blow;
　　The few late beauties that remain

Are tossed by rough winds to and fro,
And all their fragrant leaves laid low
And scattered by the latter rain.

Like some old limner's quaint design
    The sunlight's checkered play doth seem,
And through the clusters on the vine,
As through a goblet filled with wine,
    Soft, shimmering sparkles gleam.

The red-cheeked apples thickly grow
    About the orchard's leafy mass,
But when they hear the tempest blow,
Through twisted boughs they sliding go
    And hide within the tangled grass.

No more the partridge's whistle rings;
    The dove her plaintive cry has ceased,—
From tree to tree, on restless wings,
The mock-bird flits, but never sings:
    The west wind rocks an empty nest.

All harmonies of Summer fail!
    The vaulting insects cease to sport;
The songs of bees alone prevail,
The wingèd traffickers that sail
    From flowery port to port.

Upon the hills and in the fields
    A few pale flowers begin to blow;
A few pale buds the garden yields,
A few pale blooms the hedge-row shields;
    Summer consents not yet to go.

O yellow leaf amid the green!
    Sad presage of the coming fall,
Soon where your withered tent is seen
Shall Autumn's gorgeous banners screen
    The incipient ruin over all!

Though sadly to ourselves we say,
    "The summer days will soon be o'er,"
Yet who may tell the very day
Whereon the Summer went away,
    Though closely watching evermore?

With sailing clouds the heavens teem,
  That beckon like impatient guides,
And like the gliding of a stream,
Like thoughts that mingle in a dream,
  The Summer into Autumn glides.

She goes! and leaves the woods forlorn:
  For grief the birds refuse to sing;
Bare lie the fields that laughed with corn;
But of each garnered grain is born
  The certain promise of the Spring.

MISS MARY A. CRUSE.

MISS CRUSE is a native of Huntsville, Alabama, one of the most beautiful and hospitable little cities of the "Southland." Charles Lanman, in one of his volumes, thus alludes to this little city:

"It occupies an elevated position, and is hemmed in with high hills, from the summit of which it presents an uncommonly picturesque appearance. . . . . It is supplied with the best of water from a mammoth spring, which gushes from a rock in the centre of the town; and this, with the array of from one to two hundred saddle-horses which are daily collected around the county court-house square, ought to be mentioned as among the features of the place. But on becoming acquainted with the people of Huntsville, the stranger will find that they are the leading character."

This was an *ante-bellum* view, yet in this latter particular the people are not changed. The Cruse family are from Maryland, and one that would take position anywhere for their refinement and peculiar sprightliness of intellect. Sam Cruse, as he was universally termed, Miss Mary Anne's father, was a man of great probity and manliness of character, one of the first citizens of Huntsville. In the person of Mr. William Cruse, an odd old-bachelor uncle, the town of Huntsville will long remember an unfailing fund of witticisms and quaint peculiarities which will render his memory delightful. "Billy Cruse" was a curiosity, an oddity, a genius, but leaving his fame, however, entirely to tradition.

Miss Cruse, even at school, began to distinguish herself, by the studiousness of her deportment and the rapidity with which she acquired her tasks. Even then the germ of the future authoress might be discovered. She frequently indulged in poetic flights when very young, in which the partial eye of friendship found buds of future promise, though I believe she has not in maturer years given any of her poetry publicity. She is highly cultivated and a fine classical scholar. She is a woman of warm friendships, rather secluded, however, in her tastes; lavishing her sentiments upon a choice few, of great uprightness and enthusiasm of character. It was in part through her exertion and earnest work in the cause that the Sunday-school and Church of the Nativity, at Huntsville, have increased in numbers and usefulness. Her books, entitled "The Little Episcopalian," and "Bessie Melville," a sequel to the former, show the beauties of religion, are pleasingly written, and were and are very popular among Sabbath-school scholars and children of a larger growth. The writer acknowledges to have read those volumes with pleasure and profit not many years ago. These tales were written more especially for the Sabbath-school of the Church of the Nativity.

During the "war," when Huntsville was occupied by Federal troops, Mr. Sam Cruse was one of the old citizens who was sent to "Dixie" on very short notice, because he loved his Southern country too well to declare himself against it. We believe Miss Cruse accompanied him, and they were "refugees" for many months.

Since the close of the war, (1866,) Miss Cruse has published her most ambitious work, "Cameron Hall: A Story of the Civil War."

"A story," the author modestly tells the reader, "which was completed before the termination of the war, the result of which, so different from our anticipations, seemed at first to necessitate a change, or at least a modification of many of the opinions and hopes confidently expressed by some of the characters. Upon reflection, however, it was decided to leave it as it is; a truthful picture, as it is believed to be, not only of the scenes and events which occurred immediately around the author's home, but also of the inner thoughts and feelings, the hopes and expectations, in a word, the *animus* of the Southern heart."

And "Cameron Hall," which we are pleased to say was a success, is, as the author says, "a work belonging rather to truth than to fiction, — a claim which will be acknowledged by thousands of hearts in our 'Southland.'"

"Cameron Hall" would be improved by judicious pruning: there is too much of it — yet it is so pure and fresh. To read it after reading a sensation novel, is like getting up early in the morning: it was very hard to start, and awful dull and sleepy to dress in the shuttered, dark room; but once up and out, how fresh and pure and sweet! There is something so earnest and unsullied in it.

Miss Cruse, like all Southern women, was a loser by the war; but she wasted no time in idly repining, and is teaching the "young idea how to shoot" in her pleasant home at the foot of "Monte Saño." And she is appreciated and loved, quietly going on the even tenor of her way.

THE WAKING OF THE BLIND GIRL BY THE TONES OF THE GRAND ORGAN.

"Have you ever been to Switzerland, Charles?" asked Uncle John.

"No, sir."

"Then it will be worth while for you to go with us. I will tell you, Charles, and would have told you before; but I don't want Agnes to know what she is going for, since surprise will add to her pleasure. In the quiet old town of Fribourg there is a cathedral containing an organ which has but one superior in Europe, and an organist whose marvellous execution is quite as wonderful. It is the only pleasure that I know on the Continent that can be enjoyed by the blind as much as by those who can see; and I am especially anxious that the child, who has been disappointed in being able to recover her sight, should at least enjoy that. Were it not for this, I would go home in the next steamer."

.   .   .   .

They reached Fribourg early in the afternoon, and Uncle John was rejoiced that they had at last arrived at their destination, and he determined to remain there until Agnes should be thoroughly rested.

As they drove rapidly through the streets, Charles saw enough to excite his curiosity, and make him anxious to study in detail the features of this singular-looking place. Its situation is most romantic, the town being divided by immense ravines, spanned by bridges, two of which are suspension bridges, the only link to bind this quaint old town to the present. Everything else seems to belong to the far-distant past, and is black with the smoke, and dust, and mould of age. Upon one of these bridges Charles

33

stood, and looked with wonder into the ravine below, where men looked almost as small as children. The bridge is said to be as high above the street underneath it as the precipice of Niagara, and it certainly seemed to our traveller to be a dizzy height. He was so absorbed that the gathering clouds failed to attract his attention, when all at once he was aroused by the large, heavy drops of rain. The storm came as suddenly and violently as only it can come in mountain countries, and by the time he reached the hotel it was pouring in torrents, with severe thunder and lightning.

He found Agnes asleep upon the sofa, and Uncle John watching her anxiously.

"I am uneasy about her, Charles," he said. "She was so bright and well at Chamouni, I thought that the Swiss air was going to work wonders for her; but to-day she has been more languid than I have seen her since she left home."

"That is nothing. The child is tired, and a few days' rest will make her as strong as ever."

"Everything is adverse to my plans to-night, Charles," said Uncle John, going to the window, and looking out at the pouring rain and the flooded streets. "The rain and her indisposition combine to upset a favorite project of mine."

"What is that, sir?"

"It is an old man's whim, which I know will excite a smile, even if it does not awaken a doubt with regard to my sanity. For days I have been indulging a pleasant sort of dream about taking her asleep to the cathedral and having her awakened by that wonderful organ-music. It would be such a delightful surprise to the child! You don't know how much I dislike to give up the idea."

"The plan is rather impracticable, sir," answered Charles, smiling, "especially on such a night as this."

"Her condition, Charles, alone renders it impracticable. If I were certain that she was only tired, and not sick, I would not hesitate to try it, for I know that I could protect her from the rain."

"Why not wait until to-morrow night, as we are to stay here some days?"

"Because the organist will not play again, either to-morrow or the next night. He is a professor of music in Berne, and only comes here on certain nights in the week to play for the benefit of travellers, for many lovers of music come to Fribourg especially to hear its wonderful performance. Besides, I want Agnes to hear the music before she knows what I brought her here for."

"How is she to get to the cathedral?"

"In my arms."

.   .   .   .

The rain had temporarily ceased, and Charles said if they would go at once they could perhaps reach the cathedral before it rained again.

It was very dark when they went into the street, and the feeble light of the lantern was almost quenched in the surrounding gloom. Uncle John carried Agnes with gentleness and dexterity, that showed he knew how to take care of her. When they reached the cathedral, they found the doors not yet opened, and they were compelled to stand and wait. As one and another were added to the waiting group, they looked with wonder and curiosity upon the foreigner with his singular burden; but, unconscious that he was the object of interest or remark, he leaned against the heavily carved portal, and in his anxiety to keep Agnes from being awakened, he forgot all else. Presently the crowd gave way to a man who approached with a lantern, and motioning Uncle John aside, he swung open the heavy doors. All was black darkness within, except that in the dim distance Uncle John and Charles saw one feeble ray, which they followed, until they found it was the sexton's lantern, by the light of which he was seating persons in the other end of the church. By degrees, their eyes became accustomed to the darkness, and looking around and above them, where two or three glimmering lights betrayed the position of the organ, they selected a seat at a proper distance.

It was a strange audience that was assembled in the Fribourg Cathedral on that stormy night — men and women, and one blind child; some from a distant continent beyond the sea; from Britannia's Isle; and others who were born and reared in the same old town which had singularly enough produced the sweetest of organs and the most gifted of musicians. There they all sat in the stillness and darkness of midnight. Scarcely a whisper was heard, and a reverent silence pervaded the assembly.

Presently the deep, trembling notes of the organ broke the stillness, and deeper, and louder, and more tremulous they grew, until it was difficult to believe that the rushing wind, of which it was so wonderful an imitation, was not sweeping wildly through the cathedral aisles. Uncle John felt a thrill pass through Agnes's frame as she sprang up and called aloud:

"Uncle John!"

He clasped her hand tightly, and whispered:

"Here I am, Agnes."

She was satisfied. She knew not, cared not where she was, or how she had come there; she knew that Uncle John was with her, and that she was listening to her own dear organ, and she was happy.

The strange performance went on. Thunder, lightning, wind, and storm exhausted themselves in wild unearthly music, and then died away in a strain so sweet and low that it might almost have been mistaken for an angel's whisper. Quicker and quicker grew the throb of the childish heart, and tighter was the grasp with which she clung to Uncle John, but she did not speak. It was a double spell that bound him, for he heard the music through Agnes's ears and felt it through her soul. Sometimes its crushing power made the stone walls tremble, and then gradually the strain wandered farther and farther away, until all that was left was a soft, sweet echo, so pure and so distant that it might have been awakened in the snowy bosom of the far-away Mont Blanc.

At length there was a long pause: artist and instrument seemed alike to have exhausted their wealth of harmony. Uncle John's hand had grasped Agnes's shawl, when there stole through the gloom such a strain of heavenly sweetness that his outstretched arm was arrested, and though he was not unfamiliar with this strange music, still he listened in breathless wonder, as he had done the first time that he ever heard it.

Sweeter than the softest flute it floated through the air, and presently another strain was interwoven with it — a low, subdued, liquid tone of the human voice, that blended with each organ-note the most exquisite harmony. It did not strike the ear; the listener knew not that it reached the heart through the medium of a bodily organ; it seemed to melt and flow at once into the very soul.

Agnes was very still; she clung closely to Uncle John, and scarcely dared to breathe.

At length it was all over; the last note died away, and they waited, but in vain, for another awakening. Presently a soft whisper said:

" Uncle John, come close."

He leaned down, and she asked, softly:·

" Uncle John, is it heaven ? "

He did not reply, but the tears sprang to his eyes — tears of pleasure at the thought that he should have given her so much happiness.

The audience quietly dispersed. The storm was over; the elements had ceased their strife, as if to listen, and the spirit of sweet peace had been wafted upon the wings of that music until it seemed to rest upon earth, and air, and sky.

LILIAN ROZELL MESSENGER.

LILIAN T. ROZELL was born in Kentucky; her parents were Virginians, and were both fond of Poetry and Music. Hence it is not difficult to conjecture whence the daughter's genius, for at the parent fount her young soul quaffed. Her love of nature, of the beautiful, the grand and weird, was manifested at an age when most children think of toys and sweets. When a little child, she delighted in oratory, in climbing some elevation and imitating speakers she had heard, in either prose or verse; and when not roaming the shades of moss-haunted woody places, she loved to fly a kite and to shoot a bow and arrow. From these early years she was a poet, for of all features of nature's glory, the clouds always furnished her more exquisite enjoyment; and the study of astronomy and natural philosophy dispelled so many fond illusions concerning the mystery of the clouds, that she almost regretted knowledge, and looked back on ignorance *then* as bliss.

All of Miss Rozell's family are of a melancholy, sensitive, musical temperament; and she is not sanguine, and is often and suddenly the victim of most depressing melancholy: in this particular she is said to be completely Byronic, if not his counterpart in genius.

Considering that Miss Rozell has never had the aid of a large library, or the advantages to be derived from literary groups, but worked in silent gloom and isolation without help or practical aid, her verse cannot be expected to be of a very hopeful strain.

The death of her father caused a change in her prospects, inasmuch as it was the reason for the shortening of her school-days; but she expects to study all her lifetime — not always to sing her lays like the mountain streams, but aim to mount higher and higher.

It was after her father's death, when everything seemed dark indeed around the young girl, that she wrote her first verses, and the subject was "Night." She was in her sixteenth year when the first publicity was made of her poems. Colonel M. C. Gallaway was her "Fidus Achates." That true-hearted gentleman was the first to offer the young poetess and orphan a sympathetic hand. Her maiden effusions

261

appeared in the "Memphis Avalanche," under the *nom de plume* of "Zena Clifton."

Miss Rozell was married in her seventeenth year to Mr. Messenger, editor of a newspaper at Tuscumbia, North Alabama — a man of strong, clear understanding, blameless as a man and as a politician. He died in 1865, four years after their marriage, leaving his young widow and one son.

During the war, when the Federal troops plundered Tuscumbia, they took a journal of manuscripts, principally lyrics, belonging to Mrs. Messenger. General Dodge tried to recover it, but did not succeed.

Mrs. Messenger has contributed many beautiful poems to the "Louisville Journal," Memphis papers, and "New York Home Journal." Her most ambitious poems are lengthy, narrative poems, yet unpublished. One of these poems purports to be an epic, and has for its subject "Columbus the Discoverer." The theme of a second is "Charlotte Corday;" and "Penelope, the Wife of Ulysses," is the subject of a third.

Mrs. Messenger is a very sweet and earnest poet; and I verily believe, had she been in a Northern literary clique, with all the advantages to be derived therefrom, she would now be a particular star in the firmament of poesy.

She is yet in her youth; and, with a desire to become a worthy contributor to her country's literature, to be recognized as a devout worshipper in the sacred temple of the Muses, she must succeed. Says she: "If I can aid in soothing any hearts, or help to inspire noble ambitious souls, it will be a sweet reward."

Mrs. Messenger possesses good musical talents, and has fine talent for landscape painting. "Next to being a great poet, I should love to be a glorious painter," says she.

Mrs. Messenger's home is in Tuscumbia, a small town in the northern part of Alabama.

1869.

THE OLD WHARF.

AT PINE BLUFF, ARK.

Sad, broken, and scarred, with a careworn look,
It is never a place that a fay might haunt,
　This brown old wharf, where the murky waves
Forever in idle monotone chaunt

A story which seems but nothing sometimes,
Save a babble of foolish and quaint old rhymes;
Like the broken fragments of winds that fell
With sweet spring, swept to her flowery dell,
    Or yet to their deep-toned caves,
Whose soft blue gloom hath defied the sun,
But the love-warm rays of the moonlight won.

Sad, broken, and scarred, with its careworn look —
    And no one thinks it can ever be more
Than the brown old wharf by the idle waves,
    With hurrying cloudlets passing o'er;
But I often think if these could speak,
How its mummied secrets would crumbling break,
And tell of the thousand steps that passed,
(In a day near by, in a far-off day,
Which may never return, or which may be the last,)
    And whisper of farewells again,
That divided true hearts, and severed true hands,
When over the South and its sweet summer-lands
    Hung the fiery Cross of Pain.

On the grim, gory mount of war it gleamed,
And woman, the weeper, was mourning there,
One farewell cleaving brave hearts and brave hands,
And fate seemed bound in the bands of prayer —
But only seemed; and the same waves tell,
By the old wharf brown, whatever befell,
When their barks drew near, and others sailed out,
    Far off in the far-away!
Eyes there are, yet gazing through time's dim gray,
That is flecked with the gold of that dawning day.

Four times and three, at the old wharf brown,
    With a cloven heart have I said good-bye,
And my secret left, and dreamed it the last,
    While the slow sad waves passed on with a sigh.
But once they bore off a form enshrined
In death's dim dusk; and once they chimed
    To a marriage-bell, on a blue June-day;
    That, too, passed out in the far-away.
And I sometimes fear that a welcome more
Will never come back from the brown old shore,
Though an army with banners of joy stood there,
Where the phantoms of hundred farewells are.

SARAH E. PECK.

MRS. PECK has, since the close of the war, contributed many interesting sketches to the literary journals of the South; and principally excelled in sketches for children — writing like a good, true mother.

Sarah Elizabeth Peck is a native of Morgan County, Alabama.

She was educated principally at Columbia, Tennessee. She was eminently successful in drawing and painting, as well as in tastefully modelling figures in wax. Several years previous to the war, while in wretched health, confined to her room most of the time, she amused the tedium of her confinement by making extracts from her readings. These she arranged alphabetically under different heads. The title was, "A Dictionary of Similes, Figures, Images, Metaphors, etc." She has been engaged for some time in preparing this work for the press. A friend of this lady, alluding to this work, says:

"This is truly an eclectic work. It is too large for a bouquet; shall I say that it is a garden into whose rich soil she has transplanted the choicest cuttings of the most celebrated rosaries?"

Mrs. Peck's home is near Trinity Station, on the Memphis and Charleston Railroad. She proposes to publish a novel, originally appearing in "Burke's Weekly for Boys and Girls."

1869.

JULIA L. KEYES

IS the eldest daughter of Prof. N. M. Hentz and Mrs. Caroline Lee
Hentz, and was born at Chapel Hill, N. C., in the year 1829. At
the time of her birth, her father filled the chair of modern languages
in the University of North Carolina, but, while Julia was yet an infant, he resigned his professorship and removed to Cincinnati. He did
not, however, remain here long, but finally located in Florence, Ala.,
and in connection with Mrs. Hentz, opened a school for young ladies.
It was called Locust Dell Academy, and soon became one of the most
popular institutions in the South. Locust Dell! ah! it is music to
the ear of many matrons throughout the South.

It was at Locust Dell that the larger portion of Julia's childhood
was spent. She was an artless, happy little girl, beloved by her associates, and admired by all who knew her for the simplicity of her nature. With such associations, and with such a mother, it is not singular that she should, even at an early age, have imbibed a literary
taste; and yet whatever distinction she may have attained has been done
without the slightest expectation that her name would be mentioned
among the female writers of the South. No such ambition has ever
moved her heart and pen. From Florence, her parents removed to
Tuscaloosa, Ala., in the year 1842, and took charge of the Female
Institute at that place. Tuscaloosa was then the capital of the State,
besides being the seat of the University. The period during which
her parents resided there were days of pleasantness to Julia. They
were perhaps the very happiest of her girlhood. Beloved and admired
by all, with scarcely a care to disturb her peace, her young imagination
painted the future with hues even brighter and more beautiful than
those that then adorned her sky, for a vision of the Land of Flowers
was ever in her heart. She knew that an abode would be prepared
for her in that sunnier clime, for there was one, the object of her own
and her parents' choice, who would there make himself a home.

From Tuscaloosa, Professor Hentz, in 1846, removed to Tuskegee,
Ala., where, in the same year, Julia was united to Dr. J. W. Keyes,
to whom for several years her hand and heart had been plighted.

Soon after, she bade adieu to parents and home, and went with her husband to Florida, at that time the place of his residence. It was here, in the early years of her marriage, amid the mournful music of the pines and the bright flowers of the far South, she wrote some of her sweetest poems. She wrote, as we have already intimated, not for gain or glory, but from that poetic impulse of which all true poetry is born. It was, we believe, in the third or fourth year of her marriage she composed those beautiful lines, "To My Absent Husband." We append a few stanzas:

> "Why does my spirit now so oft
>   In fancy backward rove?
> As beautiful in mist appears
>   That golden year of love.
> Why do I love to live again
>   My first year's wedded life?
> Oh! I was then so young and glad —
>   A childlike, happy wife.
>
> "Swiftly these few short years have fled,
>   And I am happy yet;
> But oh! those bright and sunny days
>   My heart will not forget.
> No care had I to make me look
>   Beyond those hours of bliss,
> No griefs that only mothers have,
>   No moments such as this.
>
> "And these dear little ones, that bind
>   My heart so near to earth,
> So twine around me that I bless
>   The hour that gave them birth.
> And then, my husband, thou hast been
>   Kind, gentle, true to me,
> And these bright living links have drawn
>   Me nearer unto thee.
>
> "This happiness is sweet and pure;
>   But then so much of pain
> Is mingled with our love and joy
>   In this domestic chain,
> That I am wont to wander
>   To those bright sunny hours
> When life was joyous, and my path
>   Was ever strewn with flowers.

"But think not that I would again
    My girlhood's hours recall;
I'd rather bear life's ills with thee
    Than to be freed from all,
And be without thy loving care,
    Thy fond, protecting arm,
Thine ever constant, anxious wish
    To shelter me from harm."

A few years passed quietly away, and she who had been the happy, hopeful girl was now a matron, immersed in the cares of a household, and that tender solicitude which never sleeps in a mother's breast was hers; and yet in that land where the birds sing and the flowers bloom always, and where the stars from the deep azure sky seem to look so dimly and sadly over the stillness of earth, and where, too, the sound of the sighing pines and surf-beaten shores is heard, her feelings would oft constrain her to give expression to them in verse. Few, however, of the many poems written at that period of her life have ever been given to the public.

The year of 1856 was an eventful one, and one, too, of great sorrow to Mrs. Keyes; for in that year she lost her gifted mother. She, too, had wandered to this beautiful land; for the remaining members of the family followed soon after Julia's marriage. In one of those rare and fatal spells of cold which cut down the orange and lime trees, Mrs. Hentz was attacked with pneumonia — her last illness. Nor was this Mrs. Keyes's only bereavement. In the latter part of the same year her father, who for several years had been in feeble health, died, and on the same day a beautiful and interesting little boy of five years, to whom her heart most tenderly clung. And yet she bore all these heavy afflictions in the spirit of meekness and humble reliance upon the goodness of Him who "doeth all things well."

In the year 1857, Dr. Keyes removed to Montgomery, Ala., where he had his home until the close of the war. During her residence in this city of the South, so "lovely for its situation," her time was greatly occupied in household affairs; yet some of her best poems were written in the midst of these domestic cares. The writer of this sketch, who was an inmate of her home, has often wondered at her economy of time. After doing a large amount of sewing in the day, she would sometimes give us a poem, composed while plying the needle, and written down at odd moments.

We may here remark that her poetical talent would probably never have been known beyond the home circle, had not her husband drawn from her portfolio her fugitive pieces and given them to the public, he being, perhaps, her greatest admirer. This, as we may suppose, has given her a stimulus, without which her pen would remain idle.

In 1859, she obtained the prize for the best poem under sixty lines of the "Southern Field and Fireside." The poem is called "A Dream of Locust Dell," and is considered the most touchingly beautiful of all her published productions. Certainly, few can read it without being touched by its beauty and pathos.

During the "war," Doctor Keyes was absent from home — an officer in the army — and Mrs. Keyes was left with all the cares of a large family upon her; and she patiently and cheerfully bore up under all her burdens, for her soul was strengthened and nerved by that holy and active patriotism which clothed with such undying glory our "women of the South."

The fate of war was adverse to the cause he advocated, and Dr. Keyes felt that the South, under the rule of its conquerors, was no home for his family, and he went to Brazil, where he resided for three years. Not satisfied with the educational advantages for a large family of children, he returned to Montgomery in 1870.

1870.   G. P. K.

A DREAM OF LOCUST DELL.

What spell of enchantment is that which enthralls me
    When winding the mystical mazes of dreams?
What spirit is that which alluringly calls me,
    And leads me away over mountain and streams?

I see from afar a rich landscape unfolding —
    A beautiful grove — a lake sleeping below —
'T is my own Locust Dell once more I 'm beholding,
    As on wings of the zephyr there floating I go.

I have reached it again, and the misty reflection
    Of childhood o'erpowers me with pleasure and pain;
These musings — they seem but a dim recollection
    Of something I 've lost that I cannot regain.

I wander along in this lethean existence;
    I weep, and my tears fall like dew on the grass;

I see a white mansion, not now in the distance;
　I touch my own gate-latch, and entering I pass.

So lightly and cautiously treading, I enter
　The hall where my voice in its infancy rung;
I pause for a moment when reaching the centre,
　And list for the sound of some welcoming tongue.

The quivering moonbeams and shadows are falling
　Like ghostly illusions along the dark floor:
Why suddenly thus is that vision appalling?
　Why throbs my wild heart as it ne'er throbbed before?

To open the chambers I now am unwilling;
　No farther the mansion I wish to explore;
I feel a strange dampness the atmosphere filling —
　The cold wind is rushing within the hall-door.

Oh! where are the loved ones? Oh! where have they wandered?
　Why stands the dear homestead thus bared to the blast?
'T was thus, while weak, fainting with anguish, I pondered,
　That memory appeared with a scroll of the past.

The spirit of slumber still did not forsake me —
　Again, as on wings of the zephyr, I flew;
The cool, vap'rous breath of the morn did not wake me;
　I threaded the labyrinth of dreaming anew.

I saw by a clear gushing fountain a flower —
　On its bosom a drop of the crystalline spray;
I stooped, but the spell of some magical power
　Prevented my taking the blossom away.

I watched the bright pearl-drop; it slowly distended —
　The blush of the rose seemed the hue of the sky;
I saw a new world in the ether suspended —
　Its groves and its lakes I could faintly espy.

Amid clustering trees a white mansion was gleaming —
　Two wandered together beneath the soft shade;
The pearl-drop has fallen — I wake from my dreaming
　To see the long shadows the sunbeams have made.

Oh! I know 't is the absent I've seen in my sleeping!
　Unto mansions our Saviour prepared they are gone;
Love's vigilance still o'er their child they are keeping;
　When I pass the dark valley I'll not be alone.

AUGUSTA J. EVANS.

SOME critics of the sterner sex profess to believe that female writers skim over the surface of thought; jump at conclusions without pausing to note the various steps or arguments by which those conclusions were attained; exercise imagination more than reason; and address themselves to the emotions rather than the intellect. That this is true in some instances cannot be denied, but it is far from being universal. Examples to the contrary cluster around us "thick as leaves at Vallambrosa," among whom the subject of this sketch stands foremost. But even admitting the truth of the above proposition for the sake of argument, are we not creatures of feeling as well as of thought, and are the affections *less* important in the economy of nature than the intellect? Do not our spirits crave the beautiful as well as the useful? What would the world gain by turning its flowers into forest-oaks, or its sweet green hills into impregnable mountains?

I would refer all who imagine that women are incapable of deep metaphysical research and close logical reasoning, to the writings of Miss Evans, who, in grappling with infidelity — the hydra-monster of the present age — has placed herself among the first in point of polemic ability and literary acumen, and justly merits the title of the De Staël of the South. Like the author of "Corinne," she approaches a subject with a fearless, independent spirit, and gives it the whole energies of her mind.

Augusta J. Evans is the eldest child of the late M. R. Evans, formerly a merchant of Mobile; and connected on her mother's side with the Howards, a prominent family of Georgia. She was born near Columbus, Georgia, but while she was yet a child, her parents moved to Texas. The subsequent year they divided between Galveston and Houston, and early in 1847 removed to the then frontier town of San Antonio. The Mexican war was just then at its height, and this was a place of "rendezvous" for the soldiers sent out to reinforce General Taylor. Here, between the lawlessness of the soldiery and the mixed character of the inhabitants, society was completely disorganized. There were no schools worthy of the name, and the

270

education of the little Augusta was conducted entirely by her mother, a lady of great moral and intellectual worth. Like Madame Le Vert and Mrs. Mary E. Bryan, Miss Evans owes everything to her mother, and is withal a bright example of the efficiency of home culture.

Amid the wild, uncultivated scenes around San Antonio, with scarcely a companion but her mother, (for her brothers were some years younger than herself,) she imbibed that strong, free spirit which breathes through all her works. Here she delighted to ramble about the crumbling walls of the Alamo, with her hand clasped in her mother's; while nature's grand and gloomy solitude, and the dark and bloody tragedy which had so recently been enacted in and around those walls, stirred up the latent enthusiasm of her precocious young soul. There she first dreamed of authorship. She longed to describe the wide-spread Alameda, and tell of the treachery and cruelty that marked the fall of the Alamo and the brave men who perished in that fall.

After a residence of two years in San Antonio, Mr. Evans and family removed to Alabama, and settled in Mobile, where they have resided ever since. There Miss Augusta entered school, but her health failing from the confinement, she returned to her first *alma mater*, her much revered and excellent mother.

At the age of seventeen she wrote " Inez: A Tale of the Alamo," designed to show the errors and abuses of Papacy as revealed to her in San Antonio, and to embody the principal features of the Texan war of independence. "Inez" was published anonymously in 1855, by Harpers, New York: while hardly a "success," it was not a failure. Since Miss Evans has become famous, a New York firm has published " Inez " without her consent—at least, the " copyright " had, we believe, passed from her control. For several years after the publication of " Inez," she wrote nothing, except a few book-notices for the papers. And consequently great was the surprise when " Beulah " appeared, creating a sensation throughout the country. It was published in 1859, by Derby & Jackson, New York. This book immortalized Miss Evans's name, a book much abused by certain critics, and much admired and read by everybody else. Its merit is abundantly shown in the fact that, coming from an unknown girl of twenty-three, it ran through editions of twenty-one thousand copies in little over a year.* Its great popularity is to be attributed, in some degree, to the original-

* Since the publication of " Macaria " and " St. Elmo," there has been a great demand for " Beulah," and even " Inez."

ity of its principal characters. Beulah Benton is not exactly like any girl who ever lived; and yet when we remember the bitter sufferings of her early life, her subsequent opportunities for mental culture, her genius, and the seclusion in which she lived, her character is perfectly natural. She is not as gentle, amiable, and *loving* as we could wish her to be; and the possession of some of those "amiable weaknesses" so charming in pretty women would make her much more lovable; but if this were the case, the book would be without those strong peculiarities which are its most attractive features. Had Beulah's mind been less imbittered by early wrongs, she might not have struggled with those doubts which constitute the groundwork of the book; she most probably would never have groped through the labyrinth of infidelity, and learned by experience that the weary soul can find no rest but in the religion of the Bible.

Miss Evans's home is in Summerville, about three miles from the city of Mobile, on one of the city railways. "There is nothing dreamy or eccentric about her. She is a healthy, practical, straightforward, Christian woman." She is a member of the Methodist Church, and we believe is the leader of the choir in the St. Francis Street church of Mobile. Dr. Jerome Cochran, of Mobile, says:

"Her most remarkable characteristics seem to me to be an enthusiasm, at the same time simple and childlike, and large and generous to a degree not very common among women; and a resolute, energetic will, that will not allow her to swerve from any enterprise she has once deliberately undertaken. She has an immense capacity for work. Her genius is the same triumphant faculty that has made so many people famous in this world's history — the genius of labor. Her fluency of speech is sometimes a matter of legitimate astonishment; and yet, I believe, she does not compose very rapidly. She copies her manuscript with a great deal of care, in very clear, regular, legible chirography, with hardly a blot or an interlineation on hundreds of pages. She is a very womanly woman, and is an unwavering opponent of all the new-fangled doctrines that would lead the sex to invade the time-honored prerogatives of masculine humanity. She has her faults and her weaknesses, no doubt; else she would not be human. But she is a genuine woman, and no counterfeit imitation of one — a woman full of generous feeling and high aspirations, and who is most highly esteemed by those who know her best."

During the days of the Confederacy, Miss Evans was devoted to the cause of the South and to the soldiers. An encampment a short distance from her residence was entitled, in her honor, "Camp Beulah."

Here she was a constant visitor. "While the soldiers lived, one bright spirit never forsook them; when they died, her eloquent tongue gave them counsel and comfort." It was a rare treat to pass the evening at Miss Evans's home; and her parlors and piazza never lacked for guests highly entertained by her conversation and that of her sisters.

It became a "military necessity" to destroy the beautiful trees about Summerville, as it was expected that there might be fighting in that direction, and it was thought advisable for Mr. Evans's family to remove to the city. Mobile was crowded with people, and house-room was in demand, and they fixed up the second and third floors of their father's store, fronting the river, and for several months occupied the same in a kind of "camping-out style." In the popular acceptation of the term, Miss Evans is not a *bas bleu;* for, as some one humorously remarked, "like the girls in the history of 'Sergeant Dale,' she sings psalms and darns stockings equally well."

In 1864, West & Johnston, Richmond, published "Macaria; or, Altars of Sacrifice." The motto of which was, "We have all to be laid upon an altar; we have all, as it were, to be subjected to the action of fire." By many persons this is considered Miss Evans's best book. No man or woman ever had such a subject as that, or ever will have again.

J. R. Randall, the poet, author of "Maryland, my Maryland," reviewed "Macaria" in a Georgia paper as follows:

"In 'Macaria,' the authoress of 'Beulah' has ventured on a dangerous experiment. She has endeavored to write a story of American life — our hard, bare, prosaic, unnovelistic American life — in an ultra classic and super-erudite style, and has failed. It was necessary from the very nature of things that she must have failed — but has at least done as well as any, where none could fully succeed. The narration of life in the New World is not to be written in Græcisms, or told by all the recondite philosophizing of science. We are neither a classic nor a profound people, and any attempt to portray us by a style appropriate to such, must strike us with as painful incongruity as those French melodramas where Hannibal wears red-heeled shoes and Cato harangues in a *roquelaire* and a tie-wig. The characters in 'Macaria,' or the main characters at least, are three in number — for, disdaining even the traditional duality, perhaps because it is traditional, the authoress has given us a trinity of chief personages. There is Russell Aubrey — the very type of the American self-made man. There is Irene Huntingdon, the self-poised, 'faultily faultless' daughter of a stern millionaire; and there is Electra

35

Gray, a large-eyed, fervid devotee of Art. Russell Aubrey is, when the scene opens, a dry-goods clerk, and Irene and Electra, school-girls. Prompted by pride and ambition, the hero devotes his spare hours to study, is received into a lawyer's office, goes to Europe, returns, is admitted to the bar and prospers, dabbles in politics, and 'in the course of the political cataclysm' (*Macaria*) is elected to the legislature. He loves Irene, and Electra loves him. Feelings conflict, strange love-experiences occur. Aubrey has ambition to distract him; Electra also serves two masters — Love and Art; and Irene, who finally discovers her heart is Aubrey's, mingles with her contemplations on that subject the astronomical contemplation of the heavens. The plot thickens. The triple, or rather sextuple thread of the tale becomes inextricably involved. Then the war breaks out, and the Gordian knot is — as is classically proper — cut by the sword. Aubrey becomes a soldier, and proves himself a good one. He serves faithfully, is wounded unto death, and expires in Irene's clasping arms, a noble victim offered up on a pure 'altar of sacrifice.' At his death the proper duality is restored — though that duality is of one sex, for 'Macaria' is strange to the last. Irene and Electra become heart-sisters, one ministering to the soldier and the poor, and the other pouring out her artist soul over a high-art painting, *The Modern Macaria* — a battle-scene, where the Federal flag trails in the dust, and the white-robed Angel of Peace stops the touch-hole of a cannon.

"Such is a rapid enumeration of 'Macaria's' salient points. The design of the work we have already characterized as impossible of accomplishment, and the conduct of the story is marred by a flashy show of erudition. These are grave defects — exceedingly grave, as affecting equally design and execution; and yet, in spite of all, 'Macaria' is a fine book. It is thoroughly readable, it will be productive of good, and has not a few most tender and graceful passages — so tender and so graceful that we could wish to have heard less of *æons* and *chiliasms*, and more of love and duty. Here the authoress excels. The heart — the great, loving, clinging, lovable heart — is peculiarly the province of woman, and few there be who can touch its softest chords like the authoress of 'Beulah.' Striking those chords as she did in 'Beulah,' many will hang upon her words and bless her for the comfort and happiness they bring. Forsaking the substance for the shadow, and striving to reach the head rather than touch the heart, there are few who will not feel that she is giving but husks to the hungry. Classic allusion and metaphysic theory are 'caviare to the general,' and it is for the general the novelist should write. Those who love the classics will not look for their beauties in a modern romance; and the devotees of science are still less likely to forsake the tomes of fact for the *brochures* of fancy.

"But *cuique in sua arte credendum est* — let credit be given every one in his own craft. It may be thought that we speak too harshly of 'Macaria;' and 'Macaria' shall speak for itself.

" Here is the passage which describes the star-gazing of Irene. It is night, and she watches the heavens :

" ' In panoramic vision she crossed the dusty desert of centuries, and watched with Chaldean shepherds the pale, sickly light of waning moons on Shinar's plains ; welcomed the gnomon (first-born of the great family of astronomic apparatus) ; toiled over and gloried in the Zaros ; stood at the armillary sphere of Ju, in the days of Confucius ; studied with Thales, Anaximander, and Pythagoras ; entered the sacred precincts of the school of Crotona, hand-in-hand with Damo, the earliest woman who bowed a devotee at the starry shrine, and, with her, was initiated into its esoteric doctrines ; puzzled with Meton over his lunar cycle ; exulted in Hipparchus's gigantic labor, the first collection of tables, the earliest reliable catalogues ; walked through the Alexandrine school of *savans*, misled by Ptolemy ; and bent with Uliegh Beigh over the charts of Samarcand. In imagination she accompanied Copernicus and Tycho-Brahe, and wrestled with Kepler in the Titanic struggle that ended in the discovery of the magnificent trinity of astronomic laws framed by the Divine Architect when the first star threw its faint shimmer through the silent waste of space. Kepler's three laws were an unceasing wonder and joy to her, and with a fond, womanly pride she was wont to recur to a lonely observatory in Silesia, where, before Newton rose upon the world, one of her own sex, Maria Cunitz, launched upon the stormy sea of scientific literature the '*Urania Propitia.*' The Congress of Lilienthal possessed far more of interest for her than any which ever sat in august council over the fate of nations, and the names of Herschel, Bessel, Argelander, Struve, Arago, Leverrier, and Maedler were sacred as Persian *telefin*. From the 'Almagest' of Ptolemy, and the 'Cométographie' of Pingré, to the 'Mécanique Celeste,' she had searched and toiled : and now the sublime and almost bewildering speculations of Maedler held her spell-bound.'

" This is the style we dislike — the false, strained, would-be Frenchy, ready-made scientific style, distressing to the reader, and unworthy the writer. It glitters, yet it is not gold. But here is the pure gold itself— pray that the successors of ' Macaria ' have more of it. Russell Aubrey is dying. They have brought him to the rear, and as his life is fleeting fast away in Irene's arms, he speaks :

" ' " I should like to have seen the end of the struggle — but Thy will, O my God ! not mine."

" ' He lifted his eyes toward heaven, and for some moments his lips moved inaudibly in prayer. Gradually a tranquil expression settled on his features, and as his eyes closed again he murmured faintly :

" ' " Irene — darling — raise me a little."

" ' They lifted him and rested his head against her shoulder.

" ' " Irene !"

" ' " I am here, Russell ; my arms are around you."

" ' She laid her cheek on his, and listened to catch the words ; but none came. The lips parted once, and a soft fluttering breath swept across them. Dr. Arnold put his hand over the heart — no pulsation greeted him ; and, turning away, the old man covered his face with his handkerchief.

" ' " Russell, speak to me once more."

" 'There was no sound — no motion. She knew then that the soldier's spirit had soared to the shores of Everlasting Peace, and that not until she joined him there would the loved tones again make music in her heart. She tightened her arms around the still form and nestled her cheek closer to his, now growing cold. No burst of grief escaped her, to tell of agony and despair:

> "But, like a statue solid set,
> And moulded in colossal calm,"

she sat mute and resigned, at the foot of the Red Dripping Altar of Patriotism, where lay in hallowed sacrifice her noble, darling dead.'

"Bating the poetry and the many capitals at the close — for human extremity never quotes poetry or employs capitals — this is nobly written. It is true, and therefore touching. It is feeling, and therefore felt. It is worthy of the authoress of 'Beulah,' and as far superior to the stringing together of *microcosm* and *macrocosm*, *almagest* and *telefin*, *chiliasm* and *adyta* as the eloquence of Pericles surpassed the mouthings of Cleon."

"St. Elmo" was published in 1867, by Carleton & Co., New York, and soon acquired the reputation of being the "most praised and best-abused novel" ever published in this country by a woman.

The "Round Table," in a lengthy notice of this book, says:

" 'St. Elmo' is a curious mixture of power and weakness — of insight and superficiality — of creative vigor, and of tame imitation; and while it evinces of real merit sufficient to stock half a dozen of the domestic fictions from female hands to which we are so well accustomed, it at once falls short of the ideal the writer herself unquestionably had in view, and persuades us that with time, perseverance, and a rigid chastening of style, she can produce something far better. . . . .

" 'St. Elmo' is an interesting story, if it is in some respects a stilted and pretentious one. It is a promising story, if not a particularly robust or original one."

From the many reviews and notices that have appeared of "St. Elmo," we have selected one, written by Dr. Jerome Cochran, of Mobile, and printed in the "Home Monthly," Nashville, to make our extracts :

"It is not necessary to read the title-page to know that 'St. Elmo' is the work of the same warm, true heart, and of the same resolute, aspiring mind to which the world is indebted for 'Beulah' and 'Macaria.' We have here, in still higher development, the excellences for which those two books were remarkable; the same love of inanimate nature; the same confident assertion of the dignity and blessedness of labor; the same impatience of all servility, meanness, and duplicity; the same immaculate purity of conception, thought, feeling, expression; the same beautiful sympathy with all the forms and phases of self-abnegation and self-sacrifice; the same reverent appreciation of the metaphysical and ethical doctrines of the Christian religion; the same unswerving devotion to Duty — stern daughter of the voice of God; and, in a word, the same abounding enthusiasm, the same abiding faith in all things beautiful, and true, and good. . . . . .

"In spite of all its faults, 'St. Elmo' is a genuine, earnest book; a strong, honest, rich book; a book brimful of fine thought, graceful feeling, and brilliant imagination; a book which no other woman could have written, and of which it may be safely said that in its day and generation it will do some good in the world. In the ordinary sense of the word, it is not a sensational book. It derives no part of its interest from perverse ingenuity of plot, nor from the skilful management of some tantalizing and perplexing mystery, with its customary train of evanescent and shadowy fascinations. And yet it throws over the reader a spell which he cannot shake off, which enchains his attention from the first chapter to the last, and will not allow him to stop until the end is reached.

"It is easy to say that the style is inflated and ambitious; but more than this is necessary to describe it fitly. It is always clear and strong, and rich with every variety of rhetorical embellishment. Sometimes it is imbued with the truest and tenderest pathos, and affluent of music as the song of the nightingale. Sometimes it is all aglow with the fire of eloquence, and gleams and flashes like a sky all stars. And this is its fault. It is too rich, too brilliant, too liberally garnished with those ambitious polysyllables, words sesquipedalian of learned strength and thundering sound, which were such favorites with Dr. Johnson and Dr. Parr. It seems at times to walk on stilts; and very often, in passages which are in other respects beautiful exceedingly, we come across some verbal monstrosity, or some incongruous comparison dragged in by the heels, which provokes us beyond measure. There is too much glitter. We grow weary of the unchanging splendor — of the prodigal opulence of similes, metaphors, and recondite allusions.

"The plot is extremely simple. Edna Earl — this name, by the way, is not musically correct — Edna Earl, the heroine, is a simple country-girl, the daughter of a carpenter. Bereft in early childhood of both father and mother, she grew up, until her twelfth year, near Chattanooga, Tennessee, ignorant of worldly knowledge, and of the guile which so often keeps it company, under the shadow of Mount Lookout, and the care of her grandfather, Aaron Hunt, the blacksmith, when, he also dying, she is left alone in the world, without kith or kin, and takes the cars for Columbus, Georgia, with the intention of working in the factory for a living, and of educating herself as she best can. Providence, which watches over the sparrows when they fall, does not favor the factory scheme, having quite other fortune in store for the stricken wanderer; and the train which carries Edna collides with another, with the usual quota of broken heads and limbs. Edna, badly hurt, but with some life left in her, is taken to Le Bocage, the palatial residence of the Murrays, to be watched and tended until she recovers from her injuries. Her sweet, patient temper, together with her gifts of mind and body, wins so much of Mrs. Murray's good opinion, that it is arranged that she shall remain at Le Bocage until she is qualified to teach; and her education is intrusted to Mr. Hammond, the venerable pastor of the village church, under whose care her hungry intellect devours an immense amount of miscellaneous mental food, including Greek and Latin, and even a little of Hebrew and Chaldee, her unfeminine curiosity perversely leading her to seek acquaintance with Eddas, Sagas, Talmuds, Targums, and Egyptian, Greek, Roman, and Scandinavian mythologies, instead of resting satisfied with the usual feminine varieties. At Le Bocage she makes the acquaintance of St. Elmo Murray, the hero of the book, the master of the house, and the only son of her benefactress. St. Elmo, like Phillips' Napoleon, is grand, gloomy, and peculiar. He is also handsome and rich — his beauty, to borrow a simile from Edgar Poe, dark and splendid, like that ebony to which has been likened the eloquence of Tertullian — his wealth of such fabulous abundance as to enable him to gratify the most extravagant whims of his extravagant imagination. He had grown up with his heart full of generous sympathy for humanity's toiling and suffering millions, and with his head full of philanthropic schemes for the amelioration of humanity's abounding miseries. The darling friend of his youth, Mr. Hammond's son, whom he had overwhelmed with benefactions, betrayed his confidence with treachery most foul. The beautiful woman whom he loved with all the fervor of his passionate nature was cruelly unfaithful to her vows. He tore the false woman from his heart with scorn and loathing; the false friend he killed in a duel. Soured into misanthropy and skepticism, fierce, moody, implacable, taking no delight in man, nor woman either, he heaped bitterest maledictions and anathemas upon the whole hated race of human beings, and devoted himself, soul and body, heart, mind, and estate, to the service of the infernal gods. This man, trampling all the charities and nobilities of human nature under his irreverent feet, Edna regards, first with fear and aversion, then with pitying wonder, and then — inexorable, inevitable fatality — with blind, passionate love; illustrating the truth of Pope's familiar lines:

> " ' Vice is a monster of such frightful mien,
>   As to be hated needs but to be seen;
>   But seen too oft, familiar with its face,
>   We first endure, then pity, then embrace.'

"And how does St. Elmo feel, think, act toward the poor orphan girl whom accident had thrown under his roof? She was human, and therefore, in his opinion, vile. She was woman, and therefore, according to his philosophy, false. But when he found her always clinging resolutely to the right; when years of temptation and trial left her always faithful and true— always 'pure, womanly'— his stoical misanthropy gave way. The love that had been cast out of his fierce heart, and buried out of sight for so many years, revisited the glimpses of the moon. He struggled against it; but it would not down at his bidding. At last, clasping her in his arms, covering her lips with passionate kisses, he poured into her ear the dark history of his life, into her heart the perilous burden of his passionate love. Here is the crisis of the book. For a weak woman, under the circumstances, there would have been no hope. But Edna is not weak. In spite of the mesmeric fascinations which invested her lover as he stood before her like an arch-angel fallen—in spite of the love that pleaded for him out of the depths of her woman's heart—she will be none of his; she will not degrade her womanhood by marrying a man whom she knows is not worthy of her.

"They parted; she to pursue a brilliant literary career in New York—to win money, reputation, hosts of friends, everything necessary to gratify her ambition. She is admired and praised, and her hand is sought by men most brilliantly endowed in mind and person and in this world's perishable goods. But her heart still clings, with unreasoning affection, to St. Elmo; and so, poor, proud, honest woman that she is, the flattering offers are all declined. In the mean time, Edna's love of St. Elmo—for well the wicked man knows she cannot help but love him—is the one star, radiant of hope, which shines in the dark sky that overshadows him. He will make himself worthy of Edna; with that prize before him, his lexicon has in it no such word as fail. He mends his ways. The lips that have so often uttered God's name in curses, now tremble in pious supplications. All that he can do to atone for the folly and wickedness of his misspent life he does. And the peace that passeth all understanding descends from the heaven of heavens into his heart once more. He is ordained to the ministry. Mr. Hammond's venerable hands are laid upon him in benediction, and his mother's heart blossoms like the rose. Rehabilitated in the sight of men and of angels, he seeks Edna Earl. She cannot be more just than God—cannot condemn the man whom God has pardoned; and so she takes him 'the usual way, for bet-ter or for worse, to love, honor, and obey. . . . .

"The character of Edna has at least one of the merits which criticism demands—it is true to nature. Miss Evans puts herself, more or less, into every book she writes. Beulah is like her in many things; Irene is like her in many things; but Edna is her finished and authentic portrait of herself. The biographical details of Edna's life are not applicable to Miss Evans, and in personal appearance they are widely different; but in moral and intel-lectual character they are precisely the same. As Edna feels and thinks, so feels and thinks Miss Evans; and just as Edna talks, Miss Evans talks. The most dazzling conversational bravura of Edna in the book is not one whit more keen, polished, and brilliant than Miss Evans's impromptu conversations in real life; and Edna's self is not more worthy to be loved and honored than the gifted lady whose fancy painted her.

"Miss Evans has done well in 'St. Elmo;' but she can do better. She has the native power of thought, the energy of will, the shaping-power of imagination, and the triumphant faculty of labor, which sweeps all difficulties from its path, all the qualifications that are necessary to produce a truly great book — a book that will deserve to live, and that will live."

Miss Evans was married, on the 1st of December, 1868, to Mr. L. M. Wilson, of Mobile. Her residence is at Summerville, about four miles from the city of Mobile.

In 1870, Carleton, publisher, New York, purchased from Mrs. Wilson, at the extremely liberal price of fifteen thousand dollars, the copyright of "Vashti; or, Until Death us do Part" — Mrs. Wilson's last novel. Like "St. Elmo," this was much abused; and, unlike that fine work, "little praised." It was not equal to the former productions of Miss Evans's pen; and, although having a large sale, was not as successful as her former novels.

The preface to "Vashti" is from Lessing: "Every man has his own style, as he has his own nose; and it is neither polite nor Christian to rally an honest man about his nose, however singular it may be. How can I help that my style is not different? That there is no affectation in it, I am very certain."

1870.

I. M. PORTER HENRY.

MRS. HENRY is perhaps best known as a contributor to General Hill's magazine, "The Land we Love," and other Southern papers and magazines, under her maiden name of Ina M. Porter, also publishing under the *nom de plume* of "Ethel Hope." She is a native of Tuscaloosa, Ala., a daughter of Judge B. F. Porter, a South Carolinian by birth, and the writer of occasional verses of considerable poetic merit. Mrs. Henry from a very early age indulged in literature, always happy when she was able to sit near her father and write.

For several years, her "youthful" muse sang Indian legends, vague fancies, the beauties of her mountain home, and revelled in the mists which shrouded the rolling hills, or grew ecstatic on the bosom of the lovely Tennessee River; yet she wandered, sighing for some deeper song to sing. She felt that power within her which must be perfected through deeper emotions than those called forth by the calm beauty of nature, some key-note more sublime than caves, chasms, and mighty waters. It came — when the war-cry sounded through our land, she knew that the "South" was her theme.

Through the sufferings of her countrymen and women, she learned that poets could find no higher strain than love of right and hate of wrong — no holier subject than truth.

Judge Porter made his home in Greenville; now a thriving little town, on the line of the Mobile and Montgomery Railroad.

Miss Porter wrote a play during the second year of the war, entitled "None but the Brave Deserve the Fair," which was performed at the Mobile Theatre, and subsequently at Greenville, for the benefit of the "Confederate Soldiers." In Simms's "War Poetry of the South," "Lament for Mumford" and several other poems commemorative of the struggle of the South appear from this drama. Miss Porter's prose articles during the war were mostly on topics of local interest, or upon some practical question applicable to the wants and means of aiding our soldiers.

The "Roadside Stories," appearing in "The Land we Love," were truly excellent pictures of "life in Dixie." Few, to read them, would think they were written under adverse circumstances — written during that period of desolation which followed the surrender of the "Confederate cause."

Judge Porter's family shared the common heritage of Southrons, and were left with little to wear and little to eat; and to add to these "evils," sickness surrounded them.

A friend tells me that Miss Ina Porter and her mother were the only available workers on the place — all the others sick, and the servants all left, except one, a girl, who had the small-pox, and was of no assistance. Mrs. Porter was physician and nurse, and Miss Ina cook and maid of all work. Under these circumstances, not favorable to literary labors, the "Roadside Stories" were written. We mention these facts to show the heroic spirit that animated one of *our* bright stars among "Southland Writers," and can truly say she is but a representative of the many in her "will to do."

In October, 1867, Miss Porter was married to Mr. George L. Henry, and continues to reside near Greenville, Butler County, Ala. She continues to "wield her pen" when other duties and health permit — for, we regret to say, her health has not been good, and the death of her father was a severe blow. Mr. and Mrs. Henry have begun the battle of life with "Confederate weapons," warm hearts and strong wills; and success and happiness must crown their hearth-stone.

1869.

RIMMER.

I stand before thee, Rimmer,
    And as thy chosen wife
Am exultant in the glory —
    Crowning glory of my life.

Wind no rosy veil about me,
    My actual self to hide;
As a real — not ideal —
    Look upon your future bride.

You smile at my odd fancies;
    Smile — but know me as I am,
Or our voices ne'er can mingle
    In the holy marriage-psalm.

You flatter me, gay Rimmer;
    You call my eyes sky-bright!
Have you seen the blue skies darken
    At the falling of the night?

You vow my cheeks are petals
　　From living roses rent;
Ah, the roses wither, Rimmer,
　　When the summer shine is spent!

There! my unbound hair you're calling
　　Golden eddies of the morn!
Do you know the dawn-waves whiten
　　When the yellow sun is gone?

If you love me, if you trust me,
　　Erring, human, as you see,
Give your honor to my keeping,
　　As I give my own to thee.

My life I cast before thee;
　　Its pages lie unclaspt;
Read from alpha to omega,
　　Judge the future by the past.

Canst thou mete as I have measured
　　Truth as boundless as the sea?
Speak! my heart will not be broken —
　　Ha! 'tis glorious to be free!

Oh, forgive me, noble Rimmer!
　　No love nor faith I lack;
But the wedding robes are holy
　　As the coffin's solemn black!

Our souls are God's, not ours —
　　My heart is all I bring;
Lift me higher, royal lover;
　　I crown thee — O my king!

CATHERINE W. TOWLES.

AMONG the writers of the "Southland" who have labored in the
"heat of the day," never ceasing in the good work of providing
interesting, instructive, and moral literature for her countrywomen,
may be named Miss C. W. Barber; for by her familiar maiden name
is she best known to the readers of Southern periodical literature.

Miss Barber was born in Charlemont, a romantic little town in Northern Massachusetts, on the 25th day of October, 1823. She was the daughter of a farmer, and her earliest recollections are of green pastures, where fed herds and flocks; rich meadows, where waved the tall grass ready for the mower's scythe, and fields of golden grain ripening in the sunshine. She early began her literary career, sending verses to the country newspapers while yet a mere child. These verses were favorably received by the reading public, and were frequently copied into other journals. Hon. Whiting Griswold, now of Greenfield, Mass., was her principal teacher; he was at the time a student in Amherst College. He brought her books to read from the college library, and encouraged her to study and literary effort.

In 1846, soon after the death of her father, she came South to reside in the family of her brother. Her literary reputation followed her, and contributions were solicited of her by Southern journals.

In 1849, she received two prizes, one for the best tale, and one for the best poem, written for the "Madison Family Visitor," a literary and family journal started in Morgan County, Geo., and was solicited to take charge of its literary department; and did so, and continued editress of this paper for three years. It was during this period that she wrote a series of tales for the "Masonic Signet and Journal," which were so well received by the fraternity that they were collected into a volume, and published in New York under the title of "Tales for the Freemason's Fireside." Shortly afterward she wrote a series of "Odd-Fellow Tales," which were published in a volume, entitled "The Three Golden Links."

In 1861, Miss Barber became connected with the "Southern Literary Companion," a paper published by I. N. Davis, a blind man, in the town of Newnan, Georgia. To this journal she contributed novelettes, and articles on subjects "humorous, grave, and severe." Her connection with this paper continued until the close of the war. In the spring of 1866, she became editress and proprietress of a literary paper published in Newnan, called "Miss Barber's Weekly," which was continued until August 29th, 1867, when Miss C. W. Barber became the wife of Hon. John C. Towles, of Lafayette, Ala. She now resides on her husband's plantation near that place.

Although of Northern birth, Mrs. Towles is Southern by acclimation and long residence, and she considers Alabama her home; for to her it is now "a land of rest."

1869.

MRS. JULIA SHELTON.

("Laura Lorrimer.")

" GENIUS — native talent."

LAURA LORRIMER possesses "genius of a rare order," and several years ago was noted as one of the most promising of the young writers of the South. In December, 1855, she married Mr. J. A. Shelton, of Bellefonte, Alabama, at which place she resides at the present time, having two children, a son and daughter.

Julia Finley was born on the Cumberland River, Tennessee, and at an early age commenced "poetizing." She was one of George D. Prentice's galaxy of poets — of which Amelia Welby was probably the best known. The South, and indeed the whole country, owe much to this gifted and noble Kentuckian, for his helping hand and encouraging words to young aspirants for literary fame.

" Laura Lorrimer " was a contributor to the various journals and magazines, North and South — Godey's "Lady's Book," "Louisville Journal," and "Field and Fireside," among others.

THE FEVER–SLEEP.

A PRIZE POEM.

There was a Hecla raging in my soul,
Of wild emotions which might not be stilled.
Through its dim arcades flashed the murky light,
In fitful corruscations, and each niche
Grew all irradiate. On the year's broad breast
Four months had wreathed their coronals and died,
For it was May, but in my fevered soul
The sweet May flowers had withered, and upon
Its myrtle garland slept a mildew blight.

One year ago that very May, I bent,
In love and faith, beneath the deep-blue heaven,

And as the stars went floating up its arch,
My soul was floating on the passionate breath
Of new, strange music to a fairy land.
Life then was golden-tinted: I had not
One unbelieving thought; I could not link
The purple glory of my dreams in one;
They wavered, flashed, and paled like sunset gleams,
Through the proud arches and pilastered domes
Of Southern climes.   Oh! I had never known
Aught half so blissful, and I lived an age
In every breath which chronicled that hour
Of my existence.   Immortality
Seemed charactered upon it, and I heard
The low, sweet chiming of a thousand streams,
Which swept their crystal through the amaranth bowers
Of Aiden, and the mystic language grew
Articulate.   I seemed to hear them say
That love like this could never die; that through
The march of centuries to Eternity,
Its hymn of adoration still would rise
And tremble on the air.   I have had dreams
Which crowned my spirit as I walked amid
The shadowy vale of visions, with a band
Of all unearthly radiance, but, oh! none
So bright as those which clustered round me on
That sweet May midnight, when my eyelids drooped,
Dank with the dews of slumber on my cheek,
And the soft echo of love's thrilling words
Still lingering around me.   How my soul
Grew gently luminous with gleaming wings,
As the night-sky with stars!
                              May came again;
But my hot brow seemed banded with a chain
Of living fire.   My senses all were bound
In the dread fetters of a fever-sleep.
I struggled with my thraldom, and my thoughts
Wandered within a narrow, darkened cell—
Pale, wingless phantoms, striving to unlock
The gates of destiny.   Then strange, wild birds,
With eyes of fire and wings of lurid flame,
Perched close beside me, and, from time to time,
Sank deep their vulture beaks into my heart.
I knew they were my incarnated passions, which
The fever-demon mockingly had called

Into a fierce existence. Closer still
They flocked around me, and I was upborne
Upon their rushing pinions through the stars,
On, on to " outer darkness." There are orbs,
Which ages since flashed down a golden ray,
Whose earthward journey yet is scarce begun,
And we had passed the farthest; now we stood
At the closed gates of dread, eternal Night.
" *Room,*" shrieked, half humanly, each vulture throat,
" *Room for our burden.*" Fetterless, the winds
Roamed the abyss, and answered, " *There is none !* "

Time had not winged another moment ere
Light flashed upon my eyelids. On the earth
How one short moment oft has crowned my soul
With years of rapture, and I have grown old,
Even in the folding of one warm caress!
Another moment, and a star-throned isle
Gleamed in the blue beneath us. " We must rest,"
Moaned my fierce carriers; " *room is for us here,*
In this fair planet; *here* our weary wings
Shall leave their burden." Wooingly the waves,
From their blue, throbbing bosoms, whispered " *Come.*"
It was a lovely world: its temples lay
Like heavy snow-rifts, in the gentle light
Of seven bright moons. It was a paradise,
Which I had never imaged, even amid
My wildest visions. Opiate incense rose
From nameless flower-buds, like the heavy mists
From the damp earth, and every nerve grew faint
With dreamy languor. I was all alone,
That star-world's sovereign. It had never yet
Felt the soft stirring of an angel-plume
In its calm air. The chiming of the wave,
The wind's low footstep, and the wild bird's song,
Were all its music. But my heart-strings still
Were linked to earth, and to earth's passion-dreams.

One cloud may veil the " day-god's " fiery steeds,
Even in the zenith of their blue-arched path;
And now earth-shadows severed from my soul
The soft, gold arms of the caressing light.
Wiser than I have tangled up their prayers
In the dark tresses of a haughty head.

And sung a hymn to clay instead of God ;
And I — am but a mortal ; so I had
An *idol* with me, e'en among the stars,
A name to which my soul forever sang
As to a deity, and whispered words
Of half-unearthly worship.

      Hours or months,
It might have been, grew gray and died, but yet
There came no day. My spirit could not count
Time's heavy throbbings, but the very air
Seemed faint and tremulous with an unseen
And mighty presence. Four bright pinions came
Floating above me, and then wavered down,
Like the gold leaves of autumn, by my side.
Beautiful angels were they, Love and Faith,
But Love stood nearest, bending o'er my heart,
As if to count its throbbings. God had sent
Visible angels, thus to symbol forth
The thoughts invisible which filled my soul.
Oh, in the heavens, Israfel's sweet lute
Ne'er to his fingers thrilled as did my heart
To the soft music of their murmured words —
That angel lullaby ! My lids drooped down,
Charmed with its opiate. To the land of dreams,
I bore the vague, sweet echoes of the song :

   Slumbers be thine,
    Gentle and deep ;
   Queen of the star-isle,
    Rest in our keep !

   Chased by our pinions,
    Trouble shall fly,
   Ever around thee
    Rise Love's lullaby.

   Faith ever near thee
    Guardian shall stand,
   Love round thy forehead
    Twine her bright band.

The music died in wailings. O'er the sky
Swept a dark tempest, and my star-isle shook
To its foundations ; fiery lavas rolled
In desolating fury down the slopes

So grand with beauty, and the temples fell
In shapeless masses on the trembling earth.
My angel guards had fled; beside me stood
A demon presence, giant-like and stern.
Fearfully beautiful twined the iris crown
In the black billowy locks which swept away
From the lost angelhood of his broad brow —
Fit rival for the passions glowing fierce
And tiger-like in the wild orbs beneath.
Silent in demon majesty he stood,
But ever and anon the heavy wings
Shook almost to unfolding, and the mists
Dropped from them, leadenly, upon my brow.
All, all was silence, save the wild heart-throbs
Which strove to burst their prison; for I shrank
In voiceless terror from the bitter smile
Which curved the haughty lips, and from the stern
And blasting gaze of those dark, fiery eyes.

I rose and strove to fly; but demon wings
Flapped heavily around me, and a voice
Which filled the universe hissed in my ear
The awful words: "Down! down! to meet thy doom.
Thou hast lost heaven for earth, and staked thy soul
Against a mortal's love. For one whose brow
Is crowned with amaranth, thou hast flung down
The gauntlet to Omnipotence. Depart!"
I was a wanderer. A mark was set,
Like Cain's, upon my forehead; and alone,
Amidst the mighty forests of the West,
I writhed my way. Like sleeping Titans lay
The mountain ranges in the dim gray light
Which heralded the dawn. Before me rolled
The ocean, with its hungry waves astir,
Leaping in eager bounds upon the strand,
Like wild beasts on their prey.
                              "Alas," I cried,
"Alas for thee! my own sweet spirit-love!
Thou art not now beside me; but thy deep
And passionate words are floating round my heart
Like angels in the darkness, and again
I drink a haunting music from their swell;
Their memory comes like echoes from the past,

37

The blessed past. Will no one ope the gates,
And lead me backward to that glorious state,
And to the idol of my girlhood dreams
And their wild fervor?"
                              Then a genius came,
And he unlocked the caverns of the deep;
Then bore me downward to the blue-sea halls,
And midst those coral grottos cooled my hands
In crystal vases. There the opal shone
With mystic radiance, and the emerald wreathed
The pale, dead brows, which gleamed up white and strange
Amid the sea-weed. Oh! they slept with pearls
And all things beautiful, and the great waves
Forever pealed a requiem o'er them, and
Thus shall they sleep until time's dying throbs
Shall shake the universe.
                              "Go seek thy love,"
Whispered the spirit, and a mocking smile
Bent his red lip; "perchance he sleepeth here
In Neptune's regal palace."
                              One by one
I numbered o'er the dead, and wandered on
For weary miles. I lifted raven curls
From many a brow, and bent o'er many a lip;
But yet saw none which bore the spell of his
For whom I sought with hopeless, patient love.
Soft through the waters, gleaming like a star,
Flashed a clear ray. "Sweet love!" I murmured then,
"Be this the guide to lead my steps to him."
Fresh glories gleamed around me. Rainbow-hued
And crimson sea-flowers climbed a coral arch,
And draped a regal couch; and there he lay,
Not pale and dead, but warm and rich with life.
Age yet had pressed but lightly on the brow
So glorious in its beauty, and those curls
Of raven darkness swept its marble breadth
In shadowy magnificence. The eyes
Had learned not coldness from the frozen years
Which rolled their heights between us; the full lips
Were curving their rich crimson in a smile,
And angel pinions drooped with silvery sheen
From the broad shoulders. Like a peal of bells,
He syllabled my name. I never thought
If he had wings on earth, or was so fair,

But still I nestled in his warm embrace;
And then he said, one cabalistic word
From him would ope those portals as the sun
Unbars the gates of day. With trumpet-voice
He breathed the mystic spell. A thousand flowers
Seemed blending all their blossoms into one;
A thousand music-echoes seemed to sweep
Into infinitude, and dazzling rings
Of golden light, in widening circles, flashed
Athwart my vision, and my fever-dreams
Were torn apart, as by a wizard spell.
Yet one remained — the sweetest one — to be
A sweet *reality*. A proud face bent
O'er my pale brow, and wooing, loving words
Charmed my weak senses. All athirst, I drank
The God-sent nectar, and my pulses beat
With healthful throbbings. Life to me once more
Was beautiful, and the great boundary-line
Which spanned my Eden was Eternity.

———•◦⟡◦○———

MRS. OCTAVIA WALTON LE VERT.

MADAME LE VERT is more widely known in a social than in a literary way. She was born near Augusta, Georgia, — the grandchild of that Walton who was both sage and soldier in the Revolution, one of the signers of the Declaration of Independence. Reared in Pensacola, Florida, (whither she was removed in infancy,) she received the most thorough instruction, and became fully versed in several languages. The presence of naval officers at Pensacola gave a charm to society there; and under these most propitious auspices, Miss Walton made her *début* into society. Her intellectual accomplishments and the perpetual sunshine of a gay and glad spirit, always amiable, kind, and considerate, were her charms. Visiting the principal points of fashionable resort and the principal cities of the Union, Miss Walton became widely known and admired.

In 1836, Miss Walton became the wife of Dr. Henry S. Le Vert, an eminent physician of Mobile. Their home on Government Street was, until after her husband's death and the close of the late war, the resort of all strangers of distinction visiting Mobile; and here Mrs. Le Vert dispensed the most enlarged hospitality.

Mrs. Le Vert twice travelled in Europe; and in 1858, S. H. Goetzel & Co., of Mobile, published, in two duodecimo volumes, "Souvenirs of Travel." This work was eminently successful. These volumes con. sist chiefly of private letters, journals, and sketches during her two visits to "Over the Sea," and are rich in brilliant descriptions, and picturesque and glowing in style and arrangement of particulars.

Mrs. Le Vert makes her home equally in New York and with a married daughter near her own birthplace, and occasionally writes for the literary journals of the Metropolis. She is of that happy disposition that never takes on the years, but seems ever youthful and full of life and joyousness.

In 1866, Carleton, New York, issued a new edition of "Souvenirs of Travel," two volumes in one.

1871.

———oo꞉ౖ౦꞉oo———

MARY WARE.

THE blue hills of Tennessee encircle no lovelier gem than the beautiful vale of "Sweet Water." Here, in the midst of the most picturesque scenery, Mary Harris passed her childhood's morn, her soul imbibing a love for all things beautiful in nature. Her brother Edmund was her constant companion: they read together, rambled together, and their thoughts and feelings entwined around the same objects and desires. When they were on the verge of manhood and womanhood, their parents removed to Alabama. Edmund commenced writing for the press; and Mary, enjoying her brother's productions, ventured to do likewise. Her first verses appeared in the "Mobile Advertiser," in 1852.

Brother and sister became regular contributors to the "Home Circle," (Nashville,) and other Southern journals, and also for "Godey's Lady's Book,"— Miss Harris writing over the pseudonym of "Gertrude Glenn."

About 1854, Mr. Edmund Harris removed to Mobile, and became associate editor of one of the city papers. He died in 1859.

In 1864, Miss Harris was married to Mr. Horace Ware. She resides in Columbiana, Alabama.

She has written in prose and verse for various magazines, and is a favorite writer for children in "Burke's Weekly," (Macon, Ga.) She has about two hundred short poems of her own, and quite a collection of her brother's, which she expects to publish in book-form.

1871.   S. E. PECK.

CONSOLATION.

I'm gazing far back in life's morning,
　Through the shadows that sleep on the hills,
To the beautiful sunlight of childhood
　That lay on the valleys and rills.

I've travelled a wearisome journey,
　I'm footsore and longing for rest;
But I think of the glory of morning,
　And hope it may gild the far West.

Yes, I think of that beautiful islet
　That sleeps on the bosom of Time;
And am straining my vision to catch but
　A glimpse of its sweet, sunny clime!

But mine eyes are now weary with weeping,
　And shadows have grown up between;
So I know that I'm groping in darkness,
　Away from that beautiful scene.

Ah, never again can the sunlight
　That sleeps on those beautiful hills
Cheer my lone heart till it blossom,
　Or waken its musical rills.

But sometimes I hear in the distance
　A faint sound of music so sweet!
And I know that behind the dark river
　There are some I am longing to meet.

MRS. E. L. SAXON.

THE parents of Mrs. Saxon were Virginians. She was born in Tennessee in 1832. The following year her father moved to Alabama. Her mother lived little over a year in her new home. Mrs. Saxon came thus early under the especial care and training of her father, a man well read in ancient and modern literature, and combining with this thoroughly practical ideas and a love of nature. He early imbued his youthful charge with his man's love of reading, and his favorite works soon became her favorites. With him she read, rode, and hunted: her out-door life in the forests of Alabama was free and untrammelled, as was her in-door mental one. In the domains of thought, her peculiar training served to feed the flames of a vivid imagination, and the practical and ideal met in her, harmonious as night and day.

> "Her father wrapped his little daughter
> In his large man's doublet,
> Careless if it fit or no."

This masculine teaching never for a moment detracted from her true feminine dignity, only giving grace of action and vigor of body and intellect. In addition to her father's teaching, she shared the instruction of village schools until the age of fourteen, when she was sent to the school of Mrs. Caroline Lee Hentz, then teaching in Alabama. Mrs. Saxon married, at the age of sixteen, Mr. Lydell Saxon, of South Carolina.

She had written prose sketches and some creditable poetry before her marriage. She contributed poems and sketches to the "American Courier" (Philadelphia), over the signature of "Annot Lyle," which was her maiden name. She also published under various names; and several long stories, viz., "Judith," "Life's Changes," "The Trials of an Orphan," etc., appeared over her own name in the "Columbia Banner," of South Carolina, edited by Dr. R. W. Gibbs. About the same time she published, in the "Louisville Courier," several serial stories, which were well received.

294

Few Southern writers had fairer prospects of success, but near this time domestic afflictions caused her to cease publishing.

During the last twelve or fourteen years she has lived in New York, Memphis, Mobile, and now resides in New Orleans. This has given her a varied experience, not unprofitable to her observing mind. She has in her portfolio a large amount of MSS.

Within the last two years she has regularly contributed, prose and poetry, to the New Orleans "Picayune" and "Times," over the signature "E. L. S." She has in MS. a novel, which, we think, must establish her claims as an author beyond all dispute. Her style of writing is simple and direct, mostly from the plane of feeling, which in all cases is power, touching the heart and inspiring love for the author.

On her mother's side, Mrs. Saxon is related to Miss Mollie E. Moore, of Texas. Mrs. Saxon has ever been the centre of her home circle, never seeking the outside world, and in her charming family she finds her reward.

1870.

MY VINE.

My vine I planted in the days
　　When April's tears fell soft and warm —
Our love was in its blooming time,
　　And life was in its morning charm.
It grew so fast, the tendrils strong
　　Crept up and round the lattice clung,
Shading the little cosy bench
　　O'er which my gay canary hung.

Oh, there you whispered words of love —
　　Told all you meant to do for me;
Called me all pet names, "child and dove,"
　　Wove bright threads in my destiny.
I was a silly, simple child —
　　All girls are foolish when they love —
I only looked, believed, and smiled,
　　And told how faithful I would prove.

I loved you, and I wore my heart
　　Careless, that all the world should see
I did not know the coy, sweet art
　　To hold in thrall a man like thee.

The autumn days have dulled the green
    That gave my vine its beauty rare,
And doubts have come our hearts between
    Since last we sat together there.

Next spring will give the vine its green,
    Send all its beauty back once more;
Will nature bless her other child,
    And her lost girlish dreams restore?
The same buds never bloom again,
    But others just as fair will spring —
Kind nature learns her children well,
    Some vine about my life will cling.

S. S. CRUTE.

MRS. SALLIE SPOTSWOOD CRUTE, in 1871, announced for
publication, by subscription, a volume entitled "Buds from the
Wreath of Memory." Mrs. Crute is a native and resident of Huntsville, Ala., only daughter of Dr. John C. Spotswood, an old citizen
of that city.

ANNA FREDAIR.

MINOR PLACE," a novel, by "Anna Fredair." New York. E.
J. Hale & Son. 1869.
Miss Walker, of Tuscaloosa, was the author of this book.

CAROLINE THERESA BRANCH.

MRS. BRANCH, younger daughter of Marcellus N. and Caroline
Lee Hentz, was born in Cincinnati, Ohio, in December, 1833.
Her mother's name will at once be recognized as "a household word"
in the South. Caroline, reared in a literary circle, found herself an

author, in print, in early girlhood; and as she grew to womanhood, her pen was enlisted in adorning the pages of the most popular literary journals with novelettes, etc. In 1858, Miss Hentz was married to the Rev. James O. Branch; and, as the wife of a faithful itinerant Methodist minister, *going about* doing the Master's work, she has been denied that leisure for the use of her pen, and many of those surroundings which stimulate and assist literary labor, that a settled home-life would have afforded. Hence, unfortunately, she has not put forth her strength in the service of letters, but has made herself rich instead in that "good name" as a wife and mother which the wise man pronounces the truest wealth.

Mrs. Branch's productions are of such a character that it is difficult to make extracts from them, without giving the barest fragments and breaking up their unity.

She is at this time (1871) residing at Macon, Ga.

REV. DR. MYERS.

BETTIE KEYES HUNTER.

MRS. HUNTER'S tales and verses, published in the New Orleans "Picayune," Baltimore "Home Journal," and other periodicals, display considerable talent. She is the daughter of Colonel Washington Keyes, who was, at the time of her birth, cashier of a bank at Decatur, Ala., where she was born, March 20th, 1834. Both parents died when Bettie was only five years old.

Miss Keyes, at an early age, married her cousin, Joseph M. Keyes, of New Orleans, who died a few years afterward, leaving her with two daughters. In 1864, Mrs. Keyes married Mr. A. M. Hunter, of Claiborne County, Mississippi. Her residence is near Grand Gulf.

Mrs. Hunter's most noted publication is "A Letter addressed to Mrs. Woodhull," in the name of the "Women of the South," to whom she had appealed to clamor for the right of suffrage.

We append one of Mrs. Hunter's poems.

A MOTHER'S WISH.

Come tune, my muse, thy sweetest lyre,
And let its richest music swell:

Within me, like Promethean fire,
  Are burning thoughts I cannot quell!
For I would rend the misty veil
  That shrouds my children's future path;
Although perhaps my cheeks would pale
  At visions which that vista hath!

Two gentle girls, whose childish brow,
  Unwrinkled, fair, and innocent,
I fain would keep as smooth as now,
  If wishes were not impotent.
I would that I their fragile bark
  Might steer from all life's dangerous shoals,
Whereon, when hope's light groweth dark,
  Are wrecked so many human souls.

I cannot bear to think there lies
  Deep fountains of misfortune's tears
Within my darling's sweet blue eyes,
  To be unsealed in future years;
O'er wasted hopes and pain to see
  Their heart's rich treasure cast away,
And love's bright glow a mockery,
  Like glist'ning seaweed wet with spray!

Oh, would my eyes might shed their tears,
  And would my heart their griefs might bear!
I'd shield them through their future years
  From every woe, from every care!
My gentle Zella's soft brown hair
  Should never grow less dark than now;
And darling Lillie's curls so fair
  Should never silver o'er her brow!

It may not be!—however kind
  Our yearning hearts, God gives to each
A different fate; nor can we find
  A way through other lives to reach.
We can but pray hope's beacon light
  Shall never o'er life's sea grow dim;
And strive to guide our own course right,
  Then trust the rest in faith to Him!

MISSISSIPPI.

SALLIE ADA VANCE.

SALLIE ADA REEDY was born in Northern Alabama Captain James Reedy, her father, removed to Lexington, Mississippi, during her infancy.

Miss Reedy was early inclined to study; was passionately fond of reading, and had the advantage of careful and judicious culture.

While a child in years, she began to write in verse, and her early poems exhibit the same thoughtful tone, the same impassioned tenderness which can be seen, ripened and refined, in her later writings.

In 1860, her poems, which had appeared from time to time in the various periodicals of the South, were collected for publication in bookform. The " war " caused the idea to be abandoned for more auspicious times.

In 1865, about the close of the war, Miss Reedy entered upon a new phase of womanhood : she was married to Mr. Vance, and resided in Lexington, the home of her childhood.

The character of Mrs. Vance's poetry is subjective — her thoughts most frequently introverted — finding their field of research in the infinitely varied human heart. Yet she feels the charm of nature with all a poet's sensitive organization ; and she describes the beauty of earth, sky, and ocean with the vivid truthfulness of an appreciative as well as imaginative mind. Her melody of versification is remarkable. Her thoughts ripple away into rhyme so easily that we perceive it to be their natural vehicle. Her words are always musical and well chosen.

But there are depths in her nature which have not been stirred : there are chords which have not been sounded. When these have been awakened by the hand of a larger experience, we shall see the poetry of Mrs. Vance take a wider range — a deeper and more earnest tone.

She has recently finished a poem, longer than any she ever published, which is considered by judges to be the best she has ever written.

Mrs. Vance lost her husband in December, 1868.

"Beautiful as a poet's dream" is an old saying — but here is a poet's dream that is more than beautiful:

THE TWO ANGELS.

A boy at midnight sat alone,
  And quick throbs o'er his being stole,
Like those to graver manhood known
  When high resolves are in the soul.
Two winged angels softly leave
  The brightest star in all the sky,
And one is fair as sinless Eve —
  The other has the serpent's eye.

Now to the boy they softly glide,
  And fold their starry wings unseen,
Then rest them, one on either side,
  And watch him as he sits between.
Each angel holds within her hand
  A spotless scroll of purest white,
For God has sent them with command
  To write the boy's resolves that night.

"I will be great!" his hot cheek burned —
  "That men shall shout in ecstasy,
When first their wondering souls have learned
  How like the gods a man may be."
The angel on the left hand smiled,
  And wrote it with suspended breath;
She knew ambition oft beguiled
  To sin and sacrifice and death.

"I shall have foes, as greatness hath,
  Whate'er may be its brilliant sphere;
But I will sweep them from my path,
  Or maim their puny souls with fear."
The angel on the left hand caught
  And wrote the proud boast with a sneer;
The angel on the right had nought
  Upon her page but one bright tear.

"Love, still the poet's chosen theme,
  Shall be a thing abjured by me;

And yet — my childhood's happiest dream
  Came to me on my mother's knee.
My mother's knee! Why what is this
  That on my lips is trembling now?
A prayer? I almost feel the kiss
  Her dying lips left on my brow.

"She'd rather hear her name and mine
  In some poor creature's night-prayer told,
Than have the proud world rear a shrine
  And write it there in burning gold."
The angel on the left awhile
  Seemed half in doubt and half in rage;
The other smiled a warm, bright smile
  That dried the tear upon her page.

"I will be brave, and ask each heart
  That faints in life to lean on mine,
And strive to do that better part
  That makes a mortal feel divine;
And, if my faults should win a foe
  Relentless through all coming time,
I'll pity you who may not know
  Compassion makes this life sublime."

The boy looked upward to the sky;
  But ere his vow was halfway done,
And ere the light passed from his eye,
  The angel on the left had flown:
The angel on the right was there,
  And for one joyful moment stood,
Then waved her bright wings on the air,
  And bore her message back to God.

Very seldom, in all the range of poetry, do we find anything so
perfect in all respects as the following gem. It is unexceptionable in
every respect — a lesson for life, to be conned every day by those who
would worship the good, the beautiful, and the true:

GUARD THINE ACTION.

When you meet with one suspected
  Of some secret deed of shame,
And for this by all rejected
  As a thing of evil fame —

Guard thine every look and action:
  Speak no heartless word of blame;
For the slanderer's vile detraction
  Yet may spoil thy goodly name.

When you meet a brow that's awing
  With its wrinkled lines of gloom,
And a haughty step that's drawing
  To a solitary tomb —
Guard thine action: some great sorrow
  Made that man a spectre grim;
And the sunset of to-morrow
  May have left thee like to him.

When you meet with one pursuing
  Paths the lost have entered in,
Working out his own undoing
  With his recklessness and sin —
Think, if placed in his condition,
  Would a kind word be in vain?
Or a look of cold suspicion
  Win thee back to truth again?

There are spots that bear no flowers —
  Not because the soil is bad;
But that summer's gentle showers
  Never made their bosoms glad:
Better have an act that's kindly
  Treated sometimes with disdain,
Than, by judging others blindly,
  Doom the innocent to pain.

1869.   M. E. B.

MRS. MARY STANFORD.

"Ah, the most loved are they of whom Fame speaks not with her clarion voice."

ALTHOUGH few of Mrs. Stanford's productions have reached the public eye, her genius has long been acknowledged and admired by a large circle of friends. Her poetic faculty was a gift of nature, which received culture in her early education in the nunnery, near Bardstown, Kentucky. Under the oaks and magnolias of Claiborne County, Mississippi, she was born, and her maiden name of Mary Patterson will thrill the hearts and memories of many old associates and contemporaries. Her girlhood was passed amid scenes of gayety and pleasure; her ready wit, vivacity, and poetic taste, together with a graceful, petite physique, making her a charming companion and ornament to society. Her parents died when she was very young, leaving her two brothers and herself, and their estate, to the care of a relative.

Mrs. Stanford was twice married and widowed. An only son was the fruit of her first marriage; and in that son she "lived, moved, and had her being." "The ocean to the river of her thoughts," he grew to be an idol, worshipped with a devotion few mothers have given their offspring. He was her inspiration, the polar star of her life.

Freely were her private interests sacrificed in raising and equipping a battery, of which her son was first lieutenant, and subsequently captain; and no more manly, noble, and splendid talent was given the cause of the South, than when FERDINAND CLAIBORNE enlisted, and bravely fought and fell, a martyr to that cause, leaving in the memory of his mother and countrymen a monument of honor and chivalry more bright and enduring than the marble erected by his comrades on the spot where he fell. And this little tablet, pure and white and glistening, embowered in roses, and embalmed by a mother's daily kisses and tears, tells to the lingerer in the quiet little cemetery of Port Gibson the same history it told at the fortifications of Vicksburg, where, like a sentinel at his post, it guarded the lonely mound where a martyred hero slept.

303

Mrs. Stanford was for many years a resident of New Orleans. While the guns at Fort Sumter were still reverberating in our hearts, she pressed the farewell kisses on the lips of her son, from whom she had never been separated.

About this period, Mrs. Stanford contributed several lively tales of life in the Crescent City, and poems to the "Southern Monthly," published in Memphis.

Says she: "My writings are only to be considered for the idolatrous love that inspires them." And few mothers in our land can read her "lines" without deep feeling.

When New Orleans fell, feeling that by remaining there she could no longer guard and protect her son's pecuniary interests, she felt that the one thing left for her to do was to find her child, to be where she might at an instant's notice seek him. She had a motherless niece to care for; and not wishing to proceed on a wild, blind search for her boy, she went to the old home of her girlhood, (Port Gibson,) and found rest and sympathy with those who had loved her in the long-ago. For weeks she had not heard from her son, until she reached this place, and some returning soldiers told her of his whereabouts. When he wrote to her, he forbade her attempting to join him, urging her to remain with her old friends, "and perhaps they might meet again — perhaps he might be ordered farther South — *but he could not ask for a furlough.*"

At last, the mother's patient waiting was rewarded. Her son, who had been for over a year in East Tennessee, and in Kentucky with General Bragg, was ordered to Vicksburg with General Stevenson's Division — ordered where his mother waited for him. Need we say that the mother was soon with her son? Some months before this, finding her resources fail, being able to get nothing from New Orleans, she had opened a school for the support of her niece and self, that *she might not take from her son,* and this was in successful operation when she visited him. She found him all that a mother's loving heart could hope or pray for, but so wedded to his duties, so proud of the noble battery he commanded, that again, as he had done before, he kissed her and blessed her, and *gave her to another's charge,* and left her, to go where she could not follow. The long siege of Vicksburg succeeded.

What the year is to a mother, what it is to the country, is well told to the heart, in these few artless, plain verses:

MY NEW-YEAR'S PRAYER.

New-Year's Day! Alas! the New-Year's days
   That stalk like troubled ghosts before my sight,
From happy youth, through weary years, till now,
   When my life's sun must soon be lost in night,
And I, in death's untroubled, tranquil sleep,
Shall learn how sweet it is to cease to weep!

New-Year's Day! Yes, I remember one —
   The day I watched a little rosy face
Of six months old, with dimpling smiles
   Peep out from under folds of silk and lace:
That face, the sweetest to a mother's eyes
That ever made of earth a paradise.

And then another New-Year I recall,
   Bringing sweet prattlings I so loved to hear;
The only music I could understand,
   The only notes that ever charmed my ear,
Save th' accompaniment to this sweet song —
The steps that bore my tottering boy along.

Then, New-Year's days in numbers pass me by,
   Bearing new beauties both to heart and mind,
And adding graces to the manly form —
   I did not wonder in the three to find
All I once hoped to see united there —
My son's young promise was so passing fair.

But where, in this dark, cheerless New-Year's day,
   In thy full manhood, must I look for thee?
I shall not find in that worn face such smiles
   As dimpled through the folds of lace for me;
And stern, harsh lines are on the once smooth brow,
Babe so beloved! — a man and soldier now!

Ah! since thy mother's arms were round thee last,
   Since thou wert folded to thy mother's breast,
Since her appealing voice hath met thine ear,
   Since her last kisses on thy lips were prest,
My son, my darling, what has chanced to thee?
Loving as then wilt thou return to me?

39

Ghosts of the New Years! with them come the hopes
　　That made the promise of thy youth more fair,
Whispering how thy manhood's love would guard
　　A mother's age from every grief and care.
How canst thou be to me this guard and shield,
　　Thou — in constant change from tent to battle-field?

Ghosts of the New Years, visit him to-day,
　　My baby once! — my country's soldier now!
Paint to his memory the unselfish love
　　That, since a mother's lips first touched his brow,
Till now, when such despairing words are said,
　　A mother's heart has showered on his head.

Spirit of to-day! breathe in his ear the prayers
　　That day and night ascend on high for him;
Unceasing, hopeful, trustful, brave and strong!
　　Earth's dreams delude — its brightest hopes grow dim —
But from the ruins soars, fresh, undefiled,
　　The mother's prayer — " GOD BLESS AND SAVE MY CHILD."

When the siege of Vicksburg was over, and for weeks after, there was no one hardy enough to tell her "she was childless!" Weeks of darkness came, after this; but there was one thing to live for—to find the grave of her son. Once more, for one night the same roof sheltered mother and son — he in his coffin, into which she dared not look! And through the Federal army, and down the river, and amid perils and sufferings, and hardships that it is a wonder, now, she could ever endure, she brought her darling to Port Gibson — there, to live and die beside him — to be buried in his grave — in his arms, if it could be.

Mrs. Stanford has a collection of her tales and poems in preparation in book-form, to be sold by subscription.

1870.

MRS. S. B. COX.

MRS. COX, whose maiden name was Hughes, was born in Warren County, Mississippi, five miles from Vicksburg. Her parents were Virginians, but adopted Alabama as their home, where her father, Judge Beverley Hughes, presided at the bar with distinction. They removed to Mississippi six months before the birth of the subject of this sketch, and eighteen months before the death of her father. A lady friend says: "Unfortunately for Miss Hughes, in the death of her father she lost the hand which would have been the fashioning and guiding power of her life."

Her mother married a second time — a man chilling in his manner — and her childhood passed without one genial ray of warmth to expand and open the hidden nature within her, save rare interviews with her mother, full of love and tenderness, and usually embracing one theme that was exhaustless — the virtues and graces of her father. Says Mrs. Cox, alluding to this:

"These conversations about my father were so colored by the admiration of a devoted wife, that he alone seemed to fill my idea of God's nobleman, and early became the inspiration of my life. To be worthy of being his daughter, enlisted all my faculties in every effort I made for good; no temptation beset me that I was not fortified against it by the thought, that, to yield to it would be unworthy the daughter of my father. My successes at school were alike due to this single inspiration of my life."

Miss Hughes was married very young — fourteen years and three months old on her wedding-day. Her life became very checkered: at the age of twenty-eight, when life is bright and full of joyousness to many, she became hopelessly bedridden. The trials of her life were numerous; but, to use her own language — breathings of the mother: "I was a mother, and this bore me up to live and labor for the immortal ones God had intrusted to my care."

For eight years she could not take a step, or even stand alone; and she says:

"Yet, amid all, God was very good in preserving my mind clear, and strengthening my will to conquer every repining for myself, and devote my remaining energies to the training and cultivation of my four little daughters. Up to the opening of the war, my world was found in these, my life centred in them; but a mightier appeal thrilled my being; my country called, and my whole heart responded. I felt that even the claim of my children was secondary to it, and devoted my time, my purse, and my strength, without reserve, to the sick of the Confederate army."

A friend, who is indebted to an eye-witness for his information, says:

"At one time the enemy shelled the hospital, which was near her residence. Her house, though within reach, was out of range of their guns, and she opened her doors to the inmates of the hospital, and for several weeks there were three hundred soldiers with her."

At the raising of the siege, her means were exhausted; and at the commencement of the second siege, General M. L. Smith informed her that her house had fallen within the line of fortifications, and would have to be destroyed. The Father seems strangely to provide for his creatures in the very darkest moments of their lives. Just at this crisis with Mrs. Cox, homeless and without money, her husband was discharged from active duty on account of failing health, and returned from Virginia in time to prevent her despairing, if such a hopeful mind as that of Mrs. Cox can be looked upon as "giving up." Her husband applied for and obtained government employment in the Trans-Mississippi Department, and they removed to Shreveport. The reaction from active excitement to comparative quiet prostrated Mrs. Cox again entirely to bed, and thus it was with her until the news of the fall of Vicksburg fell like a leaden weight upon her. Says she:

"For the first time, woe took the place of full confidence, and never again was the bow of hope unclouded in my heart; yet when the fall of the Confederacy was told to me, I reeled and staggered under the blow, not aware for weeks if my vitality would survive it."

The superior facilities to be found in the public schools of New Orleans for educating their daughters, decided Mr. and Mrs. Cox to make that city their home. They were scantily supplied with the "world's goods." Mr. Cox, over fifty years of age, without a son to assist him, had to begin anew the world, and for nearly two years they struggled for the necessaries of life — "a struggle such as cannot be conceived of unless felt."

Mrs. Cox had contributed to the papers of Vicksburg and Shreveport, among other articles, several appeals to the Southern people upon subjects pertaining to the war. These were published over the *nom de plume* of "Beverley." Now, in the terrible strait of poverty, the idea of writing for money came to her. Says she: " I caught at it as a drowning man clutches at a straw, and almost as hopelessly and desperately. Without an introduction to the press of New Orleans, I made my way into the journals." A writer in the "Crescent" thus refers to her:

"We think a woman, even an invalid, who can neither sit in anything but a *robe de chambre*, nor stand long enough to have her hair frizzed, like our own 'Beverley;' whose pathos moves to tears; whose philosophy makes us proud of our own sex; whose wit and sarcasms few would wish to encounter; whose faith has for years irradiated her sick-chamber with a hallowed light, is infinitely superior to a lady whose highest acquisitions are moire-antiques, thule, coiffures, tinsel, or even diamonds; whose resources for happiness are theatres, masquerades, and dancing; whose faith exhibits itself in a few Lenten visits to church; whose self-abnegation and humiliation are the changing from one luxurious diet to another perhaps a little more delicate."

In the Spring of 1869, Mrs. Cox lost the use of her right hand and arm from paralysis,—her physician ascribing it to the incessant writing for weeks to meet her engagements, for she supported her family with her brain-work.

Mrs. Cox continues to contribute to the various papers of New Orleans, and to several Northern journals, particularly to the Sunday edition of the "Times" newspaper, to which she is a regular contributor to each issue. A daughter contributes to the last-named journal under signature of Beverley, Jr.

1871.

SPIRIT-WHISPERINGS.

Philosophy stands up in the severe, grave dignity of truth, and demands demonstrable facts in all things. But is there nothing within us, to the intellect vague, shadowy, and undefined, which may not be reasoned upon, yet is a feeling, a consciousness from which we may reason and deduce facts as clearly as from anything material? Surely this is evident to all.

We may draw from every created thing or being an undeniable evidence of a Great First Cause or Creator. From the delicate violet, which opens its beautiful petals out upon the bosom of the brown earth, up to the dewy kisses of the night-winds; to the stone-girt mountain, which, from its burning caldron of boiling lava, hurls forth destruction and death for miles around; from the tiny insect to his own image in man,— all proclaim most unmistakably the existence of a God, the Creator of all things, and the Ruler of his creation. But perhaps the most satisfying evidence to man is the demand in his own being for a God — that universal reaching out of the soul which is found in the breast of the most benighted heathen.

Of the inspiration of the Bible, but slight evidence is given by historians since the advent of the Saviour; but it is when we compare its high and holy truths with the self-evident facts of man's life, that we find the first positive proof which is apt to be taken hold of by man. Let the unprejudiced thinker turn his mind in upon his own soul, and compare its aspirations and its longings with the truths of the Bible, and therefrom will he draw evidence beyond refutation; and therein is the mystical chain of spirit with spirit; that half-hidden, half-defined something which baffles the lore of philosophy, yet enchants and delights man.

Trouble upon trouble enters in upon the heart of man; care upon care silvers the dark threads, and bends the head low upon the stooped shoulders; the weary, aching thought of the brain, which brings no fruition; the half-requited labor, the heart-sickening disappointment in friendship and love; and man grows weary and faint, and cries out for the waters of oblivion to sweep over his soul in this dark hour of woe and despair. Then comes the small, still voice of the Spirit, and whispers: "All of earth is passing away, and heaven is eternal!"

Death lays its icy touch upon our idol, and our heart is torn until every fibre is bleeding out its own vitality, and reason staggers upon its throne. Then whispers the Spirit: "Be still, and rest in the hands of thy God." It is only a little while sooner than you that the spirit has bid adieu to the troubles of life.

A little white bird wafted its downward way from paradise, and, finding its tiny, delicate form growing cold and numb in this bleak world's grasp, sought refuge in my quiet home — for a few brief hours folded its snowy wings gently and lovingly upon my breast; but though I nestled it warmly within my bosom, and wooed it to linger with me, it gave a few farewell moans, and, softly gliding from its earthly casket, took its returning flight to paradise. Thus came and went our little babe. But a cell had been opened up in our hearts for love of her; and though we consigned to the dark earth that beautiful waxen form of purest whiteness, and other children have been born to us, love for her is still warm within my heart. That heart beats still for the angel one. Her little baby form, her eyes of heavenly blue, her mouth of sweetest mould, are yet fresh within my memory. Ah! who can doubt that we two will meet again? My spirit whispers that my heart-throbs are not for nought, but will beat on throughout eternal ages.

Ah! yes, let us listen to these sweet whisperings of the Spirit, and they will breathe into our souls strength to conquer, strength to bear. Listen to them, confide in them, and they will rob death of its sting, and open out to us a great, broad vista of ages of eternal bliss. Wife, by the death-bed of thy husband; mother, by thy dead child, take comfort from it to hush thy grief.

There is a Spirit whispering of warning and hope to the young man in a career of sin and profligacy, bidding him pause, reflect, and follow its promptings.

To the old man tottering upon the verge of a dishonored grave, it says: "Even now listen to me."

Frail woman, in thy fall and degradation, listen to it; hush it not in thy poor, sin-stained soul. When all the world turn from thee, and only sin and shame clasp hands with thee, it will prove thy best friend. It is sent to such as thee by God.

ELIZA J. POITEVENT.

PEARL RIVERS, as by her pseudonym is the "sweet singer" best known, takes her name from that beautiful stream, Pearl River, near the banks of which she was born.

Miss Poitevent is a maiden, hardly of adult years; the daughter of Captain W. J. Poitevent, a builder and owner of steamboats, and a manufacturer of lumber at Gainesville, on that river, about twenty-five miles across the plain from the Bay of St. Louis, which is now, as Gainesville formerly was, the seat of justice of Hancock County, Mississippi.

On her father's side, Miss Poitevent is of French descent; on the mother's, she is connected with the Russ family — of the Florida parishes of Louisiana and Southeastern Mississippi. Shortly after the birth of Eliza, her mother's health was so delicate that she was advised by her physician to travel, and it was decided that the "babe" should be left with her aunt, Mrs. Leonard Kimball. When Mrs. Poitevent returned, she found her babe, a healthy, rosy little girl, taking her first steps — who did not want to leave her aunt for her mother. Mrs. Kimball was childless, and had become so much attached to "little Pearl," that she earnestly entreated that she might be left with her. It was finally decided that "Pearl" should remain with her aunt.

And on the banks of the Hobolochitto, with her aunt and uncle, "Pearl Rivers" spent her pure and happy childhood. She had no playmates, and roamed the meadows and fields in search of companions. There was not a narrow path that trailed its way through the dense forest of pines that she did not know; and flowers, birds, and insects were *more* than flowers, birds, and insects to her. They were her friends and companions, and she talked to them and sang with them through many a happy day.

When thirteen years of age, Pearl was sent to the Amite Female Seminary, in Amite County, Miss., where her many merry pranks soon won for her the name of "the wildest girl in school." She graduated at the age of "sweet sixteen," excelling in composition.

A stanch "little rebel," her first attempt at verse was to write patriotic words to several patriotic airs, which she sang to a circle of not critical, but admiring friends.

It was not until the "first year of the war" that any of her productions appeared in print.

Seeing a copy of "The South," a weekly paper published in New Orleans by John W. Overall, Esq., she was much pleased with the bold, dashing editorials, and sent several of her poems to him, trembling at the boldness of the step. Her poems were not only published, but were favorably noticed, and a friendly, encouraging letter from Mr. Overall followed. She received little or no encouragement from the members of her own family, and she considers that she owes much to her first literary friend and patient critic, John W. Overall, who introduced her to the public.

Since that time, her gift of song has won her many appreciative friends among the literati of our country, but she looks back with grateful remembrance to the one who caught the first, faint, trembling notes of her lyre.

After the discontinuance of "The South," "Pearl Rivers" contributed to the "New Orleans Sunday Times," and now contributes to the "Picayune," "New York Home Journal," and other journals.

A lady who knows her, says, "She always carries her scrap-book and pencil with her, and writes at all times."

She is one of Nature's sweetest poets, and as pure-hearted as the blue river from which she takes her name — a wild-wood warbler, knowing how to sing of birds and flowers and flowing brooks, and all things beautiful.

Wm. Hand Browne, the critic, says: " When larger experience and opportunities of culture have increased her knowledge and widened her sympathies — when she has learned the tragic as well as the sportive side of human life — we doubt not that Miss Poitevent will produce poetry which even the most rigid critic will pronounce worthy of the name."

A CHIRP FROM MOTHER ROBIN.

See yon little Mother Robin,
    Sitting on her humble nest:
Learn from her my poem-lesson;
    Nature's teachers are the best.

Other nests are lined more softly —
    Larger nests than hers she sees;
Other nests are swinging higher
    In the summer's gentle breeze; —

But the Robin is contented;
    Mine is warm enough, she says —
Large enough to hold my birdies
    Through their tender nesting-days.

Smaller cradle, warmer cover!
    For my little ones, she sings;
Four there are, but see how snugly
    They are tucked beneath my wings.

And I envy not my neighbors,
    Redbird, Bluebird, Lark, or Thrush;
For the breeze that rocks the tree-tops
    Rocks my cradle in the bush.

And the same bright sunshine warms me —
    By the same kind hand I 'm fed;
With the same green earth around me,
    And the same sky overhead.

Though my dress is something plainer
    Than my cousin's, Madame Red;
Though I have no vest of crimson,
    And no gay hood on my head; —

Still, my robe of graver colors
    Suits my station and my nest;
And the Master knows what costume
    Would become a Robin best.

THE ROYAL CAVALCADE.

Spring is coming, Spring is coming,
  Through the arch of Pleasant Days,
With the harps of all her minstrels
  Tuned to warble forth her praise.

In her rosy car of Pleasure,
  Drawn by nimble-footed Hours,
With a royal guard of Sunbeams,
  And a host of white-plumed Flowers,

From the busy Court of Nature
  Rides the fair young Queen in state,
O'er the road of Perfect Weather,
  Leading down to Summer Gate.

Brave old March rides proudly forward,
  With her heralds, Wind and Rain;
He will plant her standard firmly
  On King Winter's bleak domain.

Young Lord Zephyr fans her gently,
  And Sir Dewdrop's diamonds shine;
Lady May and Lady April
  By her Majesty recline.

Lady April's face is tearful,
  And she pouts and frets the while,
But her lips will part with laughter
  Ere she rides another mile.

Lady May is blushing deeply,
  As she fits her rosy gloves;
She is dreaming of the meeting
  With her waiting Poet-loves.

Over meadow, hill and valley
  Winds the Royal Cavalcade,
And, behind, green leaves are springing
  In the tracks the car-wheels made.

And her Majesty rides slowly
  Through the humble State of Grass,

Speaking kindly to the Peasants
  As they crowd to see her pass.

In the corners of the fences
  Hide the little Daisy-spies,
Peeping shyly through the bushes,
  Full of childish, glad surprise;

And her gentle Maids of Honor,
  Modest Violets, are seen
In their gala-dresses waiting,
  By the road-side, for their Queen.

By her own bright light of Beauty
  Does she travel through the day;
And at night her Glowworm Footmen
  With their lanterns guide the way.

She is coming, nearer! nearer!
  Hark the sound of chariot-wheels!
Fly to welcome her, young minstrel,
  Sing the joy your spirit feels.

MARY W. LOUGHBOROUGH

IS the author of "My Cave Life in Vicksburg," published by
D. Appleton & Co., New York, 1867. A sprightly and well-
written book, full of graphic and interesting pictures of scenes within
the city of Vicksburg during the "siege."

She has also contributed to various magazines — generally anonymously. Her home is now, I believe, St. Louis.

1868.

FLORIDA.

MARY E. BRYAN.

HERE is not a name among the literary stars of the "South-land" that fills a warmer place in every heart than that of Mary E. Bryan. Tastes differ about literature as about everything else; but there are somethings which challenge the universal admiration of mankind: some faces — some forms — as the "Venus de Medicis" and the "Apollo Belvidere" — and some books, although the latter are most rare. Mrs. Bryan comes as near filling this exclusive niche in the gallery of letters as any *woman of her age* who ever wrote. She does not dazzle, like the fitful light of the "Borealis race," nor sparkle like sunset on a summer sea — neither does she charm us by the smoothness and polish of her style; but she manages to creep into the hearts of her readers, as few young writers have ever done. This comes of her own earnestness — that deep, thrilling earnestness which marks all her writings, and especially her poetry. There her thoughts well up fresh and warm from the depths of a passionate heart, and never fail to meet a responsive throb in the hearts of her readers.

> "Bryan — hers the words that glisten,
>   Opal gems of sunlit rain!
> So much the woman, you may listen
>   Heart-beats pulsing in her brain!
> She upon her songs has won
>   Hybla's honey undistilled;
> And 'from wine-vats of the sun,'
>   With bright nectar overrun,
>   Her urns of eloquence are filled!"*

She is a poetess by nature. Largely endowed with that sense of the beautiful, which Poe called "an immortal instinct deep within the

* Mrs. L. Virginia French.

316

spirit of man," she gives us glimpses of the loveliness which lies beyond the common sight, and "whose very elements, perhaps, appertain to eternity alone."

Mrs. Bryan has taken no care of her literary fame; she has been at no pains whatever to extend it. She has scattered the brilliant productions of her intellect hither and thither among the periodicals of the South, as a tree flings its superabundant blossoms to the breeze; and she has taken no thought of them afterward. Whatever she writes, she finishes with care, being led to do so out of respect and love for her profession; but when written and sent to the press, it is forgotten — scarcely even being read over by her after its publication. To one who has studied her closely, the reason of this is obvious. Mrs. Bryan possesses true genius — hers is the real artist-feeling, which judges of the attained by the attempted; and nobly as she writes, she has written nothing to satisfy her own high-placed ideal — nothing that seems "worthy of her hope and aim more highly mated."

Mrs. Bryan is a native of Florida — daughter of Major John D. Edwards, an early settler of that State, and among the first and most honored members of its Legislature. Both on the paternal and maternal sides, she belongs to excellent and honorable families. Her mother, whose maiden name was Houghton, was herself an accomplished and talented lady. She lived in retirement, devoting her time principally to the education of her daughter. Mrs. Edwards was a charming woman and model mother. She made herself the companion of her daughters, (three in number,) won their confidence by her forbearing gentleness, and sympathy with their little cares, thoughts, and aspirations. She was never too much engaged to answer their inquiries, or give them any information they desired. Mary's mind opened early — too early, perhaps, for a cheerful and healthy youth. While other children played with their dolls, she roamed through the beautiful solitudes around her home, or wandered alone on the shores of the beautiful Gulf, where her parents were accustomed to spend their summers — her mind filled with dreams and yearnings that bewildered her by their vagueness. She discovered in part what these yearnings meant, when, at the age of ten years, she was sent on a visit to her aunt, Mrs. Julia McBride, so well known in Florida for her piety and philanthropy. The family of this aunt (her husband and a noble group of grown-up sons and daughters) lay at rest in the church-yard

on a neighboring hill; and but for the occasional companionship of
her brother, the lady lived alone.   Mary could wander at will in her
poetic reveries through the groves of orange and crape myrtle that
embowered "Salubrity," and through the wide old gardens, scattered
over with half ruined summer-houses, and enclosed by palings hung
with the Multiflora and Cherokee Rose.   She was never lonely; for, as
she has written since:

> " The poet never is alone;
>   The stars, the breeze, the flowers,
> All lovely things, his kindred are
>   And charm his loneliest hours."

But this insensate companionship did not satisfy.   She longed for
more intelligent teachers, with a vague yearning, which she did not
comprehend, until one day she chanced to gain access to the library
of her uncle — Col. R. B. Houghton — who was absent on professional
duties.   It was the opening of a fairy world to the imaginative mind
of the child.   In that shadowy, green-curtained library-room, with
the orange-branches brushing against the window-panes, she entered
upon a new life.   Her reading had been hitherto confined to her text-
books, and now she revelled in the poetry of the masters, and in romances of another age.   Much of what she read she understood through
her mind's early development, no less than through the intuition of
genius; and what her young reason could not fathom was absorbed
by feeling and imagination, as one catches the tune of a song, though
it is sung too far off for the words to be understood.

She read as a gifted child would do — losing her own personality in
that of the characters delineated, feeling every emotion as though it
were a personal experience, thrilling over deeds of heroism, shuddering
over those of crime, burning with indignation as she read of cruelty
and injustice, and weeping passionately over the pictures of wrong
and suffering and undeserved doom.   She mused and dreamed continually over the revelations thus suddenly opened to her.   None
guessed what influences were moulding the mind of the precocious
child.

Could they not read the secret in her dreamy eyes and abstracted
manner?

Her uncle did so when he returned home, and he closed his library-
doors resolutely against the little, pale, wistful face.

Years after, in the prime of her womanhood, she declared to him*
that those hours of stolen communion with the "spirits of the library" were more a blessing than a bane. Perhaps they were — perhaps
it was to these she owed the early maturity of her mind and the variety of her style.

At eleven years old, she was sent to a boarding-school in Thomasville, Georgia. Here the shy little recluse, who had been at home
among the "stately-stepping fancies" conjured up from the pages of
romance and history, experienced a shrinking timidity when brought
into intimate contact with girls of her own age. To her surprise she
found herself far in advance of these in her studies — so efficient had
been her mother's teaching, so ready her own receptive powers. She
was placed in a class of young ladies, and, says Col. Houghton:

"I remember to have seen her during an examination of the school — a
slender little figure at the head of the class of grown-up girls, her pale face
lit up resplendently by dark, earnest eyes, as she repeated page after page
of intellectual philosophy, or musically rendered the Eclogues of Virgil.
She was a special object of interest and curiosity to most of the audience
there assembled, for she was known to be a religious enthusiast. A 'revi-
val' had not long before 'converted' a majority of the girls of the boarding-
school: many of them had 'backslided,' some still held to the faith in a
quiet, commonplace way; only this one, prone to extremes through her
ardent, impulsive nature, became a fanatic, refraining from joining in the
sports and pastimes of her playmates, refusing to answer a question positively lest there might be room for a doubt, giving all her pocket-money to
the poor children of the school, and (greatest sacrifice of all, to one whose
love for the beautiful made her delight in bright colors and lovely apparel)
rejecting the pretty garments sent her from home, and appearing, in the
midst of her gayly-dressed class, in a plain, faded frock.

"Her composition upon this occasion had for its theme, 'The Shadows
and Sunshine of Life.' I have before me, now, a mental picture of that
rapt, young face — so child-like in its contour, so old in the expression of the
large thoughtful eyes, that were lighted with enthusiasm as she concluded
with a brief but glowing vision of the 'land beyond the vale of shadows
and fleeting sunshine.'"

This fanatical tendency, peculiarly strange in so young a child,

* We are indebted for many facts in this sketch to Col. R. B. Houghton, of Florida,
formerly well known as an accomplished writer and eloquent public speaker. He has
known Mrs. Bryan from her earliest youth, and by his example first gave a literary
turn to her mind, that, in fertility of imagination and ease of expression, bears a considerable resemblance to his own.

greatly troubled Mary's parents, who were proud of her brilliant talents. It must have been a deep impression, for, gentle and yielding as her nature was, easily influenced by those she loved, and most sensitive to ridicule, it yet resisted entreaties, expostulation, and ridicule. In time it wore away.

"Only once," says Col. Houghton, "did she speak to me of this period of her life. 'It contained,' she said, 'agonies, that I could not again bear and live. For the least venial sin — real or imagined — I was visited by pangs of remorse. Often have I passed whole nights on my knees in prayer, unconscious of cold or fatigue in the more acute mental anguish I endured. Yet, after the long wrestle, the agonizing doubt and despair, there would come a wonderful reaction, and I would experience moments of ecstasy indescribable. I cannot understand it. It is a mystery to my maturer years.'"

Mary was then only twelve years old. A short time afterward her parents removed to Thomasville, for the purpose of educating their daughters, and made for themselves a suburban home, beautiful with vineyards, gardens, and orchards. In the years that followed, Mary wrote, and published in a Thomasville paper, poems, and a story that ran through several numbers of the paper. She was still a school-girl, hardly sixteen, when her friends were surprised to hear that she was married — married to the son of a Louisiana planter. Her marriage was as unexpected to her as it was to her friends and relatives. An hour before she took upon herself the irrevocable vows, she was sitting, school-girl fashion, on the rug before the fire in her own room, quietly studying her Latin lesson. Two hours afterward, she had bidden adieu to her girlish pursuits, to her parents, sisters, and friends, and was on her way to her husband's home on the banks of Red River. During the first year of her marriage she passed through some bitter experiences — experiences which one so young, so sensitive, and so ignorant of life, was illy prepared to meet. At the end of a year, she was visited by her father, who thought best that she should accompany him back to her old home. Of the partial separation that ensued, (partial, because she was constantly visited by her husband, who was devoted to her, and no estrangement ever existed between them,) it is not necessary to say any more than that it was deemed advisable by her father, a just man as well as an affectionate parent. There were peculiar circumstances which, in his opinion and that of her friends, made it judicious for her to postpone a return to her husband's home in Louisiana.

To divert her mind from painful thought, her father advised a renewal of her studies, with a view to completing her education; and she turned to her old text-books — sadly and listlessly at first, afterward with new energy and zeal for knowledge. She now resumed her writing for the press, and became a regular contributor to several periodicals. Among these was the "Literary Crusader," published by Mr. John Seals, at Penfield, Georgia. After writing for this paper for two years, it was removed to Atlanta, greatly enlarged and improved, and she was solicited to take part in its editorial management. She accepted the offer, went to Atlanta, and entered upon her new duties with the ardor and energy which are her distinguishing traits. She succeeded in giving to the "Crusader" an individuality it *had* not before possessed, and in making it widely and popularly known, not only throughout the South, but in the Middle and Northern States.

During the year in which she edited the "Crusader" in Atlanta, I believe that Mrs. Bryan performed more literary work and of a more varied character than any female of her age (twenty years) ever accomplished in the same length of time. The expenses of removing the "Crusader" to Atlanta, of purchasing new type and press, etc., were *so great* that the proprietor did not *consider that his finances justified his paying for contributions;* still he wished to make his paper interesting and to have it contain a variety of original reading-matter. Mrs. Bryan was equal to this emergency. She determined to the best of her ability to supply the place of contributors. She called in play for the first time her remarkable versatility, her power of changing her style "from grave to gay, from lively to severe," and she filled a page of the "Crusader" every week with the required variety of original reading-matter from her own pen. Every number contained one or more columns of "editorial" upon subjects of present interest. Then a group of sparkling paragraphs, local or critical — essays, thoughtful or humorous, and sometimes scintillating with wit — a poem — a sketch or story, and often one or more chapters of a serial tale.

In addition to the weekly task of filling so many columns of a large literary paper, and also to the trouble of proof-reading, selecting, and other duties connected with her office, Mrs. Bryan found time to pursue, at intervals, the course of reading and study she had marked out for herself. But she did so by encroaching largely upon the hours allotted to rest. Even the Sabbath was no day of relaxation, since it

41

brought its own duties, in the care of her Bible class, of her younger band of Sunday-school scholars, and in an unfailing attendance upon divine service in the Methodist church, of which she was a faithful member.

In November of this year, she was invited to read a poem at the Commencement of College Temple, Newnan, Georgia. Her poem was an eloquent delineation of true womanhood — its sphere, its mission, and its aspirations; and it was read in her own rich, magnetic voice. After she had taken her seat, she was recalled and complimented with a diploma from the president of the college.

Before the close of the year, Mrs. Bryan felt that the unremitting toil was telling upon her health. She needed rest, and returned home, determined to write less than she had been doing. Several propositions were made for her services the next year. She accepted the offer of Col. James Gardner, proprietor of the "Field and Fireside," as being not only most liberal in salary, but most generous in its privileges. He expressly insisted that she should rest, should write at her leisure, and write with care and correction. How well she followed the latter suggestion, was shown in her first contributions to the "Field and Fireside," the noble essay, "How should Women Write," the pathetic sketch, "Cutting Robbie's Hair," and the fine poem, "The Hour when we shall Meet." (The sketch and poem are to be found in Mary Forrest's "Distinguished Women of the South.") She contributed novelettes, stories, essays, and poems. About this time she decided to return with her husband to Louisiana, and we next find her in her own quiet home, isolated from literary society, from the stimulus of applause and encouragement, and from those influences which quicken the energies and sharpen the mental faculties. Notwithstanding this, she completed her engagement with the "Field and Fireside," and entered upon a new year, beginning it with the initial chapters of "Haywood Lodge." This is a beau-ideal of a novel — "a striking fiction." The characters are as distinctly and as graphically drawn as any in "Adam Bede," or "Mill on the Floss." The scenes are sprightly and lifelike, and the plot one of intense interest. Mrs. Bryan promised a sequel to this novel — a second volume, so to speak — which has been from time to time demanded by the public, but is not yet forthcoming.

When she commenced her second engagement with the "Field and Fireside," it was at the commencement of the late war. Her husband enlisted in the service of his country, and to Mrs. Bryan was left the superintendence of the household and plantation. With these domestic duties she had little leisure for writing, yet she wrote a series of articles, vigorous in style and caustic in their satire, denouncing and exposing the system of extortion, speculation, and fraud which was undermining the Southern interest. These articles appeared in the parish paper, having a local circulation only.

When the war ended, Mr. Bryan had only honorable scars and comparative poverty. In order to contribute her mite toward rebuilding their fallen fortunes, Mrs. Bryan accepted the editorship of the "Semi-weekly Times," published in Natchitoches. She removed temporarily to Natchitoches for the purpose of superintending the paper in person, and entered upon the work with her accustomed energy and earnestness. She was now required to try her versatile powers in a direction in which they had never essayed. The "Times" was a political paper, and Mrs. Bryan's leading articles were required by its proprietor to be discussions of the grave political questions agitating the public mind. This was by no means a congenial task, but none would have guessed it from reading the bold and vigorous "leaders" which appeared twice a week in the columns of the "Times," or the pungent paragraphs, the witty and satirical comments upon contemporary opinions, or upon the ludicrous aspect of "African sovereignty."

Her work was attended by the most disheartening drawbacks. She wrote under the disadvantages of ill health, of sickness in her family, and of the necessity of devoting much of her time to the care of three young children — the eldest only five years old. In spite of these adverse circumstances, she furnished to the "Times," twice a week, not only the required columns of "editorial" and editorial paragraphs, but one or more essays, and usually a sketch, a story, or a poem.

Mrs. Bryan's stay in Natchitoches was one of misfortune, and it was terminated by an affliction — the most bitter she had ever been called upon to endure — the long, painful illness and death of her youngest child — her baby, her darling. The little sufferer (who had been a bright and beautiful boy) was suddenly and mysteriously afflicted, and lay for many weeks in the "death in life" of paralysis. It was during one of her anguished watches by that bed of silent suffering that Mrs. Bryan wrote the poem which she has called "Miserere." During the illness of her child, Mrs. Bryan exerted herself to continue her editorial duties — writing while the little one slept in her lap, or upon the bed, beside which she kept her unremitting watch; but when the little coffin was carried out from the room, and she sat down with aching heart to supply the remorseless demand for "copy," she found it impossible to collect her thoughts. The reaction had come; the long strain upon her feelings and energies showed its effects, and all she wrote was a brief adieu to the patrons of the paper.

She returned to her plantation home, but continued to contribute to the "Times." In 1868, she went on a visit to her relatives in Florida, and while there formed an engagement with "Scott's Magazine," (Atlanta.) In this magazine she published a novel, entitled "The Mystery of Cedar Bay," which will appear probably in book-form. This serial is original and thrillingly interesting.

It is difficult to convey an adequate idea of Mrs. Bryan's powers by means of extracts, owing to the variety of style. Ease and grace characterize her lighter compositions, force and vigor distinguish her graver productions.

Mrs. Bryan has frequently been called "the most gifted female writer which the South has produced." She is certainly the most versatile. It is in her power to make herself the most widely known. To do this, she must show more appreciation of her own powers — she must concentrate her energies upon some *one* work.

September, 1869.

ANACREON.

Yon sea-like slope of darkening pines
  Is surging with the tempest's power,
And not one star of promise shines
  Upon the twilight hour;
With wailing sounds the blast is rife,
  And wilder yet the echoes roll
Up from the scenes where want and strife
  Convulse the human soul.
'T is madness rules the fateful hour;
Let me forget its fearful power;
Drop low the curtains of my room,
And in the green and purple gloom
Lose sight of angry men and stormy skies,
Gazing, Anacreon, on thy splendid eyes.

My grand old Greek! far back in time
   Thy glorious birth-hour lies;
Thy shade has heard the tread sublime
   Of passing centuries.
And yet the soul that thrilled thy lyre
   Has power to charm us still,
And with its vivid light and fire
   Our duller spirits fill.
Breathe on me, spirit rare and fine,
Buoyant with energy divine:
The light and joy of other days
Live in those blue eyes' dazzling rays;
They lift my soul from its confining cage,
The barriers of this dull and sordid age.

I dream I am a girl of Greece,
   With pliant shape and foam-white arms,
And locks that fall in bright release
   To veil my bosom's charms.
The skies of Greece above me bend —
   The Ægean winds are in my hair;
I hear gay songs, and shoutings send
   Their music on the air.
I see a bright procession pass —
The girls throw garlands on the grass —
And, crowned with myrtle and with bay,
I see thee pass that flowery way,
While swim before me smiling fields and skies,
Dimmed by a glance of thy resplendent eyes.

Prince of the Lyre! thy locks are white
   As Blanc's untrodden snow;
But, quenchless in their fire and light,
   Thy blue eye beams below,
And well the myrtle gleams among
   Thy bays, like stars of truth;
The poet's soul is ever young —
   His is immortal youth.
He dwells within that border-land
Where innocence and passion stand —
Ardent, yet pure, clasped hand in hand —
And years but add a richer grace,
A higher charm to mind and face,
While youth and beauty that his dreams eclipse,
Bend to the magic of his eyes and lips.

Oh! heart of love and soul of fire!
　My spirit bows to thee;
Type of the ideals that inspire
　My dreams eternally,
I'd be a slave to such as thou,
　And deem myself a queen,
If sometimes to my kneeling brow
　Those perfect lips might lean.
High hopes and aims within my breast
Would spring from their despairing rest,
And the wild energies that sleep
Like prisoned genii might out leap,
And bid my name among th' immortal shine,
If *fame*, to me, could mean such love as thine.

MISERERE.

Alone with night and silence, and those strange,
Those bright, unseeing, sleepless eyes, whose depth
I have searched vainly, weary days and nights,
For some sweet gleam of consciousness, some ray
Of tender recognition to break forth —
Sudden and starlike — from the vacant cloud.
It does not come; the sweet soul that looked forth
From those deep eyes wanders mysteriously
In some dim land that borders upon death,
And I sit watching, after many days,
With the tears dried upon my pallid cheeks,
Their fountains dried within my hopeless heart,
Waiting for death to make me desolate.

The roses of a lovely May breathe out
Their souls of fragrance underneath the moon;
The wind comes down from the wild grove of pines,
Vocal with wordless mysteries; I see
Its fingers toying with yon delicate leaves,
Touched with faint silver by the midnight moon;
I see the dew-gleam on the tender grass,
The thousand starry sentinels that watch
Upon the battlements of heaven; I see
All these, as if I saw not; for those eyes
Haunt me forever, turn upon me still,
Through the blank darkness made by clasping hands,

By blinding tears, and clouds of falling hair,
As with bowed head I strive to shut the sight
From the o'ertortured sense.

                  Oh! what to me
Is it how many flowers the May shall blow
Into young bloom with her sweet breath, since I
Must lay mine low beneath the chilly sod,
And watch the grass grow green between my heart
And the sweet face I cradled on my breast?
What is it to me how many singing larks
The morn may send to gild their soaring wings
With the unrisen sun? the voice that was
The sweetest under heaven to me is still!
I would not turn from the pale lips, whereon
Cruel paralysis — that death in life —
Has laid his numbing seal, to list the strains
The sirens sang across the classic seas.

My child, my child! my beautiful, bright boy!
In whose large eyes I dreamed that genius slept;
For whose broad brow my fancy twined the bays
That I had ceased to strive for; my fair flower,
That came when life seemed the most desolate,
And shed a brightness round its lonely waste,
And weaned the heart from the wild love of death,
And rest, and deep forgetfulness; thy lip,
Ere it could speak, quivered in sympathy
With my hot tears that fell upon thy face;
Thy baby hand lay softly on my heart
Like a charmed flower, and soothed its wild unrest.
What hopes have I not built for thee? what dreams
Of future greatness has my fancy reared,
Kneeling beside thy cradle, stroking back
The locks from thy broad temples?

                Well I knew
That *my* own life had failed; that the bright hopes
And untamed aspirations of my youth,
Met by the storm of fate, had drooped their wing,
And fallen back, cold and dying, to the heart·
That was their nest. Alas! I felt the cord
Of iron circumstance upon my life,
And knew that woman's sorrowful fate was mine;
That the wild energies that thrilled my being

Must throb themselves to silence; that with me
Ambition must mean only grief; but thou,
No robes of womanhood could trip thy steps
Upon the mountain-paths of fame, my child;
Thou couldst be free and fearless; thou mightst win
The goal I could not touch; mightst boldly speak
The truths I dared not utter.

       Ay, I dreamed
Thy voice might thrill the great soul of the world;
And strong for truth, and brave for truth, might lead,
With clarion peal, the march of Right, and bid
Hoary Oppression tremble on his throne —
And Wrong, and Bigotry, and Hatred quail
Before its fearless utterance; that should drown
The hiss of malice, and the carping cry
Of Envy and weak Fear.

      So I have dreamed,
When hope and love beat time within my breast,
And ideal visions passed with prophecies
In their deep eyes. Yet more; when I beheld
The fair land of my love laid low, and made
A land of graves and woful memories —
A slaved and conquered land, that scarcely dares
To quiver underneath th' oppressor's heel —
I did not weep; for what avail were tears,
E'en from the depths of a "divine despair,"
Before such wrong, such woe, such wretchedness,
Such desolation? So I did not weep.
A woman's tears fit only to keep warm
And moist the sod of graves; I only knelt,
With beating heart and burning cheek, above
The fair child of my hopes, and thought to breathe
And mould into his unformed being my own
Deep love, and pity, and devotedness,
And passionate sense of wrong. In time, they might
Produce the fruits I should not see: the soul
That looked forth radiantly from the clear eyes,
The hand that lay so flower-like within mine,
Might aid to win his land's deliverance,
And break the thraldom his free soul would scorn.

Alas! to-night how vain and wild they seem —
Those earthly visions — those proud hopes and dreams —;

For thee, my darling, lying like a flower,
The flames have scathed in passing, and have left
Blighted and dying, — vain and wild they seem,
As kneeling thus, I hold in mine that hand
My fancy clothed with manhood's strength and grace,
Now pale and paralyzed, while the bright mind
That was my joy and pride, alas! they say,
It will not shine again in the sweet face,
And give its radiance to the eyes I loved;
That e'en if life creeps back, and the fell fiend
Of fever quits his victim, that the mind
Will never more leap from the eyes in light,
But stay within its cell, the brain, a dim
And dreaming prisoner.
                  Oh! I dare not dwell
Upon the thought; better for thee and me
Were death, my darling; better this dear head
Were lain beneath the shadows of the pines
That oversweep yon City of the Dead.
And thus I give thee up, my child, my life,
To the great God who lent thee. Go, and be
Tended by angels in the land where pain
Comes not to rack the brain; from angel lips
Of loveliest music, angel eyes and brows,
Divinely calm with *love*, and bright with thought,
Learn the deep lore of heaven, and forget
The brief and pain-fraught life that only saw
The roses of one summer fade away.

BY THE SEA.

Once more, once more
Beneath the golden skies I loved so well,
Listening once more to the blue billows' swell
    Upon the sandy shore —
The blue, bright waves, that in the sunlight shine
Through vistas of the feathery palm and pine.

Land of my love, once more
Thy beauty is around me : on my brow
Thy pine-trees fling their shifting shadows now,
    And when the day-beams pour

Across the cloud, my steed's swift gallop shakes
The scarlet berries in thy lonely brakes.

And when the noon is high,
I see the yellowing lime and orange swinging
On branches where the wild bird's notes are ringing,
While all neglected lie
The purple figs dropped in the plumy grass,
The wild grapes hanging where cool waters pass.

And when the planets burn,
The fairest of the long-haired Naiad daughters
Holds upward, through her lake's pellucid waters,
The water-lily's urn,
And floats its broad, green leaf upon the tide,
To form an isle, where fairies might abide.

Yet strange to me they seem —
These glories of my native tropic clime;
No more its silver-flowing waters rhyme
With my own spirit's dream.
The charm has vanished, broken is the spell;
And in the woods and in the hollow dell
Strange echoes seem to shape the word farewell.

I would rebind the spell
About my brow; fling off the chain of years.
Say, what should check me?   Why should time and tears
The *spirit* sear or quell?
Snatch me a wreath from yonder blooming vine!
Here let me lie, where morning-glories twine,
And round me call my olden dreams divine.

Vain! vain! the broken spell
Can never be renewed; the vanished charm
I 've vainly sought — in jessamines breathing warm;
In the magnolia's bell;
In deep ravines, where mystic waters pour
Through the cleft earth, and reappear no more.

But yesternight I stole
Down to the sea — down to the lonely sea,
Where but the starlight shone mysteriously;
And *there*, my listening soul
Heard, through the silence, every solemn wave
Speak, in deep, mournful whispers of *a grave*.

And now I know that here,
Even here — across the glory and the bloom —
There falls the shadow of that little tomb —
    The grave they made last year,
Hiding beneath the sodden earth forlorn
The flower of love, my desolate life had borne.

    Oh! not for me, for me,
Does the pale Naiad hold her lily-urn,
And not for me the starry jessamines burn;
    Only the dreary sea
Brings *me* a message — on each solemn wave
Bearing the mournful story of a grave.

THE FATAL BRACELET.

It wanted a half-hour to midnight. The marriage ceremony had long been over, and the bride had been gayest among her guests. There was a pause in the dance just now. Vane had gone below — called down upon some business that would not wait even for bridal festivities. Flushed and sparkling, Coralyn stood at a retired window beside her partner, resting from the exercise of the dance. The night was warm, and her companion proffered to go for a glass of iced water. When he had quitted her side, she leaned from the window, drinking in the fresh air, whose balm cooled the hot glow upon her cheeks, and quieted the feverish unrest of her heart. She did not hear a stealthy step approach her; she had no warning of the proximity of danger, until a voice said in her ear: "I am late with my congratulations for such an old friend."

She turned instantly, and confronted him face to face. It was he! He was not dead. It was the dark, handsome face of the picture — darker and more sinister than ever. Had the earth opened at her feet, she could not have been more stunned, more stupefied — could not have grown whiter, or felt her brain reel with more deadly sickness.

"Do not faint!" he whispered, with a scornful smile half defined on his full lips. "What would be thought?"

The necessity for self-control brought back consciousness and strength. She glanced around — she was not observed.

"I thought —" she faltered.

"That I was dead. Very distressing thought, no doubt, to you. Happy to relieve your mind by affording you ocular proof of my existence. Probably, you thought that death alone should have kept me away from your arms. Really, you must blame the importunities of friends, which it was out of my power to resist. They kindly obliged me to accept the privilege

of their residence and the society of their select guests, and insisted so stren-
uously upon my partaking of their hospitality for the term of my natural
life, that it was only by stratagem and the devil's help that I at last got rid
of the burden of their excessive kindness. See; I have brought away a
token of their affection." And the escaped convict unfastened his jewelled
sleeve-button, and rolling back his sleeve a little way, showed the deep scars
of handcuffs on his wrist. He smiled as he saw her shudder. Then, as` he
quietly buttoned his cuff again, the partner of Coralyn returned with the
glass of water. She would have sprung forward eagerly to his side, but a
glance from the eyes she feared, restrained her. The dark stranger stepped
gracefully forward.

"Permit me," he said, taking the glass from the gentleman with bland
politeness, and placing it in her hand.

It would have fallen from her cold fingers, but he held it, while she drained
the last crystal drop. The glass was returned to the gentleman. He was
her husband's dearest friend. He would have remained by her side, had he
seen or interpreted the mute, imploring look she cast upon him. He did not
see it. He turned away, and left her with the man, whose easy familiarity
seemed to betoken him an old friend.

She cast her eyes over the crowd — fearing and yet blindly wishing to see
her husband's tall figure, and meet his eyes in search of her. Yet how
could he help her? What would she dare to say to him? If he knew all,
would he not fling her from him in horror? Oh! what should she do? what
would become of her? Why had she ever deceived him and yielded to the
temptation of securing herself within the safe, sweet shelter of home and
love? What right had she to home or love? — she — she — she dared not
whisper it to herself. It was horrible — horrible! True, she had been so
young, so utterly ignorant; and then that cruel, terrible Margery — and
her son — the fiendish being who stood now gloating upon her beauty and
her terror. Could it be she had ever loved him — had trembled and blushed
when he spoke to her — had watched him (the first young man she had ever
seen) with a fearful, fascinated gaze, and a feeling of mingled abhorrence
and admiration?

Why had he come here to-night? What would he dare to tell of her past
life, when it must involve an exposure of himself — he, the escaped felon,
doubtless with a price upon his head? Did he read the rapid thoughts that
rushed through her brain? He stood there, watching her with folded arms,
and a smile on his lips. His eyes drank in her beauty, and burned upon her
with the blended fire of love and hate. The band began playing a waltz —
the dancers gathered upon the floor. "Let us waltz," he said suddenly,
proffering his hand. She made an involuntary gesture of loathing, and her
lips syllabled a refusal. His dark brow grew blacker as he saw the abhorrence she could not conceal. His eyes flashed luridly; he bent down and
whispered a word in her ear. She grew livid to the lips; her eyes fell, her

hands dropped at her side. He watched her with his shining, serpent eyes and half-formed smile.

"Shall we waltz now?" he asked gayly; and passing his arm around her waist, they floated into the centre of the room among the dancers.

The music was at first slow and soft. As they swam through its languid mazes, he kept his basilisk eyes fixed upon her.

"You wear my gift," he said, tightening his grasp upon her wrist that was circled by the coiled serpent.

"Yours?" she uttered. "Nurse Margery's —"

"No; mine. The note was only a ruse to make sure of your wearing the bracelet. Margery is dead."

"Dead?"

"Dead — starved to death in a gutter, thanks to the gratitude of her foster-child." He hissed out the words between his teeth. His lips parted, and the white, carnivorous teeth shone beneath the black moustache like the teeth of a wild beast.

"Her foster-child," he continued, "that she fed when a pauper, and who, when her heirship was discovered, drove her off to starve."

"Not I, not I — it was my aunt. God forgive me, I had not courage —"

"Hush speaking of God. What is God to us? My mother will not forgive. She will torture you for it in the regions of the damned."

She cowered under the dark words and the threatening brow and eyes. What a mockery it was to be whirling round to the quickening music, flower-crowned and festally arrayed, while her spirit shrank within her through terrible shame, and her brain reeled with dizzy torture.

"And you?" she found voice to say; "why are you here to-night?"

"To crush a worm that has dared to sting me. Ha! did you think I could be deceived and trifled with, without my revenge?"

As he spoke, bending his lips so close to hers that the fiery breath was on her cheek, he grasped the serpent-bound arm so tightly, that she uttered a faint exclamation. It was drowned by the music, that now rose wilder and faster, while the dancers whirled in rapid circles over the floor, that shook with the beating of their feet.

"Scream," he whispered; "draw the crowd around you. I will then have a fine opportunity of explaining old matters."

"Have mercy," she moaned, as he whirled her relentlessly around. "Loose your grasp upon my arm. The bracelet is piercing my flesh. I am suffering intensely."

"It is the cobra's tooth," he answered, with the malignant smile of a fiend. "The bracelet is bewitched. My touch endues it with life and venom. Its head is lifted no longer; the blow is struck; the fangs are in your flesh."

"O God! I am ill. I am in terrible pain! in mercy let me stop!"

But round and round he whirled her — supporting her slender figure almost wholly by his muscular arm.

"Spare me! spare me!" she groaned. "In mercy, in mercy!"

"Did you think of mercy when you broke your faith with me? — taught yourself to scorn and hate me; drove my old mother, who had nursed you, from your presence, and deceived an honorable man into taking you as his wife — *you*, a wife! ha! ha! impostor! I would have found my sweetest revenge by exposing all — holding you up to his scorn and the contempt of the world you love so well; but I look to my own safety. I am not ready to swing just yet, or to go back to that devil's hole of punishment. I have taken a safer mode to secure my revenge."

"O God! I suffer, I suffer!"

Her head fell back heavily against him.

"Water!" he cried, "a lady has fainted."

"She has fainted! the bride has fainted!" repeated a score of voices, and the throng pressed around her in helpless bewilderment.

Vane heard the words, as he came bounding up the steps.

He strode into the room. The crowd made way as he came. He took her into his arms. He flung back the rich hair until it swept rippling to the floor. He called her by all the sweet, endearing names of love, as he applied one restorative after another. But there came no sign of life. The lips were closely crushed together, and lurid circles were darkening under the eyes.

"A physician!" he cried huskily. One stood beside him now — holding the slender wrist, which the serpent bracelet no longer clasped. He knelt down and examined her attentively. He was a man of science and experience — long a sojourner in Eastern lands.

"It is death," he said solemnly.

Vane was speechless. They took her from him to another room, and he followed like a child. As the body was borne past the physician, he pointed to the livid spots gathering upon the marble of the breast, arms, and forehead, and said: "If this were in the East, I should swear that she died from the bite of the cobra da Capelli."

And where was the murderer? — where was he with that fatal bracelet, with its concealed spring and its slender, poisoned blade — dipped in the poison of the cobra — the speediest and deadliest?

No one knew. He had disappeared in the confusion of the crowd. Only one suspected him of being a murderer.

The next day the civil authorities searched the neighborhood for an escaped convict — a desperate felon, committed for life. They went away without finding him; but some days afterward, a party of hunters in the mountains saw the vultures gathered around something at the foot of the precipice. They reached the place by a circuitous path, and found the body of a human being: the wrists and ankles were scarred as if by heavy irons, the clothing was rich, and in the pocket of the coat was found a curious bracelet of gold — in semblance a cobra serpent, in the attitude of striking, with eyes of emeralds and hood studded with rubies; on touching a secret spring, it was found that the cobra's head sprang suddenly forward, and a tiny blade leaped out from its jaws!

"Do not touch it," said the physician. "It has been dipped in the poison of the cobra."

HOW SHOULD WOMEN WRITE?

The idea of women writing books! There were no prophets in the days of King John to predict an event so far removed from probability. The women of the household sat by their distaffs, or toiled in the fields, or busied themselves in roasting and brewing for their guzzling lords. If ever a poetic vision or a half-defined thought floated through their minds, they sang it out to their busy wheels, or murmured it in rude sentences to lull the babies upon their bosoms, or silently wove it into their lives to manifest itself in patient love and gentleness. And it was all as it should have been; there was need for nothing more. Physical labor was then all that was required of woman; and to "act well her part," meant but to perform the domestic duties which were given her. Life was less complex then than now — the intellectual part of man's twofold nature being but unequally developed, while the absence of labor-saving implements demanded a greater amount of manual toil from men as well as from women.

It is different now. Modern ingenuity and Protean appliances of machinery have lessened the necessity of actual physical labor; and, in the constant progress of the human race, new fields have been opened, and new social needs and requirements are calling for workers in other and higher departments.

There is a cry now for intellectual food through the length and breadth of the land. The old oracles of the past, the mummied literary remains of a dead age, will not satisfy a generation that is pressing so vigorously forward. They want books imbued with the strong vitality and energy of the present. And as it is a moving, hurrying, changing time, with new influences and opinions constantly rising like stars above the horizon, men want books to keep pace with their progress — nay, to go before and guide them, as the pillar of fire and cloud did the Israelites in the desert. So they want books for every year, for every month — mirrors to "catch the manners living as they rise," lenses to concentrate the rays of the new stars that dawn upon them.

There is a call for workers; and woman, true to her mission as the help-meet for man, steps forward to take her part in the intellectual labor, as she did when only manual toil was required at her hands. The pen has become the mighty instrument of reform and rebuke; the press is the teacher and the preacher of the world; and it is not only the privilege, but the duty of woman to aid in extending this influence of letters, and in supplying the intellectual demands of society, when she has been endowed with the power. Let her assure herself that she has been called to the task, and then grasp her pen firmly, with the stimulating consciousness that she is performing the work assigned to her.

Thus is apparent what has been gradually admitted, that it is woman's duty to write — but how and what? This is yet a mooted question. Men, after much demur and hesitation, have given women liberty to write; but they cannot yet consent to allow them full freedom. They may flutter out of the cage, but it must be with clipped wings; they may hop about the smooth-shaven lawn, but must, on no account, fly. With metaphysics they have nothing to do; it is too deep a sea for their lead to sound; nor must they grapple with those great social and moral problems with which every strong soul is now wrestling. They must not go beyond the surface of life, lest they should stir the impure sediment that lurks beneath. They may whiten the outside of the sepulchre, but must not soil their kidded hands by essaying to cleanse the inside of its rottenness and dead men's bones.

Nature, indeed, is given them to fustianize over, and religion allowed them as their chief capital — the orthodox religion, that says its prayers out of a prayer-book, and goes to church on Sabbaths; but on no account the higher, truer religion, that, despising cant and hypocrisy, and scorning forms and conventionalisms, seeks to cure, not to cloak the plague-spots of society — the self-forgetting, self-abnegating religion that shrinks not from following in the steps of Christ, that curls not its lip at the touch of poverty and shame, nor fears to call crime by its right name, though it wear a gilded mask, nor to cry out earnestly and bravely, "Away with it! away with it!" No! not such religion as this. It is *unfeminine;* women have no business with it whatever, though they may ring changes as often as they please upon the "crowns of gold," the "jasper walls," and "seraph harps."

Having prescribed these bounds to the female pen, men are the first to condemn her efforts as tame and commonplace, because they lack earnestness and strength.

If she writes of birds, of flowers, sunshine, and *id omne genus*, as did Amelia Welby, noses are elevated superbly, and the effusions are said to smack of bread and butter.

If love, religion, and domestic obligations are her theme, as with Mrs. Hentz, "namby-pamby" is the word contemptuously applied to her productions. If, like Mrs. Southworth, she reproduces Mrs. Radcliffe in her possibility — scorning romances, her nonsensical clap-trap is said to be "beneath criticism;" and if, with Patty Pepper, she gossips harmlessly of fashions and fashionables, of the opera and Laura Keene's, of watering-places, lectures, and a railroad trip, she is "*pish*"-ed aside as silly and childish; while those who seek to go beyond the boundary-line are put down with the stigma of "*strong-minded.*" Fanny Fern, who, though actuated by no fixed purpose, was yet more earnest than the majority of her sisterhood, heard the word hissed in her ears whenever she essayed to strike a blow at the root of social sin and inconsistency, and had whatever there was of noble and philanthropic impulse in her nature annihilated by the epithets of "bold" and "indelicate," which were hurled at her like poisoned arrows.

It will not do. Such dallying with surface-bubbles, as we find in much of our periodical literature, might have sufficed for another age, but not for this. We want a deeper troubling of the waters, that we may go down into the pool and be healed. It is an earnest age we live in. Life means more than it did in other days; it is an intense reality, crowded thick with eager, questioning thoughts and passionate resolves; with burning aspirations and agonized doubts. There are active influences at work, all tending to one grand object — moral, social, and physical advancement. The pen is the compass-needle that points to this pole. Shall woman dream on violet banks, while this great work of reformation is needing her talents and her energies? Shall she prate prettily of moonlight, music, love, and flowers, while the world of stern, staring, pressing realities of wrong and woe, of shame and toil, surrounds her? Shall she stifle the voice in her soul for fear of being sneered at as *strong-minded*, and shall her great heart throb and heave as did the mountain of Æsop, only to bring forth such insignificant mice — such productions — more paltry in purpose than in style and conception — which she gives to the world as the offspring of her brain?

It will not long be so. Women are already forming higher standards for themselves, learning that genius has no sex, and that, so the truth be told, it matters not whether the pen is wielded by a masculine or a female hand. The active, earnest, fearless spirit of the age, which sends the blood thrilling through the veins of women, will flow out through their pens, and give color to the pictures they delineate, to the principles they affirm. Literature must embody the prominent feeling of the age on which it is engrafted. It is only an isolated, excepted spirit, like Keats's, which can close its eyes to outward influences, and, amid the roar of gathering political storms, and the distant thunderings of the French Revolution, lie down among the sweet, wild English flowers, and dream out its dream of the old Greek beauty.

How should a woman write? I answer, as men, as all should write to whom the power of expression has been given — *honestly and without fear.* Let them write what they feel and think, even if there be errors in the thought and the feeling — better that than the lifeless inanities of which literature, and especially periodical literature, furnishes so many deplorable samples.

Our opinions on ethical and social questions change continually as the mind develops, and the light of knowledge shines more broadly through the far-off opening in the labyrinth of inquiry through which we wander,

43

seeking for truth. Thus, even when writers are most honest, their opinions written at different times, often appear contradictory. This the discerning reader will readily understand. He will know that in ascending the ladder, upon whose top the angels stand, the prospect widens and changes continually as newer heights are won. Emerson, indeed, tells us that "a foolish consistency is the hobgoblin of little minds. With consistency, a great soul has simply nothing to do. Speak what you think now in hard words; and to-morrow, speak what to-morrow thinks in hard words again, though it contradict everything you said to-day."

This is strong — perhaps too unqualified; but even inconsistency is better than the dull, donkey-like obstinacy which refuses to move from one position, though the wooing spirit of inquiry beckon it onward, and winged speculation tempt it to scale the clouds.

Still, there should be in writing, as in acting, a fixed and distinct purpose to which everything should tend. If this be to elevate and refine the human race, the purpose will gradually and unconsciously work out its own accomplishment. Not, indeed, through didactic homilies only; every image of beauty or sublimity crystallized in words, every philosophic truth, and every thought that has a tendency to expand the mind or enlarge the range of spiritual vision, will aid in advancing this purpose, will be as oil to the lamp we carry to light the footsteps of others.

As to the subjects that should be written upon, they are many and varied; there is no exhausting them while nature teems with beauty — while men live, and act, and love, and suffer — while the murmurs of the great ocean of the *Infinite* come to us in times when the soul is stillest, like music that is played too far off for us to catch the tune. Broad fields of thought lie before us, traversed, indeed, by many feet, but each season brings fresh fruits to gather and new flowers to crop.

Genius, like light, shines upon all things — upon the muck-heap as upon the gilded cupola.

As to the wrong and wretchedness which the novelist lays bare — it will not be denied that such really exists in this sin-beleaguered world. Wherefore shrink and cover our eyes when these social ulcers are probed? Better earnestly endeavor to eradicate the evil, than seek to conceal or ignore its existence. Be sure this will not prevent it eating deeper and deeper into the heart.

Genius, when true and earnest, will not be circumscribed. No power shall say to it: "Thus far shalt thou go, and no farther." Its province is, in part, to daguerreotype the shifting influences, feelings, and tendencies at work in the age in which it exists — and sin, and grief, and suffering, as well as hope, and love, and joy, and star-eyed aspiration, pass across its pages as phantoms across the charmed mirror of the magician. Genius thrills along "the electric chain wherewith we are darkly bound," from the highest to the lowest link of the social ligature; for true genius is Christ-like; *it scorns nothing;* calls nothing that God made common or unclean, because of its great yearning over mankind, its longing to lift them up from the sordid things of sense in which they grovel to its own higher and purer intellectual or spiritual atmosphere. The noblest woman of us all, Mrs. Elizabeth Browning, whom I hold to have written, in "Aurora Leigh," the greatest book of this century, — the greatest, not from the wealth of its imagery, or the vigor of its thoughts, but because of the moral grandeur of its purpose, — Mrs. Browning, I say, has not shrunk from going down, with her purity encircling her, like the halo around the Saviour's head, to the abodes of shame and degradation for materials to aid in elucidating the serious truths she seeks to impress for sorrowful examples of the evils for which she endeavors to find some remedy. She is led to this through that love which is inseparable from the higher order of genius. That noblest form of genius which generates the truest poetry — the poetry of feeling rather than of imagination — warm with human life, but uncolored by voluptuous passion — is strongly connected with love. Not the sentiment which dances through the world to the music of marriage-bells; but that divine, self-ignoring, universal love of which the inspired apostle wrote so burningly, when, caught up in the fiery chariot of the Holy Ghost, he looked down upon the selfish considerations of common humanity: the love (or charity) "which beareth all things, endureth all things, which suffereth long and is kind," — the love which, looking to heaven, stretches its arms to enfold the whole human brotherhood.

This is the love which, hand in hand with genius, is yet to work out the redemption of society. I have faith to believe it; and sometimes, when the tide of hope and enthusiasm is high, I have thought that woman, with the patience and the long-suffering of her love, the purity of her intellect, her instinctive sympathy and her soul of poetry, might be God's chosen instrument in this work of gradual reformation, this reconciling of the harsh contrasts in society that jar so upon our sense of harmony, this righting of the grievous wrongs and evils over which we weep and pray, this final uniting of men into one common brotherhood by the bonds of sympathy and affection.

It may be but a Utopian dream; but the faith is better than hopelessness; it is elevating and cheering to believe it. It is well to aspire, though the aspiration be unfulfilled. It is better to look up at the stars, though they dazzle, than down at the vermin beneath our feet.

FANNY E. HERRON.

MISS HERRON'S publications have been few, and yet we rank her among the "promising writers of the sunny South." In February, 1867, a poem of four hundred lines appeared in the "Mobile Sunday Times," entitled "The Siege of Murany," which was Miss Herron's first contribution to that journal. "Glenelglen," a romance of other days, and an excellent tale, her first attempt in prose, was written to compete for the prize offered by the "Times;" and, after appearing in that journal, was published in book-form.

Though originally a resident of Virginia, the father of Miss Herron, the late James Herron, civil engineer, was for a number of years in charge of the public works at the Pensacola Navy Yard. Miss Herron is a graduate of the Academy of the Visitation, Mount de Sales, in Baltimore County, Maryland, taking first premiums and gold medal.

Miss Herron resides in Pensacola.

1868.

EXTRACTS FROM

THE SIEGE OF MURANY.

But see, on yonder neighboring plains,
　　Where lingers still the day,
Each silvered helm, each burnished shield
　　Has caught its latest ray,
And flashes back in mimic light
　　The glory Sol had given,
Before the spangled flag of night
　　Had draped the dome of heaven.
Whence came yon band in martial gear?
　　What daring chieftain led
Yon royal host where Muran's guns
　　Rain vengeance on his head?

'T is he! 't is he, with eagle glance,
  And forehead bold and fair,
With cheek sun-kissed to olive hue,
  And waving, midnight hair;
'T is he, with martial step and mien,
  Whose deep-toned voice's sound
Might vie with lyre by Orpheus touched
  T' enchant the groves around;
'T is he, whose mouth of stern resolve
  Can melt in smiles so rare,
So soft, so sweet, his men forget
  Their months of toil and care,
And rush to death in countless forms
  Whene'er he leads the way:
'T is Wesselengi — he who sits
  In tent at close of day.
Though young in years, in deeds of arms
  Full many score is he,
As foe hath never yet beheld
  Him dastard turn to flee.
Yet when yon dark, stupendous pile
  Upon his vision rose,
The evil fortune he deplored
  That peopled it with foes.
By nature it was rendered strong,
  Impregnable by art;
Yet felt he, never from those walls
  With honor he'd depart,
Until time-hallowed Murany
  Had owned the kingly power,
Until his monarch's standard waved
  Triumphant o'er each tower.
In sullen floods these sombre thoughts
  Fast o'er his spirit roll,
Till thus he vented to the night,
  The anguish of his soul:

"Oh! must the laurels hardly earned,
  Which long have wreathed my brow,
Be tarnished by defeat or flight?
  Yield to a woman now?
I've led my hosts o'er mountain snow,
  By prestige of my name;
Was 't but to watch in darkness set
  The day-star of my fame?

No! brighter yet that star shall glow,
And laurels fresh I'll reap;
Again shall fortune greet her son,
Or with my dead I'll sleep."

.   .   .   .   .   .

O Wesselengi, was it pride,
And loyalty alone,
To keep undimmed thy martial fame,
And stay thy monarch's throne,
That made thee hazard freedom sweet—
Nay, tempt a darker fate —
By venturing unattended thus
Within that massive gate?
Or had the charms of her who dwelt
In yonder turret old
Been whispered in thy midnight dreams,
To make thee rashly bold?

MRS. M. LOUISE CROSSLEY.

ATHENS, Georgia, was the birthplace of Mrs. Crossley, whose maiden name was M. Louise Rogers.

In her childhood, Miss Rogers was left much to herself; her best teachers were nature and experience. The first published pen-work of Miss Rogers was written while she was in Southwestern Georgia, an inmate of the home of Major Edwards. Mrs. Edwards, her aunt on the maternal side, was the mother of Mrs. Mary E. Bryan. There are critical times in almost every life, when the slightest circumstance may serve to change the current of destiny; and it was probably owing to this summer visit that Miss Rogers turned her attention to author-ship so soon. For, like Miss Edgeworth, her "great respect for the public" would have made her timid about publishing, unless stimu-lated by the example of one her opposite in this particular. Such an one she found in her cousin. Although so young, Mrs. Bryan had already sounded nearly the whole gamut of feeling, and now she was reproducing her experiences through the medium of her pen. Pas-sionate, impetuous, and bold, she was rapidly throwing off her daring opinions and sentiments, more from the feverish unrest and turbulent fulness of her mind than from any fixed purpose or reverent devotion to art, (such as may have afterward come to be her motive,) and publishing with the indifference of one not troubled with any overpowering "respect for the public." The contagious quality of the *cacoethes scribendi* is proverbial. The daily sight of manuscript, the indifference with which scribbled sheets were despatched to various editors, had their influence upon Louise Rogers. Her first article, whose theme was "Beauty," was published. The ice broken, Miss Rogers published in the newspapers frequently under the *nom de guerre* of "Rena." She contributed to the "Literary Companion," published in Newnan, Ga., as "Currer Lyle." During the war she contributed, under her own name, to the "Southern Illustrated News."

In May, 1866, Miss Rogers was married to J. T. Crossley, Esq., and is resident at Columbus, Florida.

Mrs. Crossley is engaged in collecting and composing materials for a volume, to contain her best productions that have been printed, and two novelettes that have never been published.

1869.

———oo⚬⚬oo———

AUGUSTA DE MILLY.

IN Confederate literature, the signature of "Ethel Deen" and the initials "A. D." were pleasant sights; for the article to which they were attached, whether prose or verse, was always readable.

Augusta De Milly is a native of New York city, but having many Southern connections, and the greater portion of her life having been passed in the State of Florida, she claims to be a Southern woman by residence, as she is by feeling.

During the war, Mrs. De Milly contributed to the literary journals of "Dixie," principally the "Southern Field and Fireside," (Augusta,) and "Magnolia Weekly," (Richmond,) under signatures alluded to, and many of her articles, written in a careless and desultory manner, were excellent and much praised. Since the close of the war, her attempts in the writing line have been few: as she expresses it, "a school-teacher has little time to gossip with the Muses." The prose productions of Mrs. De Milly are short sketches, well written and interesting; but, as she says in a note to the writer, "Never having made any sustained effort, I can point to no effort which would at all afford a foundation for a literary reputation."

Her home is in the "land of flowers," where the "fount of perpetual youth" was said to be in ancient days, and indeed where sunshine and beautiful blooms are perennial. "Jacksonville, Florida," is her address.

1868.

"IMPLORA PACE."

The most frequent inscription on the tombs in Italy is the above petition.

The spring-time died — so would I gladly die
　　And be at rest; for life brings but remorse:
I'd welcome thee, dread Azrael, fearlessly,
　　Nor once bewail my yet unfinished course.
Come, dreamless sleep; no phosphorescent spark
Can lure me then to wander in the dark.

Germs wither, buds pale at their birth,
　　The chilling winds stab blossoms without ruth,
The grain must lie among the tares of earth,
　　And scudding vapors hide the heaven of truth.
Must I, whose soon maturity was vain,
Take up the burden of my life again?

The summer died — and fain would I too rest
　　Within thy pitying arms; quick tempests drown
Me with their tears — fierce lightnings scathe my breast,
　　And the rich treasures of my heart go down.
Oh, be not thou inexorable, Death!
Kiss on my lips thine all-availing breath.

Come thou! the orchid's eyes are calm
　　That look from the greensward — the shade
Of feathery cedars woos me with its balm,
　　And the eternal stars smile ever overhead.
How can I hush my heart that moans its pain?
How take the burden of my life again?

See! even the autumn lies beneath his pall
　　Heraldic. O ye winds that round him sweep,
Could ye, like his, my spirit disenthrall,
　　Then would I calmly lie — and calmly sleep.
Dews of the mocking vine but parch my lips;
I'd quaff, O Death! thy cup's nepenthean deeps.

Must I, pale king! so weary of the strife
   For fame, for wealth, for fruits that ever cloy,—
I, who had sown the affluence of my life,
   And built wide barns for harvestings of joy,—
Must I, who garner blight, not laughing grain,
Take up the burden of such life again?

Between white hills, within his nest of snows
   Plucked from the bosom of the brooding cloud,
Dead winter lies — so peaceful his repose,
   No royal robes could lure me like his shroud;
My blooms like his are fettered for all time,
Prisoned in bars of ice, and frost, and rime.

Why should I live? My heart is stark and dead
   To all sweet influence. Never love-bird's lays
Wake tuneful carols there — such songs have fled
   To where are verdant boughs and blossoming sprays.
Hold out thy sceptre, Death! — if thou dost reign,
Nor bid me bear life's burden yet again.

FLORIDA CAPTA.

Leaning her fair head against the pines,
   Like some faint lily resting on the waves,
In the clear waters — where a white moon shines —
   Idle and dreaming, either hand she laves.

Her listless cheek the green palmetto fans;
   The blue-eyed vine her sighing lips has kissed;
The pitying rivers, from their reedy bands
   Loosening their tresses, fold her in the mist.

And over her the sobbing roses bend,
   Dropping their fragrant tears upon her face;
For her wan temples, with a trembling hand,
   The jasmine breaks her alabaster vase.

In vain, from every sprouting screen around,
   A sweet-voiced bird her plaintive love-song sings;
With the soft moonlight linked and interwound,
   Rippling the air in bright harmonic rings.

44

A tender memory haunts her where she lies —
   The beauteous Florida! — the queen uncrowned!
And dims the light in her sweet, mournful eyes,
   That see not wave, nor moon, nor aught around.

She feels again upon her bosom bare
   The milky teeth of the young laughing corn;
Her fingers stray among the tangled hair,
   Silken and white, of one yet later born.

No more! no more on any summer night
   They 'll draw their nurture from her crescive breast;
No more the breathings of their soft delight
   Shall lull their mother into blissful rest.

Above her, O ye fauns! bend branch and bough;
   Shield her fair form 'gainst the chill, blighting dew;
Pity her dolor, and on her pale brow
   Bind your gray pearls of beaded mistletoe.

For from the dusk in her sweet, mournful eyes,
   That see not moon, nor wave, nor aught around,
Never again shall full-orbed hope arise
   To shine on her — on Florida uncrowned.

TENNESSEE.

MRS. L. VIRGINIA FRENCH.

MRS. FRENCH'S birth and education are the best the country affords. *Poeta nascitur*, and Mrs. French, aside from being a "born" poet, is a "born" lady. She knows it as well.

Her family, early incidents of her life, and romantic marriage are piquantly spoken of in "Mary Forrest's" elegant work, "Women of the South." Born on the fair shores of Virginia, educated in Pennsylvania, and married in Tennessee, her life has been like herself, varied and cosmopolitan. She is, nevertheless, a true daughter of the Old Dominion; a fair representative of its gay grace, its cordial hospitality, its love of luxury, and its indomitable pride.

The personal appearance of Mrs. French is highly prepossessing, and her manner so gifted with repose as to be unusually tranquillizing in its social influence. Yet there are seasons when the blue eyes flash, and the lips are wreathed in smiles so vivid and genial, that one can scarcely understand how the quiet lady, a moment before sitting so restfully, and listening so patiently, can be the same as she, so suddenly stirred to interest and emotion.

That rarest of all American gifts — wit — has been conferred upon her, in conjunction with poetic genius of no common order; and it is delightful to hear her low, rich laugh rippling out in ready recognition of some point of humor, obtuse to most listeners, and to find her arrow of repartee always on the string, though its point is never envenomed by the poison of bitterness.

Mrs. French possesses a noble nature; full of generous emotions and fine impulses; turning away from all wrong; not so much, perhaps, because of the wickedness of wrong; but because wrong implies something low and mean; and to do wrong, therefore, would be too deep a condescension; — large-hearted and liberal-minded; taking broad views of life and humanity; possessed of a catholic charity which "circles all the human race," and a nature with but one "prejudice," *i. e.*, a

347

healthy and well-developed hatred of all Puritanism—Puritanism, as she understands it, viz., the embodiment of hypocrisy and cant;—radically independent in all things; doing each day "whatever duty lies next to her," leaving the results with God.

"In 1848," says 'Mary Forrest,'* "Virginia Smith and her sister returned from school to their father's house. But a new spirit was rife in the old home; its lares and penates had been displaced, and the two sisters, ever united by the tenderest ties of sympathy, determined to go forth into the world and shape their own destinies. Before the close of the year, they were established in Memphis, Tennessee, as teachers.

"Strangers in a strange city, they put themselves bravely to their self-appointed work, and by their energetic perseverance, no less than their personal and intellectual charms, soon won the confidence of all.

"Having achieved a social and tutorial position, the elder sister began to turn her attention to literary pursuits, contributing occasional articles to the journals and magazines of that region under the name of 'L'Inconnue.'

"In 1852, she became associated with some gentlemen of New Orleans in the publication of the 'Southern Ladies' Book.'

"On the 12th of January, 1853, she was married to Mr. John H. French, of McMinnville, Tennessee."

Mrs. French has published one volume — a collection of her poems, under the title of "Wind Whispers"—in 1856; and a tragedy, in five acts, under the title of "Iztalilxo, the Lady of Tula." She has written enough for half a dozen volumes, or more. She takes all criticism in the proper spirit, having no fear of the "small snarlers," but little reverence for the great ones, and no ambition to become a "serf of the booksellers."

But few ladies whom "we read about" have any deficiencies. Mrs. French is the exception which proves the rule. A serious defect in her organization is want of application. Had she never married, but devoted herself to literature and art, she would assuredly have been eminently successful. But her life is too full of other attractions — home, and home happiness. She entirely repudiates the name of "*littérateur;*" loves books, but cares no more for being put into them than the lark cares for seeing his morning hymn written out on a musical score. A great deficiency this want of ambition; this lack of interest

* "Women of the South," page 440.

in her own reputation. She has no consideration for any work that is *done.* An article completed, the excitement of writing it over, is thought of no more. Literature, which with her should occupy the front rank, does not even take a secondary place in her life and estimation; it is merely a kind of little by-play while the real drama of life goes on. She scatters here and there the effervescence of an affluent intellect, the deeps of which are still clear, calm, and undrawn upon. What the public sees of her writings as yet are merely "gold-blossoms," sparkling quartz, which indicate the precious ore that lies below; the mine itself is unworked, almost untouched. Emphatically a child of the sun, her fancies, bright and beautiful as foam-bells on the deep, never suggest to you the thought of effort or exhaustion, any more than the sigh of an Æolian lyre when "the breeze is spent, intimates that the mighty billows of the air shall surge no more." Her weakness, therefore, so to speak, lies not in any lack of power; but in a lamentable want of exertion. There is no deficiency of nerve to grasp a subject, or of power to discuss, or of keen acumen to analyze it; but there is indifference; and I think it reprehensible to give us merely the spicy fragrance flung off from the cinnamon-tree of genius, while the principle of sweetness in concentrated strength still lies hidden in the heart. Yet if you should undertake to impress upon her the wrong she does herself by trifling away gifts so precious, she would probably laugh archly in your face, and say, with the philosophy of a nature rather Sybaritic in its composition, "It is pleasanter to enjoy than to labor, more especially when both amount to the same thing at last."

As a *littérateur?* If (to borrow the simile of a famous critic) the gifts of others resemble wealth, hers "is an alchemy. If others, so to speak, go out into the mind's Australia, and collect its ores, lying thick as morning dews, she remains at home, transmitting all she touches into gold." Her language, in its elegance and rhythmic flow, is clear and lucid as the pleasant rush of a summer stream; and it has been said that her absolute command of comprehensible words is such that many might, with advantage, employ her to translate their Pedantese into plain English. I have seriously objected to her want of study; yet I must confess that what she writes, most of us can comprehend. We are not compelled to sit down over any poem of hers, gazing with portentous visage and a critic's eye at its obscurity; whispering at last under our breath: "There are sunbeams in this cucum-

ber, if we could but extract them." But she does not put her sunbeams into the cucumber form. No; by all means let us take our
cucumbers and our sunshine separately.

"Lady Tranquilla's" chief characteristic in literature is a wonderful versatility, to which scarce any vein of writing comes amiss, as is
shown by poems, tales, sketches, letters, etc., written not only at her
desk "*en grande tenue,*" but scribbled in pencil under some wide-
spreading tree, by garden-bound or riverside; in short, anywhere and
everywhere, as the spirit moves her. This versatility is acknowledged
by our people in the calls they make upon her powers. It fits her
also to supply that large and constant drain made upon her time and
talents, of which the world knows nothing. You might be in her
house for months, and never know she wrote a line, for aught you
heard or saw; yet she seems to be a species of perennial fountain,
from which hundreds of people who never saw her draw supplies of
strength and comfort; never dreaming, doubtless, of the drain they
make upon this "sweet water spring," which gives out its supplies
freshly and freely; which asks no return, and thinks of no replenish-
ing, save what it draws from heaven. A lady, a thousand miles away,
wants a May-day speech for some young favorite; an agricultural editor wants an essay on a given topic; a political friend wants a letter
written which shall "bring out all the points;" a stranger widow
wants five dollars; a young lady wants a situation as teacher; a novelist wants a book noticed; and so on, almost *ad infinitum;* yet all these
applications are answered with a tranquillity equal to the fountain's,
and a patience enduring as Job's. I have expected ere this to see her
grow rather *blasé;* and she has sufficient knowledge of the world to
make her so. I have expected to see her grow weary of its

> "Dust and decay,
> Weary of throwing her soul-wealth away,
> Weary of sowing for others to reap;"

but that time seems as yet to linger by the way. In this connection,
it may be well to say that "Lady Tranquilla" is accused of being a
great favorite with contemporary *littérateurs.* She has probably been
more be-rhymed and be-sonneted than any other poetess. Her popularity arises from the fact that she claims no especial literary honors,
and thus arouses no jealousies. Then, too, she is ever ready to extend
favors, but asks none in return. She receives innumerable confidences,

but never confides. N. P. Willis says that "to listen to the confidences of others, without ever thinking it worth while to burden them with yours, is a very good basis for a friendship. Nothing bores people more than to return their secrets with your own."

Yes, versatility is the "Lady Tranquilla's" *forte*. It makes her a general favorite. It renders her *par excellence* the journalist. It causes her critics to take each a different view. As for instance, Mrs. C. A. Warfield regards poetry as Mrs. French's strong point, and says of that stinging tribute, "Shermanized:" "Never sprang cooler and keener sarcasm from more tranquil lips. It is the flash of the yataghan from a velvet sheath — the cold, clear gleam of the sword from a silver scabbard."

Mrs. Julia Pleasants Creswell takes the opposite view, and insists that "Mrs. French writes the best prose, with the strongest sense in it, of any Southern writer."

That enchanting poetess, Amelia Welby, for years previous to her death, ceased to write. It is affirmed that she gave as a reason, that she had lost the power, the "faculty divine." It is more than probable that as her mind matured and expanded, she felt that she had not the power to express what she had keen ability to feel, and I have imagined that Mrs. French too has grown away from the past. A revolution has changed us as a people, and she feels that our present needs can scarce be "bodied forth in song." She feels also that she has power to write for a *purpose*, and the fact that those seem to succeed best who write for *no purpose*, keeps her comparatively silent. Her broad views and catholicity of character fit her to grapple strongly with many moral and social evils. This breadth and cosmopolitanism fits her for "shooting her soul" into a score of contradictory characters at once, and a novel from her pen would be unique.

During the late war, by which she in common with all of her Southern sisters was a sufferer and a loser, she wrote many poems and pieces of choice prose on the subjects of common interest — distinguished from most of contemporaneous writing by their tone of graceful and scornful satire, and entire freedom from harshness and vituperation.

Mrs. French has in MS. a valuable addition to Southern literature, in the shape of a novel written during and about the war.

Still in the prime of life, and happy in her domestic relations, as well as comparatively prosperous — for she retains her delightful "Forest Home" and landed possessions, it is sincerely hoped that she may put forth her wing once more, and cleave new heights of unexplored atmosphere.*

We confidently believe that Mrs. French is capable, in her maturity of mind, of higher successes than she has yet achieved; and that her imagination, like Burke's, grows and strengthens with her years.

This gradual culmination of powers belongs only to strong natures, which grow like the oak-tree, slowly and surely, and remain vigorous and green when their frailer companions of the forest lie in ruins.

1869.

"MAMMY."

A Home Picture of 1860.

Where the broad mulberry branches hang a canopy of leaves,
Like an avalanche of verdure, drooping o'er the kitchen eaves;
And the sunshine and the shadow dainty arabesques have made
On the quaint, old oak settle, standing in the pleasant shade;
Sits good "Mammy," with the child'un," while the summer afternoon
Wears the dewy veil of April o'er the brilliancy of June.

Smooth and snowy is the kerchief, lying folded with an air
Of matron dignity above her silver-sprinkled hair;
Blue and white the beaded necklace, used "of Sundays" to bedeck
(A dearly cherished amulet) her plump and dusky neck;
Dark her neatly-ironed apron, of a broad and ample size,
Spreading o'er the dress of "homespun," with its many-colored dyes.

True, her lips are all untutored; yet how genially they smile,
And how eloquent their fervor, praying, "Jesus bless de chile!"
True, her voice is hoarse and broken; but how tender its replies!
True, her hands are brown and withered; yet how loving are her eyes!
She has thoughts both high and holy, though her brow is dark and low,
And her face is dusk and wrinkled, but her soul as white as snow.

An "aristocrat" is "Mammy," in her dignity sedate;
"Haught as Lucifer" to "white trash," whom she cannot tolerate;
Patronizing, too, to "Master," for she "nussed 'im when a boy;"
Familiar, yet respectful to the "Mistis;" but the joy
Of her bosom is "de child'un," and delightedly she'll boast
Of the "born blood" of her darlings — "good as kings and queens a'most."

---

* Claxton, Remsen & Haffelfinger, Philadelphia, have recently published (1871) "My Roses: a Romance of a June Day," — an interesting novel in Mrs. French's peculiar style, — written before the late war.

There she sits beneath the shadow, crooning o'er some olden hymn,
Watching earnestly and willingly, although her eyes are dim;
Laughing in her heart sincerely, yet with countenance demure,
Holding out before "her babies" every tempting little lure —
Noting all their merry frolics with a quiet, loving gaze,
Telling o'er at night to "Mistis" all their "cunnin' little ways."

Now and then her glance will wander o'er the pastures far away,
Where the tasselled corn-fields waving, to the breezes rock and sway,
To the river's gleaming silver, and the hazy distance where
Giant mountain-peaks are peering through an azure veil of air;
But the thrill of baby voices — baby laughter, low and sweet,
Recall her in a moment to the treasures at her feet.

So "rascally," so rollicking, our bold and sturdy boy,
In all his tricksy waywardness, is still her boast and joy;
She'll chase him through the shrubberies — his mischief mood to cure;
" Hi! whar dat little rascal now? — de b'ars will git 'im shure!"
When caught, she'll stoutly swing him to her shoulder, and in pride
Go marching round the pathways — "jus' to see how gran' he ride."

And the "Birdie" of our bosoms — ah! how soft and tenderly
Bows good "Mammy's" mother-spirit to her baby witchery!
(*All* to her is dear devotion whom the angels bend to bless,
All our thoughts of her are blended with a holy tenderness;)
Coaxing now, and now caressing — saying, with a smile and kiss,
" Jus' for Mammy — dat's a lady — will it now?" do that or this.

On the sweet, white-tufted clover, worn and weary with their play,
Toying with the creamy blossoms, now my little children lay;
Harnessed up with crimson ribbons, wooden horses, side by side,
" Make believe" to eat their "fodder" — (blossoms to their noses tied.)
Near them stands the willow wagon — in it "Birdie's" mammoth doll,
And our faithful "Brave" beside them, noble guardian over all.

Above them float the butterflies, around them hum the bees,
And birdlings warble, darting in and out among the trees;
The kitten sleeps at "Mammy's" side, and two grown rabbits pass,
Hopping close along the paling, stealing through the waving grass;
Gladsome tears blue eyes are filling, and a watching mother prays,
"God bless 'Mammy' and my children in these happy, halcyon days."

45

THE BROKEN SENTENCE.

A Tribute to the late Lieutenant Herndon.

" A ship went out upon the sea,
    A noble bark, with a gallant crew " —

And in herself a richly-freighted argosy of life and love — the ill-fated
" Central America." That dark and terrible picture of her going down
amid surging, midnight seas, which has been painted by inexorable fate, and
hung upon the walls of time's proud temple, is one upon which our whole
country has looked with "bated breath" and tear-dimmed eyes. Then, afar
over the ocean waves, "sailed the corsair, death," and, gathered in that
dread night-picture, there is the armada of the storm-king — the wrathful
sky above, and the black goal of doom "a hundred fathoms down." But,
notwithstanding all their terrific grandeur, how small, comparatively, is the
meed of attention given to those dread details! Columbia's eagle eye is
upon her noble son ; the brave commander, the gallant seaman, the humble
Christian, the immortal HERNDON. It is as though that great picture contained but one solitary human figure — one single object of interest whereon
the soul may centre her intensest gaze. We see him, as, with that heroic devotion to woman, which was one of his first characteristics, he provides for
their safety, until every woman and child has left his shattered vessel; we
see him don his uniform, the garb in which he so long had served his country, and take his last stand at the wheel-house ; we see him uncover to the
king of terrors, as the doomed ship fetches her last lurch; with tearful,
straining gaze, we see him signal an approaching boat, and order her to
keep off and *be saved*, while he himself went down ; to the last, mindful of
others and forgetful of self — the soul of a warrior, and the heart of a woman !

Beautiful, heroic, and self-sacrificing are such scenes; but there is, in this
connection, another still more beautiful and sublime; it is thus related by
his kinsman, Lieutenant Maury :

" As one of the last boats was about to leave the ship, her commander gave his watch
to a passenger, with the request that it might be delivered to his wife. He wished to
charge him with a message to her also, but his utterance was choked. ' Tell her — ' he
said: unable to proceed, he bent down his head, and buried his face in his hands for a
moment, as if in prayer, for he was a devout man, and a true Christian. In that moment, brief as it was, he endured the greatest agony. But it was over now. His crowd-
ing thoughts no doubt had been of friends and home; its desolation ; a beloved wife
and lovely daughter, dependent alone for support upon him. God and his country
would care for them now. Honor and duty required him to stick to his ship, and he
saw that she must go down."

"Tell her — " he began, but the thousand waves of an overflowing heart came rushing over him, like "high, fierce tides trampling in upon low, lee shores," and the last cry of his great soul was drowned amid the tumult. Then and there he had "tasted of the bitterness of death," and it was past. As we look upon him now, we pause in actual awe before the picture imaged in the mind. "Tell her — " said he, but human language had no words to body forth the love, the aspiration, the anguish of that noble soul in this, its hour of terrible trial. And so the strong man bowed his head upon his hands, and bent like a reed before the tempest, feeling only how, in such an hour, heart-throbs scorn the mockery of words. Undaunted by the dread danger — undismayed when all hearts were failing — gazing unblenching in the very face of destruction — ready to take death by the hand and disarm him of his terrors, he bowed down unmanned, and overwhelmed by one simple, loving memory of *her*. And now what remains to be said? What *could* be said, which in pathos and in power would not fall far, far below the single and simple reality of that broken and *forever unfinished* sentence — " *Tell her — " ?*

"Tell her" — *what?* Ah! in vain we speculate. In vain we strive through blinding tears to read his heart, and say for him what he could not say for himself. And it is best as it is. Let us leave it so, nor dare to desecrate with our poor surmises the broken column which the master artist was unable to complete. But, do we say *forever unfinished?* Will he *never* tell her?

Far away in some sun-bright "Isle of Balm," more beautiful and more radiant than the Amazonian forests through which he once wandered, will not the language of the *immortal* give him power to utter all that which the *mortal* had essayed in vain? Or in that better land will there be a "fulness of joy" so soul-absorbing, so complete and perfect, that no remembrance of a troubled past, no memory of an unfinished mission, no shadow of our imperfect life shall ever dare intrude? Who of us can tell?

Said his wife, upon the first tidings of the shipwreck: "I know he has perished. He will stand by his ship to the last, and save others by the sacrifice of himself!" A noble trust — and right nobly redeemed! *She* knew he could not be among the rescued, and still be "himself." And what must be her feelings now, as she gazes upon that parting memento, as she thinks of the last time he held it in his hand — the wild, terrific scene around him, and those two solitary syllables which constitute his dying words! To her, now it is as silent as the loved lips of him who sent it from that scene of death; and justly so — for why should it mark time to her whose eternity began with his, who was the life of her life, and soul of her soul?

We leave her with her treasures — a broken sentence and a silent keepsake — the first sounding ever in her heart like the murmur of an ocean-shell cast forth upon a lonely shore, while the slender hands of the last, having ceased to chronicle the flight of time, are ever pointing her away into the opening ages of eternity.

And have we yet no word to say for him? The "heart grows full to weeping" as we linger above his honored memory — but a nation's acclaim is his proudest eulogium, and woman's tears his most fitting epitaph. As Nelson fell, he exclaimed: "Thank God! I have done my duty!" As Webster passed the dread portal which opens into the valley of shadows, he murmured: "I still live!" As Napoleon gathered up life's failing forces to battle with the last enemy, he shouted feebly: "*Tête d'armée!*" But what said the heroic Herndon of *himself?* Nothing. He neither encourages himself with the knowledge of duties well performed — no, he leaves his deeds to speak for him; nor solaces himself with the idea that he will hereafter live in the hearts of his countrymen — no, he leaves that for *them* to say; nor does he proudly assume his province of command, and go forth to meet death as king meets king in battle; nay, he uncovers to the last conqueror, acknowledging him the vicegerent of God, and with a brave heart and firm faith goes down with him silently, and grandly too, into the dark abyss of ocean, and the darker abyss of an unknown eternity.

Silent — silent all! And if we say to the great sea, and the wild winds, and the overlooking skies, "Where is he now?" they are silent also. Perhaps, like drifting sea-weed, cast upon some distant strand, his bones bleach beneath the fiery sun of the tropics; perhaps laid softly down by gently bearing waters, where

> "coral reefs lie bare,
> And the cold sea-maids sit to sun their streaming hair;"

perhaps carried away by the impetuous surge to regions where "night and death" have built their thrones — where giant icebergs go thundering down the deep — where Euroclydon rolls forth its "stern triumphant psalms," and beneath shattered mast and mouldering sail sleep the old Vikings of the Northern Sea. In our cemeteries, "stone spells to stone its weary tale" — we read records of the loved and lost as the long funeral train is passing by, and the dirge is wailing for the dead; but who dares follow *him* to the grave, who went down to death amid the battle of the elements; whose funeral train was long lines of marching billows, and whose burial psalm was the volleying thunder and the sounding storm? We may enter the city's splendid mausoleums, and read engraven on brass and marble the virtues of the dead; we may sit down by some lone grave in the forest, whose only monument is a cluster of snowy lilies, on which the morning dewdrops write their transient epitaph; but who shall venture down, even in thought, to the "dark, unfathomed caves of ocean," where now sleeps the heart which bore up bravely against terror, and danger, and death, but broke in the struggle to utter one little sentence in loving guise, and so left it forever unsaid? The winds and the waves will bring no answer to the questioning voice: "Where is he now?" but we may lay our hands upon our hearts, and answer softly and truly too: "He is here! he dwells forever in the great heart of his country;" and while we answer thus, we also murmur meekly: "Our God has taken that noble spirit into his eternal rest!"

MRS. ANNIE CHAMBERS KETCHUM.

IF genuine admiration for Mrs. Ketchum's genius, and the same admiration mingled with warm personal regard for herself as a Christian gentlewoman and ardent friend, could constitute fitness for the labor of love through courtesy assigned me, then this sketch would be among the most interesting of all these narratives of "Southern Writers."

It has never been the present writer's good fortune to meet in person the lady whose name stands at the head of the present article, but several years of familiar correspondence originating in a business way, when Mrs. Ketchum was at the head of the "Lotus," (an entertaining magazine established at Memphis in 1858 or '59,) has afforded more than a passing glimpse of that earnest, fervent nature which appears in everything that emanates from her pen, and constitutes her, according to my ability of criticism, the first poetess of the South — unless we may place Margaret J. Preston in the same rank with her.

Of Mrs. Ketchum's prose-writings, I am not qualified to speak in detail. The "Ladies' Home," edited jointly by Mrs. French and Dr. Powell, gave us, indeed, extracts from "Nelly Bracken," her only published prose volume, unless I mistake, containing specimens of a style simple, terse, vigorous, and devoid of mannerism; the "Lotus" editorials were, oftentimes, tender and touching — imbued with a delicate pathos, whatever the theme; and of her letters — enchanting, artless, soul-breathing — I can only say that they seem to me the perfection of epistolary writing. Poetry, however, seems to be Mrs. Ketchum's natural element, and it is in rhythm that her peculiar bent of mind and feeling seeks its outlet.

My first acquaintance with her name and writings was through a poem which appeared in the "Richmond Enquirer" — copied into that paper from the "New York Churchman," to which it was originally contributed.

The lines struck me as breathing the very soul of poetry and fervent prayer; and, by the way, this religious element pervades almost every-

thing she has written, exerting, as I have cause to believe, a wide influence upon her daily life.   The article alluded to is copied entire,
thus:

A MOTHER'S PRAYER.

They sleep. Athwart my white
Moon-marbled casement, with her solemn mien
Silently watching o'er their rest serene,
 Gazeth the star-eyed night.

My girl — sedate, or wild,
By turns — as playful as a summer breeze,
Or grave as night on starlit Southern seas,
 Serene, strange woman-child.

My boy, my trembling star!
The whitest lamb in April's tenderest fold,
The bluest flower-bell in the shadiest wold,
 His gentle emblems are.

They are but two, and all
My lonely heart's arithmetic is done
When these are counted. High and holy One,
 Oh, hear my trembling call!

I ask not wealth nor fame
For these my jewels. Diadem and wreath
Soothe not the aching brow that throbs beneath,
 Nor cool its fever-flame.

I ask not length of life
Nor earthly honors. Weary are the ways
The gifted tread, unsafe the world's best praise,
 And keen its strife.

I ask not that to me
Thou spare them, though they dearer, dearer be
Than rain to deserts, spring-flowers to the bee,
 Or sunshine to the sea.

But kneeling at their feet,
While smiles like summer-light on shaded streams
Are gleaming from their glad and sinless dreams,
 I would my prayer repeat.

In that alluring land,
The future — where, amid green, stately bowers,
Ornate with proud and crimson-flushing flowers,
    Pleasure, with smooth white hand,

    Beckons the young away
From glen and hill-side to her banquet fair —
Sin, the grim she-wolf, coucheth in her lair,
    Ready to seize her prey.

    The bright and purpling bloom
Of nightshade and acanthus cannot hide
The charred and bleaching bones that are denied
    Taper, and chrism, and tomb.

    Lord, in this midnight hour
I bring my lambs to thee. Oh! by thy truth,
Thy mercy, save them from th' envenomed tooth
    And tempting poison-flower!

    O Crucified and Crowned,
Keep us! We have no shield, no guide but thee.
Let sorrows come — let Hope's last blossom be
    By Grief's dark tempest drowned;

    But lead us by thy hand,
O gentlest Shepherd, till we rest beside
The still, clear waters, in the pastures wide
    Of thine own sinless land!

The "Home Journal" published Mrs. Ketchum's "Christmas Ballad," of which her beloved "Benny" was the infant hero — Benny,
whose pious youth gave such high promise of future usefulness and
parental satisfaction in his career through life, whose last Christmas
(of 1857) found him keeping the great birthday in his Father's house
of "many mansions." While he sang the angel's song there, was
there not one on earth whose heart-throbs kept time to the beat of
that Christmas carol in its concluding lines?

    "He is sleeping — brown and silken
        Lie the lashes, long and meek,
    Like caressing, clinging shadows,
        On his plump and peachy cheek;

> And I bend above him, weeping
> Thankful tears, oh, undefiled!
> For a woman's crown of glory,
> For the blessing of a child!"*

I think it will be perceived by the specimens already quoted, and others which I shall proceed to quote, that Mrs. Ketchum ignores mere verbiage in expression; that each word has its corresponding idea, and that — to use a homely, but it seems to me expressive phrase — her writings contain no words or phrases thrown in for stuffing. She is exceedingly accurate, saying all she means, and no more — a style impossible of acquisition to a writer less thoroughly imbued with the spirit of his subject. Those who give us sentiment at second-hand always betray themselves, if in no other way, by the employment of some vehicle of speech a little the worse for long use — some pet phrase in demand of poetasters since time, or at least rhyme began. Mrs. Ketchum does not dally to adapt these to her thoughts, seeming to feel that fresh, strong conception is best expressed in the language it originally inspires, and that it confers its own picturesqueness and acceptability on its peculiar spontaneous forms of speech.

In "word-painting," I have thought she rivalled Ruskin at times in his peculiar gift. Who — beyond sympathy with the pathetic beauty of this "Requiem" — but can see therein the chameleon-tinted forests, the "setting" to this central object — the new-made grave? Who but breathes the breath of the autumn flowers, and sees their tantalizing, brilliant beauty — witnesses the white-winged spirit sweep through the "valley's" expanse — and later, the warder-stars come out to guard the battlements she has passed, and passed forever?

> Leaves of the autumn time,
> Crimson and golden, opalesque and brown,
> To this new grave-heap slowly rustling down,
> Come with your low, low chime
> And sing of her, who, spring and summer past,
> In her calm autumn went to heaven at last,
> Where there is no more rime.
>
> Flowers of the autumn days,
> Bright lingering roses, asters white as snow,
> And purple violets on the winds that go
> Sighing their sad, sad lays,

* Published in handsome style by S. R. Wells. New York. 1870.

Tell with your sweet breath how her spirit fair
Through life's declining kept its fragrance rare,
    Fresher amid decays.

    Birds of the autumn eves,
Warbling your last song ere ye plume your wing
For milder climes, stay awhile and sing
    Where the lone willow grieves;
Tell of a nest secure from storm and blast,
Where her white wing — the shadowy valley past —
    Rests under heavenly eaves.

    Stars of the autumn night —
Crowned warders on the rampart of the skies,
With your bright lances holy mysteries
    Upon the gravestone write;
Tell of the *new name* given to the free
In that fair land beyond the silent sea,
    Where Christ is Lord and Light.

    God of the wind and rain,
Seed-time and harvest, summer-time and sleet!
Stricken and woful, at Thy kingly feet
    We bow amid our pain!
Help us to find her where no falling leaf
Nor parting bird doth tell of death and grief,
    Where Thou alone dost reign،

Mrs. Ketchum was born and her early life passed in that picturesque portion of her State among the crags of the old Elkhorn River.
But I must let her tell something of herself:

"We were three, we fatherless sisters — three little ones in the old Kentucky
home, watched over by three older grown-up sisters, to whom we were seve-
rally awarded by our dear widowed mother, when our father was called home
to heaven. Day by day, when dismissed from the study where our elder sisters taught us, we shouted among the hills, we plashed in the flashing streams.
Night after night, in the long, snowy winters, we knotted ourselves in the
chimney corner, and listened with wide-open eyes to our dear black nurse's
marvellous tales, or, covered up in the warm nursery bed, whispered together
of Sinbad the Sailor, with half-closed, sleepy eyes, and at last went off from
the fairy world of child romance into the fantastic realm of dreams."

The above prefaced a sad narration of domestic affliction, the loss
of one of the devoted trio of sisters above spoken of; and in connection with it, I copy one of the "Lotus" editorials, "Under the Leaves,"

which I think (without any authority whatever) had for its subject the lamented one just mentioned.

"We have a pleasant shade now, children, under the leaves. There are delicate buds peering out from the leaves of the rose, and glistening emerald beads on the jasmine sprays, almost bursting to display their golden cups. See, out on the slopes, and under the budding trees, the fresh young grass lies like a velvet carpet. The weeping-willows that lean over the high, white wall of the cemetery are fringed with tender leaves; and yellow jonquils, growing on the graves, are tolling their golden bells in every breeze that whispers among the cedars. It is spring-time, and you know all the world is gay in the spring; but the Lotus cannot dance with Laeta now, when the March wind blows his merry, boisterous fife, and the hyacinths, awakened from their sleep, nod and swing in the gamesome frolic.

"There is a gentle river far away, where the rock-moss clings to the tall, gray cliffs, where the wild rose climbs like a fearless child, and over whose clear, murmuring waters the sycamore-trees stretch out their long, white arms in silent benediction. Its waters flow into the Kentucky, the Kentucky bears them to the Ohio, and the Ohio leads them at last to join the armied waves of this grand old river marching to the sea, on whose banks our leafy bower is built. The waters of that far-off stream are singing a death-song now: they have murmured it all the way from the far Kentucky hills, past cities and towns and plantations, where light-hearted children were playing, but none of them understood its meaning—its story was not for them. It tells to the trembling Lotus, as she leans to the solemn water, how the tall, red mountain-pinks will lift their heads on those distant crags, watching in vain for the pleasant eyes that sought them every spring; how the sycamore leaves will stop their whisperings to listen for the light footfall that will rustle the dead leaves at their hoary roots no more; and day and night the Lotus will kiss the blessed waves that a little while ago bathed fair and dainty feet that were whiter than her petals, and mirrored a face that is hid beneath the violets now.

"Laeta, joyful Laeta, has an elder sister, with soft, brown eyes and sweet, majestic manners. Her name is Lucia. She is wise and thoughtful. Through deepest darkness of sorrow she opens a path of light, and where there are only thorny thickets, she can show us safe and pleasant passages. She has sung with the night-wind in the ear of the sorrowing Lotus the story of One who taught the whole world patience in the garden of Gethsemane; she has written on the morning clouds the wondrous legend of the King's Daughter, whose raiment is of wrought gold, and on whose forehead shines the morning-star. Laeta is singing with the mocking-birds; we can hear them in the wood. It is her office to rejoice with every joyful thing. She is good and innocent, and always lovely and unselfish; but Lucia is wiser and knows better what to say when the white rabbit strays away, and the rain washes up the newly-planted flower-seeds, and the black crape hangs at the silent door."

I cannot better conclude this imperfect narration than by adding that the fortunes of our late civil contest left this lady bereft of most her worldly goods, if not all; and that, with true courage, and zeal, and faith, she set herself to the practical work of earning her own living. Her fine mind found employment in the duties of a teacher in the large female school or college conducted in Memphis by a brother of General J. E. B. Stuart; and until an almost ruined state of health incapacitated her for the exertion, she remained in the institution, illustrating the worthlessness of the doctrine that literary women are an incubus upon the body social, separate from their pens and ink; and, moreover, substantiating the fact that Southern women are worthy of all that has been ascribed to them in high heroism — true adaptation of themselves to the changed circumstances their mother-land's misfortunes have brought peculiarly home to them.

1868.   MARY J. S. UPSHUR.

MRS. CLARA COLES.

IN 1861, J. B. Lippincott & Co., Philadelphia, published a beautiful volume, entitled "Clara's Poems." "Clara" is Mrs. Coles, at that time and now residing in the city of Nashville.

"These poems are in many respects well worthy the mechanical labor expended upon their proper presentation; for though they cannot claim, and never were meant to claim a place amid the standard poetry of the language, they are worth, well worth perusal and preservation. Classic in structure, thought, or imagery, they are far from being; elaborateness of verbal finish has not been bestowed upon them; they neither paint nor awaken any of those undeveloped passions, or even sentiments, the revelation of which entitles the poet to the proud title of "original;" but they deal simply and chastely, yet often warmly, with those tender sorrows and feminine fancies felt and nursed by most cultured females, especially by those who have passed much of life far from the frivolities of good society, and dreamed, amid crowds, of heart experiences never realized save to those whose solitariness of sentiment is by circumstances wedded to solitariness of life. The conclusion is forced on the reader of these poems, that the writer had a vague consciousness of possessing a fund of poesy, but had never developed it.

"The very simplicity attained, seems to arise from a dread of using powers, thoughts, and imagery of whose real worth and meaning she was timidly dubious. She is a pleasing versifier, possessed of poetic instincts, but lacking poetic power. She might have been a poet and a *good* one: her book reveals this pleasingly and clearly, but it does no more. This is one side of the verdict of strict impartiality, and were we to stop here it were partiality itself, for we should omit the better features of the poems — music, morality, and a prevailing tone of religious effect, unobtruded, yet, unconsciously to the writer herself pervading the whole book, and fitting it admirably for the parlor table, or what-not — a book that may ever safely and profitably be placed within easy reach of young lovers of poesy, in the certainty of

364

yielding pleasure, inflicting no pain and teaching no error. Would we could say the same of greater poets!" Thus said a critic in the "Southern Monthly," 1861.

John T. Edgar, D. D., in an "introductory" to "Clara's Poems," says:

"'Clara' is truly retiring, and as delicate in her claims to attention, as she is in the sweet images which are so meekly and touchingly conspicuous in many of the more tenderly pathetic of her pieces. It will be seen that the great charm of her verse is found, not in their classical allusions or romantic imagery, but in the simple appeals which they so winningly make to all that is unartificial, uncorrupted, truthful, and responsive in the more pure and gentle emotions of every unsophisticated heart. She has had no learned resources from which to draw her inspirations. To such fountains, no former familiarity or more recent acquaintance could have enabled her to resort. The school in which many of her most impressive lessons have been taught has been that of disappointment and sorrow; and to such lessons we are indebted for many of the finest and most thrilling stanzas of her often plaintive and pensive muse."

1869.

SABBATH MORN.

Bathed in the orient flush of morn,
    How lovely earth appears!
New tints the opening rose adorn,
    Gemm'd with night's dewy tears.
Soft, whispering breezes sigh around,
    And snowy cloudlets lie
Like angel watchers, floating through
    The calm, pure, azure sky.

The mountain-tops reflect the rays
    That usher in the day-god's beams;
The birds trill forth their songs of praise;
    The wave in gold and crimson gleams:
Oh, beautiful! My spirit drinks
    In copious draughts of love divine,
While gazing on this glorious scene,
    And worships at a holier shrine

Than mortal hands could ever rear,
    Or mortal language e'er portray;
For angel voices, murmuring near,
    Seem wafting my glad soul away.

Sweet, tranquil morn! so clear, so calm;
What soft emotions fill my breast!
Bright emblem of that glorious dawn —
A Sabbath of eternal rest!

————o⚬⦂⚬⦂o⚬o————

ADELIA C. GRAVES.

THE stone on which it is written that such a one was born, lived so many years, and died, often furnishes the only record of a long and useful life, of patient suffering and unrequited toil; yet even this is frequently more than the great world cares to read.

The life that has in it no thrilling incident, no wonderful event, no startling tragedy, or mirth-exciting comedy, but which is spent in the quiet performance of every-day duties, has little in it to attract attention from those outside the circle of personal friends.

Such a life is that of Mrs. Adelia C. Graves, the devoted wife, the self-sacrificing mother, the accomplished teacher, and the gifted poet. Had she persisted in following the impulses of her early years, and devoted her life entirely to the pursuits of literature, something would doubtless have been accomplished which would have caused the world to feel much interest in her biography.

She was born March 17th, 1821, at Kingsville, Ashtabula County, in the State of Ohio, and spent her early life upon the romantic shores of Lake Erie. Her father, Dr. D. M. Spencer, was a physician of ability and reputation. He was a man of uncommon mental power, and at one time exerted no small influence in the political circles of his State. But his friends having been defeated in their endeavors to secure his nomination to Congress by the wire-working of his anti-slavery opponent, the noted Joshua R. Giddings, he withdrew from further participation in a conflict where success could be gained only by the use of such means as neither he nor his friends were willing to employ. When Mr. Giddings was elected, Dr. Spencer declared that the ultimate result would be the dissolution of the Union, and a fratricidal war between the North and South. About a quarter of a century has elapsed since that prediction, then denounced as the insane ravings of disappointed ambition.

The children of Dr. Spencer, one by one, as they were free to do so, came and united their destinies with the South. Three of them are buried in Southern soil, and the subject of this sketch is the only one left.

Miss Spencer had in her early girlhood resolved to devote her life to literature. The Muses had been the companions of her childhood. Stanzas written before she was nine years old are models of correct versification, and exhibit the beautiful simplicity of expression and happy choice of words which characterize the productions of her more mature years. She wrote because she could not restrain the flow of bright and beautiful thoughts that were forever welling up from her young heart, and taking shape in simple, child-like rhymes.

She loved to be *alone* — passing her time on the pebbly beach, or in the grand old forests that had stood a thousand years near where she had been born. There she could commune with the invisible. There, with no mortal ear to heed, and no tongue to criticize or blame, she could warble out the extemporized lays which *would* be ever coming to her tongue. Her love of nature was a passion, the record of which is beautifully given in some of her earliest unpublished poems.

Miss Spencer married a teacher, Z. C. Graves, President at that time of Kingsville Academy, since founder and President of Mary Sharpe College, Winchester, Tenn.

To Mr. Graves, the highest of all employments, save one, the Gospel ministry, was that of training the minds of the young. The goal of his ambition was to become the greatest of living teachers: not greatest in the amount of money he might amass by teaching, nor yet in the reputation he might gain as the manager of a school; but greatest in his capacity to communicate knowledge, and secure the very highest possible development of the moral and intellectual powers of those who should be objects of his care. In this he was at once seconded by his wife with all the energy of her soul. So long as health and strength permitted, she was with him in the school-room, sharing fully with her husband, not only in its labors, but in all its responsibilities.

A few years after her marriage, Mrs. Graves received a sad injury, which has crippled her physical energies ever since. For five years, at first, she could not walk across her room; and oftentimes now, she is unable to walk a short distance.

In 1850, Mr. Graves, as President, laid the foundation of the Mary Sharpe College, at Winchester. It was designed to be an institution in which the daughters of the South could secure, not merely the fashionable accomplishments of an ordinary boarding-school education, but the same mental discipline and extensive knowledge of ancient and modern languages, the higher mathematics, and the natural sciences which our sons could gain at the very best colleges or universities of the land. The wonderful success of this institution depended, for the first few years, very much upon the patient labor, the indefatigable energy, and the judicious counsels of Mrs. Graves.

That characteristic of Mrs. Graves's poetry which most commends it to our taste, is its extreme naturalness and simplicity of expression. They are beautiful word-paintings, in which every line of light and shade is distinct upon the mental canvas; yet there is no labor for effect, no straining after rhymes, no far-fetched similes; but the verse is in simple Anglo-Saxon words, with a predominance of monosyllables, singing its music as it goes. The rhyming words are there simply because no other words would so well express the thought. Yet while it is thus unstudied and simple, thus devoid of all artistic display, it is full of

" Thoughts not thought before,"

full of the beautiful and the grand.

Mrs. Graves's first-born — the child of hope and promise — fills a soldier's grave! The war and its consequences nearly ruined them pecuniarily. Mrs. Graves at the present time occupies the position of Matron and Professor of Rhetoric in the College. She was formerly Professor of Latin and Belles-lettres.

The Baptist Sunday School Union have published eight little volumes for Sunday-school children, mostly selected from the "Children's Book," which Mrs. Graves edited for several years, and for which she wrote a great deal. These books, at the request of the "committee of the Union," she compiled from her sketches therein published. She has contributed to different periodicals, mostly fugitive poems, and two prose tales, one a prize tale; and "Ruined Lives," published in the "Southern Repository," Memphis, constitute, with the drama of "Jephthah's Daughter," her published works. She has a quantity of MSS. on hand, written as a pleasure and a solace; in fact, because she could not help writing. She is engaged now on a work, entitled "Seclusaval; or, The Arts of Romanism," several chapters of which have been published in the "Baptist," at Memphis.

Mrs. Graves's aim is to instruct and to do good with her pen; consequently, she has tried rather to repress a somewhat exuberant youthful fancy. If Mrs. Graves's health will admit, she hopes to publish several volumes, and also to collect her published and unpublished poems.   She has a work on "Woman: Her Education, Aims, Sphere, Influence, and Destiny," (which has been delivered as lectures to the pupils of the college;) "A Guide and Assistant to Composition;" and a poem, entitled "Alma Grey" — all of which we hope to see in print.

1868.

HUMAN SOVEREIGNTY; OR, EVERY MAN A KING.

To the young men of our beloved Southland, who, repining not at the past, or despond-
ingly brooding over what might have been, have yet the courage to accept their situation as it is, and the energetic exercise of whose wisdom, goodness, and virtue is yet
to constitute the true wealth and freedom of a fallen people, the following poem is
most respectfully dedicated, with the assurance that gold, bank-stock, lands, cotton-
bales, and negroes make no man rich or great; but the real wealth of any country is
to be estimated by the amount of the active intelligence and virtue of its sons and
daughters.   RESURGAMUS.

Victoria sitteth on a throne, with thronging nobles round,
And with a rich and jewelled crown her queenly brow is bound,
While thousand hands, at her behest, perform her slightest will,
And only wait a wish to know, with pleasure to fulfil.

Her kingdom is the sea-girt isles, and far-off India's shore,
And stretches from the northern snows to great Niagara's roar;
While ocean-gems are crouching low her lion arms to greet,
And strong Gibraltar humbly kneels a subject at her feet.

Queen of a mighty realm, she rules o'er lands so widely spread,
And fearful weight of royalty resteth upon her head;
Millions of beings yield to her their life-career to guide,
While Wisdom, with its hoary hairs, must her decrees abide.

But thou, young man, with sun-browned cheek, a tiller of the soil,
Which, with the fruits it yieldeth thee, rewardeth all thy toil —
The labor-gems that gird thy brow have value rich and great
As diadems of jewels rare that burden by their weight.

Thy God hath given to *thee* a realm, and made thee, too, a king;
And willing subjects unto thee their votive offerings bring;
While thou must reign a sovereign lord, with undisputed sway,
Or yield the master-spirit's rule the subject to obey.

"My mind to me a kingdom is," * wrote one who suffered long
Within the Bastile's gloomy walls, 'mid gratings high and strong;

---

* Madame Guyon, confined on account of her religion.

47

And, like a bird, she sat and sang to him who placed her there;
Although a bird shut from the fields of sunlight and of air.

Well was that inborn realm subdued, thus faithfully to bring
The fruits of joy and sweet content, and pleasant memories fling
Among the hopes that budded thick within that grated room,
Where yet the sunlight of the heart in gushing floods could come.

Youth, with the generous impulses that crowd thy opening way,
Thou 'rt each a king — monarch supreme — an empire owns thy sway:
'T is true thou wear'st no purple robe, no glittering, golden crown,
Nor bear'st a jewelled sceptre's wand t' enforce thy haughty frown:

Thy kingdom is no wide-spread land, girt by the heaving wave;
But of thyself thou 'rt ruler all, from childhood to the grave;
And he who hath a high-born soul, a true and kindly heart,
Addeth to "human sovereignty" its most distinguished part.

No princely dome is thine to boast, no costly marble walls
Reared by the sweat of toiling men, who must obey thy calls;
No pictures of proud artists' skill, no tessellated floors
That echo to the courtly tread of those within thy doors.

Thy palace is the wide-spread earth, its dome the arching sky;
And far more bright than gorgeous lamps the light that meets thy eye —
The glorious sun at morning's hour, the flashing stars at eve,
Among whose rays the moonbeams too their silver tissue weave.

The Architect who built for thee hath fashioned for thy view
Full many a scene of beauty rare, bright flowers of Eden hue,
The greenwood shade, the waterfall, the mountain tipped with mist,
Whose sunny heights and dusky grots the amber clouds have kissed.

What though earth trumpet not thy fame across her lakes and seas,
Nor silken banner waft it forth upon the floating breeze?
If in thy peaceful breast there lives the consciousness of right,
Thou 'rt happier than a CONQUEROR returning from the fight.

What though no herald's blazonry trace back thy ancient name,
And find unmixed with vulgar blood thy royal lineage came?
Man's acts proclaim nobility, and not the kingly crest;
For he 's the noblest who performs life's trying duties best.

And should men scorn thy mean attire, and dare to call thee "*slave*,"
Hold up thy head, *king of thyself*, and be thou truly brave;
For God hath given thee sovereignty of soul, and mind, and heart,
And absolute thy power must be till life itself depart.

Then arm that soul with heaven-born truth, with justice, and with love;
And fill thy mind with knowledge too, foul error to remove;
Stir well the ground of thy young heart, that it produce no weeds,
But precious fruits of charity, and treasures of good deeds.

Ay, let thy bosom wear the robe of high-born honesty,
And truth gird e'en thy secret acts with its pure panoply;
Then, knowledge-crowned, thy brow serene with holy light shall glow,
And rays of living radiance o'er a darkened world shall throw.

And thou 'lt so rule this precious realm bestowed, fair youth, on thee,
That when is asked thy last account thou 'lt give it joyfully;
Nor fear abash thy pallid cheek, nor tremble on thy tongue,
To meet the Universal King and mingle with his throng.

Prince of humanity! self's rightful, heaven-born lord!
Virtue and goodness bring their own exceeding great reward:
Be free from passion's rule, from ignorance and pride,
And *there 's no nobler work than man, the Godhead's self beside.*

MRS. MARY E. POPE.

MRS. POPE'S maiden name was Mary E. Foote. She is a native of Huntsville, Ala. She married, when young, Mr. Leroy Pope. Mr. and Mrs. Pope made their home in Memphis, where she has resided since. Her life has been chequered by misfortune and sorrow, which have only seemed to give occasion for the development of the lofty and noble qualities of her nature. Mrs. Pope is the mother of Lieutenant W. S. Pope, killed at Tishemingo Creek, and mentioned in the life of General Bedford Forrest.

Mrs. Pope has grappled with adversity with a bold, unquailing spirit, and ridden triumphant over the storms of life. She has charge of a flourishing school for young ladies in Memphis, which sufficiently attests the indomitable energy dwelling in her slender and fragile figure.

The sweet murmurings of her muse may be frequently heard floating on the breeze, in the Memphis journals.

THE GIFT OF SONG.

If, when bright visions o'er thee throng,
They clothe themselves in words of song,
And strengthen and refresh thy soul;
Though weak and faint the numbers roll,
    Yet fear not thou to sing.
If common life to thee keep tune
Unto thy spirit's chaunting rune,
And all the actual grows bright
'Neath fancy's soft ideal light,
    Thou hast the power to sing.
If in each living, human face,
Thy unsealed eye doth love to trace,
Through sin's dark, loathsome, outward form,
God's image, ever pure and warm,
    Thou art a poet; sing.
When sorrow bows thy burdened head,
And lurid clouds thy path o'erspread,
If in thy grief, on radiant wing,
The muse doth woo thee to her spring,
    Fear not to sip and sing.
When life blooms like a new-made bride,
With hope and love and grateful pride,
And earth to thy illumined eye
With Aiden seems in sheen to vie;
    If joy is tuneful, sing.
When morning blushes o'er the earth
With rosy softness, bloom, and mirth,
And birdlings from each jewelled spray
Woo thee to hail the new-born day;
    If music haunt thee, sing.
If, when thy glances seek the sky,
Where sunset hues its pavement dye,
Thy fettered spirit clank its chain,
Struggling to make its utterance plain;
    Unbind the links and sing.
It may be that thy lyre's faint tone
No magic master-key may own;
Thy falt'ring steps may fail to reach
In fame's great temple-shrine a niche;
    But yet fear not to sing.

As well the twitt'ring wren might fear
With his soft strain the day to cheer
Because the nightingale's rich note
More proudly sweet at eve doth float,
    And thus refuse to sing,
As thou, because on stronger wing
Thy brothers scale fame's height and sing —
Their grand, immortal harps will wake
A thousand lesser shells to take
    Part in creation's hymn.
The heaven-descended, god-like power
To mortals is a priceless dower.
Some hearts in silent grief may ache;
But some, if mute, e'en joy would break,
    And, sad or glad, must sing.
But if to thee no radiant sheen
Light up the roughest human mien;
If life wear not a glorious light,
Beyond what beams on common sight,
    Be still, nor dare to sing.
If human faith and human love
In thee no sacred worship move;
If in bright nature's open eye
No great, eternal beauty lie,
    Be sure thou canst not sing.
If thy calm pulse and even blood
Course not at times a lava flood,
With suffocating rush of thought,
By noble deeds or evil brought,
    Such cool blood cannot sing.
Touch not with hand profane the lyre,
Unbaptized with the sacred fire.
Study may give the tricks of art,
But cannot the bard's power impart
    To other souls to sing.

MARTHA W. BROWN.

"ESTELLE."

MARTHA W. FRAZER was born in Alabama, from which State her parents emigrated in her infancy to Memphis, at that time a small town. Old Court Square was the playground of Martha's earliest school-days; under its ancient trees she had many a frolic with girls and boys whose silvery hair now tells the tale of many winters, but the most of whom have passed to the "other shore."

In those early days, Memphis was a commercial rather than a literary place, and the schools were deficient; and, in order better to secure the education of his children, on which he was steadfastly determined, Mr. Frazer removed to La Grange, at that time considered the Lyceum of the West. After several years at this town, Mr. Frazer removed to Holly Springs — a rising and progressive town at that time, and it was here that the greater portion of Martha Frazer's education was accomplished, and here the "poet fledgling took wing." "It is pleasant to see one's verse in print," and Miss Frazer published numerous poems in "Southern Literary Messenger," &c., and, wielding an easy and graceful pen, she had cause for encouragement for the future. But "love" supplanted "fame," and, in 1849, she became the wife of R. B. Brown, a lawyer by profession. Mr. Brown died in 1864.

The most auspicious period of Mrs. Brown's literary career was under the genial patronage of the late Colonel J. H. McMahon. To his warm friendship and encouragement the world owes many of "Estelle's" poems. To the timid and doubtful, a kind word and encouraging smile are the waft of a fairy's wand, bringing to life beautiful creations that else might have slumbered in darkness and oblivion forever.

Mrs. Brown's residence is in Memphis. It has been beautifully said of the following lines, "They are of the very essence of the poetry of the heart."

THOU ART GROWING OLD, MOTHER.

Thou art growing old, mother,
  Thy voice is gentler now
Than when a little child, mother,
  I gazed upon thy brow.

For thou art nearer home, mother,
  And music, soft and bland,
Has wakened in thy heart, mother,
  Dreams of the "better land."

Thou art growing old, mother,
  That measured step of thine
Was once as free and light, mother,
  As full of life as mine.
I hear its fall e'en now, mother,
  I know its quiet air,
And standing by my side, mother,
  I feel that thou art there.

Thou art growing old, mother,
  The dark and glossy hair
That, clambering on thy knee, mother,
  I've stroked with so much care,
Waves still as softly now, mother,
  Yet higher on thy head,
And 't is sprinkled over now, mother,
  With many a silver thread.

Thou art growing old, mother,
  Yet do we love thee less?
Do we not feel for thee, mother,
  A deeper tenderness?
The never-tiring form, mother,
  The pale and careworn brow,
That nursed our helpless years, mother,
  Ah, we will cherish now.

Thou art growing old, mother,
  But soon the vernal bloom
Of life's eternal morn, mother,
  Will burst upon thy tomb.
And on the "other side," mother,
  Beyond the stormy swell,
Of Jordan's death-cold stream, mother,
  Is one who loves thee well.

He waiteth for the bride, mother,
  That blest his manhood's prime.

The pilgrim by his side, mother,
　Adown the stream of time.
He waiteth for the wife, mother,
　Faithful and true to him,
And constant to the last, mother,
　When life in death grew dim.

Then let the dream of life, mother,
　Close softly round thy heart,
As evening's gentle dews, mother,
　When clouds and storms depart;
Believing that the sun, mother,
　That rises on that night,
Brings all that loved ones home, motner,
　To their father's home of light.

───oo⦂⦂oo───

AMANDA M. BRIGHT.

AMANDA METCALFE was born in Lexington, Ky., 1822. While she was an infant, Mr. Barnett Metcalfe, her father, removed to Huntsville, Ala. In the female seminary of that city, Amanda received a portion of her limited education. At the age of twelve her school-days ended; but, inheriting from her father a love for books, she read and studied without the help of a teacher. She was married to Mr. Bright at the age of sixteen, and entered at this early age into many trials of a domestic character, that palsied her natural abilities, and "shut the hatches" upon those importunate promptings to write which were not gratified until a recent date.

Mrs. Bright was separated from her husband in 1860. Her eldest son was killed at the battle of "Seven Pines," and less than two years thereafter her only child died. The incentives to action of any kind were now wanting; but she conceived the design of writing a book, hoping to realize a sufficient sum from the sale of the same to erect a monument to her son. Of this design was born "The Three Bernices; or, Ansermo of the Crag," Philadelphia, 1869. Thus reviewed by the "Round Table," New York:

" . . . The task the lady has assumed is not an easy one. Few writers succeed in investing the dry bones of ancient history with life and reality; and when the drapery of fiction has been successfully adopted to hide the bare, hard outline, the writers of historic romances have put together graphic and entertaining stories — which is not the case in the present instance — by means of which they have brought home to their readers the everyday features of past ages, investing them with vitality, and affording information as well as amusement. The present author contents herself with giving a succession of striking and varied pictures of Roman life in the reign of Agrippa, without much compunction concerning the inroads she makes upon historical probability; and, upon the presumption that ancient history is a 'tolerable pattern for guess-work,' she undertakes the 'rehabilitation' of Bernice, by assuming that there were three persons of that name who lived about the same period, and that some of the acts charged to one may justly be laid on the shoulders of the other two. The infamous Agrippina's memory is in like manner rescued from obloquy by taking up her story where the Roman historian leaves it, and causing her to repent of her crimes and become a Christian. . . .

"Mrs. Bright is by no means deficient in imagination, nor in the capacity for weaving plots; her fault is that she weaves too many, and gets them confused. But, with the aid of experience, we doubt not that her next story will be more worthy of perusal, and in every respect more satisfactory to herself. She must learn, however, to chasten the richness and exuberance of her style."

Mrs. Bright has been an occasional contributor to several weekly journals, in prose and verse. She has in preparation several stories: "The Prince of Seir" is the title of one. Like her first book, this is a "historical" romance. Her home is Fayetteville, Tennessee.

1871.

———∘∘⟨°⟩∘∘———

MISS ANNIE E. LAW

IS of English birth. She is now a resident of Philadelphia, East Tennessee. Her poetical abilities are of rare order, and give promise of excellence as a writer hereafter.

1870.   W. G. M.

MEMORIES.

Oh, there are memories that linger in the heart,
 And oft awake with warm and gushing tide;
Thoughts of the past from which we would not part
 For all the illusive Future gives beside.

48

Once more — once more — to wander by the river
  That winds among the gently sloping hills,
To see again the lights and shades that quiver
  In bright mirrors of the ever-sparkling rills.

Oh, for the path meandering o'er the mountain,
  The tangled vines and branches by its side,
The mosses creeping in the shaded fountain,
  The woodland nooks where fairest flowerets hide!

The old oak-tree that stands before the door
  Will keep its corner in my heart forever;
Though home it shelters I may see no more
  While life remains, I can forget it never.

The blissful memories of our earlier years
  In silence haunt the soul through joy or pain;
And on their mighty stream, the smiles and tears
  Of happy childhood o'er us sweep again.

VIRGINIA.

MRS. MARGARET J. PRESTON.

MARGARET JUNKIN is the second daughter of the Rev. George Junkin, D. D., a Presbyterian divine of some note in the Southern portion of that Church. Dr. Junkin was President of Lafayette College, Easton, Pa., and of Washington College, Lexington, Va. The successor of the Rev. Dr. Junkin in the presidential chair of the latter College was Robert E. Lee. "Stonewall" Jackson was one of its professors in the term of Dr. Junkin, whose eldest daughter was the wife of the famous Confederate leader.

Miss Junkin was a frequent contributor to the "Southern Literary Messenger" during the editorship of John R. Thompson.

In 1870, J. B. Lippincott & Co., Philadelphia, published "Old Songs and New," a collection of Mrs. Preston's poems, which were reviewed in the London "Saturday Review" thus:

"'OLD SONGS AND NEW' is the title of one of the best volumes of American poetry that have lately appeared. The authoress has not the fire of Whittier, the scholarship of Bryant, or the originality and power of Lowell, and most of her poems appear to have a certain imitative character, as if the subject and mode of treatment had been suggested by her admiration of some well-known models. Nevertheless, her thoughts and expression are her own; and though, perhaps, we should never have seen her pieces on classical themes if she had not made acquaintance with Mr. Lowell's 'Rhœcus,' and Lord Lytton's 'Tales of Miletus,' we cannot fairly rank her best 'Greek Stories' much below their prototypes. Her domestic pieces are marked by a grave and truly feminine tenderness, and are likely to be read with pleasure by hundreds who, if they would own it, are more capable of appreciating their simple beauties than the splendor and majesty of the masterpieces of English poetry."

In 1857, she published a volume, entitled "Silverwood : A Book of Memories."

Colonel J. T. L. Preston, the husband of the subject of this article, is one of the faculty of the Virginia Military Institute, at Lexington.

Mrs. Preston's most ambitious effort is the poem of "Beechenbrook : A Rhyme of the War."

Mrs. Preston has written because she "thought in numbers, and the numbers came," not for popular notice, nor from necessity, as, alas ! so many of her countrywomen have been forced to do since the war, by the reverses of fortune. She is so happy as to be lifted above want or accidents of poverty. She has written for pastime and from patriotism, as the amusement in the pleasant idleness of a life devoted not to literature, but to the womanly cares and pleasures which a large establishment, husband, children, and "society" force upon her.

Mrs. Preston was a frequent contributor from its commencement to the "Land we Love;" General Hill, its editor, being a warm personal friend of hers. She also contributes to various other Southern journals. We subjoin some critiques, Northern and Southern, of "Beechenbrook "— the first taken from the "Round Table," the second from the "Field and Fireside:"

"BEECHENBROOK: A RHYME OF THE WAR. — A publisher's printed estimate of the sale of his publications is usually somewhat imaginative ; to use a threadbare but serviceable quotation, 'The wish is often father to the thought.' Yet in this case we see no reason to doubt the entire veracity of Messrs. Kelly & Piet in announcing 'fifth thousand' on the title-page of this volume. It is one which, we should judge, would be immensely popular among the people for whom it was written, and to whose sectional pride and prejudices it appeals in more ways than one. In all respects it is essentially Southern, and in most it is praiseworthy. Its press-work especially shows a standard of excellence which we were not prepared to look for below Philadelphia ; and the poems themselves, if they do not quite deserve, still do not altogether disgrace their handsome setting. In two points particularly they challenge Southern admiration : in the first place, they are not absolutely trash, which is quite an advance on the majority of Southern verse ; and in the second place, their merit is even sufficient to dimly foreshadow a time when the sunny South shall achieve intellectual emancipation in a literature of its own, and be no longer dependent on New England for poetry, as well as piety, politics, and prints. To the author's own people, therefore, unjaded as yet by the worship of many literary idols, her book must be peculiarly grateful : even we of the North, who are not tainted by that sombre fanaticism that sees no good in Nazareth, may find in it much to admire and applaud. The verse is graceful and flowing, and the language and sentiment prove the author to be a lady of refined and cultivated taste. '*Dulce et decus*' is rather an indecorous liberty with Horace, and we should greatly prefer that Miss (or Mrs. ?) Preston had not linked 'breast' with 'caress,' nor turned 'hárassing' and 'suppórt' into 'harássing' and 'súpport.' But after all, we are not so much concerned with Miss (or Mrs. ?) Preston's Latin and orthoepy, which might be better, as with her poetry, which might be decidedly worse. The story of 'Beechenbrook'—a story mournfully trite to thousands of aching hearts — is simply and gracefully told; and some of the shorter poems interspersed —'Only a Private' and 'Slain in Battle'— are not without pathos. Of course, the war is regarded from the Confederate standpoint, and equally, of course, there is the usual amount of Southern devotion and Southern invincibility — Miss (or Mrs. ?) Preston's rebels being easily victorious against anything less than quadruple odds, which is a rather perplexing statement, considering that Northern bards assure us of its exact converse. But to offset these very natural and not unpardonable flights of fancy, we have much less than the usual amount of 'vandal hordes' and 'despot's heels' that generally trample through and make gory the war-poetry of Dixie, just as the strains of the Federal minstrel are enlivened by the dismal howl of the bondman. The most flagrant error in this direction is a rather invidious comparison of the vulture and the eagle in what is one of the best poems in the book, 'Stonewall Jackson's Grave;' but it is suggested only to be deprecated and dismissed. The stanza will bear quoting :

> ' The largess of their praise is flung
>   With bounty rare and regal;
> Is it because the vulture fears
>   No longer the dead eagle?
> Nay, rather far accept it thus —
>   An homage true and tender,
> As soldier unto soldier worth,
>   As brave to brave will render.'

" The last stanza is even better :

> ' Rare fame! rare name! If chanted praise,
>   With all the world to listen;
> If pride that swells a nation's soul,
>   If foemen's tears that glisten;
> If pilgrim's shrining love — if grief,
>   Which nought may soothe or sever;
> If THESE can consecrate — this spot
>   Is sacred ground forever!'

" The political tone, if we may so call it, of these poems, is much higher and healthier throughout than we could have expected, or than we were warranted in hoping for by any example of moderation that loyal muses have set. Southern women, we are told, still cherish in their hearts that bitterness of hatred and that stubbornness of rebellion that did so much to prolong the late conflict, and which their husbands and brothers, we believe, have more wisely and nobly dismissed; but if we interpret this volume rightly, if it has not been deftly doctored for the Northern market, we take it as a sign, that, even among the women of the South, at least the more cultivated portion, the right feeling, the true patriotism, is gradually re-asserting itself. The concluding poem, entitled 'Acceptation,' expresses best the spirit which should animate the Southern people; a spirit wherein a very intelligible regret for the past is tempered by submission in the pre-sent, and abiding hope for the future:

> 'We do accept thee, heavenly peace!
> Albeit thou comest in a guise
> Unlooked for — undesired; our eyes
> Welcome through tears the sweet release
> From war, and woe, and want — surcease
> For which we bless thee, blessèd peace!'

"These lines have the true ring; and an extension of the feeling which prompted them will do more to hasten reconstruction than the harangues of a dozen Senators, and the Freedmen's Bureau to boot. The women of the South have done much to destroy the Union; they can certainly do as much to rebuild it."

"It is to be sincerely hoped that the war which has so severely scourged the South will bring some good to the country, beside the lessons of political economy it has impressed upon us all. It is cheering to begin to see already some marked signs of fruition of this hope in the matter of the literary sta-mina, and taste, and ambition of our people. It has always seemed to us that whatever of genius there is in the South, there has always been wanting some great necessity, some great pressure of circumstances, some great awak-ening cause to arouse and develop it; and it would seem that the war, in its progress and final effect, is the first gleam of the dawning. It certainly has kindled a poetic fire that has never burned before; and now, while the great avalanche of worthless rhymes which it forced out upon the seething surface are being sunk into their proper places in the dark waters of oblivion, a pearl here and an opal there are being fished out, burnished, and set ablazing in tissues of beautiful gold.

" At first, some good things will be lost in the scramble with the bad; some bad things will be saved in the shadow of the good. At last, all the bad will filter through, and most of the good, and the good only, will be saved.

"Messrs. Kelly & Piet, of Baltimore, have executed a commendable piece of workmanship in bringing out, from all this rubbish, the poems of Mrs.

Preston.* We like the book. It contains some elegant touches that should not be lost.

"To begin with the beginning, and end with the ending, as we propose to do, the leading poem covers seventy-five pages, and is styled 'A Rhyme of the War.' An appropriate title, it is true; but we wish it did not have this double name at all — we have had too much of the war. It is written in the anapestic measure, which is so beautifully employed in the splendid ballads of Scott and Macaulay, and is interspersed with several animated odes in the Pindaric style. The hero is a Colonel Dunbar, and the introductory scene portrays the parting of husband from wife and children, and the sorrow which overspreads his hitherto happy home, Beechenbrook Cottage, when war's rude alarms burst over Virginia, in 1861, on 'a day bright with the earliest glory of May,' and when

> 'The blue of the sky is as tender a blue
> As ever the sunshine came shimmering through.'

The wife, after she prepared the few little articles belonging to a soldier's wardrobe, and after he was ready to leave,

> 'On the fresh, shining knapsack she pillows her head,
> And weeps as a mourner might weep for the dead.
> . . . .
> And the stout-hearted man is as weak as a girl.'

And then the good wife rouses herself, and, in the very midst of her overpowering paroxysm of grief, throws her arms around her husband's neck, and leaning upon his breast,

> 'She raises her eyes with a softened control,
> And through them her husband looks into her soul,'

while she speaks, with a steady and clear voice, the sentiment of a Macedonian mother to her son, when she told him to 'Go: return with your shield, or on it;' but the griefful wife makes this uninterrupted speech, *twenty-six lines long*, hardly stopping to take breath. It is the heaviest part of the poem. If she had said what she did say with more brevity and more vim, it would have been better. It is a good scene, too much drawn out.

"Beechenbrook Cottage is situate within hearing of the booming of the guns in the battle of Manassas. Mother, daughter, and little son seek a green hillock, and pause to listen:

> 'Again and again the reverberant sound
> Is fearfully felt in the tremulous ground;
> Again and again on their senses it thrills,
> Like thunderous echoes astray in the hills.'

That is certainly very fine.

* Mrs. Preston is a sister-in-law of Stonewall Jackson.

"Again:

> ' On tiptoe — the summer wind lifting his hair,
>   With nostrils expanded, and scenting the air,
>   Like a mettled young war-horse that tosses his mane,
>   And frettingly champs at the bit and the rein,
>   Stands eager, exultant —'

"What? who?

> ' — *a twelve year old boy,*
>   His face all aflame with a rapturous joy.'

It is really to be regretted that the author should have attempted to fill such a magnificent background for a superb picture with '*a twelve year old boy.*'

"Many and many an eye that peruses this paper will recognize a scene portrayed in Mrs. Dunbar's letter to her husband. It is not hard to find the beauty in these lines: whether it is hard or not to find any truth — and how much of truth — in them we leave the reader to determine. Here is what she writes to him:

> ' Our beautiful home — as I write it, I weep —
>   Our beautiful home is a smouldering heap!
>   And blackened and blasted, and grim and forlorn,
>   Its chimneys stand stark in the mists of the morn!

> ' I stood, in my womanly helplessness, weak,
>   Though I felt a brave color was kindling my cheek,
>   And I plead by the sacredest things of their lives —
>   By the love that they bore to their children — their wives —
>   By the homes left behind them, whose joys they had shared —
>   By the God that should judge them — that mine should be spared.

> ' As well might I plead with the whirlwind to stay,
>   As it crashingly cuts through the forest its way!
>   I know that my eye flashed a passionate ire,
>   As they scornfully flung me their answer of — fire!'

" The hero of the rhyme is once wounded ere he receives the fatal shot that deprived his cause of his gallant services, and his bereaved widow and orphans of their husband and father. The allusions to the fields which were fought in the Old Dominion are but incidental, and perhaps, on this account, are more interesting and artistic.

" The poem is a very fair reflection of the feelings of our people, both men and women, during the progress of the war, telling how the women urged the men forward to the front, and wrote them kind letters, burning with patriotic zeal — how the men marched through snows and ice without shoes, and fought battle after battle, with never enough to eat — how the mothers, wives, sisters, and sweethearts toiled day in and day out for the soldiers, the sick and the wounded, their hearts writhing the while with a terrible doubting, hoping, fearing.

"The last two stanzas of this poem are full of vigor and earnestness — a fire that will kindle life enough, even where the process of freezing has been quite completed, to make one appreciate the lines on page 42 :

> 'The crash of the onset — the plunge and the roll
> Reach down to the depths of each patriot soul;
> *It quivers — for since it is human, it must,*' etc.

"Besides 'Beechenbrook,' this volume contains 'Virginia,' a sonnet; 'Jackson,' a sonnet; 'Dirge for Ashby,' 'Stonewall Jackson's Grave,' 'When the War is over,' and 'Virginia Capta.'

"There have been but few poems produced by the war so exquisite and thrilling as the 'Dirge for Ashby;' perhaps it has not its equal, if we except Harry Flash's 'Zollicoffer.'

"We cannot resist the temptation to quote a stanza or two from 'Virginia Capta;' they have so much of sublime submission — the conquered to the conqueror — in them :

> 'The arm that wore the shield, strip bare ;
>   The hand that held the martial rein,
>   And hurled the spear on many a plain —
> Stretch — till they clasp the shackles there !
>   .   .   .   .   .   .
> 'Bend though thou must beneath his will,
>   Let not one abject moan have place ;
>   But with majestic, silent grace,
> Maintain thy regal bearing still.
>   .   .   .   .   .   .
> 'Weep, if thou wilt, with proud, sad mien
>   Thy blasted hopes — thy peace undone —
>   Yet brave live on, nor seek to shun
> Thy fate, like Egypt's conquer'd Queen.
>
> 'Though forced a captive's place to fill
>   In the triumphal train, yet there,
>   Superbly, like Zenobia, wear
> Thy chains — *Virginia Victrix* still !'"

Wm. Hand Browne thus criticizes Mrs. Preston :

"To pronounce her the first female poet of the South would be arrogating too much to our own judgment; but we know of none we could place before her. The critical reader of Mrs. Preston's poems is first struck by the dignity of the thoughts and the simplicity of the style. She never writes

49

without a worthy theme, nor handles any theme slightly and carelessly. The poet's art with her is not a mere elegant accomplishment, or a convenient outlet for a lively fancy, but a noble art, which none have a right to essay but those who know that they have received the divine gift of poesy, and feel that they are answerable for its worthy use. Hence in her poetry, while we may have our preferences, there is nothing that we could wish away — nothing that is discordant with the rest, or that does not justify its poetic treatment. At the same time she rarely, if ever, soars into the higher regions of the imagination; her poems have all a direct human interest, and are treated with a firm, what we may call a conscientious, realism. In many of her pieces there is a noble pathos and a grand tenderness, only surpassed by the greatest masters of emotion.

"Her style is chastened almost to severity, every word being weighed and chosen for its place; giving a sharp distinctness to her thought, which is the very opposite of the vague, nebulistic, epithetic style of too many of her contemporaries, who seem aiming at they know not precisely what; like Orbaneja, the painter of Ubeda, of whom it is recorded that when asked what he was painting, he used to answer, 'Whatever it turns out.' In a word, we find in Mrs. Preston, if not the most splendid, a pure and noble imagination, combined with and ruled by a clear judgment and refined taste; quick sympathies for all that is good and lovely; deep, but unobtrusive piety, and an admirable gift of expression — qualities, when united, sufficient to form a poet of whom we may well be proud, and whose works will be read with perpetual pleasure by all lovers of true poetry."

NON DOLET.

A SONNET.

When doubt, defeat, and dangers sore beset
   The Roman Arria, yielding to the tide
   Of ills that overwhelmed on every side,
With unheroic heart, that could forget
'T was cowardice to die, she dared and met
   The easier fate; and luring, sought to hide
(For her beloved's sake — true woman yet!)
   The inward anguish, with a wifely pride.
Not so our Southern Arria! In the face
   Of deadlier woes, she dared to live, and wring
      Hope out of havoc; till the brave control,
Pathetic courage, and most tender grace
      Of her " *Non dolet*" nerved her husband's soul,
   Won him to life, and dulled even failure's sting!

UNDERTOW.

A SONNET.

It is a gift for which to render praise,
  Ceaseless and fervent, that our troubled hearts
  Can hide the harrowing grief that chafes and smarts,
And shut themselves from all intrusive gaze.
  Oft when the murmur of the world grows low,
And the felt silence broods serene and still,
  The inward ear is listening to the flow
Of eddying memories, that flood and fill
  The soul with tumult. Then how blest to wear,
In eyes that yield no sympathizing look,
  A face of tidal quiet, that shall bear
No hint of undercurrents! Who could brook
  That even our nearest, dearest, best should know
  The secret springs of many an hour of woe?

ACCEPTATION.

We do accept thee, heavenly Peace!
  Albeit thou comest in a guise
  Unlooked for — undesired; our eyes
Welcome through tears the kind release
From war, and woe, and want — surcease
For which we bless thee, holy Peace!

We lift our foreheads from the dust;
  And as we meet thy brow's clear calm,
  There falls a freshening sense of balm
Upon our spirits. Fear — distrust —
The hopeless present on us thrust —
We'll front them as we can, and *must*.

War has not wholly wrecked us; still
  Strong hands, grand hearts, stern souls are ours —
  Proud consciousness of quenchless powers —
A past whose memory makes us thrill —
Futures uncharactered, to fill
With heroisms, if we will!

Then courage, brothers! Though our breast
 Ache with that rankling thorn, despair,
 That failure plants so sharply there —
No pang, no pain shall be confessed:
We'll work and watch the brightening west,
And leave to God and heaven the rest!

THE LADY HILDEGARDE'S WEDDING.

"I dare not doubt his word," she said,
 With steadfast voice and clear;
"For sure as knight did ever plight
 True faith, he will be here.

"He sware it on this crested ring,
 That by our Lord's dear leave,
He'd wed me here at Lyndismere,
 This blesséd Christmas Eve."

— Sir Walter dallied with his blade,
 And his steel eyne grew wroth:
"Nay, sweetheart, see! — it cannot be:
 Thy knight hath broke his troth."

Out spake the Lady Hildegarde,
 With grieved, reproachful air:
"None other may such slander say, —
 My father only dare!

"My bower-maids all await my call,
 My bridesmen will be here;
And merry throngs with wedding songs
 Shall bide at Lyndismere."

"Now out upon thee, — simple lass!"
 With heat Sir Walter cried;
"To-morrow e'en, with seas between,
 How can'st thou be a bride?

"The Nether-land is far o'erseas,
  And angry storms may roar;
Or war may send (which Heaven forfend!)
  Tidings to vex thee sore.

"Forbear, until the galliot drop
  Anchor at Malden-head,
To fix the day, and yea or nay,
  Proclaim thou wilt be wed.

"Let the old Hall ring loud and high
  With roistering Twelfth Night cheer;
Bring holly-glow and mistletoe
  To garland Lyndismere.

"Let frolic mummers don their masks,
  Let morris-dancers come
And reel and sing in jocund ring,
  With rebeck, pipe, and drum.

"Of capons, boar's-head, nut-brown ale,
  Let liberal store be shown;
And wassail-shout shall make the bout
  The merriest ever known.

"The jesters with their bells shall plot
  All mirth-provoking pranks:
So ... let me sue; — forget Sir Hugh,
  And take thy father's thanks!"

She heard, the Lady Hildegarde,
  With firm, unflinching eye;
Then forth she stepped, and onward swept,
  Disdainful of reply.

— The snows lay deep round Lyndismere,
  But generous fires blazed free,
And casements clear flashed far and near
  Their gleams across the lea.

Retainers filled the ancient Hall,
  Guests thronged as fell the night,
And rare to see, right gorgeously,
  The chapel streamed with light.

"Be brave Sir Hugh come back?" they asked
  The gray-haired seneschal:
"Not yet?" — "'Twas said to-night he'd wed
  Our Lady of the Hall."

Sir Walter chafed and strode apart;
  The cassock'd priest was seen;
And maidens fair came pair by pair . . .
  "What could the folly mean?"

A sudden vision hushed the mirth, —
  Sir Walter's breath came hard;
For last of all adown the Hall
  Swept Lady Hildegarde.

"Saint Agnes! — but she's comely!" quoth
  The parti-color'd clown;
"And by the rood! in bridal hood
  And bridal veil and gown!

"Sir Hugh should e'en be here to mark
  The orange posies bloom;
Will proxy due for stout Sir Hugh?
  Then *I* would fain be groom!"

Straight onward to the chancel-rails
  The snooded maidens passed;
When suddenly the companie
  Was startled by a blast, —

A blast that echoed loud and shrill
  Without the castle gate,
As though the train that passed amain
  Was sorely loth to wait.

Unmoved stood Lady Hildegarde,
  Nor seemed to hear nor feel,
Till up the floor, one moment more,
  There tramped a clanking heel.

"*Beloved!*" — With one bound they met!
  Then, dashing off a tear,
She turned and said, with lifted head, —
  "*Father, — Sir Hugh is here!*"

MRS. S. A. WEISS.

SUSAN ARCHER TALLEY is descended, on the paternal side, from a Huguenot refugee, who settled in Hanover County, Virginia. In an old homestead on an estate in this county the subject of this article was born, and passed the years of childhood.

We are indebted to "Mary Forrest's" volume, "Women of the South," for the following:

"Among the traits earliest developed in Miss Talley were extreme fearlessness and love of liberty. . . . .

"It is said that she was never known to betray a sign of fear; and at the age of five years, in her visits to the neighbors, she would unhesitatingly face and subdue by her caresses the fiercest dogs, which even grown persons dared not approach. A singular power of will and magnetism, like that ascribed to the author of 'Wuthering Heights,' seems to have possessed her. She rode with a graceful, fearless abandon, and loved nothing better than to float away by herself in a frail boat. She was the frequent companion of her father and grandfather in their walks, rides, and hunting and fishing excursions; yet with all these influences, she was ever a gentle child, and remarkable for extreme sensibility and refinement. She delighted in all sights and sounds of beauty, and would sit for hours watching the sky in storm and sunshine, or listening to the wind among the trees, the plashing of a waterfall, or the cry of a whip-poor-will. This life familiarized her with all the voices of nature. A sound once heard she never forgot, but could, years after, imitate with surprising exactness.

"When she was eight years of age, her father removed to Richmond, and she then entered school. . . . . When in her eleventh year, she was released from the thraldom of the school-room by an unexpected dispensation. It had been remarked that for some days she had appeared singularly absent and inattentive when spoken to; being at length reproved, she burst into tears, exclaiming, 'I can't hear you.' It was then discovered that her hearing was greatly impaired. She was placed under the care of the most eminent physicians of the country; but their varied efforts resulted, as is too often the case, only in an aggravation of the evil. She lost the power to distinguish conversation, though carried on in a loud key; a power which she has not wholly recovered. . . . .

"Her parents were at first greatly at loss as to the manner of conducting her education. Fortunately, she was advanced far beyond most children of her age; and now, released from the discipline of school, her natural love of study deepened into a passion. It was soon found sufficient to throw suitable books in her way, and thus, unassisted, she completed a thorough scholastic course. She also acquired an extensive acquaintance with the literature of the day, and her correct taste and critical discrimination elicited the warmest encomiums from that prince of critics, Edgar A. Poe.

"It was not until Miss Talley had entered her thirteenth year that her poetic faculty became apparent to her family; she having, through modesty, carefully concealed all proofs of its development. Some specimens of her verse then falling under the eye of her father, he at once recognized in them the flow of true genius, and very wisely, with a few encouraging words, left her to the guidance of her own inspiration. In her sixteenth year, some of her poems appeared in the 'Southern Literary Messenger.'"

In September, 1859, a collection of her poems was issued by Rudd & Carleton, of New York. This volume secured for her a distinction of which she may well be proud. For rhythmic melody, for sustained imagination, for depth of feeling, and purity and elevation of sentiment, these poems are equalled by few, and surpassed by none of the productions of our poets. They are rich also in those qualities of mind and heart, which, apart from any literary prestige, win for Miss Talley the esteem and affection of all who are admitted within the choice circle of her friendship.

Miss Talley was imprisoned at Fort McHenry during the war, on the charge of being a spy — refusing to take the oath of allegiance to the United States Government. It was while imprisoned at Fort McHenry that Miss Talley was married to Lieut. Weiss, of the Federal army.

It was upon her return to Richmond, after her imprisonment, that she commenced writing for the "Magnolia Weekly" and the "Southern Illustrated News." Up to the time of her commencing to write for the two named journals, she had never been able to write, satisfactorily, a line of prose. Poetry had been to her as the breath of life; and her poems had occurred to her almost as inspirations, conceived and written out on a moment's impulse, without labor or difficulty whatever, and in several cases (as, for instance, in the case of "Summer Noonday Dreams,") without a word being altered. Then, about three years before the war, this power seemed to desert her entirely; and in this interval she wrote nothing. It returned as suddenly upon the inspiration of the war; but again as suddenly departed. For over three years she has not written a line of poetry; but, strangely enough, prose now flows readily, and almost without the labor of thinking, from her pen. Providence seems thus to have provided for Mrs. Weiss at the very moment when she needed this capacity as a sole means of support.

Mrs. Weiss is, and has been for several years, a regular contributor to the New York "Sunday Times."

1869.   C. D.

THE BATTLE EVE.

I see the broad, red, setting sun
  Sink slowly down the sky;
I see, amid the cloud-built tents,
  His blood-red standard fly;
And mournfully the pallid moon
  Looks from her place on high.

O setting sun, awhile delay;
  Linger on sea and shore;
For thousand eyes now gaze on thee,
  That shall not see thee more;
A thousand hearts beat proudly now,
  Whose race, like thine, is o'er!

O ghastly moon, thy pallid ray
  On paler brows shall lie,
On many a torn and bleeding breast,
  On many a glazing eye;
And breaking hearts shall live to mourn,
  For whom 't were bliss to die.

CON ELGIN.

Con Elgin was a horseman bold,
   A chief of high degree,
And he hath gone with twenty men
   A-sailing on the sea;
Now woe the hour and woe the strand
When Elgin with his men shall land,
   Wherever that may be.

Con Elgin sought the stormy isle
   Across the foaming flood,
And he hath marched with all his men
   Into the Druid wood,
Where dark beneath the ancient oaks
   The Christian temple stood.

Con Elgin slew the old Culdee —
   The priest with silver hair;
He slew him at the altar-stone
   In sacerdotal gear;
He slew the half-baptizèd babe,
   And its mother, young and fair.

He seized the sacramental cup
   The blessed wine to drain;
He mixed it with the Christian's blood
   And quaffed it yet again;
Then, while his eyes in fury roll,
His beard he cleanses in the bowl —,
But there is on his blackened soul
   An everlasting stain.

Con Elgin lies in troubled sleep
   Beneath a Druid oak:
Was it the whisper of the wind,
   Or a voice to him that spoke?
"Oh, hard of heart and fierce of hand
   I sign thee with a sign:
Where'er thou goest, on land or flood,
O'er icy plain, through dusky wood,
   Shall loneliness be thine!"

Uprose the bloody horseman then,
  And loudly laughèd he:
"I bear the spell and wear the sign,
  Thou old and weird Culdee!
Now by the shades of Odin's hall,
That such an ill should me befall,
  That such a curse should be!"

And loudly laughed his followers
  As round about they stood:
But a sudden thrill and a whisper ran
  Through the ancient Druid wood;
And trembled all the Valkyrmen
  As round about they stood.

And now they are upon the sea,
  And far and fast they go;
For lo! the storm is on their track —
The waves are white — the clouds are black,
  And the icy breezes blow.
Oh, that the storm would wear away,
  And the winds would cease to blow!

Yet darker grows the fearful night,
  And loud the tempest's shriek;
They cannot see each other's forms,
  Or hear each other speak:
But though the waves the wilder grow,
And though the winds the fiercer blow,
With stately mast and steady prow
  The vessel onward rides:
They know that some unearthly hand
  The broken rudder guides.

A sudden lull — and in the south
  There dawns a misty day;
There is no cloud, there is no breeze,
But far away o'er frozen seas
  The Borealis' play —
A ghastly light, like that which lies
Within the dying's glazing eyes.

There is no life in all the scene,
  There is no breath — no sound;

But slowly o'er the glassy deep
The icy bars in silence creep,
  And clasp the ship around,
Till mast and sail and deck alike
  In icy chains are bound.

Gloom on the vast, unbroken sky,
  And stillness on the air,
And loneliness upon the sea,
  And silence everywhere;
And in Con Elgin's hardened heart
  A stern and cold despair.

He shrank to see the famished crew,
  So gaunt were they and grim;
He gazed where, sea and sky between,
In lurid haze was ever seen
  The sun's unsetting rim;
But evermore those stony eyes
  Glared fixedly on him.

He spake to them — he called to them —
  Then came a silence dread;
For lo, upon the northern skies
Strange gleams of lurid light arise,
  And gather overhead;
They gleam upon the frozen ship,
  And on the frozen dead.

The faces of the dead were they,
  So rigid, wan, and blue;
Oh, 't was a fearful thing to stand
  Amid that lifeless crew!
And thrice Con Elgin drew his blade,
And thrice his iron hand was stayed:
  Ah, well the grasp he knew!

He paces on the icy deck,
  He chants a mystic rune;
He cursed the long and weary day,
  Yet ended all too soon,
As the lurid disk of the blood-red sun
  Sinks suddenly at noon.

The ghastly dead — the ghastly dead —
  They chill him with their eyes;
The silent ship — the lonely sea —
  The far and boundless skies!
Oh, that some little breeze would stir,
  Some little cloud arise!

And then uprose a little cloud —
  Uprose a little breeze —
And came a low and slumberous sound,
Like moaning waves that break around
  The stormy Hebrides:
The ice is rent — the ship is free,
  And on the open seas!

He saw the land upon his lee —
  He strove the shore to gain;
And wild and fierce his efforts grew,
  But strength and skill were vain;
Still onward ploughed the fated ship
  Unto the outer main.

A sail, a sail! "What ho! what ho!"
  He shouted from the mast;
And back there came a cheering cry
  Upon the rushing blast:
Their very life-blood chilled with dread —
They saw the living and the dead
  As swift they hurried past!

And long upon those Northern seas,
  At silent dead of night,
A cry would echo on the blast,
And a phantom ship go hurrying past —
  A strange and fearful sight!
And well the trembling sailors knew
Con Elgin and his ghastly crew.

MRS. CONSTANCE CARY HARRISON.

THE subject of this short sketch, whose maiden name was Constance Cary, and who is best known to Southern literature under her *nom de plume* of "Refugitta," is the daughter of the late Archibald Cary and of Monimia Fairfax, his wife, both representatives of ancient families of Virginia. Mrs. Harrison is the elder of two children, and was born, we believe, in Mississippi, to which State her father had removed, shortly after his marriage, for the purpose of practising his profession, the law. Mr. Cary was a gentleman of fine literary abilities, and during his residence in Mississippi was associated in the editorship of a newspaper at Port Gibson, the place of his residence. Mr. Cary subsequently removed to Cumberland, Maryland, where he became proprietor and editor of the "Cumberland Civilian," which journal he edited up to the time of his death.

At the breaking out of the war, Miss Cary was residing with her mother at "Vancluse," about three miles from Alexandria, Virginia, for many years the country-seat of the Fairfax family, and the former home of her maternal grandfather, Thomas Fairfax. Like many others, overtaken by the coming of war, Miss Cary became a "refugee," a term understood with a mournful distinctness by thousands of the best and noblest of the South, and sought shelter, accompanied by her mother, in Richmond, in which city she remained until the close of the war.

It was in Richmond that Miss Cary first wrote under the name of "Refugitta." From both father and mother she had inherited a decided literary taste and aptitude; and hence the lively, sparkling sketches which appeared under that name in the literary papers of the Confederate capital, displayed a more than usual vigor, and their vivacity of style earned for their fair author no little reputation and applause. Among the writers of the four years of warfare that befell the South, none was more popular than "Refugitta," especially in Richmond, where were published most of her writings.

In the autumn of 1865, Miss Cary went to Europe with her mother, remaining there about a year. Some time after her return to the United States, she was married to Mr. Burton N. Harrison, who, during the war, was attached to the person of Mr. Jefferson Davis in the capacity of private secretary. Mr. and Mrs. Harrison at present reside in New York.

1870.   C. D.

M. J. HAW.

IN the fall of 1863, the "Southern Illustrated News," published in Richmond, had the following announcement:

"AN ILLUSTRATED ROMANCE!
"PRIZE OF ONE THOUSAND DOLLARS!

"Having engaged the services of a corps of competent engravers, who are confidently expected to arrive in the Confederacy in a few weeks, the proprietors of the 'Illustrated News' will award a prize of one thousand dollars to the author of the best illustrated romance, to be submitted to them between the present date and the 1st of November next.

"September 5th, 1863."

The time was extended to the 1st of December.

March 1st, 1864, the "News" announced that the prize for the best romance had been awarded to Miss M. J. Haw, of Hanover County, Virginia, for her story, entitled "The Rivals: A Tale of the Chickahominy."

The "committee" stated that, "in recommending the superiority of 'The Rivals,' they base their preference upon the fact that to its other excellences is added that of unity. The story itself is written with a pleasing simplicity of style and a freshness of interest."

Miss Haw had been a contributor to the "Magnolia Weekly," of tales, etc., signed with her initials, the only objection to which were the sombre backgrounds. "The Beechwood Tragedy" was the title of the first story we ever read from "M. J. H.'s" pen. The prize romance was her most ambitious and most successful effort.

Miss Haw had the misfortune to reside during the war "in the midst of battle-fields," and suffered from marauders and so-called scouting parties. The close of the war found her "moneyless," and since that time she has written for the "Christian Observer," and other Southern journals and magazines. Her post-office address is Old Church, Va.

1868.

MRS. MARY WILEY,

(" *Margaret Stilling.*")

A *NOM DE PLUME*, in my opinion, should express character.
Now, the best that I have seen in the South is that one of ' Margaret Stilling.' It attracted my attention at once." "Margaret Stilling" (the *nom de plume* of Miss Mary Evans) is a native and resident of Amelia County, Virginia. Her father, Dr. M. H. Evans, was a physician of some eminence in his profession. Her mother, who contributed poems to the "Southern Literary Messenger," many years ago, and published a volume of poems at Philadelphia in 1851, was of Northern birth — a Miss Stockton, related, I believe, to the celebrated Commodore Stockton.

The subject of this sketch was educated at the North, and is an elegant, accomplished woman, of high intellectual and musical culture, and a brilliant conversationist.

During the war, Miss Evans was a teacher, yet found time to cultivate the muses, to the pleasure of the "blockaded" Southrons, contributing her productions in prose and verse to the "Confederate" literary journals. Since the war, she has become Mrs. William Wiley, and only occasionally does she publish.

A BUNCH OF FLOWERS.

Across the leaves bright sunshine fell,
Touching their green with gold,
And tingeing, as some lustrous shell,
Each rosebud's crimson fold

A dewy network's pearly bands
Set, diamond-like, with light,
Stretched o'er each flower its gleaming strands,
With moonlight radiance bright.

While many a tiny, trembling spray,
  Some liquid star-drop brushing,
Would flash from thence one silver ray,
  And show a rosebud's blushing.

With mute delight I gazed on all,
  Some charm my spirit thrilling,
Hearing His voice through nature call,
  Each mystic yearning stilling.

Then 'gainst the wall the shadow fell,
  An outline dim and strange,
As if the colors, limned so well,
  Had known some wondrous change.

'T is thus, O heaven, thy glories bright,
  Fairer than star-gemmed skies,
Fall, shadowed with uncertain light,
  Before our sin-stained eyes.

MISS M. E. HEATH.

THE *nom de plume* of "Nettie Neale" was favorably known to the readers of the "Field and Fireside," a weekly literary journal published at Raleigh, N. C. A novelette, entitled "Eoland," which ran through a dozen issues of that journal, was favorably received.

Maggie E. Heath is a native of Petersburg, Va. She contributed to the Richmond "Christian Advocate" and "Home Circle" (Nashville), under the pseudonym of "Miriam," both prose and verse.

Miss Heath resides at Oakland. Her post-office address is Disputanta, Va. She has ready for publication a volume entitled "Under the Oaks."

1868.

MISS VIRGINIA E. DAVIDSON.

THE subject of this notice has always been an invalid. Says she, in an elegant letter to the writer: "On this account I have had the misfortune to be uneducated, except so far as a fine private library and an extraordinarily intelligent father's conversation and explanations could supply the painful deficiency."

She is the daughter of Colonel James Davidson, who was well known in Petersburg, Virginia, (the home of Miss Davidson,) as a man of remarkably varied information upon all subjects and sciences, and who occasionally wrote verses. On her mother's side she is, by affinity, connected with the Harrisons, of James River; and the Claibornes, Maurys, and Fontaines, of this State. Her brother, W. F. Davidson, was an officer in the United States Navy, and was considered one of the finest mathematicians in that highly educated branch of the service: he also wrote poetry; and a sister has also evinced the same talent.

To best illustrate a determined spirit, and showing what can be done when one places their might at the wheel, we would mention that, at the age of sixteen, to use her own words, "I was so illiterate, I did not know or even understand the commonest branches of education, until one night a friend, younger than I, came to spend the evening. She contended with my father about a difference of opinion of Hector, and then of Ajax, Theseus, and Marc Antony. I sat fearful, lest they should call upon me as umpire; for I was entirely ignorant of these heroes. Fortunately, the conversation turned upon the beauties of poetry: upon this subject I knew a little, and gladly did I avail myself of my superficial knowledge. Ignorance was abashed, and I at once commenced, without consultation with any one, a three-hours' task of ancient history and mythological reading, until history became a mania and an idol. This was the commencement of my education."

At the close of the war, Miss Davidson was no better off than the majority of her Southern sisters. "Necessity is the mother of invention, and poverty is the fruitful mother of energies," and at once in

402

Miss Davidson brain and will and determination awoke, and she wove the incidents detailed to her during social hours of pleasant association *during the war* into book-form, under the title of "Bloody Footprints." Some of the incidents of this volume were published in the "Southern Opinion," Richmond, under the name of "Virginia." Miss Davidson has also written a novel, entitled "Philanthropist," and one which she has called "Principle and Policy." The last named is now in the hands of publishers in New York.

1868.

MRS. J. W. McGUIRE.

DIARY OF A SOUTHERN REFUGEE DURING THE WAR; by a lady of Virginia. New York. 1867.

The above is the title of Mrs. McGuire's only book. This work was not written with the intention of publication. It is a diary, written between the 4th of May, 1861, and the 4th of May, 1865, — while Mrs. McGuire was a "refugee" from her home, — for the benefit of the younger members of her family, who would naturally desire to know something of the inner life of their relatives during the terrible years indicated.

Mrs. McGuire's maiden name was Brockenborough. Her father was Judge of the Court of Appeals of Virginia. Richmond was the place of her nativity and early years.

After becoming the wife of Rev. John P. McGuire, an Episcopal clergyman, she lived for many years in the county of Essex. Her husband became rector of the Episcopal High School, near Alexandria, Va., where they lived until they became "refugees," as set forth in the "Diary." After the war, they moved into the village of Tappahannock, where Mrs. McGuire has ever since been the principal of a female school.

1871.

MISS SALLIE A. BROCK

IS the author of "Richmond During the War: Four Years of Personal Observation," a work which, had she written nothing else, would deservably give her a prominent place among the first female writers of the country. A reviewer in a Northern journal says:

"It is characterized by a purity of style and thought, a delicacy of sentiment, and an earnestness of conviction that are too rarely found in the publications of the day. The hopes and fears, the resolution and self-sacrifice, the sufferings and privations, the heroism and courage displayed by the Southern people, are described with all the warm affection and loving reverence of a true woman's heart — a heart whose every throb beat in sympathy with the cause of the South. The generous and noble impulses by which, in common with tens of thousands of her Southern sisters, the fair authoress was actuated, are manifested in the general style and character of the subjects treated. She brings to her task a mind fully stored with the most minute information on the principles in controversy. She is thoroughly conversant with the causes that led to the conflict, and this knowledge is employed with admirable judgment during the progress of the work for the enlightenment of the reader. The style is peculiarly pleasing, and the literary character of the book is of the highest order. Full of incident, and of stirring, striking, and often thrilling scenes, the interest of the work never flags. All the joyousness of victory and the gloom of defeat, all the glory and all the horrors of war, are depicted with a lifelike vividness; and the leading characters that appear upon the stage are painted with the fidelity of truth itself. The title of the volume would convey the impression that the scope is limited to Richmond; but this is not so, for the fair authoress takes in the whole range of the Confederacy, and describes the influence of this or that event as affecting the general progress of the contest. There are no less than seventy-six chapters in the book, a fact which will serve to convey some idea of its varied interest. The first opens with the secession of Virginia; and the last, entitled "Life in the Old Land Yet," breathes forth words of hope and encouragement, giving a glowing picture of the future of the South, rousing the faint-hearted, and inspiring the despondent with new life and courage. We heartily commend 'Richmond During the War' as one of the most interesting, valuable, and best written volumes that has appeared since the close of the great struggle."

404

Sallie A. Brock is a native of Madison Court House, Virginia, an obscure little hamlet among the hills of Piedmont, and overhung by jutting spurs of the Blue Ridge. This little village is distinguished for the wild and romantic character of the surrounding scenery, and the fair intelligence and high moral standard of its inhabitants; and Miss Brock's attachment to her birthplace is shown in the pseudonym for her literary efforts, "Virginia Madison." And this very appropriate *nom de plume* calls particular attention to the many inappropriate ones; and it is a cause for conjecture why so many elegant writers show such questionable taste in their pseudonyms.

Miss Brock, on her father's side, is of Welsh descent. In England, the Brocks were staunch Royalists; and one of the name sealed his devotion to his country and his crown by his blood, upon the Heights of Queenstown, in Canada.

Her mother, whose maiden name was Buckner, was a descendant, from her father, of the Beverlys and the Chews; and from her mother, of the Burtons, the Heads, and the Marshalls, all names inseparably connected with the colonial and revolutionary history of Virginia.

Miss Brock's childhood was passed in her native village, under the tutelage of her father exclusively; and later, under tutors and governesses. She is ignorant of what is usually called "boarding-school experience."

In her childhood, she was fond of study, and devoted to æsthetical pursuits, whether growing out of nature or of art, in the circumscribed sphere of her acquaintance, and was possessed of a passionate fondness for military display, in which her taste was fully gratified during the late war.

In the fall of 1850, Mr. Brock removed to the University of Virginia, where his daughter spent the following eight years of her life. There her sphere for improvement was sensibly enlarged, and she enjoyed the advantages of society as moral, refined, highly cultivated, and intellectual as can be found in the country. Her fondness for books grew upon her; in the course of time, she devoted herself to studying oil-painting, and then she indulged the dream of *authorship*.

In the winter of 1858, the Brock family removed to Richmond, and were living in that city when the news from Sumter announced the breaking out of hostilities. Miss Brock's course of life from that time was changed. Dreams of distinction were hushed before the stern demands of duty. There was much for her to do, in common with all of her Southern sisters. She sewed and knitted, and nursed and cooked, and watched and prayed, during the four years of the war, in service for the South and her soldiers; while the delicate health of her mother, and the frequent and necessary absences from home of her father and younger brother, threw upon her the cares of the family. They were severe and onerous, and she bore them with fortitude, feeble enough as she watched her mother's decline to the grave. This was her first personal sorrow; and the only drop of consolation she tastes is in the remembrance that she has been rescued from the great national sorrow, which, like the raven, "never flitting, still is sitting, still is sitting," brooding over the wreck of the buried hopes of a nation. A total change in circumstances and family changes have drifted Miss Brock away from home and friends; and she is now residing in the city of New York, which is the "literary emporium" of the country, where authors much do congregate.

"Virginia Madison's" muse is a busy one, and is becoming to be appreciated by the reading world. Writing gives Miss Brock intense pleasure, and her writings give her readers no less delight.

Her second volume, a collection of poems from Southern poets, is entitled "The Southern Amaranth," published for the benefit of the "Ladies' Memorial Association," (1869.) This volume contains many poems furnished expressly for this work by the authors; also, many beautiful poems from the muse of the gifted editress. Miss Brock's talents are of a versatile order, excelling in fiction, in poetry, and in what a woman seldom does well, political topics, which she discusses and argues knowingly and eloquently. She has established a reputation as a writer, of which she may well be proud, and which must increase with time: thus considered, her first volume may be looked upon as a bud which must be followed by many magnificent blossoms, which we firmly hope may be fadeless.

In 1869–70 Miss Brock travelled in Europe, and her letters were very extensively published. She has several novels in MSS. and a large and valuable work on the "American Poets and their Favorite Poems," will be published shortly.

April, 1871.

WHAT IS LIFE?

"What is Life?" I asked of a wanton child,
    As he chased a butterfly;
And his laugh gushed out all joyous and wild,
    As the insect flitted by.
"What is Life?" I asked; "oh, tell me, I pray!"
His echoes rang merrily, "Life is PLAY!"

"What is Life?" I asked of the maiden fair,
    And I watched her glowing cheek
As the blushes deepened and softened there,
    And the dimples played "hide and seek."
"What is Life? Can you tell me its fullest measure?"
She smilingly answered, "Life is PLEASURE!"

"What is Life?" I asked of a soldier brave,
    As he grasped the hilt of his sword;
He planted his foot on a foeman's grave,
    And looked "creation's lord."
"What is Life?" I queried; "oh, tell me its story."
His brow grew bright as he answered, "GLORY!"

"What is Life?" I asked a mother proud,
    As she bent o'er her babe asleep,
With a low, hushed tone, lest a thought aloud
    Might waken its slumber deep.
Her smile turned grave, though wondrous in beauty,
While she made reply, "Life—life is DUTY!"

I turned to the father, who stood near by
    And gazed on his wife with pride;
Then a tear of joy shone bright in his eye
    For the treasure that lay at her side.
I listened well for the tale that should come:
"My life!" he cried, "my life is HOME!"

"What is Life?" I asked of the infidel;
    His eyes were haggard and bleared;
Fierce, mocking sneers from his thin lips swell,
    And his heart with vice was seared.
"What is Life," I asked, "in its ebb and flow?"
With an oath he muttered, "Life is WOE!"

"What is Life?" I asked of the invalid wan,
    As he wheeled to the grate his chair,

And frowned as through the casement there ran
A fluttering breath of air.
"What is Life?" I asked — I asked again:
He languidly coughed, and answered, "PAIN!"

"What is Life?" I asked of the statesman grand,
The idol of the hour;
The fate of a nation was in his hand —
His word was the breath of power.
He, sickening, turned from the world's caress·:
"'T is a bubble!" he cried — "'t is EMPTINESS!"

"What is Life?" I asked of the miser grim,
As he clutched his well-filled bag;
His features were gaunt and his figure slim,
His garment a tattered rag.
"What is Life?" I asked, "the story unfold."
"Life," he chuckled, "life is GOLD!"

"What is Life?" I asked of the student of books,
Exploring a ponderous tome;
There are curious things in the rare old nooks
Whence the records of science come.
For a moment he turned from his learnèd perch,
And quickly answered, "Life is RESEARCH!"

"What is Life?" I asked of a Christian meek,
As she knelt before a shrine;
The impress of Heaven was on her cheek,
In her eyes a light divine.
"What is life?" I questioned, "oh! trace me its path!"
She pointed upward, and whispered, "FAITH!"

"What is Life?" I asked of a man of care,
Bending under the load of years:
He ran his fingers through his thin gray hair,
And his eyelids were humid with tears.
His voice trembled, "I once was brave;
Life is a shadow that points to the GRAVE!"

I turned and asked of my inner heart
What story it could unfold?
It bounded quick in its pulses' start,
As the record it unrolled.
I read on the page, "Love, Hope, Joy, Strife!
What the heart would make it, such is LIFE!"

MISS SUSAN C. HOOPER.

A QUIET home-existence up to the close, or rather beginning of the war—for "quiet" was hardly to be found in Richmond during the time the "City on the James" was capital of the Confederate States—was that of Susan C. Hooper.

Miss Hooper's father, on the death of his wife and an infant daughter, which occurred shortly after the second birthday of the subject of this article, discontinued housekeeping, and the subsequent life of father and daughter was spent as boarders in the home of one or another of their kindred. Says the lady:

"My earliest *distinct* recollection is of a character rather different, I opine, from that of most girls. I could not have numbered more than three or four years, at farthest, when our city had the honor of a visit from the Sage of Marshfield. Reared in the Slashes of Hanover, familiar with the scenes of Clay's early life, and bred in the same school of politics, it was always a marvel to me that Harry of the West was not my father's favorite leader. But, no; it was Webster, from the colder latitude and granite hills of New England. Well, my father could not permit so golden an opportunity of his child's seeing his political idol to pass unimproved; so, girl, almost baby as I was, he hurried me down to the honorable gentleman's reception on the portico of the old Powhatan, then a leading hotel, held me in his arms above the heads of the populace, that in after years I might boast of having heard Webster, the immortal. My impressions of that hour were a source of infinite amusement to my father to the day of his death. Mr. Webster was welcomed by James Lyons, Esq., a prominent member of the Richmond Bar, afterward a representative of that district in the Confederate Congress; and I, after an impartial hearing of both speeches, boldly avowed the opinion that Mr. Lyons was the greater orator of the two, in my infantile judgment. It may have been the elegance and grace of our fellow-citizen, or his sonorous, Ciceronian periods, or perhaps both united, as compared with the stout, portly figure and short, pithy sentences of the New-Englander, as my dim, shadowy remembrance now paints him, which captivated my childish fancy; but there was evidently something in his manner, or appearance, or rhetoric, which indelibly stamped itself upon my mind, and made Mr. Lyons, for a long period, my beau ideal of an orator."

The childhood of Miss Hooper was passed with her maternal grandmother, a woman of strong and well-cultivated mind for the ante-revolutionary period. Politics was her forte. She was never quite so near the climax of happiness as when she could engage a Democrat in controversy, and overthrow (as she conceived) some of his pet theories, by a womanly thrust, or an apt quotation from the Sage of Ashland, her paragon of statesmanship. Who can aver that these surroundings had no influence in shaping the habits of thought and manner of writing of Miss Hooper?

Miss Hooper's father made her, his *only one*, a companion from infancy; taught her to read at an early age, years before she was old enough to go to school; interested himself in her childish pleasures and pursuits. Mr. Hooper was a man of sound judgment and superior practical sense, and was always very ambitious for his daughter.

In her childhood, authorship had been Miss Hooper's hobby; but emancipated from the restraints of the school-room, for several years she had no ambition beyond present enjoyment. It is to Reviews, of which department of literature she is particularly fond, that Miss Hooper is indebted for most of her knowledge of authors, never having had access to a library.

Her first article was published in the "Religious Herald," Richmond, under the *nom de plume* of "Adrienne," which she still retains.

Her first story was published in a literary weekly of Richmond, and was much complimented by the editress; since which time she has contributed to Southern and Northern literary journals. During the war, "Adrienne" was one of the most prominent contributors to the "Magnolia Weekly," Richmond. Her novelettes were lacking in vivacity, and the characters were similar. "Ashes of Roses" we consider her cleverest novelette; some of the scenes being not only lifelike, but capitally delineated. Her best productions will shortly be given to the public.

Shortly before the close of the war, Mr. Hooper died; and with the downfall of the Confederacy, *her* property was all swept away; and single-handed, this true Christian woman prepared to contend with the "cold charities of the world in the battle of life."

A Virginian by birth, having ever resided within the borders of the "mother of States," Miss Hooper is proud of the "Old Dominion," and clings to her, "desolated," as she rejoiced in her "pomp and beauty." She converses fluently and elegantly. As a correspondent, Miss

Hooper is to be praised; her letters are natural and interesting, an index of the character of the writer.

In the writings of Miss Hooper, the defects are those that are inherent in her nature and surroundings. Having never travelled or mingled in "society," so called, her novelettes are necessarily plain, unvarnished records of home-life in the middle class of society; in which, perhaps, the *religious* element predominates too strongly for the mass of readers. We think Miss Hooper has erred in too little following Longfellow's suggestion, "to look into her heart and write."

Miss Hooper is at this time (1871) an assistant teacher in the Richmond Female Institute.

THE OCCUPATION OF RICHMOND.

I do not believe there ever was a more panic-stricken woman than I, the first day, and, indeed, the first week of the occupation of Richmond by the Federal troops; but, upon present reflection, I admit that the causes for alarm existed more in my imagination than in reality.

Sunday was the loveliest of April days, the morning as quiet as any within four years; and worshippers wended their way to church as peacefully as if "wars and rumors of wars" were mere abstractions. In the afternoon, there were whisperings of evacuation; and, toward evening, elongated visages, the constant whistle of locomotives, and fugitive inhabitants, betokened some unusual commotion; but I remembered the gun-boat panic in '62, and persistently refused to credit the evidence of my senses. Such was my confidence in the success of our cause, that it was not until eleven o'clock that night, when it was positively asserted that our pickets were to be withdrawn two hours thereafter, that I began to realize the situation. That slumber visited not my eyes you will readily believe; but it is too much for your credulity to believe that hope was still inspired by my reflections upon the numerous miraculous interpositions of Providence in behalf of God's chosen people in ancient times, particularly the deliverance of Hezekiah from the hosts of Sennacherib; and I fondly dreamed, even then, that the enemy would never be permitted to enter our "beautiful, seven-hilled city." This delusion was dispelled about dawn by an explosion which shook the house to its very foundation, and I sprang up, exclaiming to my room-mate, "Oh, L——, the Yankees are shelling us!" and shortly after, there was another report more terrific still, which fully convinced me that the enemy had opened a bombardment. These reports we soon ascertained to be from the destruction of the "Patrick Henry," at the Rockets, and the powder magazine, almost in our immediate vicinity; and were but the beginning of the explosions, which were continued throughout the morning at the armory and the arsenal. About sunrise, the mob, who had been sacking the stores all night, completed their work by firing the houses they had rifled. The brooding wing of the destroying angel seemed to hover over us in the dense clouds of smoke which obscured the sun, and made almost a twilight darkness at midday.   The fire raged furiously all day, and by night at least one-half of the business portion of the city was in ashes.

About eight o'clock in the morning, in the midst of the consternation about the conflagration, there was a general stampede of the pillagers from "down town," fleeing before the enemy. As everything was remarkably quiet, except in the burning district, and I expected they would enter with "a great flourish of trumpets," I pronounced it all a hoax, until one of our neighbors assured me "he had seen the Yankees on the Square." My first view of them was about ten o'clock, when two regiments of fine-looking, soldierly fellows, whom, but for their splendid uniforms, I might have imagined some of our own brave boys, advanced up the street with a firm, steady tread, and a dignified, martial air. I confess, until then, anxiety for my personal safety had absorbed every other feeling; but when I descried through the closed blinds the "stars and stripes" waving in the Confederate capital, I burst into tears.

The first freshet of my grief having subsided, I became tolerably composed; but, in the afternoon, was again precipitated into a panic by the approach of a colored brigade, who rushed pellmell past our residence, singing, shouting, yelling, firing, the white officers not even endeavoring to restrain them.   We anticipated such scenes that night as marked the occupation of Columbia, S. C.; and as these black fiends were encamped only two squares beyond us, we apprehended danger to our neighborhood from their proximity. However, everything passed off quietly, and we scarcely heard a footfall on the street after nightfall.

"Our friends, the enemy," (to quote the polite language of the *late* Mr. Daniel, of the "Examiner," who *fortunately* died the week before the evacuation,) have preserved very good order ever since their occupation. There have been some irregularities and depredations in the vicinity of the camps, particularly before the removal of the negro troops; but, as far as possible, they have been promptly punished. Indeed, *ma chère*, I thought I never knew what gratitude was until the first week of the Federal rule here: every hour we were protected from violence seemed a miracle of grace.   The authorities and the soldiery, in the main, have pursued a conciliatory course toward our citizens, and have carefully refrained from any exultation over a fallen foe. At church they are exceedingly respectful and devotional; they have been particularly courteous to ladies; don't even glance at us in the street, except to move aside to allow us to pass. . . . .

An amusing incident occurred not long since on Franklin Street, the fashionable promenade of the city. A belle, in meeting a Federal officer, doubled her veil; but just as he passed, a gust of wind drifted it at his feet.

He picked it up and presented it very gallantly, meanwhile concealing his face with his hat — a suitable reproof for her silly affectation.

Another incident, more interesting still, as showing the temper of the people: Last week, several young ladies, at the passport office, while awaiting their passports, entered into a cheerful conversation, but carefully abstaining from any allusion to the Yankees or the state of the country. An officer in the crowd appeared interested in their discourse, and presently made a casual inquiry. He was answered civilly, but coldly; but, not regarding his repulse, he pursued his interrogatories on indifferent topics. Finding he could elicit no reference to politics or the war, he pertly asked: "Well, what do you think of the success of your Confederacy now?" "Sir," replied one of the girls, "with God nothing is impossible; and I believe with his assistance we shall yet achieve our independence; for we are assured that 'whom the Lord loveth He chasteneth.'" Her questioner, crest-fallen and abashed, hung his head, and was soon lost in the crowd.

We are allowed considerable latitude of speech, of which we are not slow to avail ourselves. Treasonable utterances are not tolerated in the pulpit; but some of our ministers, even in conversation with the Federals, "use great plainness of speech," with perfect impunity. . . . .

On the 29th of April, an order was promulgated by General Halleck, to take effect on the 1st of May, that no minister would be allowed to perform a marriage ceremony without having taken the oath, and the parties contracting marriage should also be required to take the oath. Two of our wealthy young ladies of the *beau monde* were engaged to be married to a pair of North Carolina officers the first week in May; but, upon the appearance of this order, the parties "out-heroded Herod," by being united in Hymen's silken tie on Sunday morning, April 30th — Rev. Dr. Burrows, of the First Baptist Church, officiating. It is said there were at least fifty marriages in Richmond that day.

MATILDA S. EDWARDS.

MATILDA CAROLINE SMILEY ·was the youngest of twelve children: six sons and six daughters made the old homestead a very bright and happy place.

Matilda was left pretty much to her own inclinations in childhood, and spent many hours wandering through the woods around Grape Hill, (Nelson County, Virginia,) gathering flowers, and listening to the birds and the rippling of the bright waters that sparkled in the sunshine. It was a happy childhood, full of bright, sweet memories. She wrote a great deal; and her compositions, although hidden away, as she thought, securely, were often found by her sisters, who made them subjects of amusement, to her great mortification. One day, the presiding elder of the Virginia Conference, Rev. George W. Nalley, was stopping at the "homestead," and her sister found her blank book and showed it to him. The gentleman saw much good in these juvenile productions, and took them with him, reading them to his friends, and some of the poems appeared in the "Richmond Advocate," then edited by Rev. S. M. Lee. Not long afterward, Mr. Nalley and Bishop Dogget selected poems from the MSS. book, and a volume was published.

About that time, Mr. Nalley persuaded Mrs. Smiley to send Matilda to the Rockingham Institute, presided over by that good man and eminent educator, Rev. John C. Blackwell; a portion of the proceeds of the book of poems was used to defray some of the expenses of her schooling. She spent nearly three years at the Institute.

One by one her sisters left home as brides, until the youngest only was left. She kept up her studies and writings, publishing her articles in the "Louisville Journal," "The Home Circle," and various other Southern journals.

Just before the war, she married Rev. A. S. Edwards, son of General S. M. Edwards, of Washington. City.

Life in Richmond was one of few pleasures and many privations to any, unless they had many "blue-backed promises to pay." Mrs. Edwards, used to the free and open-hearted hospitality of the country with the pure air and green woods, suffered many privations — one month staying in the house of a rich acquaintance, who let rooms cheaper to them on score of friendship; another month in a damp basement room; and another in the third story of one of the Richmond hotels, then used as a hospital — living on pork, beans, and rye coffee, without sugar. And so life went by from year to year, until the Confederacy ended, and the drama closed with the fall and burning of Richmond.

After the fall of the Confederacy, Mrs. Edwards went back to her childhood's home, "Grape Hill," and opened a female school; but the country was so poor that it did not succeed, and the school was closed.

Mrs. Edwards has little time for writing, surrounded by a family of small children; and like all Southern women, she has many small cares upon her hands. She anticipates publishing a poem this fall.

William Archer Cocke, Esq., the author of "Constitutional History of the United States," a work which attracted considerable attention, enriching our literature, and placing the author high upon the list of Southern authors, in "Sketches of Southern Literature," published in 1863, notices the volume of poems of Matilda "as an agreeable volume of minor poems, which has much of womanly tenderness and delicate sweetness."

1868.

MRS. MARY McCABE.

AMONG the prominent contributors of prose and verse to the "Magnolia Weekly" — the most prominent literary journal of the "Confederate States," published in Richmond from 1863 to the close of the war — was "Miss Courtland."

She married Mr. James D. McCabe, Jr., at the time editor of the "Magnolia Weekly," and one of the few successful young authors of the South. Mr. McCabe, Jr. is the author of several books. The best known, probably, is his "Life and Campaigns of General Lee," published in 1867.

Mrs. McCabe is residing in Brooklyn, N. Y.

1869.

MARY J. S. UPSHUR.

MISS UPSHUR, well known under her pseudonym of "Fanny Fielding," has written for nearly every literary journal of the South, prose and poetry. She is one of the few writers who entertain the strictest ideas of the responsibility of writers for the press, in any capacity whatever; aiming to be useful in her sphere — "to leave no line which, dying, she would wish to blot."

Miss Upshur's birthplace is in Accomac County, Virginia, on the wave-washed Eastern Shore, where, almost literally, the Atlantic billows rocked her cradle, and the ocean waves sung lullaby. She was removed from here, in childhood, to Norfolk. She is a daughter of William Stith Upshur, (at one time a lawyer of the Accomac Bar, a contemporary of the Hons. H. A Wise and Thomas H. Bayly,) and a niece of Judge Abel P. Upshur, who was Secretary of State during President Tyler's Administration.

Miss Upshur has an inherent fondness for books — could read "handsomely," it has been remarked, at four years old. Though, when a child, devoted to play, she would frequently indulge in seasons of retirement in a dimly-lighted closet, poring over "Pilgrim's Progress," and other books of a serious character. Much of her childhood was spent in lonely, old country-houses, with little company and many books.

She commenced writing for the press at an early age. Her ambition was to be identified with the "literature of the South." Her first story, of any length, was a novelette, entitled "Florine de Genlis," and appeared in a Norfolk paper. Miss Upshur has written generally over the signature of "Fanny Fielding;" but sometimes over other assumed names, and frequently without any *nom de plume.*

Like Miss Evans, the author of "Beulah," etc., Miss Upshur was educated entirely at home; the difference being that the former was educated by her mother, while the latter lost her mother early, had no elder sister, and was the feminine head of the family from her very juvenile years, and was educated principally by her father.

416

Miss Upshur's most ambitious prose work, that has been published, appeared in the "Home Monthly," Nashville, 1867, entitled "Confederate Notes," the "prefatory" to which was in the following strain:

"Yes, despite whatever odium may attach to the term, thus is baptized this desultory record, which, written out from an irregular journal of the late war time, and immediately antecedent period, seems not thus misnamed.

"Those blue-backed 'promises to pay' are significant of a grander venture and a nobler hope than mines of gold can express; and exalted in such association, we brave the pronunciamento 'below par,' only wishing the new namesake merited, equally with its original, exemption therefrom.

"Critics of a different turn of mind may vote these 'Notes' discordant, and assign them one characteristic in common with those of the dying swan, whose 'last' are traditionally 'best.' Humoring the metaphor, we feel that not a few are left, yet, upon whose ear the sound will fall like a bar of some old, familiar strain in music, and to whom, though the original melody has died out in air, each echo is a memory of the sweetest song that was ever sung in vain."

"Confederate Notes," said a critic noted for his fairness and clearness of thought, "is a work of great power and deep, earnest thought. The style is terse, graphic, and idiomatic. This work will place the writer indisputably among the leading writers of the South."

The "Richmond Whig" said: "Confederate Notes," (it was published anonymously,) "in a strictly literary sense, and apart from any sectional or political significance contained in its title, is destined, we believe, to make its mark upon the comparatively fallow field of what is called Southern authorship."

The following extract from a letter from Miss Upshur is a picture of her every-day life, showing she is no *bas bleu*, in the popular acceptation of the term:

"A just report of my literary career could, I feel, scarcely be made without some allusion to the peculiar circumstances preventing that entire *abandon* to study and contemplation almost necessary to insure high excellence in one who designs making authorship a profession."

Of the poem "Margaret," given hereafter, she writes:

"I perhaps should tell you that it was written, as so many of my efforts were, disjointed—that is, at odd times, when I was busy with other matters, and yet felt 'a call,' as the Quakers says, 'to write.' I kept pencil and paper in my work-basket, and jotted down a verse at intervals while engaged with a pressing job of sewing.

53

"Well, I fancy I see certain household achievements interrupting," writes she, "gleaming here and there through breaks — very plain to me, in most things I have accomplished; pots of jam perceptible between stanzas of poems; seams of sheets, of carpets, disjointing the general narrative and final catastrophe of some heroic tale. I do not sigh for more poetic surroundings, or that my lot *is as it is*. There is no poetry without beauty, and use is beauty. A woman can have no higher appointment, I hold, than the keeper of a home. Her first duty is here: if she can shine abroad after this, all well; but this God intended as the centre of her warmth and light. So I believe."

The following poem was extensively copied by the newspapers throughout the country. The "Norfolk Herald" thus prefaces it:

"We take much pleasure in transferring the following beautiful stanzas from the pages of the 'Southern Literary Messenger,' for April, (1859.) They are the production, it seems, of one of the most gifted of the young ladies of Virginia, and one who should rank higher than many whose names have become famous. . . . We commend them to the lovers of the beautiful; for they will find, under their simple style, exquisite figures, conceived in the very spirit of poesy's self."

MARGARET.

Oh! Margaret, pretty Margaret!
  I pray ye linger yet
At the stile beyond the hay-field,
  When the summer sun is set;
And I'll tell ye in the twilight
  What ye never shall forget.

Oh! Margaret, sweet Margaret!
  With face so lily fair,
The sunbeams loved to nestle
  In the meshes of her hair,
And gleam and gleam more golden
  From the light they borrowed there.

Oh! Margaret, sweet Margaret!
  With eyes of violet blue;
Or, when she looked most lovingly,
  Of that celestial hue
The heavens show when cloud gates ope
  To let the good pass through.

Oh! Margaret, merry Margaret!
  Beyond the meadow mill,
My heart will listen, listen
  For your gentle tripping still;
All its pit-pat echoes waking,
  As of old, at your sweet will.

But Margaret, sweet Margaret!
  Ye'll never come again,
Like the spring-time after winter,
  Like the sunshine after rain;
But I could kiss the blessèd dust
  Where your sweet form hath lain.

But Margaret, sainted Margaret!
  The hay-field and the mill,
The meadow-path, its windings,
  And its little running rill,
Will speak more lovingly of you
  Than the grave-yard, all so still.

And Margaret, blessed Margaret!
  In my heart's love-lacking dearth,
I'll look upon the sunshine,
  And the flowers that strew the earth,
And I'll think I see in each of them
  The types of your new birth.

Then Margaret, sweet Margaret!
  Like sunshine after rain,
Like summer after winter,
  Ye will glad my heart again;
For I'll say they are your messengers,
  And they shall not speak in vain.

Miss Upshur has completed and expects to publish a novel, entitled
"Mabbit Thorn;" and "Confederate Notes" will also probably appear
in book-form.

In 1869, Miss Upshur lost her father, and shortly afterwards made
New York her home. She has recently married a Mr. Sturges, of New
York City.

1870.

MISS SARAH J. C. WHITTLESEY.

THE subject of this sketch, familiarly known to the readers of magazines and weekly journals, for which she has contributed both prose and verse, was born in Williamstown, Martin County, North Carolina, came to Virginia in 1848, and now resides at Alexandria.

Miss Whittlesey commenced rhyming at an early age, and published her first article in the "Edenton (North Carolina) Sentinel," in 1846. She published a book of poems, entitled "Heart Drops from Memory's Urn," in 1852; and through M. W. Dodd, New York, 1860, a volume of prose novelettes, entitled "The Stranger's Stratagem; or, The Double Deceit; and other Stories." She received a prize from a North Carolina paper for a novelette, entitled "Reginald's Revenge;" also, from the same journal, a prize for a novelette, entitled "The Hidden Heart." She again was the successful competitor for a prize offered by "The American Union," of Boston, "The Maid of Myrtle Vale" being the title of the successful tale.

In 1866, the publishers in New York of a series of Dime Novels appropriated one of Miss Whittlesey's stories, "The Bug Oracle," and published it without her knowledge or consent.

We believe she has recently, or is about to publish, a novel, entitled 'Herbert Hamilton; or, The Bas Bleu." Her longest, and we think most successful novel, appeared in the "Field and Fireside," entitled "Bertha, the Beauty."

420

HELEN G. BEALE,

THE author of "Lansdowne," is a young lady of the "Old Dominion State," a daughter of William C. Beale, a merchant of Fredericksburg, where she was born and has lived always, with the exception of two years spent in the "Old North State," after the bombardment of Fredericksburg during the war. She spent the day of the bombardment in a cellar at her home. Her father died when she was fourteen years of age. Her education was conducted by Rev. G. Wilson McPhail, now President of Davidson College, North Carolina, until she was sixteen, at which time she began the duties of life as a teacher, and has since spent the largest portion of her life in a school-room. Her aim during these years has been, and still is, to perfect herself as a teacher. Being thus occupied all day, she wrote "Lansdowne" one winter, in the evenings, after tea, for amusement.

A lady, who has had close association with Miss Beale, so as to afford her the best facilities for observing the springs of thought and action to which *we* are indebted for "Lansdowne," her first literary effort, writes to me:

"While reading 'Lansdowne,' both in MS. and print, I was confirmed in my idea that *worthy* persons, who are impelled to put their thoughts on paper, throw into their creations their own mental and spiritual life, however unconscious they may be of producing any transcript of themselves. This is seen in the analysis of the *two* most prominent characters of the story.

"We all see, daily, persons resembling the other characters: their traits may have been personified from observations of common life; but *these two* are pure creations of the author's brain — the hero, Theodore Lansdowne, loving, sensitive, tender, and beautiful, being the type of the æsthetic portion of the writer's human emotional economy — an acknowledgment of homage to the truth of the saying, 'A thing of beauty is a joy forever;' while Horace Ashton is a portrayal of another side of her character. In him, we find a crucifixion of *self*, in giving up not only worldly ease and secular ambition, but even love itself, held in abeyance to the call of Divine truth. Here is the culmination, that defines more faithfully than wordy sketch of mine could give, the calibre of the author of 'Lansdowne :' so does she 'ful-fil her God-given hest.'

"In person, Miss Beale is very slight, of medium stature, fine skin, bright brown hair, and broad, high forehead; but the eye is a mystery I have not yet fathomed, beautiful, clear brown, calm almost to sadness, as the 'mist resembles the rain;' though if she be moved to mirth, sunshine breaks through the mist, and a most quick, nimble spirit peeps out, full of humor, which has the gift of speech. This lady has written a book worthy of her-self, and which, like the companionship of the author, makes

> ' The cares that invest the day,
>   Fold their tents like the Arabs,
>   And as silently steal away.' "

"Lansdowne" was published serially in a weekly journal published in Baltimore — "Southern Society;" and as a narrative of Southern society, it was an ornament to the pages of any journal, and particu-larly suited to the *one* in which it appeared. Like many illy-managed Southern periodicals, "Southern Society" existed for less than a year.

Professor F. A. March, of Easton, Pennsylvania, (a gentleman of reputation for learning, in Europe as well as in this country,) thus alludes to "Lansdowne": "Over and above its merits as a story, it is decidedly worthy of the honor of appearing in book form, on the score of its value as a memorial of the society which it depicts."

1868.

MRS. CORNELIA J. M. JORDAN.

THE subject of this notice was born in the ancient and romantic city of Lynchburg, Virginia, on the 11th of January, 1830.

The maiden name of Mrs. Jordan was Cornelia Jane Matthews. She was the eldest of the three daughters of Mr. Edwin Matthews, at one time mayor of the city; a citizen of sincerest worth, intelligence, and character, highly respected by the entire community, and frequently honored and rewarded with positions of public responsibility. The wife of Mr. Matthews was a sister of the Hon. William L. Goggin, of Bedford County, and was a lady of rare accomplishments, of great personal beauty, and of many marked traits of amiability and excellence. She died when her eldest child was but five years old. Her husband, faithful to her memory, never married again; but devoted himself to the care and training of his children, and sustained toward them, as far as was possible, the relation of father and mother united in one. The three daughters, after their mother's death, lived with their maternal grandmother in Bedford County, till the youngest was old enough to attend school, and then they were placed in charge of the Sisters of Visitation, Georgetown, D. C. It was while in Georgetown that the first attempts of Miss Cornelia to compose, in verse, in accordance with the rules of prosody and composition, were made. Heretofore, she had written "as the spirit moved"—a spontaneous and impulsive utterance. She had sung as a bird, but was now to sing as a trained and cultivated musician. Her "wood-notes wild," which had been merely soliloquies, assumed the form of May-day addresses, verses to her schoolmates, album addresses, etc. These efforts were crowned with the grateful guerdon of flattery and praise: their author began to be known as the "poet laureate," and was always in requisition whenever anything metrical was needed. At the commencement of 1846, the highest prize in poetry and prose was conferred upon her, amidst admiring plaudits. Perhaps no other evidence of triumph ever gave her half the pride and pleasure conveyed by the simple and sincere assurance of her teacher's appreciation and her friends' approval and satisfaction.

The death of Emily, the youngest sister, occurred at this period. She was only fourteen years of age; but united to great liveliness a richly endowed mind and noble heart, which won the affection of all her companions, and the almost idolatrous love of her elder sister The fair unfolding of a flower so sweet and rare was watched with almost maternal solicitude, and the sudden blighting of the beautiful blossom inflicted a deep wound, whose scar will ever remain to witness its cruel severity. This was the first great sorrow of the poetess. It made a profound impression on her nature, and imparted — unconsciously, no doubt — a melancholy character to many of her pieces. It was in memory of her dead darling that she dedicated her first book, many years after, to "The Fireside and the Grave: the Living and Dead of a Broken Home Circle." The consolation of an assured hope and the gracious promises of the Divine faith were not wanting. But even these could not soothe the great sorrow which despoiled so early the tenderest emotions and aspirations.

The two surviving daughters returned, in 1846, to their grief-stricken father. The spring of 1851 found the elder daughter the happy bride of Mr. Francis H. Jordan, of Page County, a distinguished and accomplished member of the Bar, and afterward commonwealth's attorney. A beautiful home in the Valley of Virginia became now the centre of her affections and the object of her care. It was the fit seat of the Muses, presenting a rare and unrivalled combination of mountain and water scenery. Various poems embalmed its beauties, and evidenced the happiness and tranquil joy which awoke in the married heart of the poetess.

The early years of Mrs. Jordan's married life were spent in the Valley of Virginia; but in the first year of the war, she was called upon to mourn a double loss — that of her only surviving parent and her only child, both of whom died in the short space of one year.

Shortly before the commencement of the war, Mrs. Jordan published a collection of her fugitive poems, under the title of "Flowers of Hope and Memory." The book included the poems which, from time to time, she had written, and which had "gone the rounds" of the newspaper world — waifs upon the sea of journalistic literature. The book was brought out by Mr. A. Morris, of Richmond, Virginia, at a time which was sadly unpropitious; for no sooner was it issued than communication between the sections was at an end and all the horrors of war inaugurated.

About this time, Mrs. Jordan's health became seriously impaired, and she was debarred from writing by a disease of the visional nerve, which had previously threatened her with blindness. However, with the assistance of an amanuensis, she managed to maintain a correspondence with several journals. In April, 1863, she visited Corinth, Mississippi, where her husband held a staff appointment under General Beauregard. It was here that she wrote her poem, entitled "Corinth," which, on its publication after the surrender, was suppressed and burned by order of one General Terry, at that time commanding in Richmond. Mrs. Jordan made this vandalism the subject of a sarcastic communication to one of the newspapers of New York, and detailed how her little pamphlet, entitled "Corinth, and other Poems," of which an edition of about five hundred copies only was printed, had been seized by the timorous military commander as dangerous and heretical. Mrs. Jordan had lost all her possessions by the war, and she had hoped, by the sale of her poems, to obtain return at least sufficient to meet her pressing needs, in that moment of general prostration and ruin. How her hopes were frustrated is shown in the facts that have just been recited.

During the existence of the bazaar held in Richmond by the "Hollywood Memorial Association," about two years ago, the Association published a poem of Mrs. Jordan's, entitled "Richmond: Her Glory and her Graves," the last of any length from her pen.

Mrs. Jordan has always been, even from early childhood, a devotee of the poetic impulse. She is of an essentially poetic temperament. She was especially partial to the poetry of Mrs. Hemans; and she still retains in her possession an old volume of Mrs. Hemans's poetry, thumbworn, faded, and much abused, which has been her inseparable companion for years. A little incident connected with the childhood of our poetess, will show how strongly her nature was wedded to the divine gift of poetry, even at a time when the could have but a faint conception of the poet's mission. On one occasion, an old phrenologist — at a time when phrenology was the fashion — came to her grandmother's residence in Bedford County. Casting his eye around for a subject, he selected the little Cornelia. Running his hand over her head in a very knowing manner, he observed, with a smile: "A pretty *hard* head, to be sure; but one that will some of these days make a poet." The child's heart throbbed wildly at the announcement; and often, in the years that have since passed, has the memory

54

of the old man's words come back to her to give her courage and confidence.

Mrs. Jordan resides at present in Lynchburg. Though her fortunes are altered by the war, and by the result of the unfortunate investment of a large estate left by her father, she still finds a mother's consolation in training and caring for her only child, a bright little girl of six years of age.

It is to be hoped that ere long Mrs. Jordan will give to the world a volume containing all her poems, and especially that entitled "Corinth," the published edition of which, at the behest of a backward civilization, was so wantonly destroyed.

1869.   CHARLES DIMITRY.

FALL SOFTLY, WINTER SNOW, TO-NIGHT.

Fall softly, winter snow, to-night,
  Upon my baby's grave,
Where withered violets faded lie,
  And cypress branches wave.
Ye bright flakes, as ye touch the ground,
Oh! kiss for me that little mound.

Beneath it lies a waxen form
  Of boyish beauty rare —
The dust upon his eyes of blue,
  And on his shining hair.
Above his little heart so low,
Fall gently, gently, winter snow!

We laid him there when summer flowers
  Gave out their fragrant breath,
And pale white roses watched beside
  That narrow bed of death.
One soft curl from his sunny brow
Is all of him that's left me now.

Ethereal snow, fit mantle thou
  For one so pure and fair;
Fit emblem of the spotless robe
  His baby soul doth wear:
As stormy night-winds howl and rave,
Oh! gently wrap his little grave.

FLOWERS FOR A WOUNDED SOLDIER.

Go, gentle flowers!
Go light the soldier's room,
Go banish care and gloom,
Go, with a voice of home
    Gladden his hours.
Tell him of woods and fields,
Tell him of hearts and shields,
Tell him that sadness yields
    Kindly to you.
Bear in your sunny smile
Hopes that all cares beguile,
Faith in All-Good the while
    Fervent and true.
Go in your beauty drest,
Types of the pure and blest;
Bear to the weary rest,
    Holy and calm.
Soothe, soothe his bosom's smart,
Gladness and joy impart;
Breathe o'er the fevered heart
    Comfort and balm.
Go in your summer bloom,
Light up the soldier's room,
Drive thence all care and gloom,
    Brighten his hours.
Cheer him with memory-gleams —
Pictures of woods and streams,
Boy-haunts and childhood-dreams —
    Go, gentle flowers!

LAURA R. FEWELL.

MISS FEWELL was born in Brentsville, Prince William County, Virginia, and has spent the greater portion of her life there. Her father died when she was sixteen years of age, and immediately after she commenced teaching, and by her exertions in that way she has educated a younger brother and sister.

She commenced writing during her school-days, when she was chief contributor to a school paper published in the institution where she was educated. She has written a great deal, occasionally publishing in various journals — contributing to Godey's "Lady's Book" under the *nom de plume* of "Parke Richards."

During the war she wrote a novel, "Neria," which has not been published. In 1866, she came to Clark County, Georgia, and established a school, and contributed to "Scott's Magazine" and other journals.

A VIRGINIA VILLAGE.—1861.

Who does not distinctly remember the spring of 1861? Not for the beauty of the season, though that was as lovely as smiling skies, balmy winds, and odorous flower-cups could make it; but for the cloud, at first scarcely larger than a man's hand, that began to loom up in the political horizon, and the distant mutterings of the storm so soon to burst upon the land. . . . . . Then came the call for troops, and soon the earth resounded with the tramp of armed men. . . . . There was a glory and enthusiasm about the whole thing — in the waving banners, the glittering uniforms, and nodding plumes — that led captive the imagination and silenced reason. In every town where troops were quartered the ladies were affected with "button on the brain;" and seemed to think life was only made to be spent in walking, riding, dancing, and flirting with the young officers. Youth and gayety were everywhere uppermost, unappalled by the spectacle of national distraction.

To a little village situated in the lovely valley lying between the Bull Run and Blue Ridge Mountains, only a faint echo of the din of war had penetrated. Not a single company of soldiers had ever passed through or been camped in its vicinity; and more than one of its young belles read with envious feelings the accounts of the brilliant conquests achieved over the hearts of the Carolinians and other Southern troops by their correspondents in more fortunate towns, and sighed over the hard fate which condemned them to "waste their sweetness on the desert air," for in that light they regarded the members of the county companies, most of whom they had known from their childhood.

This little village merits a description: — It figured in more than one official bulletin during the war. It consisted of one long street, through the middle of which ran the turnpike, and on either side of this the houses — some very pretentious-looking structures of stucco and brick, others frame buildings, stained and weather-beaten — stretched for nearly a mile. Some few houses were situated on side streets crossing the main one at right angles, and there was a pleasant tradition among the people that their town had once rejoiced in back streets, but these, by common consent, were now given up to the hogs and nettles. In spite of these drawbacks, it was a quiet, cosey-looking place, especially when the trees that shaded it were in full foliage, and every garden and door-yard was flushed with flowers whose fragrance filled the air.

A stranger would have thought that this little village, lying in the lap of verdant meadows, encircled by the Briarean arms of the mountains, and so remote from all busy thoroughfares of trade, would have escaped the corruptions of larger towns, and its inhabitants, if not retaining the simplicity of country manners, would, at least, be free from the pride and exclusiveness of city life. But a short residence there would have taught him the fallacy of this opinion. Not in Washington, that modern Gomorrha of pride and vanity, did the strife for fashion and pre-eminence rage higher than in the little village of which we write. It might justly be called the town of cliques, for it boasted as many as any fashionable city extant.

First, forming the *élite* of the place, were the families of the military and professional men, and those of the large landed proprietors residing on estates, and a few aspirants after aristocracy, who kept up an uncertain footing upon the outer bounds, but were not allowed to enter the arena of this charmed circle, from which all new-comers, whatever their personal merits, were rigorously excluded, unless they could exhibit a long list of illustrious ancestors. From this apex — this *crème de la crème* — society descended, in graduating circles, to the lowest phase of social life, which, strangely enough, was found in a *castle;* for so the inhabitant, who had aspirations above her station, termed the mud walls which formed her home. Except a few loiterers, mere lookers-on at life, all the inhabitants of the village belonged to some one of these circles, which were entirely separate and distinct, never infringing on each other's privileges, save in the manner of scandal and backbiting — those time-honored adjuncts of village-life — except when some stray cow or pig trespassed on neighboring property, when there was apt to be an outbreak between the plebeians and patricians, sometimes coming to blows.

MRS. LIZZIE PETIT CUTLER.

LIZZIE PETIT was born in the town of Milton, Virginia, a place of some importance formerly, but which has been swallowed up by the increasing power and wealth of its more widely-known neighbor, Charlottesville. Her ancestry, on the paternal side, consisted of respectable farmers; on the mother's side, she boasted of descent from Monsieur Jean Jacques Marie Réné de Motteville Bernard, an early *emigré* to the colonies, driven from France by political disabilities.

Monsieur de Bernard married in Virginia, and lived on his wife's estates on the James River. Miss Petit had the great misfortune to be left motherless in her early childhood. She was brought up by her grandmother and aunt with tender care and affection, upon one of the beautiful farms lying under the shadow of the Blue Ridge Mountains, in that most picturesque portion of the State of Virginia, near Charlottesville. She was a sprightly child, very precocious, sensitive, and of very delicate beauty. She very soon began to scribble rhymes and write little stories for her own and her cousin's amusement. At the age of thirteen she removed to Charlottesville, where the chaperonage of her aunt enabled her to mingle in the gay society of the city. She was very bright, and a belle among the students at an age when most girls are scarcely released from their pinafores. She was soon trammelled in Cupid's fetters. But accident produced estrangement between her lover and herself, and he departed, to die in Alabama; while she, in the shadow of this disappointment, found relief in the absorption of literary labor. She wrote here her first novel, "Light and Darkness." It was brought out by the Messrs. Appleton, and had very considerable success, both in this country and in England, where it ran through several editions. "Household Mysteries" was her second novel, written at the suggestion of Mr. Appleton. This book was written in the vortex of New York society.

After eighteen months' rest, Miss Petit wrote again; but being advised unwisely, forsook her steadfast friends, the Appletons, and proffered her MS. to the Harpers, who rejected her work. After this, the Messrs. Appleton also refused it. This was a great disappointment to the young girl; and her means becoming limited, she was induced to give a series of dramatic readings, which were so successful that she was thinking of going upon the stage, encouraged by the applause of connoisseurs in the histrionic art. While preparing herself for a "star engagement" proffered her, she nearly lost her life by her gown taking fire accidentally. She was saved by the presence of mind of her friend Mr. Oakley. This severe affliction caused her to pass several months of suffering on her couch; but she was gradually restored to health by the affectionate care of her many friends; one among whom so endeared himself by his assiduous and constant attentions, that upon her recovery she became his wife. She lives now at her husband's residence, near New York, where she enjoys a tranquil domestic peace, and employs her leisure hours in the use of her pen. She is engaged in writing a novel, which will embrace the period of the war.

Mrs. Cutler's sympathies, like those of all the true daughters of Virginia, were with her own people in their recent struggle; but powerless to aid, she could only weep over the misfortunes of her country. Her husband has been a prominent member of the Bar in New York.

1869. ——————— S. A. D.

SPIRIT-MATES.

I always endeavor to preserve, in every character and circumstance portrayed, the strict unities of truth and human nature.

To a casual observer, the love existing between two such opposites as my hero and heroine may seem rather opposed to probability; but I am sure one who looks farther into cause and effect, will agree with me in pronouncing it the most natural thing in the world.

Ida herself, the perfect type of all that was feminine, delicate in organization, and timid, notwithstanding her sometime flashes of spirit, worshipped in Cameron the type of manliness, bravery, health, strength, and energy. Perhaps, in some respects, the intellect of the woman was superior — that is, she had more of those finer gifts of genius to which men, in all ages, have yielded homage; more of that rare union of ideality and passion, which gives to the harp of poesy the chord which vibrates in the hearts of the multitude; and it was better so: for these qualities, in the exquisite fineness of their moral texture, suit better a woman than a man.

The world may drink in the passionate incense which genius burns on the shrine of feeling, until their whole moral nature becomes purified and elevated; but the "spirits finely moulded," which have given birth to thoughts like these, suit not to come in contact with the jagged edges and rude paths of common life.

Within the world of her own home, a woman of fine intellect and feelings may, unless opposed by extraordinary adverse influences, create an atmosphere redolent of all that the most dreamy and ideal worshipper of the holy and beautiful could desire; but a man must tread rough paths; he must come in contact with the coarse and vulgar elements which compose a portion of the world; and alas! it needs not to tell how often the children of poesy have laved their spirit-plumes in the muddy, turbid waters of the world's recklessness and vice.

It needs not to tell; for their fall, like that of the children of light in the olden time, is never forgotten. The remembrance, like a shadowy pall, darkens future ages with its influence.

But to return to the more immediate theory of our present discussion.

Nature created men and women in pairs. There can be no more doubt of this than the laws of affinity in the science of chemistry. There is the essence of truth in the homely saying, "Matches were made in heaven; but they get terribly mixed coming down."

There is for every one a spirit-mate; one who, morally, mentally, and physically, must gratify every necessity of our being; with whom to live would be happiness: such happiness as would at once ennoble and elevate our nature, bringing it nearer to that of the angels.

And in our search for a being like this, we often pass them in our own blind folly, rather than through the influence of that fabled power men call destiny.

Allured by some passing meteor, turned aside by convenience, caprice, passion, we wander from the star whose light, in after years, we remember with the vain prayer:

> "Oh! would it shone to guide us still,
> Although to death or deadliest ill."

What is the ideal cherished, even though vaguely, in the mind of every one, but a dreamy sense, an unconscious divination — if I may so express it — of the existence of a being formed by nature to blend with and become a part of ourselves?

The loves of a lifetime — what are they but the illusions of an hour, when, deceived by some passing resemblance, we cry, Eureka! and think the bourne is found — until the heart, disappointed, recoils upon itself, or circumstance mercifully tears the counterfeit from our clinging grasp.

God forbid that there should be many loves in a lifetime; for 't is a sad thing, nay, 't is a sin, to waste on many feelings which should be the hoarded wealth of one; like the scattering drops of a rare perfume, which sweeten the common atmosphere, but can never return to the source from whence they emanated.

I have sometimes thought there might be an inner fount shut deep in the soul, never to be unsealed save at the magic touch; never to give forth its wealth of thrilling bliss and unalloyed sweetness to aught save *the one*.

'T is a blessed belief! And yet how sad it is to reflect that many live who are destined never to have the seal removed from the lip of the fountain; many, too, who are surrounded by all the nearer ties of life — ties formed in haste by the force of circumstance, convenience, expediency! Far better to live and die alone, than thus to rebel against the good angel of our nature, clasping the cold corpse of happiness, while its soul sleeps in the unsealed fount of our own bosom, or animates the form of the far-off unseen being, between whom and ourselves we have opened an impassable gulf.

————∘o̶◦⚬◦o̶∘————

MARY E. WOODSON.

MISS WOODSON is a native of Goochland County, Virginia, where her parents still reside. She has contributed to various papers and magazines under different *noms de plume*. Her first published novel — for she has her juvenile productions in manuscript — was published in 1860, by A. Morris, Richmond, anonymously. It was an interesting and well-sustained novel for so young a girl, and was entitled "The Way it all Ended." The Richmond "Dispatch," in a notice of this book, speaks of it "as a truly astonishing production for a girl who had never been five miles from home, and over whose head but fifteen summers had passed."

After the war, Miss Woodson published a novel in the Montgomery "Ledger," entitled "Perdita: a Romance of the War." This serial was very flatteringly received. Her address is Issaquena P. O., Goochland Co., Va.

1871.

————∘o̶◦⚬◦o̶∘————

M. VIRGINIA TERHUNE.

M. VIRGINIA HAWES (the maiden name of the well-known and well-beloved "Marian Harland," whose pseudonym has become "as familiar as a household word") is the second daughter of the late Samuel P. Hawes, of Richmond — deceased in 1868 — and Mrs.

Hawes, *née* Smith, a near relative of Rev. Dr. B. M. Smith, of the Presbyterian Church.

M. Virginia Hawes's early days were passed in Powhatan County, the residence of her parents at that time. About 1850, Mr. Hawes removed to Richmond, where he was engaged in merchandising. At the age of fourteen, Virginia contributed, under an assumed name, a series of sketches to a city journal. The commendations bestowed upon these articles were precious encouragement to the young author; and she continued to write, contributing anonymously tales and poems to the different periodicals of the day.

In 1854, assuming the name of "Marian Harland," Miss Hawes sent forth her first book with the imprint of A. Morris, Richmond. "Alone" was a most decided success; edition after edition was called for. In 1856 appeared "The Hidden Path," Marian Harland's most charming novel — my favorite of all of her books. Shortly after the publication of this book, Miss Hawes was married to Rev. E. P. Terhune, in charge of a church in one of the central counties of Virginia. "Moss-Side," her next volume, was written in her Virginia home; and in 1858, Rev. Mr. Terhune was called to take pastoral charge of the First Reformed Dutch Church, Newark, New Jersey, where they have resided ever since.

Mrs. Terhune's younger sister, Alice Hawes, several years her junior, early evinced a talent for literature, but native timidity prevented her appearing before the public. Her only published tale was forwarded anonymously to the "Southern Literary Messenger," and appeared after her death; for she died in the Christmas tide of 1863, in the "gladness of youth." The title of this tale was "Yule."

Marian Harland has been a most industrious writer. Her tales and novelettes furnished to the magazines and literary journals of the country would form many volumes.

The following comprise her books:

Alone. 1854.

Hidden Path. 1856.

Moss-Side. 1857.

Nemesis. 1859.

Miriam. 1864.

Husks. 1864.

Husbands and Homes. 1865.

Sunnybank. 1866.

Helen Gardner's Wedding-Day.   1867.
Ruby's Husband.   1868.
The Christmas Holly.   1868.
Phemie's Temptation.   1869.
At Last.   1870.
The Empty Heart.   1871.
Common Sense in the Household.   1871.

"Sunnybank"—published a short time after the close of the war, purporting to be a sequel to "Alone," her first book — was criticized more than any of "Marian Harland's" novels, and was bitterly denounced by several Southern journals, who fabricated absurd reports in regard to the political status of the family of Mrs. Terhune. Although residing in Newark, N. J., throughout the war, "Marian Harland's" husband was a "man of peace," and preaching "tidings of peace and good-will." Mrs. Terhune's youngest brothers were in the Confederate army. The eldest brother, to whom "Alone" was dedicated, is a Presbyterian clergyman, stationed in the interior of Virginia.

Mrs. Terhune has quite a number of "olive plants round her table."

The following notice of "Sunnybank" is from the New York "Round Table:"

" . . . This work is undertaken and executed in the same conscientious and painstaking spirit which characterized the author's earlier productions. With a simple love story she has interwoven an interesting portraiture of the trials experienced by those who bore the burden of the severe conflict from which this country has so recently emerged; and she has so far succeeded in rendering justice to the heroic devotion displayed on both sides, as to satisfy the reader that she has endeavored to prevent any partisan spirit from warping her judgment or tinging her writing with bitterness or extravagance. The incidents are narrated in the form of a double journal, or series of letters,—Eleanor and Agatha furnishing alternate chapters, and each taking up the thread of the story in such a manner that the interest is maintained throughout without flagging.

"That this book will fail to satisfy the intellectual taste of many of our readers must be obvious: the style is faulty, and there is occasionally a disregard for grammatical rules scarcely pardonable in an experienced writer. But while it is impossible to accord the authoress of 'Sunnybank' a place among the first female novelists of the day, we cheerfully acknowledge that she appeals to a very large class of society by omitting all that runs counter to its prejudices, and by carefully avoiding the strongly sensational scenes of crimes and passion which render the writings of some women obnoxious to censure. To this her popularity is mainly attributable."

"Marian Harland's" recent novels are of a domestic character, as are her numerous novelettes in the "Lady's Book."

"'Ruby's Husband' exposes with power and dramatic management the evils arising from a hastily contracted marriage between a man who, in the best sense of the word, is a gentleman, and a woman who, with some beauty and a superficial education, is vulgar, vain, and selfish at heart. The hero, Louis Suydam, is introduced as a melancholy, reserved, ambitious young student of medicine, whose family have both wealth and aristocratic tastes. In consequence of a severe wound from the accidental discharge of his gun, while hunting, he falls, for ten days, under the charge and care of the family of Nick Slocum, a rude, shiftless, sporting Anak, whose wife — a woman of real refinement, long-suffering, and Christian resignation — had eked out of their slender means enough to give an education to her daughter. The latter, Ruby, avails herself of the opportunity to win the disabled young student's fancy, and is successful. After a semi-romantic courtship, Louis marries her, but secretly, for the fear of the displeasure of his father. During the period which intervenes between the marriage and its public avowal, Louis suffers the natural consequence of an alliance with a woman inherently coarse and mean, and of a perpetual hypocrisy toward his family and the world. His sufferings are intensified when, after discovering his wife's unworthiness, he meets and falls in love with one who, in refinement, delicate sentiment, and every noble quality, is the reverse of his wife. Without following the plot, we will merely say that the development of this complicated situation is skilfully managed." — "The Galaxy," December, 1868.

MRS. WILLIAM C. RIVES.

THIS accomplished lady — one of the most distinguished of American ladies — is the widow of the Hon. William Cabell Rives, who was twice United States Minister to France, 1829 to '32 and 1849 to '53, and United States Senator from Virginia in 1832. He was a member of the Confederate Congress; and died at his home in Virginia, April 26th, 1868, — she was born at Castle Hill, Albemarle Co., Va., in 1802.

Mrs. Rives was Miss Judith Page Walker, daughter of Col. Francis

Walker, a gentleman of ancient descent and large means. She married Mr. Rives when quite young and still under the guidance of Mr. Jefferson. She accompanied him to Washington, and later to France, where he was sent as Minister. His influence at the time of the July Revolution of 1820 being exercised in behalf of the Orleans family, he became a great favorite with the royal household. Mrs. Rives was of eminent service to him there, — as everywhere; — and when her first daughter was born, she received the name of Amitie Louise from her godmother, the Queen of France. Upon her return home Mrs. Rives published her first novel, "Souvenirs of a Residence in Europe," by a Lady of Virginia, Philadelphia, 1842: many pictures in which were taken from life, as most of the characters were real personages. "This book," (I quote from a review published at the time this work appeared,) "is distinguished throughout for its moral and elevated tone. Its style, which perhaps in some instances may be rather luxuriant, is generally chaste, fluent, and graceful. The first and longest story in the volume, 'A Tale of our Ancestors,' is founded, we are told, on truth. The scene is first laid in Europe, in the age of Louis XV., but is subsequently shifted to our own mountains and valleys. Some of the scenes in this tale are exceedingly well depicted, and some of the characters, of which there is no lack of variety, are drawn with a skilful pencil. Following the 'Tale of our Ancestors,' the authoress has given us 'Fragments' of her own journal in Switzerland and a part of Italy; and very acceptable fragments they are. . . . Interwoven with the incidents which the authoress has journalized are two tales: the 'Soldier's Bride,' and the 'Valley of Goldan.' The volume concludes by a successful imitation of an old English ballad."

After some years of happy life on their immense estate, Castle Hill, Mr. and Mrs. Rives found themselves once more in Paris, where the American Minister was once more called upon to throw the weight of his influence in behalf of the new Government of France. The memoirs of that time, still to be written, will show how efficiently he was assisted by the rare gifts and the admirable tact of his wife.

After her second return from Paris, she published a work called "Home and Abroad," New York, 1857, — abounding, like her former book, with graphic sketches of foreign society and valuable comparisons with the state of things in America.

Mrs. Rives's deep and earnest religious convictions led her to devote much of her time, and occasionally her talents, to efforts in behalf of

the church and its faith. Thus she built, entirely by her own exertions, a beautiful church near her paternal home.

Since her husband's death, Mrs. Rives has led a quiet but useful life
on her estate, devoting herself with unabated energy to the duties of
a Virginia matron, and occasionally visiting her children, who have
founded new homes at the North and abroad.

A most useful helpmeet to her distinguished husband, a faithful
mother, a prominent and yet ever beneficent leader in society, and an
author of more than ordinary ability and popularity, Mrs. Rives has,
during her long life, been privileged to exercise a wide-spread, healthful influence like few women in the Republic.

Mrs. Rives resides at Castle Hill. Her post-office is Cobham
Station.

March, 1871.

MARY TUCKER MAGILL.

M ISS MAGILL gets a love for literature, and a desire to aspire to its
laurels, by inheritance. Judge St. George Tucker, of Virginia,
her great-grandfather, was not without acknowledged merit in the
literary world of his time, and several of his poetical pieces have out-
lived his generation, — "Days of my Youth," &c., for instance. His
two sons, Judge Henry St. George Tucker, Miss Magill's grandfather,
and Judge Beverly Tucker, improved upon the reputation of their
father ; the latter is the author of "George Balcombe," "a bold,
highly-spirited, and very graceful border story, true to life; a fine
picture of society and manners on the frontier, animated and full of
interest." — *W. G. Simms*. Also of "The Partisan Leader," published
in 1837, and reprinted in New York and Richmond in 1861 : this is
a curious anticipative political history.

St. George Tucker, son of Henry St. George Tucker, and the uncle
of the subject of this notice, was the author of "Hansford," a successful
novel, and many poetical pieces of exquisite taste and genius. He
died during the *late war*.

Miss Magill has from early girlhood looked forward to a literary
life. She weaved stories in childhood. Of a sensitive disposition, she
never attempted anything of more importance than stories for maga-

zines, which were published under an assumed name, and were received with some favor. During the years 1860 to 1865, Miss Magill's whole heart was completely absorbed in the stirring events, leaving no room from the stern reality to cultivate fancy. "After the war" she returned to Winchester, her once beautiful home, to find her house sacked and destroyed. Now her pen was called into requisition, and she was for several months special correspondent for the New York "News." The following fall, Mrs. Magill and her two daughters, of whom Mary Tucker Magill is the elder, opened a school at Winchester, which for four years has been very successful.

Last year, Miss Magill wrote "The Holcombes," a story of Virginia home life, published recently (1871) by Lippincott & Co., Philadelphia. This story is more subservient to the scenes and characters portrayed than they are to the story. The author designs to present a history of Virginia life in the slave days just anterior to the war.

This, Miss Magill's first book, is dedicated to "Virginia — my native State."

In "The Holcombes," she presents to view "Virginia in her palmiest days, as she was when she first bared her bosom to the sword, and opened her gates to present her soil as the battle-field."

March, 1871.

MISS EMILY V. MASON.

MISS MASON is prominent in all noble works, as she has been in society, by right of intellectual gifts and charming manners. Her parents were Virginians, descended from the best stock in the "Old Dominion." Her mother was of the Marshall and Nicholson families; her paternal grandfather and uncle were both United States Senators from that State. Her father, General Mason, removed to Kentucky some years after his marriage, and Emily was born in Lexington.

"During the war, Miss Mason devoted her energies to active usefulness in the hospitals in Richmond. Her spirit of benevolent enterprise survived the war. Since its close, she has worked even more indefatigably than ever in the cause of humanity. She has been the benefactress of Southern orphans, solicitous to provide for them the means of education, that they may be enabled in time to earn their own living." *

Miss Mason collected and arranged "The Southern Poems of the War," published by John Murphy & Co., Baltimore, 1867, and a second edition, revised and enlarged, was issued in the following year. This book was warmly received everywhere, and was the most popular of the several collections of the war muse of the South. Part of the profits of this volume were dedicated to the noble charity of educating the children of fallen Confederate soldiers, and twenty-five have, by this means, been provided for.

"In Miss Mason's collection of 'Southern War Poems,' we have gems from nearly all of the poets of the South — the stirring lyrics of Randall, the sweet and mournful verses of Father Ryan, the sternly defiant songs of Mrs. Warfield, the eloquent appeals of the lamented Timrod, the touching lines of Mrs. Preston, poems of joy and songs of sorrow, the shouts of triumph, the wailings of despair, the sweet and tender grace of Southern women, the chivalrous courage and unparalleled endurance of the Southern men, are here immortalized in melodious numbers which the world 'will not willingly let die,' for they commemorate a cause which is eternal."

Miss Mason's residence is in Baltimore. She has several books in preparation; among them, a "Popular Life of General Robert E. Lee," is now in the press of J. Murphy & Co., Baltimore.

1871.

MARY EUGENIE McKINNE.

MRS. McKINNE was born in Southampton County, Va. She is of Scottish descent. Her father, Capt. Joseph Vick (of the family who founded the city of Vicksburg) was a gentleman of high standing, both as a soldier and citizen. Her mother was the third wife of her father, and quite young enough to have been his daughter. Of Capt. Vick's twenty-one children by his three marriages, Mary, the child of his old age, alone survives. Bereft of both her parents at an early age, the subject of this notice was adopted into the family of her maternal uncle, Mr. John Waddell, of North Carolina, under whose

* Abridged from "Queens of American Society," by Mrs. E. F. Ellett.

fostering care the young orphan developed into a womanhood of uncommon loveliness and promise.

Miss Vick began her career as a writer when very young: at first writing for the amusement of the home circle, verses, romances, plays, etc. For the composition of plays she displayed a remarkable talent, and several of her dramatic pieces were acted on the stage. She contributed to newspapers and magazines prose and poetry, under *noms de plume.*

Becoming a wife, Mrs. McKinne made a nest for herself in south Alabama; and from her beautiful sylvan home came, through the press, now a love story, a fantastic sketch, or a poem, "like music upon the waters," or a graphic description of the enchanting springs and customs of that beautiful Southern land where Nature is so beneficent.

She began writing for the juvenile world; and thousands of little readers have, we trust, been made wiser and better and happier for the sweet lessons of love, gentleness, and truth emanating from her pen. As a writer for children, she is exceedingly popular with both young and old. There is a freshness and naturalness about her little men and women peculiarly attractive and charming.

Mrs. McKinne now resides near Marianna, in the State of Florida.

March 15th, 1871.   A. W. H.

NORTH CAROLINA.

MARY BAYARD CLARKE.

BY JUDGE EDWIN G. READE.

NE of the sweetest poets and truest women of America is Mrs. Mary Bayard Clarke, a native of Raleigh, North Carolina. Her prose writings, as well as her poems, are characterized chiefly by simplicity, power, and naturalness. Hearing Daniel Webster speak, one was apt to feel, "That is just what ought to be said on the subject; and I could say it just as he has done." The like may truly be said of Mrs. Clarke's poetry: there is no straining after effect — no doubling and twisting to make a rhyme — no climbing after a sentiment, or ranting over a passion — no gaudy dress or want of neat attire. It is just what you would feel; and just what you, or anybody else, would say — as you think. But try it — and it will prove to be just what you *cannot* say. This simplicity and power makes her poetry in the parlor what Daniel Webster's speeches were in the Senate.

Mrs. Clarke is a daughter of Thomas P. Devereux, an eminent lawyer and large Roanoke planter: her grandmother, Mrs. Frances Devereux, a granddaughter of the celebrated logician, Jonathan Edwards, President of Princeton College, was a woman of remarkable intellectual endowments, and well known in the Presbyterian Church.

Reared in affluence, thoroughly educated, and highly accomplished, the subject of our notice married, at an early age, William J. Clarke, Esq., of North Carolina, who had entered the United States Army at the beginning of the Mexican war; and after being brevetted as a major for gallant conduct at the battles of the National Bridge, Paso Ovejas, and Cerro Gordo, had retired from the army on a pension granted him for wounds received in the service of his country, and resumed the practice of the law in his native State.

Her position in society was one of ease and elegance; and her contributions to literature were induced by the love of the beautiful and

442

intellectual, and by the ease with which she composed, both in prose and poetry. Her productions were mere pastimes — the pleasures of thought and the scintillations of genius. Her fragile form was soon, however, seen by her husband to be drooping: consumption was hereditary in her mother's family; and, to save her from falling a victim to it, he carried her, first to the West Indies, and finally to the salubrious climate of Western Texas, where she resided, with her little family, at San Antonio de Bexar, until the beginning of the late war, when they returned to North Carolina, and Major Clarke took command of the 24th North Carolina Regiment, and served during the whole war as its colonel. The long and "cruel war" brought adversities in fortune, and then came out all the force of Mrs. Clarke's character, the brilliancy of her genius, and the nobleness of her soul, in educating her children, sustaining her family, and inspiriting her countrymen. Her pen was constantly busy in correspondence, in poetry, and in translations from the French; in which latter she is considered by the best judges — educated Frenchmen — to be particularly happy.

Some of her poems were collected and published in a volume called "Mosses from a Rolling Stone; or, The Idle Moments of a Busy Woman," which was sold for the benefit of the fund for the *Stonewall Cemetery*, in Winchester, Va.; but much the larger, and, her friends say, much the better portion of them have only appeared in the periodicals of the day.

What Mrs. Clarke was some few years ago, is very graphically and truthfully portrayed in a sketch which appeared not long since, from the pen of some unknown admirer who met her in Havana. All her faculties are now matured. Not so beautiful, of course, as when younger, she is yet far more interesting. Her conversational powers are remarkable, and her manners distinguished by their graceful ease and playfulness. Sparkling and impulsive, she is also gentle, amiable, pious, and industrious beyond her strength.

In all she has written, there cannot be found a sentiment that is not as pure as snow, nor an expression unsuited for the ear of the most delicate refinement. Though much of her own history and many of her trials are necessarily shadowed forth in her poetry, there is no appearance in it of an effort to "serve up her own heart with brain-sauce" for the taste of the public.

"The Mother's Dream," in which she says "conflicting duties wore away her strength and life," though doubtless a page from her own experience, speaks directly to the heart of every conscientious mother, and is but a leaf from the life of all who, like her, resolve to climb the hill of maternal duty,

> " Unmurmuring at the petty round she daily trod,
> But doing what came first, and leaving all to God."

" My Children " were emphatically *her* children.   It was published first in the New Orleans " Picayune," anonymously, and as many as a dozen friends, in different parts of the United States, cut it out and sent it to her, because it so exactly suited her and her two little ones. Who, that knows them, can doubt that she expresses her own feelings, when she says,

> " Though many other blessings
> Around my footsteps fall,
> My children and their father
> Are brightest of them all"?

How beautiful is her description of " the sweet notes of memory: "

> " Like the perfume that lingers where roses are crushed,
> The echo of song when the music is hushed!"

And how chaste and poetic the discrimination in " Smiles and Roses," where she says:

> "A smile may be given to many —
> 'T is only of friendship a part;
> But I give not a kiss unto any
> Who has not the love of my heart!"

These selections are all from her earlier poems: those written later in life have more concentrated force, and more passionate depth of feeling, with equal sweetness and simplicity.

Her lines to General Robert E. Lee are highly poetical and finished; so much is seldom found concentrated and clearly expressed in such a short space:

> "You lay your sword with honor down,
> And wear defeat as 't were a crown,
> Nor sit, like Marius, brooding o'er
> A ruin which can rise no more;
> But from your Pavia bear away
> A glory brightening every day"—

describes General Lee's deportment and conduct since the surrender most accurately; while the closing lines show an appreciation of the feelings hidden under his dignified serenity which must have touched his heart when he read them:

> "But who can tell how deep the dart
> Is rankling in your noble heart,
> Or dare to pull the robe aside
> Which Cæsar draws his wounds to hide?"

"Must I Forget?" which was by mistake put among the translations from the French, is not excelled by anything Byron ever wrote for the strong expression of a deep passion; while "It Might Have Been," "Under the Lava," and "Grief," have a depth and force of feeling, with a clearness and terseness of expression seldom found in the writings of a woman. This is but a tame criticism of what will in future be cherished as part of the purest and brightest literature of the age; but space beyond the limits of this article would be needed to do justice to the subject.

The following is a sketch of Mrs. Clarke, taken from a Baltimore paper:

"LA TENELLA.

"Some years ago, during a 'health-trip to the tropics,' it was my good fortune to spend four months in the company of a lady who is now well known in Southern literature, not only as 'Tenella,' the *nom de plume* she first adopted, but also by her real name of Mrs. Mary Bayard Clarke. Sprightly, intellectual, and remarkable, not only for her easy, graceful manners, but also for her delicate, fragile beauty, she was the acknowledged 'queen of society' in the circle in which she moved. The Spanish Creoles are very frank in their admiration of beauty, which they regard as the gift of God, not only to the possessor, but to the admirer of it; and nothing like the *furore* created among them by the blue eyes, fair complexion, masses of soft, sunny curls, and clear-cut, intellectual features of this lady can be conceived of in this country.

"The first time I ever saw her was at the Tacon Theatre. She was leaning on the arm of Mr. Gales Seaton, of the 'National Intelligencer,' and surrounded by three or four British naval and Spanish army officers, in full uniform; and as the party walked into the private box of the Spanish admiral, every eye was turned upon them, and a hum of admiration rose from the spectators, such as could only be heard, in similar circumstances, from a Spanish audience.

"Shortly after this, I met her at a ball given by the British consul-general at the Aldama Palace, and was presented to her by Mr. Seaton, and, from that time, saw her almost daily for the four months during which she reigned the acknowledged queen of the small but select circle of English and Americans residing in the city of Havana; increased, as it is every winter, by visitors from every part of the United States, English, American, and French naval officers, and such other foreigners as speak English. A more brilliant circle than it was that winter it would be hard to find anywhere.

"But while to casual observers Mrs. Clarke was but the *enfant gaté* of society, to those who looked further she was also the highly cultivated, intellectual woman. The Honorable Miss Murray, then on her American tour, was charmed with her, and said she was the only woman she had met in America, who, without being a blue-stocking, was yet thoroughly educated. 'She has not an accomplishment,' said that lady, 'beyond her highly cultivated conversational powers; but they, with her beauty and graceful manners, would render her an ornament to any circle in which she might move.'

"But the lady-in-waiting of Queen Victoria was mistaken, for Mrs. Clarke had two accomplishments rarely found in perfection among ladies: she was a bold, fearless, and remarkably graceful horsewoman, and played an admirable game of chess.

"Speaking one day to Mr. Seaton of her quickness, and the felicitous skill with which she threw off little *jeu d'esprits*, in the shape of *vers de société*, he replied: 'She is capable of better things than she has yet done; and, if she lives long enough, will, I predict, make a name for herself among the poets of our country. I may not live to see the noontide of her success, but I already discern its dawn.' He did not live to see much more than this dawn, but he instigated and suggested much that has brightened that success. Walking one day in the *Quinta del Obispo* with Mrs. Clarke, he said to her, 'I shall expect a poem from you, describing these triumphs of summer as beautifully as you have already described the "Triumphs of Spring." ' It was not until years after that 'Gan Eden' appeared in the 'Southern Literary Messenger:' and, although my poor friend had long before died of the disease with which he was threatened when he uttered these words, I saw the effect of them as soon as I read that poem, which is one of the most truthful as well as poetic descriptions of the tropical beauties of the 'Isle of Flowers:'

> "'T is the Queen of the Antilles
> Seated on her emerald throne,
> Crowned with ever-blooming flowers
> And a beauty all her own.
> With a grace that's truly regal,
> Sits she in her lofty seat,
> Watching o'er the subject islands
> In the ocean at her feet.

> ' While its waters, blue as heaven,
>   Laughing, leap upon her breast,
> Where all nature ever seemeth
>   For a happy bridal drest.
> Truly is it called " Gan Eden,"
>   'T is a garden of delight;
> But, alas! the serpent's trailing
>   O'er the beauty casts a blight.'

" All can realize the beauty of these lines; but none but one who has seen 'a stately ceyba-tree' in 'the poisonous embraces' of a 'deadly *Jagua Chacho*' — a creeping vine of exquisite beauty, which destroys all life in the tree to which it clings — can fully realize the beauty as well as the force of the simile which follows it. Neither can justice be done to the verse,

> ' Where the cucullos at even —
>   Insect watchmen of the night —
> On the sleeping leaves and flowers
>   Shed their emerald-tinted light,'

by one who has never seen the long files of watchmen, each with his lantern lighted, start from the Plaza, and scatter over the city of Havana just as the short tropic twilight begins, nor marked the beautiful, pale, green-tinted glow cast by the Cuban fire-flies — cucullos — over the object on which they light.

" Several of the poems in Mrs. Clarke's last book, 'Mosses from a Rolling Stone,' show, to one intimate with him, that Mr. Seaton, who was a man of rare taste and great originality of thought, had at this time much influence in developing the powers which he saw were unknown in their full force to their possessor. Let me not, however, be understood as detracting from Mrs. Clarke's originality by this remark. It is the attribute of art to suggest infinitely more than it expresses, and of genius to catch suggestions, no matter from what source, and reproduce them stamped with its own unmistakable mark; and one of the chief beauties of Mrs. Clarke's poetry lies in her ability to invest with a new and poetic beauty the common things of every-day life. Who can read without emotion those exquisite lines of hers, 'The Rain upon the Hills'? or that beautiful household-poem 'The Mother's Dream'? She is as remarkable for strength as for richness of imagery: there is nothing weak in any of her poems, and some passages of great force and depth of feeling. Take, for instance, 'Aphrodite' and 'It Might ‚Have Been:' when I read them, I felt that Mr. Seaton's prophecy was fulfilled, and she had indeed 'made herself a name among the poets of our land,' and was a literary as well as a social queen.

" I cannot better close this short and imperfect sketch than by giving you an account of the reading of her magnificent poem, 'The Battle of Manassas,' among the prisoners of Fort Warren. Mr. S. Teakle Wallis, of Baltimore, was the first to get the paper in which it was published. It was the hour for exercise, and most of the Confederate prisoners were in the court. Rushing down among them, Mr. Wallis jumped on a barrel and exclaimed, 'Boys, I have something to read to you.' From the animation of his manner, and the sparkle of his eye, they knew it was something they would like, and instantly gathered around him, when he read, with all the emphasis of a poet who feels every word that he utters:

'Now glory to the Lord of Hosts! oh, bless and praise His Name!
For he has battled in our cause, and brought our foes to shame.
And honor to our Beauregard, who conquered in His might,
And for our children's children won Manassas' bloody fight.
Oh! let our thankful prayers ascend, our joyous praise resound,
For God — the God of victory — our untried flag hath crowned.'

" Before he had half finished reading there was not one of those strong men who did not shed tears; and when he had finished, such a shout went up from them that the guards came running out to see if there was not an outbreak among the prisoners.

" I have never seen Mrs. Clarke since we parted on the 'Isle of Flowers,' but I have watched her literary career ever since, and eagerly read all the poems under the signature of 'Tenella.' Latterly, she has turned her attention more to prose than poetry, and is a contributor to 'The Land we Love,' as well as several other periodicals. Her 'Aunt Abby the Irrepressible,' in the first-mentioned magazine, has rendered her name a household word among all its readers. After several years spent in Texas, she returned to her native State, and at present resides in North Carolina. She has won considerable reputation by her translations from the French, and some of her translations of Victor Hugo's poems have been republished in England, where they attracted attention by the beauty of the rhythm into which they are so truthfully rendered.

But her 'Battle of Manassas,' 'Battle of Hampton Roads,' and her 'Rebel Sock,' together with other of her war poems, have given her a home reputation which renders her poems 'household words' by many a Southern hearth."

Mrs. Clarke seldom signs her name to her prose articles. Shortly after her return from Havana, she wrote " Reminiscences of Cuba," for the "Southern Literary Messenger," 1855. She translated from the French for a Confederate publication, "Marguerite; or, Two Loves," and has published considerably under the pseudonym of "Stuart Leigh." " General Sherman in Raleigh," " The South Expects Every Woman to do her Duty," and other sketches, appearing in the " Old Guard," New York, with "The Divining Rod," in Demorest's "Monthly" in the fall of 1867, and a novelette in " Peterson's Magazine," and " Social

Reminiscences of Noted North-Carolinians," appearing in " The Land we Love"—beside contributing as editress to the " Literary Pastime," a weekly journal published in Richmond—show she is an elegant prose writer.

In 1854, Mrs. Clarke published "Wood-Notes," a collection of North Carolina verse. In 1871, an elegant volume entitled "Clytie and Zenobia; or, The Lily and the Palm: a Poem." She resides in Newberne, N. C.

1871.

APHRODITE.

'T was in the spring-time of the world,
The sun's red banners were unfurled,
And slanting rays of golden light
Just kissed the billows tipped with white,
And through the waters' limpid blue
Flashed down to where the sea-weed grew,
While rainbow hues of every shade
Across the restless surface played.
Then, as the rays grew stronger still,
They sought the sea-girt caves to fill,
And sparkled on the treasures rare
That all unknown were hidden there.
Roused by their warm, electric kiss,
The ocean thrilled with wak'ning bliss:
Its gasping sob and heaving breast
The power of inborn life confest;
But, though their waves were tossed ashore,
Upon their crests no life they bore.

Deep hidden in its deepest cave,
Unmoved by current, wind, or wave,
A purple shell, of changing shade,
By nature's careful hand was laid:
The clinging sea-weed, green and brown,
With fibrous grasp still held it down
Despite the waters' restless flow;
But when they caught that deep'ning glow,
They flushed with crimson, pink, and gold,
And from the shell unclasped their hold
Its shadowy bonds thus drawn aside,
It upward floated on the tide;
But still its valves refused to yield,
And still its treasure was concealed.

Close shut upon the waves it lay
Till warmly kissed by one bright ray;
When, lo! its pearly tips unclose,
As ope the petals of the rose,
And pure and fresh as morning dew
Fair Aphrodite rose to view.
First — like a startled child amazed —
On earth and air and sea she gazed;
Then shook the wavy locks of gold
That o'er her neck and bosom rolled,
Loosened the cestus on her breast,
'Gainst which her throbbing heart now prest;
For, ah! its clasp could not restrain
The new-born life that thrilled each vein,
Flushed to her rosy fingers' tips,
And deeply dyed her parted lips,
Spread o'er her cheek its crimson glow,
And tinged her heaving bosom's snow.

Conscious of beauty and its power,
She owns the influence of the hour —
Instinct with life, attempts to rise:
Her quick-drawn breath melts into sighs,
Her half-closed eyes in moisture swim,
And languid droops each rounded limb;
With yielding grace her lovely head
Sinks back upon its pearly bed,
Where changing shades of pink attest
The spot her glowing cheek hath prest.
There all entranced she silent lay,
Borne on 'mid showers of silvery spray,
Which caught the light and backward fell
In sparkling diamonds round her shell.
Thus, wafted by the western breeze,
Cytherea's flowery isle she sees:
Its spicy odors round her float,
And thither glides her purple boat;
And, when its prow had touched the land,
There stepped upon the golden.sand,
With life and love and beauty warm,
A perfect woman's matchless form.

The tale is old, yet always new,
To every heart which proves it true:
The limpid waters of the soul
In snow-crowned waves of feeling roll,

Until love's soft, pervading light
Has into color kissed the white,
And in its deep recesses shown
Rich treasures to itself unknown —
Though many restless sob and sigh,
Nor ever learn the reason why;
While others wake with sudden start
To feel the glow pervade their heart,
Flash down beneath its surface swell
And shine on Passion's purple shell,
Change to the rainbow's varying hue
The ties it may not rend in two;
Till doubts and fears, which held it fast,
Beneath love's glow relax their grasp:
Slowly the network fades away,
Like fleecy clouds at opening day,
And Passion, woke by warmth and light,
In deep'ning shades springs into sight.

But man the shell too often holds
Nor sees the beauty it unfolds;
Its close-shut valves refuse to part,
And show the depths of woman's heart.
And tossing on life's billows high,
The purple shell unoped may lie,
Till cast on Death's cold, rocky shore,
Its life and longing both are o'er.
But if Love's warm, entrancing light
Shall kiss the parting lips aright,
And wake to life the beauty rare
Which nature's self hath hidden there,
Beneath his soft, enraptured smile
'T is wafted to the flowery isle,
And Aphrodite steps ashore
A perfect woman — nothing more.

GRIEF.

"A great calamity is as old as the trilobites an hour after it has happened. It stains backward, through all the leaves we have turned over in the book of life, before its blot of tears, or of blood, is dry on the page we are turning." — *Autocrat of the Breakfast Table.*

'T was such a grief — too deep for tears —
Which aged my heart far more than years;

How old it seemed, e'en when 't was new,
Backward it stained life's pages through,
And, ere another leaf I turned,
On all my past its impress burned.
My happy days a mock'ry seemed —
I had not lived, but only dreamed;
And then, when first I wished it done,
Life seemed to me but just begun:
Begun in bitter unbelief
That Time could dull the edge of grief —
Could give me back my hope and faith,
Or bring me any good but death.
'T was but a moment; yet to me
It seemed a whole eternity!
I felt how gray my heart had grown;
Its plastic way was changed to stone
When Mis'ry there her signet set,
Impressing lines which linger yet.
In each fresh leaf of life I find
The shadow of this grief behind;
For though the page at first appears
Unsullied by the mark of tears,
They 'll blister through before 't is read:
A real grief is never dead!
Its iron finger, stern and dark,
Leaves on the face and heart its mark,
As quickly cut — as plainly told
As that the die stamps on the gold;
Though read aright, perchance, alone
By those who kindred grief have known —
Like Masons' signs, which seem but nought,
Although with deepest meaning fraught.
The grief which kills is silent grief;
For words, like tears, will bring relief:
Husband and wife from each conceal
The wounds which are too deep to heal.
But, oh! when Hope and Faith seem dead,
While many a page must yet be read,
And in despair the heart doth sigh
And wish with them it too might die,
Remember that no night's so dark
But we can see some little spark,
And patient wait till dawning day
Shall its red line of light display:

For if we keep our love alive,
Our hope and faith will both revive.
Thus, as life's ladder we ascend,
Our hope shall in fruition end —
Our faith be lost in sight at length —
Our charity increase in strength;
And grief, which stamps the heart and mind,
But coin the gold Love has refined.

LIFE'S FIG-LEAVES.

Life's fig-leaves! Tell me, are not they
The outside beauties of our way,
The pleasant things beneath whose shade
Our inner — spirit-life — is laid?
I own they oft give promise fair
Of fruit which never ripens there;
For though we seek with earnest hope
Some tiny bud that yet may ope,
'T is all in vain — for fruit or flower
The tree has not sufficient power.
And still the earnest spirit grieves,
Which, seeking fruit, finds only leaves.
When such I meet, it calls to mind
The Saviour's warning to mankind:
"The time for fruit was not yet nigh."
Then wherefore must the fig-tree die?
Nature demanded leaves alone;
But yet He said, in solemn tone,
"Let no more fruit upon thee grow,"
That He to us this truth might show:
All life for some good end is given,
And should bear fruit on earth for heaven;
Its leaves and blossoms go for nought,
Unless they are with promise fraught:
No buds for fruit the fig-tree bore,
Hence it was blighted evermore,
And unto man still mutely saith,
A barren life is living death.
And so the parable should teach
That soul which does not upward reach.

MARY MASON.

MRS. MASON is the wife of Rev. Dr. Mason, of Raleigh. She has written several books for children. She is entirely self-taught, and her works are remarkable from that fact, besides possessing considerable literary merit. She cuts cameos and moulds faces; and, for a self-taught artist, her "likenesses" are excellent. Had she made "sculpture" a study from early youth, we warrant that the name of Mary Mason would have been as familiar to the world as is that of "Harriet Hosmer."

A head of General Lee, cut in cameo by her, is said to be exquisite.

She has recently published a book entitled "The Young Housewife's Counsellor and Friend." Philadelphia, 1871. This book will give directions in every department of household duty; with ample receipts of the choicest kinds tried, and improved by Mrs. Mason, and very many of them originating with herself.

CORNELIA PHILLIPS SPENCER.

MRS. SPENCER is a daughter of Prof. Phillips, of the University, and resides at Chapel Hill, North Carolina. She contributed a series of articles to the "Watchman," a weekly journal published in New York, in 1866, by Rev. Dr. Deems, of North Carolina. These articles were published in a volume, entitled "The Last Ninety Days of the War in North Carolina." This volume is a narrative of events in detail of the war, and personal sketches, showing, says a would-be facetious reviewer, "how the people of the Old North State ate, drank, and were clothed; and telling how the fowls were foully appropriated by vile marauders." The last chapter of the book is devoted to a history of the University of North Carolina.

1868.

FANNY MURDAUGH DOWNING.

BY H. W. HUSTED, ESQ.

HIGH blood runs in the veins of this gifted lady, and she came honestly by the talents for which she is so eminently distinguished. She was born in Portsmouth, Virginia, and her literary life commenced in North Carolina, in 1863. The Old North State awards to Virginia the honor of her birth, but cannot waive claim to her literary labors.

She is the daughter of the late Hon. John. W. Murdaugh, a distinguished name in the Old Dominion. She was married, in 1851, to Charles W. Downing, Esq., of Florida, and at that time its Secretary of State; and she is blessed in four bright and beautiful children.

Another writer has said of her, and said truly: "Her eyes are black," (they are large and lustrous too,) "her hair of a magnificent, glossy blackness," (and a glorious flood of hair it is!) "her carriage stately, queen-like, and graceful, and in conversational powers she has few equals."

Her health is extremely delicate, but her spirits are always bright, and her heart brave and buoyant.

Many of her works are composed while too weak to leave her bed; and a jolly comedy of three acts, called "Nobody Hurt," was thus dashed off in ten hours. Daniel Webster has been called "a steam-engine in breeches;" but Daniel was a man, almost as strong in body as he was in mind. Mrs. Downing, fragile as she is, has performed an amount of intellectual literary labor which may well entitle her to be saluted as (with reverence be it spoken) a steam-engine in crinoline. When she began to write for the public, which she did with the *nom de plume* of "Viola," she announced her intention in a letter to a friend in these words:

"I shall write first to see if I can write; then for money, and then for fame!"

She has proved to the perfect satisfaction of the court and jury by which her merits were tried that she "can write," and write well. At present, she says, she is in the second-stage of her programme; and, in catering to the general public taste, is compelled to bow to its decrees, in instances where her purer Southern taste would suggest a far different and less sentimental style.

One of these days, we trust the land we love will be able to foster, cherish, and *pay for* a literature of its own, and then our authors may write at the same time for money *and* fame. This one of them, in yielding to stern necessity and writing for money, has also achieved ample fame.

Mrs. Downing's first publication was a poem entitled "Folia Autumni," and its success was so great that it was rapidly followed by numerous other poetical effusions, most of which have a religious tinge, and seem the breathings of a subdued and pure spirit. They are all remarkable for musical rhythm, and the easy and graceful flow of feelings which can never be spoken so well as in the language of song.

Among the best of these are her "Egomet Ipse," a terrible heart-searcher; "Faithful unto Death," full of a wild and nameless pathos; and "Desolate," which is not exceeded by any elegiac poem in the language. As a specimen of her minor poems, we select

SUNSET MUSINGS.

Love of mine, the day is done —
All the long, hot summer day;
In the west, the golden sun
Sinks in purple clouds away;
Nature rests in soft repose,
Not a zephyr rocks the rose,
Not a ripple on the tide,
And the little boats, that glide
Lazily along the stream,
Flit like shadows in a dream.
Not one drooping leaf is stirred;
Bee, and butterfly, and bird
Silence keep. Above, around
Hangs a stillness so profound,
That the spirit, awe-struck, shrinks,
As of Eden days it thinks,
Half expectant here to see
The descending Deity!

Love of mine, when life's fierce sun
  To its final setting goes,
Its terrestrial journey run,
  Varied course of joys and woes,

May there come a quiet calm,
Bringing on its wings a balm
To our hearts, which aching feel
"Sorrow here has set its seal!"
May a stillness soft as this
Soothe our souls in purest bliss,
Till the worry and the strife
Of this fever we call life,
With its pain and passion cease,
And we rest in perfect peace.
Love of mine, may we behold
Eden's visitant of old,
When our last breath dies away,
By us at the close of day!

These poems were followed by "Nameless," a novel of merit, filled with sprightly descriptions and delineations of character, but which was, from some unexplained reason, too suddenly crowded to a close, before its plot could be evolved and completed. It is said to have been hastily written in ten days, as a proof whether or not she could write prose. She had already written good poetry which was appreciated and applauded, and her next venture was in prose fiction. "*Tentanda via est*," quoth Mrs. Downing, and spread her trial wings. This trial proved the existence of high power, which has since been wonderfully improved, developed, and matured in her excellent novels, "Perfect through Suffering" and "Florida." Then came a series of poems of a sterner sort, which were deemed by some to be just a trifle rebellious, but which found a responsive feeling deep in the hearts of thousands of true men, who are not willing to wear chains without giving them an occasional shake. Of this style are "Confederate Gray," "Holly and Cypress," "Prometheus Vinctus," "Memorial Flowers," "Our President," "Two Years Ago," "Sic Semper Tyrannis," a majestic lyric, which thrills each Virginian heart to the core, and glorious little "Dixie," which stirs to its fountains every Southern soul, and teaches it

"To live for Dixie! Harder part!
To stay the hand—to still the heart—
To seal the lips, enshroud the past—
To have no future—all o'ercast—
To knit life's broken threads again,
And keep her mem'ry pure from stain—
This is to live for Dixie!"

In very playfulness, and as if to show her great diversity of talent and her surprising power of writing by antagonism instead of sympathy, and conceiving what could have only existed with her by the aid of a most lively and exuberant fancy, she has written some of the most musical and genial poems of love and wine since the grapestone choked the old Teian bard.

It may be said of her as of the celebrated French authoress, that she "writes by her imagination, and lives by her judgment." In truth, she seems to rejoice in a sort of "double life" of her own, and to sport *ad lib.* in whichever she pleases. One is the life common to us all; the other, such as poetical fancy alone can build up and people with its own bright and beautiful creations, and which she has described in her poem, "The Realm of Enchantment."

Mrs. Downing's home is in Charlotte, N. C.

January, 1869.

————o∘⦂⦂⦂∘o————

VIRGINIA DURANT COVINGTON.

M RS. COVINGTON is a native of Marion, South Carolina. Her home is now Rockingham, Richmond County, North Carolina. During the late war, Mrs. Covington made her *début* as a writer in the "Southern Field and Fireside," published at Augusta, Ga., as "Fabian." Since that time she has been a frequent contributor to Southern periodicals, under the assumed names of "Casper," "Popinack," and under her own name. She has published enough to fill several large volumes. Her most ambitious production appeared serially in the "XIX Century," a Charleston magazine, (1870,) entitled "Morna Elverley; or, Outlines of Life." We are not able to give lengthy extracts, and a brief one would not do justice to the writer. The work will probably appear in a volume.

1871.

MRS. MARY AYER MILLER,

(*Luola.*)

THE subject of this sketch was born in Fayetteville, North Carolina, but on the death of her father, General Henry Ayer, removed with her mother, when only eight years old, to Lexington, North Carolina, for the purpose of being educated by her uncle, the Rev. Jesse Rankin, a divine of the Presbyterian Church, who had a classical school at that place.

She received the same education given to the boys of her uncle's school, which was preparatory for the University of North Carolina, and began as early as her fourteenth year to show signs of the poetic talent which she has since cultivated with success. She married early a young lawyer, Mr. Willis M. Miller, who gave promise of making a reputation at the Bar, but abandoned his profession about a year after his marriage, and commenced studying for the Presbyterian ministry. This change in the plan of his life, after taking on himself the cares of a family, involved a change in his style of living, which drew his wife almost entirely from literary to domestic pursuits, as his salary, after being licensed to preach, was too small to allow much leisure to the mother of his rapidly increasing family. Consequently, her pen was laid aside for the needle just when her poems, under the signature of "Luola," were beginning to attract attention by the smoothness of their flow and the purity and tenderness of their sentiment. But the spirit of song was latent in her heart, and burst forth, from time to time, in little gushes, which kept her memory alive in the hearts of those who had already begun to appreciate her poetry. In a letter to a friend, she says: "I have never made the slightest effort for popularity, but set my little songs afloat as children do their paper boats: if they had sail and ballast enough, to float; if not, to sink."

Some have sunk; for, like most women who write *con amore*, and not for publication, she does not always give her poems the after critical supervision of the scholar, but is content to throw them off with the easy rapidity of the poet.

459

But many of them show the fire of genius; and, like the love-boats of the Hindoo girls on the Ganges, cast a light on the waters as they float down the stream of Time, and all are distinguished by some grace which touches the heart, or pleases the fancy for the moment.

As a writer for children, Mrs. Miller has been very successful. The Presbyterian Board of Publication has issued several of her works as Sunday-school books; and her poems in the youth's department of the "North Carolina Presbyterian," and the "Central Presbyterian," published in Richmond, Virginia, have rendered her a favorite among the little ones, who have as keen an appreciation of what is suited to their taste and capacity as older readers have of what pleases them; and such happy conceits as that of "Linda Lee" speak directly, not only to their fancy, but also to their hearts.

Mrs. Miller resides at present in Charlotte, North Carolina, writing occasionally for publication, but as often carrying her poems for days in her memory, until she can steal time from the duties and cares of a wife and mother to commit them to paper.

A few of her poems are preserved in "Wood Notes," a collection of North Carolina poetry made by Mrs. Mary Bayard Clarke, and published in 1854; but most of them have appeared only in the newspapers.

1868.   M. B. C.

MRS. SARAH A. ELLIOTT

IS the author of "Mrs. Elliott's Housewife," containing practical receipts in cookery and valuable suggestions for young housekeepers. In one volume, 12mo. Published by Hurd & Houghton, New York, 1870.

This is an excellent collection of practical receipts in cookery, nearly all of which have been tested and approved by the author, a well-known lady of Oxford, North Carolina.

1871.

FRANCES C. FISHER.

"CHRISTIAN REID," the author of "Valerie Aylmer," a novel. New York, 1870.

"Valerie Aylmer," the first book of Miss Fisher, written for amusement, proved the most successful first effort of any Southern writer.

Miss Fisher is the eldest daughter of Col. **Charles** F. Fisher, who lost his life on the battle-field of Manassas. She is **a** native of Salisbury, N. C., which is her home.

She has recently published, in "Appleton's Journal," "Morton House," a story of Southern life of thirty years ago.

From a criticism of "Valerie Aylmer," by Mr. T. C. De Leon, in the "Mobile Register," I quote:

"Since the older novelists of America left the scene, — since Hawthorne, Cooper, Simms, and their peers, made the lighter part of our literature respectable, — the production of home-made works of fiction has dwindled into a mere farce. Since before the war, the novels by American authors that have attracted great attention and enforced respectful criticism can be counted on the fingers of one hand. Three of these works have been of Southern birth. The last of the trio is 'Valerie Aylmer;' and no work of the day has called forth more general, and apparently more honest, criticism. And the gross result of this has been highly commendatory, notwithstanding the fact that the work is plainly from the hand of a woman, undoubtedly a *Southern* woman, and almost as perceptibly an untried one in that most difficult field she has chosen — character romance; for ' Valerie Aylmer' depends for its power far less upon plot than it does upon character drawing. In the story itself there is little novelty of construction or development. The heroine, a Southern creole, is about to lose a fortune, expected from her grandfather, through the unlooked-for appearance of Maurice Darcy, a cousin, to whose parents the rich grandfather had done great wrong. In his reparation, M. Vacquant strives to combine justice and inclination by ' making a match ' between Valerie and Maurice. Upon this hinges the whole story. Noble, strong, and of iron will that knows no yielding, even to powerful urging from his own heart, Darcy spurns the fortune and the wife, on suspicion of the latter's falsity. Valerie, proud, and with strength to suffer, though not to resist, the effects upon her physical and moral nature, separates from Darcy, and eats her own heart in silence, until accident, and the patient endurance of his crippled brother, Gaston, melts her resolve, and she goes forth to seek him in the midst of the Maximilian troubles in Mexico. Such is the idea of the work; and it is well carried out by many characters, some of them too sketchy to make deep impression, and all of them rather types of their class than emphasized photographs of individuals. Valerie herself is perhaps the most detailed picture; and she is the true Southern girl that buds into womanhood under our passion-producing sun, with the dangerous nourishment of flattery and full freedom of action. Superficial pride, reckless love of power, and carelessness of result, almost cover up the true womanhood, and possibility of deep, enduring, womanly love in her heart. Time and trouble kill the dangerous weeds, and bring the real flower into the one light which can make it — even amid the ruins of her power and her happiness, as it seems —

'Smell sweet, and blossom in the dust.'

"Dealing with people of wealth and fashion, and of the highest refinement, the story carries us from Louisiana to Baltimore; then, rather unfortunately, we think, to the south of France; and back, for the *dénouement*, to Havana. In all its scenes, sensation is never introduced; and the reaching after dramatic effect, naturally weak in the unpractised hand, is ever subordinated to good taste. The style is pure, clear, and free from most affectations of a young — especially of a young female — writer; and the absence of pedantry is refreshing in promise of a vigor that can but grow in such good soil into a brilliant future. The sentiment is strongly Southern; but it never hurries our author into forgetfulness that the war is over; but its history is not yet ready. On the whole, the work is one of graceful and pleasant description; not without rare strength in character outlining, and with promise — when time shall have steadied the hand — of powerful shading in the most difficult of society picturing."

The New York "Evening Post" reviews the book:

"'Valerie Aylmer' is undeniably quite charming; the plot interests and the style delights us; there is much excellence in its dramatic construction, and in its delineation of character, and, as a literary work, it is altogether worthy of praise. 'Christian Reid,' the pseudonymous author, betrays on almost every page a wide acquaintance with literature; not that encyclopædic pedantry which is so wearisomely manifested by certain popular novelists, and which ranges from the Talmud to Tennyson, but an easy familiarity with the best authors, and a love for whatever in them is pure and lovely and of good report. Many passages there are that run unconsciously into the earnestness of true eloquence, but we see no deliberate attempts at 'fine writing,' and we are never let fall from the clouds by a helpless anti-climax. No reader of 'Valerie Aylmer,' we are sure, will lay down the book without sharing in our own desire to hear from 'Christian Reid' again."

SOUTH CAROLINA.

SUE PETIGRU KING.

MRS. S. P. KING has been complimented by being called the "female Thackeray of America." She is a native of South Carolina — a daughter of the late Hon. James L. Petigru, a prominent lawyer of Charleston. She was early married to Mr. Henry King, a lawyer, and son of Judge Mitchell King, of Charleston. Her husband lost his life in defence of his native city during the late war.

Mrs. King's first book was "Busy Moments of an Idle Woman," this was followed by "Lily." The former was successful, and both were pictures of society. She collected a series of tales she had written for "Russell's Magazine," called "Crimes that the Law does not Reach," to which she added a longer story, "The Heart History of a Heartless Woman," published originally in the "Knickerbocker Magazine," and, under the title of "Sylvia's World," it was published by Derby & Jackson, New York, (1860.) This was the most popular of Mrs. King's books, although her last work, published during the war in the "Southern Field and Fireside," and afterward in pamphlet form, entitled "Gerald Gray's Wife," is her *chef-d'œuvre*. The characters in this novel *are* real people, breathing Charleston air, and were immediately recognized by the *élite* in Charleston society. We know of no book or writer that we can compare Mrs. King to. She is highly original, witty, satirical, and deeply interesting. Her writings are all pictures of society. It is said that her "Heartless Woman of the World" is herself. In society, Mrs. King was always surrounded by a group, who listened with interest to her brilliant flow of conversation. She could talk for hours without tiring her hearers with her sparkling scintillations. Repartee, as may be imagined from her books, is her forte. When William Makepeace Thackeray lectured in this country, and met Mrs. King, he said to her in a brusque manner: "Mrs. King, I am agreeably disappointed in you; I heard you were the fastest woman in America, and I detest fast women." She replied: "And I am agreeably surprised in you, Mr. Thackeray; for I heard you were no gentleman."

Mrs. King is below the medium height, fair; brilliant, variable eyes, black and gray and blue in turn; hair dark, and worn banded across a brow like her father's, high and broad, rarely seen in a woman; lips never ·at rest, showing superbly white teeth; hands and feet perfect; arms, bust, and shoulders polished ivory, and yet withal not beautiful as a whole; slightly lisping accent; and dress so artistic and ultra-fashionable that nature seemed buried in flowers.

Mrs. King despises foolish sentimentalism, and shows up human vice in all of her books. All of her characters are true to nature. Bertha St. Clair, who is one of the *dramatis personæ* in "Sylvia's World," and also in "Gerald Gray's Wife," is an exquisite portraiture. In the latter the characters are, as we have mentioned, from life—the false Gerald Gray still breathes the air of Charleston. That piece of insipidity, or "skim-milk, *soft* Cissy Clare," is strikingly true to nature, as are pompous Mr. Clare, sturdy old Jacob Desborough, scheming Phillis, and the gallant Josselyn.

The transforming power of love, as displayed in the metamorphosis of plain Ruth Desborough to beautiful Ruth Grey, is very charmingly wrought out.

Mrs. King has published nothing since the close of the war; but shortly after the downfall of the Confederacy, she gave dramatic readings in various parts of the North, and is, we believe, now residing in Washington City.

A LOVERS' QUARREL.

There was not a more beautiful avenue of trees in all the world than that which led to the front entrance of Oaklevel. They were very old—they met overhead, and enlaced themselves with wreaths of moss; the sunlight came flickering through the branches, and fell stealthily and tremblingly upon the clean, smooth ground; little heaps of dead leaves lay here and there, scattered by each breath of the December breeze, and forming their tiny mounds in fresh places as the wind trundled them along.

On a fine, bright morning, some years since, two persons were slowly pacing up and down this grand, majestic walk. They were both young, and both were handsome. She was blonde, and he a dark, grave-looking man.

"Nelly, I don't like flirts."

"Yes, you do—you like me, don't you?"

"I don't like flirting."

"What do you call flirting? If I am to be serious, and answer your questions, and admit your reproofs and heed them, pray begin by answering me a little. Where and when do I flirt?"

"Everywhere, and at all times."

"Be more particular, if you please. Name, sir, name!"

"I am not jesting, Nelly. Yesterday, at that picnic, you talked in a whisper to John Ford, you wore Ned Laurens's flowers stuck in your belt-ribbon, you danced two waltzes with that idiot, Percy Forest, and you sat for a full hour *tête à tête* with Walter James, and then rode home with him. I wish he had broken his neck, —— him!" and a low-muttered curse ended the catalogue.

"If he had broken his neck, very probably he would have cracked mine; so, thank you; and please, Harry, don't swear: it is such an ungentlemanly habit, I wonder that you should have it. And now for the list of my errors and crimes. The mysterious whisper to John Ford was to ask him if he would not invite Miss Ellis to dance; I had noticed that no one had yet done so. You gave me no flowers, although your sister's garden is full of them this week; so I very naturally wore Ned Laurens's *galanterie*, in the shape of half a dozen rosebuds. Percy Forest may be a goose, but he waltzes, certainly, with clever feet; one of those waltzes I had offered early in the day to you, and you said you preferred a polka. Walter James is an old friend of mine, and, for the matter of that, of yours too. We talked very soberly: I think that his most desperate speech was the original discovery that I have pretty blonde ringlets, and when he falls in love, it shall be with a woman who has curls like mine. You best know whether papa allows me to drive with you since our accident: my choice lay between a stuffy, stupid carriage, full of dull people, and a nice, breezy drive in an open wagon, with a good, jolly creature like Walter, whom you and I know to be, despite his compliments to my Eve-like coloring, *eperdument amoureaux* of Mary Turner's dark beauty. Now, Harry, have you not been unreasonable?"

"How can I help being so, Nelly, darling, when I am kept in this state of misery?" answered Harry, whose frowning brow had gradually smoothed itself into a more placable expression. "What man on earth could patiently endure seeing the woman he adores free to be sought by every one — feeling himself bound to her, body and soul, and yet not being able to claim her in the slightest way — made to pass his life in solitary wretchedness because an old lady and gentleman are too selfish —"

"Hush, hush, Harry! You are forgetting. I am very young; papa and mamma think me too young to bind myself by any engagement."

"It is not that. They choose to keep you, as long as they can, mouldering with themselves in this old house."

"Harry!"

"Or else it is I whom they dislike, and refuse to receive as a son. Too young? why, you are nineteen. It is an infamous shame!"

"I will not speak to you, if you go on in this way. You know just as well

59

as I do what their reasons are. My poor sister Emily made a love-match at eighteen, and died, broken-hearted, at twenty-three. Her husband was a violent, jealous man, who gave her neither peace nor valuable affection. He looked upon her as a pretty toy, petted her, and was raging if a gentleman spoke more than ten words by her side, so long as her beauty and novelty lasted. Her health failed, her delicate loveliness departed, and with these went his worthless passion. I was a mere child then — the last living blossom of a long garland of household flowers — when my father laid his beloved Emily in her early grave. I stood by his great chair that sad evening in my little black gown when he returned from the funeral, and he placed his hands upon my head and made a vow that never, with his consent, should his only remaining darling follow in the steps of the lost one. 'No man shall have her who has not proved himself worthy to win her. As Jacob served Laban shall her future husband serve for her, if it please God that she live and that she have suitors.' Day by day, year by year, he has but strengthened himself in this determination; and when, last spring, you applied to him for my hand, he told you frankly that if you had patience to wait, and were convinced of the strength of our mutual attachment, on my twenty-third birthday you might claim a Mrs. Harry Trevor from his fireside."

"But, Nelly, four years to wait! and all because poor Mrs. Vernon had weak lungs — forgive me, dearest Helen, dearest Helen!" But Helen walked on and away from him, with proper indignation.

With impatient strides he passed her, just as they reached the lawn which bordered the avenue and surrounded the house. Extending his arms to bar her passage, "Listen to me, my own dear Nelly," he pleaded. "I was wrong to say that; but you cannot understand, my angel, how furious and intractable I become when I think of those incalculable days between this time and the blessed moment when I shall be sure of you."

"If you are not sure of me now, you do not fancy that you will be any more so then, do you?" asked Helen, gravely; but she permitted him to lead her away from the stone steps that she was about mounting, and back to the quiet alley under the old oaks.

He drew her arm through his, gently stroking her gloved hand as it rested in his own.

"If there is no truth and belief between us to-day, there will be none then," Helen pursued. "I am, in the sight of heaven, by my own free will and wish, your affianced wife. All the priests on earth would not make me more so, in spirit, than I am now. But I respect my father's wishes and feelings; and you must do so too," she added, lifting her eyes with such a lovely look of tenderness that Harry, as he pressed her hand with renewed fervor, murmured a blessing in quite a different tone from the one which he had devoted to the now forgotten Walter James.

He glanced around, and was about to seal his happiness upon the dainty pink lips, smiling so sweetly and confidingly; but Helen, blushing and laughing, said: "Take care: papa is reading yesterday's paper at the left-hand window of the dining-room; and I think, if one eye is deciding upon the political crisis, the other is directed this way."

"We are watched, then!" exclaimed Trevor, passionately, all his short-lived good-humor again flown. "This is worse and worse."

Helen looked at her lover with a calm, searching expression in her blue eyes. "Perhaps papa is right. He has a terror of violent men, and he may like to see if you are always as mild as he sees you in his presence."

Trevor bit his lip and stamped his foot impatiently. Helen hummed a tune, and settled her belt-ribbon with one hand, while she played the notes she was murmuring on the young gentleman's coat sleeve with the other.

He let the mischievous fingers slide through his arm, and "thought it was going to rain, and he had better be thinking of his ride to the city."

Nelly looked up at the blue heavens, where not a speck of a cloud was visible, and gravely congratulated him on a weather-wisdom which was equally rare and incomprehensible.

"But your season, my dear Harry, is always April. Sunshine and storm succeed so rapidly, that you can never take in the unbroken calm of this — December, for instance. Beside, I thought you were to stay all night with us? I know mamma expects you to do so."

"I am very much obliged," said Mr. Trevor, haughtily; "I have business in town."

"Clients? court sitting?" asked Nelly, innocently, and demurely lifting her pretty eyebrows.

"No. There is a party at Lou Wilson's, and I half promised to go. We are to try some new figures of the German."

"Indeed!" Nelly's eyes flashed, and the color stole up deeper to her cheek. "I won't detain you."

She bowed, and turned from him with a cold good-morning. Her heart was beating, and the tears were very near; but she managed to still the one, and send back the others, so as to say indifferently, over her shoulder: "Should you see Walter James, pray tell him that I shall be happy to learn that accompaniment by this evening; and, as there is a moon, (in spite of your storm,) he can ride out after business hours and practise the song. But, however, I won't trouble you; mamma is to send a servant to Mrs. James's some time to-day, and I will write a note."

"I think it will be useless. He is going to Miss Wilson's."

"Not if he can come here, I fancy," said the wilful little beauty, with a significant tone; and then, repeating her cool "Good-by — let us see you soon," she sauntered into the house, elaborately pausing to pick off some dead leaves from the geraniums that were sunning themselves on the broad steps by which she entered.

Thus parted two foolish children, one of whom had a moment before expressed the most overwhelming passion, and the other had avowed herself, "in the sight of heaven, his affianced wife!"

CAROLINE GILMAN.

MRS. GILMAN is the daughter of Samuel Howard, and was born in Boston, Mass., October 8th, 1794.

In 1819, Miss Howard married Samuel Gilman, who came to Charleston, S. C., where he was ordained pastor of the Unitarian Church, which pulpit he filled until his death in 1858.

In 1832, Mrs. Gilman commenced editing the "Rose-Bud," the pioneer juvenile *newspaper* of the United States. From this periodical she has printed at various times the following volumes:

Recollections of a New England Housekeeper.

Recollections of a Southern Matron.

Ruth Raymond; or, Love's Progress.

Poetry of Travelling in the United States.

Tales and Ballads.

Verses of a Lifetime.

Letters of Eliza Wilkinson during the invasion of Charleston.

Also, several volumes for youth, collected into one volume, and published as "Mrs. Gilman's Gift-Book."

Mrs. Gilman's life has been a long and useful one; and of her writings can be truly said, "she has written not one line she would wish to blot." For nearly half a century Charleston has been her home; and her wish is to make her final resting-place in the cemetery adjoining the church of which her husband was pastor.

March 31st, 1871.

468

MRS. CAROLINE H. JERVEY.

CAROLINE HOWARD GILMAN, the daughter of Rev. Samuel Gilman, a Unitarian clergyman, and Mrs. Caroline Gilman, the celebrated authoress, was born in Charleston, South Carolina, in 1823.

In 1840, Miss Gilman married Mr. Wilson Glover, a South Carolina planter, and was left a widow in 1846, with three children, one son and two daughters. She returned to her father's house, and immediately began to teach, and for fifteen years carried on a successful school in Charleston.

While engaged in teaching, she wrote papers for magazines, also poems, over the signature of "Caroline Howard;" and finally her novel, "Vernon Grove; or, Hearts as they Are," which appeared serially in the "Southern Literary Messenger," and was afterward published by Rudd & Carleton, New York, passing through several editions, and warmly received by the critics. "Vernon Grove" was copied for the press at night, after being in the school-room all day; and yet Mrs. Glover kept up all her social duties, visiting, entertaining, and seeming always to be as completely the mistress of her own hours as the idlest fine lady.

She is fastidiously neat and particular in all her surroundings, and a wonder for arranging and contriving. While in Greenville, during the war, says a friend, where her apartments and premises were unavoidably small, they were miracles of ingenuity and order.

In ——, 1865, Mrs. Glover married Mr. Louis Jervey, of Charleston, who had been devotedly attached to her for many years. By this marriage she has one daughter. Her son is married; and her eldest daughter has been, like herself, left a youthful widow, with two little children.

In Mrs. Jervey's home circle she is idolized; her temper is perfectly even and self-controlled, her judgment good and ready, and her unfailing cheerfulness and flow of pleasing conversation make her a charming companion. She talks even more cleverly than she writes, and has a vein of humor in speaking which does not appear at all in her novels. Mrs. Jervey is uncommonly youthful in appearance, is above the middle height, with a fine, full figure, and an erect, commanding carriage. Her hair is golden-red and abundant; her complexion is very fair, and with dark eyebrows and lashes she would be lovely: as it is, she is at times indisputably handsome. Her manner is striking, lady-like, perfectly self-possessed — not exactly *studied;* but " her memory is extremely good, and she never forgets to be graceful," never seems to give way to an awkward impulse, and is *always posed* and seen to advantage. A friend says: "I was constantly reminded of Mrs. Jervey by Ristori's attitudes and gestures."

We are sorry to say that this accomplished lady is at present in ill health — prohibited any literary labor, even the most careless letter-writing. Her latest novel, "Helen Courtenay's Promise," (published by George W. Carleton, New York, 1866,) was prepared for the press by dictation of an hour a day to one of her daughters. This novel has been styled the "production of a brilliant, creative fancy."

1869.   JEANIE A. DICKSON.

JULIA SLEEPING.

Hush! let the baby sleep!
Mark her hand so white and slender,
Note her red lip full and tender,
And her breathing, like the motion
Which the waves of calmest ocean
　　In their peaceful throbbings keep.

Hush! let the baby rest!
Who would wake from blissful sleeping,
To this world so filled with weeping,
Those sweet eyes, like stars o'erclouded,
Those calm eyes with dark fringe shrouded,
　　Those crossed hands upon her breast?

Hush! let the baby rest!
See each white and taper finger,
Where a rose-tint loves to linger,
As the sun at evening dying
Leaves a flush all warmly lying
　　In the bosom of the west!

See on her lips a smile!
'T is the light of dreamland gleaming
Like to morning's first faint beaming:
Hush! still solemn silence keeping,
Watch her, watch her in her sleeping,
 As she smiles in dreams the while.

I would paint her as she lies,
With brown ringlets damply clinging
To her forehead, shadows flinging
On its whiteness — or where tracings
Of the blue veins' interlacings
 On its snowy surface rise.

God hear our fervent prayer!
Through the whole of life's commotion,
As she stems the troubled ocean,
Give her calm and peaceful slumber;
And may sorrow not encumber
 Her unfolding years with care.

Ah, see, her sleep is o'er!
Flushed her cheek is: she is holding
Mystic converse with the folding
Of the curtains o'er her drooping:
What beholds she in their looping
 Mortals ne'er beheld before?

Now from her bath of sleep,
Many a deep'ning dimple showing,
She hath risen fresh and glowing,
Like a flower that rain hath brightened,
Or a heart that tears have lightened,
 Tears the weary sometimes weep.

Herself the silence breaks!
Hear her laugh, so rich and ringing!
Hear her small voice quaintly singing!
She hath won us by caressings:
We exhaust all words in blessings
 When this precious baby wakes.

A SUMMER MEMORY.

Beloved, 't was a night to shrine
   In happy thought *for years,*
A memory of certain joy,
   A spell 'gainst woe and tears.

And why? Was it because the moon,
   More bright than e'er before,
Stooped from her throne to kiss the waves
   That rippled to the shore?

Or was it that the gentle breeze,
   With whispers fond and sweet,
Brought fragrance from some spicy land
   And laid it at our feet?

Ah! never since primeval time
   Was night so fair as this —
So filled with joy, so fraught with peace,
   So marked with perfect bliss.

I seemed to live a fresh, new life,
   A life almost divine,
As on the glittering shore we sat,
   Thy meek eyes raised to mine.

Was it the *night* that brightened all?
   Oft comes the question now —
The *night* that brought such blest content?
   No, dearest, it was *thou.*

CAROLINE A. BALL.

MRS. BALL is the daughter of the late Rev. Edward Rutledge, an Episcopal clergyman of Charleston. Her early life was passed at the North, having been educated at the seminary of the Misses Edwards, in New Haven. Her first poem, or rather the first which caused any sensation, was written when she was sixteen, and was a satirical piece, in answer to an impertinent attack on woman in the "Yale Literary Magazine." It was published anonymously, and was freely discussed, in the presence of the fair author, by the students of her acquaintance, in terms of high compliment, or in condemnation of its severity.

Mrs. Ball is the wife of Mr. Isaac Ball, of Charleston. She never published under her own name until the struggle for "Southern independence" commenced. The poems she wrote were very popular: coming, as they did, from a heart full of love for her fatherland, they spoke to the hearts of the Southern people, inspired by the same mighty love.

Her poems are not studied efforts; but of and from the heart.

In 1866, a number of her poems on the war, originally published in the "Charleston Daily News," were printed in pamphlet form —

IN MEMORIAM

OF

OUR LOVED AND LOST CAUSE,

AND

OUR MARTYRED DEAD:

"Outnumbered — not outbraved."

This book was entitled "The Jacket of Gray, and Other Fugitive Poems."

THE JACKET OF GRAY.

Fold it up carefully, lay it aside,
Tenderly touch it, look on it with pride;
For dear must it be to our hearts evermore,
The jacket of gray our loved soldier-boy wore.

Can we ever forget when he joined the brave band
Who rose in defence of our dear Southern land,
And in his bright youth hurried on to the fray,
How proudly he donned it, the jacket of gray?

His fond mother blessed him, and looked up above,
Commending to Heaven the child of her love:
What anguish was hers mortal tongue cannot say,
When he passed from her sight in the jacket of gray.

But her country had called, and she would not repine,
Though costly the sacrifice placed on its shrine;
Her heart's dearest hopes on its altar she lay
When she sent out her boy in the jacket of gray.

Months passed, and war's thunders rolled over the land;
Unsheathed was the sword and lighted the brand;
We heard in the distance the sounds of the fray,
And prayed for our boy in the jacket of gray.

Ah! vain, all, all vain were our prayers and our tears;
The glad shout of victory rang in our ears;
But our treasured one on the red battle-field lay,
While the life-blood oozed out on the jacket of gray.

His young comrades found him, and tenderly bore
The cold, lifeless form to his home by the shore;
Oh! dark were our hearts on that terrible day,
When we saw our dead boy in the jacket of gray.

Ah! spotted and tattered, and stained now with gore
Was the garment which once he so proudly wore;
We bitterly wept as we took it away,
And replaced with death's white robes the jacket of gray.

We laid him to rest in his cold, narrow bed,
And graved on the marble we placed o'er his head,
As the proudest tribute our sad hearts could pay,
He never disgraced the jacket of gray.

Then fold it up carefully, lay it aside,
Tenderly touch it, look on it with pride;
For dear must it be to our hearts evermore,
The jacket of gray our loved soldier-boy wore.

MRS. MARY S. B. SHINDLER.

MARY STANLY BUNCE PALMER is a native of Beaufort, S. C., but removed while very young to the city of Charleston, where her father, the Rev. B. M. Palmer, was the highly honored pastor of the Independent Church on Meeting Street. She was chiefly educated at the seminary of the Misses Ramsay, in that city; but, in consequence of the delicate health which so often accompanies the delicate organism of the gifted children of song, she was sent for a short period to complete her studies in the more bracing climate of the North. She gave early evidence of poetic genius, and many of her school-mates remember with pleasure her impromptu and mirthful efforts in childhood. After her return to Carolina, Miss Palmer became known as a contributor to the "Rosebud" and other similar periodicals. Her graceful manners and sprightly conversation made her at all times a desirable companion; while her ready sympathy and thorough appreciation of the feelings of others rendered her a warmly cherished friend.

In 1835, Miss Palmer was united in marriage to Mr. Charles E. Dana, and accompanied him to the city of New York, where they spent three years, and then removed to the West. They were but a short time located in their new home, when one of those singular epidemics that sometimes sweep over the rich prairies, and enter (none know how) into the new settlements that populate that vast region of country, appeared in the vicinity of their residence, and in two short days Mr. Dana and their only child were numbered among its victims.

Alone, among comparative strangers, Mrs. Dana, rousing into action the latent energy of her character, sought and gained once more her Southern home. As the wearied birdling returns to the parent nest for rest and comfort, so this heart-stricken wanderer came back to the bosom of her family, and, amid the ties of kindred and associations of her girlhood, found consolation for her grief and strength for the duties yet before her.

From early youth she had written, for amusement, occasional contributions for various publications, but now she devoted her fine talents to the task as a regular occupation; and in 1841 published that happy combination of music and poetry known as "The Southern Harp." A similar volume soon followed from her pen, under the title of "The Northern Harp," which met as warm a welcome as her first attempt to adapt her own pure thoughts to the secular music familiar to all. Then came "The Parted Family, and Other Poems," also a success. About the year 1844, Mrs. Dana published a succession of short prose stories, and, soon after, her largest and most remarkable prose work, entitled "Letters to Relatives and Friends," written to defend her changed opinions on the subject of religious faith. Doubts of the creed she had inherited had arisen in her mind, and investigation had strengthened them into a conviction that she had mistaken the denomination to which she should attach herself: therefore she became a Unitarian. The work was well written, and immediately republished in London.

In 1847, Mrs. Dana suffered another most deeply-felt bereavement, in the death of both of her parents, and it required all the support of that religion which she had still continued to investigate, to enable her to bear up under the renewed trial; and, happily for her, light and strength crowned her efforts.

In May, 1848, she married the Rev. Robert D. Shindler, of the Episcopal Church.

> "Alas for those who love,
> Yet may not join in prayer!"

sings Mrs. Hemans, in her "Forest Sanctuary." But Mrs. Dana-Shindler was spared this bitter experience, for she had once more returned to her belief in the Holy Trinity, and could unite with her husband in all his offerings of praise and prayer, while the Angel of Peace folded its white wings over her chastened, but loving heart.

During the late war, Rev. Mr. and Mrs. Shindler experienced many trials incident to the condition of the country. They were in the neighborhood of the famous "Fort Pillow," and saw and heard enough of bloodshed and suffering to harrow up their hearts. Mrs. Shindler *could* tell some thrilling tales; but she tries to forget, or to regard it as some horrible dream which has passed away.

Her writings, since her marriage to Rev. Mr. Shindler, have been published in magazines and newspapers, and for several years have been almost entirely on church subjects. In 1869, Rev. Mr. and Mrs. Shindler were residing in Nacogdoches, Texas.

The following is a list of Mrs. Shindler's books:

1. The Southern Harp. Original sacred and moral songs, adapted to the piano-forte and guitar. Boston. 1840.
2. The Northern Harp. New York. 1841.
3. The Parted Family, and other Poems. 1842.
4. The Temperance Lyre. 1842.
5. Charles Morton; or, The Young Patriot. 1843.
6. The Young Sailor. 1844.
7. Forecastle Tom. 1844.
8. Letters to Relatives and Friends on the Trinity. 1845.

———o-o-:-o:-o-o———

JULIA C. R. DORR.

JULIA CAROLINE RIPLEY was born February 13th, 1825, at Charleston, S. C. While she was in early childhood her mother died, and shortly afterward her father, William Y. Ripley, removed to New York City. Mr. Ripley is a native of Vermont: his wife was the daughter of French *emigrês*, who, residing in the island of San Domingo, fled to Charleston at the time of the insurrection of slaves in that island.

In 1830, Mr. Ripley, quitting business in New York, removed to Vermont. Hence the subject of this sketch is generally styled "a Vermont authoress."

February 22d, 1847, Miss Ripley was married to Seneca M. Dorr, of Columbia County, New York.

Mrs. Dorr has been a most industrious writer. Her tales, novelettes, and poems, published in various first-class literary journals and magazines from 1848 to the present time, would form a score of medium-sized volumes.

Her last published volume — "Sybil Huntingdon," a novel, New York, 1870 — was much praised.

Mrs. Dorr has a daughter, Zulma, who promises to attain the same rank in art her mother has reached in literature.

MISS ESSIE B. CHEESBOROUGH.

ESSIE B. CHEESBOROUGH is a daughter of the late John W. Cheesborough, a prominent shipping merchant of Charleston, South Carolina. Her mother is a native of Liverpool, England. Miss Cheesborough was educated in Philadelphia and in her native city, Charleston, South Carolina.

She commenced her literary career at an early age, writing under the *noms de plume* of "Motte Hall," "Elma South," "Ide Delmar," and the now well-known initials of "E. B. C."

She was a regular contributor to the "Southern Literary Gazette," published in Charleston, and edited by the Rev. William C. Richards; and when Mr. Paul Hayne assumed the editorship, she continued her contributions. She was also a contributor to "Russell's Magazine," one of the best magazines ever published in the "Southland," and to various other Southern literary journals of the past, and to the "Land we Love," of the present era. After the war she was a regular contributor to the "Watchman," a weekly journal, edited and published in New York by the Rev. Dr. Deems, of North Carolina, with which journal she was connected until its discontinuance.

Miss Cheesborough's style is fluent and easy, and she does not pander to the sensational, but is natural, truthful, and earnest, never egotistical, or guilty of "fine writing." She has never published a book, although her writings on various subjects, political, literary, and religious, would fill several volumes.

1868.

RENUNCIATION.

I know that thou art beautiful:
  The glory of thy face
Are those dark eyes of witchery,
  That certain nameless grace.
Old Titian would have painted thee
  With joy too deep for telling —

That ivory cheek, the lustrous light
  In golden tresses dwelling.

But, manacled by solemn fate,
  I cannot burst the fetters;
Or write the story of my life
  In precious, golden letters:
Love's star for me can never shine;
  Its trembling light grows dimmer,
As through the dusky veil of grief
  Hope sends a feeble glimmer.

Then go; and in thy happy fate
  Of womanly completeness,
Make strong a husband's loving heart
  With all thy woman's sweetness.
But I must stand without the gate,
  While Eden's glowing splendor
Lights up with its aurora smile
  The glories I surrender.

MISS ALICE F. SIMONS.

MISS SIMONS was born and reared in Charleston. Her mother's maiden name was Wigfall,—a connection of ex-Senator Wigfall, of Texas, and a niece of the late Washington Alston, artist and author. Mrs. Simons has weaved "fictions" from early childhood; and her published novelettes, appearing anonymously, give promise of success in the field she has chosen. "Destiny," a tale of before the war, published in the Yorkville "Enquirer" is her most ambitious publication.

Her home is that of her birth.

1871.

MARY SCRIMZEOUR WHITAKER.

THE author of "Albert Hastings" and various productions, prose and poetical, is a native of Beaufort District, South Carolina. Her father, Rev. Professor Samuel Furman, son of the Rev. Dr. Richard Furman, of Charleston, South Carolina, is a clergyman of the Baptist persuasion, still living at the advanced age of seventy-seven years, and famed for his learning, eloquence, and piety. Her mother, whose maiden name was Scrimzeour, is of Scottish descent, and·traces back her lineage to Sir Alexander Scrimzeour, celebrated in Scottish story, whose descendants, in the male line, were hereditary standard-bearers of the kings of Scotland.

Her father having removed from Beaufort to Sumter District, she passed the early part of her life at the High Hills of Santee, probably the most beautiful and romantic portion of South Carolina.

The critical articles on the poets from the days of Dryden to those of Tennyson, which appeared editorially in the Sunday issue of the "Times" newspaper in New Orleans during the year 1866, were from her pen.

Previous to the late war, she was, for some time, a regular contributor to the Philadelphia magazines, writing under her own name, regarding a *nom de plume* as a foolish species of affectation, and not being ashamed to claim the authorship of anything she wrote herself, nor willing that it should be claimed by others.

In 1837, she, with her parents and two of her brothers, visited Edinburgh, her mother being entitled to a large estate in Scotland, then in litigation, and which she finally recovered. They took lodgings in a fashionable portion of the New Town of Edinburgh, characterized by the elegance and massive character of its private edifices and the beauty of its gardens. Here she passed her time surrounded by friends, among whom were some of the most distinguished literati of that ancient metropolis, such as Campbell, the poet; the Messrs. Chambers, editors of "Chambers's Journal;" Professor Wilson, editor of "Blackwood's Magazine;" Professor Moir, (the "Delta" of that work;) Mr. Tait, editor of "Tait's Magazine;" Burton, the historian; Mary Howitt, and other notables. Campbell was so pleased with her poetry that he encouraged her not to neglect her gift, and compli-mented her highly, calling her "his spiritual daughter." Some of her fugitive pieces were published, at the time, in the journals of Great Britain.

While in Edinburgh, she formed an acquaintance with a young advocate of the Scottish Bar, John Miller, Esq., (brother of Hon. Wil-liam Miller, now member of the British Parliament,) whom she subse-quently married. Having received the appointment of Attorney-Gen-eral of the British West Indies, he embarked for Nassau, N. P., with his young wife, but immediately after his arrival there, he was seized with yellow fever, and fell a victim to its insidious attacks. Mrs. Miller, assailed by the same fearful disease, recovered from it, and, with a heavy heart, returned in a Government vessel to South Carolina.

Her descriptions of the scenery of the West Indies, and of the epi-demics which annually sweep off so many of its inhabitants, contained in "Albert Hastings," were doubtless suggested by her visit to that beautiful but fatal region.

After twelve years passed in widowhood, almost exclusively devoted to literary studies and pursuits, she married Daniel K. Whitaker, Esq., a gentleman not undistinguished in the world of letters, the editor for many years of the "Southern Quarterly Review," and a fine scholar.

In 1850, Mrs. Whitaker published a volume of her poems. There are pieces in the collection characterized by spirit and fire; but the majority of her effusions are deeply tinged with the seriousness that naturally resulted from passages in her early history. The tributes to "Scott," "Byron," "Campbell," "Caravaggio," "Miss Landon," and "Mrs. Hemans," are among the most finished of her compositions. Many of her best pieces, written since this volume was published, (several of them elicited by the scenes of the late war and the gallantry of our generals upon the battle-field,) are scattered in the newspapers and periodicals of the day.

In 1868 appeared "Albert Hastings," her first extended effort in the de-partment of novel-writing. The scene of the novel, commencing in the Southern States, ends in England, the birthplace of the ancestors of the hero, where, after struggling manfully with many difficulties which beset him in the outset of his career in this country, he inherits a princely fortune. This work is the precursor of others, which, the writer of this sketch understands, are either finished or in course of preparation.

Mrs. Whitaker resides in New Orleans, and is a regular contributor to the "Sunday Times" of that city. Her daughter Lily possesses considerable poetic talent, and several of her published poems have been extensively copied.   W. K. D.

1870.

THE SUMMER RETREAT OF A SOUTHERN PLANTER.

Noonday sun fell in gorgeous effulgence over a field where long maize-leaves drooped like those of the Indian banana, when salt sea-breezes cease to fan them, and vertical rays glitter on white rocks, burn into the bosom of earth, and blind the eye of the beholder by their intenseness. But this is no tropical scene. On the declivity of a green hill-side rises a rude dwelling, composed of logs, built after the fashion of a pen. A wide passage separates two apartments. This passage, or corridor, is floored with pine boards, which, having been often scoured with sand and the shucks of Indian corn, has assumed an aspect of purity and whiteness truly refreshing. It extends from the front to the back of the house, and whenever there is the least atmospheric agitation, here the wind plays in cooling gusts.

But, as before said, it is noontide now, and stagnation pervades all, both within and without. Great hickory-trees and oaks seem to be sleeping a luxuriant sleep, brooded over by the day-king, as purple wild grapes ripen in luscious clusters on tangling vines, which form untrained arcades down a steep declivity, terminating in a dingle, or branch, cool, and sheltered by tall, magnificent pines, unlike those of the uplands. High wave their green crests, in fine contrasts to rich, blue, cloudless summer heavens, dominating a less stately growth of fragrant gum-trees, cedars, dogwood, and black walnut.

Here the cool spring-house is built over a running stream; and earthen pans, disposed on either side, are crusted over by cream, which will to-morrow be converted into healthy buttermilk and yellow butter, fresh and pure as the stream that wanders beneath, and rich as the golden sky that gleams above them. A large orchard extends on the right side of the dwelling. There the ruddy peach, Tyrian damson plum, large purple fig, and humble melon, lying on the earth, striped with green and white, nestling under grass, and its peculiar serrated leaves, await the hand of the gatherer. Tall sunflowers rise amid these Southern productions, and, ever turning their attention toward their potent lord, stand bravely forth, as though they said, "Perfect love casteth out fear." And so they follow his grand march over the blue empyrean down to his setting, when, their graceful adieu being made, they await to-morrow's sunrise ere, like adoring Persians, they turn them to the east and drink in his morning light.

A large dog lies dozing in the shade of a flower-shaped catalpa. Lazily he slumbers, and from gnats and flies occasionally attempts to relieve himself; flaps his huge ears, whisks his tail, and shows his glittering teeth. A lofty pole, planted firmly in the ground, is hung about with dry calabashes, each presenting an open aperture in front, which has been cut for the admission of swallows and martins, these birds being esteemed as denizens of a farm at the South, for no reason that I could ever ascertain, save that the old African crones, who preside over the plantations in matters of superstitious belief, reverence them.

A farm in South Carolina engages our attention, or rather the summer residence of one of her sometime princely planters. It was the custom of these gentlemen to retire from their plantation, usually situated in the low country, at this season. Their operatives, of African descent, whose lineage and constitution prevented them from incurring the least risk by continued residence in lowland sections during midsummer heats, remained on rice-plantations, on the seaboard and in river-swamps, where cotton was cultivated, while their Anglo-Saxon masters sought refuge amidst pine-barren wastes or on the apex of elevated hills.

The house now introduced on the scene was one in the latter-named region, the dwelling of Mr. Campbell — Scotch, as his name imports, and a true son of that land which not only gives birth to heroes of the sword and autocrats of the great mental republic of the world, but to good citizens, honest, industrious, and enterprising, all the world over. A love of his native land, or at least a memory of it, was traceable in the objects which, on entering either of the apartments separated by the wide passage before alluded to, met the eye. On unplastered walls were Highland scenes, depicted with graphic skill. Falls of the Clyde, Covalinn, Tantallon Castle, and Highland trosacks looked in speaking semblance from rich frames; and disposed on tables, in the midst, were "Blackwood," the "Edinburgh Review," and various periodicals fraught with that sound sense and discriminating intelligence which made Walter Scott the wonder of his age as a novelist, Thomas Campbell the legitimate successor of Dryden and Pope, and a long line of historians, orators, and statesmen the exemplars of their country's glory.

Bating the indications stated, this was a truly American establishment, or rather a sample of Southern summer residences among the wealthy. The house, being plain almost to rudeness, did not lack any accommodation consonant with free ventilation, a warm season, comfort, and use. The stables were as large as the dwelling, and under one extended roof were elegant vehicles, English horses, and attendant grooms, black as ebony, whistling and happy, very cheerfully performing the duties of that fraternity — chopping oats, currying sleek steeds, or putting in order trapping and harness.

Around the low-built but wide house were bare poles supporting a shed covered with green pine boughs, which emitted a healthful odor, and when dried in the sun were removed and replaced by others fresh and verdant.

Coral woodbine and many-flowered convolvulus with passion-flower and yellow jessamine twine around these rude posts and garland with beauty their lofty pilasters.   Here humming-birds expand gossamer plumage, hover over India creeper, and insert their long spiral bills into the heart of each fragile and fairy flower.   Great black butterflies, with silver-spotted wings, flit from lilac and white althea to scarlet verbena beds, from forest honey-suckle to crimson butterfly-weed, from wild thyme to those unnoted children of our American flora which rejoice in Southern suns and bloom like Eden beneath Southern dews.   The grasshopper sings his shrill song, the bluejay whisks amidst sycamore leaves, and the speckled woodpecker rings his horny beak against decaying bark, as, perched midway on some ancient trunk, he plies his ceaseless task.   Yet there is silence.   All things own the might of heat — all save wild songsters and the busy hostler's whistle.

Down sinks day's grand luminary !   Above his evening couch is gathered the glorious drapery of the skies drawn over a cerulean expanse.   His lingering beams shoot yellow lustre over the scene.   Shadows are being lengthened from skyey tops of towering pines to the lower altitude of man's dwelling.   That, with light, is insensibly withdrawn, and soon the chick-will-willow, whip-poor-will, and night-hawk raise their voices, while locusts and katydids chirp in unison, and the harsh-throated swamp-frog sends a hoarse cry from the dingle below.

--------oo؛ө؛oo--------

FANNY M. P. DEAS.

THE efforts of this lady in the literary line have been limited, and chiefly directed to the entertainment of the domestic circle.   The maiden name of Mrs. Deas was Wigfall; both parents were Carolinians: her mother of English descent.   Her father was a nephew of Washington Alston.   Mrs. Deas possesses considerable talent for drawing and painting.   She lives in Charleston.   "The Little Match-Girl," versified from Hans Anderson's story of that name, a poem with the imprint of J. B. Lippincott & Co., Philadelphia, 1870, is her only published volume.

She is the author of a prize novelette, published in the Yorkville "Enquirer," (1871,) entitled "The Lost Diamond."

MARGARET MAXWELL MARTIN.

THE subject of this sketch was born in Dumfries, Scotland, in 1807, and when eight years of age, accompanied her parents to America. They settled in North Carolina, at Fayetteville; but afterward removed to the beautiful city of Columbia, S. C.

In 1836, she married the Rev. William Martin, of the Methodist Episcopal Church, and shared with him the life of an itinerant missionary.

Mrs. Martin has taught a large female seminary in Columbia for nearly a quarter of a century. Her occupation has not been writing, but teaching, which has occupied her life's prime. Conscientiously she felt that she could not give the Muse her strength — her school had first claims; consequently, her poems have been recreation, and her themes chiefly religious, for she felt she owed God a peculiar debt, that she could only pay by devoting to Him her "one talent," along with all else she possessed.

The late William Gilmore Simms said:

"Mrs. Martin partakes of the missionary spirit with her husband; and, while he illustrates the Scriptures in sermons which bear glad tidings of salvation to hungering souls, she clothes like lessons in the more melodious garments of poesie, which appeal equally to the affections, the necessities and tastes. . . . .

"In her various wanderings as a missionary's wife, our author has been brought into neighborhoods which should have with us a classical and patriotic distinction. She has sought out and explored their place of mark, and caught up and woven into graceful verse or no less graceful prose the legends and the histories of our colonial and Revolutionary periods. The fields distinguished by the storm of battle, the ruins which mark the decayed or devastated settlement, the noble heroism which makes obscure places famous forever — these she has explored with something of the mood of 'Old Mortality,' and with her pen she has brightened the ancient memories, while newly recording the ancient deeds of heroism or simple virtue. We commend her writings as always possessing a value for the reader who desires truth in its simplicity, character in its purity, and heroism when addressed to patriotic objects."

Among Mrs. Martin's publications are "Day-Spring," "Methodism, or Christianity in Earnest," "The Sabbath-school Offering," a collection of poems and true stories, and two volumes of poetry — "Religious Poems" and "Flowers and Fruits."

That scholarly lady and graceful writer, Mrs. E. F. Ellet, is the author of the following genial notice of "Religious Poems:"

"The author of this book is an accomplished lady of Columbia, the wife of a clergyman of the Methodist Episcopal Church. She has for many years been engaged in teaching, and communion with the Muse has formed the recreation of her useful life. It is a spirit like David's, 'after God's own heart,' that here outpours itself in melody. Rare indeed is the sight of a mind attuned to all things bright and lovely and tender and sweet in nature, consecrating all its powers to the worship and service of God. Such poems, even were they not marked by high literary ability, are fragments of the language of heaven, because they breathe the life and illustrate the grace of Christianity. Faith, childlike and pure; hope, exalted; love, ardent and enduring; patience, humility, and a fair sisterhood of virtues, are reflected in these simple strains. The reader will feel a benign and holy influence stealing into his heart, and will find solace for almost every pang 'entailed on human hearts,' if he reads with a true sympathy. It would be a blessed thing if our poetical literature were more generally imbued with this fervor of religious feeling — this deep love of truth.

"The longest poem in the collection is an epic of the 'Progress of Christianity,' exhibiting God's dealings with His church, from the days of the apostles until now. The second part of this poem illustrates the power which has accompanied the progress of the religion of our Redeemer. Viewing briefly its influence in Scotland, the hallowed Sabbath of the Puritans is considered, and various pictures of human life represented, in which piety has triumphed over trial, sorrow, and death. The following are of them:

> 'Gaze on that lovely one: consumption's doom
> Is hastening her to an untimely tomb:
> Hers fortune, friends, and genius; yet all
> Must yield her up at Death's relentless call;
> Fades day by day the rose-tint from her cheek,
> And daily grows she weaker; and, thus weak,
> Is she not daunted at the approach of him —
> The "King of Terrors," horrible and grim?

Will she not shrink from his unyielding clutch,
Nor seek to evade his blighting, withering touch?
Thus fragile, the last conflict will she dare?
Has she been nerved by mighty faith and prayer?
What words? "I'm ready!" 'T is her own dear voice;
She's more than conqueror — rejoice! rejoice!

. . . .

'See ye yon widowed mother o'er the bier
Of her fair babe, so precious and so dear?
'T was her sole solace since the dreadful day
When death removed her partner and her stay:
This little one, e'en sleeping or awake,
Sweet solace to the poor bereavèd spake.
It lay upon her bosom, and its breath
Was redolent of health — none dreamed of death;
When suddenly 't was from the bosom torn
Of that fond mother, now indeed forlorn;
Yet mark her faith: "The Lord is true and just;
Although he slay me, yet in him I'll trust!"'

The remaining two-thirds of the volume are composed of "Poems by the Lamplight," as the author felicitously calls her paraphrases of Scripture passages. These are applied to the incidents and interests of daily and practical life. "The Beatitudes" form a series, and seldom has sacred truth been more gratefully made familiar to the soul than in the stanzas headed "Blessed are they that Mourn."

MY SAVIOUR, THEE!

When the paths of life's young morning
  First I enter'd on, unheeding
Wisdom's well-weighed words of warning;
  When my feet were torn and bleeding
  With the way, then I was needing
    My Saviour, thee!

When the bright sun's daily duty
  Lighted life's meridian, beading
That life's slender thread with beauty;
  When, by that light, I was reading
  Life, then, oh! how I was needing
    My Saviour, thee!

When the autumn, mellow, sombre,
  Came, with all earth's hopes receding,
Casting shadows without number;
  When the signs my soul was heeding,
  Of that searing, I was needing
    My Saviour, thee!

When shall come death's midnight awful,
  And my parting soul is deeding
All its sins and sorrows woful
  To the past, dead past, when pleading
  But thy merits, I'll be needing,
    My Saviour, thee!

———oo°o°oo———

MRS. M. A. EWART RIPLEY.

MRS. RIPLEY is a writer of novelettes of some considerable local reputation. A novelette written by her, entitled " Ellen Campbell; or, King's Mountain," — a Revolutionary tale, which was published in the Yorkville (S. C.) " Enquirer" during the war, — created a furore, and doubled the subscription of the paper.

Mary Ann McMahon was born in Ireland, but removed to the United States in early childhood; and when she was five years old, her parents removed to Columbia, S. C., where she was educated. It was not until after her marriage with James B. Ewart, of Columbia, that she published any of her writings. The maiden novelette was a prize story for a literary journal published by Dr. Gibbs, of Columbia.

Mr. Ewart dying in 1857, leaving his widow with a young family, she removed to Hendersonville, N. C., in 1861, and took charge of a school at that place. She wrote at this time a series of Sunday-school stories for the " Southern Presbyterian."

In 1862, she married Colonel V. Ripley, of Hendersonville, where she resides.

Her last publication is " Avlona," a prize novelette published in the Yorkville " Enquirer," 1871.

Mrs. Ripley is in the prime of life, possessing that vivacity of which her writings are characteristic.

1871.

MRS. CATHARINE LADD.

THE name that heads this article will call a thrill of pleasure to many hearts — for this lady is "one of the most noted and successful of the teachers of the State of South Carolina," and hundreds of her old pupils, many of them now "teaching," scattered throughout the land, remember her kindness and entire unselfishness. "She is the most generous of women; her time, her talents, her worldly goods are at the command of all her friends," says one of her ex-pupils.

Mrs. Ladd is a native of Virginia — was born in October, 1810 — married when eighteen years old to Mr. Ladd, a portrait and miniature painter. Her maiden name was Catharine Stratton.

For several years after her marriage Mrs. Ladd wrote poetry, which was published in the various periodicals of the day. For three years she was a regular correspondent of several newspapers, and published a series of articles on drawing, painting, and education, which attracted considerable attention.

In 1842, Mrs. Ladd permanently settled in the town of Winnsboro', South Carolina, where she established one of the largest institutions of learning in the State, which sustained its well-deserved reputation until closed, in 1861.

Mrs. Ladd has contributed tales, sketches, essays, and poems to various journals under different *noms de plume* — as "Minnie Mayflower," "Arcturus," "Alida," and "Morna."

During the existence of the "Floral Wreath," published in Charleston by Mr. Edwin Heriott, Mrs. Ladd was a regular contributor. Mr. Heriott, in a notice of the literary talent of the South, speaking of Mrs. Ladd's poetical works, said: "They were sweet, smooth, and flowing, particularly so; but, like Scotch music, their gayest notes were sad."

In 1851, she with ardor took up the subject of education, home manufactories, and encouragement of white labor, believing that the ultimate prosperity of South Carolina would depend on it. She reasoned from a conviction that South Carolina could not long compete with the more Southern and Southwestern States in raising cotton, and an extensive system of slave labor would realize no profit.

Mrs. Ladd's plays, written at the solicitation of friends, and performed by them, were very popular. The "Grand Scheme" and "Honeymoon" were celebrated far and wide. The incidents and introduction of characters showed that she had more than ordinary talent for that species of composition. Mrs. Ladd has a wonderful knack of managing young people.

After the commencement of the war, Mrs. Ladd gave up everything to devote herself to the cause of the South. She lived for the soldiers! was elected President of the "Soldiers' Aid Association," which office she retained until the close of the war, and by her untiring exertions kept the society well supplied with clothing. Her pen was unused during the war, the needle and her personal supervision being constantly in demand. In Winnsboro', no church is built, no charity solicited, no ball, concert, tableaux, or fair — *nothing* goes on without her cheerful and ever-ready aid.

Mrs. Ladd is said to be "homely," and dresses to suit herself, never caring about the "latest fashions," ignores "hoops," and always wears her hair short. Her manner is abrupt and decided; but one instinctively feels it to be "kind."

The "Confederate flag" is said to have originated with Mrs. Ladd; the first one, we allude to. The fire of February 21st, 1865, destroyed the literary labor of thirty years. With the assistance of a Federal officer, Mrs. Ladd saved the jewels of the Masonic Lodge in the next house to hers; but the flame and smoke prevented her finding the "charter." By this time the fire had got so much ahead on her own premises, and the confusion was so great, that she lost everything.

It is said that outside of the walls of her school, Mrs. Ladd was the gay, social companion of every young lady under her charge. Following her to the school-room, you instantly felt the change: though not perhaps a word was spoken, every young lady felt it. She has a powerful will and habit of centring every thought and feeling instantly on the occupation of the moment. The confusion of voices or passing objects never seemed to disturb her when writing.

A friend of Mrs. Ladd says: "Her quick motions show the rapidity of thought. Even now, at the age of fifty-eight, were you walking behind her, you might mistake her, from the light buoyancy of step, for a young girl."

1869.   ◇

CLARA V. DARGAN.

FILLED with aspirations after the true and the beautiful—enthusiastic about music—with *a something* so bright, so star-like about her that we conceive she must be all that is fair and "lovely, and of good report"—few young writers, who have written as much as Miss Dargan, have uniformly written so well, and with so little effort. Says she, "If I did not write *de mon cœur*, I should not be able to write at all."

The subject of this sketch was born near Winnsboro', S. C. Her father, Dr. K. S. Dargan, was descended from an old Virginia family, and was noted for his extremely elegant manners and unrivalled conversational powers. Her mother was a native Charlestonian, of French Huguenot blood, a remarkably handsome and graceful lady. Clara inherits her mother's vivacity and love of repartee, fondness for society, her enthusiasm and romance, and her father's manners and conversational powers. For some years the family lived on a plantation in Fairfield, and removed to Columbia in 1852, noted as one of the most beautiful cities in the whole country *then!*

At the capital of South Carolina, with the exception of a year or so, resided Miss Dargan, until the death of her parents, her father dying in 1865, and the mother two years afterward, scattering the once happy and united family — for with the fall of the Confederacy their wealth vanished.

Miss Dargan was for a time a pupil of Mrs. C. Ladd, who says: "She commenced writing when about ten years of age. I read a story written by her when about eleven ; it was worthy of the matured pen of twenty. Nature has endowed her with many rich gifts, which she has not failed to improve; the budding promise of childhood has expanded, scattering many literary gems over her pathway."

Her first publication was a poem, "Forever Thine," in the "Courant," a journal which flourished a brief time under the editorship of the lamented Howard H. Caldwell. It was signed "Claudia," and appeared in 1859. During the following year she wrote several stories for the "Southern Guardian," published in Columbia, under the *nom de plume* of "Esther Chesney," under which name she wrote for the "Southern Field and Fireside" in 1861. In this year she was a successful competitor for the prize offered by the "Field and Fireside" for the best novelette —her story, "Helen Howard," sharing the honors with a novelette entitled "Our Little Annie."

Encouraged by this success, she competed for the prize offered by the "Darlington Southerner," and was successful.

In 1863, she edited the literary department of the "Edgefield Advertiser," then under the control of that elegant scholar and gentleman, Colonel Arthur Simkins: his death dissolved her connection with it. She wrote for the "Field and Fireside" during the war, and after the close of the same was a contributor to the "Crescent Monthly," the ablest periodical ever published in the South, which was edited and published in New Orleans, by William Evelyn, for a short time only. In this magazine appeared "Philip: My Son," considered by many her best story. The late Henry Timrod said "that he considered it equal to any story in 'Blackwood's.'"

Miss Dargan never mixes "ego" with her stories. They are told so naturally that the writer is forgotten entirely in the narrative. As far as a "title" is an index to a story, we append the titles of a few of Miss Dargan's tales: "Nothing Unusual," "Still Faithful," "Coming Home," "Come to Life," "Judith," "Riverlands."

"Charles Auchester," that delightful work of Miss Elizabeth Sara Sheppard, whose short life is one of the saddest of stories, is a great favorite with Miss Dargan. She considers it one of the few books that can be placed next to the "Holy Word." "It is a rare gem, an amethyst of the richest purple, set in the purest gold, chastely carved. It was and is a text-book on more subjects than music to me. So pure and earnest and calm and deep!"

Says she, in speaking of "Mendelssohn's Songs:"

"All he ever wrote, is there such music anywhere, except in heaven? People talk senselessly about Italian operas, and English and Scotch and Irish ballads; these are all very well. I think there is an air or two from 'Lucia,' and one from 'Lucretia Borgia,' and several from 'Ernani,' that are beautiful; but none will compare with those sublime, those soul-full creations."

We have noticed Miss Dargan's musical talents, and music is a highly-developed talent in the family. Clara's two brothers and sisters are not only fine singers, but perform on several instruments; and of course she is a poet. The critic and talented gentleman, author (among other things) of a series of articles on "Southern Littérateurs" — Mr. J. W. Davidson, who was Miss Dargan's literary sponsor — says: "I rank Miss Dargan first in promise among the Southern daughters of song." In person, Miss Dargan is a tall, graceful figure, good eye, and expressive face when conversing.

Said the late Henry Timrod: "If simplicity and pathos be poetry, 'Jean to Jamie' is poetry of the most genuine stamp. The verses flow with the softness of a woman's tears." (1866.)

Miss Dargan is teaching in Yorkville, S. C.

1871.

JEAN TO JAMIE.

What do you think now, Jamie,
    What do you think now?
'T is many a long year since we parted:
Do you still believe Jean honest-hearted —
    Do you think so now?

You did think so once, Jamie,
    In the blithe spring-time:
"There 's never a star in the blue sky
That 's half sae true as my Jamie," quo' I —
    Do you mind the time?

We were happy then, Jamie,
    Too happy, I fear;
Sae we kissed farewell at the cottage door —
I never hae seen you since at that door
    This many a year.

For they told you lies, Jamie:
    You believed them a'!
You, who had promised to trust me true
Before the whole world — what did you do?
    You believed them a'!

When they called you fause, Jamie,
    And argued it sair,
I flashed wi' anger — I kindled wi' scorn,
Less at you than at them; I was sae lorn,
    I couldna do mair.

After a bit while, Jamie, —
    After a while,
I heard a the cruel words you had said —
The cruel, hard words; sae I bowed my head —
    Na tear — na smile —

And took your letters, Jamie,
    Gathered them a',
And burnt them one by one in the fire,
And watched the bright blaze leaping higher —
    Burnt ringlet and a'!

Then back to the world, Jamie,
    Laughing went I;
There ne'er was a merrier laugh than mine:
What foot could outdance me — what eye outshine?
    "Puir fool!" laughed I.

But I'm weary o' mirth, Jamie —
    'T is hollowness a';
And in these long years sin' we were parted,
I fear I'm growing aye colder-hearted
    Than you thought ava!

I hae many lovers, Jamie,
    But I dinna care;
I canna abide a' the nonsense they speak —
Yet I'd go on my knees o'er Arran's gray peak
    To see *thee* ance mair!

I long for you back, Jamie,
    But that canna be;
I sit sll alone by the ingle at e'en,
And think o' those sad words: "It might hae been" —
    Yet never can be!

D'ye think o' the past, Jamie?
    D'ye think o' it now?
'T wad be a bit comfort to know that ye did —
Oh, sair would I greet to know that ye did,
    My dear, dear Jamie!

SLEEPING.

Go down, thou sun, nor rise again;
　　Sink low behind the purple hills,
　　And shimmer over western rills,
And gild the dusky moor and plain.

Chant low, ye wildwood birds, chant low;
　　The cooing ringdove, so forlorn,
　　Her parted mate as gently mourn,
And thou, sad river, calmly flow.

I sit beside the mossy mound
　　That gently lies upon my dead;
　　And violets wave above his head,
And daisies gem the dewy ground.

The willow, like a mourning veil,
　　Waves quietly above my grief:
　　The very rustling of the leaf
Against the ruined garden-pale

Murmurs of him who sleepeth here
　　As sweetly in his narrow bed,
　　With roses pressed beneath his head,
As if his mother's arms were there.

FLIRTING WITH PHILIP.*

I saw my boy growing rapidly into manhood with the growth of his love. It was the first love of a strong and passionate nature, and a young man's first love so seldom has root in anything deeper than mere physical beauty. Margaret Thorpe was a woman to infatuate enthusiastic natures, especially of boys or very young men. There was a peculiar fascination about her rare loveliness — her manner, half childlike, half dignified — her winning voice, and willowy, graceful figure. At times I believed her utterly unconscious of Philip's sentiments toward her; she seemed to meet his impulsive demonstrations so calmly, and look almost with surprise at any sudden outburst of earnestness: but anon this changed; and when I saw her sitting with downcast eyes and drooping lash under the gaze which he fixed upon her, listening with that peculiar manner she knew so well to assume, and

* From " Philip : My Son," (1866.)

replying in a voice so tenderly cadenced, lifting her violet eyes to his, *then* I knew she felt and believed it. No woman could doubt such evidence.

Philip seemed to grow taller and grander. There was a pride in his bearing; the splendid Antinous-like head, the flashing eagle eye, the quivering finely-cut nostril, the mouth and chin shaped like a woman's in its delicate curves — all were touched with new fire, undying, immortal. As he dismounted from his horse at the gate and walked up the garden-path with his stately step, I heard Margaret, who was watching him from the window, murmur to herself, " *Philip, my king !* " Long years after I heard that same voice, broken by tears, chaunt an exquisite home-lyric, bearing a similar burden of love and pride, as she folded a tiny, white-robed Philip in her arms.

They went out often together, sometimes on horseback, sometimes walking. On these latter excursions, Margaret frequently carried a little basket on her arm, filled with sandwiches and cake, and a bottle of home-made wine; and Philip would take a fishing-rod, while out of the breast-pocket of his coat would peer the azure binding of Tennyson, the inevitable and invariable companion on all occasions, though I heard Philip declare laughingly he could not comprehend one word from preface to finis of the volume, except the poem quoted daily to the praise of his idol, " Margaret." What all this tended to I could not tell. I did not even know if Philip had declared his affection. Like one in a dream, I was content for all things to go on as they had done, and dreaded a change: but it came at last.

Late one evening I was half dozing in my arm-chair by the sitting-room window. The day had been intensely warm, and the entire household appeared overpowered by some influence in the atmosphere. Philip had ridden off before sunset. I saw him dashing down the avenue like one mad, and presently Margaret went up stairs with her light step, humming, in a mocking voice it seemed to me, a foolish little French *chanson*. I had left the two very good friends, in the veranda, after dinner, Philip smoking and playing with Margaret's ball of gold thread, while she sat demurely netting on that wonderful piece of work, half smoking-cap, half turban; but somehow, these latter days, there was a provoking air about Margaret that seemed at times to goad Philip almost to desperation. I knew now she had been teasing him again — my poor boy, who had never been denied the smallest boon in all his short, bright life.

From where I sat, I could see Margaret's white dress gleaming between the rose-vines as she sat on the steps of the piazza, half hid from view by thick clusters of multiflora and drooping sprays of clematis. She had a manuscript book in her hand — while her chin rested in the palm of the other, and her head was bowed in deep revery. There was a step on the gravel, and I heard her say, without raising her head, " Come here, Philip ! I have something to read to you ; " and she read in a low, steady monotone, peculiarly impressive in its exquisite modulation — flowing on like the sound of water afar off. . . . .

She stopped, and it seemed like the breaking of a dream. Philip sat at her feet: I could not see his face, but I heard his quick breath come and go, as if he panted for relief.

"Margaret," he exclaimed, in a hoarse voice, "don't torture me!"

"Torture you, Philip?"

"Yes, you know you do! Margaret, you have won me with your syren songs, and now you wreck me without a shadow of remorse or feeling."

"It is not my fault that you love me; I never encouraged you."

"Not your fault!" he exclaimed, in that passionate, uncontrollable manner which he so often used of late. "Not your fault? Did you not look up into my face with those beautiful eyes, and say plainly with them, again and again, that you accepted my love? Did you not flatter me with every cadence of your voice, every smile so deadly sweet, to believe that you knew and requited it? And now you call me to fawn at your feet, and listen to verses you knew would craze my very brain, and say it is not your fault that I love you! Oh, Margaret! Margaret!"

"Philip, you wrong me. Listen, for I *will* speak —"

He interrupted her with a gesture eloquent of despair. "Don't, Margaret! I know you are going all over those cruel words again — about my being younger than you, and how I surprise you, and the utter absurdity. All those words mean nothing to me. I don't believe any of it! Just tell me now, once and forever, do you not love me at all — not at all?"

He leaned forward eagerly, and caught her hand. There was a brief silence; and I waited to hear Margaret Thorpe speak. She only said, in a half-suppressed, breathless way, "I am engaged."

I could not endure it. I rose from my seat and went out into the piazza, where the moon, lately risen, shed her clear, pure light over the two figures on the steps; and I saw my boy sitting there as one stunned, looking straight into the false face before him — so fair, and yet so false.

"Margaret Thorpe," I said, "may God deal with you as you have dealt with my son."

MISS MARIAN C. LEGARE REEVES.

"FADETTE" — the author of "Ingemisco" — is Miss Reeves. Her father is a native South Carolinian, and her mother of the Reed family of Delaware. She is a niece of Gen. Samuel Jones, of the late C. S. A., and a niece of the Rev. Dr. Palmer, of the old Circular Church of Charleston; consequently, a cousin of his nephew, the present Dr. B. M. Palmer, of New Orleans, to whom her book is dedicated. "Ingemisco" was published by Blelock & Co., New York, 1867. To quote from a poet critic of our "Southland" (C. Woodward Hutson):

"'Ingemisco' is the tale of a travelling party in Germany. Some of the descriptions are very able, picturesque in scenery-painting, and nervously sketched. The scene of the danger and rescue in the Alpine storm is admirable. The style is good, very fair indeed, with only a touch of feminine affectation, which will wear off as she writes more. There is plenty of that sweet glimmer and soft air-music of romance which we miss so much in most of the fiction of modern days; and much that reminds of the pleasant mirth and genial love that charm us so gladsomely in 'Quits' and the 'Initials.' There is a wild legend, too, told by the Swiss peasant-girl, Luise, of the ancient monastery and the anchorite's cave, which are connected with the fate of Margaret Ross, the heroine of the present tale. It is worthy of the wonderful legendary lore of old Deutschland, and is well told. It is something, in these dull, unbelieving days, to catch into the nostrils of the soul a breath of the witching fragrance of those delicious old superstitions; and I bless the charming craftswoman that she has allowed this quaint embroidery of Sir Walter's magic mantle to linger on her fair shoulder. Thank heaven, there is no pedantry! It is all true woman throughout, with not a bit of the blue-stocking, only traces in plenty of close and artist-like observation in travel and taste in reading. Knowledge is never obtruded. It is a great relief in these days to read clear English, unbroken by huge scientific technicalities or mythological allusions *ad nauseam*, as if the reader were to be put to school again through the medium of a book pretending to be one of amusement.

"The characters are well conceived, and painted with great power. I mean the *two*, the only ones we ever care a button about in a real warm romance of love. Margaret is a proud, high-souled woman, a superb nature, with a world of tenderness in her heart, but with a world of scorn for any baseness, even though born of passionate love for her. The wrong done her by her lover in marrying her against her will, thus forcing her to break her plighted

498

word, rouses her strong nature, and shows the true woman better than almost any other trial of trust could show that wonderful mechanism of the affections. Her Ernst, the gallant Polish exile, Count Zalkiewski, despite his one great error, for which he paid so dearly in her heart's estrangement from him, is a noble being, and interests the reader deeply. It is truly a wonderful book for the first. Much as I admire it, it is not half so good as she is. That winter visit I made to the great river region is bright in my memory with many a picture of the pleasant and hospitable homes of transplanted Carolina families. Among those carefully kept visions of a most charming tour, not the least refreshing is that which was lit by the smile of one who is now a princess in Parnassus. As I read her book I could not but rejoice that so true a heart-tale was written by neither Titanide nor Encyclopæde, but by a quiet, *natural* maiden, sweet and modest as the violet she loves."

The "Round Table," New York, in a review of "Ingemisco," concludes by saying:

"As a whole, this book contains so much that gives promise of future excellence, that we hope the authoress will not shrink from that steadfast and patient toil which alone can insure her, in the sequel, that enviable position to which, no doubt, she aspires."

Another Northern reviewer says :

"This book, if we do not greatly mistake, marks the advent of a new and very conspicuous star in the firmament of letters. 'Ingemisco' is an exceedingly clever performance in itself, and involves a promise of richer fruits in the future. The plot is conceived with originality and developed with skill, the characters are drawn with a bold and symmetrical pencil, the descriptions of still life are painted with peculiar gorgeousness of coloring, the dialogue is animated, and some of the situations strikingly dramatic, and the work is illuminated throughout with those subtle glimpses of scholarship which signalize a genuine culture as contradistinguished from the inapposite *sputter* of encyclopædic empiricism. We wish to mark this last statement with the stress of a strong emphasis. In casually turning over the leaves of this book, the eye cannot fail of catching brief and pertinent citations from the most beautiful things in French, Italian, and German literature, and occasionally—as if with a hand deliberately restrained—from the ancient classics. In every instance, these citations are exactly and nicely appropriate to the person, the situation, and the circumstances—are, in short, an unpremeditated outburst of the author's culture, at the point where they spontaneously arise, and not an unnaturally contrived occasion for a palpably meretricious display. To say of a young American author that he brings to his initial effort in the department of fiction a highly-cultivated mind, is to mark an exceptional advantage, whose influence is second only to the possession of genius. But this last great quality is really the dominating feature of this book. It appears in every page, equally attested by colloquy, characterization, or description. In the very first chapter there is a description of an Alpine storm, in which the life of the heroine is almost hopelessly involved, which we do not hesitate to affirm is one of the finest we have ever perused, notwithstanding the subject is equally attractive and familiar, and has exercised all manner of pens, from the 'Great Unknown' to that vast company of little ones who yearly travel the road to oblivion, and contribute to the manufacture of trunks.

" ' Ingemisco' will remind every discriminating reader of those beautiful creations which shed, a few years ago, a splendid but fugitive halo around the world of letters — 'Initials' and 'Quits.' It is conceived mainly in the same vein as these charming productions. But the pen of 'Fadette' is clearly distinguished from that of the gifted daughter of Lord Erskine, and is, in no respect that we can discover, imitative. On the contrary, its individuality asserts itself constantly, almost to the degree of harshness. We mention the resemblance in question only to indicate what seems to us the great fault of this book. The writer has attempted to condense an interesting story and a book of travels into the same volume. This will not do; it never has done. And, so long as a person engaged in the perusal of a narrative dramatically conceived and evolved must consider it a nuisance to be abruptly interrupted by substituting a book of travels (however well written) for the one in his hands, it never will do. No examples, however distinguished, can justify such a departure from the fundamental laws of art. A novelist is entitled to incorporate into his story just so much of the merely outward conditions of the selected theatre of his fable as is indispensably necessary to the illustration of the supposed facts thereof: if he go beyond this, he is irrelevant — the interest flags — Homer sings of ships — the reader sleeps.

" With this exception, we have only commendation for this admirable book; and we cordially greet — shall we say, the fair authoress, as her *nom de plume* implies ? — into the 'magic circle' where fairies dance upon the greensward and imagination weaves into forms palpable and real the colors of the rainbow."

"Randolph Honor"· was published by Richardson & Co., New York, (1868,) and was cordially welcomed by the reading world and literary journals. The "Round Table" said:

" In 'Randolph Honor' we have pictures of life which are not wanting in power, and descriptions of scenery drawn with truth and delicacy. The story is not sensational, and its moral tone is unexceptionable; but the plot is meagre, and the great difficulties of character-painting the authoress has not yet mastered. . . . .

" In this work, as in ' Ingemisco,' there appears so fair a promise of future excellence, that we feel justified in saying that the young authoress who produced them is capable, with increased cultivation and mature thought, of achieving something much better than she has yet offered to the public."

And the "poet critic" must have his delightful talk about this delightful second book recorded:

"'Randolph Honor' is a marked improvement on 'Ingemisco.' The characters are ably drawn; and, what is particularly pleasant in this age that gives us spasmodic portraitures for real dramatic delineation, they are ladies and gentlemen. The story is of the war, and is staunchly Southern, true to the ring of those noble tones that died away only when smothered in blood.

"The style *is* faulty. It is injured by a somewhat glaring mannerism, resulting from a tendency to poetic inversion in the mode of expression. But this blemish will wear away as the young writer grows in practice. She is certainly versatile. This last work is totally different from 'Ingemisco.' She is clear, so far, of that vice of the too rapidly productive writers of fiction, whose novels troop out from the publishing-houses in such numbers we cannot keep the run of them — she does not repeat herself. There is, too, great variety in the story, and frequent changes of the locality, perhaps too frequent for the maintenance of the spell upon the reader; for the attachment we form for places in actual life we carry with us into our ideal life, and we like fiction to hallow for us certain spots in association with the persons of the story who have won our liking, and not remove us too capriciously from the scenes thus endeared to us.

"This principle is violated here. We are hurried from the charming Maryland manor-house, Randolph Honor, to Baltimore; from Baltimore to the Steamer 'St. Nicholas,' (the capture of which, by the way, is graphically described); from there and thereabouts to Charleston; from Charleston to Arkansas; and from Arkansas to all sorts of places—the prairies and elsewhere. But the novelty of scenery and of mode of life, I must say, compensate in a great measure for the distracted feeling one experiences in this flitting to and fro. The dramatic action is full of fire and motion. The lady is loved to the heart's content of the reader bent on his heroine's being duly honored. The young men are dashing cavaliers, worthy of the sunny soil they fight for; and 'Miss Charley' is a dashing damsel, much nearer to Joan of Arc and the Maid of Saragossa than Dr. Simms' famous swamp-rider, 'Hurricane Nell.' The life in the West is a fine picture, and shows up well the strong contrasts of culture and roughness in a country of comparatively recent settlement. The darkey wedding is pleasantly described, and the feudal picture it presents of mutual good feeling between beneficent suzerain and attached retainers, readily recognized by us, who have lived under the system, as truth itself, will do well to put alongside the present rancorous hate that glows from the pages of such as Helper of 'No-Joque.'

"Need I say to you who have read the earlier work that the poetic soul of this lady delights in the sweet tenderness and fragrance and the bright bloom of the out-door world, which ought always to lift our hearts to the God who made it so lovely for us. Yes, she loves the good creatures that are so eloquent, though to the material organ they may seem dull. She is of those 'Sunday children' who have the poetic instinct, and to whom nothing that the Divine artist has made is ever mute. Nature, with all its fulness of life and light and freshness, she dearly loves; and the blessed beauty and radiance and vocal melody with which it surges on the soul in a thousand soft wavelets of light and scent and sound, rippling rare undertones of harmony into the dreamy recesses of the heart, draw from her ever and anon tributes of love and praise, and a glad poetic dallying with its wondrous richness in change and varying form."

"Ingemisco" was written with no idea of publication — merely to lighten some heavy hours of the war-time for the author's home circle; and "Randolph Honor," though with imaginary characters, is, regarding war-incidents, drawn from sketches of that which came within the author's own experience or knowledge.

"Fadette's" last publication bears the imprint of Claxton, Remsen & Haffelfinger, and is called "Sea-Drift."

Miss Reeves is residing in New Castle, Delaware.

1869.

----o◦⦂◉⦂◦o----

FLORIDE CLEMSON.

MISS CLEMSON is a granddaughter of John C. Calhoun, and a native of Pendleton Village, S. C. She is the author of a little work entitled "Poet-Skies, and other Experiments in Versification," by "C. de Flori."

Miss Clemson is married to a Mr. Lea, and is residing in New York.

1870.

ANNIE M. BARNWELL.

MISS BARNWELL is one of the youngest of our "Southland Writers," and one who desires to make "literature" her profession.

Annie M. Barnwell is a native of Beaufort, S. C., the eldest daughter of Thomas Osborn Barnwell — until the war, a planter of that place. She was educated entirely in the quiet town of her birth, and, until the war, had seldom quitted it.

From earliest childhood she was passionately fond of reading, and the world of books was a delightful reality to her. Her life has been spent in a narrow circle; and, until the war, it was a very quiet one; but no Southerner can have passed through the last eight years without thinking and feeling deeply and passionately.

Although fond of writing from childhood, noted as the best composition writer in school, she never published anything until 1864, when a poem appeared in a local journal. In the spring of 1866, encouraged by the approval of Rev. George G. Smith, of Georgia, she wrote for publication under the *nom de plume* of "Leroy," a name chosen as a slight tribute of love and respect to the memory of one who held the first place on her list of friends, the late accomplished Dr. Leroy H. Anderson, of Gainesville, Alabama.

Under this signature she has been a frequent contributor to "Scott's Magazine," (Atlanta,) and the "Land we Love," (Charlotte, N. C.) To the kind and generous conduct of General D. H. Hill, editor of the latter-named magazine, Miss Barnwell owes much, for it encouraged her to persevere in her intention of becoming an author, when the difficulties which lie in the path of every beginner would otherwise, perhaps, have frightened her into turning back.

Miss Barnwell's style is easy and graceful, with the fault of young writers generally, using the "adjectives" profusely. Her most ambitious effort is a tale, entitled "Triumphant," which we hope may be the beginning of many triumphs in the path she has chosen. She is teaching in Waynesboro, Burke County, Georgia.

1871.

ON SOUTHERN LITERATURE.

Hitherto the South has contributed a comparatively small share to the great mass of American publications. This was, perhaps, owing to the truth of that old opinion that poverty is the soil best calculated to render talent and genius fruitful, not to produce them, for they are rare plants, peculiar to no soil, no climate, and no season ; but merely to stimulate them to a fairer growth, and to ripen their rich and varied fruit. We were a prosperous people ; our slaves were carefully housed, fed, and clothed by the masters, who were their protection from those blessings of the free children of poverty, exposure, starvation, and nakedness. We were not obliged to write for our daily bread, and so many who, under other circumstances, would have wielded a successful pen, were content, instead, to satisfy the cravings of their intellect with copious draughts from the cup of knowledge prepared by other hands. Now the case is widely different. Never, perhaps, in the annals of the world, were there so many people of education, culture, and refinement suddenly reduced at the same moment to such a state of absolute and painful poverty. In this condition there is but one alternative — we must work or starve : but where is work to be obtained such as we can perform ? Many of us have received the best advantages of education, and with such, food for the mind is a necessity second only to that of food for the body. They cannot get books ; and if they could, time is too needful for the task of earning bread, to be spent in anything which does not aid in that object. In this emergency, they seize the pen, and become authors. Eagerly, hungrily they write, striving to feed body and mind at once ; now disheartened by the frequent failure of their efforts, now cheered by a feeble gleam of success, but always struggling on for bare existence. Chatterton, poor, lonely, gifted boy, insulted, proud, and shut in by so dark a sky, might well serve as the type of those who will one day be remembered and honored as the founders of a Southern literature.

And it is now, while we are thus at the commencement of our work, that no effort should be spared to lay a sure and strong and pure foundation, that will resist time and change and decay. Is it poetry that is needed to call forth our highest efforts ? Surely, we can scarcely have it in a fuller measure than at present. Is it education and refinement ? We will never have more than is ours to-day. Is it love of country, and the wish to twine a wreath of immortal bays to crown her brow ? Ah ! never in her brighter days of pride and hope did we love our sunny land as now, in her hour of woe and desolation — never did we long more eagerly to do her honor. Is it a noble, animating spirit, the sight of gallant deeds and priceless sacrifices, of heroes and of martyrs ? Surely, surely the memory of our glorious struggle has not faded yet — we have not yet forgotten the heroes and martyrs, the victories and the sacrifices, the noble deeds and the fearless deaths that marked our brief day of freedom. Or is it examples of faith and trust and self-forgetfulness, of dignity, manliness, and stainless honor that we crave? Look, oh! look around you, and in the lives of thousands of our suffering people you will find examples of all these as fair and as bright as the record of the heroes and martyrs of other days — the Cranmers, Ridleys, and Latimers, the Hoopers, John Bradfords, and Anne Askews, whose names shine like stars amidst the darkness of cruelty, sin, and oppression by which they are surrounded.

MARY CAROLINE GRISWOLD.

IN 1864, the "Southern Field and Fireside" published several novelettes and poems, by "Carrie," which were interesting and naturally written, and consequently popular. "Zaidee: A Tale of the Early Christians," was a very pleasing story; as was "Bannockburn," the longest of these novelettes.

"Carrie," or, rather, Miss Griswold, is rather young, as yet, to have made much progress in the literary line; although, from her published novelettes, etc., we feel warranted in giving her a place among "Southland Writers," as a writer of much promise.

Miss Griswold is a resident of Charleston, S. C.

THE WHITE CAMELIA.

Circled with glossy leaves, in queenly power
Rested in its purity the marble flower:
No balmy fragrance swept the silent air,
A *dream* of sweetness only lingered there,
Like to a loving heart that stands alone
With o'er each gushing thought a silence thrown:
'Neath the snow-drifts of pride it calmly lies,
Lives in the world awhile, then droops and dies;
Alone with an inward grief that none divine,
It, like the flower, falls without a sign:
Fit emblem thus of pride in all its power,
In dreamy stillness lay — the *marble flower!*

MISS JULIA C. MINTZING.

JULIA CAROLINE MINTZING, the subject of this sketch, comes from one of the most prominent and highly respected families of South Carolina. She is a thorough Southern woman, and she has that intensity of character that distinguishes those women of the South who are truly representatives of their section. By ancestry and nativity a South-Carolinian — her father and mother both having been born in that State — it is not strange that Miss Mintzing should possess that self-consciousness of the Carolinian, which, carried in the persons of statesmen into the political arena of the country, has done so much to mould the public opinion of the South, and, indeed, of Democrats everywhere. In these days of woman-rightism — when the weaker sex tilt against the sterner, mounted upon the hobby of Reform — it would perhaps seem invidious to refer to our sister as one who has always taken a deep and absorbing interest in the politics of the country. But the interest which Miss Mintzing, even from early childhood, has ever manifested in the political questions of the day, has arisen, we may presume, from the necessities of the case. Reared in that fierce school of States Rights which admits of no parleying and no compromise, it would not be singular to find one embodying in herself all the proud traditions of her State, giving to the cause, which in South Carolina partakes almost of the sanctity of a religious creed, her enthusiastic reverence. As the French would say, *ça va sans dire.* This, however, in passing.

In contemplating Miss Mintzing as a writer — our main purpose — we must judge her not so much by what she has done as by her capabilities and her promise of future performance. Her writings, up to within a recent period, have not been voluminous. Circumstances which so many tenderly nurtured of the South have had reason to deplore — the desolations produced by war and rapine — have had much to do with Miss Mintzing's literary efforts. The losses sustained by her family during the war were severe. Happily, the subject of this sketch has found it within her power to call upon her mental armory for weapons wherewith to resist the too pressing encroachments of pecuniary adversity. She has found place for her writings in some of the best magazines and literary papers of the country, and in the pages and columns of these has laid the seeds of a reputation which only needs time to insure its blossoming into fame.

From Miss Mintzing's writings we give two selections, one of poetry, and the other of prose. We commence with the poem:

VICTOR AND VICTIM.

Only a lance in her quivering breast,
Fatally poised in the tourney's jest,
Only a wreck on life's stormiest sea
Wildly adrift for Eternity!
Only a shade on a summer sky,
Only the break of a careless tie,
Only a prayer — O Father — God!
Her passionate cry beneath the rod!
　　Comfort her, Lord!
　　Shield with thy sword
　　　From all who oppress,
　　　From all who distress.
　　Man and his falsity,
　　Pettiest mockery!
　　Woman the slanderer,
　　Friend, foe, and panderer —
　　　Grant her redress!

Why did she pause for the Lorelei's song?
Why did she listen and dream so long?
Why was she blind to the dazzling snare
That lured her on to the end so sair?
Why were the eyes so tender and blue —
And the trysting vows that seemed so true!
Why the soft touch — the passionate thrill,
And the lips that kissed away reason's will!
　　Back, ye sweet memories!
　　Off, ye fond reveries!
　　　Hark to the world!
　　She is but human —
　　Only a woman!
　　So crush all feeling,
　　Weakness revealing,
　　For we are maskers,
　　Hypocrite taskers!

> Life a poor summer day,
> And we the potter's clay
> Toys to be hurled!

> Was he so brave thus to tilt for her life —
> Was he a man in this dalliance-strife?
> Flash shield and buckler — blaze helmet and lance
> Quick to this tourney — valiant advance!
> But the hand that is poising with steadiest aim
> Shall quiver with weakness and tremble with pain
> When the ghosts of those moments swoop fierce from unrest,
> And falsehood's Nemesis holds hell in his breast!

> > True, 't is but a lance
> > In the road's advance,
> > And but a woman
> > Proves to be human!
> > Only a heart
> > Breaks in the jesting;
> > 'T is but a part
> > Played in life's testing!
> > Then pity her, God,
> > As faint, 'neath Thy rod,
> > Weary in the agony,
> > She treads her Calvary!

As a writer of prose, Miss Mintzing is just as earnest in her style and in her manner of expressing herself as she shows herself to be in her poetry. Indeed, this earnestness of character is one of her marked attributes. We can well imagine that she would be one to rejoice in the courage of Joan of Arc and in the devoted patriotism of Charlotte Corday — choosing these as memorable examples of the heroism of her sex.

In an article upon Gœthe and Schiller, the illustrious German authors, published in the "Land we Love," Miss Mintzing compares these two masters of the literature of Germany. The following passages from the article in question will afford a fair understanding of Miss Mintzing's characteristics as a writer of prose:

The old city of Frankfort on the Main claims the birth of Johann Wolfgang Von Gœthe, August 28th, 1749. Sprung from the aristocracy, nursed and petted by his beautiful child-mother, his bright, sunny childhood passed.

Impressionable and fiery, we find him, while yet a boy, agonized by the intensity of his first love.

But the heart that through a long life was only to dispense successively, did not break; though the boy-love has, with the boy-faith, so exquisitely idealized the heroine's name in that Faust which thrilled all Germany. Despite the ethics of the poem-drama, which the "rigid righteous" so vehemently decry, the sweet, girlish trust, the faith and pathos of Margaret's love, hold the heart against all judgment.

The pretty poetry of Mignon's episode in Wilhelm Meister pleases, and the refrain of her child-sorrow is still echoing in our hearts, as she pleads for her return to that sunny land where "the gold-orange blooms;" but Margaret, man's spiritualized earth-love, attracts with a sad, sweet witchery which holds us spell-bound as only Gœthe's genius can — lifts us far above the fault, and wrong, and sin, though the hard world thundered its code as the organ rolled the "Dies Iræ," and faint and weary the broken lily fell at the cathedral gates.

But the perfection of Gœthe's womanhood is seen in his conception of Clara — the Clara of "Egmont." Here again the characteristic rather than the morale must appeal! — aye the strength of the passionate devotion of this Amy Robsart of Germany wakens for her an all-absorbing interest. In Margaret, the trust, and clinging, girlish love, are most prominent — the development born of the dangerous guile of the accomplished man of the world; but in Clara it is Egmont's inspiration — the passion called to life by the gallant soldier, brilliant noble, and impetuous lover. Her little songs are exquisite; breathing sometimes a witching coquetry, and always her unselfish devotion. In this drama, less metaphysical than Faust, the scenes are graphic, and the stirring history of the revolt of the Netherlands moves almost as a living spectacle.

Some of Egmont's soliloquies rise into all the grandeur of the truly majestic German, and the famous prison reflection is unsurpassed by anything which even Shakspeare has left to us.

An English writer, comparing the Juliet of Shakspeare with Schiller's Thekla, has remarked that in Juliet is found an "infinity of love," but in Thekla "an eternity;" and in truth the womanly characteristics are wonderfully developed in this rare gallery. Sweet, trustful Margaret pleads her faith-love — for even when dying, her lips fashion the name of her beloved; Clarchen, with more of the strength of passion, exhibits the fathomless depths of her intenser nature; while Thekla, Schiller's pure, self-sacrificing girl-patriot, passes away in the music of her broken heart, as she murmurs her exquisite farewell, in the sweet, sad line,

"Ich habe gelebt, und geliebet!"

And this, his earliest and most spirituelle creation, recalls another of the great lights which brightened the eighteenth century.

John Christopher Frederic Von Schiller was born on the tenth of November, 1759, at Marbach on the Neckar. And what a contrast his infancy and boyhood present, when compared with the cloudless happiness of Gœthe's life. Born in poverty, and educated at a military-monastic school, he was restricted from all intercourse with women; for Charles, Duke of Wurtemberg, thought it most conducive to the intellectual development of his beneficiaries to allow only the visits of mothers and very young sisters. Heart-food and brain-food were alike dusty books; and we find the talent which, in the future, was to give us Don Carlos, Marie Stuart, Thekla, and the thrilling drama of William Tell, diligent in the study of physic and jurisprudence.

But the soul of the thirsting neophyte panted for its native element, and we watch him through the stolen hours of the night, revelling in what was to make his fame throughout the world.

And now the student-life passes away, and we find the independent German spirit boldly and bravely struggling for freedom of thought; and unwilling to submit to the sway and espionage of his old patron, he escaped from the army, and then appeared "The Robbers," the first-born of that wonderful intellect, and a drama of rare talent and marvellous power.

Afterward came Don Carlos, Marie Stuart, Wallenstein, Piccolomini, Revolt of United Netherlands, and, as the last effort and crowning glory, William Tell. The story of Don Carlos, as told by Prescott, in his simple and beautiful English, is familiar to all; but the grace and eloquence of the love-passages in the drama require all the fiery imagination of this grand old master. Marie Stuart, as portrayed by Schiller, has all the womanly dignity with which we love to associate the beautiful Queen of Scotland. The garden scene has become world-renowned since Ristori's perfect rendering and gentle accents have thrilled two continents with their eloquence.

In preparing himself for Wallenstein and the Piccolomini, Schiller collected material for the Revolt of the United Netherlands, a period with which we are now well acquainted through the researches of the terse and elegant Prescott and tireless Motley.

Schiller's life differs entirely from that of his great compeer; for Gœthe, with his rare beauty, seemed born to happiness; while his joyous, expansive heart, ever life-giving, received and gave forth without ceasing, emphatically an absolvent, and, whirled on by destiny, he dispensed what might be called his life-charities: receiving always a more costly recompense, as Gretchen, Frederica, and a hundred others answer to the roll-call of his unresisting and irresistible heart.

But of all the many, the history of Frederica, the timid, shy, yet loving maiden, stands conspicuous in her sweet, forgiving sorrow; a mute, appealing rebuke to the faithless poet. Through long years of neglect and forgetfulness, still she clung to this grand passion of her life: and when wooed, her reply was,

" The heart that has once been Gœthe's, can never be another's."

Schiller, differently situated, had life's hard realities to struggle against; for poverty, with its iron grasp, had seized him, and he had little time for love's dalliance or its joys; in fact, his early isolation from women told plainly in his writings, and his heart-impressions were neither many nor inspiring: therefore we are not surprised at his friendship — love-marriage. Whether the heart of this mighty German could have been otherwise wakened, remains a mystery; but certainly the perfection of womanly passion has never been evidenced in his heroines.

Schiller generally wrote at night, strengthened by very strong coffee: this was the habit of a lifetime, and to and fro, through the cold German midnights, would he pace his room, while the grand conceptions of his magnificent intellect were dreamed into realities.

But the battle, the toil, and the wear of a troubled existence told upon him while yet in the flush of his manhood. An earnest spirit, disdaining the mean and the sensual, his strivings were after the pure, the true, and the good; and as his last-born, his farewell benison to his fatherland, he bequeathed his great drama of William Tell.

Who that has read this does not feel his pulses quicken, as the splendid talent of the author does noble battling for the right? and, as the last flush on the Rütli dies along the Swiss heavens, we feel Schiller's spirit floating upward in its light.

As the one illustrates the German genius, so the other stands colossal as the German talent.

Even the personal appearance of the men seems to speak their especial characteristics. Gœthe was tall and majestic, the handsome man of Germany; with that marvellous beauty which lit every lineament with the reflex of his soul: and Schiller, towering in his rugged outlines, large-featured and irregular, yet always bearing the impress of the great intellect that swayed him with imperial rule.

But they both have passed where, to use Schiller's own language,

"Word is kept with Hope, and to wild Belief a *lovely truth* is given."

And the old German is singing still their echoes — the delicious thrilling minor, and the vibrating, heart-stirring bass — a grandly weird symphony, born in the wild German mountains, and nursed by the blue, rippling Rhine.

Again we listen to the sweet Minnesingers, and again we bow in reverence to the magnificent hymns of the seventeenth century: now the spell of Gœthe's genius lures us, and anon Heine's silvery music wilders, as did his own beautiful Lorelei. The soul-chants of Schiller waken and vibrate to the very depths of the spirit; while Kremer, fiery, impassioned, freedom-loving Kremer, shields us with that last hymn, born while his immortality hovered on the brink of destiny.

And so the mighty host passes onward, onward! marshalled into the far eternity ; but their teachings remain forever in our hearts, and as an inspiration from them echoes the sentiment,

> "Whoever with an earnest soul
> Strives for some end, from this low world afar
> Still upward travels though he miss the goal,
> And strays — but toward a star!"

Miss Mintzing's personal presence is very attractive. She is of a *distingue* appearance, somewhat above the medium height, graceful in the extreme, and denotes in every gesture the lady of culture and refinement. In conversation, she is earnest; bordering, sometimes, on the enthusiastic — especially upon subjects connected with her State and section — and dispenses a great deal of her own magnetism to those with whom she converses. Her social tastes lead her to pleasure and gayety; and in the drawing-room she is an acknowledged ornament. She is rather of an Italian type, being a brunette of a clear and soft complexion. Her eyes are dark, and her hair is dark-brown and lustrous.

Since the war, Miss Mintzing has resided chiefly in New York. As a writer, her future lies before her. We do not doubt, if she should choose to follow the thorny paths of literature, that she will establish herself among the authors of the South whose reputations will be something more than ephemeral. Hitherto she has never published under her own name.

1869.   CHARLES DIMITRY.

————◦○○◦○○————

JEANIE A. DICKSON.

MISS DICKSON, daughter of Dr. Samuel Henry Dickson, an eminent physician, formerly of Charleston, has published considerable in prose and verse in different magazines. She was among the contributors to "Russell's Magazine," Charleston, and recently to several Southern journals. Her residence is in Philadelphia.

1870.

MRS. LAURA GWYN.

THE life of this gifted lady has been as remarkable as her poetry has been sweet and brilliant. Without ambition, without seeming to be conscious of her genius, her days have been spent in seclusion from society, and devoted to her household affairs.

Her father, Samuel G. McClanahan, was related to Chief Justice Marshall. Laura was born in Greenville, S. C., September 18th, 1833. She was educated at the academy of her native place. While at school, at the age of twelve years, she began to write in verse, and would present her compositions in verse instead of prose; and a number of years ago published a volume of poems, which attracted attention.

Hon. Wm. C. Preston, and Paul H. Hayne, the poet, have spoken in terms of praise of her poems and genius.

Mrs. Gwyn has a large number of poems in manuscript.

At a youthful age she married the Rev. T. D. Gwyn, a Baptist clergyman. They reside on a farm near Greenville.

1871.   Ex-Gov. B. F. Perry.

MY PALACE OF DREAMS.

Far hidden away from the pomp and glare
  Of this dreary world where we droop and pine,
Wrapt in soft shadows and balmy air,
In a land that is always green and fair
  Stands my palace of dreams divine!
And whatsoever of change or woe
The years may bring me, I know, I know
  They never can darken my palace of dreams!
For e'en as a cloud in the sunset rolled,
Is turned to colors of crimson and gold,
  So each thought-flower that hither I bear
  Drinks the dew and is kissed by the air,
Spreads its petal, and glows and gleams
With the magical hue of my palace of dreams,
  My beautiful palace of dreams.

In this charmed palace, so fair, so fair,
  A wonderful spring-time reigns alway:

65   513

Here are sweet June roses to wreathe the hair,
  Buds of April, and flowers of May!
Flowers, flowers with dewdrops deftly hung —
  Under their jewels they glisten and glow,
Under their jewels they sparkle and quiver —
  And wearing these I forget that ever
    Hearts were broken or hopes laid low —
  I forget all sorrow, and only know
That life was sweet when I was young!
  For deep in the shade, with a liquid flow,
  The beautiful fabled Lethean river
    Goes by my palace of dreams.

The voice of a bird in the twilight singing
  Its early song with dewy throat,
The drowsy hum of a glad bee winging
  Its homeward flight from flowers remote,
Is not more sweet than the sounds that float,
    Moving wind-like, evermore
    Through each long shady corridor —
Soft echoes borne from the vale of youth,
  Voices that gladdened me long ago,
  Passionate vows that were murmured low,
Full of tenderness, love, and truth!
  But all things evil that darken my soul —
  Thoughts of sorrow and sounds of dole —
Can enter not: they have found a grave
Under the shimmering Lethean wave
    That flows by my palace of dreams.

Clothed with soft raiment of poesy,
    There are forms that move with stately paces!
And looking forth from each niche I see,
Smiling welcome and love to me,
    Wonderful faces! wonderful faces!
And lo! through all this palace of mine
    The sweet rhymes wander — ballad and song,
Quaint and merry, and many a time,
    On the wings of some melody glad and strong,
My soul is borne to the innermost shrine,
    To the chambers fair that are furnished meet
    With Lydian music faint and sweet,
    For the ingoing of Love's light feet
      In my beautiful palace of dreams!

The silken poppy with drooping head,
    The lotus blossom and myrtle spray,
And heavy roses of white and red
        Hang over the portals cool and gray
        Of my beautiful palace of dreams!
And tenderly, tenderly evermore,
Love meets my soul at the open door—
The sweet, lost love of the days of yore,
        That lives in my palace of dreams!

There, served forever by memory,
    The fair immutable love of mine,
Forgotten by all the world save me,
Weareth its immortality,
Is crowned with its immortality
        In my palace of dreams divine!
In this world of shadows alone, alone,
    Whatever of sorrow or pain I dree,
    Let no soft heart have pity for me,
Let no sweet soul for me make moan,
    For have I not Love in my palace of dreams!
All gorgeous music 'tis mine to hear!
All pleasure roses 'tis mine to wear!
And I softly live and I daintily fare
        With Love in my palace of dreams!

MISS CATHARINE GENDRON POYAS.

THE author of the "Year of Grief," (published in 1870 by Walker, Evans & Cogswell, Charleston,) is not a literary character, but a woman who, from the shade of retired life, has ventured twice to launch a little skiff on the ocean of letters, leaving them to float or sink at the mercy of the wind and wave.

Her first volume, entitled "Huguenot Daughters, and other Poems," was published in 1849; but few copies were read beyond Charleston, or the shores of South Carolina, Miss Poyas' native State.

Miss Catharine G. Poyas was born in Charleston, a daughter of the "Ancient Lady," who, it will be remembered by many Charlestonians, was held in high estimation, under that *nom de plume*, for her literary attainments and popular contributions to the leading journals of her day. The subject of this sketch was educated in Charleston, first by the Misses Ramsay, and afterward by the South Carolina Society School, under that accomplished teacher, Miss Anna Frances Simonton, of New York. This lady dying of yellow fever in 1827 or '28, Miss Poyas then left school and continued her studies alone, her own energy and love of learning supplying the need of a school-mistress.

At an early age she began to make verses, which were circulated among admiring friends. It was not, however, by impulse of genius alone, that she became a poetess; reading with her being not a mere pastime, but a study for mental improvement: she cultivated her mind diligently by devoting herself to English literature, not skimming over, but mastering works of history, theology, biography, and poetry — these were her chief studies, the fruits of which are offered to the public in her interesting volume, "The Year of Grief."

This volume seems to have been chiefly produced during and since the late war; and a very large proportion of the poems have been inspired by the events in its progress; sometimes full of hope and exultation, but more frequently a wail over its disastrous incidents and deadly results. It records, indeed, many years of grief instead of one. The first poem in the collection, which gives its title to the book, consists of a series of memorial sonnets, in which the author laments the losses in a single year of the good and great which her circle had known. These sonnets are all graceful of expression, tender, feeling, and deeply suffused with religious sentiment — a sentiment, by the way, which infuses every verse issuing from the author's pen.

The sonnet which follows is one of the prettiest and most perfect things in the volume; very sweet, graceful, and fanciful, the religious sentiment being still happily blended with the poetical. Indeed, in none of the verses of our author do we ever find them separated. She sings always either before the altar or at the grave.

> "Pure as a moonbeam sleeping on the sea,
>   Or playing in the chalice of a flower
>   In some romantic fairy-cultured bower,
> Seems thy sweet maiden presence unto me,
> With its soft light, and holy witchery
>   Of Christian graces; the peculiar dower
>   Of stern affliction, which in Life's young bower
> Put out the sun and left sad night to thee,

Yet not a night of darkness and of gloom —
Bright, solemn stars look from its deep blue sky,
And silvery moonbeams ripple and illume
Thy path else dreary, and allure thine eye
To where *thy friend*, amid perpetual bloom,
Awaits thy coming in the realm on high."

1870.

SELINA E. MEANS.

THE future will discover the justice in admitting Mrs. Means among the " Writers of the South."

" Reminiscences of York, by a Septuagenarian," is Mrs. Means most popular contribution to the literature of the day. The material for these reminiscences Mrs. Means gathered from her father, Dr. Moore, who for years has been a collator of Revolutionary anecdotes, and is the author of a pamphlet of considerable historical value, " A Life of Gen. Edward Lacey," forming a nucleus for the history of the partisan warfare of Upper Carolina in the Revolutionary war.

The style and matter of these " Reminiscences " proving popular, Mrs. Means became a competitor for a prize offered by a Carolina literary paper. Her novelette did not receive the prize, but was accepted and paid for by the proprietor. The title of this story is " Unknown." She has other and more ambitious literary ventures completed and in preparation.

Mrs. Means was born April 21st, 1840, in Union District, S. C. From both parents she has a right to the pen of a ready writer. Her father's literary talent has been alluded to ; and her mother was a sister of Dr. Josiah C. Nott, now of New York, formerly of Mobile, a distinguished physician and surgeon, and author of " The Types of Mankind," etc., etc., and of the late Prof. Henry Junius Nott, of the College of South Carolina, and author of two volumes of tales, called " Novelettes of a Traveller; or, Odds and Ends from the Knapsack of Thomas Singularity, Journeyman Printer." These tales were taken from life, and exhibit in a style of much humor the happy faculty possessed by Mr. Nott of catching every odd trait of character that presented itself. Prof. Nott and his wife were lost in the wreck of the unfortunate steamer " The Home," off the coast of North Carolina, October 13th, 1837.

Mrs. Means is the wife of Dr. T. Sumter Means, of Glenn's Spring, South Carolina.

1871.

———oo:o:oo———

LOUISA S. McCORD.

MRS. McCORD, the daughter of Langdon Cheves, Esq., well known in the public and political history of the State, was born December 3d, 1810, in Charleston. She was educated in Philadelphia. In 1840, Miss Cheves was married to D. J. McCord, of Columbia, S. C. In 1855 Mrs. McCord became a widow. Her residence is Columbia, South Carolina.

Mrs. McCord's writings have consisted principally of essays and reviews, and she has written well on the difficult subject of political economy.

Her published volumes are:

My Dreams. A volume of poems, published in Philadelphia in 1848.

Sophisms of the Protective Policy. A translation from the French of Bastiat. Published in New York. 1848.

Caius Gracchus. A five-act tragedy. New York. 1851.

Mrs. McCord was a contributor to the "Southern Quarterly Review," and the "Southern Literary Messenger," for a number of years from 1849.

"Mrs. McCord's poetry is simply and clearly uttered, and is the expression of a healthful nature. Her tragedy of 'Caius Gracchus,' a dramatic poem for the closet, is balanced in its philosophy and argument, Cornelia wisely tempering the democratic fervor of her son. Many sound, pithy aphorisms of conduct may be extracted from this piece; all expressed with purity and precision. The character of Cornelia is well sustained."

1871.

———oo:o:oo———

MRS. MARY C. RION.

MRS. RION resides in Winnsboro, S. C. Has published one volume on floriculture, entitled "The Ladies' Southern Florist." 12mo. Columbia, 1860.

1871.

MARYLAND.

ANNE MONCURE CRANE.

 NEW and Original Novel" was the heading of an article in the "Boston Transcript," written by E. P. Whipple, the essayist, in which he says:

"The most notable characteristic of this book, published by Ticknor & Fields, entitled 'Emily Chester,' is its originality, and it will give novel-readers a really novel impression. All the usual elements of romantic interest are avoided, and new elements, heretofore but slightly hinted in English novels, are made the substance of the work. Since Gœthe's 'Elective Affinities,' we are aware of no story in which the psychology of exceptional sentiment and passion is represented with such keenness and force as in 'Emily Chester.' The play of sympathy and antipathy, in recesses of the mind where will exerts no controlling influence, is exhibited with a patient, penetrating, and intense power, which fastens the reader's somewhat reluctant and resisting attention, and compels him to take interest in what has no natural hold on his healthy sympathies. The character of Emily Chester is not a pleasing one, but it is deeply conceived and vigorously developed. Max Crampton and Frederic Hastings are also types of character strongly individualized, and the contrasted magnetism they exert on the mind and heart of the heroine is **vividly** represented. The interest and power of the novel are concentrated **in** these three persons. The other characters are rather commonplace, and seem to be thrown in simply to give relief to the passions of the principal personages. In those parts in which the author is not analyzing and representing the strange mental phenomena which constitute the fascination of the book, she shows immaturity both of thought and observation. . . . . 'Emily Chester' exhibits such palpable mastery of illusive phases of passion difficult to fix and portray, that it cannot fail to make a profound impression on the public."

"Emily Chester" was published without a word of preface to give the least hint of the whereabouts of the author, and was not covered with the pall of "Great Southern Novel!" as is usually the mode novels by Southern writers are announced. It had made a reputation in the North, in Boston, the "Athens of America," before it was announced that the author was a lady of Baltimore.

The Hon. George H. Hilliard thus reviews the book:

. . . . "We have a work of remarkable originality and power, certainly in these qualities entitled to rank side by side with the best productions of American genius in the department of fiction. The interest of the book is entirely derived from psychological sources, that is, from the delineation of character, and not from the incidents of the narrative, which are of a commonplace character, and with hardly the merit of probability. It reminds us of two works of fiction of a past age, Godwin's 'Caleb Williams,' and Gœthe's 'Elective Affinities,' but more of the latter than of the former. Indeed, 'Emily Chester' could hardly have been written had not the 'Elective Affinities' been written before it. We may be sure that the writer of the former is familiar with the latter. Imagine the 'Elective Affinities,' with a distinct moral aim superadded, and written with the intensity and consecration of Godwin, and we get a tolerably fair impression of 'Emily Chester.' . . . . Emily Chester is a young woman of radiant beauty and extraordinary mental powers. One of her lovers is a man of iron will and commanding intellect, from whom she nevertheless recoils with an unconquerable physical or spontaneous repulsion. The temperament of the other is in harmony with her wn; she is happy in his presence, and yet she is ever conscious of his intellectual inferiority, and thus resists the influence of his nature upon hers. Here is the whole web and the woof of the novel. . . . . It is unquestionably a work of genius. It is fair to add that it is a very sad story throughout, and thus not to be recommended to those who have sorrows enough of their own not to make them crave the books that make them grieve. It is a web in which flowers of gold and purple are wrought into a funeral shroud of deepest black. . . . .

"The heroine is an impossible creature. She is a combination of Cleopatra, Harriet Martineau, and Florence Nightingale. She is a being as supernatural or preternatural as a centaur or griffin. She is a blending of irreconcilable elements. She is represented as choosing between one lover who satisfies her intellect, and another who gratifies her temperament, as coolly as she would between a pear and a peach at a dessert. Human beings are not so made. You cannot run a knife between the intellect and the sensuous nature in this way; nor can we think Max Crampton and Frederic Hastings are true to nature. They are to real men what Ben Jonson's characters are to Shakspeare's: they are embodiments of humors, and not living flesh and blood. . . . . And we need hardly add that it is not a healthy book. We lay it down with a feeling in the mind similar to that produced on the body by sitting in a room heated by an air-tight stove. . . . . But, as has been said, there is only one kind of book which cannot be endured, and that is the stupid kind, the book that bores you. 'Emily Chester' will never fall under this condemnation, for it is a book of absorbing interest. From the first chapter the author seizes the attention with the strong grasp of genius, and holds it unbroken to the last. And when the end comes, we lay the book down with a sort of sigh of relief at the relaxation of fibres stretched to a painful degree of tension."

To show plainly the attention this novel attracted among the intellectual portion of the North, I give a criticism from the pen of a female genius of New England, widely known under her pseudonym of "Gail Hamilton":

"The very common, fault of this book will have a tendency to conceal from the popular gaze its uncommon excellence. It has all the millinery of a third-rate American novel—the most abounding beauty in its women, perfect manly grace in its men, fabulous wealth surrounding the important personages, with a profusion of elegant appurtenances which, at the present rates of gold, reads like an Arabian Night's entertainment. In style it is sometimes careless, sometimes slightly coarse, and not unfrequently labored. It constantly falls into the vulgar error of making all of its outside women pretty, gossiping, envious, malignant, and hateful, with only here and there a gleam of faint and altogether flickering sunshine, as if womanly splendor were not sufficient of its own shining, but must be set off against a black background. The conversations are sometimes spun out to undue length, and it indulges too largely in philosophy and generalizations. Yet even these drawbacks have their own compensations. The remarks and reflections, if sometimes a little impertinent, are generally sensible and shrewd, indicating an uncommon depth and clearness of insight. The conversations would occasionally be improved by abridgment; but they are earnest and high-toned. . . . .

"I do not know that American novel literature has produced any other work of the kind. Miss Sheppard's 'Counterparts' offers, so far as I can recollect, the only resemblance to be found in the English language. But discarding all resort to hard-featured fathers, mercenary mothers, family feuds, and all manner of *circumstances*, go directly inward, and find in the internal mystery of the complex human being all the obstacle, the passion and purpose which life requires. This will not, perhaps, add to the popularity of the book; but it makes its power. It may, indeed, be a stone of stumbling and a rock of offence to those conservative novel-readers who love to have a story go on in the good old paths, with which they have become so familiar that they can see the end from the beginning. It is so comfortable to know of a surety that the villain will come to grief, and the knight to joy, however stormy may be the sea of troubles on which he is tossed. All present pain is viewed with a tranquillity inspired by foreknowledge of future happiness. But this book thrusts in upon all these easy-going ways. A beautiful woman, of her own free will, marries a man who is passionately and most unselfishly devoted to her, whom she holds in profound respect and reverence, yet with a feeling little short of loathing. What newfangled notion is this? Alas! it is newfangled only in novels, not in life, and it is only by failing to recognize these subtle yet all-powerful facts, that life has so much confusion. The most careful students, as well as mere casual observers, may fail to comprehend them; but we have learned much when we have learned that there is mystery, that nature has her laws, impalpable but imperative, by obedience to which life is perfected, and by disobedience destroyed; that, deeper down in the heart of man than any words can penetrate, are forces against which it is useless for even the will to contend.

"'Emily Chester' presents this theory in what seems to be an exaggerated form. Perhaps, to state a truth, it is necessary to overstate it. The motto of the title-page avows this: 'It is in her monstrosities that nature discloses to us her secrets.' Max and Emily are scarcely so much man and woman as an impersonation of magnetism. But granting their existence, they act according to rigid natural laws. They are often melo-dramatic; there is a certain overdoing of attitude, gesture, and expression, as if a youthful hand had traced the windings of Emily's inward experience, her changing relations to Max, the effects of his absence and presence, the mingled distrust, repentance, regard, and gratitude. Such things come by special revelation. Emily herself is pure, and pure womanly, an intensified woman drawn with much skill and an infinite pity, sympathy, and tenderness. Her mirth, her coquetry, her gentleness and wilfulness, her great heart-hunger and brain-power, her passionate tastes and distastes, are a mighty relief after the bread-and-butter heroines who mostly trip it through even our good novels. Max is as great an anomaly, in his way, as Emily in hers. From time immemorial the self-immolation has been appointed to woman; but this man, opening his eyes to the evil his indomitable will had wrought upon the woman most dear to him, gave himself a living sacrifice for atonement. With stern, unwearied self-denial, he bore the sharpest pain, if so he may bring to her a gleam of peace. He will have more disciples in his sin than in his suffering; but it is well to know that such a thing is possible, even in conception."

Who is the author of this wonderful book?

Miss Anne Moncure Crane, a young lady of Baltimore, and her first attempt at writing.

Miss Anne Moncure Crane is from a talented family. The best translation in English of the celebrated German poem, "Körner's Battle Hymn," I know of, was made by a younger sister — never pub-

lished. The author of "Emily Chester" was born in the city of Baltimore, and has ever resided in that "city of beauty and talent."
"Emily Chester" was her first attempt at writing. She became an
authoress by the merest accident. Had any one told her a month
before she began *the* book that she would ever write a novel, she would
have laughed at the idea. She was twenty years old when her book
was written. How true is it "that great events arise from trivial
causes!" One evening some one carelessly suggested that a circle of
friends should form an original composition class, upon the plan of a
reading class — and Miss Crane contribute a novel. The plan was not
carried out, but the idea of "writing" had fallen upon fertile soil, and
before the next day Miss Crane resolved to seriously attempt to write
a book for publication. She began it, and "Emily Chester" was the
result — she says, "a greater surprise to me than it could have been
to any one else." A very unusual case was that of the publication
of this book, and "as an act of justice to the much-maligned race of
publishers," we state the case. When "Emily Chester" was completed,
it was taken to Messrs. Ticknor & Fields by a lady who was a
stranger to them. She was told that they could not even entertain
the idea of publishing it, as they were overcrowded with previous engagements; but upon her urging the point, she was politely allowed to
leave the book for inspection. Within two weeks from that time they
sent a contract for its publication, addressed to the "Author of 'Emily
Chester;'" and it was not until Miss Crane returned the paper signed in
full that they knew the name of the writer whose novel they had bound
themselves to publish. They were aware that it was a first attempt,
and that the author was a woman. Miss Crane's literary life has been
peculiarly exempt from those trials and discouragements which tradition has led us to believe are almost inseparable from the career of a
young, unknown author. Miss Crane is a contributor of brilliant
stories and poems to our magazines — among others to the "Galaxy"
and "Putnam's Monthly."

Her second book, entitled "Opportunity," was published at the close
of 1867, and was welcomed by the many admirers of "Emily Chester," although it did not create such a furore. It is thus noticed in
a Southern journal, by Paul H. Hayne, the poet:

"This is no common romance. Depending but slightly upon the nature
of its plot and outward incidents, its power is almost wholly concentrated

upon a deep, faithful, subtle analysis of character. Indeed, it is rather a series of peculiar psychological studies, than a novel in the ordinary sense of the term. True insight, genuine imagination, a somewhat unique experience of life, are everywhere apparent in its elaborate, careful, and not unfrequently profound portraitures. Even the faults of the work are such as could scarcely have had their origin in a commonplace mind. A morbid, exaggerated force of introspection, laying bare to their very roots the motives of human action, strikes the reader sometimes with a shuddering distaste, the sort of feeling one would experience in beholding too deep and merciless a dissection of any diseased condition, whether of body or heart! Yet how can one fail to admire the strong and subtle gifts by which such results are attained? Moreover, the *general* purpose of the story is noble and exalted. A purity of aim some might call transcendental distinguishes its central *morale*. But its unworldly suggestiveness is charming. Two male characters — brothers — divide the reader's interest. One is a brilliant, susceptible, but frivolous nature, possessing, no doubt, capacities for good, yet too feeble to arrest and to develop them. The other is a strong, passionate, manly, upright soul, who, in the blackest hours of misfortune and doubt, feels (as that gallant Christian gentleman, Frederick Robinson, was wont to observe) that there are instinctive spiritual truths — the 'great landmarks of morality' — which a man (in the midnight of skepticism) must cling to, would he avoid destruction. These brothers, so diverse in temperament, encounter and fall in love with the same woman. She is little more than a girl in years, but her heart and intellect are strangely precocious : and not merely precocious, but wonderful in the exceptional character of their endowments. Her fascination radiates chiefly from *within*. To Grahame Ferguson — the elder and weaker brother — she is led unconsciously to give her affection.

> " 'Ah!' says the author, referring to this singular heroine — 'Ah! the marvellous fascination of these beautiful-ugly women. To watch the loveliness they seem to keep as too sacred for ordinary eyes, slowly dawn and reach a divine perfection in your sight, what mortal man *can* withstand? If it be only a faint, momentary wild-rose flush upon the usually colorless cheek, a single flash or passing gleam in the lustreless eyes, if you know it to be your very own, that *you* alone have created it, no glory of Greek art can so stir you! This was the miracle Grahame wrought daily, and yet so differently, that he waited each time in expectancy as uncertain as intense. "This is the true, essential beauty!" he was tempted to exclaim. Another truth he awoke to, as he listened to her careless talking, with ever-increasing wonder. Not only was it that *he* recognized her absolute originality, her large structure of mind, but that her thoughts seemed radiant with *that* gleam which "never was on sea or land," her sentences musical with nature's own harmony.'

"Very speedily, however, the shallow, sensuous nature of the man betrays itself by an irrecoverable act of self-committal, and there is a passionate though secret renunciation of him on the part of Harvey Berney, (the heroine's name,) which is depicted with a refined and searching skill, a degree of mind-knowledge and soul-knowledge that are unquestionably remarkable. We cannot follow the various complications of the narrative. It is at a later date that Grahame's brother, Douglas, makes the acquaintance of Miss Berney. These two were evidently fitted for each other; strength to strength, purity to purity, passion to passion. But one of those errors, apparently so trifling, in reality pregnant with fate and death, came between and separated them.

"Douglas was not permitted even to tell his love. Yet how the true, loyal, noble spirit rises gradually from the depression of the blow, and finds comfort in the arms of *duty*, which are finally transformed into the arms of *happiness!*

"Grahame's destiny is of another and sadder kind. It never occurred to him that

'To bear is to conquer our fate.'

Therefore he yields to disappointment and all its insidious temptations, sinks lower and lower in the moral scale, and may finally be regarded as one of those dead souls which, though freed from absolute sensuality, are yet the 'bounden slaves' of *ennui*, sloth, discontent, and that host of effeminate vices which in certain moods are more revolting to us than downright, monstrous, satanic wickedness.

"Underneath the surface of Miss Crane's story and its characterizations, there runs a vein of meaning which only the attentive reader will clearly comprehend. She shows how 'opportunities' may be neglected to the utter misery of the individual; but she rightly and philosophically represents these 'opportunities' as often coming in such 'questionable guise,' that an inspired foresight alone could be expected to take advantage of them. Thus, it is not in the ignorant neglect of 'opportunity' that she pretends to find the seeds of guilt or folly, but in *that illogical and disloyal faithlessness* which sinks weakly under the ban of circumstance, accepts tamely its awards, and never, with the superb audacity of the 'GREAT HEART,' strives to force a way upward, in the very teeth of what we are too apt to call falsely 'providential decrees.' In this way the unlucky Grahame sinks to a level below our contempt. Pursuing an opposite course, his brother not only vanquishes the desperation and despair which beset his reason, but grasps, finally, the serene rewards of an unselfish, manful endurance.

"We close our notice of Miss Crane's production with the remark that no tale has recently appeared, North or South, which is so full of rich evidences of genuine psychological power, a profound study of character in some of its most unique spiritual and mental manifestations, and fervid artistic aspirations, destined to embody themselves gloriously in the future."

Miss Crane looks the "woman of genius," having large features, her nose aquiline and prominent, her mouth large, but rather pleasant, her chin firm, her brow moderate and well arched : her eyes are dark, and have a bright outlook on this world ; her hair is dark and very luxuriant—she wears it piled up according to the present " Japanese " style. She is tall, but not ungraceful. She prides herself on making all her own clothes, and being able to do *everything* for herself, which is very commendable. A friend calls her " an universal genius " who is very ambitious, thinking " an intellectual woman ought to do everything." The following characteristic paragraph expresses so much, that we give it place here, against our better judgment perhaps : " In fact, the author of ' Emily Chester' is a steam-engine of a woman, a regular locomotive, and flies desperately along the railroad of life; and one must either subside into the train of cars she leads quietly, or be run over, perhaps crushed to infinitesimal atoms." Miss Crane has formed an " *ideal* " of what an " authoress " ought to be, and she tries to be it.

In the fall of 1869, Miss Crane was married to Mr. Seemuller, of New York.

J. R. Osgood & Co., Boston, published a sensational novel from her pen, (1871,) entitled, " Reginald Archer."

WORDS TO A "LIED OHNE WORTE."

All earth has that is rare or is treasurable :
  Long I searched for a token, in vain,
Worthy to speak of this love so immeasurable,
  Worthy to be both my gift and her gain.
      Nor palace nor glory,
      Nor name high in story,
These, not these would I bring to my love;
      But what God gave me
      To raise and to save me,
This, 't is this I would bring to my love.

Years go by, and they take what is perishing,
  This world's fashion, which passeth away;
That which I give will need but love's cherishing,
  Ever to live and to bloom as to-day.
      Love's silver lining
      Through life's dark clouds shining,
This, 't is this I would bring to my love;
      All I have shared with none,
      All I have dared with none,
This, all this I would bring to my love.

Pleasure lures, and we follow its beckoning;
　Fame and honor seem life's best ends;
Aught that may stand in our way little reckoning,
　Onward we press, whomsoe'er it offends.
　　But when Love's star rises,
　　Nought else the soul prizes,
As earth sinks to darkness when heaven shows light,
　　Then seem these empty hands
　　Richer than golden strands,
With love, and love only, to bring to my love.

WINTER WIND.

　Restless wind of drear December,
　Listened to by dying ember,
Do you hold the same sad meaning to all other hearts this night?
　Sweeping over land and ocean
　With your mighty, rhythmic motion,
Has your hasting brought swift wasting to their hope and joy and light?

　To them, does your passing darken
　Night's black shadow as they hearken;
Filling it with mystic phantoms, such as throng some haunted spot,
　With the ghosts of joys and pleasures,
　Tortures now that once were treasures?
Does your sighing seem the crying of a soul for what is not?

　Does the same weird, weary moaning
　Seem to underlie your toning,
Whether risen in your strength, or sunk to wailing, fitful blast?
　Do they hear wild, distant dirges
　In your falls or in your surges?
Does your swelling seem the knelling for a dead, unburied Past?

"FAITH AND HOPE."

That night, after her mother had fallen asleep, Harvey, scenting tobacco-
smoke upon the porch, stole down stairs for a quiet talk with Dr. Dan, or
perhaps an hour of silent sitting, as of yore. At first, it proved to be the
latter; for, taking her childish place at his feet, and laying her head upon
his knee, he put out his hand, and softly stroked her hair with the familiar

gesture, but said nothing. Except the necessary aging with years, Dr. Dan was just the Dr. Dan of old. Presently, he began asking questions about her future plans; and then the conversation came back to the present, and even to the past.

"Harvey," he asked at last, "do you ever intend to marry?"

The inquiry had arisen somewhat naturally from others which he had put concerning a strong, true-hearted gentleman, whose apparently hopeless devotion to Harvey seemed but to deepen and strengthen with the deepening and strengthening of his nature.

"That is as God pleases," she answered, rather sadly. "Uncle," she continued presently, and her voice had changed perceptibly, "I was wounded terribly, early in the battle of life, and since then I have been among the halt and maimed."

"Yes, I know it," he replied, and his thoughts went sorrowfully and silently back to those early days.

"Harvey," he said at last, and there was something like despair in his tone, "I want you to answer me one question truthfully. You have worked and won; you have been faithful to what God gave you, and have striven hard to choose the better part: now tell me, has anything in existence yielded you real satisfaction? I frittered away my strength and purpose; I wasted my substance of heart and soul in riotous living, and the punishment of spiritual starvation rests rightfully upon me: you did none of these things; yet tell me what essential, soul-satisfying element has life ever brought you?"

For a moment or two the woman sat motionless, not looking at him, nor at the broad, moonlit heavens above her; but with eyes fixed upon the low, dark horizon, and filled with a hungry, wistful light.

"I shall be satisfied when I awake with His likeness."

This faith and hope were all she had rescued from that failure which she called her life. Ah, me! from the beginning, has any human heart ever truly rescued more?

LYDIA CRANE.

NOT noted in the "literature" of our country, yet we cannot conscientiously omit a place in our volume to the translator of the beautiful "Battle Prayer" that we give. If she so desired, she could occupy a high position among our "Southland Writers," as a translator and as an "original writer."

Miss Lydia Crane is a daughter of the late Mr. William Crane, for many years a merchant in the city of Baltimore; a man of wealth, noted for his extensive contributions to the Baptist Church and charitable institutions. She is a younger sister of the authoress of "Emily Chester" and "Opportunity."

Says a lady who has reverence, admiration, and true, respectful affection for *her :* "Lydia Crane is a noble, suffering woman, a martyr all her life to nervous disease and curvature of the spine, but who rises above pain and wretched health, and studies mathematics when every nerve is quivering with anguish."

KÖRNER'S BATTLE PRAYER.

Gebet in der Schlacht.

Father, I cry to Thee!
Rolling around me the smoke of the battle,
Lightnings surround me and war's thunders rattle,
    Leader of armies, I cry to Thee!
      Father, lead Thou me!

Father, lead Thou me!
Lead me to victory, lead me to dying;
Lord, by Thy word, be my labor and trying;
    Through this world's strife my guide deign to be.
      My God, I discern Thee!

My God, I discern Thee!
As in the murmur of leaves that are falling,
So in the thunder of battle appalling,
    Fountain of Mercy, I recognize Thee!
      Father, bless Thou me!

Father, bless Thou me!
To Thy hands alone my life is commended;
That Thou hast ordained, by Thee must be ended:
    In life and in death wilt Thou bless me!
      Father, I praise Thee!

Father, I praise Thee!
If war ever good to the earth has afforded,
The holiest cause we have saved and rewarded:
    Failing or conquering, I praise Thee!
      To Thee all surrendered be!

To Thee all surrendered be!
Though from my heart my life-blood be flowing,
When from my lips my last prayer is going,
    To Thee, my God, I surrender me!
      Father, I cry to Thee!

ELLIE LEE HARDENBROOK.

MRS. HARDENBROOK, born Lee, is a native of Baltimore, and younger sister of Mrs. J. W. Palmer. Since her girlhood, — she was born in 1836, — Mrs. Hardenbrook has been a brilliant and versatile writer for the press; although she has never published a book. For several years she was editress of a New York "weekly." She has published many continued stories, — novelettes, in fact, remarkable for imaginative power and skilful construction, — together with letters and weekly gossip on the social and æsthetic topics of the day, for New York, Philadelphia, and Baltimore papers.

GEORGIE A. HULSE McLEOD.

MRS. McLEOD is well known as presiding over the "Southern Literary Institute," of Baltimore, Maryland — a seminary for young ladies which is well known throughout the United States. That Mrs. McLeod is a generous, noble-souled lady, the fact that she gives free tuition to one young lady, the daughter of a deceased Confederate soldier, from each Southern State, amply attests.

Mrs. McLeod was born in Florida, at the Naval Hospital near Pensacola, of which her father, Dr. Isaac Hulse, was then surgeon. She was left an orphan in infancy.

Her first books, "Sunbeams and Shadows" and "Buds and Blossoms," were published in New York, in 1851. Two years after the appearance of her books, she was married to Dr. A. W. McLeod, of Halifax, N. S., where they resided for some time. Her first volume after her marriage was "Ivy Leaves from an Old Homestead," which was followed by "Thine and Mine; or, The Step-mother's Reward," published by Derby & Jackson, in 1857 — a book that was received with much favor, and inculcating an excellent moral, showing that a step-mother may supply a mother's place in kindness and care.

Mrs. McLeod, since the close of the war, has published two little volumes, "Sea-Drift" and "Bright Memories." The former is a little story, dealing mainly with school-girls, their ways and thoughts, their joys and trials — a charming book, pure, healthful, and inspiring.

Mrs. McLeod has been a constant contributor to magazines, etc., North and South, under the signature of "Flora Neale," and other *noms de plume.*

Mrs. McLeod is a very industrious writer, conducting a large school successfully, and considering her pen-work as a recreation.

She has recently completed a book for juveniles, entitled "Standing Guard," and a novel, the title of which is very inviting, viz., "The Old, Old Story."

Mrs. McLeod also has in preparation a First-Class Reader, intended for the senior class of the Southern Literary Institute, for which some of the most noted writers have contributed.

MINE!

The fresh green robes spring had given to the earth became gorgeous with the many-colored blossoms springing up everywhere. The June roses clambered over the lattice-work, and sent in on the breath of the south wind a perfumed greeting, to woo into the summer air the happy-hearted.

Never, to Mrs. Rivers, had the summer been so fair, the flowers so lovely. A joy within had shed an influence over outward things — a new, deep joy; for, with the summer blossoms, a bud of beauty, a living floweret, gave an added charm to home. A murmur of praise trembled on her lips, and a happy light was in the soft, dark eyes, as she folded the unconscious little one so lovingly to her heart, murmuring, "*Mine*, all my own!"

A little child! How the memory of Him who was cradled in a manger comes back upon us when we look upon such helplessness! Its very weakness has the power of twining about proud hearts a chain of love and pity, that even man's strong hand may not unbind.

We bless little children, for their presence bringeth purity and joy. Around them cluster affections that are nearer to the love of heaven; and when, from one dwelling and another, the timid doves are won heavenward, their flitting leaves a void which may not easily be filled.

"*Mine!*" What a spell in that simple word — a strangely solemn influence. So to Grace it was. "Mine" is an added charge — an immortal spirit, which must learn through me the way to live — the how to die. Far away into the future her thoughts were fast flitting, weaving, thus early, visions of beauty yet to open upon the baby dreamer. But as shades shut out the sunlight, so darker thoughts were blending with them. What if she were called away ere it should learn to tread life's changing way? Even thus another had been taken from those leaning upon her love — even thus, for the young voices that were echoing around gave to *her* the name lisped *first* to one departed. It was a sad memory, but one which made them seem the dearer, a more precious charge. The new tie that so blessed her should not weaken their claim, but, as a pure and cherished link, bind them more closely together.

THE LOST TREASURE.

The blue fades out from the fair summer sky,
  And my flowers have drooped their bright buds;
The winds of the autumn are scattering the leaves,
  And chanting a dirge o'er their heads.
So the love that made earth always summer to me,
  Has failed me and left me alone;

I sit by the ashes all cold on the hearth,
   And weep for the light that is gone.

I set up, unseen by a stranger's cold eye,
   A stone in my heart's secret shrine:
"In memory of"—and a name is thereon,
   The name of this lost love of mine.
I prayed for him nightly; I blessed him each day,
   The love and the blessing he scorns;
He has crushed from my path the roses I loved,
   And leaves me all pierced by the thorns.

But murmur not, heart—poor, sorrowful heart:
   We will keep loving vigil together;
It may be some day he will seek us again,
   When with him 't is less sunshiny weather.
Let us patiently wait, and pray, and love on;
   Kindly welcome him back, should he come;
But if not, the rich treasures we lose here on earth,
   May be found in a heavenly home.

EMMA ALICE BROWNE.

MISS BROWNE was born in Cecil, Maryland, on Christmas day, 1840. Her father, from whom she inherits her poetical gift, died when she was a child.

The late poet and journalist George D. Prentice termed Emma Alice Browne "the sweetest song-bird in all the land." Every line she has written bears the imprint of genius.

Fatherless at an early age, Miss Browne has carved her own way in the world with her pen.

She has been for a number of years a contributor to the principal literary journals of the United States. Her poems have never been collected into a volume.

Her home is at Woodville, Rappahannock County, Virginia.

ESTELLA ANNA LEWIS.

WHEN we say that this poet is decidedly the most eminent literary woman of her time, we do not mean to deny that there are others whose writings are distinguished by more justness and sobriety of thought, by more directness, and more practicable utility; but we mean to say that she has pursued a more lofty and dangerous career. Like Sappho of Lesbos, of whom she has so eloquently written, she has dared to enter the race for fame with the strongest, and to pluck the laurel from the very summit of Olympus.

"Jupiter," says an eminent critic, speaking of her poetic powers, "is usually represented as sitting on a golden throne, holding in the one hand thunder-bolts, and in the other a sceptre of cypress. We do not say that Stella plays with the lyric fires as did Jupiter with thunder-bolts, but we do assert that her powers are great, and that her versatility is wonderful. At times she soars into the regions of the grand and imposing, and again, waves a wand as gentle and persuasive as the cypress."

Estella was born in Baltimore, Md., and is the only child of Delmonte Robinson, a West Indian planter, by his second wife, Anna Estella Butler, daughter of Col. Butler, of Washington, a descendant of the heroes of Wyoming of that name, who, as history tells us, were descended from the House of Ormond. After the death of her father, she was confided to a maternal uncle, who placed her at the Troy Female Seminary, where she was an ardent student from ten to fifteen, and where she won, at that tender age, the title of " the *tenth muse.*" Her compositions were always in poetry; and when asked by her skeptical teacher where she found such pretty poems, she replied, " *In my own heart!* " On one occasion an impromptu poem found its way into a daily paper before she had read it in the class, and she was accused of having taken it verbatim from said paper, and was obliged to call in the editor to prove her innocence.

On leaving the seminary she was married to S. D. Lewis, Counsellor-at-Law, and immediately afterward the Appletons, of New York, published her " Records of the Heart," (1844,) which was received by the press with universal applause. No first volume of poems ever gained a wider popularity. Edgar A. Poe was so pleased with many of the poems that it contained that he immediately made the author's acquaintance, and constantly wrote and talked of the young poetess. He recited " The Forsaken " on several public occasions, and in his " Literati " thus speaks of it :

"The popular as well as the critical voice ranks 'The Forsaken' as the most beautiful ballad of its kind ever written. . . . We have read it more than twenty times, and always with increasing admiration. *It is inexpressibly beautiful.* No one of real feeling can peruse it without a strong inclination to tears. Its irresistible charm is its absolute truth — the unaffected naturalness of its thought."

We give it entire.

THE FORSAKEN.

It hath been said — for all who die
　　There is a tear ;
Some pining, bleeding heart to sigh
　　O'er every bier.
But in that hour of pain and dread,
　　Who will draw near
Around my humble couch and shed
　　One farewell tear?

Who watch life's last departing ray
　　In deep despair,
And soothe my spirit on its way
　　With holy prayer?
What mourner round my bier will come
　　In weeds of woe,
And follow me to my long home —
　　Solemn and slow?

When lying on my clayey bed,
　　In icy sleep,
Who there by pure affection led
　　Will come and weep ;
By the pale moon implant the rose
　　Upon my breast,
And bid it cheer my dark repose,
　　My lowly rest?

Could I but know when I am sleeping
　　Low in the ground,

One faithful heart would there be keeping
    Watch all night round,
As if some gem lay shrined beneath
    That sod's cold gloom,
'T would mitigate the pangs of death,
    And light the tomb.

Yes, in that hour if I could feel,
    From halls of glee
And Beauty's presence one would steal
    In, secrecy,
And come and sit and weep by me
    In night's deep noon —
Oh! I would ask of memory
    No other boon.

But, ah! a lonelier fate is mine,
    A deeper woe:
From all I love in youth's sweet time
    I soon must go:
Drawn round me my pale robes of white,
    In a dark spot
To sleep through death's long, dreamless night
    Lone and forgot.

This little poem of such rigid simplicity and tearful pathos was composed at the age of fourteen, on hearing the doctor tell her nurse, in the evening, that she could not live till the morning. Ah! what a night was this for a child full of hope and ambition, and of a naturally melancholy temperament! With her long brown curls flowing over the pillow, all night she lay bidding adieu to earth, and in the morning recited to her nurse "The Forsaken." The next volume of Mrs. Lewis was "The Child of the Sea, and other Poems," (1845,) which was received with still more favor than her first volume, and of which Lamartine thus speaks in one of his notices of the author:

"In dramatic movement and graphic description, "The Child of the Sea" will compare with any similar poem in any language. It is a beautiful novel in verse."

Two years after this volume followed the "Myths of the Minstrels," which included those sonnets to "Adhemar," so widely known and admired, and of which the great French poet thus speaks in his critique.

"The sonnets to 'Adhemar' entitle the author to the appellation of the 'Female Petrarch,' and the 'Sappho of America,' a title which her compatriots have justly given her. We agree with M. Edgar Poe, who has said, in his critique on the young poetess, that she is endowed with the truest poetic genius of any woman since the poetess of Lesbos."

In 1858 the Appletons issued a collection of "Stella's" poems in one magnificently illustrated volume; and soon afterward the poetess went to Europe, a widow, where she has since resided, with the exception of one short visit to the United States.

In Paris she resided in a fashionable hotel, where she gave weekly receptions, and had on her list of visitors the *élite* of American and English society then in Paris, and such Frenchmen of genius as Lamartine, Guizot, and Dumas.

From Paris she went to Italy, where she passed two years, mostly in Florence and Rome.

In 1863 she published, in New York, "Helemar; or, The Fall of Montezuma:" a tragedy in five acts, written while she was in Italy. We quote the following from a long critique in Sear's "National Quarterly Review" for October, 1863.

"Helemar is written with great power, and will add much to the author's reputation, as well as to the honor of American literature. In subject and treatment it is similar to the 'Alzire' of Voltaire, the 'Cid' of Corneille, and the 'Cromwell' of Victor Hugo; and it is by no means unworthy of a comparison with those great historical dramas."

We quote from the "Review" a single passage, where Helemar enters, and discovers the bodies of the Aztec noblemen who have been slain by the Spaniards.

HELEMAR [*recoiling aghast*].
    Horror of horrors! O grim-visaged horror!
    Pale, ghastly death! Thrice damn'd inebriate murder!
    That couldst not slake thy thirst with common blood,
    But needs drain Anahuac's royal rivers dry! —
    O Reason, keep thy throne! Judgment, thy seat!
    Until I fling my soul on this rank deed,
    And with its lightning wither up the foemen,
    As the great tempest crisps the autumn leaves!
               [*He approaches the dead bodies.*

O most untimely harvest! Glorious sheaves!
Unripely gathered to Death's granary! —
Burst — burst, big heart, and let thy great grief forth,
As from volcano's bosom lava leaps,
Into pale faces of affrighted stars!
What instigated this foul, bloody murder?
This deed, so red it scents the world with gore,
And sets all cannibals in earth a howling!
My noble brothers — Anahuac's young oaks —
The very nerves and sinews of the State —
Untimely felled — hewn down before their heads
Had glittered in the glory of the sun.
Ope earth! gape hell! and swallow up the white man!
Are ye all dead, my brothers — all so mute
Ye cannot tell me wherefore ye were slain?
Is there no lingering pulse — no throbbing heart —
No mouth wherein is breath enough for speech? —
Awake! arise! To thirsty vengeance give
These thrice ten thousand hydra-headed fiends! "

At Nice, in the winter of 1868, Mrs. Lewis finished "Sappho of
Lesbos," a tragedy which has been successfully produced at the Lyceum
Theatre, London; and in the summer of 1869, at St. Adresse, Upper
Normandie, she wrote "The King's Stratagem," a tragedy in five
acts. Besides these elaborate works, she has furnished to the New
York "Home Journal," and other papers, during her residence
abroad, "The Stella Letters," a piquant correspondence on society,
literature, and art. She is about to publish in London, in two volumes,
these letters, under the title of "Ten Years Outre Mer."

The following, from the tragedy of "Sappho," has been much read
and admired in London theatrical circles:

THE GRIEF OF ALCÆUS.

"SAPPHO."—ACT II.

Where am I? Whence this sable pε⸮,
Whose inky folks around me fall,
Shutting the day-god from my sight?
Just now the world was full of light,
And now to me 't is starless night.

What have I done, ye gods? Oh say!
That ye should snatch from me the day,

And from my life its beacon bright?
Just now the world was full of light,
And now to me 't is starless night.

Mine arms I put forth like the blind,
And only empty darkness find;
Sun, moon, and stars have taken their flight:
Just now the world was full of light,
And now to me 't is starless night.

Must I thus grope along the stream
Of life without a beacon-beam
To guide my lonely steps aright?
Just now the world was full of light,
And now to me 't is starless night.

Pitying, O Jove, take me from earth!
Allay' this bosom's gnawing dearth!
Translate to heaven my beacon bright!
Just now the world was full of light,
And now to me 't is starless night.

———o○¦●¦○o———

HENRIETTA LEE PALMER.

MISS HENRIETTA LEE was born in Baltimore, Md., February
6th, 1834. She enjoyed the advantages of the famous "Patapsco
Institute," established by Mrs. Lincoln Phelps, and the educational
home of many Southern girls from Maryland to Texas. Miss Lee
was married in 1855 to Dr. J. W. Palmer, of Baltimore, author of
several successful books of California life, translator of Michelet's
"L'Amour," etc., and compiler of "Folk Songs for the Popular
Heart," an elegant gift-book published in 1860; and also the author
of that popular poem of the war, "Stonewall Jackson's Way." Dr.
Palmer is at this time (1871) editing a literary weekly in his native
city.

Mrs. Palmer's writings consist of contributions, stories, letters, etc.,
etc., to various New York, Philadelphia, and Baltimore papers, and to
the "Young Folks' Magazine." She translated for Rachel, "The Lady
Tartuffe." In 1858, Appleton & Co., New York, published in elegant

style, "The Stratford Gallery; or, The Shakspeare Sisterhood, comprising forty-five ideal portraits, described by Henrietta Lee Palmer." I append a critical notice of this work from high authority, "Atlantic Monthly," January, 1859.

"This book is what it purports to be, — not a collection of elaborate essays devoted to metaphysical analysis or to conjectural emendations of doubtful lines, but a series of ideal portraits of the women of Shakspeare's plays. The reader may fancy himself led by an intelligent cicerone, who pauses before each picture, and with well-chosen words tells enough of the story to present the heroine, and then gives her own conception of the character, with such hints concerning manners and personal peculiarities as a careful study of the play may furnish. The narrations are models of neatness and brevity, yet full enough to give a clear understanding of the situation to any one unacquainted with it. The creations of Shakspeare have a wonderful completeness and vitality; and yet the elements of character are often mingled so subtilely that the sharpest critics differ widely in their estimates. Nothing can be more fascinating than to follow closely the great dramatist, picking out from the dialogue a trait of form here, a whim of color there, and at last combining them into an harmonious whole, with the truth of outline, hue, and bearing preserved. Often as this has been done, there is room still for new observers, provided they bring their own eyes to the task, and do not depend upon the dim and warped lenses of the commentators.

"It is very rarely that we meet with so fresh, so acute, and so entertaining a student of Shakspeare as the author of this volume. Her observations, whether invariably just or not, are generally taken from a new standpoint. She is led to her conclusions rather by instinct than by reason. She makes no apology for her judgments:

'I have no reason but a woman's reason:
I think her so because I think her so."

And it would not be strange if womanly instinct were to prove oftentimes a truer guide in following the waywardness of a woman's nature than the cold, logical processes of merely intellectual men.

"To the heroines who are most truly *women*, the author's loyalty is pure and intense. Imogen, the 'chaste, ardent, devoted, beautiful' wife, — Juliet, whose 'ingenuousness and almost infantile simplicity' endear her to all hearts, — Miranda, that most ethereal creation, type of virgin innocence, — Cordelia, with her pure, filial devotion — are painted with loving, sympathetic tenderness.

"Altogether, this is a book which any admirer of the poet may read with pleasure; and especially to those who have not ventured to think wholly for themselves, it will prove a most useful and agreeable companion."

EMMA D. E. N. SOUTHWORTH.

MRS. SOUTHWORTH is best known among the general public, of all writers of Southern birth. Her numerous thrilling romances have many fond readers in England as well as in this country.

Emma D. E. Neville Southworth, as she has informed the world in an autobiographical notice, was born in Washington, D. C., December 26th, 1818. The eldest daughter of her parents. She has a half-sister, Mrs. Frances Henshaw Baden, who is a favorite contributor to the "New York Ledger," and in connection with whom she published "The Christmas Guest, and other Stories," Philadelphia, 1870.

Mrs. Southworth's history is so well known that it is not necessary to quote it here. In 1849 Mrs. Southworth, then a teacher in a primary school in Washington, wrote her first novel, "Retribution," originally written for and published in the "National Era," of that city. This novel was published in a volume by Harper & Brothers, and Mrs. Southworth, who, before the publication of this novel, "had been poor, ill, forsaken, *killed* by sorrow, privation, toil, and friendlessness, found herself born, as it were, into a new life; found independence, sympathy, friendship, and honor, and an occupation in which she could delight." She has by her efforts achieved competence, and resides in a charming home in Georgetown, D. C. She has a son who inherits his mother's talent.

Mrs. Southworth has published more than any Southern writer. She has published thirty-three large volumes in twenty years. I append the titles of her novels:

Retribution. The Deserted Wife. The Missing Bride. Love's Labor Won. The Lost Heiress. Fallen Pride. Curse of Clifton. Bridal Eve. Allworth Abbey. The Wife's Victory. The Gipsy's Prophecy. The Two Sisters. Discarded Daughter. Three Beauties. Haunted Homestead. Vivia; or, The Secret of Power. India; or, The Pearl of Pearl River. The Fatal Marriage. The Lady of the Isle. The Fortune Seeker. The Bride of Llewellyn. The Mother-in-Law. The Widow's Son. How He Won Her. The Changed Brides. The Bride's Fate. The Prince of Darkness. The Family

Doom.   The Maiden Widow.   The Christmas Guest.   Fair Play.
Cruel as the Grave.   Tried for her Life.

May, 1871.

———o○;○;○●———

MISS ELIZA SPENCER

IN 1867–68, "Mary Ashburton: a Tale of Maryland Life, by Elise
Beverly," appeared serially in Gen. Hill's magazine, " The Land
we Love." This novel attracted considerable attention.

"Elise Beverly" was the pseudonym of Miss Eliza Spencer, of
Skipton, Maryland.   In 1869, she was residing at New Castle, Delaware, where her brother was rector of a flourishing church.

We give from the " Tale of Maryland Life," the following graphic
picture of a Maryland farm-house of years ago :

"An old-fashioned farm-house in the eastern part of Maryland, ochre-
washed into a delicate straw color, a tall yellow chimney peering above the
trees, a little attic window peeping out from the great gable end, and where
rose-vines are clambering and tumbling over, except where caught by strips
of morocco mellowed by time and the rust of the nails almost into the hues
of the walls ; here and there deep-seated dormer-windows, front and back,
where the bees are swarming in at the dishes of dried fruit therein displayed ;
old gnarled apple-trees lovingly kissing each other over the high shelving
roof, and almost covering it with their sweet white blossoms ; pear- and
cherry-trees mingling their odoriferous flowers on the deep, grassy carpeting
of the enclosure ; a wilderness of jessamine and honeysuckle growing on the
walls ; a long, large garden behind, luxuriating in the dear old-fashioned
flowers, not forming squares or triangles in stiff, prim lines, but springing up
everywhere, contrasting their colors in the richest, gayest confusion, evidently
not suffering for want of attention, for the ground about them is carefully
worked, and all weeds and briers most promptly removed.   No prim walks
glistening with sand and gravel, but a rich green sod on which the fruit-
blossoms lay their sweet little white cheeks, or the lovely pink flowers of the
peach embroidered it in charming patterns.   In front spread a long enclosure
lined with fruit-trees, and interspersed with them, so as to form an almost
uninterrupted shade about the house, though the sunlight fell in golden
patches on the grass and penetrated through the leaves and branches,
glinting and sparkling amid the vegetation till lost in its deepening laby-
rinths.   A well-sweep, suspending an 'iron-bound bucket,' arose from a well
on whose oaken sides the green moss of ages seemed collected, and, glancing
over into its clear depths, the water looked so pure and cool that it tempted

you to drink whether thirsty or not. Then the apple-blossoms fell about it, and seemed to make it the sweeter for their breath. An old love of a picturesque well it was, suggestive of pretty maids tripping there with their pitchers on their shoulders, while the traveller quenched his thirst by their kind assistance."

———○○⊶∘⊶∘○———

MISS TAMAR A. KERMODE.

MISS TAMAR ANNE KERMODE was born in Liverpool, England. Came to Baltimore in 1853. Has resided there since. She has contributed poems and prose to the "New York Ledger," Godey's "Lady's Book," and other papers and magazines, North and South.

"GIVE US THIS PEACE."

"The peace of God, which passeth all understanding."

These words fell softly on my ear, and so I prayed —
 Give *us* this peace, O God, and in each breast
All stormy thoughts and feelings shall be stayed,
 And we shall find in thee our perfect rest.
We're weary of the care, and toil, and strife,
 These dark attendants of our onward way —
Still cast their dreary mists o'er all our life:
 Look down, O Lord, and send them all away.
And then a voice, soft, solemn, low, and sweet,
 Seem'd to my fancy whispering in my ear,
"Be not cast down nor troubled 't is but meet
 That thou shouldest bear thy cross — then wherefore fear
The trials in thy path? Our Saviour looketh down,
 And those who work with patience win at last a crown.

1871.

ELEANOR FULLERTON.

"VIOLET FULLER" is the *nom de plume* of this lady. Her occasional poems have been widely copied. Mrs. Fullerton, whose maiden name was Hollins, is of English birth: her parents removed to the United States when she was quite young. She was educated in Baltimore, and has always resided there. Miss Hollins had every advantage wealth could command. She travelled in Europe while in the flush of youth, with her mind beginning to expand to all that was beautiful in nature and art. On her return home she commenced to write poetry, but did not publish for seven years. She was married in 1860.

Her poems and prose sketches have generally appeared in Baltimore journals.

Mrs. Fullerton has recently (May, 1871,) published a volume of her poems, through Sampson Low & Son, London.

The following verses give an idea of her graceful style: —

SO LONG AGO.

Oh, youth and love! the golden time
When life was in its joyous prime;
How fair each flower, how green each tree,
As, hand in hand, I walked with thee
      So long ago.

Beneath the beauty of thy brows
Thine eyes shone soft; thy whispered vows,
As on mine ear their accents fell,
I loved their music passing well
      So long ago.

And I looked love into thine eyes,
While brightly beamed the summer skies,—
Around us sighed the sweet perfume
Of summer roses, rich in bloom
      So long ago.

'Tis past, as summer roses die,
As fades the light from earth and sky
When night comes on, so beauty goes,
And withers, like the radiant rose
　　　So long ago.

Yet think not that I blame thee, dear;
'Tis but the fate of mortals here,
To lose their charm, when no more lies
The light of youth in once-loved eyes
　　　So long ago.

There is a light that's better far,—
A holy light that, like a star,
When the dark night of life comes on,
Beams in the eyes whence youth has flown
　　　So long ago.

The light of Heaven! Oh may it shine
On thee, and may a grace divine
On thee be shed when fades away
The tender radiance of the May
　　　So long ago.

69

TEXAS.

FANNY A. D. DARDEN.

HE subject of this brief article is a native of Texas. She belongs to a thoroughly Southern stock. Her father, General Mosely Baker, a native of the "Old Dominion State," was one of Texas's most distinguished soldiers during her struggle with Mexico for independence, and, after peace was declared, was her bright, particular star of legal acumen and forensic eloquence. Her mother was the only daughter of Colonel Pickett, of North Carolina, and sister of the historian of Alabama, in which State Fannie was educated.

As a lady of birth and culture, as a *littérateur* of taste and genius, as a native Southerner, and true, unswerving "daughter of the Confederacy," as the wife of a gallant officer — Captain William Darden, of Hood's Texas Brigade — Mrs. Darden's patent of nobility is clear and unmistakable, and therefore, with pride and pleasure, Texas presents her among "Southland Writers" as one of her representative women.

THE OLD BRIGADE.

Hood's gallant old brigade!
Ah! how the heart thrills, and the pulses leap
  When once again those well-known words are spoken,
Rending aside the clouds that darkly keep
  The present from the past, and bring a token
  From that weird, shadowy land, whose silence is unbroken!
Hood's gallant old brigade! what memories throng
  With the swift rush as of a torrent leaping;
And far-off strains of high, heroic song
  Come like a rolling wave majestic sweeping,
  When that mute chord is struck which stirs our souls to weeping!

And was it not a dream, those glorious days
   When hope her banner proudly waved before us;
When, in the genial light of freedom's blaze,
   We lived and breathed with her bright heaven o'er us,
   While every hill and vale rang out her lofty chorus?
When our loved State (whose one bright, glorious star
   Her lonely vigil keeps o'er earth and ocean)
Poured forth her sons at the first cry of war,
   Which thrilled each soul with patriot emotion,
   And claimed from those brave hearts their loftiest devotion.

Nay, 'twas no dream, those four long years, when war
With gloating triumph rode her bloody car,
Dragging, enchained, o'er fierce and stormy fields,
Her bleeding victims at her chariot wheels.
Nay, 'twas no dream, though vanished are the days
   When glory's splendid pageant moved before us,
Though now no more is seen the lurid blaze
   Which from each gory field lit up the heaven o'er us —
Though fallen is that flag, once proudly floating
   Above the battle's roar where heroes fought
With more than Spartan valor, there devoting
   Those hearts, whose flame from freedom's shrine was caught,
   To that loved cause, the freedom which they sought.

Hood's gallant old brigade! where are they now?
   Those souls of fire, who on the bloody plain
Of proud Manassas swept the usurping foe
   Before them, as the rushing hurricane
Its fatal vengeance wreaks and spreads its mighty woe.
Oh! where are those whose blood baptized the soil
   Of Sharpsburg and the sombre Wilderness,
Who, through long years of strife, and pain, and toil,
   No want could sadden, and no power depress —
Who charged the foe on Malvern's fatal hill,
   And where the mountain's brow frowns darkly down
On Boonsboro', and on the historic field
   Where Richmond looked on deeds whose high renown
Amazed the world, and in the valley deep
Where Chickamauga's heroes gently sleep?

But few remain of those, who, side by side,
Together braved the storm; and far and wide

Hood's Texans sleep a dreamless sleep, nor mark
The times nor changes, nor the heavy cloud
  That wraps their once-loved land in pall so dark.
The past has fled, but thickly memories crowd
  Upon us, and the phantom years return
With distant echoes from its shadowy shore.
  Our bosoms throb, our hearts within us burn;
We hear again the deep artillery's roar,
  And see our banner in the light of day
Borne high aloft upon the buoyant air;
  And columns deep of those who wore the gray
Are marshalled as of yore — the foe to dare.
  The past comes once again, and memories throng
With the swift rush as of a torrent leaping;
  And far-off strains of high, heroic song
Come like a rolling wave majestic sweeping,
When that mute chord is struck which stirs our souls to weeping.
  The past comes once again, but stays not long;
Its forms dissolve, its glorious splendors fade.
  But still is heard the burden of its song:
  And distant ages shall the strain prolong,
Which tells thy immortal deeds, Hood's gallant old brigade!

CHECKMATE.

They sat beneath the lamp-light's glow, —
  He was dark and she was fair, —
And chess was the game that they played; but oh,
Often a furtive glance he threw
  At her rippling waves of hair.

And she, with looks bent on the game,
  Seemed not to mark the roving glance;
But her cheek bore a blush of maiden shame,
And it told that treacherous "tell-tale" flame,
  Her dream of soft romance.

Rippling waves of golden hair
  Sparkled in the lamp-light's glow,
Around her forehead, without compare,
Over her shoulders, so snowy fair,
  To her waist, in billowy flow.

Now on the board with eager look,
　　Where kings and queens, in mimic war,
With knights and bishops their lances broke,
They gazed, while not a word was spoke
　　By each would-be conqueror.

But Fate was there with mystic spell,
　　And silently her web she wove,
And the maid's bright hair as it waving fell,
She knew would soon his heart impel
　　To her mesh, whose woof was love.

"Checkmate!" he cried, "you've lost at last;"
　　But she, with meek, unconscious air,
Was smiling at Fate, who, with wise forecast,
In her golden mesh had caught him fast,
　　Entangled by her hair.

COLUMBUS, April, 1870.

———o-o:o-:oo———

MRS. S. E. MAYNARD.

SARAH ELIZABETH HILLYER is a native of Eatonton,
Putnam Co., Georgia. Was born in 1841, daughter of Rev.
John F. Hillyer, a Baptist minister.

When she was six years old, her family removed to the "Lone Star"
State. From a very early age, Sarah was given to rhymes; exciting
the fear that "she would become a poet, and be utterlv worthless."

At the age of fifteen, Miss Hillyer was married to Mr. J. J. Ballard,
of Halletsville, Texas. After her marriage, Mrs. Ballard published
poems in various papers, under the signature of "Kaloolah." Her husband died five years after the marriage. During her widowhood she
published under her name, Sallie E. Ballard, — her articles meeting
with much favor.

She has nearly ready for publication a novel, entitled "The Two
Heroines; or, Freaks of Fortune."

She has recently married Mr. Maynard, and they reside near
Bastrop, Texas.

CLEOPATRA TO MARC ANTONY.*

Oh! my Antony, look on me!
  Let me gaze into those eyes;
Let me revel in their radiance
  Till the light within them dies;
Let their starry brightness, beaming
  O'er my tranced soul once more,
Thrill me with the wild emotions
  Which they woke in days of yore.

Oh! my Antony, look on me!
  Raise thy worshipped eyes to mine;
Let my soul hold sweet communion
  Through those crystal doors with thine;
Let our loving spirits mingle
  Till the icy clasp of death
Shuts those eyes on me forever —
  Stops that music-waking breath.

Thou art dying, my proud Roman!
  Dying!—when thou might'st have been
Monarch of a world, but gave it
  For a smile from Egypt's queen.
Fatal smile! to win thy spirit
  From its glorious eagle flight:
Mark me, Antony, my Roman,
  It shall fade in endless night.

Egypt's queen is throneless, fallen;
  But she hath a soul of pride.
Hark! the victors! they are coming!
  How they'll mock me and deride!
One more look, my dying Roman;
  One more lingering, fond embrace.
Cæsar comes! but Cæsar's triumph
  Egypt's queen shall never grace.

He is dead! But died Triumvir.
  Cleopatra dies — a queen!
Back to Rome, steel-hearted victor,
  Tell them there what thou hast seen;
Tell the fair and chaste Octavia
  Antony has scorned a crown;
Tell her how, for him, and with him,
  Egypt's royal star went down.

* Written after reading Lyttle's "I am dying, Egypt, dying!"

MRS. MAUD J. YOUNG.

MRS. M. J. YOUNG, daughter of Col. N. Fuller, Houston, Texas, is a native of North Carolina. Through her father she is a lineal descendant of John Rolf and his wife, Pocahontas, and blood kindred of the Randolphs of "Turkey Island" and "Roanoke," and of the Bollings, of Virginia. Her great-grandfather, Michael Pacquenett, a Huguenot from Bordeaux, France, came to this country after the revocation of the Edict of Nantes, and is mentioned in Hawkes's History of North Carolina as a freeholder in that State in 1723.

On her mother's side she is descended from the Dunbars, Braggs, and Braxtons, of Maryland and Virginia ; and the Marshalls, of Marsh Place, Essex, England. Her grandfather, Dr. John Marshall, a man of vast erudition and finished accomplishments of mind and manner, was educated at Eton and Oxford; Trinity College, Oxford, conferring upon him two degrees. After completing his education, during a travelling tour in this country, he met Miss Mary Bragg, (aunt of General Bragg, of the Confederate Army,) and became so enamored of the fair American that he did not return to England until he had wooed and won her for his wife. Their youngest daughter is the mother of the subject of this sketch.

Miss Fuller was married in her twentieth year to Dr. S. O. Young, of South Carolina, a man of superior mind, thorough cultivation, and elegant address. His family are connected by ties of blood and frequent intermarriage with the Bonners, Lees, Pressleys, Calhouns, and Bonhams, families whose names are interwoven with the literary, political, judicial, religious, and military history of South Carolina since the first Revolution. He died the first year of their marriage, leaving an only son, to whose education and training Mrs. Young's life has been devoted. This son is now, after having completed his college studies under General Lee at Lexington, pursuing the study of his profession at the Medical School in New Orleans, and bids fair to be a worthy representative of his family name and honors.

After showing Mrs. Young to be so truly a daughter of the South, it need scarcely be added that she was true to the traditions of her race in the late struggle. During the war, her pen, guided by the thrilling impulses of her soul, dropped words of comfort and songs of fire that soothed the souls and inspired the hearts of her countrymen from the Potomac to the Rio Grande. The 5th Regiment of Hood's Texas Brigade sent their worn and bloody flag home to her, after it had been covered with glory on a hundred battle-fields. She was enshrined in thousands of stern, true hearts, under the title of " The Confederate Lady " and " The Soldier's Friend." The commanding general of the Trans-Mississippi Department caused her appeals to be published by thousands and distributed through the army during the dark days after Lee's surrender, when it was still hoped that Texas would constitute herself the refuge and bulwark of that cause which none could deem then " lost." General Kirby Smith, General Magruder, General Joseph Shelby, and " The Confederate Lady " came out in a paper addressed to the " Soldiers and Citizens of Texas, New Mexico, and Arizona." This sheet, whose thrilling and soul-stirring appeals were enough to have created heroic resolutions under the very ribs of death, was printed by military command, and posted in the towns and served broadcast over camps and country.

Since the war, Mrs. Young has in all her writings made more or less practical application of her subjects to the times ; comforting, consoling, and encouraging her people — yet never bating one jot or tittle of her convictions concerning the past. To fail is not to be wrong, we can acknowledge defeat without believing ourselves in error, is her maxim. A distinguished officer of General " Stonewall " Jackson's regiment, after a visit to Texas, writes of her as " the vestal matron, guarding with religious and patriotic devotion the home-altars of her beloved State."

In an essay entitled " Weimar," she exclaims :

"Shall any young Southron fall into despair, or feel that he can never achieve greatness or distinction, now that his patrimonial acres and slaves are gone, when he reads the great Schiller congratulating himself upon the possession of an income of one hundred and twenty dollars? Go to your libraries, my young countrymen, and read the splendid thoughts that God sent Schiller in his poverty, and see how, in his humble cottage, in the capital of a duchy whose entire territory is scarcely larger than your plantation, he made a glorious fame, and crowned the brow of his native land with wreaths as immortal as her mountains, and beautiful and bright as the sparkling waves of her broad, blue Rhine! "

Again she writes:

"To contemplate Weimar, her insignificant territory, her poverty, her weakness, her dependence, and to see her become the nursing mother of the whole German Empire, and that too, not by wealth, or arms, or diplomacy, but simply through the mental powers of her children, we are constrained to admit that the grandest possibilities of humanity lie within the grasp of every condition; and that the watchword of youth should be that terse but comprehensive command of the Bible, 'Despise not the day of small things.' The best things of this world have owed nothing to extraneous circumstances — the power has been from within — fashioning, elevating, and purifying the individual, then the masses. No thought of failure should weaken your energies. 'Heart within, and God overhead.' You have not only a right to the brightest hopes, but a solemn duty to make those hopes verities."

Mrs. Young has written under several *noms de plume.* Her two works of greatest length are "Cordova," a religious novel, and a work on botany, soon to be issued, illustrative principally of the flora of Texas. Essays, short poems, and stories for magazines and newspaper publications, make up the bulk of her writings.

Simms, in his volume of Southern poems, has her "Song of the Texas Ranger." It was published originally without her name, as the most of her war poems were.

She has embodied in stories several of the legends of her State — among them, one of the famous watering-place, Sour Lake. Under the garb of a fairy story, she relates the story of secession, and the downfall of the Confederacy, pointing, in conclusion, to the only hope of happiness left us — *labor, and an unselfish devotion to the welfare of each other.*

A leading paper, in speaking of this, says:

"'The Legend of Sour Lake,' by M. J. Y., is really one of the finest prose poems we have read for many a day. Though not in verse, it is genuine poetry from beginning to end. Would that all the wild and beautiful legends of our wide field of poetic treasures — Texas — could be put in enduring form by the literary artist. This romantic Indian tradition, so beautifully rendered, and whose glorious symbolisms are so happily applied to the instruction of the Southern people, will not die."

Rev. Mr. Carnes, himself one of the purest and most talented of writers, says that the "'Legend of Sour Lake' is a tale worthy the

70

author of Undine itself," etc. The proprietors of the Lake presented the writer with the freedom of the springs.

One of Mrs. Young's best productions is an essay upon the relative character of the mind of man and woman. She takes ground against the "New School lights," denying woman's mental equality in kind, though she claims it for her in degree. She has chosen Milton and his "Paradise Lost," and Mrs. Browning and her "Drama of the Exile," as illustrations of her theory. The essay is too long to give entire, and to make quotations would only be an unsatisfactory marring of the whole. The "Telegraph" has been the most frequent medium of her communications, Mr. Cushing, its editor, being the Nestor of the press in her State, and the kindly guardian of every genius in its boundaries.

The writer of this sketch is reluctant to leave her pleasant task without making some mention of the sweet atmosphere of sympathy and feeling which emanates from and surrounds Mrs. Young in her social and private life, and of the brilliant light which her genius sheds upon those who come in immediate contact with her. Not only are her conversational powers incomparable and her manners perfect, but she has that silent tact and ready understanding which brings forward the *best* that is in those about her, and makes them feel, after leaving her, that they have themselves shone in truer and sweeter colors than their every-day garb. She is enveloped in incense from grateful hearts day by day; she is the "comforter," the "Christian," to those who come within her orbit. In her town, and in the country surrounding, no bride is pleased with the adjustment of her orange-blossoms unless Mrs. Young's fingers have helped to arrange them; no schoolboy is satisfied with his prize until she has smiled upon it. Grief comes to be folded to her heart, and happiness begs for her smile. She has drunk herself most deeply of the cup of sorrow — she has been scorched by the flames of affliction; but she has risen refreshed and strong from the bitter draught; she has come out brightened and purified, "even as refined gold" from the heat of the furnace.

In person, Mrs. Young is tall, with a commanding grace. She has beautiful dark eyes, an expressive mouth, and a soft, clear voice. Clad always in soft, black, flowing robes, and moving, as she does, like a dream, her memory haunts all who have once seen her, and her wonderful presence leaves a sense of itself wherever she has been.

1869.   * * *

MISS MOLLIE E. MOORE.

NATURE has wrought such profusion of beauty over the prairies of Western Texas, that the lover of the romantic and picturesque is often too much bewildered, as he travels the rolling hills and mimic mountains about the upper tributaries of the Colorado and the Guadalupe, to decide where she has been most lavish of her exquisite touches.

But would you find yourself lost in a Western Eden, and believe that you had passed, unwitting, into the spirit-land? Then pause in your travels amid the hills of the "Rio San Marcos."

Ask you how, away in this solitude, the mocking-bird learns to sing the thousand songs she never heard of bird, or instrument, or human voice?

Answer your own question, by finding the forest, prairie, flower and foliage, the winds and waters burdened with the very spirit of song: the vocal organs of the happy bird are only the instrument through which the music gushes.

And here it was, before she was nine years old, our Texas poetess, Mollie E. Moore, first sang her tuneful songs — and, without a master other than nature's voice, learned, like her feathered friend, to sing the songs she never heard; and, like that mistress of the winged minstrels, she sang "because she could not help it." Poetry gushed from her *pen* as the mere instrument of utterance. *She* is our "Texas Mocking-bird."

Dr. Moore emigrated from the banks of the Coosa, in the State of Alabama, where "Mollie" was born, when she was a mere child, and found a home in Texas such as we have described. Here he resided till his child, the only daughter of a large family, had imbibed the elements of poesy. He could command but few advantages of education for his children beyond their home circle; but he had some books, and a taste for natural beauty and natural science. His wife, too, had a gift for song and versification, readily caught by their little darling. No bird sang, or wind sighed, or grasshopper chirruped, or prairie-plume nodded, that Mollie's heart did not respond; and the passion for natural beauty, in all its thousand phases, that she sketches now with the hand of magic, was so deeply inwoven with her very being, that she lived a kind of fairy-life during her few years on the banks of the "Rio San Marcos." But read her own sweet song of her childhood's home:

"THE RIVER SAN MARCOS."

Far o'er the hills and toward the dying day,
Set like a heart — a living heart — deep, deep
Within the bosom of its wide prairies,
Lies the valley of San Marcos. And there,
A princess, roused from slumber by the kiss
Of balmy southern skies, the river springs
From out her rocky bed, and hastens on,
Far down the vale, to give her royal hand
In marriage to the waiting Guadalupe.

Like some grim giant keeping silent watch,
While from his feet some recreant daughter flies,
Above, the hoary mountain stands, his head
Encircled by an emerald-pointed crown
Of cedars, strong as those of Lebanon,
That bow their sombre crests, and woo the wind,
Drunken with fragrance, from the vale below.
About his brow, set like a dusky chain,
The mystic race-paths run — his amulet —
And nestled squarely 'gainst his rugged breast.
Perched quaintly 'mong the great, scarred rocks that hang
Like tombstones on the mountain-side, the nest
The falcon built still lingers, though the wing
That swept the gathering dust from off our shield
Hath long since drooped to dust!
         .   .   .   .   .   .

And here, down sloping to the water's marge,
The fields, all golden with the harvest, come:
And here, the horseman, reining in his steed
At eve, will pause, and mark the village spires
Gleam golden in the setting sun, and far
Across a deeply-furrowed field will glance
With idle eye upon a stately hill,
That, girt with cedars, rises like a king
To mark the farther limit of the field.
'T was here, between the hill and river, stood

A shaded cottage; and its roof was low
And dark, and vines that twined the porch but served
To hide the blackness of its wall. But then
'T was home, and "heaven is near us in our childhood.
And I was but a child; and summer days,
That since have oftentimes seemed long and sad,
Were fleeter then than even the morning winds
That sent my brother's fairy bark, well balanced,
In safety down the river's tide. Alas!
Is there, can there be aught in all the world
To soothe the sick soul to such perfect rest
As filled its early dreams? Is there no fount,
Like that of old, so madly sought by Leon,
Where the worn soul may bathe and rise renewed?

.   .   .   .
                    Well I remember,
Down where the river makes a sudden bend,
Below the ford, and near the dusky road,
Upon her bosom sleeps a fairy isle,
Enwreathed about with snowy alder-boughs,
And tapestried with vines that bore a flower
Whose petals looked like drops of blood —
We called it "Lady of the Bleeding Heart" —
And through it wandered little careless paths.

.   .   .   .
                    And o'er this living gem
The very skies seemed bluer, and the waves
That rippled round it threw up brighter spray.
Upon the banks for hours I've stood, and longed
To bask amid its shades; and when at last
My brother dragged, with wondrous care, his boat —
Rude-fashioned, small, and furnished with one oar —
Across the long slope from the stately hill
Where it was built, ne'er did Columbus' heart
Beat with a throb so wild upon that shore
Unknown to any save to him, as ours
When, with o'erwearied hands and labored breath,
We steered in safety o'er the dangerous way,
And stood, the monarchs of that fairy realm!
My brother! how I wish our wayward feet
Once more could feel that lordly pride — our hearts
Once more know all their cravings satisfied!

Sweet valley of San Marcos! few are the years
That since have linked their golden hands and fled

Like spirits down the valley of the past;
And yet it seems a weary time to me!
Sweet river of San Marcos! the openings seen
Between thy moss-hung trees, like golden paths
That lead through Eden to heaven's fairer fields,
Show glimpses of the broad, free, boundless plains
That circle thee around.   Thine own prairies!
How my sad spirit would exult to bathe
Its wings, all heavy with the dust of care,
Deep in their glowing beauty!   How my heart,
O'ershadowed with the cloud of gloom, would wake
To life anew beneath those summer skies!

. . . .

Oh, river of my childhood! fair valley-queen!
Within thy bosom yet at morn the sun
Dips deep his golden beams, and on thy tide,
At night, the stars — the silver stars — are mirrored;
Through emerald marshes yet thine eddies curl,
And yet that fairy isle in beauty sleeps,
(Like her of old who waits the wakening kiss
Of some true knight to break her magic sleep;)
And yet, heavy with purple cups, the flags
Droop down toward the mill; but I — oh! I
No more will wander by thy shores, nor float
At twilight down thy glassy tide! — no more.
And yet, San Marcos, when some river-flower,
All swooning with its nectar-drops, is laid
Before my eyes, its beauty scarce is seen
For tears which stain my eyelids, and for dreams
Which glide before me of thy fairy charms,
And swell my heart with longing,
            Sweet river of San Marcos!

Dr. Moore afterward removed to near Tyler, in Smith County, Texas, where a more cultured association soon developed another phase of his daughter's life; and the many modest verses that never expected to see the light, but which the poet always retains with affection, as bearing with them the history of the spirit's joys in its buddings, found their way, through admiring friends, to the light they would scarcely bear without the photograph of the girlish writer to vindicate their unpretending juvenility.

It was not long (in her fifteenth year) till some of her verses found their way into the "Houston Telegraph," then under the editorship of the acute and scholarly E. H. Cushing, Esq. With the ready appreciation of a man of wit and letters, Mr. Cushing encouraged and invited the contributions of the young and gifted writer, without knowing how young and uninstructed she was. Further information induced Mr. Cushing to invite, and procured a visit to his family of his youthful contributor. Like the true patron of genius, he sought, by every proper aid, to afford it the means of development. He and his noble-hearted wife prevailed upon her parents to allow their daughter to become a member of their family whenever they could part with her society at home, and, in the absence of good schools, (all broken up by the events of the war,) avail herself of the use of his personal instruction, and his extensive and well-selected library.

Thus for three years, until after the close of the war, our young writer spent a large portion of her time in the city of Houston, in association with ladies and gentlemen of cultured intellect, and in the reading and study that have developed her taste, and made her the true poetess and the elegant and charming woman — a favorite in every circle in which she moves. Somewhat subsequent to this period, we believe it was, she received the aid in her selections of reading and study of the somewhat mystic and profound critic and theologian, Rev. J. E. Carnes.

Miss Moore's pen has never been long idle; and although but few of her productions have seen the light, her literary correspondence has widened, and her prose as well as poetic writings have grown voluminous for one still so young.

In 1866, her father removed, with his family, to Galveston, thus bringing his daughter's two homes within a few hours of each other, and giving her additional advantages of society and the seaside promptings to her muse.

A season of travel through the East and North with Mr. Cushing's family and some other friends, the meeting with many writers of note, and, above all, that monster to all young authors, the publisher, and seeing a volume of her own thoughts collected and published by her friend and patron, were the prominent events of the next season. Then came that terrible shock — her first great grief — the death of her loving and excellent mother, each event, in its turn, giving a new tinge to her productions, or hushing her muse to silence in the presence of unutterable thoughts and emotions.

Thus a large family of brothers, the younger ones scarcely beyond infancy, together with her widowed and stricken father, were thrown entirely upon the care and affection of this slender and frail girl of books and poetic vocation. Yet, as if with one of her own intuitions, she adapted herself to the necessities around her with a maturity and earnestness beyond praise. Yet never has her life appeared more beautiful, nor her pen gushed with a more full and genuine inspiration, than when discharging, with such tender devotion, all these onerous cares thus devolving upon her.

It must not be inferred, because Miss Moore's very versatile muse oft grapples with the grave and the lofty, or weeps in sadness, draped in gloom, that her life and manners are usually austere, or her pen always clothed in mourning. On the contrary, she illustrates a trait not uncommon with poets and persons of exalted fancy. In conversation with friends, in society, and in the hospitalities of her own house, she wears a cheerfulness and humor that would leave an impression of the happy girl taking life and its cares rather lightly. Many of her fugitive pieces illustrate this joyous temper, and prove her humor to be genuine. The poem which follows contains the scintillations of a merry heart:

STEALING ROSES THROUGH THE GATE.

Long ago, do you remember,
  When we sauntered home from school,
As the silent gloaming settled,
  With its breezes light and cool?
When we passed a stately mansion,
  And we stopped, remember, Kate,
How we spent a trembling moment
  Stealing roses through the gate?

But they hung so very tempting,
  And our eager hands were small,
And the bars were wide—oh! Kate,
  We trembled; but we took them all!
And we turned with fearful footsteps,
  For you know 'twas growing late;
But the flowers, we hugged them closely,
  Roses stolen through the gate!

Well, the years have hasted onward,
  And those happy days are flown;

Golden prime of early childhood,
   Laughing moments spent and gone!
But yester e'en I passed your cottage,
   And I saw, oh! careless Kate,
Handsome Percy bending downward —
   Stealing roses through the gate!

Stealing roses where the willow
   O'er the street its long bough dips!
Stealing roses — yes, I'd swear it —
   Stealing roses from your lips!
And I heard a dainty murmur,
   Cooing round some blessed fate:
Don't deny it! was n't Percy
   Stealing roses through the gate?

We do not propose writing a critique upon her productions, but must make note of a few pieces that show her versatility. We open the volume of poems, that casket of jewels, ("Minding the Gap, and Other Poems,") presented to the public by Cushing & Cave, Houston, 1867, the first literary production (we believe) ever published in Texas; and the very dedication to her friend and patron will indicate the originality, the tenderness, and poetic beauty of Miss Moore's mental constitution. First in the compilation is "Minding the Gap," which is suggested by a custom prevalent in the rural districts of Texas, which may not be understood elsewhere. At harvest-time, a length of the fence is let down to allow the wagons to pass to and fro. To keep cattle out, the children are set "minding the gap." It evinces one of her strong peculiarities. Its description is exceedingly graphic and beautiful, while the style of transition, from the simple idea of "minding the gap" in the field-fence, to the heartful reflections upon those "open places of the heart," where, in maturer life, the spirit's foes are ever seeking such wily entrance, is not only tender to tears, but may be said to be one of Miss Moore's decided individualities.

MINDING THE GAP.

There is a radiant beauty on the hills —
   The year before us walks with added bloom;
But, ah! 't is but the hectic flush that lights
   The pale consumptive to an early tomb —

71

The dying glory that plays round the day,
Where that which made it bright hath passed away.

A mistiness broods in the air — the swell
  Of east winds, slowly wearing autumn's pale
With dirge-like sadness, wanders up the dell;
  And red leaves from the maple branches fall
With scarce a sound. This strange, mysterious rest!
Hath nature bound the Lotus to her breast?

But hark! a long and mellow cadence wakes
  The echoes from their rocks! How clear and high,
Among the rounded hills, its gladness breaks,
  And floats like incense toward the vaulted sky!

It is the harvest-hymn! a triumph tone;
  It rises like those swelling notes of old
That welcomed Ceres to her golden throne,
  When through the crowded streets her chariot rolled.
It is the laborer's chorus! for the reign
Of plenty hath begun — of golden grain.

How cheeks are flushed with triumph, as the fields
  Bow to our feet with riches! How the eyes
Grow full with gladness, as they yield
  Their ready treasures! How hearts arise
To join with gladness in the mellow chime —
"The harvest-time! the glorious harvest-time!"

It is the harvest, and the gathered corn
  Is piled in yellow heaps about the field;
And homely wagons, from the break of morn
  Until the sun glows like a crimson shield
In the far west, go staggering homeward-bound,
And with the dry husks strew the trampled ground.

It is the harvest; and an hour ago
  I sat with half-closed eyes beside the "spring,"
And listened idly to its dreamy flow;
  And heard afar the gay and ceaseless ring
Of song and labor from the harvesters —
Heard faint and careless, as a sleeper hears.

My little brother came with bounding step,
  And bent him low beside the shaded stream,

And from the fountain drank with eager lip;·
　While I, half rousing from my dream,
Asked where he'd spent this still September day —
"Chasing the birds, or on the hills at play?"

Backward he tossed his golden head, and threw
　A glance disdainful on my idle hands;
And, with a proud light in his eye of blue,
　Answered, as deep his bare feet in the sands
He thrust, and waved his baby hand in scorn:
"Ah! no: down in the cornfield, since the morn,
　　　I've been mindin' the gap!"

"Minding the gap!" My former dream was gone!
　Another in its place: I saw a scene
As fair as e'er an autumn sun shone on —
　Down by a meadow, large and smooth and green,
Two little barefoot boys, sturdy and strong
And fair, here in the corn, the whole day long,
　　　Lay on the curling grass
　　　Minding the gap!

Minding the gap! And as the years swept by
　Like moments, I beheld those boys again;
And patriot hearts within their breasts beat high,
　And on their brows was set the seal of men;
And guns were on their shoulders, and they trod
Back and forth, with measured tread, upon the sod,
　　　Near where our army slept,
　　　Minding the gaps!

Minding the gaps! My brothers, while you guard
　The open places where a foe might creep —
A mortal foe — oh! mind those *other gaps* —
　The open places of the heart! My brothers, keep
　　　Watch over them!

The open places of the heart — the gaps
　Made by the restless hands of doubt and care —
Could we but keep, like holy sentinels,
　Innocence and faith forever guarding there,
Ah! how much of shame and woe would flee,
Affrighted, back from their blest purity!

No gloom or sadness from the outer world
  With feet unholy then would enter in,
To grasp the golden treasures of the soul,
  And bear them forth to sorrow and to sin!
The heart's proud fields — its harvests full and fair!
Innocence and love, could we but keep them there,
      Minding the gaps!

One turns the leaves of the volume, and finds they would select almost each piece they read as sample of Miss Moore's poetic gifts.

"The Departing Soul," in its dialogue with the body, has a depth of thought that would do credit to the maturer minds of the great poets. It depends not at all upon its special rhythm, for you read its blank verse as if following the thoughts of Bryant or Cowper, without seeing the words, only living and wrestling with the searching and thrilling conceptions.

"Reaping the Whirlwind" is powerfully presented. The religious lesson is developed in an allegory as original as it is truthful and poetic. This spiritual trait, that is usually deemed a great beautifier of the female character, runs like a modest silver thread through the whole web of her poetic constructions. But the intellectual trait, that will at least rank second in the estimation of cultured minds, is the *reflective*. And in this class you might rank nearly every piece she writes. The original and independent manner in which our poetess weaves the reflective into her verses, even on the tritest themes, is fast asserting her claim to fame. She has no mentor, no model, no guide but her own perception of the lofty, the true, and the beautiful. She wrote before she knew there were models; and still she writes, with an untrammelled independence, the thoughts, the reflections, the fancies, just as they flow through the mind of this "our Texas Mocking-bird," our own "Mollie Moore."

The patriotic is a large element in her earlier writings. It found ample promptings just as her mind was developing into the open world. It glows in many of her longer poems, and often creeps in by stealth as she writes upon other themes. The deep impressions made by the sufferings of her people, her friends and family, up to the close of the war, have tinged her mental character for life.

Taking Miss Moore's poems all in all, they indicate a wide range of excellence, a lofty sweep of thought, a subtle gift in allegory and personification, and richness in exquisite fancies.

An engraving of Miss Moore is the frontispiece to her volume of poems. It is an excellent likeness, having the fault of looking too stern, and much too old. "Looking at this engraving, we see a girl hardly out of her teens, with a face 'which evinces refinement and culture of the highest order: it is not beautiful, nor would we consider it pretty; but it is a face altogether remarkable — of the kind you love to look at, return to again and again; and having seen it, it is not easily forgotten."

No great poem has yet been given to the public by Miss Moore; but we shall hope, from the promise given in many fugitive and a few more lengthy poems, that as years flow on, and her mental character ripens in its development, her spirit-fancies may find utterance in elaborate works of genius.

1869.   COL. C. G. FORSHEY.

——◦◦⟡◦◦——

FLORENCE D. WEST.

MRS. WEST, whose maiden name was Duval, was born in Tallahassee, Florida. Her grandfather was Governor of Florida. Her father moved to Texas when she was a child, and settled in Austin, where she has ever since resided. Her father now holds the position of Federal Judge. Mrs. West has written considerable verse, and what she has published has been favorably noticed. Poetry has been her recreation, and not her study. The following poem originally appeared in Gen. Hill's magazine:

THE MARBLE LILY.

Shaking the clouds of marble dust away,
  A youthful sculptor wanders forth alone
While twilight, rosy with the kiss of day,
  Glows like a wondrous flower but newly blown.
There lives within his deep and mystic eyes,
  The magic light of true and happy love —
Tranquil his bosom as the undimmed skies
  Smiling so gently from the depths above.

All Nature whispers sweet and blissful things
  To this young heart, rich with emotions warm:

Ah, rarely happy is the song it sings!
   Ah, strangely tender is its witching charm!
He wanders to the margin of a lake
   Whose placid waves lie hushed in sleeping calm —
So faint the breeze, it may not bid them wake,
   Tho' breathing thro' their dreams its odorous balm.

A regal lily stands upon the shore,
   Dropping her dew-pearls on the mosses green:
Her stately forehead, and her bosom pure,
   Veiled in the moonlight's pale and silver sheen.
The sculptor gazes on the queenly flower
   Until his white cheek burns with crimson flame,
And his heart owns a sweet and subtile power,
   Breathing like music through his weary frame.

The magic influence of his mighty art —
   The magic influence of his mighty love —
Their mingled passion to his life impart,
   And his deep nature each can wildly move.
These passions sway his inmost being now —
   His art, his love, are all the world to him:
Before the stately flower behold him bow;
   Speaking the love that makes his dark eyes dim.

"Thou art the emblem of my bosom's queen;
   And she, as thou, is formed with perfect grace —
Stately she moves, with lofty air serene,
   And pure thoughts beaming from her angel face.
While yet thy bosom holds this silver dew,
   And moonbeams pale with passion for thy sake,
In fairest marble I'll thy life renew,
   Ere the young daylight bids my love awake."

A wondrous flower shone upon the dark —
   A lily-bloom of marble, pure and cold —
Perfected in its beauty as the lark
   Soared to the drifting clouds of ruddy gold.
The sculptor proudly clasped the image fair
   To his young ardent heart, then swiftly passed
To where a lovely face, 'mid floating hair,
   A splendor o'er the dewy morning cast.

She beamed upon him from the casement's height —
   The fairest thing that greeted the new day —

He held aloft the lily gleaming white,
   While tender smiles o'er her sweet features play.
Presenting his fair gift on bended knee —
   "Wilt thou, beloved, cherish this pure flower?
'T was born of moonlight, and a thought of thee,
   And well will grace this cool and verdant bower.

"And when these blushing blossoms droop and pine,
   Chilled by the cruel north wind's icy breath,
Unwithered still these marble leaves will shine
   Calm and serene, untouched by awful death."
The summer days flew by like bright-winged dreams,
   Filling those hearts with fancies fond and sweet;
But when the first frost cooled the sun's warm beam,
   The purest, gentlest one had ceased to beat.

How like she seemed — clad in her churchyard dress —
   To that cold flower he chiselled for her sake!
What wild despairing kisses did he press
   On those sealed eyes that never more will wake!
His clinging arms enfold her once again,
   In one long, hopeless, passionate embrace —
Then that fair child, who knew no earthly guile,
   Hid 'neath the flowers her sad and wistful face.

The world that once was fairy-land to him,
   Now seemed a dreary waste — of verdure bare —
He only walked abroad in moonlight dim,
   And shunned the gaudy sun's unwelcome glare.
Each night he sits beside a small green mound
   O'er which a marble lily lifts its head
With trembling dews and pearly moonbeams crowned,
   Fit emblem of the calm and sinless dead.

He never tires of this sad trysting-place,
   But waits and listens through the quiet night —
"Surely she comes from mystic realms of space,
   To bid my darkened spirit seek the light.
Be patient, my wild heart! yon glowing star
   Wears the fond look of her soft, pleading eyes;
Gently she draws me to that world afar,
   And bids me hush these sad and longing sighs.

Thus mused he, as the solemn nights passed by,
   Still folding that sweet hope within his soul,

And always peering in the tender sky
  With earnest longings for that distant goal.
One radiant night, when summer ruled the land,
  He sought the darling's bed of dreamless rest —
The wooing breeze his pale cheek softly fanned
  With balmy sighs from gardens of the blest.

A witching spell o'er that fair scene was cast,
  Thrilling his sad heart with a wild delight;
And steeped in visions of the blessed past,
  He gazed upon the lily, gleaming white.
Jewels of diamond-dew glowed on its breast,
  And the rich moonlight, mellow and intense,
In golden robes the quiet churchyard dressed,
  Pouring its glory through the shadows dense.

A nightingale flew from a neighboring tree,
  And on the marble lily folds his wings —
His full heart trembles with its melody —
  Of love and heaven he passionately sings.
The sculptor, gazing through his happy tears,
  Feels his whole being thrilled with sudden bliss —
An angel voice in accents soft he hears,
  And trembles on his lips a tender kiss.

His hope has bloomed! above the marble flower,
  Radiant with heavenly beauty, see her stand!
His heart makes music like a silver shower,
  As fondly beckons that soft snowy hand.
The golden moon paints in the crimson sky,
  And morning's blushes burn o'er land and sea,
Staining a cold, cold cheek with rosy dye:
  The sculptor's weary, waiting soul is free!

Onward glide the years through bloom and blight;
  Unchanged, the marble lily lifts its head:
Through summer's glow, through winter's snow, so white,
  Unheeding sleep the calm and blessed dead.
Wherever falls the pure and pearly dew,
  Wherever blooms the fresh and fragrant rose,
In that far world removed from mortal view
  Two loving souls in perfect bliss repose.

THE END.